THE COLLAPSE OF VENEZUELA

RECENT TITLES FROM THE HELEN KELLOGG INSTITUTE SERIES ON DEMOCRACY AND DEVELOPMENT

Paolo G. Carozza and Aníbal Pérez-Liñan, series editors

The University of Notre Dame Press gratefully thanks the Helen Kellogg Institute for International Studies for its support in the publication of titles in this series.

Roxana Barbulescu
Migrant Integration in a Changing Europe: Migrants, European Citizens, and Co-ethnics in Italy and Spain (2019)

Matthew C. Ingram and Diana Kapiszewski
Beyond High Courts: The Justice Complex in Latin America (2019)

Kenneth P. Serbin
From Revolution to Power in Brazil: How Radical Leftists Embraced Capitalism and Struggled with Leadership (2019)

Manuel Balán and Françoise Montambeault
Legacies of the Left Turn in Latin America: The Promise of Inclusive Citizenship (2020)

Ligia Castaldi
Abortion in Latin America and the Caribbean: The Legal Impact of the American Convention on Human Rights (2020)

Paolo Carozza and Clemens Sedmak
The Practice of Human Development and Dignity (2020)

Amber R. Reed
Nostalgia after Apartheid: Disillusinment, Youth, and Democracy in South Africa (2020)

James J. Sheehan
Making a Modern Political Order: The Problem of the Nation State (2023)

Séverine Deneulin and Clemens Sedmak
Integral Human Development: Catholic Social Teaching and the Capability Approach (2023)

Kathleen Bruhn
Politics and the Pink Tide: A Comparative Analysis of Protest in Latin America (2024)

Tiago Fernandes
Democratic Quality in Southern Europe: France, Greece, Italy, Portugal, and Spain (2024)

Orçun Selçuk
The Authoritarian Divide: Populism, Propaganda, and Polarization (2024)

For a complete list of titles from the Helen Kellogg Institute for International Studies, see www.undpress.nd.edu.

THE COLLAPSE OF VENEZUELA

SCORCHED EARTH POLITICS AND ECONOMIC DECLINE, 2012–2020

FRANCISCO RODRÍGUEZ

University of Notre Dame Press
Notre Dame, Indiana

University of Notre Dame Press
Notre Dame, Indiana 46556
undpress.nd.edu

Published in the United States of America

Library of Congress Control Number: 2024947147

ISBN: 978-0-268-20901-8 (Hardback)
ISBN: 978-0-268-20903-2 (WebPDF)
ISBN: 978-0-268-20904-9 (Epub3)

GPSR Compliance Inquiries:
Lightning Source France, 1 Av. Johannes Gutenberg, 78310 Maurepas, France
compliance@lightningsource.fr | Phone: +33 1 30 49 23 42

To María Eugenia, my fiercest and most loving critic

They both want to reign.

—Cicero, *Letters to Atticus*, 49 BCE

CONTENTS

PART III. THE DESCENT INTO ECONOMICALLY DESTRUCTIVE POLITICAL CONFLICT, 2016–2020

PART IV. EXTENDING THE FRAMEWORK

FIGURES

TABLES

ABBREVIATIONS

AD	Acción Democrática
Adem	Alianza Democrática
AFL-CIO	American Federation of Labor and Congress of Industrial Organizations
ANC	Asamblea Nacional Constituyente
AP	Avanzada Progresista
BCV	Banco Central de Venezuela
Bs	bolivars
CADIVI	Comisión Nacional de Administración de Divisas
CDS	credit default swap
CLAP	Comités Locales de Abastecimiento y Producción
CNE	Consejo Nacional Electoral
CPI	Consumer Price Index
ENCOVI	Encuesta Nacional de Condiciones de Vida
FDI	foreign direct investment
Fedecámaras	Federación de Cámaras y Asociaciones de Comercio y Producción de Venezuela
FONDEN	Fondo Nacional de Desarrollo
GDP	gross domestic product
HDI	Human Development Index
IMF	International Monetary Fund
JV	joint venture
MDC	Movement for Democratic Change
MDN	Mesa de Diálogo Nacional
MPSD	Social Democratic Party of Germany
MSE	mean-squared error
MUD	Mesa de la Unidad Democrática

MVR	Movimiento Quinta República
OAS	Organization of American States
OECD	Organization for Economic Co-operation and Development
OFAC	Office of Foreign Assets Control
OHCHR	Office of the High Commissioner for Human Rights
OPEC	Organization of the Petroleum Exporting Countries
PDVSA	Petróleos de Venezuela, S.A.
PJ	Primero Justicia
PPP	purchasing power parity
PRI	Partido Revolucionario Institucional
PSUV	Partido Socialista Unido de Venezuela
PU	Plataforma Unitaria
PWT	Penn World Table
PZPR	Polska Zjednoczona Partia Robotnicza
RCF	Rapid Credit Facility
RFI	Rapid Financing Instrument
SDN	Specially Designated Nationals
SFV	special financing vehicle
SITME	Sistema de Transacciones con Títulos en Moneda Extranjera
SPD	Sozialdemokratische Partei Deutschlands
SSPNE	symmetric subgame-perfect Nash equilibrium
tbd	thousand barrels per day
TFP	total factor productivity
UN	United Nations
UNASUR	Union of South American Countries
UNCTAD	United Nations Trade and Development
UNDP	United Nations Development Programme
UN IGME	United Nations Inter-Agency Group for Child Mortality Estimation
UNT	Un Nuevo Tiempo
VP	Voluntad Popular
VV	Vente Venezuela
WTI	West Texas Intermediate
ZANU-PF	Zimbabwe African National Union

PREFACE

Studying the Venezuelan economy is the social science equivalent of being a rare disease specialist. Colleagues will listen to you discuss your research with a mixture of fascination and amazement, yet invariably end the conversation by telling you that your findings, while interesting, are irrelevant. Venezuela is too atypical and unique, they will say. It cannot be considered a practical guide to the experiences of other countries.

One of the key challenges that Venezuela researchers must face is the readiness with which some of our colleagues will appeal to Venezuelan exceptionalism—the belief that Venezuela is so idiosyncratic that understanding it is useless for explaining anything else. Chávez, they will state, was unique. As—they will argue without perceiving a contradiction—is Maduro. The country sits atop huge oil deposits, with an economy totally distorted by its resource wealth. It is a pariah state whose leaders speak as if reading badly translated versions of Soviet Cold War–era pamphlets. If there were a country equivalent of Christiane Kerner—the East German mother who wakes up from a coma without realizing that the Berlin wall has fallen in Wolfgang Becker's 2003 masterpiece, *Goodbye Lenin*—it would be Venezuela.

Of course, as the pandemic years grimly reminded us, sometimes it comes in handy to have rare disease specialists around. Even if we don't ever have to contend with a Venezuelan disease epidemic, there are plenty of good reasons to study the outliers of any process. This is because understanding the reasons that make a particular case anomalous may yield important insights as to the mechanisms that operate in more typical cases. In the same way in which understanding the reaction of immunocompromised individuals to infections can teach us about the role played by a functioning immune system in fighting disease, understanding the causes of economic and political collapses can yield valuable insights into the role institutional arrangements play in impeding functioning market economies from descending into chaos.

Venezuelan exceptionalists, however, face a problem when trying to account for the country's impressive record as a harbinger of what is to come in the region. When Venezuela began its experiment with democracy in 1958, only a small group of countries in the region held competitive elections. In fact, Venezuela still holds the record for the longest-lasting streak of competitive presidential elections in South America (the second longest after Costa Rica in all Latin America).[1] Venezuela was also the first country in the region in which a leftist political movement with an anti–Washington Consensus platform rose to power through elections, sparking the "Pink Tide" phenomenon. It pioneered the use of constitutional conventions to help chief executives gain control over other branches of government in 1999, a move that would be followed later by other elected governments in the region, including Bolivia, Ecuador, and the Dominican Republic. When Venezuela began its slide into autocracy, few scholars saw democratic backsliding as a serious problem for consolidated democracies; today scholars worry about the risk of backsliding in the United States and Europe.

This book is an attempt to make sense of the Venezuelan experience using the analytical tools and insights of modern economics and political science. I believe, and strive to show, that there is nothing exceptional about the mechanisms that led to the spectacular collapse of the country's economy and society. On the contrary, Venezuela's implosion is the result of the breaking of the fail-safe mechanisms that protect modern market democracies from descending into destructive political conflict. Venezuela is a cautionary tale of what happens when the institutions that are designed to manage and limit conflict between political actors stop working. It is not an exception that proves the rule but rather an example of how the breaking of the rules produces the exceptions.

Venezuela is only an anomaly if we view it from the myopic perspective that the past fifty years of world history are all that matters. As Cicero's epigraph to this volume reminds us, destructive political conflict has been with us for pretty much as long as we have written memory. Even the United States, with two and a half centuries of democracy, is a toddler compared to Cicero's Rome, with five hundred years of republican governance, a system that ultimately descended into internecine conflict ending in the consolidation of an autocratic regime. At the root of the stability of Rome's republican arrangements, the historian Edward Watts tells us, were the norms that circumscribed conflict between its political actors. When the Republic lost its ability to regulate political conflict, "politics became a zero-sum game in which the winner reaped massive rewards and the losers often paid with their lives" (Watts 2018, 9). Quite obviously, no one who reaches power in that type of system will be eager to willingly give it up.

Venezuela's economic collapse, I argue, is the result of a similar descent into destructive political conflict. This is not to minimize the effect of mistaken economic policies, corruption, and mismanagement, all of which play important roles in the story I tell in these pages. Yet even corrupt and inept leaders rarely launch a campaign to exterminate the geese that lays the golden eggs. In contrast, I argue that a large part of Venezuela's spectacular economic implosion can be traced to the severing of its financial and trade linkages with the world economy, a severing that is itself the result of actions and strategies adopted by its political actors in their fight for power.

Modern societies display an impressive variety of mechanisms for mediating political conflict. At one extreme we find democracies in which the sphere of political competition is clearly delimited and settled through competitive elections and separation of powers; at the other extreme we have autocracies in which political competition is severely restricted and authority is highly concentrated. When the institutions that manage conflict in the former begin to break down, but the concentrated authority of the latter has yet to develop, we find ourselves in spaces of political conflict like those of Cicero's Rome, where the stakes are high and so is the power of political contenders. It is this fight for absolute power among forces that cannot both prevail, yet can both cause substantial harm, that has the potential for bringing down an economy. Where absolute power corrupts, contested absolute power destroys.

Venezuela is an example of what happens when institutions fail to effectively mediate political conflict. At the root of the country's economic collapse, I argue, was a set of reforms initiated in the late 1990s that considerably strengthened the power of the winners of the political contest. Political scientists have long known that raising the stakes of power creates incentives for politicians to take actions that ultimately threaten democratic stability. I argue that they also create incentives for them to target the economy in their fight for power, thus undermining economic stability. As politicians descend into a no-holds-barred conflict for absolute power, they become increasingly likely to appeal to scorched earth strategies that turn the economy into a political battlefield.

Venezuela's spiral into scorched earth political conflict took place when its high-stakes political system proved unable to manage the large negative external shock brought about by the decline by more than two-thirds of oil prices that began in 2014. That system of political competition could survive only as long as high oil revenues allowed political actors to be responsive to both the needs of the electorate and those of the groups whose support they needed to protect their control over the spoils of power. When oil revenues were no longer there, contending forces shifted to scorched earth tactics, opting for strategies that improved their prospects of reaching or holding on to power, even at the cost of damaging the economy and sacrificing popular support.

Venezuela's descent into economic chaos is a result neither of the incompetence of those who managed its economy, as alleged by their right-wing critics, nor of their struggle to redirect oil wealth to their constituents, as claimed by their left-wing supporters. After managing to stay in power for more than a decade, weathering all types of political storms and systematically outwitting the country's opposition, Nicolás Maduro is not the best candidate for the charge of being incompetent or foolish. Class conflict perspectives, on the other hand, are particularly problematic for understanding the genesis of a collapse in which both capitalists and workers end up suffering large losses. Instead, I argue, Venezuela's collapse is an example of how the struggle for power between competing elites can cause economic destruction. Politically induced economic collapses occur not because politicians misunderstand the economy but because they understand all too well how to manipulate it to enhance their chances of attaining or holding on to power.

—In his remarkable work exposing the suppression of the role of Africans in historical accounts of the Haitian Revolution, the Haitian American anthropologist Michel-Rolph Trouillot (2015, 140) reminds us that "the inability to step out of history in order to write it or rewrite it applies to all actors and narrators." It is a warning that we all too often ignore at our own peril. Nowhere does it ring more relevant than in writing and thinking about conflicts in which we ourselves take part.

Friends who remember my father from the 1950s recall a quick thinker and fiery orator whom many saw as a possible future leader of the Venezuelan left. I remember a very different man. My memory has held on to images of him at his study poring over books and statistics into the night; or sitting at the dinner table with family in conversations that would last for hours and range over every conceivable topic, from nineteenth-century Venezuelan caudillos to the best way to make Margaritan fish stew. It also brings me recollections of his deep-seated concept of personal loyalty and the way in which he would call up friends and colleagues to rally help for his friend Carlos Andrés Pérez, the two-time Venezuelan president for whom he served as planning minister and who was impeached on trumped-up allegations of wrongdoing that brought out the worst in the country's political class.

Much like my father, I have never felt totally at home in academia, politics, or policy making. Rather, the more time I spend in one of them, the more I feel the urge to go back to one of the others. To a great extent that accounts for an eclectic professional career that has seen me go back and forth from US campuses to the Venezuelan public sector and to international organisms, with an additional stint in financial markets. Having done so has its benefits and its drawbacks. On the plus side is having lived through many of the events chronicled in this book and having directly observed some of the country's key political actors take some of the decisions that I discuss in the following pages. On the minus side is the difficulty of detaching myself enough from the object of my study to have any claim at impartiality.

—The first time I decided to take one of these jumps was in 2000, just two years after I had earned my PhD at Harvard and joined the faculty of the University of Maryland at College Park as an assistant professor in the economics department. During a trip to give a talk in Caracas, I got a call from a friend close to the new president of the National Assembly, Venezuela's unicameral legislature. The body needed to appoint someone to head Venezuela's Congressional Budget Office and had encountered a problem. The institution's bylaws specified that the director of the office had to be appointed with a two-thirds majority of the National Assembly, and the government coalition had fallen short of that supermajority in the 2000 parliamentary election. The two-thirds rule had been a precondition of the Inter-American Development Bank when it approved a loan to fund its operation in 1997. That meant that the government needed a compromise candidate whom the opposition would also agree to, and they thought I could be that person.

My wife, María Eugenia, and I had a long talk about the decision in the living room of our Maryland home as soon as I got back from my trip. The decision had huge uncertainty associated with it, but in the end there were two reasons to accept. One was the possibility of making a direct contribution to the well-being of my country in an institution that had been designed to operate with independence. The other was that, in a country where deep polarization between government supporters and opponents was already visible, my appointment by consensus to head an autonomous institution would give me the opportunity to show how it was possible to bridge the divide between both sides for the good of the country.

I served as director of Venezuela's Congressional Budget Office for three and a half years, during which time my office built a first-class team of economists who produced in-depth analyses of the economic and budget impact of proposed legislation and published numerous reports on the country's economy and reform proposals. However, our technical autonomy and independence would put us on a collision course with the country's government. Many in the government were incensed when they realized that our reports could and often would be critical of proposed government legislation.

I recall one day receiving a call from the office of the Social Development Commission to the National Assembly. The president of the commission, I was told, wanted to meet with me to discuss a report that my office had submitted on the commission's proposal for a reform of the country's social security law. Our report had shown that the project's attempt to maintain a pay-as-you-go system without adjusting the contribution rates or retirement age would lead to the accumulation of an unsustainable deficit, which would ultimately have to be assumed by future taxpayers (the need to pay for the commitments of this pension system ended up being one of the drivers of the country's later hyperinflation).

The commission's president was a young rising star within the government party who had led the organization of trade union movements in support of Hugo Chávez's campaign. He had convened all the legislators of the government party in the commission to the meeting. When I walked in, I found him leafing through a copy of our report. He asked me to sit and told me that he was concerned about the report's potential repercussions. The actuarial analysis that we presented would be used by the opposition to attack the law project, he said. I should consider withdrawing the section dealing with economic and financial sustainability from the report.

Taken aback, I answered that I could not do what he was asking for two simple reasons. First, he had given me no substantive reasons that would lead me to change any of the conclusions in the report. Second, I respected the autonomy of my team's economists to carry out their analysis independently and could not order them to change their results based on political considerations. Nevertheless, I invited him and the other legislators in the meeting to join our team for a technical discussion of the report and promised that if arguments came to light that led us to reconsider our results, we would of course do so.

Neither the commission president nor any of the other legislators heeded that invitation, but I learned several weeks later that he had proposed to the party leadership that I be fired from my position. However, the same two-thirds rule with which I had been elected also applied to my removal from office, and the government did not have the two-thirds majority necessary for my removal. The government then tried to restrict the disbursement of the funds necessary for the operation of our office but found that its control of these funds was limited precisely because they came from a loan granted by the Inter-American Development Bank.

However, I didn't just manage to incense leaders of the government. It was in early 2003 when I received some calls from opposition lawmakers who had supported our office in the midst of the conflict with the government party and who were puzzled at a report that we had just issued concluding that the 2002 to 2003 general strike called by the opposition had generated output losses for the economy of approximately 9% of gross domestic product (GDP). In fact, Chávez himself had cited the report to assail the opposition for the harm that it was causing to the economy. My response was that our report had not engaged in any normative assessment of whether the strike was justified but that as part of our monitoring of the economy, it was fundamental to try to assess the effect of factors that had large impacts on it, and this was one of them.

Despite their discontent at this publication, opposition legislators were all in all much more respectful of our office's autonomy and sided with us when the government tried to close us down. In March 2004, the government majority in the National Assembly voted to oust me, after having used their simple majority to change the two-thirds majority rule for the hiring and firing of the office's director to a simple majority. I argued that such a change could not be retroactive and won the case in court, but the government ultimately appealed the case to the Supreme Court, which it controlled and which of course ruled in its favor.

Those three and a half years gave me a crash course in Venezuelan politics. They also allowed me to meet and interact on a daily basis with some of the figures on both the government and opposition sides who would play determinant roles in the next two decades of Venezuela's history. Some of them would later rise to high-level positions and ultimately would be responsible for many of the policy decisions that I discuss in this book. One of them was the commission president and former union organizer who tried to get my office to withdraw its assessment of the social security law. His name is Nicolás Maduro.

—In September 2011, I took my first job in the private sector. Earlier that year, I had been approached by two economists who had been tapped by Bank of America (BofA) to lead a group of emerging markets researchers. Venezuelan debt had become a hot topic given the large levels of bond issuance carried out by Chávez, and they were looking for an economist with expertise in Venezuelan and other Latin American economies.

After coming back from my job at the National Assembly, I had returned to academia, joining the economics faculty at Wesleyan University in Connecticut. I was happy to go back into academic research and was full of ideas inspired by my experience in Venezuela. Together with colleagues at Berkeley and IESA, I started thinking about ways in which we could evaluate the effect of the social policies launched by Chávez, as well as the instruments for social control that had been developed by his government (Rodríguez 2008; Ortega and Rodríguez 2008; Hsieh et al. 2011). I was also puzzled by Venezuela's poor economic performance compared to the rest of the region even before Chávez reached office and teamed up with Ricardo Hausmann, a longtime friend and mentor, to try to understand that puzzle (Hausmann and Rodríguez 2014). Some years later, I moved to the Human Development Report Office at the United Nations Development Programme, where I led the research team of the organization's flagship publication for three years.

The idea of moving to the private sector was intriguing. I had always seen myself as someone devoted to public service in way or another—either by implementing public policies directly or by producing socially valuable research. On the other hand, I felt that understanding financial markets was fundamental to running economic policy and that the experience I could gain in a job like this would be invaluable. In the end, it seemed to me that I could learn much from changing tracks and viewing my country from a perspective different from the one that I was used to, so I took the leap.

In fact, the job was surprisingly similar to an academic job. I spent most of my time analyzing data, estimating models, and writing research notes. The research was much more focused on events with potential market impact, and thus the time span for writing was much shorter: you couldn't afford the luxury that you have in academia of spending three years writing a research paper. Surely this meant different standards of evidence, but it also meant greater and different analytical challenges.

Analysts are evaluated by their predictions. Macroeconomic analysts are expected to maintain and publish updated forecasts of all relevant economic data releases in their countries of coverage; it is not unusual for analysts to be ranked according to the average accuracy of their forecasts. In academia, your writing is judged by the standards that the scientific community sets. In finance, your analysis is judged by its ability to help you make the correct calls.

Just over a year after I joined BofA, Venezuela held its 2012 presidential elections. This was a particularly important election for markets: were Chávez to lose his reelection bid, Venezuela's economic model could change dramatically. Henrique Capriles, the challenger, was running on a platform of economic openness and liberalization that would have been cheered by markets. Venezuelan bonds began to rally whenever news came out suggesting that Capriles could win.

One of my first tasks was to take a serious look at the likely outcome of this election. At first sight, the idea that Chávez could lose seemed counterintuitive to me: the economy was growing strongly, and I knew that incumbents rarely lose elections in Latin America. I also had good reasons to be cautious: I remembered the overoptimism of the opposition in previous elections that it had ended up losing to Chávez.

Polling data was all over the place: some pollsters were predicting a very tight race, some were even calling a Capriles win, while others were seeing Chávez ahead by a comfortable margin. The first thing I did was build a database of the historical predictions of all Venezuelan polling companies and measured the average forecast error of each one. I then used those errors to construct a bias-corrected polling aggregate. The results, which I published in a research report two weeks ahead of the election, indicated that Chávez would win by 12.6 percentage points. In the end he won by 10.7 points, making my forecast the most accurate among my competitors, most of whom had said the election was too close to call, and some of whom had predicted a Capriles win.

Forecasting forces you to have a particular type of discipline. One thing that I found during my time in finance is that market analysts are much more likely than academics to change their minds. Once an academic has been identified with a theory, they will go to great lengths to prove that theory right. But if you're a forecaster and you find reason to believe that you were wrong in what you told your clients, you'll do everything possible to try to change your call before events prove you wrong. It is much better to change your call the day before an event and to get it right belatedly than to stick to it and have everyone remember you were wrong.

But in the polarized world of Venezuelan politics, it was sometimes hard to explain this to my friends and colleagues. We all wanted Capriles to win, so why was I saying that Chávez would prevail? Did that mean I was on the government's side? One commentator even hatched a far-fetched conspiracy theory about why I was making this forecast. BofA was in dire straits after the 2008 financial crisis and had found a way to make a quick buck: convince the market that Chávez would win, force a sell-off in Venezuela bonds, and buy them all back at cheap prices to make a killing after the opposition won (Runrun.es 2012).

In the end, one makes an effort to remain unfazed by this type of critique. But what I began to see at the time was that making systematic, unbiased forecasts of the Venezuelan economy was going to be a thorny road. In the end, many of us have a hard time distinguishing between what we want to happen and what we expect to happen, and it is not uncommon for people to lash out against someone who tells them something different from what they want to hear.

The American journalist Sydney Harris (1986, 7) once wrote that "we believe what we want to believe, what we like to believe, what suits our prejudices and fuels our passions." Yet the more strongly people want to hold these beliefs, the more difficult it is to provide them with the unbiased and objective analysis that they need to rely on if they want to change reality.

—Lake Valencia in northern Venezuela is home to one of the region's worst environmental disasters. Poorly designed water management systems have caused rising water levels, forcing twelve thousand families to lose their homes; the rest live in dwellings that are continuously inundated when sewer systems overflow during rainy season. Residents suffer from endemic skin diseases and respiratory infections and complain that a constant stench permeates the floors and walls of their homes regardless of how often they wash them. Many families could have resettled if the government had complied with a 2007 Venezuelan Supreme Court decision to compensate and relocate residents. Instead of seeking a structural solution, the government built an overpriced containment wall that continuously overflows.

I visited Lake Valencia as policy director for the presidential campaign of Henri Falcón, a popular former governor who tried unsuccessfully to unseat Maduro in the 2018 presidential election. Just a few months earlier, I had left Wall Street to work in Falcón's campaign, convinced that the 2018 election was the best opportunity that the country had yet had to change its course and put an end to Chávez's and Maduro's disastrous socialist experiment. I accepted Falcón's invitation to coordinate a team of specialists tasked with creating a road map for Venezuela to construct a modern inclusive democracy and rebuild the country's institutions. The results and recommendations of our work are summarized in the candidate's 2018 platform, which we called, in honor of the Hungarian economist Karl Polanyi's treatise on the formation of market institutions, "the Great Transformation" (Falcón 2018).

Regrettably, on election day, more than half of voters stayed home, permitting Maduro to coast to another six-year term in office. A postelection survey found that 62% of voters who saw themselves as pro-opposition or nonaligned—but only 10% of pro-government voters—abstained in the election. When they voted, opposition and nonaligned voters, who make up 78% of the electorate, were three times more likely to vote for Falcón than for Maduro (Datanálisis 2018). Had turnout rates been the same across different political groups, Falcón would have easily won.

Most opposition and nonaligned voters stayed home because Venezuela's mainstream opposition parties called for an electoral boycott. Supporters of the boycott argued that participating in the elections was tantamount to legitimizing them. The argument made little sense to me. Did Chileans legitimize Pinochet's dictatorship by voting to oust him in the 1988 plebiscite? In politics, however, sometimes noise speaks louder than logic. As a result, a president who was reviled by three-quarters of the electorate effortlessly renewed his lease on power when most of the people who opposed him decided to stay home on election day.

The decision to boycott the election, despite the significant amount of empirical evidence indicating that boycotts are rarely successful and often lead opposition movements to lose key spaces of power (Frankel 2010; Gordji, Askari, and Abdi 2018), would usher in a new period of radicalization of the Venezuelan opposition's political strategy. Buoyed by the strong support of hawks at the helm of foreign policy in the Trump administration, Venezuela's opposition began lobbying for draconian sanctions to be imposed on the Venezuelan economy. In January 2019, shortly after his election as president of the opposition-controlled National Assembly, the opposition legislator Juan Guaidó announced that because of the illegitimacy of Maduro's 2018 reelection, he was assuming the position of interim president. The United States, with the support of Europe and several Latin American countries, immediately recognized the Guaidó government, handing it control of the country's offshore assets.

In an op-ed published in February 2019 in the *New York Times*, the Columbia economist Jeffrey Sachs (my dissertation advisor at Harvard in the 1990s) and I argued that this approach entailed extraordinary risks and could end up helping Maduro consolidate political control (Rodríguez and Sachs 2019b). By cutting off the country's access to oil resources, we warned, the United States was risking "an economic and humanitarian catastrophe of a dimension never seen in our hemisphere." We urged both sides to find common ground in a negotiated solution that would involve joint management of oil funds under the supervision of the United Nations and handing over control of key economic and social policy decisions to an interim government of experts.

Our calls were ignored as the United States and the opposition forged ahead with the "maximum pressure" strategy that they believed would drive Maduro from power in days. This overestimation of the capacity of the United States to provoke regime change proved to be an egregious miscalculation—one that, sadly, is all too common in the history of US foreign policy. The conviction that the United States would drive Maduro from power through economic pressure also began to reshape political forces in the country. Opposition politicians became more adept at lobbying Washington than at doing the hard work of mobilizing voters to oppose Maduro. Corruption scandals involving the management of offshore assets by the interim government began to surface, feeding into a growing disenchantment among Venezuelans with the opposition leadership. The US government threw its support behind hard-liners more interested in wresting power from Maduro than addressing Venezuela's humanitarian crisis. Doing so only helped convince many Venezuelans that a change in government would simply trade an authoritarian left-wing government for a right-wing one.

The strategy ended in an unmitigated disaster. The military leadership dug in its heels in support of Maduro, while China and Russia lent him crucial support. As Dorothy Kronick noted in February 2019, at the height of enthusiasm for sanctions, "Nicolás Maduro has a knack for surviving prophecies of his demise." The prolonged economic and humanitarian crisis further demobilized civil society, as Venezuelans struggling to cope with the crisis began to disengage from politics. An estimated seven million Venezuelans—nearly one-fourth of the population—left the country in the largest documented migration exodus in the history of the western hemisphere. Those who remained began to see the opposition leadership as increasingly disconnected from people's main problems. When in November 2021 the mainstream opposition coalition reversed its four-year strategy of electoral boycotts and fielded candidates in mayoral and gubernatorial elections, they managed to receive only two-fifths of votes cast against the government. One year later, the opposition-controlled National Assembly elected in 2015 put an end to Guaidó's interim government in a heated and acrimonious debate that evidenced its effective splintering.

In the 2024 presidential elections, the main opposition coalition made a 180-degree turn in strategy and decided to challenge Maduro at the ballot box. This decision occurred even though electoral rules are indisputably much more biased in favor of the government than they were six years previously. That the return to an electoral path energized millions of voters who want to put an end to the Maduro government is the best demonstration that it should never have been abandoned. Yet during the intervening six years, Venezuela's economy spiraled into disaster, nearly six million Venezuelans left the country, political polarization deepened, and Maduro was able to further consolidate his control over the country's institutions, making the prospects for a peaceful and democratic change appear even more distant.

The following pages contain the sum of my efforts to understand what happened in Venezuela during this period. How did a strong and united opposition movement that was able to capture a supermajority of the country's legislature in 2015 implode over the following years? Why did some key actors in that coalition decide that it made sense to pursue strategies—such as lobbying for economic sanctions or advocating for a US invasion—that were highly unpopular among Venezuelans and that would only contribute to deepening the country's crisis and sowing distrust among voters? Why did Maduro ignore calls for a more rational macroeconomic policy that would have helped reduce the depth of the economic contraction? Why did the opposition leadership discard calls for negotiation when it had the full support of the international community, unrealistically demanding that Maduro step down as a precondition of any deal, and only accept the need to negotiate after Maduro had consolidated his hold on power? How did these key strategic decisions by both government and opposition actors contribute to the deepening of the country's economic and humanitarian catastrophe?

In the following pages, I argue that Venezuela's economic collapse was driven by the decision of political actors from both the government and the opposition to adopt political strategies in their struggle for power that generated severe negative externalities on the economy. Doing so made sense strategically because the institutions that constrained executive authority had been systematically dismantled more than a decade earlier, raising the stakes of power and turning political competition into a winner-take-all contest. My argument suggests that a necessary condition for rebuilding the country's economy is to seek to forge agreements on the creation of institutions that limit the capacity of political conflict to spill over into the economic arena and cause damage to the livelihoods of Venezuelans.

My hope is that the ideas in this book will serve Venezuelans who are trying to chart a way out of the country's current cycle of authoritarianism and stagnation. Venezuela's story can also serve as a cautionary tale that shows what happens when societies lose their ability to manage conflict. I argue that among the key risk factors for falling into politically induced growth collapses are high levels of political polarization and the prior dismantling of constraints on executive power. Yet it is not uncommon to hear even well-intentioned calls for reducing the power of the judiciary or eliminating supermajority requirements in many modern democracies that are also highly polarized. If you are among those who think that making the presidency more powerful is good for democracy, this book invites you to reconsider. There was a time when many Venezuelans thought the same.

—Stephen Marglin, whom I was fortunate to learn from at Harvard in the 1990s, used to say that one of the problems of doing economics is that we are constantly shooting at a moving target. That phrase has come to my mind time and time again while working on this book. Some nights I went to bed wishing that the country would just stay still long enough so that I wouldn't have to rewrite the chapter I had just finished, only to wake up the next morning to the realization that I would not be so lucky.

Many people have helped me make sense of this shifting reality through the years. I began writing this book when I was still working in financial markets in 2018. Through subsequent years the work evolved and morphed as I moved back to academia while keeping a foot in the policy world. Almost every other page of this book finds its inspiration in a conversation that I had with colleagues in one of those worlds. While a list like this is sure to miss some names, some of those that come to mind include Alberto Ades, Dany Bahar, Esfandyar Batmanghelidj, Marcos Buscaglia, Felipe Cala, Michael Coppedge, Javier Corrales, Gorge DiMartino, Pablo Druck, Tom Farer, Michael Galant, Nicolás Idrobo, Vitor Gaspar, Joy Gordon, Ilene Grabel, José Guerra, Ricardo Hausmann, Chang-Tai Hsieh, Patrick Imam, Claudio Irigoyen, Lakshmi Iyer, Daniel Kurtz-Phelan, Luis Vicente León, George Lopez, Luis Felipe López-Calva, Alex Main, Scott Mainwaring, Paolo Mauro, Edward Miguel, Keith Mines, Francisco Monaldi, Frank Muci, Singumbe Muyeba, William Neuman, José Antonio Ocampo, Luis Oliveros, Daniel Ortega, Michael Penfold, Anibal Pérez-Liñán, Geoff Ramsey, Sanjay Reddy, Jorge Alejandro Rodríguez, Gustavo Rojas-Matute, José Luis Saboín, Victor Sierra, Rachel Sigman, Kait Sims, Timothy Sisk, Francisco Toro, Alberto Unanue, Alejandro Velasco, Mark Weisbrot, and Eduardo Zambrano.

A small group of colleagues deserve special mention because this book would be unrecognizable without them. As my advisor at Harvard, Jeffrey Sachs was the first person to encourage me to try to understand Venezuelan macroeconomics within the framework of modern growth theory. Alberto Alesina, Stephen Marglin, and Dani Rodrik taught me that often the best insights about the determinants of economic outcomes come from looking at the motivations of the political actors that influence them. Dorothy Kronick, David Smilde, and Eduardo Zambrano provided a sounding board for many ideas and gave me extensive comments on prior drafts of the book, as did three anonymous referees.

I am especially grateful for the support of the institutions that allowed me to devote a significant part of the past five years to writing this book. These include Torino Economics, Oil for Venezuela, Tulane University's Stone Center for Latin American Studies, the University of Notre Dame's Kellogg Institute of International Studies, the Council on Foreign Relations, the International Monetary Fund's (IMF's) Fiscal Affairs Department, and my current home institution, the University of Denver's Josef Korbel School of International Studies. I was particularly fortunate to count on the help of a fabulous group of junior colleagues, students, and assistants that included Jacques Bentata, Giancarlo Bravo, Simón Call, Adolfo De Lima, Arnaldo Espinoza, Luisa García, Guillermo Guerrero, Pilar Navarro, Juan Vera, and Nicolle Yapur. Rachel Kindler, Steve Wrinn, Matthew Dowd, and Eli Bortz at the University of Notre Dame Press provided invaluable guidance on the editorial process, as did Sheila Berg on behalf of the press.

Yet if there is one person who has her stamp on every line of this book, it is my love and lifetime companion, María Eugenia. Even from the life of economic security that our professional careers have afforded us, it has been indescribably hard to watch the country in which we met and fell in love become that harrowing place where a full stomach is a luxury and violence is ubiquitous. Yet it is also with and through her that I learned to see the warmth and hope that flows from the eyes and faces of even those Venezuelans who have endured the most difficult circumstances. It is that warmth and hope that makes me certain that there is a way back from the abyss that our country has found itself in. If this book can contribute to helping find that way, my work will be more than done.

PART I

The Political Economy of Economic Collapse

ONE

How Economies Self-Destruct

War can never be separated from political intercourse.
—Carl von Clausewitz, *On War*, 1832

OUTPUT COLLAPSES AND DEVELOPMENT ECONOMICS

There is an interesting contrast between medicine and development economics. Both are concerned with improving people's lives. Yet while much of the medical literature focuses on understanding how people become ill and how to treat these illnesses, the literature on economic development centers on how to make living standards rise. Medical practitioners publish in the *Journal of Infectious Diseases* or the *Journal of Clinical Oncology*; development economists publish in the *Journal of Development Economics* or the *Journal of Economic Growth*.

Surely one can argue that declines and improvements in health or living standards are simply two sides of the same coin. Yet the differences in emphasis are nonetheless striking. Do a Google Scholar search for "health," and you will get roughly the same number of hits as you will for "sickness" and "illness" combined. Do the same for "economic development" and "economic growth," and you will get twenty-six times more hits than for "economic underdevelopment," "economic stagnation," and "economic collapse" put together. An archaeologist who sees these search results millennia into the future could well conclude that most people on earth today lived under enormous material prosperity, yet somehow managed to get sick a lot.

The canon of development economics contains a plethora of models designed for understanding how economies evolve to higher living standards. The question of what makes some economies wealthier than others is of course at the origin of classical political economy: Smith ([1776] 1982) argued that specialization and the division of labor allowed access to larger markets and thus held the key to prosperity. Rostow (1959, 1960) described development as an economy's evolution through stages that would ultimately lead to a "take-off into sustained growth" made possible by the shift from subsistence economies to a productive structure capable of generating and reinvesting surpluses. The neoclassical growth model popularized in the 1960s views economies as converging to their steady-state levels of income, accumulating capital and gradually pushing down the rate of return as diminishing returns to capital set in (Ramsey 1928; Solow 1956; Swann 1956; Cass 1965; Koopmans 1965). Endogenous growth theories argue that countries can sustain high rates of growth despite diminishing returns to capital because innovation and a growing diversity of products can generate countervailing increases in the rate of technological growth (Romer 1986; Lucas 1988). More recent debates have focused on the role that trade, institutions, and geography play in explaining differences in living standards (Acemoglu, Johnson, and Robinson 2001; Rodrik 2004; Sachs 2005, 2020; Acemoglu and Robinson 2012, 2019; DeLong 2022; Galor 2022; Koyama and Rubin 2022).

In contrast, the same canon is silent on the causes of growth collapses. At first sight, this seems surprising. If we consider our well-developed theories of how societies learn to be prosperous, the least one would expect is that we would also know how and why societies can lose that prosperity. Yet explaining long secular declines in per capita incomes has its own complexities. It is one thing to come up with a story of how people learn ideas about how to do things better; it is quite another to tell a story of how they forget them. Even growth theories that put the development of institutions at their center are hard pressed to explain why societies that were able to build institutions conducive to progress can end up dismantling them.

Macroeconomics does of course have well-laid-out theories of recessions, or short- to medium-lived negative fluctuations in income along the business cycle. Yet there are few attempts to account for more sustained or permanent declines in per capita income. One attempt to do so in the context of the neoclassical growth model was provided by Jeffrey Sachs and me when we argued in a 1999 paper that exhaustible natural resources can lead some economies to overshoot their steady-state level of income and converge to it from above (Rodríguez and Sachs 1999). Natural resource–abundant economies can thus display absolute declines in living standards in the transition to their steady state.[1] Multiple equilibria models of development can also account for economic collapses as transitions from a high-income-level to a low-income-level steady state (Murphy, Shleifer, and Vishny 1989; Boldrin 1990; Durlauf 1993). In these models, spillovers between firms and industries generate nonconvexities in the aggregate production function that make economic actors' decisions to invest or produce dependent on the decision of other actors. For example, producers may be willing to incur the costs of adopting more expensive technologies if they expect there to be a sufficiently large market for their products, which may depend on the decision by other producers to also adopt advanced technologies. In this view, development is a coordination problem writ large. Sudden changes in the expectations of actors regarding the actions of other actors in the economy (e.g., confidence crises) can make the jump to a low-investment equilibrium a self-fulfilling prophecy, driving a collapse in income per capita.

Unfortunately, testing poverty trap models of development is not easy. By definition, multiple equilibria exist when different outcomes are associated with the same parameters—that is, when two countries that are otherwise undistinguishable at the outset end up following two very different development trajectories. This feature makes the results of conventional econometric tests of comparative statistics inapplicable. Some empirical work has pointed to the bimodal distribution of per capita income across countries as evidence of multiplicity of equilibria (Quah 1996; Bloom, Canning, and Sevilla 2003; Azariadis and Stachurski 2004), but this could reflect either multiple steady states or bimodality in omitted determinants of growth. Some authors have pointed to the slow growth of some poor countries as countering the prediction of convergence that arises from the neoclassical model (Sachs et al. 2004), yet there is little evidence that this is caused by a savings-induced poverty trap since these countries do not have systematically low savings rates (Kraay and Raddatz 2005; Easterly 2006). Production function estimates from industrial survey data do not display a higher degree of increasing returns during growth accelerations and growth transitions, as would be implied by theories of poverty traps arising from increasing returns in manufacturing (Rodríguez 2008). Even very large exogenous shocks to the terms of trade are not associated with long-term increases in per capita income, in contrast to the prediction of multiple equilibria models (Rodríguez and Shelton 2013).

Only a handful of empirical papers have examined the correlates of growth collapses. In developing countries, negative shocks to exports—through production, demand, or prices—are closely related to the incidence of collapses (Becker and Mauro 2006; Hausmann, Rodríguez, and Wagner 2006). Other drivers include high dependence on primary exports, mismanagement of natural resource rents, debt crises, weak conflict management institutions, political transitions, the export sector's inability to rapidly adapt, and location (Rodrik 1999; Cerra and Saxena 2008; Reddy and Minoiu 2009; IMF 2018; Meneses and Saboin 2021; Splinter and Klomp 2021). One common finding is that there is a great incidence of collapses during armed conflict and after natural disasters. This is unsurprising, as wars and natural disasters both directly destroy the economy's productive infrastructure.

Episodes such as that of Venezuela in the period covered in this book, where massive economic collapses occur in the absence of armed conflict, natural disasters, or a major external shock, are relatively rare.[2] In chapter 2, I argue that Venezuela's collapse was driven to a large extent by the decline in output from its main export industry, yet this only pushes back the question to that of understanding the causes of the loss in oil production. Why would a country sitting on what by some accounts are the world's largest oil reserves suddenly decide to kill the goose that laid the golden eggs?

Developing an explanation for collapses that are not driven by conflict, natural disasters, or external shocks requires understanding why actors "unlearn" (or stop taking advantage of) modes of cooperation and institutional arrangements that help sustain higher living standards. The thesis developed in this book builds on a crucial insight of the Prussian general and military strategist Carl von Clausewitz (1832), which serves as the epigraph to this chapter: war and politics are at their essence very similar phenomena. Both entail the deployment of resources in the struggle to attain power. In both, the sides to the conflict can find it in their interest to destroy the economy's means of production as part of their attempt to prevail.

THE BIGGEST PEACETIME ECONOMIC COLLAPSE IN MODERN HISTORY

Between 2012 and 2020, Venezuela's per capita income fell by 71.5%—the equivalent of more than three Great Depressions. The contraction is also the largest observed in Latin America and the fifth largest observed in the world since 1950. When we only consider collapses observed during peacetime, Venezuela's is the largest worldwide in this period. It is also larger than any pre-1950 episode of collapse in per capita output documented in the historical database constructed by Bolt and van Zaden (2020), as well as during Venezuela's own violent nineteenth century according to estimates produced by Baptista (2011).

It is not unusual to see Venezuela's economic collapse explained away as the result of poor policies, mismanagement, or corruption (Abuelafia and Saboin 2020; Shabani 2020; Cheatham et al. 2021; Álvarez et al. 2022). I argue that the story is much more complex. While Venezuelan governments took numerous poor policy choices prior to and after the start of the decline in per capita income, it is hard to attribute all the country's growth collapse to them. Venezuela's mixture of state dirigisme, large relative price distortions, procyclical macroeconomic policies, failure to save the earnings from its commodity boom, and even its rampant corruption are not all that different from that seen in many other developing countries or even in Venezuela's own past. While such policies often lead to substantial productivity losses and typically end in large currency and fiscal crises, as originally described by Dornbusch and Edwards (1992), the magnitude and timing of the decline of Venezuela's per capita income suggest we need to look beyond just poor policies to explain the largest peacetime collapse in modern history.

There is nevertheless a sense in which Venezuela's collapse is not all that hard to understand. Between 2012 and 2020, Venezuela's oil exports declined by 93%. Given that oil revenues accounted for more than 95% of export revenues and around half of fiscal revenues before the collapse, it is not surprising that an external shock of this magnitude would drive the economy into a tailspin. In fact, most research on Venezuelan economic growth prior to the post-2012 collapse had emphasized how its high dependence on and near-complete specialization in oil exports made its economic performance highly dependent on oil market conditions (Rodríguez and Sachs 1999; Hausmann and Rigobón 2011; Hausmann and Rodríguez 2014). Once we know that oil revenues virtually evaporated during the 2010s, the magnitude of the country's economic contraction does not appear that anomalous.

However, acknowledging that the collapse in oil exports largely drove the decline in per capita income only serves to push the question back to one of understanding why oil exports collapsed.[3] In the following pages, I argue that the severing of the oil industry's commercial and financial ties with the rest of the world that began around 2017 had a significant impact on the country's capacity to take advantage of its abundant oil endowment. And as Venezuela's political crisis deepened, key internal and external political actors chose to target the government's access to financial and goods markets in an effort to block its ability to spend and weaken its hold on power. Venezuela's oil industry would become caught in that political cross fire, ultimately becoming the target of some of the strictest financial and trade sanctions that the United States has applied on any country.

I also argue that there is very strong evidence that sanctions and the associated toxification of dealings with the state-owned oil company were a key driving factor of the decline in Venezuelan oil production. The precipitous fall in oil production after 2016 made it impossible for Venezuela's economy to reap the benefits of the recovery in oil markets that occurred in subsequent years. In this sense, Venezuela's economic collapse is really a combination of two crises. Between 2012 and 2016, the country underwent a large recession like those that typically accompany the fiscal and balance of payments adjustments needed to correct the internal and external disequilibria caused by prolonged episodes of macroeconomic populism. From 2017 on, Venezuela was denied the recovery that it would have normally enjoyed with improving terms of trade because oil production had gone into freefall, partly as a result of the worsening political conflict.

Targeting the economy for political ends was not just something that the opposition and its allies did. In chapters 5 and 6, I document how President Maduro's economic policy decisions became increasingly subordinated to political considerations as Chavismo's ability to hold on to power through elections weakened. For example, in November 2013—one month prior to an election that was widely viewed as a referendum on his government—Maduro went on national television to accuse Daka, one of the country's largest electronics retailers, of price gouging. Maduro claimed that the retailer was selling consumers products at grossly inflated prices while at the same time using subsidized government-provided dollars to import them. He then ordered the military to organize the sale of Daka's inventory to consumers at reduced prices. The event, which would become known as the Dakazo, would provide Maduro with a large boost in public approval and allow his party to coast to victory in that year's municipal elections, at the cost of severely weakening property rights and contributing to causing a significant increase in scarcity in subsequent years.

WHEN CONFLICT DESTROYS

Sanctions and the Dakazo, I argue, are two sides of the same coin. They both reflect a strategic decision by political actors to adopt strategies in their struggle for power that generate severe negative economic externalities on society. I contend that to understand why countries like Venezuela suffer long, protracted economic crises, we need to understand how and when politicians find it in their interest to undertake actions that damage the economy.

That they will do so is not necessarily a given. Most policy makers in advanced democracies have a good reason not to wreck their economies: the fear that voters will punish them if they do so. The evidence shows that voters typically reward politicians who deliver good economic performance, building an incentive for policy makers to try to run their economy well (Kramer 1971; Arcelus and Meltzer 1975; Peltzman 1988;

Erikson 1990). Nevertheless, there are many cases in which politicians may find it in their interest to pursue policies that differ from the optimal or efficient ones, and an extensive literature in the fields of public choice and political economy has dealt with establishing the conditions under which we are likely to see them do so (Drazen 2000; Persson and Tabellini 2002).

One reason policy makers may have to harm the economy is as part of a strategy to confuse voters as to their effectiveness as public sector managers. Inflationary financing is a prime example: a well-established literature has argued that governments have an incentive to appeal to inflationary financing prior to elections to temporarily raise economic growth and convince voters that they can deliver more public goods without raising taxes (Rogoff and Siebert 1988). In chapter 7, I argue that these incentives become even stronger when the stakes of power are greater and elections become more frequent, as they did—in part as an unintended consequence of the 1999 Constitution's staggered scheduling of elections—during Nicolás Maduro's first term in office. When Maduro faced increasingly high perceived costs of losing power *and* increasingly frequent elections, his incentives to appeal to policies delivering short-term benefits at the expense of long-term efficiency costs became greater.

Under certain conditions, opposition political movements can also choose political strategies that harm the economy in their fight to reach power. Iranian oil workers aligned with leftist opposition movements brought the country's oil production to a standstill in 1979, helping drive Reza Shah Pahlavi from power and ushering in the country's Islamic Revolution (Amanat 2017, chap. 13; Jafari 2013). South Africa's opposition African National Congress effectively lobbied for a boycott on South African exports and international sanctions against the Apartheid governments in the 1980s, imposing significant costs on the economy that appear to have played an important role in forcing a transition to a multiracial democracy (Manby 1992; Jones 2015). The blocking of appropriations bills by opposition legislators in the United States has led to ten government shutdowns and two debt downgrade decisions since 1980 (Congressional Research Service 2018, 2021; Fitch Ratings 2023).

Opposition movements can have an impact on the economy under at least two conditions. One is when they have a direct impact on domestic production. This can be because opposition forces have direct control over key factors of production, as in the case of Iranian oil workers, or because they control spaces of power that can affect economic conditions, as in the case of the US Congress in times of divided government. Another is when they interfere with the economy's capacity to access global markets. That is the case of South Africa as well as that of many other countries in which diaspora movements have successfully advocated for sanctions. Both conditions—opposition control over institutions that affect economic conditions and strong international support from key trading partners—were present in Venezuela after 2016.

When both the government and the opposition can affect the economy, there is the risk that they turn the economy into a political battlefield. I argue that political actors in these settings will be faced with the choice of whether to appeal to "scorched earth" political strategies—strategies that can damage the economy while increasing their chances of gaining power—or to instead exercise self-restraint and limit their actions to those that do not generate severe economic externalities. When one or more of the actors fighting over power decides to adopt scorched earth strategies, I argue, we see the phenomenon of economically destructive political conflict emerge.

In chapter 3, I present a theoretical model that allows us to specify the conditions under which we see actors adopt scorched earth strategies and economically destructive political conflict emerge. I show that the adoption of these strategies becomes an equilibrium when the stakes of power (i.e., the inequality in the distribution of the rewards from power between winners and losers) are sufficiently large. I also show that the economy's wealth endowment has a significant effect on the propensity of actors to adopt these strategies, with poorer economies being more likely to see economically destructive conflict emerge for given levels of stakes of power. Richer economies, in contrast, are likely to be able to sustain higher stakes of power without falling into economically destructive political conflict. This introduces the possibility that in a context of high prior stakes of power large negative external shocks such as the one seen by Venezuela between 2012 and 2016 can trigger the descent into destructive conflict.

The higher likelihood of economically destructive political conflict for countries that are poor or suffer from negative income shocks in my model echoes the results of the literature on the positive relation between income and democratization (Helliwell 1994; Barro 1996; Boix 2003; Gerring et al. 2005; Przeworski 2008; Acemoglu et al. 2019). Yet while many models in this literature highlight how increasing wealth changes the relative incentives of elites to accept democratization, the intuition behind my results is different. In my model, political groups must devote resources to preparing to respond to nondemocratic threats to their power. As society becomes wealthier, high levels of deterrence investment that were previously inaccessible now become affordable. The results are analogous to findings in the crime victimization literature showing that rates of crime against property are higher in poorer neighborhoods because the poor can spend less to protect their property, making them comparatively more attractive to potential thieves (Ayres and Levitt 1998; Vollaard and van Ours 2011; Kang 2014). Similarly, the governments of poor countries may be less able than rich ones to invest in defending their governments from violent attempts to overthrow them. The government of the United States, for example, is rich enough to pay for a national security apparatus that would make an attempt to overthrow it futile without significantly affecting its capacity to provide other public goods. The government of Haiti is not.

I use this model to argue that we can understand Venezuela's descent into economically destructive political conflict as a result of two key structural forces. One is the impact of major reforms to the country's constitutional framework adopted toward the turn of the twenty-first century that significantly increased executive authority. These changes went so far as to grant the president the authority to convene elections for an all-powerful constitutional convention with the authority to dissolve other branches of government, thus effectively erasing any effective separation of powers. The other one is the large negative terms of trade shock experienced in the mid-2010s, which made the Venezuelan economy poorer and thus unable to sustain a self-enforcing democratic equilibrium for these high stakes of power. Lower income levels forced political actors to choose between continuing to devote resources to courting voters or to invest them in catering to the powerful military selectorate.

As the government and opposition began to adopt scorched earth strategies, both became increasingly less responsive to the demands of voters. Despite the fact that opinion surveys showed overwhelming opposition to sanctions among Venezuelans (Atlantic Council 2021; Datanálisis 2021; Villarreal 2022), the opposition embraced US economic sanctions in the hope that economic pressure would force Maduro to abandon power. Opposition leaders, who had been granted control over the country's main overseas assets when US president Donald Trump recognized an interim government led by National Assembly president Juan Guaidó, became more adept at courting Washington for access to resources than at mobilizing voters or protesters in Venezuela. Maduro became more repressive, with his actions to quell dissent ultimately making his government the target of an international investigation for crimes against humanity by the prosecutor of the International Criminal Court (ICC 2021). Yet somewhat ironically, even as he appeared to abandon the idea of contesting power through free elections, Maduro's macroeconomic policies improved, with the government embracing spontaneous dollarization and exchange rate unification and loosening the price controls that had hobbled economic performance during his first years in office. These policy changes, together with adaptation to sanctions and an improvement in global oil markets, helped the country emerge from its eight-year contraction in 2021.

The story of Venezuela's collapse told in this book is the story of a conflict between competing elites that turned the country's economy into a political battlefield. In that sense, my argument is fundamentally different from stories of policy failure that focus on how misguided policies generate economic distortions that impair growth. The problem, I argue, is not that politicians misunderstand the economy. It is that they understand all too well how to manipulate the economy for political gain.

My emphasis on interelite conflict is also distinct from the emphasis on class conflict that underlies recent explanations for comparative economic performance. Acemoglu and Robinson (2012), for example, argue that development failures stem from the resistance of elites to the development of inclusive institutions in which political power rests with a broad coalition or plurality of groups, allowing large segments of the population to reap the gains from exchange and innovation. They contend that Venezuela's transition to democracy after 1958 did not translate into empowerment at the grassroots level and did not create a pluralistic distribution of power, leading the country to continue to languish under extractive institutions (459). They also claim that the lack of development of pluralistic institutions gave cause to Venezuelans to support Hugo Chávez in 2012, "most likely because they thought he alone would stand up to the established elites of Venezuela" (460; though see Kronick, Plunkett, and Rodríguez 2023), but that Chávez's authoritarianism impeded the emergence of the checks on executive authority that form part of truly pluralistic and inclusive institutions.

While Acemoglu and Robinson's story may have merits for explaining Venezuela's inability to grow strongly during the latter part of the twentieth century, a focus on class conflict is unhelpful if we want to understand why the country's economy lost nearly three-fourths of its size during the past decade. Venezuelan economic institutions did not become less inclusive during this period, nor were changes in Venezuelans' ability to participate in the benefits of economic exchange a key driving factor in the reduction in living standards over this period. On the contrary, the case has been made that economic institutions are somewhat more open now than they were a decade ago (Batmanghelidj and Rodríguez 2020; Bull and Rosales 2020). The bulk of the country's economic collapse is clearly a direct consequence of the precipitous decline in the country's exports of oil, a capital-intensive industry where production is constrained by access to export markets and the availability of imported inputs and finance. Venezuela's failure to adopt more inclusive institutions is unlikely to have had any effect on the productivity of its oil industry. The cause of the decline in Venezuela's oil exports lies not in class conflict but in inter-elite conflict over the control of the country's oil wealth.

Venezuela's growth collapse, I argue, is the consequence of a pitched battle between competing elites for control of the country's oil industry and the rents that it generates. Venezuela's fundamental economic institutions continue to be as extractive today as they were in the latter part of the twentieth century. Even with those extractive institutions, the country was able to maintain living standards near the upper end of the Latin American distribution of per capita national incomes up until the past decade through the distribution of those oil rents. It is the capacity to produce those rents that evaporated when political actors decided that destroying it made sense in their fight to prevail in a winner-take-all struggle for power.

CHOOSING YOUR BATTLES

This book is a study in positive political economy. As such, it strives to explain growth collapses as a result of the interaction of both political and economic forces. The conceptual framework developed in it is born out of the combination of two distinct approaches to thinking about political conflict. One comes from the political science literature on democratization, authoritarianism, and democratic backsliding. The other one comes from the economics literature on conflict, appropriation, and rent seeking.

Understanding the conditions under which governments will give up or accept constraints on their power has been central to political science since at least the times of Thomas Hobbes ([1651] 2017). Modern theories of democratization highlight the role played by the self-interest of political actors in determining the scope for political competition. One of the central results of this literature is the idea that constraints on executive power lower the costs of conceding defeat and thus make possible the transition to self-sustaining democratic institutions (Przeworski 1991; Weingast 1997; Fearon 2011; Mittal and Weingast 2013).

Classical economists understood that the command of resources was ultimately determined by political arrangements. "Civil government," wrote Adam Smith in 1776, "is, in reality, instituted for the defence of the rich against the poor, or of those who have some property against those who have none at all" (Smith [1776] 1982, 2:715). Engels and Marx ([1848] 2015, 15) famously referred to the executive of the state as "a committee for managing the common affairs of the whole bourgeoisie." The Virginia school of political economy investigated the conditions under which the state would become the center of distributive struggle and how this contest would affect the functioning of the economy (Buchanan 1968; Krueger 1974; Tullock 1980; Coate and Morris 1995). The literature on conflict and appropriation has studied the conditions under which groups competing for the control of resources invest in technologies that allow them to forcibly seize control of assets rather than engage in exchange with their holders (Collier 2000; Garfinkel and Skaperdas 2007; Grossman and Kim 2010).

My approach is born out of combining the insights from these two strands of literature. As in standard models of democratization, I argue that politicians must make a choice as to whether to abide by established rules of the game and accept the outcome of competition governed by existing institutions (which may of course be biased in favor of some groups of actors) or to fight for control of the state outside of those institutional constraints. In doing so, they must choose what political technologies to use. Electoral competition requires investments in catering to the electorate; nonelectoral competition requires vying for the support of those who control the means to forcibly seize power. Once politicians try to seize or maintain power by force, concerns with what voters think become second order. It is then that the incentives for adopting scorched earth strategies dominate and the risk of descending into economically destructive political conflict becomes paramount.

Understanding that politics can be at the root of growth collapses is of fundamental importance for charting a strategy for economic recovery in a country riven by destructive conflict. One of the key motivations for writing this book was my frustration on observing how much of the thinking on economic strategies for Venezuela was written as if the country was in an institutional vacuum, where the only relevant questions were about the optimality and sequencing of policies in a hypothetical political transition. If there is anything that the past three decades of Latin America's economic experience should teach us, it is that the building of effective political coalitions is fundamental for the sustainability of economic reforms aimed at fostering growth. This book thus strives to produce a politically nuanced vision of the constraints that hobble Venezuela's development that can serve to inform the design of strategies for politically and socially sustainable economic transformation.

A view of economic collapses as driven by political conflict has radically different implications from those in which economic failure is caused by policy-maker ignorance. If the policy and strategic choices that caused economic harm are the consequences of rational decisions by political actors who see these choices as advantageous in their struggle for power, then bringing the economy out of crisis will require transforming the incentives of political actors to adopt these strategies. I argue that among the fundamental determinants of this incentive structure for Venezuela are the high stakes of power embodied in the constitutional and institutional rules that govern political competition. If we want to help Venezuela's economy recover, we must focus on establishing conditions that permit the coexistence and cooperation of the factions that vie for control of political power. Otherwise, we are likely to see similar political and economic dynamics emerge even if those who currently control power are made to relinquish it.

Knowing that growth collapses can be driven by political incentives can be crucial not just for helping countries mired in economically destructive political conflict to chart a way out of it but also for understanding what the countries that today enjoy political and economic stability need to do to preserve it. While the idea that restraints on executive power are vital to democratic stability is accepted by most political scientists, what is less well understood is that they may also be central to economic stability. Arguments in favor of relaxing executive constraints in both developed and developing countries are frequently voiced by those who claim that doing so is needed to improve democratic accountability and facilitate policy reforms (see, e.g., Presidential Commission on the Supreme Court of the United States 2021). This book argues that one of the main risks of lowering executive constraints is that by raising the stakes of power, such reforms may increase the incentives for political actors to adopt strategies that severely harm the economy.

METHOD, CHOICE, AND VALUES

As a study in positive political economy, this book is firmly grounded in a methodologically individualistic approach to the inquiry of the causes of social phenomena. My method for explaining Venezuela's economic collapse relies on understanding the motivations, intentions, and beliefs of the actors who made the decisions that caused the decline in the economy's ability to produce goods and services. At times this approach will require us to understand why politicians chose to adopt strategies that would cause severe negative economic externalities, such as doubling down on price and exchange controls or advocating for economic sanctions. In other instances it will imply explaining why consumers and firms reacted the way they did to government regulations, such as by reselling goods or dollars bought through official channels in the parallel black markets.

Methodological individualism is at the core of economic theory and positive political economy. It implies making the decisions of individuals, instead of those of groups or societies, the unit of analysis. As Joseph Schumpeter (1909, 215) famously argued, "Society as such, having no brains or nerves in a physical sense, cannot feel wants." Methodological individualism strongly contrasts with the functional explanations frequently found in Marxist political economy, which posit that institutions serve the purposes of certain classes without accounting for the decisions that make them fulfill these functions (Elster 1985).

A large part of the explanatory framework laid out in this work relies on game theory models of political conflict. This is a specific variant of the methodologically individualistic tradition that presumes that the actors involved in strategic interactions have well-defined preferences as to outcomes and know that they interact with actors who have similar well-defined preferences. In more technical language, actors are presumed to be rational and to share common knowledge of rationality. I see this description as a reasonable characterization of the interaction among many political actors engaged in high-stakes conflicts over power. Most importantly, I argue that this approach can explain the timing of the adoption by these actors of political strategies that imposed severe negative economic externalities on Venezuelan society, driving the intensification of the country's recession.

While game theory models of conflict can be an extraordinarily powerful tool in explaining many social and economic interactions, this does not mean that they are always right. Research in the field of behavioral economics during the past decades has shown that individuals can and often do make choices at odds with the standard axioms of rationality. As I argue in chapters 6 and 7, the Maduro government's decision to delay adjustment after the steep decline in oil prices that began in 2014 can best be understood within the framework of a government that lost its integrative capacity to make long-term economic policy choices after a succession of economic and political shocks led to very high cabinet turnover rates. Similarly, as I argue in chapter 12, the conditions for building trust among competing actors needed to make a negotiation process successful may go beyond what can be usefully illuminated by a dogmatic interpretation of the axioms of rationality.

The method of this book should thus be seen as an eclectic version of methodological individualism that accepts and incorporates different varieties of approaches in that tradition. These range from the sophisticated rational actor models of game theory to the often more realistic bounded rationality models found in modern behavioral economics. My approach is methodologically individualistic because I adopt the view that no explanation is complete unless it provides an account of why individuals make the choices that cause the phenomena that I seek to explain. Yet I don't much care whether my methodologically individualistic cat is rational or behavioral, as long as it manages to catch my causal mice.

As a study in *positive* political economy, this book is concerned with establishing causal explanations for phenomena that affect the functioning of economies through the incentives of political actors. Of course, it is also motivated by a normative preoccupation, which is the desire to help identify the policy and institutional reforms needed to avoid and help overcome politically driven economic collapses. In the concluding chapter, I discuss how the framework developed in this book suggests we should go about trying to come out of and protect against economically destructive conflict.

What this work does not attempt to do is establish the moral or ethical responsibility of political actors in the country's crisis. This point is worth underscoring because it is not uncommon to see causal explanations confounded with attributions of responsibility, and it would be natural for followers of Venezuela's politically charged debate to expect to find those attributions in this work. In fact, virtually all assignments of moral responsibility rely on some type of causal explanation, so it is at the very least natural to try to draw such implications from positive analyses. Yet the converse is not always true: not all causal explanations necessarily imply a specific attribution of responsibility, and such attribution will necessarily depend on normative value judgments that play no role in establishing a causal relationship.

By way of illustration, consider the example of a judge who sentences a convicted criminal to death.[4] That the judge's decision is a cause of the criminal's death is clear: had the judge imposed a life sentence instead, the criminal would have lived.[5] Nevertheless, we would not normally claim that the judge is morally responsible for the criminal's death. This is because we accept that judges who make sentencing decisions have a responsibility to conform to the law and existing norms, such as accepted sentencing guidelines. Depending on our value judgments, we may blame the death on the criminal, who knew that breaking the law was wrong and could bring about this consequence; on legislators, who passed a law establishing a punishment we may deem cruel and unusual; or on society, which failed to provide the support system needed to steer the criminal away from a life of crime. In this, as in many other cases, directly drawing conclusions on moral responsibility based on causal identification exercises can lead to simplistic, misguided, and wrong conclusions.

Of course, some readers of this book may attempt to use my results to buttress their claims of attribution of moral responsibility. Opposition sympathizers may point to my discussion of the political motives behind policy-imposed distortions as supporting the thesis that Chavismo is responsible for the country's economic and political crisis. Government supporters will likely cite my analysis of the economic effects of sanctions as proof that the United States and the opposition are responsible for the deterioration of the country's living standards. Those unaligned with either side may conclude that both strands of my analysis are indicative of a shared moral responsibility of the government and the opposition in the country's woes.

My decision to steer clear in this work of debates on moral attribution of responsibilities reflects the conviction that those discussions have little to add to the identification of the causal forces driving the country's economic collapse. Normative analyses are not necessary for identifying causal effects but can easily distort the positive analyses necessary to discern between alternative causal explanations. Being an economist and not a moral philosopher, I think that I can contribute most to the understanding of Venezuela's economic and political collapse by focusing on explaining the structure of incentives that led political actors to take actions that precipitated the collapse rather than on trying to establish who bears moral responsibility for it.

Nevertheless, many positive accounts of democratic backsliding in Venezuela—as well as in other settings—often emphasize the role of key actors in breaking or altering the rules that govern political competition (e.g., López-Maya 2016; Farnsworth 2018; Naím and Toro 2018).

While such analyses can prove insightful and valuable, they also run the risk of leading us into intractable questions that end up distracting us from identifying the key structural determinants of these actions. This is because they often make us focus on who broke the rules rather than on why they broke the rules.

Let us think about this issue in the context of what is perhaps the most well-known model of strategic interactions, the classic prisoner's dilemma game. The example is not casual, as the game-theoretic model of economically destructive political conflict that I present in chapter 3 shares the classic prisoner's dilemma structure in which the adoption of dominant strategies leads to Pareto-inferior outcomes. But instead of thinking of the prisoner's dilemma as a theoretical exercise, let's think about it as if it involved real people. Think of the two accused criminals who are facing life in prison, sitting in separate interrogation rooms at the side of their court-appointed defenders. Imagine the district attorney who shuttles back and forth between the two rooms trying to convince each criminal that they should be the first to confess. Visualize their nerve-wracked families sitting separately in adjoining rooms waiting to hear the news of whether and for how long their loved one will be locked away.

Imagine yourself as a social scientist doing research on police confessions. After requesting and obtaining permission from the local police chief, you interview both prisoners and their families. Both tell similar stories, blaming the other for being the first to break (or plan to break) the agreement not to confess. After they do so, both will claim that they had no choice but to confess because their partner could not be trusted.

In the end, you may find the story of one of the sides more compelling and conclude that the breakdown of the agreement was due to the actions and plans of the other prisoner. And you may well be right. Yet if you focus exclusively on answering the question of who can be blamed for breaking the rules, you may also have missed the forest for the trees. The reason that the characterization of the prisoner's dilemma is an important contribution to our understanding of the dynamics of human interaction is because it shows us how some actors can be trapped in suboptimal results because of their inability to coordinate mutually beneficial actions. This crucial insight is obtained not by asking who struck the deal with the prosecutor first. It is gained by asking why they did it.

Just as in the prisoner's dilemma case, the framework developed in this book does not rely on the sequencing of the breaking of established rules by specific actors. In other words, the predictions of the models used to explain the country's collapse are invariant to the order of movement by players. I consider this a strength of my approach, as it makes the results of the analysis independent from the often-contentious interpretation of legal and procedural issues. To name one of many possible examples, the Venezuelan Supreme Court's 2015 decision to suspend the election of four legislators from the state of Amazonas on allegations of vote buying and the decision of the opposition-controlled National Assembly to not comply with the court's order (both of which I discuss in detail in chapter 8) are important turning points in the unraveling of institutional arrangements that had previously governed political competition. Whether one attributes the responsibility for the breaking of the rules to the government (for partially annulling the results of an election) or to the opposition (for failing to abide by a decision of the judiciary) depends on one's interpretation of the evidence underlying the allegations, the soundness of the court's interpretation of vote-buying laws, and the constitutional rights and responsibilities that branches of government have in the case of conflicts between them. Because these issues of legal and constitutional interpretation are naturally contentious, explanations that do not depend on them can provide a more robust framework for predicting and understanding the breakdown of existing institutions that manage political conflict.

The fact that my explanations are robust to the sequencing of moves between political actors does not mean that they are insensitive to the asymmetries of power among them. In fact, chapter 3 develops two models of political conflict: a one-player model of politically induced distortions imposed by policy makers in response to electoral threats and a two-player model of symmetric conflict between political actors. These models span the possible characterizations of power asymmetries between the government and the opposition: in the former the government is all-powerful, while in the latter the government and the opposition are equally powerful rivals. I consider and refer to both models throughout the work and argue that the model of asymmetric conflict helps explain the pre-2017 period, during which the opposition lacked any meaningful capacity to affect the economy. The model of symmetric conflict, in turn, can help explain economic and political dynamics after the opposition gained control of the legislative branch and obtained the support of a US government willing to restrict Venezuela's access to global financial and oil markets.

A ROAD MAP

The remainder of this book seeks to provide an analytical narrative of Venezuela's descent into economic chaos.[6] The next two chapters lay out in greater detail the economic and political framework used to understand politically driven economic collapses in a resource-abundant economy. Chapter 2 begins by considering Venezuela's crisis in comparative perspective and explains how economic theory can help us make sense of an economic contraction of these dimensions. I argue that to understand why Venezuela lost nearly three-fourths of its GDP over the past eight years we need to consider that during this process it also lost what was essentially its only source of export revenue, which was its capacity to produce and sell oil. Chapter 3 sets out the theoretical model of economically destructive political conflict and explains the conditions under which political actors will decide to adopt scorched earth strategies in the fight for power, generating severe economic externalities for society. It argues that while the adoption of a highly distortionary policy response to the decline in oil revenues in the 2012 to 2016 period can be explained in the context of single-actor models of politically induced distortions commonly found in the political economy literature, a more complex model of political competition in which both sides can harm the economy is necessary to understand the evolution of the economy from 2017 on. The model of economically destructive political conflict introduced in chapter 3 shows how a country can experience a politically driven growth collapse as a result of high stakes of power combined with a negative terms of trade shock.

Parts 2 and 3 apply this conceptual framework to understand Venezuela's economic collapse. Each part is concerned with two specific subperiods: part 2 covers the period from 2012 to 2015, during which the economy saw the unraveling of a populist macroeconomic cycle after a large negative terms of trade shock. The three initial chapters in part 2 deal with the genesis of the country's fiscal and balance of payments crisis during this period and develop the argument that up until 2016 Venezuela's crisis was not too different from those that we commonly see in the unraveling of populist experiments and can be explained in the context of single-actor models of politically induced distortions. This part of the book begins with a historical recap of Chávez's fourteen years in office in chapter 4, followed by a discussion of the key economic decisions taken during Maduro's first years in office in chapters 5 and 6. The overview highlights how the changes in the political competitiveness of Chavismo led the Maduro administration to adopt increasingly distortionary economic policies, culminating in the choice to tighten price controls and increase the overvaluation of the official exchange rate in face of the 2014 to 2016 decline in terms of trade. It will be this initial economic crisis, triggered both by a plunge in oil prices and by policy responses that exacerbated the contraction, that will serve as catalysts for the political crisis that would drive the economy into a prolonged tailspin. Chapter 7 examines the economic policy decisions of the first half of the Maduro administration from a theoretical perspective. I argue there that the choice to monetize fiscal deficits makes political sense in environments of high stakes of power and intense electoral competition like the one created by the 1999 Constitution.

Part 3 covers the 2016 to 2020 period, during which the economy descends into full-blown economically destructive political conflict. Until then, the government had appealed to increasingly distortionary policies while the opposition sat on the sidelines. Yet once the opposition gained control over the National Assembly and failed in its attempt to call a recall referendum to remove Maduro from office, I argue, a major change in strategies took place. Chapter 8 traces the way in which Venezuela's opposition actors also began to use strategies that they saw as necessary in their fight for power yet that had significant collateral effects on the Venezuelan economy. I trace these decisions to specific episodes of escalation in the country's political crisis that led these actors to reassess their decisions regarding whether to cross red lines that they had previously felt compelled to respect.

One of these strategies was advocating for the adoption of financial and trade sanctions restricting the economic transactions of the Venezuelan government with the rest of the world. Chapter 9 discusses the empirical evidence regarding the effect of these sanctions on the economy and finds that they explain a significant part of the decline in Venezuelan oil output. Nevertheless, I argue that sanctions are part of a broader process of toxification that significantly raised the regulatory and reputational costs of doing business with Venezuela. Chapter 10 discusses how other policy decisions, such as the recognition of a government without de facto control over the territory, also contributed to severing Venezuela's financial and economic ties to the rest of the world.

Part 4 considers how the insights gained from this analysis can help us think about other cases and about Venezuela's future. In chapter 11, I argue that the model developed in this book can help us develop a diagnostics tool kit to assess when countries undergo economically destructive political conflict and present the cases of Zimbabwe and Weimar Germany as examples. I also explore two cases in which political actors had scorched earth strategies at their disposal but decided not to use them: Poland at the end of Communism and the United States during the recent debt ceiling crisis. Chapter 12 argues that the diagnosis presented in this book should lead to a rethinking of much of the current approach of the international community and global policy makers regarding Venezuela. Venezuela's problem, I argue in this book, is not so much one of forcing an unpopular regime to face elections but one of creating the institutional basis for the parts to its political conflict to coexist. I explore alternative proposals for reforms oriented to changing the structure of political incentives that lead actors to adopt scorched earth strategies. Without fundamental structural reform of its institutions of conflict management, I argue, Venezuela is likely to remain trapped in a cycle in which the best it can hope for is to trade one strand of authoritarianism for another. Helping Venezuelans build the institutions that make coexistence of its political factions possible is much more likely to offer a viable way out of their conflict.

TWO

The Great Contraction

As oil inflates the budget, so the body is to the shadow.
We live leaned up against a shadow.
—Valmore Rodríguez, 1940

TAILSPIN

Between 2012 and 2020, Venezuela underwent the largest peacetime economic collapse in modern world history and the largest collapse of any economy, including those that suffered a war, in modern Latin American history. GDP fell by 74.0%; per capita income, by 71.5%. The decline is even larger when calculated in purchasing power parity (PPP) adjusted income measures, though measurement problems may be much more severe in those series.[1]

Venezuela's economic collapse began looking like a standard recession. The economy slowed from 5.6% growth in 2012 (the last year of Chávez's presidency) to 1.3% in 2013 (the first of Maduro's) and turned negative the following year. Yet at -3.9%, the 2014 growth rate was still within the typical range of historical variation in this very volatile economy. What followed was not. Growth turned sharply downward in 2015 and suffered its first ever double-digit contraction in 2016,

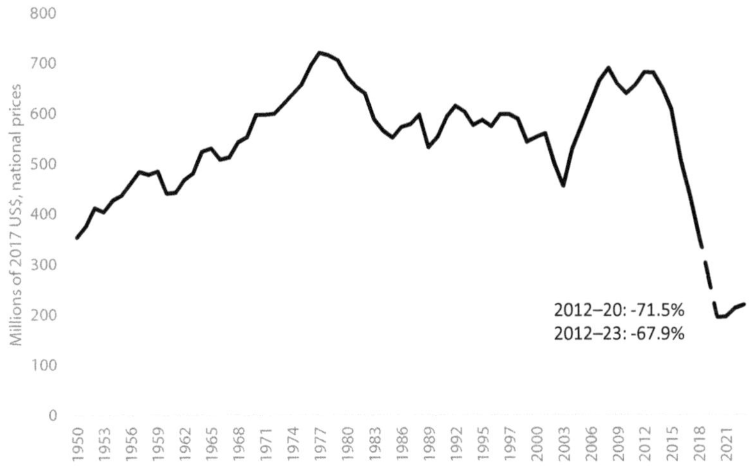

FIGURE 2.1. Venezuela's per capita GDP, 1950–2022. *Source*: Author's construction using Feenstra, Inklaar, and Timmer 2015; University of Groningen 2021; BCV 2023b; FocusEconomics 2023.

followed by another double-digit loss in 2017. By the end of 2018, the economy had shrunk by a massive 48.6%.

There was worse to come. The economy would post two more consecutive years of double-digit collapse, 2019 and 2020, bringing the cumulative contraction in GDP over the eight-year period between 2012 and 2020 to -74.0%.[2] While GDP has recovered since then, growing at an annual average rate of 4.8% from 2020 to 2023, the recovery is far from sufficient to reverse the large decline in living standards of the previous eight years: per capita income at the end of 2023 was still 67.9% below its peak in 2012 (fig. 2.1).

Measured in terms of real per capita income, living standards peaked in 2012 and fell by 71.5% between that year and 2020. (Because of the migration exodus, the drop in per capita GDP is lower than that of absolute GDP.) This is the fifth largest contraction in world history and the largest one in Latin American history since 1950. It is also the largest contraction in the world outside of war (tables 2.1, 2.2). The contraction is not only deep when measured by the trough-to-peak ratio; it is also particularly intense, with the decline occurring over a relatively reduced period, at an annual rate of 14.0%.

TABLE 2.1. Largest output contractions, world, 1950–2020

Rank	*Rank (Peacetime)*	*Country*	*Trough-to-Peak Ratio (% decline)*	*Period*	*Years*	*Average Percentage Decline*	*Cumulative Loss (% of initial GDP per capita)*	*Armed Conflict*
1	—	Liberia	–89.2	1974–95	21	–10.1	–733.7	Intrastate conflict
2	—	Kuwait	–86.8	1970–91	21	–9.2	–1,134.3	Interstate conflict
3	—	Iraq	–77.2	1979–91	12	–11.6	–365.5	Intra- and interstate conflict
4	—	DR Congo	–75.7	1974–2002	28	–4.9	–1,190.9	Intra- and interstate conflict
5	1	Venezuela	–73.0	1977–2020	43	–2.9	–874.5	Peacetime
	—	Venezuela	–71.5	2012–20	8	–14.5	–256.3	Peacetime
6	—	Tajikistan	–71.4	1990–96	6	–18.8	–289.9	Intrastate conflict
7	2	Lebanon	–70.7	1974–76	2	–45.9	–102.1	Peacetime
8	—	Georgia	–70.6	1990–94	4	–26.4	–214.8	Intrastate conflict
9	—	Iran	–66.6	1969–88	19	–5.6	–793.4	Intra- and interstate conflict
10	—	Yemen	–65.6	2010–19	9	–11.2	–386.5	Intrastate conflict
11	—	Moldova	–64.8	1990–99	9	–11.0	–474.5	Intrastate conflict
12	—	Azerbaijan	–61.0	1990–95	5	–17.2	–187.5	Intra- and interstate conflict
13	3	Djibouti	–60.8	1976–91	15	–6.1	–667.9	Peacetime
14	4	Saudi Arabia	–59.9	1974–87	13	–6.8	–358.9	Peacetime
15	—	Angola	–59.2	1973–94	21	–4.2	–678.2	Intra- and interstate conflict

Source: Author's construction using Sarkees and Wayman 2010; Feenstra, Inklaar, and Timmer 2015; University of Groningen 2021; IMF 2023b; World Bank 2023a; FocusEconomics 2023.

TABLE 2.2. Largest GDP contractions, Latin America, 1950–2020

Rank	*Country*	*Trough-to-Peak Ratio (% decline)*	*Period*	*Years*	*Average Percentage Decline*	*Cumulative Loss (% of initial GDP per capita)*	*Armed Conflict*
1	Venezuela	–73.0	1977–2020	43	–2.9	–874.5	Peacetime
—	Venezuela	–71.5	2012–20	8	–14.5	–256.3	Peacetime
2	Nicaragua	–58.4	1977–93	16	–5.3	–683.9	Intrastate conflict
3	Haiti	–45.4	1980–2010	30	–2.0	–928.3	Peacetime
4	Peru	–31.8	1981–92	11	–3.4	–184.3	Intrastate conflict
5	El Salvador	–27.9	1978–83	5	–6.3	–94.2	Intrastate conflict
6	Bolivia (Plurinational State of)	–26.1	1977–1986	9	–3.3	–114.1	Peacetime
7	Argentina	–23.6	1979–90	11	–2.4	–135.3	Interstate conflict
8	Chile	–23.0	1971–75	4	–6.3	–45.6	Intrastate conflict
9	Bolivia (Plurinational State of)	–22.5	1951–58	7	–3.6	–112.0	Intrastate conflict
10	Argentina	–21.9	1998–2002	4	–6.0	–43.9	Peacetime

Source: Author's construction using Sarkees and Wayman 2010; Feenstra, Inklaar, and Timmer 2015; University of Groningen 2021; IMF 2023b; World Bank 2023a.

The episodes of contraction shown in tables 2.1 and 2.2 are defined as episodes during which both per capita and absolute GDP fell from a historical maximum level of per capita GDP (i.e., the highest level attained to that date) and which end when the series reaches the minimum between that peak and the next historical maximum, or the end of the sample.[3] Interestingly, using this definition, Venezuela's contraction in the 2012 to 2020 period is part of a larger contraction that began in 1977 and in which per capita income dropped by 73.0%. As is evident from these magnitudes, the 2012 to 2020 contraction accounts for almost all that collapse. The reason is that by 2012 the economy had almost recovered its 1977 peak of per capita income. The purpose of this book is to understand Venezuelan economic performance in the post-2012 period, which by itself would make it onto the list of largest collapses.[4]

While information on many other socioeconomic indicators is sparse due to a nearly absolute dearth of official series, the little available official data as well as independent estimates are consistent with a decline in living standards that is unprecedented in the nation's history. For example, authorities stopped publishing income poverty data in 2015, probably a reflection of how dismal the figures had become. Yet a consortium of leading national universities estimated income poverty at 93% in 2019 and 2020, up from 48% in 2014 (ENCOVI 2022). Nearly one in three Venezuelan children have abnormally low height for their age as a result of acute malnutrition, and infant mortality rates shot up by 42% between 2009 and 2020 (ENCOVI 2020; UN IGME 2021). The country spent more than three years in hyperinflation, the third longest episode in documented history.[5]

Of course, Venezuelan data may be less than perfectly reliable. Official GDP data run up to the first quarter of 2019; the rest is inference based on forecasts, informed by data from trading partners and international organisms.[6] Hyperinflation does typically play havoc with national accounts numbers; the fact that the country's current minimum wage is approximately $5 suggests that measures that do not adjust for changes in purchasing power may overestimate the magnitude of the collapse in living standards.[7] More generally, the collapse in the state's institutional capacity is likely to have affected the quality and reliability of what remains of official, and even of unofficial, data.

Nevertheless, there is no doubt that the magnitude of Venezuela's economic collapse is unprecedented. Data from receiving countries indicate that 6.4 million Venezuelans left the country between 2015 and 2023. This would make Venezuela's the second largest absolute movement of persons in a decade or less, slightly below Syria's exodus of 7.4 million persons between 2010 and 2020, according to data from the UN's Department of Economic and Social Affairs. Even this number is possibly an underestimate of the current stock of emigrants given lags in reporting and the inability to fully capture undocumented emigration.[8] Data on trade flows also capture evidence of a collapsing economy: in 2020, Venezuela imported from its main thirty-one trading partners only 11% of what it imported in 2012.

While the scale of Venezuela's collapse is staggering, there is a dearth of academic studies attempting to explain it. Journalistic accounts and some policy-oriented research notes have pointed to the role of macroeconomic imbalances, microeconomic distortions, and economic sanctions as possible drivers (Kurmanaev 2019; Abuelafia and Saboín 2020; Harvard Kennedy School 2020). Consensus on an overarching explanation of the causes remains elusive.

This chapter considers the magnitude, nature, and correlates of the country's economic collapse and puts forward ideas about how we can begin to assess different causal hypotheses. I argue that Venezuela's collapse can to an important extent be traced to the decline in its oil revenues, with an important additional contribution from recent productivity declines. The fall in oil revenues, while sustained, is due to two factors: a decline in global oil prices between 2012 and 2016 and a decline in Venezuela's oil production between 2016 and 2020. These patterns are consistent with the story, developed in the following chapters, in which the first part of the contraction reflects the standard unraveling of a populist economic cycle caused by the accumulation of macroeconomic distortions during a temporary resource boom, while the second one reflects the escalation of political conflict into a full-fledged governance crisis that led to a severing of the country's financial and trade ties with the global economy.

Before continuing, an important methodological caveat is in order. When we ask ourselves about the causes of a country's crisis, we may be asking one of two distinct questions. One is why the country's living standards are so low; the other is why they have deteriorated so much.

That is, we can try to explain the country's current level of income or the recent changes in that level of income. These questions are conceptually different and thus can and often do yield different answers. Quite obviously, any recent deterioration in living standards will have contributed to a country's low living standards today. But there are many reasons that a country may be poor today that have little to do with the changes it has experienced in the recent past.

Consider, for example, the case of an individual who recently became unemployed. If we ask ourselves what the causes of that person's recent loss of income are, we may rapidly conclude that the main cause was the loss of their job. We may also uncover certain decisions or factors that contributed to that event. They may have had a fight with their boss, for example, or the firm they worked for may have been hurt by the pandemic. But if we want to ask ourselves why the person is poor, we must broaden our inquiry to ask additional questions. Why, for example, didn't the person acquire the level of education that could have given them access to a job with greater stability? Why didn't they save enough from their previous employment to cushion the effect of the loss of their job? Why are they having such a hard time finding a new job?

Asking ourselves why Venezuela's economy collapsed, in other words, is one way of framing the question that puts the focus on relatively recent causes of variations in income. Asking ourselves why a country with Venezuela's natural resource wealth is among the poorest nations in Latin America today, in contrast, would lead us to focus on many longer-run factors that have had an impact on past growth and thus on the country's recent living standards. Both questions are relevant, and both merit an answer. Yet not distinguishing between them can lead to substantial confusion and misinterpretation. I will return to this distinction at several moments throughout this book.

UNDERSTANDING THE DRIVERS OF THE COLLAPSE

The Venezuelan economy's outsized contraction poses a puzzle from the standpoint of economic growth research. It is obviously tempting to offer an explanation of Venezuela's collapse that traces it to the many policy failures that occurred during the past two decades. But Venezuela is not the first country to make such policy choices. Venezuela's accumulation of macroeconomic and microeconomic distortions is not dissimilar from what we have seen very often in failed state-led development strategies. Yet while it is true that the gross contours of the country's boom-and-bust experience are like those of other economies that accumulated deep macroeconomic imbalances through populist macroeconomic policies, the country's contraction is much larger than the severe recessions that usually accompany the end of those cycles. What is surprising, in other words, is not that Venezuela fell into crisis in 2014. What is surprising is how deep and sustained that crisis was.

The start of Venezuela's crisis does look remarkably like the episodes of unraveling of what Rudiger Dornbusch and Sebastián Edwards labeled the "macroeconomics of populism" in their seminal 1992 book (Dornbusch and Edwards 1992). The term described a policy mix that targeted short-run output expansions through expansionary fiscal and monetary policies and currency overvaluation, typically fueled by favorable external circumstances. This stance led over time to the accumulation of severe fiscal and external imbalances, ending in runaway inflation, falling real wages, and a drastic macroeconomic adjustment.

The problem with trying to fit Venezuela into this story is one of sheer magnitude. As tables 2.1 and 2.2 make clear, Venezuela's contraction isn't like what we see in the typical episode of macroeconomic populism; rather, it's more like what we see in highly destructive wars. The country's policy mix during the Chávez and Maduro years was not all that different from those undertaken by the first administration of Alan García in Perú (1985–90) or by the Sandinista leadership's first tenure in Nicaragua (1979–90), to cite just two of the most disastrous populist experiments in the region. Yet while both experiences ended in unmitigated disasters, the contraction of their economies (which respectively suffered declines of 30.9% and 32.1%) is well below what we saw in Venezuela during the eight-year period covered in this book. Venezuela itself had suffered several boom-bust cycles along the populist playbook in the past; the largest of those, during the 1970s and 1980s, caused a contraction of 26.1% of GDP, or only around one-fourth the size of the 2012 to 2020 contraction.[9]

Resource Curse Redux?

It is also tempting to attempt to explain Venezuela's growth collapse by the resource curse hypothesis, that is, that natural resource abundant economies have lower rates of economic growth and poorer development outcomes than other economies (Gelb 1988; Auty 2001; Humphreys, Sachs, and Stiglitz 2007; Smith and Waldner 2021). Yet while the resource curse literature offers important insights regarding the sources of structural and institutional vulnerabilities to external shocks like the one experienced by Venezuela in the mid-2010s, it tells us relatively little about the main source of the decline in incomes in the late 2010s, which is the destruction of the economy's capacity to convert its abundant endowment of oil into foreign exchange earnings and international purchasing power.

The modern resource curse literature traces its origins to the work of scholars seeking to understand the effect of the development of the Slochteren gas reserves on the Dutch economy in the 1970s (Corden and Neary 1982; Corden 1984; Neary and van Wijnbergen 1985). These researchers observed that in response to the influx of natural resource revenues, the economy's real exchange rate would tend to appreciate (i.e., the price of domestic goods in terms of imported goods would rise), leading the economy to lose competitiveness in other tradables industries such as manufacturing and thus driving an economy's potential deindustrialization.

The phenomenon quickly became known as the "Dutch disease" (*Economist* 1977). Yet this implication of natural resource booms was well known to students of the Venezuelan economy at least half a century earlier, suggesting that perhaps it would be more appropriate to call it the Venezuelan disease. The Venezuelan economist Alberto Adriani, for example, a son of Italian immigrants who would become the country's first agriculture minister, decried the effects of oil revenues on the competitiveness of the country's agriculture in a set of articles written in the 1930s. "The surge in extractive industries occurs at the expense of the decadence of our agriculture," wrote Adriani, explaining that "agriculture suffers a deterioration or a pause with the expansion of the extractive industries which absorb our workforce" (1946, 163, 351). Adriani blamed the real appreciation of the bolivar for the country's loss of competitiveness and would become a strong yet ultimately unsuccessful advocate of devaluing the currency to offset these effects.[10]

As economists writing on the Dutch case recognized at the time, in principle there is nothing wrong with an economy shifting resources out of other sectors in response to an increase in its competitiveness in a particular tradable good; in fact, this is the standard, expectable, and (in a competitive framework) optimal response of an economy that specializes in producing what it's good at following the dictum of comparative advantage (van Wijnbergen 1984). To argue that it is suboptimal for an economy to shift resources out of manufacturing and into nontradables, one must either postulate that the resource windfall is temporary and that there are adjustment costs in being left without a well-developed industrial sector once the rents come to an end or that there are other reasons, such as technological externalities, that countries lose out from a contraction in their manufacturing sector. The latter intuition was formalized by Matsuyama (1992) in a two-sector model of endogenous growth in which productivity improvements were driven by learning-by-doing in the manufacturing sector. An open economy, he argued, would display lower growth rates the higher its productivity in the resource sector, as following its comparative advantage would lead it to specialize away from manufacturing and thus lose out on opportunities for technical progress.

Whether there is a negative link between resource abundance and economic growth in the data is a contentious issue. Sachs and Warner (1995) showed that countries with a high ratio of primary exports to GDP in 1970 had lower rates of economic growth in the subsequent two decades. The results appeared to lend statistical support to the case studies of Gelb (1988) and Auty (1990), who had highlighted the poor economic and institutional outcomes of resource-abundant economies. As with much of the empirical cross-country growth literature, the results turned out to be highly sensitive to changes in specification and sample. Rodríguez and Sachs (1999) showed that the same regressions run using level of income (instead of growth rate) as the dependent variable yielded a positive coefficient on natural resource abundance, suggesting that the low growth in the 1970 to 1990 period reflected higher growth in the pre-1970 period. Lederman and Maloney (2008) argued that the Sachs and Warner results were sensitive to the specification of the independent variable and showed that once net (instead of gross) resource exports were used, the results vanished. Sala-i-Martin, Doppelhofer, and Miller (2004) found that the Sachs and Warner proxy lacked sufficient robustness to be considered as a core explanatory variable. A meta-analysis of forty-three studies conducted by Havranek et al. (2016) found that approximately 40% of studies reported a negative and significant effect of natural resources on economic growth, while 40% reported no effect and 20% reported a positive and significant effect.

Most scholars recognize that natural resources have been huge boons for some countries while appearing not to have helped, and possibly to have even hurt, other countries (Ros 2000; Wright and Czelusta 2004). One variant of the literature argues that the effect of resources on economic growth is mediated through the development of institutions. Sala-i-Martin and Subramanian (2003) contend that while the link between natural resources and growth is statistically fragile, there is a robust negative effect of resource abundance on institutional quality. Wantchekon (2002) argues that increased levels of natural resource dependence can fuel authoritarianism, particularly among countries in which initial levels of resource dependence are high to begin with.

Not surprisingly, Venezuela has been an important focus of studies of the resource curse hypothesis. Karl (1997) argues that it is a prime example of how oil-abundant economies in which the state is the main recipient of rents will have little incentive to develop independent and efficient institutions for domestic taxation. Because petrostates see less need to justify taxes to their citizens, they also tend to be much less accountable and have much lower quality of spending as a result. This becomes particularly problematic when these states are faced with declining revenues, as the lack of accountability makes it politically more difficult to introduce fiscal reforms. Coronil (1997) argues that while the resulting Venezuelan petrostate was dominant with respect to its citizens, it played a subaltern role in relation to foreign governments and transnational capital. While oil empowered the state to carry out ambitious developmental projects and allowed it to promote a vision in which instant modernization was at hand, it also reinforced its external dependence and vulnerability.

Nevertheless, once one uses a broader lens that goes beyond the post-1970 evidence, Venezuela becomes a problematic poster boy for resource curse theories. Between 1920 and 1977, Venezuela's per capita income grew more than ninefold, with its annual rate of per capita growth (4.2%) far exceeding that of any other Latin American country, as well as more than doubling the average rate for the region (1.9%). In 1977, Venezuela was the richest economy in the region, with its per capita income surpassing those of Spain, Ireland, and Portugal and only 10% lower than that of the United Kingdom.[11] In 1981, the US political scientist Peter Merkl (1981, 127) suggested that "the only trail to a democratic future for developing societies may be the one followed by Venezuela." Venezuela's dismal post-1977 development experience needs to be seen in the context of a rather stellar pre-1977 performance.

Rodríguez and Gomolin (2009) suggest that the development of a modern military and a centralized state under the Andean Hegemony of the strongmen Cipriano Castro (1900–1908) and Juan Vicente Gómez (1908–35) was key to ensuring that growing oil revenues would strengthen state structure and protect Venezuela from falling into a resource-conflict trap. Di John (2009) argues that Venezuela's consolidated state with a centralized political organization from 1920 to 1968 could handle a big push import substitution industrialization plan backed with resource rents, as patronage could be deployed through a one-party state backed by an organized military. It was after 1968 that political fragmentation made the Venezuelan state incapable of providing the level of coordination necessary to continue with a big push import substitution strategy of development. Dunning (2008) argues that increasing oil rents nearly eliminated distributive demands put on economic elites, lowering their costs of acquiescing to democratization despite the country's high level of inequality. Kronick and Rodríguez (2023) argue that interelite conflict has been a key driver of Venezuela's economic contractions since the nineteenth century.

Even if we put aside all the caveats regarding the empirical evidence of its existence, resource curse theories are ill suited to providing an explanation for Venezuela's post-2012 economic collapse. This is because, like many theories of economic growth, resource curse theses provide explanations for economic underperformance but not for economic collapse. Low rates of productivity growth or poor institutions can explain why a resource-dependent economy grows more slowly than others, but there is no simple, straightforward way in which they account for why a previously growing economy would see nearly three-fourths of its per capita income evaporate in less than a decade. Further, Venezuela's 2012 to 2020 growth collapse is not driven by the increase in oil exports but by their near-disappearance. A theory of development based on the premise that oil revenues are negative for economic growth is not very helpful in explaining why an economy goes into freefall when its oil revenues evaporate.

Yet while the resource curse thesis does not provide us with a straightforward explanation for why Venezuela's economy collapsed, it can provide us with clues as to why its economy was so vulnerable to declining oil rents. As I argue in what follows, the lack of development of alternative tradables sectors, itself the consequence of the Dutch disease phenomenon, implied that the decline of oil rents had a much larger effect on Venezuela's growth than it would have had on an economy with a different export structure. Lack of institutions to ensure accountability of spending decisions allowed Venezuela to overspend and rack up debt during the 1999 to 2012 boom, thus leaving it in a much poorer position to withstand a negative terms of trade shock. This implied that the decline in oil prices suffered by the economy in the mid-2010s led to a much larger initial decline in incomes than would have been the case under different institutions and previous policy choices, thus contributing to the shift toward scorched earth strategies and the descent into economically destructive political conflict.

Oil Dependency and Economic Growth

To understand why the Venezuelan economy contracted by as much as it did, we must start with one of its basic characteristics: extreme dependence on oil exports. One way to think about this facet of the economy is that for all relevant purposes, the only tradable goods produced by the economy are hydrocarbons. Just before the collapse started, in 2012, oil accounted for 96% of the country's exports.[12] Chemical products, metals, and mining accounted for another 3%, reflecting the economy's comparative advantage in petrochemicals and energy-intensive steel and aluminum. Non-energy-intensive exports were virtually nonexistent.

The share of oil in exports is a more adequate proxy for the country's oil dependence than the share of oil in GDP, which stands only at around 15%.[13] The reason is that most economic activity in Venezuela—or in any oil-exporting country, for that matter—is not oil production in and of itself but the production of nontradable and import-competing goods that are made possible by the acquisition of imported capital and intermediate goods paid for with the country's oil export revenues. Even in Saudi Arabia, oil accounts for only 36% of GDP (GASTAT 2023). The oil sector plays a determinant role in these economies not because it is the only provider of output—after all, there is only so much fuel people can consume—but because it is the only relevant provider of foreign exchange.[14] Put differently, even though most of Venezuela's or Saudi Arabia's output is not oil, almost all of it is *made possible* by oil since it would not exist without the oil revenues that fund it.

The simplest way to think about the Venezuelan economy is thus as an economy in which changes in the value of oil exports—measured in terms of their effect on the economy's capacity to buy imported goods—are the key determinant of changes in GDP. As oil exports rise, the economy can acquire more intermediate and capital goods, which make possible the production of goods for domestic consumption. Even direct imports of consumption goods can be drivers of growth, as large swaths of the economy, including a large retail sector, are organized around the marketing and sale of imported goods to consumers.

For reasons that I explain in more detail in the next section, this intuitive explanation of why oil revenues drive the economy may be easy to explain to a layperson but somewhat more difficult to put into workhorse economic models of growth. Some standard general equilibrium models posit no relationship between an economy's terms of trade and growth, and the empirical evidence on whether such a link exists is ambiguous at best.[15] In fact, it is not unusual for people to think about exports being *detrimental* to growth in advanced economies. When the US government accuses China of currency manipulation, to name just one example, it is because it is concerned with the effect of a flood of inexpensive Chinese goods on American industry.

However, one of the most salient characteristics of economies that are specialized in the production of nonrenewable mineral resources is that their production of other tradable goods—whether import competing or exportables—tends to become atrophied. The reason that in these countries we don't find policy makers as concerned as in other economies about the effects of imports on the national production of tradable goods is because there is little production of tradables to begin with. Even in the case of industries that are nominally import-competing—such as automobile assembly—reliance on imported inputs is so large that they are simply unviable without a source of foreign exchange.

The atrophy of tradable-producing sectors caused by resource booms turns out to be remarkably important for understanding the strong correlation between imports and growth in resource-dependent economies. As the resource-exporting sector becomes predominant, the production of other tradable goods tends to lose relevance and the economy becomes dominated by a large nontradables sector. When the economy suffers a positive terms of trade shock, this nontradables sector expands in tandem for two related reasons: first, it can benefit from access to cheaper intermediate and capital goods; and second, increased consumption will drive demand for nontradables, which will raise the returns to investment in that sector. When there is a downturn in external conditions, both forces will act in reverse, with the contraction in foreign exchange availability becoming amplified through its impact on nontradables investment and production.

The bottom line is that in an economy with the extreme oil dependence of Venezuela, we would expect changes in output to be determined to a very great extent by changes in oil exports (which could come from changes in world oil prices or the oil sector's productive capacity) and the economy's access to international financing (in itself a reflection of the country's perceived capacity to pay with its oil revenues). When these channels are open—as was the case from 2004 to 2012—the economy will expand, and when they are closed—as was the case from 2014 on—the economy will contract.

Venezuela's Boom and Bust Cycle: Some Stylized Facts

The first striking stylized fact of the Venezuelan economy is the strong correlation between imports and growth. As figure 2.2 shows, the surge and collapse of the economy are essentially reflected one-to-one in the economy's imports over the past quarter century. Growth was stagnant during a period of stagnant imports until 2003. As oil prices and export revenues rose, the economy was able to strongly ratchet up imports and experienced a period of strong growth between 2003 and 2008; GDP

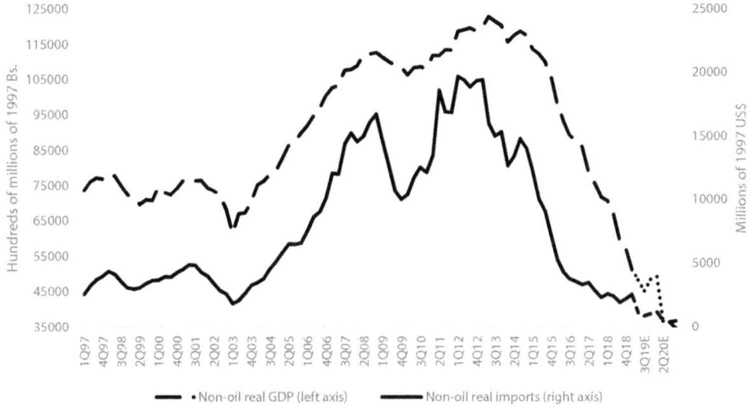

FIGURE 2.2. Non-oil imports and GDP, 1997–2020. *Source*: Author's construction using BCV 2023c. *Note*: Both series are seasonally adjusted.

peaked as imports stabilized and then began falling sharply as imports began experiencing a protracted collapse. The pairwise correlation between the seasonally adjusted log growth rates of non-oil imports and non-oil GDP is 0.71, with a one log point increase in imports associated with a 0.13 log point increase in growth.[16]

If we want to understand why Venezuela's economy collapsed during the past eight years, it thus makes sense to begin by focusing on why its capacity to import goods plummeted. It is not hard to find the answer to this: over this same period, the economy's oil exports all but disappeared. Venezuela could buy much less from the rest of the world because it was selling much less to the rest of the world than it had in the not too distant past. Between 2012 and 2020, exports fell from $98 billion to $7 billion, a 93% decline.[17] This huge decline in export revenue meant that the country simply did not have the resources to continue funding its import needs.

Therefore, there is a strong prima facie case that the proximate cause of Venezuela's economic collapse is the massive decline in oil revenues and resulting contraction in import capacity that occurred in the 2012 to 2020 period. Venezuela's boom-bust cycle in GDP correlates almost perfectly with its boom and bust cycle in imports.[18] As I argue in the rest of the chapter, macroeconomic models tailored to resource-dependent economies predict that we will see a dependence of income on resource exports much like what we see in figure 2.2.

Not all economies suffer as greatly when hit by an external shock to export revenue as that of Venezuela. For example, between 2014 and 2016, Colombia suffered a negative terms of trade shock due to the same decline in oil prices that hit Venezuela, with Colombian exports falling by 42% and the economy's imports contracting by 28% as a result. Oil accounted for around 50% of Colombia's exports at the time, so the magnitude of the shock was somewhat less than that of Venezuela, yet still sizable. Nevertheless, Colombia's economy did not go into recession. Growth slowed from 4.7% in 2014 to 1.4% in 2017, and the country did not suffer a single quarter of GDP contraction.

One of the reasons that Colombia did not contract in response to the import decline is that its export and import-competing sectors were able to expand in response to the depreciation of the real exchange rate that came with the negative shock. In 2017, when the Colombian economy was slowing down the most, non-oil exports were growing by 18% while domestic agriculture had accelerated to 5.5%—almost double its 2.9% growth of 2014. Colombia's ability to produce other tradable goods and the capacity of its domestic industry to raise production to substitute for more expensive imported goods served as insurance against negative terms of trade shocks. In contrast, Venezuela's extreme levels of oil dependence, as well as the private sector's inability to react to changes in relative prices—among other things, due to the administration's byzantine system of price and exchange controls—play an important role in explaining the economy's inability to respond in a way that would have cushioned the effect of a negative external shock.

Because of these structural impediments to growth in other sectors that could have served as automatic stabilizers to the shock, one can make the case that the reason for the economy's income collapse is not so much having received a negative shock but rather the economy's inability to adapt to it. Both a negative external shock and the economy's prior structural characteristics can be said to have a causal impact on GDP—in the same way in which, to return to the example presented at the start of this chapter, a person being fired and their inability to find other jobs can both be said to be causes of their current unemployment—and it is neither always possible nor meaningful to try to separate them.[19] This dependence on structural characteristics and initial conditions is a quite common result in empirical analyses of economic growth, which is full of examples of nonlinear and nonseparable effects.[20]

Another important qualification to the story that declining oil revenues drove the economy's collapse comes from the fact that countries with high terms of trade volatility typically build up large external reserve levels to ensure against negative shocks. However, this did not happen during Venezuela's oil boom, even though the country enjoyed the largest positive terms of trade shock of major Latin American economies (see chap. 4). On the contrary, the government's main stock of liquid international assets to face balance of payments crises, its international reserves, remained virtually unchanged despite the boom: they stood at $15 billion in 1998, when oil prices hit historic lows, yet had only risen to $21 billion by mid-2014, when oil prices were near their peak. And while the government did build up some nonreserve savings in off-budget funds (not included in the official reserve figures and some of which were extremely illiquid), it also racked up significant external liabilities. Therefore, the broader measure of net public sector external assets as captured by the public sector's international investment position rose by just $10 billion in that period (or 1.2% of the country's cumulative oil export earnings during those years).[21]

To drive home the comparison, it is instructive to note that Saudi Arabia had a similar level of reserves as Venezuela in 1998 ($16 billion) but by September 2014 had seen them increase to $745 billion (Saudi Arabia also has oil reserves similar to Venezuela, though it produced around three times as much oil in 2014). As a result, it was able to accommodate the negative shock in oil prices by spending around $250 billion of those reserves, something that Venezuela was clearly unable to do.

In other words, Venezuela's output collapse was driven by collapsing oil revenues, but the Venezuelan economy was highly sensitive to declining oil revenues both because of its extreme dependence on oil as its only meaningful export sector and because of the decision of authorities not to save the revenues generated by the 1999 to 2012 oil boom. In this book, I focus primarily on the determinants of the collapse of oil revenues because they are the factor with a causal incidence on incomes that changes during the period of study. Yet for the purposes of normative analysis, it is important not to lose sight of the fact that Venezuela would not have experienced a contraction of the magnitude observed in this period if its policy makers had made different choices in the years that preceded the onset of the collapse.

VENEZUELAN MACROECONOMICS 101

In this section, I explore further what economic theory tells us about the relationship between external shocks and economic growth in resource-exporting economies. First, I show why the traditional multisector general equilibrium model of an open economy does not provide a ready explanation for large effects of a natural resource sector on the economy's non-oil growth. Then I show how standard models have been modified to explain why some economies that export natural resources may experience significant economic fluctuations in their non-oil sector in response to external shocks and show how these models can help us make sense of the Venezuelan experience.

First, a brief nontechnical summary of my argument. An expansion of oil output will obviously affect GDP because oil is part of GDP. What is more complex is how it affects non-oil production. It is not enough to say that it makes the economy richer, because the economy could simply consume all that wealth—and because real output is measured at constant prices. The answer is that oil output drives non-oil growth by making possible higher levels of capital accumulation. This can happen through one of two channels: it can make capital goods imports cheaper, or it can increase the return to capital needed to produce goods for domestic consumption. Both effects make investment more attractive. Therefore, an oil boom will lead to a surge in imports of capital goods and/or inflows of foreign investment that will drive growth in the non-oil sector higher—producing an output boom that will be as durable as the export boom. Once export revenues disappear, so does growth. (Nonspecialists can feel free to skip the mathematics at this stage and jump to the next section.)

The Limits to Oil

Let us begin by considering a very simple trade model in which the economy produces two internationally tradable goods, 1 and 2, using two factors of production, capital (K) and labor (L). The economy can trade these goods at given international prices. Let good 1 be the numeraire, so that international prices are fully described by the relative price of good 2, $p = p_2/p_1$. Consumers thus maximize utility $U(C_1, C_2)$ such that the value of consumption is equal to that of production in international markets.

We bring in the oil (or, more generally, resource) export sector as an additional source of income in consumers' budget constraint and assume for simplicity that it does not use any capital or labor inputs. This is not an unreasonable first approximation to the reality of many resource-exporting sectors that use relatively little labor and whose capital requirements are generally quite manageable compared to the value of the output. The additional income earned by consumers as a result of these oil exports is termed G (for simplicity, I measure it directly in terms of numeraire goods).

This is just the traditional Heckscher-Ohlin model of trade, with an additional resource-export revenue term added in (see, e.g., Dixit and Norman 1980; Feenstra 2015). In formal terms, consumers solve the problem of

$$Max_{C_1,C_2}\, U(C_1,C_2) \tag{2.1}$$

Subject to

$$C_1 + pC_2 = Y = Q_1 + pQ_2 + G \tag{2.2}$$

Labor and capital are assumed to be perfectly mobile between sectors. Profit-maximizing firms will ensure to employ these factors of production up until the level at which the value of the marginal product of each factor of production equals its return in both industries, that is,

$$Q^1_L(L_1,K_1) = pQ^2_L(L_2,K_2) \tag{2.3}$$

$$Q^1_K(L_1,K_1) = pQ^2_K(L_2,K_2) \tag{2.4}$$

where $Q^i_J = \frac{\partial Q_i}{\partial J_i}$. Competitive factor markets also ensure that full-employment constraints are satisfied:

$$L_1 + L_2 = \overline{L} \tag{2.5}$$

$$K_1 + K_2 = \overline{K}. \tag{2.6}$$

What is important to note here is that equations (2.3)–(2.6) describe a system of four equations in four unknowns whose solution completely determines the level of production of goods 1 and 2. What this means is that resource rents do not affect the level of production in sectors 1 and 2 and the effect of resource rents on the economy's GDP in this simple model can be determined by taking the partial derivative of the right-hand side of equation (2.2):

$$\frac{dY}{dG} = 1 \tag{2.7}$$

In other words, the effect of a decline in resource rents on GDP will be limited to its direct effect on the resource sector's output. Shocks to G may affect consumption levels and welfare but have no effect on non-oil output $Q_1 + pQ_2$.

The result is even starker if we try to distinguish between the role of prices and production in the resource sector. If we define resource rents as the product of the price of the resource p_G and the quantity produced Q_G, then the effect of changes in p_G on nominal output is still given by equation (2.7), but its effect on real output is zero—because Q_G has not changed and real output is valued at constant prices. In other words, a price shock should have absolutely no effect on real GDP in a basic trade two-sector model of an open competitive economy.

This result is extremely problematic for our purposes because it tells us that the effect of a collapse in the country's oil sector on production will be bounded by the size of that sector in the economy (and the effect of a collapse in oil prices will be zero). Yet, as we have seen, Venezuela's oil sector represented at the start of the crisis around 15% of the economy. This means that even the complete disappearance of the oil sector can, in a conventional neoclassical trade model, explain at most a decline of 15% in Venezuela's GDP. It cannot explain the loss of more than two-thirds of output that occurred.

One intuitive direction in which the model can be made more complex is by allowing the additional imports made possible by the oil rents to be directed to the purchases of intermediate goods. Regrettably, this by itself doesn't help us address the problem. Certainly, being able to buy more imported intermediate goods will allow us to produce greater levels of output, but output is not our variable of interest when we think about improvements in living standards: it is the contribution of domestic factors of production to output, also known as value added. GDP is the sum of value added across all sectors of the economy. The contribution of intermediate inputs to GDP, at least insofar as it is measured by their cost, has already been subtracted from its calculation. In the case of domestic intermediate inputs, they form part of GDP through the value added in the process of their production. Imported intermediate inputs make no direct contribution to GDP.

This does not mean that imported intermediate inputs are completely irrelevant to growth. Intermediate products may contribute to an economy's productivity over and above what is reflected by the market value of their services. For example, it may be that the combination of different varieties of intermediate products positively impacts productivity at the aggregate level in a way that is not totally captured by their market price. This contribution of the variety of intermediate products to technological progress is at the center of many modern models of economic growth, which view innovation as the expansion of production possibilities due to growth in the number of intermediate goods. Resource rents may therefore enable an economy to "import" this technological progress, by having access to greater and better production technologies whose combination makes the economy more efficient. The use of these intermediate products produces a positive externality that can be a key channel through which they contribute to the economy's growth.[22]

One interesting implication of the externalities approach is that it suggests that we should see a direct effect of imports on productivity growth (which, as I argue below, we do see). Nevertheless, the idea that imported intermediates make the economy more productive is not without controversy. In fact, some have made the opposite argument—that by shifting relative prices against industries with greater rates of technological growth, resource rents can lead to a decline in aggregate productivity.[23]

Savings, Imports, and Capital Accumulation

Another channel through which the higher import capacity obtained from resource exports can contribute to economic growth is by improving the economy's capacity to accumulate capital. Partly because Venezuela's growth over long-run periods also seems mirrored in an increase in its capital stock and partly because of the ambiguity about the effect of imports on productivity,[24] the neoclassical models constructed to study growth in the case of the Venezuelan economy have focused on the effect of resource rents on capital accumulation.

In a 1999 paper, Jeffrey Sachs and I provided a model of economic growth modified to incorporate the role of resource rents and calibrated it to the Venezuelan economy (Rodríguez and Sachs 1999). We modeled the rents as allowing the economy to purchase an additional amount of investment goods over and above those that it accumulated through domestic savings. Our model was a modification of the workhorse Ramsey model of economic growth. A representative agent maximizes the intertemporal utility function:

$$Max \int_0^\infty e^{-\rho t} \log c_t dt \tag{2.8}$$

with ρ being the subjective discount rate and c_t denoting per capita period t consumption. Non-oil production y_t is carried out using a Cobb-Douglas technology in capital k_t and labor l_t:

$$y_t = ak_t^\alpha l_t^{1-\alpha} \tag{2.9}$$

At any given moment in time, the economy can devote its production either to investment or consumption:

$$c_t + i_t^d = y_t \tag{2.10}$$

and domestic as well as imported investment goods raise the capital stock:

$$\frac{dk}{dt} = k(1 - \delta - n) + i_t^d + i_t^m \tag{2.11}$$

Natural resource exports are brought in as allowing the economy to purchase additional imported capital goods. In other words, the economy's balance of payments constraint is

$$g = i_t^m \tag{2.12}$$

This model can be solved using standard dynamic optimization techniques, leading to a system of differential equations:

$$\frac{dc}{dt} = c(A\alpha k^{\alpha-1} - \delta - \rho) \tag{2.13}$$

$$\frac{dk}{dt} = Ak^{\alpha} - c - (n+\delta)k + g \tag{2.14}$$

This system of differential equations does not have an explicit solution, but we can solve it numerically for specific parameter values. What Sachs and I showed in our 1999 paper was that if we assume that resource rents grow less rapidly than population—an assumption that captures the history of Venezuelan oil production over most of the past century adequately—then for any parameter values the model will predict *overshooting* of per capita output and capital: the economy will experience an initial period of growth, which will lead income to surpass its steady-state level, followed by another prolonged period of negative growth in which it converges to its steady-state level of income *from above* and not—as happens in the traditional Ramsey model without natural resources—from below. The behavior of the models with and without natural resources is shown in figure 2.3. A similar pattern emerges if we simulate what happens to an economy that suffers an unexpected negative shock to its resource rents.

What is important to bear in mind is that the level of production represented in figure 2.3, which is given by equation (2.9), corresponds to non-oil output. This simple model, in other words, explains why an economy that suffers an oil boom will see a decline in its non-oil sector after an initial expansion in tandem with declining oil revenues—in contrast to the Heckscher-Ohlin trade model described in the previous subsection. This effect can be quite substantial. For example, a decline of rents accounting for around 3% of GDP a year can lead to a cumulative

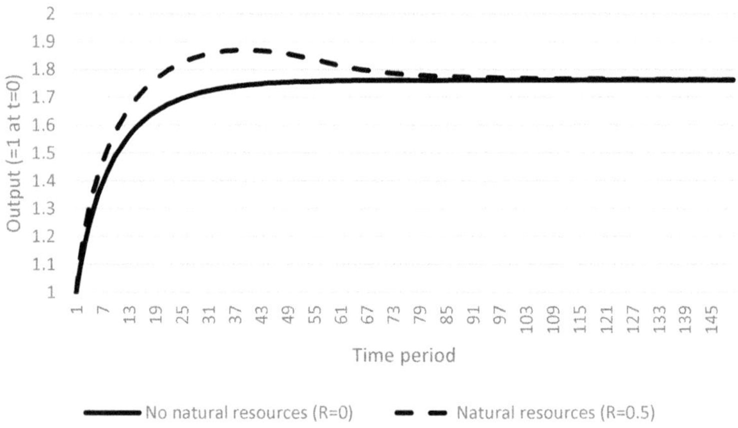

FIGURE 2.3. Non-oil output over time in regular and resource-dependent economy.
Source: Author's construction based on Rodríguez and Sachs 1999.

decline of nearly one-third of GDP over subsequent years. The reason is that while the flow of oil rents is moderate in any particular year, the amount of capital that the economy has been able to accumulate as a result of these past rents is considerably larger.

In this model, the economy's resource abundance allows it to enjoy abnormally high levels of consumption for an extended period. After the economy discovers natural resources, its consumers would like to save those resources for the future, but the only way they can do this is by investing in domestic capital, and the only way for that capital to yield returns is if it is used in producing non-oil goods. As the economy starts carrying out those investments, it pushes down its marginal product of capital and therefore raises the price of future consumption, also stimulating a consumption boom.

Note that the model predicts that we will see a strong surge of imports accompany the oil boom—and a decline in imports accompany the bust—as we saw in the data in figure 2.2. The model can thus explain the key stylized facts of Venezuelan growth in response to changes in oil revenues in a way that the traditional multisector trade model cannot do, at least in the absence of very large positive externalities from the use of imported intermediates.

One of the key assumptions of this model is that the economy cannot invest its oil wealth internationally. If consumers could, they would mortgage the future oil rents to finance a steady stream of consumption from the interest payments on it. In other words, if the economy can save the wealth in foreign assets, there is no need to invest it in domestic capital and push down the rate of return on it, which is what generates the temporary boom. Whatever the merits of this assumption—and a long tradition in economics suggests that models need to be judged on the accuracy of their predictions rather than on the realism of their assumptions[25]—the bias toward investing its proceeds in the domestic economy as opposed to international markets is undeniably an accurate description of the history of the management of Venezuela's oil wealth.[26]

Foreign Investment and Resource-Led Booms

In a 2003 paper, Ricardo Hausmann and Roberto Rigobón provided an alternative explanation of how oil could lead to resource booms in the non-oil sector (Hausmann and Rigobón 2003). In contrast to the one-sector Rodríguez-Sachs model,[27] the Hausmann-Rigobón explanation relies on the existence of a nontradables sector whose production cannot be imported but into which capital can flow. In a nutshell, their explanation is that economic growth in resource-abundant economies comes from the need to expand the nontradables sector as the economy becomes wealthier. As the economy enjoys the benefits of a resource boom, its consumers seek to consume both tradable and nontradable goods. The former can be imported, but the latter cannot. Capital will therefore flow into the economy to make possible the higher production in nontradables demanded by wealthier consumers.

The basic structure of the Hausmann-Rigobón model is that of a multisector model with an open capital account—in contrast to the Rodríguez-Sachs model, which has one sector and a closed capital account. Consumers can consume both tradables and nontradables, but the economy only produces nontradables and oil—whose revenues can be used to import tradable goods. Because the model has an open capital account, capital will flow in or out of the economy immediately to equalize any differences with international rates of return. This allows us to dispense with the dynamics and focus on the economy's steady state.

Per capita production of oil is given at g and is expressed, as above, in terms of the units of tradable goods that it allows the economy to import. The model assumes that the oil sector is owned by the government, but the rest of the economy's capital stock, which is invested in the non-tradables sector, is owned completely by foreigners.[28] This implies that consumers will spend their labor income on tradables and nontradables. The government, in contrast, spends all its oil revenues on nontradables. Consumers will thus solve

$$Max\, U = C_{NT}^{\gamma} C_{T}^{1-\gamma} \tag{2.15}$$

subject to total expenditure equaling labor income:

$$pC_{NT} + C_{T} = wl \tag{2.16}$$

where C_i denotes consumption of good i, with $i = \{T,NT\}$ denoting respectively tradable and nontradable goods, p the relative price of non-tradable goods, w the wage rate, and l the economy's stock of labor. There are perfectly competitive labor, capital, and goods markets; in addition, capital is internationally mobile with its supply perfectly elastic at rate of return $\bar{r}$. Nontradables output is produced with a Cobb-Douglas production function:

$$y = Ak^{\alpha} l^{1-\alpha} \tag{2.17}$$

Equilibrium in this economy will be given by the following three conditions:

$$w = p(1-\alpha)Ak^{\alpha} l^{-\alpha} \tag{2.18}$$

$$\bar{r} = p\alpha Ak^{\alpha-1} l^{1-\alpha} \tag{2.19}$$

$$pAk^{\alpha} l^{1-\alpha} = (\gamma w + g)\, l \tag{2.20}$$

Equations (2.18) and (2.19) are respectively the labor and capital market equilibrium conditions, while equation (2.20) is the condition for equilibrium in the nontradables sector. This is a system of three equations in three unknowns: w, p, and k (the economy's labor supply l is fixed).

Solving this system of equations for k gives us

$$k = \frac{g}{\frac{r}{\alpha}(1-\gamma(1-\alpha))} \tag{2.21}$$

and substituting in equation (2.17) gives us

$$y = A\left(\frac{g}{\frac{r}{\alpha}(1-\gamma(1-\alpha))}\right)^{\alpha} l^{1-\alpha} \tag{2.22}$$

showing the direct relationship between nontradables output y and oil exports g.

As is the case in the Rodríguez-Sachs model, the Hausmann-Rigobón model gives us a positive relationship between imports and oil rents (and therefore with the capital stock and output). This can be seen by noting that imports are equal to consumption of tradables, which are a constant fraction of labor income. Using equations (2.18) and (2.19), we can solve for imports as

$$M = (1-\gamma)wl = \frac{(1-\gamma)(1-\alpha)}{1-\gamma(1-\alpha)}g \tag{2.23}$$

This result is not exactly analogous to the Rodríguez-Sachs relationship between imports and oil rents because here imports correspond to consumer goods instead of capital goods. This economy does accumulate capital in response to increases in the oil rents, but this happens as a result of capital inflows, not imports. Thus, the correlation between imports and growth that arises in this model does not imply a causal relationship from imports to growth, as it does in the Rodríguez-Sachs model.[29]

While in the Rodríguez-Sachs model consumers are trying to accumulate more capital and would save their oil wealth internationally if they could, in the Hausmann-Rigobón model it is international capital that wants to flow into the country to take advantage of the opportunity to invest in the profitable domestic nontradables industry. Despite this difference, both models are similar in their key implications: they explain why the non-oil sector can be expected to expand in tandem with the oil sector and why this would coincide with a surge in imports. Both models thus provide potential explanatory frameworks for explaining Venezuela's growth collapse as a consequence of declining oil exports.

One interesting difference between the models is that in the Hausmann-Rigobón model oil booms are associated with capital inflows and busts are associated with capital outflows. No such phenomenon is present in the basic Rodríguez-Sachs model, where the capital account is completely closed, but modifying the model to allow for some capital mobility would produce a positive association between booms and capital outflows as consumers seek to save the oil wealth that they know to be temporary. Therefore, if the main driver of the boom-bust dynamics is the economy's desire to save, as it is in the Rodríguez-Sachs model, we would expect the economy to accumulate net external assets during boom periods and to draw down these assets during bust periods. If the main driver is demand for domestically produced nontradables, as in the Hausmann-Rigobón model, we would expect the economy's net international investment position to deteriorate during booms and to improve during busts.

On this particular issue, the data appear to be more consistent with the savings-led explanation of the Rodríguez-Sachs model (fig. 2.4). That model predicts that the economy's savings will rise with the resource boom and decline as export revenues fall. That is in fact what we see in the dynamics of the savings rate, which rises from 20% when oil prices were at their low in 1998 to 36% in the 2005 to 2006 period. After 2015, the savings rate plummets and in fact turns strongly negative for the first time in history. The data also seem to suggest that, independently of the rises and declines associated with oil revenues, there is a secular downward trend in the savings rate.[30]

Furthermore, we would expect that if the economy is trying to save its resource boom as in the Rodríguez-Sachs model, we would also in practice see an increase in external asset holdings during a boom. In contrast, the Hausmann-Rigobón model says that we should expect capital inflows into the economy, so that net external assets should turn negative during the boom. We can contrast these hypotheses with the data by looking at the evolution of the country's net international investment position, the result of subtracting external assets from external liabilities, in the 1997 to 2018 period. This is shown in figure 2.5. The upsurge in exports between 1997 and 2008 is associated with rising net international assets; these assets stabilize as exports stabilize on average from 2008 to 2012 and begin to decline in 2014 and 2015 precisely as oil exports plummet. Because these statistics value external

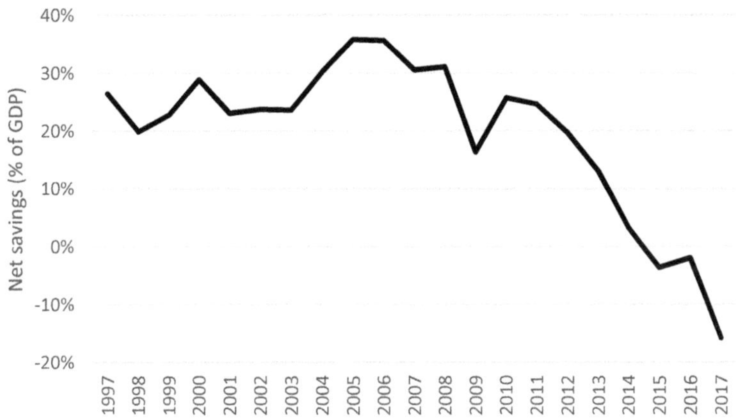

FIGURE 2.4. Net saving as % of GDP, 1997–2017. *Source*: Author's construction using BCV 2023b, 2023d.

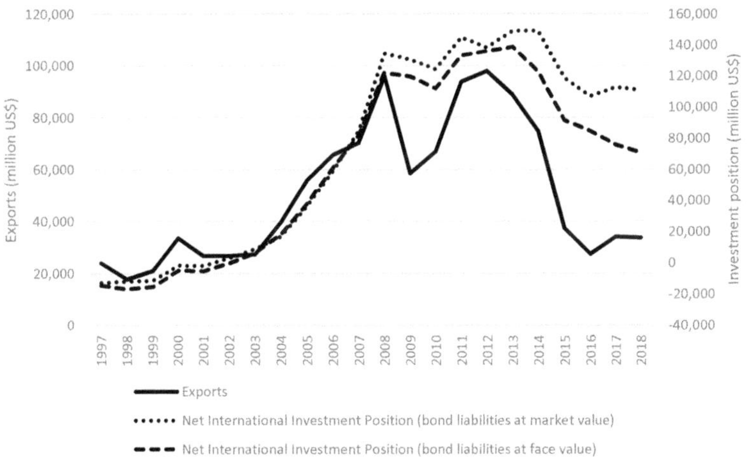

FIGURE 2.5. Exports and net asset accumulation. *Source*: Author's construction using BCV 2023e.

debt at its market value, they actually may underestimate the growth in the economy's net indebtedness, and thus the decline in the net asset position, in the post-2017 period after the government default, financial sanctions, and the collapse in Venezuelan sovereign bond prices. To account for this possibility, I provide an additional estimate that corrects for this by valuing bond liabilities at face values instead of market prices; these show an even more accentuated decline in the post-2014 period. Both the adjusted and unadjusted series are more consistent with the domestic savings–led explanation of the Rodríguez-Sachs model than the foreign investment–led explanation of the Hausmann-Rigobón model.

The Productivity Puzzle

In both models presented in the previous section, economic growth is the result of capital accumulation—whether it is driven by domestic savings from oil rents or by capital inflows attracted by growth in the demand of the consumers who are spending these rents. This leads us to expect that oil-driven economic growth should be mirrored in the data in estimates of the capital stock: oil booms should also be investment booms, and oil busts should be associated with strong disinvestment. The models, in turn, are much more ambiguous on how we should expect productivity to behave. Both the Rodríguez-Sachs and the Hausmann-Rigobón model treat productivity as a constant parameter that is unaffected by oil revenues. To bring in the effect of imports on productivity, we would have to assume that there exist external effects from imported intermediates—an assumption that, as I discussed above, is not uncontroversial.

Table 2.3 provides the results of a standard growth accounting exercise decomposing variations in GDP in the contributions of capital and labor and a productivity term. Following standard practice, productivity growth is calculated as the residual of the contributions of physical and human capital (labor force adjusted by years of schooling) weighted by their shares in national income.[31] In mathematical terms, let the economy's aggregate production be given by the standard production function

$$y_t = Ak_t^{\alpha}h_t^{1-\alpha} \tag{2.24}$$

where y is the economy's output, k is its capital stock, and h is its stock of human capital, and let the t subscript denote time. Differentiating with respect to time and reorganizing allows us to calculate productivity as a residual of the difference between growth in output and growth in inputs weighted by their respective factor shares:

$$\frac{1}{A}\frac{dA}{dt} = \frac{1}{y}\frac{dy}{dt} - \alpha\frac{1}{k}\frac{dk}{dt} - (1-\alpha)\frac{1}{h}\frac{dh}{dt} \tag{2.25}$$

The results of this decomposition, shown in table 2.3, confirm the prediction of the models discussed in the previous section: the period of increasing oil revenues (1998–2012) is associated with increasing stocks of human and physical capital, while the period of declining oil revenues (2012–19) shows a declining stock of physical capital and a strong deceleration in the growth of human capital. However, the data show that these changes in factor endowments, while important, are far from sufficient to explain the magnitude of the growth collapse. Instead, the baseline calculation identifies a huge downturn in productivity—from -0.5% to -14.1% between the two periods—as the main driver of the country's growth collapse.

TABLE 2.3A. Sources of growth decomposition, 1998–2012 (pre-collapse)

Concept	*GDP*	*Capital*	*Human Capital*	*TFP, Conventional Method*	*Imports*	*TFP, Import Effects Adjustment*
Growth (%)	2.7	2.3	4.3	–	7.1	–
Contribution (%)	2.7	1.3	1.9	–0.5	2.2	–2.6
Percentage Contribution	100.0	48.1	69.1	–17.1	79.8	97.0

TABLE 2.3B. Sources of growth decomposition, 2012–2019 (collapse)

Concept	*GDP*	*Capital*	*Human Capital*	*TFP, Conventional Method*	*Imports*	*TFP, Import Effects Adjustment*
Growth (%)	–15.7	–3.0	0.4	–	–31.1	–
Contribution (%)	–15.7	–1.7	0.2	14.1	–9.4	–4.7
Percentage Contribution	100.0	11.0	–1.0	90.0	59.8	30.2

TABLE 2.3C. Sources of growth decomposition, 1998–2016 (pre-sanctions)

Concept	*GDP*	*Capital*	*Human Capital*	*TFP, Conventional Method*	*Imports*	*TFP, Import Effects Adjustment*
Growth (%)	0.6	1.7	3.7	–	–1.6	–
Contribution (%)	0.6	0.9	1.7	–2.0	–0.5	–1.6
Percentage Contribution	100.0	163.8	300.6	–364.3	–86.4	–278.0

TABLE 2.3D. Sources of growth decomposition, 2016–2019 (sanctions)

Concept	*GDP*	*Capital*	*Human Capital*	*TFP, Conventional Method*	*Imports*	*TFP, Import Effects Adjustment*
Growth (%)	–27.3	–6.1	–1.6	–	–25.5	–
Contribution (%)	–27.3	–3.5	–0.7	–23.1	–7.7	–15.4
Percentage Contribution	100.0	12.8	2.6	84.6	28.1	56.5

Source: Author's construction using Feenstra, Inklaar, and Timmer 2015; University of Groningen 2021; BCV 2023a, 2023f.

In other words, the calculations tell us that changes in factor accumulation can only explain a part of the collapse. For example, between 2012 and 2019, the country's capital stock fell 19%. This is a large decline for sure, but it can only explain around one-tenth of the collapse in GDP. And while growth in human capital decelerated strongly, it was still mildly positive for the post-2012 period as a whole, so it cannot directly contribute to explaining a decline in living standards. Put together, the changes in the stock of human and physical capital would lead us to have expected a contraction of 10% in GDP—or around one-sixth of the 66% contraction actually observed.[32] These results are mirrored in the decline of productivity, which suffered a cumulative 63% drop in the 2012 to 2019 period. The Venezuelan economy, in other words, lost nearly two-thirds of its capacity to convert inputs into production during these seven years.

This is a puzzling result. In general, economists expect to see positive productivity growth over time, reflecting improvements in technology. Negative variations can be explained as a result of the dynamics

TABLE 2.4. Largest productivity collapses

Rank	*Country*	*Trough-to-Peak Ratio (% decline)*	*Period*	*Years*	*Average Percentage Decline*	*Years of Initial Productivity Lost (% decline)*
1	Kuwait	−91.6	1974–91	17	−14.6	−1,187.7
2	Saudi Arabia	−84.4	1974–2019	45	−4.1	−3,135.5
3	Iraq	−81.7	1979–91	12	−14.1	−543.3
4	Venezuela	−80.8	1970–2019	49	−3.4	−2,050.3
5	Iran	−79.7	1969–2019	50	−3.2	−3,439.8
6	Qatar	−75.5	1974–2019	45	−3.1	−2,140.7
7	Jordan	−67.3	1965–2019	54	−2.1	−2,721.3
8	Rwanda	−63.2	1981–94	13	−7.7	−307.9
-	Venezuela	−63.0	2012–19	7	−14.2	−192.8
9	Gabon	−62.4	1976–87	11	−8.9	−522.8
10	Bahrain	−62.4	1974–2019	45	−2.2	−2,148.9
11	Sierra Leone	−57.9	1990–99	9	−9.6	−299.6
12	Angola	−53.6	1974–94	20	−3.8	−571.8
13	Mozambique	−48.3	1964–86	22	−3.0	−445.7
14	Togo	−45.0	1980–2007	27	−2.2	−840.0
15	Cameroon	−44.8	1984–94	10	−6.0	−299.5

Note: The productivity collapses in this table are defined analogously to the per capita GDP collapses shown in tables 2.1 and 2.2. The definition, explained in Rodríguez and Imam (2022), identifies a collapse as the decline between the maximum level of income per capita reached until a certain time and the subsequent minimum prior to a new maximum being reached. It also adds a requirement that this decline coincides with a period in which absolute levels of income are declining. This last condition is not well defined for productivity, which is independent of whether the growth accounting decomposition is carried out in absolute or per capita terms, and is thus omitted from this calculation. Average percentage declines are expressed in logarithmic growth rates for comparability with table 2.3

Source: Author's construction using Feenstra, Inklaar, and Timmer 2015.

of economic cycles, but a collapse of two-thirds in productivity is highly unusual. This is confirmed in table 2.4, which compares Venezuelan total factor productivity (TFP) growth over the 2012 to 2019 period with the largest TFP declines observed in the sample. Venezuela's productivity collapse in the 2012 to 2019 period is the ninth highest observed in the world between 1950 and 2019.[33] As before, this is part of a longer-run productivity decline that begins in 1970; viewed as a whole, the productivity decline reaches 80.8%, the fourth highest in the world.

There are several potential competing explanations of the productivity collapse. I have already discussed one of them, the potential declining externalities from reduced imports. If in fact imports allow the economy to have access to a more diverse range of intermediate goods, allowing it to raise productivity by more than what is already accounted for in the GDP statistics (which, remember, subtracts the costs of intermediate goods from the value of production), then the import collapse could explain the strong changes in productivity.[34]

In other words, if we modify the production function by directly contemplating the role of imports m by modifying equation (2.24), we get

$$y_t = Ak_t^{\alpha} l_t^{1-\alpha} m_t^{\eta} \tag{2.26}$$

And the productivity residual can now be calculated as

$$\frac{1}{A}\frac{dA}{dt} = \frac{1}{y}\frac{dy}{dt} - \alpha\frac{1}{k}\frac{dk}{dt} - (1-\alpha)\frac{1}{h}\frac{dh}{dt} - \eta\frac{1}{m}\frac{dm}{dt} \tag{2.27}$$

That is, growth accounting under externalities simply requires subtracting the external effect $\eta\dot{m}_t$ from the conventional TFP estimate. In table 2.3 I have added an estimate of this import externality using an elasticity of 0.30 derived from previous published studies.[35] The results are presented under the column labeled “TFP, Import Effects Adjustment.”

Augmenting the production function to include the role of imported intermediates allows us to attribute a substantial part of the productivity decline to the import contraction. According to this calculation, import externalities were contributing 2.2 percentage points to growth over the 1998 to 2012 period, which suggests that they were essentially masking a substantial decline in productivity of 2.6% per year during the Chávez years. During the Maduro period, in contrast, the import collapse explains around three-fifths of the decline in output, with the decline in physical capital explaining around one-tenth and the decline of import-adjusted productivity—which fell at an annual rate of 4.7%—another third.

Therefore, while including imports in the growth accounting relationship goes part of the way toward explaining the productivity collapse, it still leaves an important part of it unexplained. According to the import-corrected estimates, productivity still fell by a magnitude that would have generated a contraction of 28% in GDP over this seven-year period even if imports had remained constant.

There are other explanations for this residual productivity collapse that do not rely on import externalities. Venezuela's productivity collapse could reflect, for example, our inability to capture changes in the stocks of human and physical capital and thus to adequately reflect the evolution of the stock of productive assets. Venezuela's mass process of emigration, for example, suggests that the loss of human capital may have been much more accentuated than what is captured in an aggregate measure of the labor force adjusted for average years of schooling. Residual-based productivity estimates have been famously called a "measure of our ignorance";[36] our case is no different.

Nevertheless, it is notable that the productivity collapse is concentrated just in the final years of the sample. This is shown clearly in the bottom two panels of table 2.3, where I adopt a different periodization that distinguishes between the pre-sanctions (1998–2016) and sanctions (2016–19) periods. In the conventional calculation, the decline in productivity for the sanctions period is a massive 23% a year. Even after we allow for import external effects, we estimate a productivity decline of 15% a year—enough to explain nearly two-thirds of the contraction observed during that three-year period.

This sharp discontinuity in the productivity decline suggests that disruptions to the economy's productive process during the period starting in 2017 significantly harmed its capacity to convert factors of production into outputs.[37] It is true that the economy had lower levels of human and physical capital to work with, as well as lower import levels, as a result of falling oil revenues. But it is also true that even at those lower levels of factor and intermediate good inputs, we would not have expected to see such a large decline in output. There is a large unexplained decline in productivity in the post-2016 period that cannot obviously be traced back to the collapse of the economy's capacity to access imported inputs.

In the following chapters, I suggest an alternative explanation of the productivity puzzle. I argue that the severing of the economy's financial and trade links to the rest of the world imposed significant costs on the Venezuelan public and private sectors, severely limiting their capacity to interact with the global economy. I argue that not only is this increasing economic isolation the main cause of the collapse in oil production; it also had significant effects on the productivity of the non-oil sector, thus contributing to the acceleration in the rate of decline in productivity seen over the past decade.[38]

To summarize, there are several important takeaways from this growth accounting analysis. First, we observe a continued decline in productivity for the past two decades. This sustained decline is certainly one of the most important reasons for Venezuela's low living standards today. Second, the data are consistent with the hypothesis that a significant part of the country's economic contraction since 2012 was driven by the collapse in its export revenue. Our calculations suggest that, given certain sensible assumptions, the decline in the country's import capacity can explain—both directly and through its induced effects on lower capital accumulation—up to two-thirds of the decline in GDP that has taken place since 2012.

Yet the data also show a huge decline in the economy's productivity starting in 2017. This decline is nine times as large as what the economy saw in the pre-2017 period—an unprecedented deterioration in the economy's capacity to convert productive factors into output. The magnitude and timing of this discontinuity suggests that we need to focus on the changes to the economy that took place in the period since 2017. As I explain in the rest of this book, that period coincides with a time during which Venezuela's economic links with the world economy were severely disrupted as a result of a political crisis spilling over into the economy. Understanding the damage caused by this descent into all-out political conflict is crucial to any account of the implosion of the Venezuelan economy. Before telling that story, we must first take a closer look at the factors that drove the collapse of the country's oil exports.

WHERE DID ALL THE EXPORTS GO?

The previous section argued that a large part of the economy's contraction since 2012—around two-thirds, by my calculations—can be attributed to declining export revenues. I now look in greater detail at the causes of the decline in these revenues. Figure 2.6 displays the evolution of oil export revenues between 2012 and 2020, together with Venezuelan oil prices. The figure shows that while Venezuela suffered a sustained

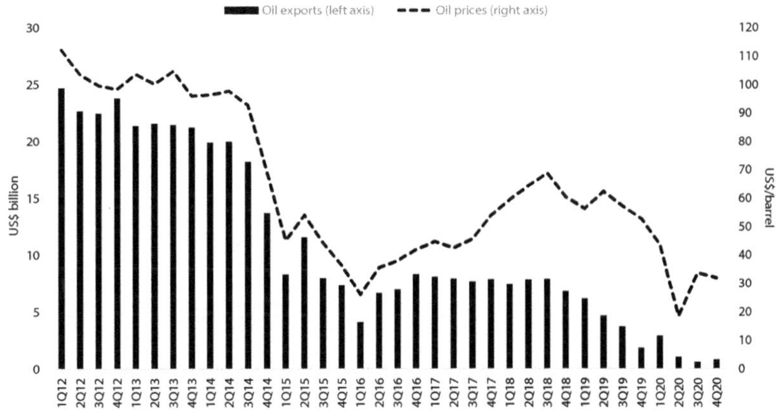

FIGURE 2.6. Venezuelan oil exports and prices, 2012–2020. *Source*: Author's construction using Bloomberg 2021b; BCV 2023c.

collapse in its foreign exchange earnings from oil revenues over this eight-year period, the decline is a combination of two very different processes. Between 2012 and 2016, oil exports are brought down by a large decline in prices. That part of the export collapse is simply a reflection of a strong negative terms of trade shock that cut the value of the country's oil sales by around two-thirds. After 2016, in contrast, we see a different phenomenon. Here oil prices begin to recover, but oil exports do not. The reason is that Venezuelan oil production had begun to fall, so that the country was selling less and less oil to the rest of the world. Figure 2.7 shows this phenomenon more directly, tracing how Venezuelan oil production plummeted by four-fifths between 2016 and 2020.[39]

These figures clearly illustrate that between 2014 and 2016, Venezuela suffered a large external terms of trade shock caused by a decline of two-thirds in the price of what is virtually its only source of export revenue. It is not surprising that the economy contracted during this period—although the magnitude of the contraction, as I already suggested and discuss in more detail in the following chapters, was surely exacerbated by poor policies both during and before the crisis. From 2017 on, the decline in foreign currency earnings continues, but the driver is different. Falling oil production, rather than declining oil prices, is from that moment on the cause of declining export revenues.

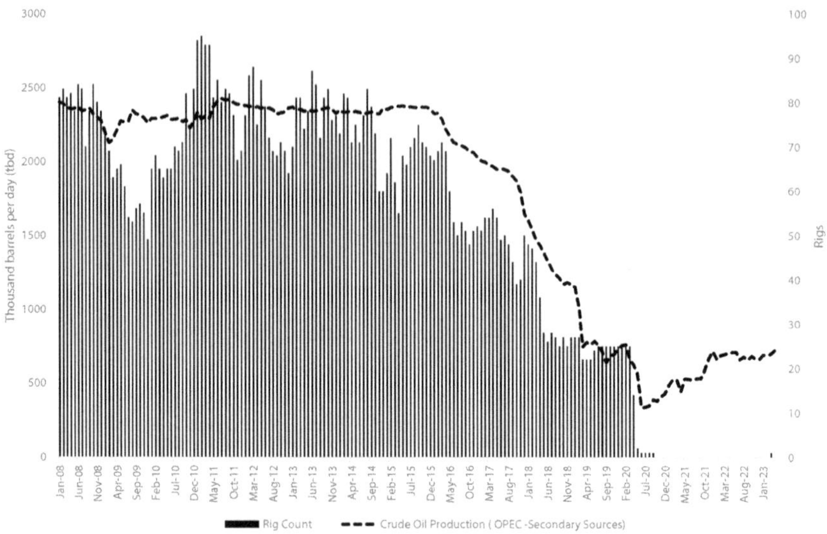

FIGURE 2.7. Venezuela crude oil production and rig count, 2012–2020. *Source*: Author's construction using OPEC 2023; Baker Hughes 2023.

To understand the magnitude of this effect, consider how much Venezuela would be earning in oil export revenue today if production had not declined. Had the country sold as many barrels to the rest of the world in 2020 as in 2015, it would have received $31 billion in oil revenues that year—more than three times what it received.

These figures also illustrate why the fact that Venezuela's economic crisis began before the imposition of the first economic sanctions in 2017—a fact that is often highlighted by authors who discount the effect of sanctions—doesn't tell us much about the relative contribution of sanctions in comparison to other potential drivers to Venezuela's economic crisis.[40] Had oil output not declined between 2016 and 2020, the recovery of oil revenues from higher oil prices would most likely have fueled an economic recovery—or at the very least allowed the economy to escape its massive contraction—as had happened in past episodes of oil price recoveries (most recently, 2010–11). Given this, it makes little sense to assume that the trend of decline in output and socioeconomic indicators of the 2014 to 2016 recession would have continued absent sanctions in the 2017 to 2019 period. Put differently, the fact that Venezuela suffered a decline in living standards in the 2014 to 2016 period due to a decline in oil prices in no way implies that it is a reasonable counterfactual to expect that decline to have continued during the subsequent recovery in oil prices. I take these points up again in chapter 9.

In the introduction of this chapter, I noted that in investigating the causes of Venezuela's crisis we needed to distinguish between questions about levels (why are Venezuelan living standards low today) and questions about changes (why have Venezuelan living standards fallen dramatically in recent years). I also noted that the distinction between these two questions is largely one of the time span over which we are willing to consider the effect of driving factors. The same distinction is applicable to questions about the performance of the country's oil industry. It is one thing to ask why Venezuela's oil production is low today relative to its potential; it is another to ask why it has declined so much in recent years. The latter requires us to focus on factors that have impacted changes in production in recent years, while the former allows us to broaden our investigation to consider factors that impacted production even before the recent decline.

The final part of this chapter discusses some of the long-run determinants of the underperformance of Venezuela's oil sector, centering on the institutional changes and policy decisions that affected the oil sector during the Chávez administration as well as the pre-sanctions period. Doing so helps us understand why Venezuela has been unable to exploit its potential as the holder of what by some estimates are the world's largest oil reserves. I leave discussion of more recent changes in the external environment to chapter 9, where I revisit the role of economic sanctions on the sector's recent decline.

GREAT EXPECTATIONS

Figure 2.8 plots Venezuela's oil production from the month that Chávez took office, January 1999, to the end of 2020. I also plot the total production of the Organization of the Petroleum Exporting Countries (OPEC) cartel, of which Venezuela is a member. OPEC quotas put a limit on the production of member countries, so it makes sense to compare Venezuela with other cartel members that are similarly constrained.

What the data show is that Venezuela consistently underperformed OPEC during Chávez's tenure, particularly in the post-2003 period

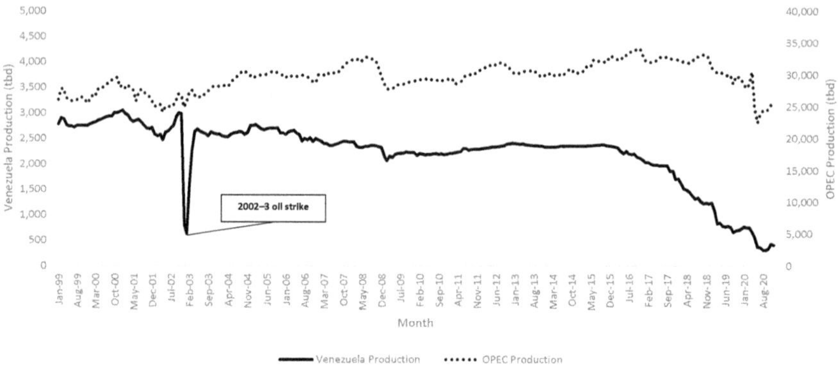

FIGURE 2.8. Venezuela and OPEC production, 1998–2020. *Source*: Author's construction using OPEC 2023.

when the government replaced most of the state-owned oil company PDVSA's management in the aftermath of the 2002 to 2003 general strike. Between 1998 and 2015, Venezuela's oil production fell by 21.5%, while OPEC's output rose by 20.5%, leading Venezuela's share of OPEC production to fall from 11.0% to 7.2%. It is worth remembering that some OPEC members, like Iraq and Libya, underwent armed conflicts during this period that hampered their production growth, so that Venezuela's underperformance is even greater when compared to other oil-producing economies in peacetime.

Venezuela's oil sector performance is also poor when measured against its potential. Venezuela is home to 20% of the world's oil reserves but—even before the recent collapse in oil production—accounted for around 2% of global oil output. Venezuela produced in 2015 around 0.3% of its proven reserves annually, as opposed to an OPEC average of 1.1% and a world average of 2.0%. Saudi Arabia, with reserves of 266 billion barrels, manages to produce 10.5 million barrels per day, while Venezuela, with 304 billion barrels in reserves, has been unable to produce more than 3 million barrels per day during the past two decades.[41]

Venezuela's inability to take advantage of its oil wealth can be traced to Hugo Chávez's decision at the start of his administration to impose high taxes on the oil industry to fund higher levels of government spending. Even though Venezuelan oil production had been in state hands since nationalization in 1976, key figures in Chavismo believed the state-owned oil company was undertaxed and accumulating surpluses that were used for the benefit of its own management. In the 1990s, Venezuela had signed operating agreements with transnational companies that allowed them to operate high-cost fields under favorable fiscal conditions. Chavismo had been highly critical of these agreements, which it saw as symptomatic of state capture by the local private sector and oil corporations (Parra 1998; Mendoza Potellá 2017).

In 2001, the Chávez government approved a controversial reform of the hydrocarbons law that significantly raised the government's participation in oil revenues. The royalty rate was raised from 17% to 30% for the industry as a whole, and the special 1% royalty rate that had been given to some private sector operators was scrapped, forcing them to adopt the 30% rate. While the oil sector income tax rate was lowered from 68% to 50%, a change that in principle was designed to offset the effect of higher royalties on PDVSA, private sector firms were forced to give up their special income tax rate of 34% and transition to the 50% rate (Key 2010; Guerra 2021; Monaldi, Hernández, and La Rosa 2021).

Perhaps even more important than changes in the tax code was the decision for PDVSA to directly finance social spending over and above its mandatory fiscal contribution. Between 2004 and 2016, the oil sector devoted $137 billion, or 12% of its gross revenues, to funding government spending over and above its statutory royalty and income tax payments, an item called "Social Development Contributions" in its financial statements. Despite its name, most of these resources did not go to fund social policy initiatives but rather to the National Development Fund, FONDEN, an opaque off-budget fund in charge of paying for large infrastructure projects.

Shortly after securing reelection in 2006, Chávez decided to further reshape the relationship with oil multinationals. When Venezuela's oil industry was nationalized in 1976, the law had left open space for the government to enter into fee-based operating service agreements and strategic associations when it concluded that doing so was in the public interest. Amid a cash crunch in the early 1990s, Venezuela had invoked this possibility to invite private sector partners to invest in the country's oil sector, an initiative that focused on developing the country's expensive extra-heavy oil reserves. In 2007, Chávez ordered these agreements to be converted into new joint ventures in which PDVSA had a minimum

60% stake (*Gaceta Oficial* 2007a). Some companies went along, since the rise in oil prices that had occurred by that time made their investments remain profitable under renegotiated conditions; others such as Conoco-Phillips and Exxon Mobil rejected the offer and took the government to arbitration tribunals. Then, in 2009, the government moved one step further, nationalizing hundreds of assets of service providers of the oil industry, including docks, shipyards and vehicles, and absorbing the employees of these firms into PDVSA's payroll (*Gaceta Oficial* 2009; *El País* 2009).

PDVSA was not just being saddled with numerous assets that it had no knowledge of how to manage; it was also taking on an increasing amount of debt. To fund higher spending, pay for many of the nationalizations, and defend an overvalued currency, the government not only used the revenues from higher oil prices but also issued new liabilities. The government's external debt rose from $29 billion when Chávez took office to $129 billion by 2017—not counting around $20 billion in expropriation debts subject to international arbitration. This included $57 billion owed directly by PDVSA (fig. 2.9).

Increasing debt meant increasing debt service needs. Had the debt been used up to build the country's infrastructure or invest in the oil

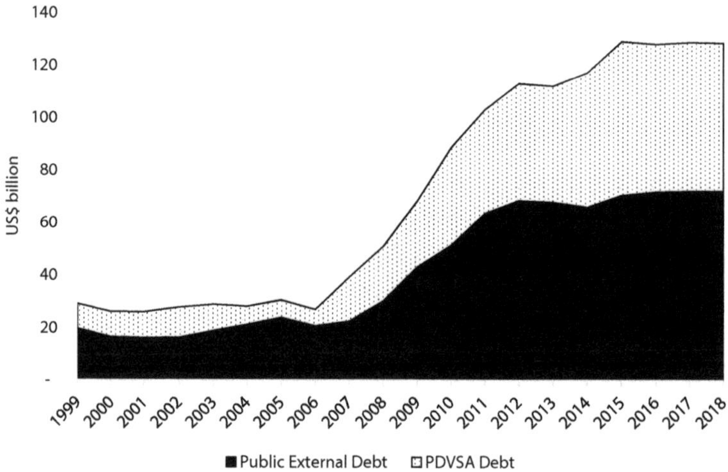

FIGURE 2.9. PDVSA and government external debt, 1999–2018. *Source*: Author's construction using BCV 2023a.

sector, then the increased revenues could have helped pay the cost of this financing. But, as we have just seen, oil output was actually lower—and the economy less productive—in 2015 than when Chávez came to power. And more money to pay debt service meant even less money that the country had to invest in oil production.

All of this meant that PDVSA was not able to maintain the investment commitments it needed to develop the use of its oil reserves. The government launched several plans for expanding oil production, but PDVSA was never allowed to invest the resources necessary to carry them out. For example, the 2005 "Plan Siembra Petrolera" laid out an investment plan of $77 billion in investments over six years to double oil production that barely materialized; by 2012, the government expanded the plan to $257 billion, 81% of which was expected to be made by PDVSA (Monaldi, Hernández, and La Rosa 2021). Yet year after year, PDVSA failed to hit its investment targets and diverted growing shares of its investment to non-oil concerns such as electricity plants purchased to alleviate the country's growing energy shortages (Hernández and Monaldi 2016). Although the amounts invested grew significantly from 2003 to 2014, some indicators of investment outcome, such as the number of wells completed, did not trend upward, suggesting increased inefficiencies, as well as probable leakages to corruption, in the company's investment activities.

Things came to a head when oil revenues collapsed in the second half of 2014. As oil prices fell, PDVSA's revenues fell from $122 billion in 2014 to $48 billion in 2016. The company slashed investment, cutting it from $25 billion in 2014 to $12 billion in 2016, the lowest level seen by the company in a decade (fig. 2.10). Oil production soon followed suit, with output falling by 324 thousand barrels per day (tbd), a decline of 14%, during 2016.

Yet the decline observed in oil production in 2016 was not completely out of the ordinary given the external environment. Faced with similar conditions, many high-cost leveraged producers were forced to cut back investment and suffered losses in production. For example, oil output in neighboring Colombia, part of whose oil industry was also highly leveraged, saw production fall by similar levels during 2016. However, oil production stabilized in Colombia in 2017 as oil prices began recovering but went into freefall in Venezuela.

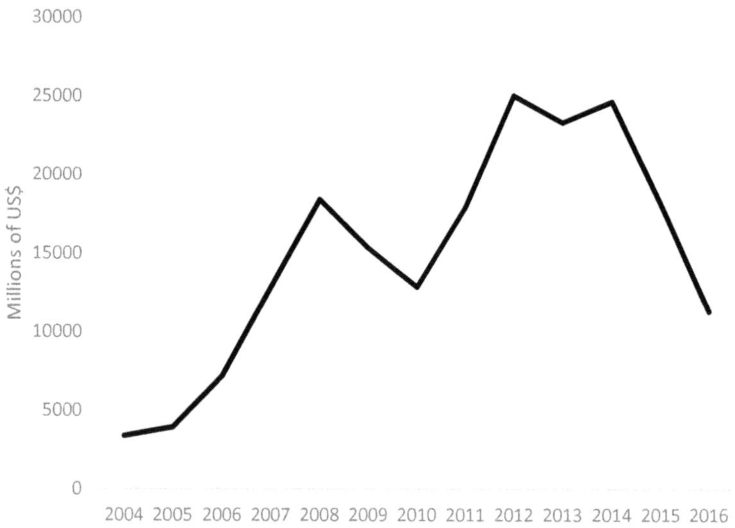

FIGURE 2.10. PDVSA fixed investment. *Source*: Author's construction using PDVSA financial statements.

Perhaps even more importantly, while the data do show that PDVSA curtailed investment spending in the face of the 2014 to 2016 decline in oil prices, they also show that those levels of investment were still similar to what it had invested in the recent past. The company's 2016 financial statements show asset acquisitions of $11 billion—an acute decline from the 2012 peak of $25 billion but very similar to the 2010 investment level of $13 billion and well above the 2004 to 2007 average of $7 billion. If we accept that these figures adequately reflect the firm's actual investment levels (admittedly a big if), then it is hard to explain an unprecedented collapse of production from the company returning to investment levels that were in line with its historical averages.

Of course, for all we know, data drawn from PDVSA financial statements may not tell us anything about its actual investment levels, since we know nothing about the efficiency of those investments. In the limit, if investment contracts are merely a way to siphon funds to cronies, then the numbers could be completely uninformative about actual investment levels (though one would have to assume that corruption systematically

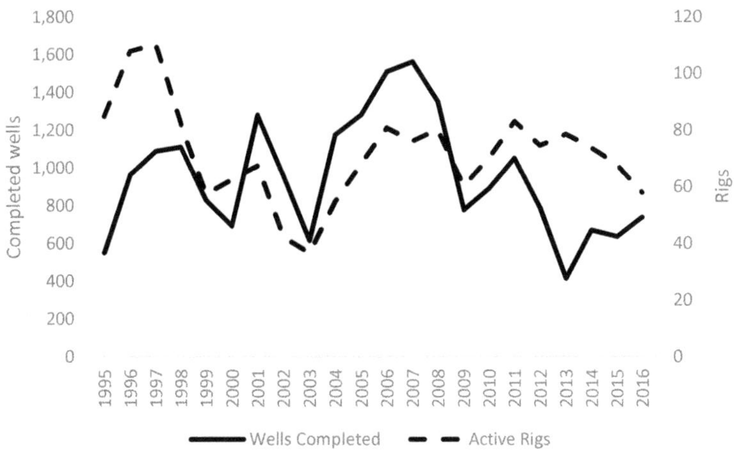

FIGURE 2.11. Oil investment indicators, 1995–2016. *Source*: Author's construction using PDVSA financial statements.

increased relative to the earlier years of Chavismo to claim that this data implies declining real investment). To address this issue, figure 2.11 plots two commonly used proxies for investment in the oil sector that depend on observed activities rather than investment figures: the number of wells completed and the number of active exploration rigs. The data shows that while active rigs did decline after the slide in oil prices, they still remained well within the range of historical variation, while completed wells actually rose between 2013 and 2016. Again, nothing in this series is indicative of the acute investment cuts that would have led us to expect a collapse in production like what took place after 2016.

Perhaps for these reasons, the magnitude of the post-August drop in production caught many observers by surprise. Writing in April 2017, IPD Latin America—perhaps the most prominent oil consultancy covering Venezuela—predicted that production would drop that year by 11% but would then stabilize and remain unchanged at 2.2 million barrels per day by 2020. Even in its most pessimistic "worst case," it saw a 13% decline in production in 2017 and an annual average rate of decline of 6% in the subsequent three years, leaving production at 1.8 million barrels per day in 2020. By contrast, production fell by 19% in 2017 and by an annual average of 36% in the subsequent three years, falling to 431 barrels per day by the end of 2020. The post-2017 plunge in oil production was unexpected even by specialists who were well aware of the cash crunch and investment cuts generated by falling oil prices.

In sum, Venezuela's economic freefall was precipitated by a decline in oil revenues. Falling oil revenues severely curtailed the economy's capacity to import capital and intermediate goods, dealing a severe blow to a highly import-dependent economy. While the decline in oil revenues was originally driven by a slide in oil prices that began in 2014, it deepened even as oil prices started to recover because of the decline in oil production.

Undeniably, Venezuela would have significantly higher levels of oil production and GDP today if it had not underinvested in and overtaxed its oil industry during the Chávez years. Dysfunctional price and exchange rate policies also strongly affected the oil sector, working as an additional mechanism of overtaxation and contributing to logistical and operational problems. And as oil prices began to fall, investment cuts made it even more difficult for PDVSA to achieve its production targets. However, the data suggest that these investment cuts were in line with historical variation and cannot easily explain the severe fall in oil output that takes place after 2016.

The post-2016 collapse in oil production took sector specialists by surprise. It also coincided with a period of acute deterioration in the economy's productivity, suggesting that the economy suffered additional disruptions after 2017 that contributed to explaining the economy's outsized growth collapse. While underinvestment and overtaxation of the oil industry can help explain why Venezuelans are not much richer today, they are not a good explanation for why they are so much poorer than they were in 2012.

In the rest of this book, I argue that to fully explain this collapse, we need to understand the nature of the political crisis that overtook the country from late 2016 on. I argue that toward the end of 2016, the country's political actors significantly escalated their conflict in a form that began generating sizable negative spillovers on the economy. These spillovers are reflected both in the post-2016 decline in oil production and exports and in the acute decline in TFP. In the end, the political conflict led to the severing of the country's financial and trade links with the world economy, with disastrous consequences for Venezuelan living standards.

Before doing this, however, let us step back and set out a conceptual framework to help us understand how and when political actors decide to adopt strategies in their fight for power that undermine general economic conditions. I take up that task in the next chapter.

THREE

Scorched Earth Politics

As long as there is a General
I won't even buy a calf,
Because, in order to steal,
They will, out of nothing, make war.
—Nineteenth-century Venezuelan grasslands couplet,
in Gil Fortoul 1907

This chapter presents an analytic framework for understanding when and why political actors choose to damage the economy. I focus on the decision by contending political forces to adopt strategies that deplete the resources they are fighting over. I argue that the actors involved in a conflict over power can choose to limit their actions to strategies that do not cause negative spillovers on the economy or to instead adopt tactics that improve their chances of capturing power while destroying economic resources. Whether they choose to use these destructive, scorched earth strategies will depend on the characteristics of the political contest, including how much they have to gain by prevailing, as well as their capacity to deter their adversaries from fighting over power using destructive means.

Two key determinants of the sustainability of nondestructive political competition in the theory laid out in this chapter are the stakes of power and the endowments of the economy. When the stakes of power are high, politicians have greater incentive to appeal to economically destructive strategies in their fight for power. Increases in the economy's endowments, on the other hand, may allow the state to deploy greater resources to deterring opponents from using destructive means of contesting power, thus reinforcing political and economic stability. External shocks can affect the incentives to adopt scorched earth strategies by affecting the ability that political actors have to deter their adversaries from engaging in destructive conflict.

I argue that this framework helps us understand why Venezuela's economic collapse occurred when it did and what forces drove it. Venezuela saw a systematic concentration of authority from the late 1990s that allowed the national executive to subordinate other branches of power to it, thus raising the relative benefit of being in power—and the relative cost of being out of it. It also suffered a massive adverse external shock in the 2014 to 2016 period, which significantly raised the cost to political actors of investing in dissuading their opponents from playing outside established rules. The combination of these two factors—increased stakes of power and declining external resources—significantly raised the incentives for both the government and the opposition to opt for political strategies capable of generating severe negative economic external effects on society, descending into an all-out political conflict that was ultimately able to bring the economy down with it.[1]

The conceptual framework offered in this chapter borrows from established literatures in economics and political science. Theories of public choice and political economy have shown us how policy makers can manipulate the economy and generate inefficient outcomes in their pursuit of political objectives. Modern democratization theories, in turn, have shown us how political actors are likely to take higher risks in their fight over power when constraints on executive power are loose and the stakes of power are high. I bring together these two insights to show that political actors may be more willing to harm the economy when they become engaged in a high-stakes fight for power, precipitating an all-out political conflict that can sow the seeds of a society's economic collapse.

The rest of the chapter proceeds as follows. In the next two sections, I present an overview and stylized description of political economy models of inefficient policies and democratic theories of high-stakes conflict. I also introduce two models that help us understand how and when political actors can decide to impose economic distortions for political gain. The first one is a distilled version of the established political economy literature that shows that politicians will be more likely to impose economic distortions when they are at risk of losing power through elections and when the stakes of power are higher. The second one is a game-theoretic model in which competing political actors must decide whether to adopt scorched earth strategies with severe negative economic externalities in their fight over power. Using the latter model, I establish the conditions under which their choice of political strategies can precipitate a decline into economically destructive political conflict. In the last section, I provide a brief summary of how this conceptual framework can help explain the evolution of Venezuela's economy and politics over the course of the past two decades.

POWER, POLITICS, AND THE ECONOMY

The idea that politicians may pursue inefficient policies to strengthen their chance to stay in power has a long history. The book of Isaiah describes the rulers of Judah as corrupt "companions of thieves" who "do not bring justice to the fatherless, and the widow's cause does not come to them" (Isaiah 1:1–31). In the first century BCE, the Roman tribune Clodius passed a law promising a free corn dole to all male citizens; the law led to the draining of the Roman treasury but allowed Clodius to reduce the power of magistrates and send his rival, Cicero, into exile (Tatum 1999; Watts 2018, 209). Holy Roman Empire princes prepared for the Thirty Years' War by paying for mercenaries with debased currency, throwing early seventeenth-century Europe into a competitive hyperinflation (Kindleberger 1991).

The view that governments should be considered not as altruistic social planners but as spaces where political actors pursue their self-interest, leading to policy decisions that are often neither economically optimal nor representative of the popular will, was brought into mainstream neoclassical economics through the contributions of the Virginia school of public choice (Buchanan and Tullock 1962; Olson 1965; Niskanen 1971). Much of the work in this tradition saw electoral politics as inextricably linked with suboptimal economic outcomes, positing that politicians would systematically try to fool voters or use the political system as a smokescreen to divert resources to special interests (Tullock 1983; Tollison 1988; Magee, Brock, and Young 1989). An alternate vision, associated with the University of Chicago economics department, viewed political competition as leading to convergence to efficient outcomes (Stigler 1971; Becker 1976).

Many contributions of the public choice school were based on the premise that voters were irrational and that politicians could systematically deceive them. For example, the earliest political business cycle models argued that the government would have an incentive to pursue expansionary policies by exploiting a short-run Philips curve to generate economic expansions ahead of elections (Nordhaus 1975). In the 1980s and 1990s, scholars working in the rational choice tradition explored ways to make the findings of systematic politically induced policy distortions consistent with the hypothesis of voter rationality. Signaling models were used to show that under asymmetric information, rational voters could be tricked into believing that some policy makers were more competent than they actually were. For example, Rogoff and Siebert (1988) show that policy makers could use inflationary financing ahead of elections to pay for a given level of public spending at lower tax rates; voters, uncertain as to whether these lower tax rates were due to the use of inflationary financing or greater policy-maker competence in turning tax revenue into public goods, would be more likely to vote for those who implemented distortionary policies ahead of elections. Alesina and Tabellini (1990) show that under electoral alternation, policy makers could accumulate debt strategically to constrain the choices of their successors, leading governments to incur suboptimally high levels of debt. Coate and Morris (1995) establish that politicians could use inefficient public spending projects to transfer income to special interests when voters were uncertain as to the returns to public investment. In their model, politicians do so because voters would be less likely to punish them for carrying out a project of uncertain returns than for directly transferring funds to the special interest—even though the direct transfer to the special interest would, strictly speaking, be more efficient.

Some contributions to the political economy literature explicitly bring in the distribution of rewards between losers and winners of the political contest and link it to the likelihood of inefficient outcomes. Alesina and Drazen (1991) model macroeconomic stabilization decisions as the outcome of a war of attrition between groups that defend alternative adjustment programs that differ in the distribution of the costs of adjustment between groups. When the costs of adjustments are equally borne among groups, then stabilization occurs immediately; the more unequal the distribution of costs, the longer the delay of stabilization and the cumulative cost of distortions from not stabilizing. Fernandez and Rodrik (1991) show that when there is uncertainty about the distribution of benefits from reform, efficiency-enhancing reforms may be rejected even when they benefit most people. This will happen when there are large groups that are uncertain as to whether they will be net gainers or losers from reform. In this case, guaranteeing a more egalitarian distribution of the benefits of reform can ensure passage of the reform and the resulting increases in economic efficiency.

How to Fool a Rational Voter

Political business cycle models hypothesize that elections increase the government's incentive to pursue short-term expansionary policies. The rational expectations version of these models relies on the idea that elected policy makers have asymmetric information on their own competence and use inflationary financing near election time to fool voters into believing that they are more competent than they actually are. Rogoff and Sibert (1988) model competence as the ability of a government to provide a given level of public goods at a lower cost to taxpayers. In one of the equilibria that emerge from their model, most policy makers generate inflation surprises in election time, and policy makers with intermediate levels of ability display the greatest bias toward inflationary policies.

In the Rogoff and Siebert (1988) model, policy makers resort to inflationary financing only ahead of elections. The reason is that it makes sense to fool voters only if doing so improves the chances of having them reelect you. If you use inflationary financing in an off-election year, by the time of the election voters will have figured out that you were not as competent as you appeared to be. The crucial assumption here is that voters observe the level of inflationary financing only after the election, an assumption that is consistent with the literature documenting the lagged effect of monetary policy on prices.[2]

A sizable empirical literature has documented evidence for the existence of a political business cycle. Shi and Svensson (2006) use a panel of eighty-five countries over a twenty-five-year period and find evidence that, on average, government fiscal deficits increase by around one percentage point of GDP in election years. They argue that the cycle is more pronounced in developing than in developed countries. Brender and Drazen (2005) argue that this effect is driven by recently established democracies and that it is stronger in weaker democracies. Chauvet and Collier (2009) attempt to empirically distinguish a cyclical from a structural effect of elections on policies: the structural effect captures how elections may improve the quality of policies via increased accountability; the cyclical effect captures the idea that policies will be of lower quality near election time. Using a panel of eighty-two countries, they find that the quality of policy is indeed highest in the middle of the electoral term. There is also a much broader literature on the effects of democracy on economic performance, as well as a long-standing debate on whether democracy is good or bad for growth.[3]

A Model of Politically Induced Distortions

We can capture some of the basic intuitions from this literature using an intuitive reduced-form model. Consider a policy maker who trades off the electoral benefits of distortionary policies against their welfare cost. Let the utility of the policy maker U be denoted as

$$U = q(P)R - \sigma W(P) \tag{3.1}$$

where q is the probability of the incumbent policymaker winning the election, P is the distortionary policy, W is the welfare cost of distortionary policies, σ is the weight that the policy maker assigns to those welfare costs, and R is the rewards from power. For simplicity, I normalize the rewards to the policy maker in case they lose the election to zero. Note that this implies that the term R should be interpreted as the benefits of being in power *relative* to those of being out of power—what I will call the stakes of power.

I assume $W' > 0, q' > 0, W'' > 0$, and $q'' < 0$. Then the equilibrium P is given by the solution to

$$q'(P)R - \sigma W'(P) = 0 \tag{3.2}$$

with the second-order condition

$$q''R - \sigma W'' < 0, \tag{3.3}$$

which is ensured for any interior solution by the assumptions $W'' > 0$ and $q'' < 0$.

Differentiating equation (3.2), we can derive the comparative statics result:

$$\frac{dP}{dR} = -\frac{q'}{q''R - \sigma W''} > 0 \tag{3.4}$$

and

$$\frac{dP}{d\sigma} = -\frac{W'}{q''R - \sigma W''} < 0 \tag{3.5}$$

Equations (3.4) and (3.5) tell us that the higher the relative returns from being in power and the lower the cost to the politician of economic distortions, the higher the incentives for policy makers to adopt distortionary policies and the higher the consequent costs to efficiency and output.

While the literature discussed above and summarized in this stylized model tells us how the risk of losing power can create a powerful incentive for politicians to adopt policies that harm the economy, it doesn't describe how the structure of political competition affects these incentives. To more fully understand the determinants of policy-maker incentives, we need to model not only what happens to politicians when they are in power, but what happens to them when they are out of power. Doing so requires understanding both what politicians do when they are in office and what their competitors do to try to replace them in office. For insights into these issues, I turn to the political science literature on electoral competition.

DEMOCRACY AS A SELF-ENFORCING EQUILIBRIUM

The central thesis of this book is that Venezuela's economic collapse was driven by the choice of political actors to adopt strategies with severe negative external effects on the economy. To explain why Venezuela's government and opposition chose to adopt these scorched earth strategies, we must understand what had stopped them from doing so previously. That is, we need to explain why political actors chose up to a certain moment of time to abide by self-imposed limits on the choice of political weapons to use in the battle of power and why they ultimately chose to abandon that self-restraint.

This question parallels one of the central issues of modern democratic theory, which is that of why actors—including governments that hold a monopoly on the use of force—choose to abide by rules of political competition that determine if and when power is transferred. The two questions—why politicians don't destroy the economy and why they accept peaceful transfers of power—are also directly related because implicit or explicit commitments not to harm the economy commonly form part of the rules governing political competition in modern democracies. Political leaders are more likely to spur their supporters to engage in strategies that harm the economy (such as general strikes, rioting, or armed insurrection) when they choose to claim that the rules of the political system are rigged against them.

Democratic political systems are governed by rules such as free and fair elections, the protection of political rights and liberties, and the existence of checks on executive discretion. These institutions regulate the relationship between those who hold power and those who do not. Like any set of rules, they have practical meaning only if the actors that they bind comply with them. Yet unlike many of the rules that humans face in their day-to-day lives, the actors that must comply with these rules often have the power to subvert them. This is the essence of the democratic compliance paradox: the puzzle that actors who hold the monopoly on power are willing to give it up when they lose elections.

Sometimes they are not. Democratic breakdown occurs when key political actors decide to stop abiding by the rules that govern political competition. Coups are the most extreme version of democratic breakdown, but there are many other ways in which politicians can decide to stop playing by the established rules of the democratic game. They can rig elections or fail to recognize valid election results; they can disobey decisions of other branches of government, or they can use their influence over the judiciary to produce politically biased court decisions. They can call for violent protests to attempt to force a government out of power, or they can use their power over security forces to repress political opponents.

Compliance with rules is often in the eye of the beholder. The winner of an election may claim that the vote count has been transparent while the loser cries fraud. Protesters accused of violence may claim that they face sham trials while their accusers will say they are upholding the rule of law and complying with the state's duty to maintain peace. A convicted political leader may claim to be a political prisoner while their accusers will say that being a politician does not entitle you to being above the law.

LOSING POWER

In November 2020, US president Donald Trump shocked the political establishment by refusing to recognize the results of that year's presidential elections. The decision not to concede defeat in a presidential election by a major party candidate was unprecedented in American politics (Vile 2002; McKeever 2021). Several weeks later, the president's supporters stormed the Capitol building during the joint session of Congress assembled to count electoral votes, in an event that some analysts labeled a coup attempt (Graham 2021; Hill 2021).

While relatively new to American politics, this type of scene is common in many other countries. The government never loses, "and when it loses it grabs," quipped a refrain used by Mexicans to refer to the Institutional Revolutionary Party (Partido Revolucionario Institucional, PRI), which held uninterrupted power through nominally competitive elections for more than seven decades. Because of this, the Peruvian writer Mario Vargas Llosa once referred to the PRI as "the perfect dictatorship" (*El País* 1990). The Russian opposition leader Gary Kasparov (2020) proposed a similar description of his country's political system: "All roads, all votes, lead to Vladimir Putin." Somewhat more crudely, faced with an opponent's accusation of ballot rigging, the Nicaraguan dictator Anastasio Somoza is said to have replied, "You won the elections, but I won the count" (Ratcliffe 2011, 141).

Many political scientists have converged over time on the idea that alternance in power is a defining characteristic of a democracy. Echoing Vargas Llosa, the political scientist Adam Przeworski (1991, 10) offered a succinct definition of democracy in 1991 as "a system in which parties lose elections." Some modern attempts at measuring democracy only classify as democratic countries those in which the government has ceded power to another party.[4]

For democracies to be sustainable, Przeworski (1991) argued, those who lose the democratic contest for power must find it in their interest to accept the results. But why would any government ever give up power? This is in fact one of the central questions of political theory. Thomas Hobbes ([1651] 2017) concluded that it would not: the only way in which societies could overcome the chaos of a state of nature where life was "nasty, brutish and short" was by handing over power to a sovereign; the catch, of course, is that such a sovereign would by design have to be unconstrained.

Yet modern democracies are the opposite of the Hobbesian Leviathan, with chief executives accepting and abiding by multiple constraints. The principles of separation of powers and divided government are enshrined in their constitutions. Recognizing this, however, only pushes the question further back: Why do actors with enough force to subvert constitutional rules decide to accept them? Why would any government choose to be constrained by the rule of law?

Sometimes they don't. Przeworski argued that incumbents losing an election would recognize the outcome only if they felt there was a reasonable chance that they would be able to accede to power again in the future. He provided a simple model in which the loser of an election would only comply with the results of the election if the benefits of compliance exceeded the benefits of subversion. In his model, the loser of an election is confronted by a choice of whether to subvert the electoral proccss and get a benefit S_t, or instead comply with the electoral result and get $C_{t+1} = pW + (1 - p)L$ in the next period, where W, L, and p respectively denote the value of winning and losing and the probability of winning the election. Assuming politicians discount the future according to a discount factor r and letting C^* and S^* respectively denote the cumulative values of compliance and subversion, some simple algebra shows that at any given moment, a losing incumbent will give up power when

$$p > \frac{1}{r}\frac{(1-r)S^* - L*}{W - L} = p^* \tag{3.6}$$

In other words, compliance requires that the loser of an election estimate that the probability of winning a future election is sufficiently high. Sustainable democracies are those that ensure that the losers will remain sufficiently competitive in future elections to have a reasonable chance of reaching power again. Democratic rules must restrain the power of the executive enough to ensure that it is not used to annul the chances of the opposition acceding to power in the future; otherwise no one would ever want to give up power.

This powerful intuition set the ground for a literature on the sustainability of democratization processes (Przeworski et al. 1996; Weingast 1997; Geddes 1999; North, Summerhill, and Weingast 1999; Lizzeri and Persico 2004; Svolik 2019). Yet before going on to explore the dimensions in which Przeworski's model can be expanded, it is important to understand some of its shortcomings. One is that the model assumes by construction that $W > S$; that is, the benefits of winning are larger than the benefits of subverting the democratic process. Therefore, winners will always accept the results of the electoral process.

If we interpret "accepting the results" of an electoral process in the narrow sense of recognizing the outcome of a vote count, then this makes sense. But if we go beyond the literal reading of a model and consider that it is often elected leaders who do much to subvert the democratic process, then the assumption begins to sound questionable. Accepting the results of an election isn't only accepting the fact that you won; that's the easy part. Accepting the results also means accepting the limitations that functioning democracies impose on officeholders, despite the fact that they have the power to subvert them. That is where the real paradox lies.

In other words, it is not hard to understand why a political actor can accept being out of power for some time given the prospects of returning to power in the future. What is not altogether clear is why winners—who gain control of a monopoly on power by accepting the result of the democratic contest—would not choose to abuse the power of the state to make sure their competitors never again have a chance to drive them out of power. We know that many leaders do precisely that: they reach power through elections and then use the control of the power of the state to undermine the democratic process. This process of what is known as democratic backsliding (Levitsky and Ziblatt 2018; Haggard and Kaufman 2021) appears to be increasing in recent years; Venezuela under Hugo Chávez and Nicolás Maduro is often cited as a prominent example (Corrales and Penfold 2015; Corrales 2023).

Constitutions play an extremely important role in restraining executive power; constitutional changes therefore are also key turning points in processes of democratic backsliding. Przewroski's (1991) conjecture was that constitutions that are observed and last for a long time are those that reduce the stakes of political battles to allow minimum conditions for political oppositions to effectively contest power. Successful democracies, he argued, are those in which institutions make it difficult to fortify a temporary advantage and turn it into a permanent one (Przeworski 1991, 34–37).

Weingast (1997) builds on Przeworski's insight to argue that democracy would emerge when leaders accepted constraints on their power; when leaders are unconstrained, they will in the final instance use their power to remain in power. North, Summerhill, and Weingast (1999) contend that high stakes of power bring leaders to sabotage constitutional and democratic rules and bring those out of power to use extraconstitutional means to try to attain power. Fearon (2011) and Mittal and Weingast (2013) develop the idea that constitutions can serve as focal points allowing citizens to coordinate when rulers transgress constitutional provisions.

The struggle for political power in a society, of course, involves much more than politicians. Indeed, many strands of political theory treat politicians as little more than a sideshow. Marx and Engels's ([1848] 2015, 15) famous dictum that the state is "but a committee for managing the common affairs of the whole bourgeoisie" is mirrored in modern rational choice political models in which politicians converge to the policies preferred by the voter whose preferences are at the median of the distribution (Downs 1957; Hinich and Munger 1997; Roemer 2006). A highly influential generation of models built on the characterization of democracy as a self-enforcing equilibrium and combined it with models of distributive conflict to derive predictions regarding when and where we could expect democratization to happen.

One strand of thinking conceived of democracy as a compromise solution to polarizing distributive conflict. Przeworski (2008) modeled political parties as representatives of the extremes of the distribution of income—the left representing the poor and the right representing the wealthy. While the left wants high levels of redistribution and the right wants little or none of it, democracy will result in the tax policies preferred by the middle class. Both the poor and the wealthy put up with democracy because such an intermediate solution is better than paying the cost—in terms of repression and absence of political rights—of a dictatorship. However, the loss of political rights is less important relative to the gains from having your preferred level of redistribution when societies are poorer, explaining why democracies are more likely to survive in wealthier countries.

Arguments along similar lines have been provided by Boix (2003) and Acemoglu and Robinson (2005). Both model the choice of elites to democratize as a strategy to avert a costly revolution. Elites balance the cost of accepting the choice of redistributive taxation that predominantly poor voters will make in a democracy with the cost of repressing the poor and the risk that revolutions will end up being successful. Boix (2003) emphasizes the role of inequality and capital mobility: more egalitarian societies will adopt lower levels of taxation in a democracy, as will societies in which capital is able to flee to lower-tax jurisdictions. The rich will have less to lose from accepting democratization where inequality is lower and capital mobility is higher. Acemoglu and Robinson (2005) highlight the capacity of democratic institutions to serve as a device to credibly commit to future pro-majority policies. They argue that development failures stem from the resistance of elites to the development of inclusive institutions in which political power rests with a broad coalition or plurality of groups, allowing large segments of the population to reap the gains from exchange and innovation.

Much as these models may help shed light on some of the cross-national patterns of democratic institutions—such as their greater prevalence in higher-income and less unequal societies—they appear limited in their capacity to explain Venezuela's descent into destructive political conflict. Surely, one can take any theory that posits a relationship between income and authoritarianism and explain Venezuela's democratic backsliding as a result of its economic collapse. Yet one would have to contend with the simple fact that Venezuela slid into authoritarianism at a time when its per capita income was not all that different from that in the 1960s, when it was beginning to build what for decades was a remarkably stable democracy. Furthermore, as I argue in chapters 8 through 10, there is strong evidence that the political crisis was a cause, rather than just a consequence, of declining living standards in the post-2016 period.

Class-conflict models of democracy posit that authoritarianisms can be of two stripes: right-wing dictatorships enshrined to protect against high levels of taxation or Marxist-inspired dictatorships of the proletariat. The Maduro regime fits neither mold. Venezuela today certainly does not look like the result of a rational choice by the country's working class to pay the cost of revolution to extract high taxes from the rich. Not only is Venezuela no socialist utopia; it doesn't even rise to the level of a minimally rational bureaucratized centrally planned economy. Rather, it is a country that has descended into dystopian chaos because the state lost both its capacity and its willingness to operate a functional economy. It is on this destruction of basic state capabilities, rather than their use to favor some groups in detriment of others, that we need to focus if we want to understand Venezuela's descent into economically destructive political conflict.

One important attempt to use the elite-led democratization framework in a way that is directly relevant to Venezuela is the work of Dunning (2008), who deploys a game-theory approach to model the effects of resource rents on the willingness of elites to democratize. Dunning argues that there are two distinct effects of rents on the benefits of democratization relative to autocracy for elites. On the one hand, greater rents mean that the state has more control over resources, increasing the attractiveness of controlling those rents through an autocratic government. On the other hand, greater rents imply lower demand for redistributive taxation from the poor, whose needs can be met by distributing rents instead of taxing the rich, thus making democracy less costly for elites. Dunning argues that this model can help explain Venezuela's early democratization as a result of the ability that it gave to elites to tolerate democracy without the risk of resulting in high levels of redistributive taxation. Declining resource rents in the 1980s and 1990s help explain the increasing salience of distributive conflict and the decline of pacted democracy.

Although the Dunning model is attractive as an explanation of the rise and decline of Venezuelan democracy, it too is inadequate for understanding the collapse of the Maduro years. As I argue in part 3, the main cause behind the magnitude of Venezuela's economic collapse is not an exogenous decline in prices; the oil price faced by Maduro is not all that different from that faced by Chávez during most of his time in power. The main cause, rather, is an endogenous collapse in production. Solving the puzzle of Venezuela's collapse requires understanding why its political actors decided to kill the goose that laid the golden eggs.

The central idea posed in this book is that Venezuela's economic collapse and growing authoritarianism can be explained as a case of the unraveling of a self-enforcing democratic equilibrium. I argue that the decision to break with preexisting democratic arrangements reflected the rising stakes of political conflict and the increasing scarcity of resources to play the democratic game caused by the 2014 to 2016 external shock. I also argue that in this breakdown, political actors had at their disposal strategies that allowed them to compete for power outside of existing institutional arrangements at the cost of inflicting severe negative economic externalities on society.

Thus, while my explanation borrows strongly from the rational choice approach of viewing democracy as a set of self-enforcing constraints on executive power, it departs from the strand of the literature that attempts to explain variations in development outcomes as a result of distributive struggle among different economic classes. While this literature may have its merits for explaining other experiences of underdevelopment, I argue that it is woefully inadequate for understanding Venezuela's economic collapse, which is essentially driven by the tug-of-war between political elites for control of the country's oil revenues.

In other words, rather than superimpose a political model of democratization on an economic model of distributive class struggle, I argue that Venezuela's economic collapse can be understood as the consequence of competition between elites for political power. At the root of the country's collapse is the inability of political elites to coordinate on obeying rules to delimit and regulate their competition for power. While both elites make claims to represent the country's poor, these claims play little role in determining their choice of political strategies with their consequent economic impacts. A model of interelite conflict, rather than a model of distributive struggle, appears better equipped to explain the main stylized facts of Venezuela's political and economic explosion.

A Model of Economically Destructive Political Conflict

In this section, I present a formal model that attempts to provide an explanation for why political elites may choose modes of confrontation that generate large negative economic externalities. This model, originally proposed in Rodríguez (2021) and developed into its current form by Rodríguez and Imam (2022), extends the framework of the one-player model of policy distortions and elections outlined at the start of this chapter to a setting in which there are two political actors, both of which can choose political strategies that harm the economy.

In the model, two competing political forces face a choice of how to fight for power. They can invest resources in campaigning for elections and accept the results of that election, or they can decide to ignore the election's results and fight for power using nonelectoral means. In other words, they can choose whether to fight for power with votes or with bullets. If they accept the election's results, they also accept the resulting distribution of the benefits of power; if they choose to disavow it, then their rewards will be determined by how many bullets they have compared to their opponents.

I show that equilibria in which losing candidates recognize the results of the election are only possible if the stakes of power are not too high. However, the viability of democracy is also affected by an economy's wealth: a richer economy may be able to sustain democracy at stakes of power that are too high for it to be viable in a poorer one. Therefore, economies in which the stakes of power are high may only descend into conflict when they experience a shock to their wealth that pushes them below a certain threshold. This, I argue, is what happened in Venezuela: a large increase in the stakes of power and a large negative terms of trade shock pushed the country into full-fledged economically destructive political conflict.

I refer to the decision to appeal to modalities of engagement that generate aggregate economic losses in the struggle for power as scorched earth strategies. The scorched earth concept has a long history in studies of warfare. While the tale of Roman soldiers "wasting the earth" in their fight against the Carthaginians may be apocryphal, there is no shortage of examples of such strategies from ancient and modern warfare, including General William T. Sherman's "March to the Sea" through the Confederacy in the US Civil War and the spraying by American forces of twelve million gallons of toxic chemical agents in Vietnam (Leebaw 2014; Murphy 2020; Kreike 2021). Scorched earth military campaigns focus on the destruction or impairment of natural resources, including agricultural land, while the terms "strategic warfare" and "strategic bombing" are often reserved for attacks on physical infrastructure (Grimsley and Rogers 2008). This distinction is often moot, as physical infrastructure and natural resources are usually interdependent. More comprehensively, the concept "total war" encompasses armed conflict where "anything and everything is the object, subject and means of war" (Kreike 2021, 37).

The model presented in this section combines two traditions of thinking about political conflict. One is the modeling of electoral competition in which politicians vie for the support of voters to win elections through the investment of resources in political campaigns (Austen-Smith 1987; Baron 1994). The other tradition is the analysis of conflict through models that emphasize the use of resources in activities aimed at appropriation (Hirshleifer 1989; Fearon 1995; Grossman and Kim 1995). In my model, politicians choose between investing in influencing voters and recognizing the legitimacy of the election results, as they do in models of electoral competition, or contesting the legitimacy of those results and directly battling over appropriation of the rents from being in power, as they do in models of conflict.

Whether to accept the rules of the democratic game or to instead act to subvert democracy is also the question at the center of the theories of democratization discussed previously in this chapter. However, the democratization literature generally models the returns to subverting the democratic process as exogenous and independent of a political actor's electoral performance. This common characterization disregards the fact that the choices that politicians must make if they wish to subvert the democratic process are often at odds with what they must do if they want to win elections. My model, in contrast, starts out from the assumption that there is a fundamental trade-off between investing in winning elections (campaigns) and investing in fighting for power through nonelectoral conflict (guns).

Consider then two political groups vying for power. Both groups compete in elections by spending resources that determine their probability of winning. Those resources could include money as well as broader political influence that allows the mobilization of votes.[5] They could also include other actions that are perceived positively by voters and that have an opportunity cost for political actors to provide. Alternatively, both groups can also spend resources in acquiring the means that will allow them to contest power independently of the vote count.

I treat the two actors as symmetric. I label each of the groups $i = \{1,2\}$, the resources they spend on electoral competition E_i, and those that they invest in conflict technology P_i. The economy has a fixed endowment R distinct from those that political groups devote to electoral and conflict investment and whose distribution between the groups is defined through the political process. If both groups accept the results of the election, the winning group will receive a fraction $\delta > 1/2$ of that endowment, while the loser will receive $1 - \delta$. I call δ the stakes of power: the higher δ, the more unequal the distribution of political rewards between winners and losers.

The utility of group i if the election result is respected by both sides will then be

$$U_i^E = q(E_i, E_j)\delta R + (1 - q(E_i, E_j))(1 - \delta)R, \tag{9.1}$$

where q denotes the probability of i winning if i spends E_i and i's opponent spends E_j. Each party makes a choice of whether to accept the election's outcome conditional on the results. I allow a party to disavow the results both of its defeat and of its victory. The reason, as discussed in the previous section, is that recognition entails accepting the distribution of rewards (δ and $1 - \delta$), and a party may decide that it prefers the rewards that it is able to reap from conflict to those that emerge even from winning an election. A winner's decision to disavow the outcome should thus be seen as a decision to take more for themselves than is accepted under existing institutional arrangements.[6]

If either party decides not to accept the election result, then the groups will enter into conflict over power. This need not be interpreted as explicit armed conflict. Rather, it involves all types of efforts at capturing power through means other than persuading voters. They can of course include armed uprisings and military coups but may also include softer means of influencing political outcomes such as fomenting unrest or calling for international sanctions. What is crucial is that the distribution of rewards will no longer be determined by the democratic institutional arrangements reflected in δ but rather through confrontation of forces in the nonelectoral arena and that this conflict will generate an adverse effect on the economy.

When groups enter conflict, the distribution of R is determined according to what is known in the literature as a *contest success function*, in which the reward of each player is a function of the investment in conflict technology by them and their opponent. I write this function, which specifies what fraction of R i receives when i spends P_i and i's opponent spends P_j, as

$$C(P_i,P_j) \tag{3.7}$$

Production is carried out by N atomistic firms, which share a common constant returns to scale production function,

$$Y_m = A(V)F(K_m,H_m) \tag{3.8}$$

where A denotes productivity, m indexes firms, and K_m and H_m respectively denote a firm's use of capital and labor. The economy has aggregate endowments of $\overline{K}$ and $\overline{H}$. Labor and capital markets are competitive and will thus clear at $K_m = \frac{\overline{K}}{N} = \overline{k}$ and $H_m = \frac{\overline{H}}{N} = \overline{h}$, so that aggregate output is given by

$$Y = A(V)NF(\overline{k},\overline{h}) \tag{3.9}$$

The externality of conflict is captured in the dependence of productivity in the sum of politician payoffs, $V = V_1 + V_2$. I describe how these are determined below. For now, it is important to note that if politicians engage in destructive political conflict, then V will decline, and so will Y.

The *C(.)* function can be interpreted in two ways: as a deterministic function setting out the distribution of rewards from power that results from the scenario of conflict or as a probabilistic function that describes the chance that each side has to capture the totality of those rewards. While both interpretations are plausible, the latter seems most relevant for my context. This is because, as a matter of practice, it is not that usual for open political conflict to lead to stalemate situations in which both sides end up with a share of power. Rather, I view the decision to enter political conflict as the ultimate raising of the stakes of power: entering a fight for absolute control, in which one side will ultimately prevail. For this reason, I characterize a conflict equilibrium as one leading to dictatorship or authoritarianism: ultimately, whoever wins gets to capture the totality of the rewards from power.

I make several assumptions about the form of the functions *C(.)* and *q(.)* that are discussed in greater detail in the online appendix. Yet one particularly important distinction between these two functions is that *C(.)* destroys output, and *q(.)* does not. It is for that same reason that I refer to the decision to disavow an election and enter conflict as a scorched earth strategy. Regardless of how much is spent on E_i and E_j, there will always be an endowment R left to distribute between the winner and loser if both accept the results of the election. In contrast, if i and j enter conflict, then their use of P will lead to a loss of aggregate output. I call these assumptions respectively the *nondestructiveness of electoral competition* and the *destructiveness of conflict*.[7] The decision to adopt scorched earth strategies is what leads a society to enter into economically destructive political conflict.

Both groups choose E and P to maximize expected utility subject to the constraint $E_i + P_i = \overline{L}_i$; that is, they decide how to allocate their initial endowment (not to be confused with the rewards allocated in the contest for power R) into electoral and conflict technologies. It is this choice of political technologies that will determine their comparative advantage in winning elections or fighting for power.

To take a specific example, consider the decision by Venezuela's opposition to lobby for sanctions or the decision by the Maduro government to strip the legislature of its budget oversight functions. Both require the investment of political capital—international lobbying efforts on the opposition's side, pressuring the judiciary on Maduro's side. Both are likely to be disliked by voters and thus to decrease their support at the voting booth. Both have a negative effect on foreign investment and thus cause aggregate economic losses. But both may also make it more likely for the actors that adopt them to prevail in the nonelectoral contest for power.

Temporally, the structure of play is as follows. First, each group selects E_i and P_i. Elections are then held and the winner and loser determined. After the election's result is known, each group decides whether to recognize or disavow the result. If neither group contests the result, then the winner of the election receives δR and the loser receives $(1-\delta)R$. If either group decides to contest the result, then group i will receive $C(P_i,P_j)R$. This structure is illustrated in figure 3.1.

I will solve this game by backward induction, that is, looking first for a Nash equilibrium of the post-election recognition game and then solving for the subgame-perfect Nash equilibrium in the pre-election game given that strategies are Nash equilibria in the post-election game. I state the main results here and leave the proof of the propositions for the online appendix.

Consider first the post-election game. Label w the winner of the election and l the loser. The winner will decide to accept the results if and only if

$$C(P_w,P_l) \leq \delta \tag{3.10}$$

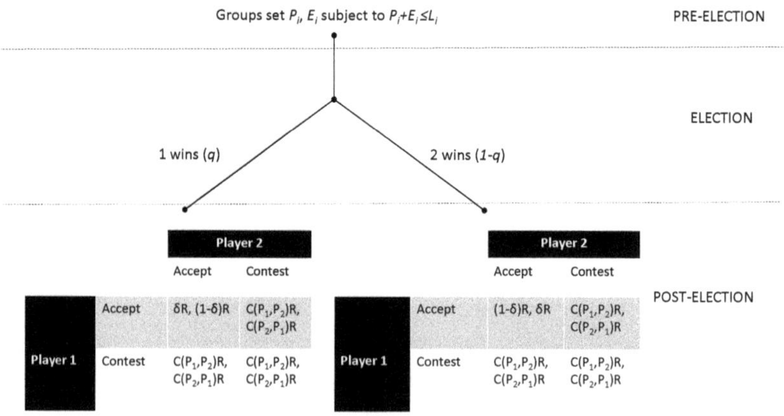

FIGURE 3.1. Temporal structure of play. *Source*: Rodríguez and Imam 2022.

that is, the expected benefit of contesting the result and having the distribution be determined through conflict must be less than that of reaping the rewards from having won the election. For the loser to recognize the result, in turn, it would have to be true that

$$C(P_l,P_w) \leq 1-\delta \tag{3.11}$$

Each group will have a piecemeal payoff function made up of four segments, depending on the decision of each actor to recognize or disavow the election result. Thus, politician payoffs V_i are determined as follows:

$$V_i = q(E_i,E_j)\delta R + (1 - q(E_i,E_j))(1 - \delta)R$$

if both sides accept i's and j's victory.

$$V_i = q(E_i,E_j)C(P_i,P_j) + (1 - q(E_i,E_j))(1 - \delta)R$$

if both sides accept j's but not i's victory.

$$V_i = q(E_i,E_j)\delta R + (1 - q(E_i,E_j))\,C(P_i,P_j)R$$

if both sides accept i's but not j's victory.

$$V_i = C(P_i,P_j)R$$

if at least one side does not accept i's victory and at least one side does not accept j's victory. (3.12)

I focus on the case in which both groups have the same endowments, that is, $\overline{L_i} = \overline{L_i} = \overline{L}$. Given that in this case actors are identical, I focus on symmetric subgame-perfect Nash equilibria (SSPNE). Symmetry implies that both sides either accept or contest their loss and accept or contest their victory, implying that the equilibrium solution must lie on either the first or the last part of equation (3.12). Therefore, there are only two types of equilibria: uncontested elections, where both the winner and the loser accept the result, and contested elections, where the loser (and possibly also the winner) contests the result.

Let P^* denote the choice of P by both parties in SSPNE where the election is uncontested and P^{**} the choice of P when it is contested. Then we can establish

Proposition 1: In any pure-strategy symmetric subgame-perfect Nash equilibrium, $C(P^*,P^*) = 1 - \delta$ if the election is uncontested and $P^{**} = Argmax_{Pi \in [0,\overline{L}_i]} C(P_i,P^{**})$ if the election is contested.[8]

Proposition 1 tells us that if the election is uncontested, then each group will spend in conflict technologies just as much as is necessary to get equation (3.11) to hold, that is, to dissuade the loser from contesting the election result. Since the election is uncontested, these conflict technologies are not used in equilibrium—the rewards to each party are determined by the electoral contest—so the only reason it makes sense for groups to spend any of their resources in developing them is that they need to dissuade their opponents from not recognizing the election's results. In other words, whoever is going to win the election must be sufficiently powerful at fighting for power through nonelectoral means to make sure that their opponent is not going to decide to take the battle to the nonelectoral terrain.

On the other hand, if we are in a contested election equilibrium, then electoral spending is irrelevant. Ultimately, the distribution of rewards will be the outcome of direct conflict, so it makes little sense for groups to devote resources to winning an election that they do not think will be honored anyway. Electoral spending does not fulfill a deterrence role here comparable to that fulfilled by conflict technologies in the uncontested elections equilibrium. Nevertheless, this does not necessarily mean that groups will spend all their resources in conflict technologies. Because of the destructiveness of conflict, it is possible that increasing conflict spending given your opponent's spending contributes to destroying output so much that it is not individually rational to do so. Therefore, here both groups will take conflict spending to the level that maximizes their rewards from conflict given the other group's spending.[9]

There are three important implications of Proposition 1.

Corollary 1: Along any pure-strategy uncontested SSPNE, P^* is an increasing function of δ. Furthermore, there will be a level $\overline{\delta}$ such that if $\delta > \overline{\delta}$ there will be no SSPNE where the election is uncontested.

As the stakes of power increase in a democratic society, two things happen. The first is that groups start spending much more resources in conflict technologies. Even though the rules of democracy are being honored, it is still the case that higher stakes of power make political actors devote more resources to deterring their opponents from deciding not to play by the rules of the game. The second is that there is a level of stakes of power at which democracy breaks down. If the stakes of power are too high, there is no level of spending in conflict technologies that will be able to deter players in equilibrium from disavowing election results.

Corollary 2: Along any pure-strategy SSPNE where the election is contested, P^{**} will be independent of δ. Furthermore, there will be a level $\underline{\delta}$ such that if $\delta \leq \underline{\delta}$, there will be no SSPNE where the election is contested.

When society falls into conflict, the stakes of power in the electoral game become irrelevant for pretty much the same reason electoral spending is irrelevant: the electoral contest is not binding once both sides know that the rewards will be distributed through conflict. Nevertheless, the stakes of power are determinant of the sustainability of conflict as an equilibrium. If the stakes of power are low enough, then conflict will not be a viable equilibrium. This result is directly related to the destructiveness of conflict. At any symmetric conflict equilibrium, each side is receiving strictly less than one-half of R because part of R is destroyed by conflict. On the other hand, at sufficiently low stakes of power, even the loser of an election is ensured of receiving close to half of R. They thus prefer accepting their electoral defeat to continuing to be immersed in conflict.

Corollary 3: There exists a $\tilde{\delta} \epsilon (\frac{1}{2},1)$ such that if $\delta < \tilde{\delta}$, there is no pure-strategy SSPNE.

Corollary 3 tells us that if the stakes of power are sufficiently low, neither democracy nor conflict is an equilibrium. This is a novel result that, to the best of my knowledge, has not been established previously. It suggests that while high stakes of power are a problem for democratic stability, very low stakes of power can also be a problem for it. The reason is that very low stakes of power can make a democratic equilibrium vulnerable to a deviation in which one player decides to invest in weapons to try to take power by force.

To understand the intuition for this result, consider what happens when the stakes of power are very low. The logic of political competition ensures that investment in guns will never be more than what is needed to deter the loser from contesting the elections. If the stakes of power are low, then the loser does relatively well, and it won't be necessary to spend too much to deter them. But if the level of investment in guns is low in equilibrium, then that means that there is an incentive for any player to decide to play an alternative strategy, which is to accumulate more guns and plan to contest the election. Only if deterrence spending is high enough in a democratic equilibrium will there be no incentive for any player to try to deviate from it by buying more guns.

Note that there is a key distinction from the unsustainability of democracy that takes place when the stakes are too high ($\delta > \overline{\delta}$) and that which occurs when they are too low ($\delta < \tilde{\delta}$). In the first of these cases, democracy is unsustainable, but conflict will be an equilibrium. This means that both groups will decide that it is in their interest to determine who has power through confrontation, with the results decided according to the conflict technology C. In the case in which $\delta < \tilde{\delta}$, in contrast, there is no equilibrium in pure strategies. What this means is that neither a democracy (where players never contest elections) nor conflict (where players always contest the elections) is sustainable as equilibria. A democratic equilibrium, as I just explained, is vulnerable to a deviation in which one actor decides to forgo electoral competition and amass weapons (i.e., invest in P), but a hypothetical conflict equilibrium is similarly vulnerable to a deviation in which the losers decide that recognizing the electoral result pays more than contesting it. The reason is that while amassing weapons may seem attractive if your opponent is not doing it in a democracy, accepting the results of low-stakes electoral competition will seem equally attractive once your opponent has responded in kind and accumulated weapons to a level at which the conflict equilibrium becomes one of mutually assured destruction.

Interpreting the absence of pure-strategy equilibria has always been a controversial issue in game-theoretic applications.[10] One potentially attractive interpretation for our purposes is that of cycling, in which actors adopt strategies that are best responses to their opponent's, only to see their opponent's strategy change over time in a way that merits a different response.[11] In our context, two actors immersed in a conflict may find that it is in their interest to recognize the election's results and forgo the costly confrontation; once they do so, they will find it optimal to maximize the amount of resources spent trying to win the electoral contest and lower spending in weapons. This in turn will open an opportunity for one of the actors to accumulate weapons and try to seize power by force, restarting the cycle of destructive conflict and unstable democracies.[12]

Therefore, my model does not predict the absence of democracy at low levels of stakes of power; it predicts its instability. What we may see is short-lived democracies giving way to conflict, with conflict often itself resolved through democratic accords to restart the cycles. When the stakes of power are high, we see conflict leading to dictatorship; when they are intermediate, we see democracy; when they are very low, we see instability.

Figure 3.2 shows the areas for each equilibrium corresponding to one parameterization of these equations (see the online appendix for greater detail). In this case, both C and q assume the power form of the contest success function, but in addition C is multiplied by an exponential term

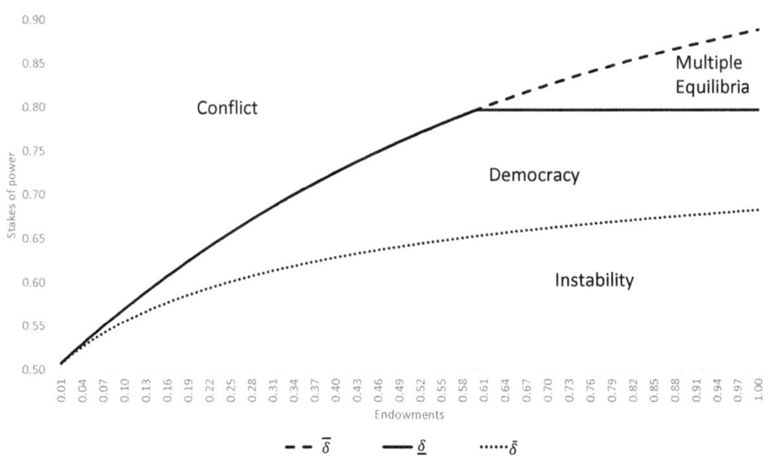

FIGURE 3.2. Endowments, stakes of power, and sustainable political regimes.
Source: Author's construction.

in the sum of conflict investments. High levels of δ are associated with a conflict equilibrium, intermediate levels with a democracy equilibrium, and low levels with a mixed-strategy equilibrium (which I describe as instability). At high levels of endowments and stakes of power, both democracy and conflict become viable.

Figure 3.3 maps out the implications of my model for output and its potential explanation for output collapses. There are only two levels of A—and thus of equilibrium output—under this model: that which corresponds to democracy, that is, nondestructive electoral competition; and that which corresponds to conflict, that is, economically destructive political conflict. Low output can only occur at high levels of δ, where conflict is an equilibrium; high output is sustainable under democracy, which is feasible at intermediate levels of output. As economies become wealthier in terms of their endowments, the range of stakes of power over which higher output is possible is larger.

A growth collapse in this model can occur for one of two reasons. The first is that an increase in the stakes of power can lead an economy to transition from a situation in which only democracy is an equilibrium to one in which only conflict is an equilibrium (panel a of fig. 3.3). The second is that an economy may be in a range of parameters in which both democracy and conflict are equilibria, and actors choose to change their strategies in a way that makes them jump from one equilibrium to another (panel b of fig. 3.3).

The fact that the width of the range over which democracy is feasible is increasing in endowments coincides with the results obtained in

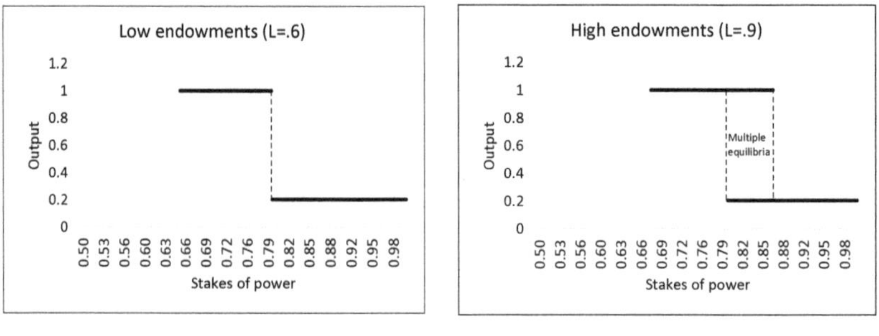

FIGURE 3.3. Equilibrium output and stakes of power under different endowments.
Source: Author's construction.

other settings such as those developed by Boix (2003) and Przeworski (2008) in which democracy is more likely to be stable at higher levels of income. It also echoes Acemoglu and Robinson's (2019) idea of a "narrow corridor" of liberal democracies that widens with the level of development. My logic, however, is somewhat different from theirs. In my model, political groups must invest in weapons, even if they are in a stable democratic equilibrium, to deter their opponents from contesting the election result when they lose. However, if the stakes of power are too high, the level of investment in weapons necessary to deter opponents from trying to grab power may be unattainable because it would exceed the resources available to each political group. As groups become wealthier, these high levels of deterrence investment that were previously inaccessible to them now become accessible.

These results are analogous to findings in the crime victimization literature. Even though richer neighborhoods are home to wealthier households that may be more attractive targets to crime, it is well known that poorer neighborhoods tend to be characterized by higher crime rates. One of the reasons is that the poor tend to spend less to protect their property, making it comparatively more attractive to potential criminals (Ayres and Levitt 1998; Vollaard and van Ours 2011; Kang 2014). For the same reason, poor countries may be less able than rich ones to invest in defending their governments from violent attempts at overthrow.

Put differently, it is much easier to overthrow the government of Haiti than that of the United States. The government of the latter can provide ample funding for its security services without significantly sacrificing the resources necessary to address the needs of its voters; the government of the former may find that it does not have enough resources to do both. There is a reason that people are willing to hire mercenaries to overthrow the government of Haiti but don't try to do the same to overthrow the government of the United States. The government of the United States is rich enough to make such an exercise futile without compromising its commitment to provide public goods to voters. The government of Haiti is not.[13]

The driver behind this result is the fact that in my model the rewards to be apportioned between political competitors, R, are unrelated to the endowment that groups can decide to spend on campaigns or weapons,

L. This assumption is not hard to justify. What is divided between political competitors is power over society, and it makes sense to think of it as a relative good. The life satisfaction of the president of Zimbabwe is likely similar to—if not higher than—that of the president of the United States. The ability of the president to purchase weapons without significantly sacrificing the provision of public goods and services, in contrast, is much lower in Zimbabwe than in the United States.

The model is consistent with some prominent stylized facts about the spread and survival of democratic regimes. First, it accounts for the widely observed fact that while some democracies exist in poor countries, they are less frequently found and tend to be more unstable than in wealthier economies. As figure 3.2 clearly shows, the space of parameters consistent with a stable democracy is much narrower in my model for poorer than for richer countries. Second, it suggests that very low stakes of power are also incompatible with political stability, a result that broadly confirms findings of the literature on power-sharing agreements (Koneska 2014; McCulloch and McGarry 2017; Jarstad and Nilsson 2018). Third, it predicts that while democracy can be stable in high-income countries, it is not the only possible equilibrium, and a descent into authoritarianism is also possible at high levels of income. This result is compatible with the concerns voiced recently by scholars regarding the stability of democratic arrangements in some of the world's most advanced economies (Acemoglu 2021), as well as the observation that some very rich countries (e.g., Saudi Arabia, Singapore) continue to be ruled by autocracies.

For the purposes of the discussion in this book, one result that is remarkably relevant is that the effect of a negative shock to endowments on the likelihood of avoiding destructive conflict will depend on the stakes of power. This explains why an economy that saw significant increases in the power of the presidency—such as Venezuela after the 1999 Constitution—may only descend into conflict once it experiences a negative shock to incomes. The high stakes may have been compatible with a stable democracy at high levels of income but not at low ones. The descent into conflict, even though made possible only by the increase in the stakes of power, may not become manifest until the economy is forced to confront lower levels of income.

EXPLAINING VENEZUELA'S IMPLOSION

This chapter has sketched two complementary models that explain how higher stakes of power can lower an economy's growth. In the first section of the chapter, I presented a stylized model of a single policy maker who can impose economic distortions on society and derive political benefits from it. That model summarizes the findings of a great part of the political economy literature about the electoral incentives of policy makers to adopt inefficient policies for political gain. As I showed, increased stakes of power in a context of electoral competition will lead policy makers in that model to adopt more distortionary policies, with a negative effect on economic growth.

While this single-actor model can explain why policy makers adopt suboptimal policies, it has a harder time explaining a full-blown economic collapse. Ultimately, politicians want to be reelected, and single-handedly causing an economic implosion is not a reasonable route to gaining voters' support. Even for authoritarian leaders whose primary goal may be to transfer rents to their supporters and key constituencies, destroying the economy is typically far from the most efficient way to do so.

Thus, while a single-actor model of politically induced distortions may be sufficient to gain insight into why and when governments adopt distortionary policies for political gain, it is incomplete for understanding the destructiveness of political conflict when both the government and the opposition can affect the state of the economy. In the second section of this chapter, I presented a more detailed model in which two political actors vying for power had the ability to adopt strategies that generated negative economic externalities on society. I characterized the equilibria arising from this type of political competition and showed that at high stakes of power and low income levels, political actors were more likely to adopt scorched earth strategies with negative impacts on the economy, precipitating society's descent into economically destructive political conflict.

The rest of this book develops a narrative of Venezuela's economic collapse that is anchored in these two complementary models of political competition. For analytic purposes, I propose to divide the period of study into two periods. The first period, 2012 to 2015, corresponds to the time during which the only political actor capable of imposing distortions on the economy was the government. In other words, I argue that until 2016, Venezuela's opposition did not have the capacity to affect the country's economic conditions. The single-actor model of politically induced distortions is well equipped to explain this period.

The first part of the collapse, between 2012 and 2015, is to a certain extent simply the standard unraveling of a prior period of macroeconomic populism that led the economy to become fiscally and externally overextended. As the economy was forced to roll back the excessive spending levels of the pre-2012 period, it embarked on import cuts and rationing of access to imported goods. Yet the magnitude of the adjustment became daunting when the economy suffered a two-thirds decline in the price of oil in the 2014 to 2016 period—a shock that years of overspending had left it unprepared to handle. Political considerations weighed heavily on Maduro's decision to delay the price adjustments that would have been needed to restore economic stability.

The intensity of political competition played a key role in determining Maduro's reticence to adopt a more conventional economic adjustment program. Chapters 5 and 6 tell the story of how the Maduro administration put off substantial economic adjustments and imposed distortionary policies during periods immediately preceding elections. They also show how the government reaped a political payoff from enforcing price and exchange controls and accusing private sector actors of price gouging ahead of key electoral contests. In chapter 7, I provide evidence that the first Maduro administration faced some of the most intense periods of electoral competition in Venezuela's democratic history and argue that, against the backdrop of high stakes of power, the intensity of political competition generated large incentives for the government to pursue policies that severely harmed the economy's long-term growth.

The second period of analysis begins in 2016 and lasts until the economy reaches its trough in 2020. I argue that beginning in 2016, Venezuela's opposition gained access to political technologies that allowed it to significantly impact the country's economic performance. One was the control of the National Assembly and its ability to constrain the government's access to external financing. The other was the election in the United States of an administration willing to take a hard line on

Venezuela in support of the opposition. This included the willingness to impose economic sanctions in support of the opposition's attempt to drive Maduro from power.

These changes in the political technologies available to the opposition profoundly affected the structure of political competition. After 2016, it was not just the government that could harm the economy for its political purposes; the opposition could also do it. I contend that the two-actor model of political competition and choice of political technologies developed in the second section of this chapter is well suited for analyzing this second period. My contention is that political actors chose to adopt strategies that created severe negative economic externalities because they concluded that those strategies would be more effective in helping them reach or hold on to power. The struggle for control of oil revenues turned the economy into a political battlefield.

My model specifies two important preconditions for the descent into economically destructive political conflict. One is that the stakes of power must be sufficiently high for the economy's level of income. I argue that the institutional reforms that took place in Venezuela around the turn of the millennium significantly raised the stakes of power, lowering the incentives of the country's political actors to abide by democratic rules (Monaldi and Penfold 2012; Carrión 2015; Corrales and Penfold 2015; Corrales 2018). By substantially increasing the power of the executive branch and giving it the mechanisms to subordinate other branches of government to the presidency, the 1999 Constitution dramatically increased the political rewards from being in power—and the cost of being out of it. Increased stakes of power made it rational for both contenders in the political contest to try to play outside the rules of the game.

According to the two-actor model presented in this chapter, increases from intermediate to high stakes of power will make democracies more fragile as they raise the incentives of the losers of the political contest to disavow electoral results.[14] If they expect to contest electoral results, political actors will invest in developing capabilities that help them prevail in the nonelectoral contest for power, even if these represent modalities of contesting power whose use is unpopular among voters. But it is not just the losers who appeal to these modalities. Once the winners understand that the losers are fighting in a political arena that is different from the electoral game, they will find it in their interest to do the same. Both sides thus end up fighting for power by nonelectoral means, appealing to scorched earth strategies that generate significant aggregate costs for society.

A second condition for economically destructive political conflict to emerge is that the economy's endowments be sufficiently low. According to my model, higher stakes of power are more sustainable in richer countries. Therefore, a major negative economic shock, such as what Venezuela saw between 2014 and 2016—could make a previously stable democratic equilibrium increasingly unstable. In my model, democratic stability requires not just a decision by actors to respect the electoral results. It also requires that actors be able to invest the resources necessary in accumulating the force needed to dissuade their political adversaries from not accepting the results of elections. When an economy becomes poorer, political actors may not be able to spend both what is needed to prevail in electoral competition and what is needed to dissuade their adversaries from contesting their electoral victory. Once that happens, they may find it optimal to simply forget about electoral competition altogether and instead spend all their resources fighting it out on the nonelectoral terrain.

It is straightforward to apply this reasoning to the strategies of Maduro and the governing United Socialist Party of Venezuela (Partido Socialista Unido de Venezuela, PSUV) after the 2014–16 shock. Faced by a huge negative terms of trade shock that the economy was unprepared to deal with, the government found it increasingly difficult to keep voters satisfied. This would become evident when it suffered the stunning political defeat in the 2015 parliamentary elections. Playing by the institutional rules of the game would have meant accepting the opposition's two-thirds majority control of the legislature and its authority to set in motion the recall referendum in what would have surely led to Maduro's loss of power. Maduro's inability to respond to those challenges after the collapse of state revenues would make it rational for him to shift strategies and begin to prioritize the support of the military instead of electoral competition. This would mean using his control of the courts to invalidate the recall referendum, giving security forces free rein in repressing protests, and allowing the military increased control over mining and oil production. None of these decisions would make him very popular; all of them would make him more likely to stay in power.

My logic also applies to the changes in opposition strategies. The opposition began boycotting elections again in 2017, returning to a strategy that it had abandoned after 2005. The strategy went as far as boycotting the 2018 presidential elections, despite polls indicating that it could defeat an unpopular Maduro.[15] The avowed rationale for this strategy was that the government was very likely to rig the vote and that internationally delegitimizing the vote would be more likely to achieve the sought-after regime change. The opposition also began to forcefully lobby for economic sanctions and against foreign investment, unpopular actions that had a cost in terms of popular support but were perceived to increase their chances of ousting Maduro from power. In other words, rather than invest its limited resources in attempting to prevail—as it had been able to do in the past—in a terrain of uneven electoral competition, the opposition chose to focus on convincing its allies to impose significant economic costs on the Maduro regime. Doing so was clearly unpopular with voters, but the opposition believed it stood a greater possibility of helping drive Maduro out of power.[16]

One of the dimensions in which the change of opposition strategy is most evident is in the transformation of the opposition coalition. The Democratic Unity Roundtable (Mesa de la Unidad Democrática, MUD), which served as the umbrella grouping of opposition political parties between 2008 and 2017, began as a broad coalition that included a diverse array of parties from across the country's ideological spectrum. While this coalition was significantly united through 2017, it lost 21 of its 112 legislators in 2018 and 2019. Some of them were expelled from the coalition either because of breaking the boycotts or because of corruption allegations; others resigned in support of the expelled lawmakers (F. Rodríguez 2020). Maduro's efforts to chip away at the MUD coalition (which allegedly included the payment of sizable bribes) almost certainly played a role in some of these decisions. Yet the fact that the desertions occurred at the moment of staunchest international support for the Venezuelan opposition (in fact, many of the dissenting legislators were ultimately sanctioned by the United States) suggests that they were also a consequence of the opposition leadership's decision to rely on the support of a narrower coalition willing to support a hard-line stance rather than the larger set of actors that it would have courted if it had seen winning elections as its main challenge.[17]

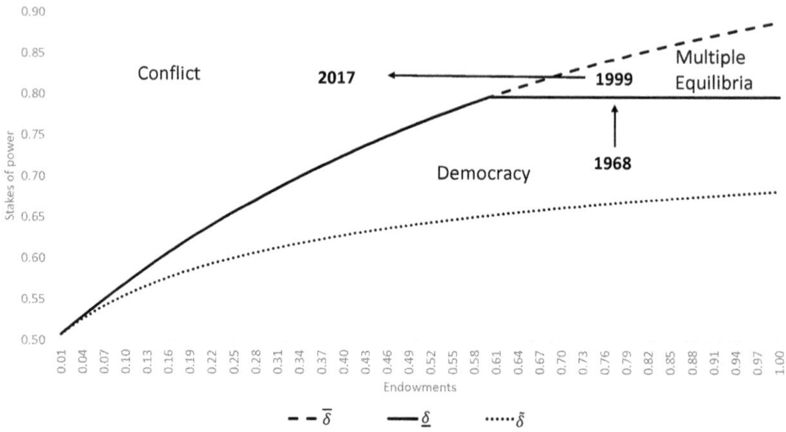

FIGURE 3.4. Hypothetical Venezuela trajectory. *Source*: Author's construction.

Figure 3.4 provides a schematic representation of my story by superimposing a hypothetical trajectory for Venezuela on the parameter areas identified in figure 3.2. Between 1968 and 1999, Venezuela's political system was characterized by moderate stakes of power and growing income per capita (Karl 1997; Di John and Putzel 2009; Kronick, Plunkett, and Rodríguez 2023).[18] As I discuss in greater detail in chapters 4 and 7, the reforms of the 1990s, in particular, the approval of the 1999 Constitution, significantly raised the stakes of power, leading political actors to take greater risks in their pursuit of power—as they did, for example, in the 2002–3 coup and strike. However, my model would suggest that the economy's oil wealth during this period of rising terms of trade made these high stakes of power compatible with both authoritarianism and democracy.

The model also suggests that a large negative shock to the economy's wealth, as occurred during the collapse in oil prices suffered between 2014 and 2016, upset the viability of the political equilibrium that the country had settled into. As parties had to make tougher choices between continuing to contend power electorally and doing so through other, nondemocratic means, they opted for the latter. This is explained in figure 3.4 as a leftward shift in endowments, out of the region compatible with both democracy and authoritarianism and into a region in which a conflict leading to dictatorship was the only viable outcome.

It is worth highlighting that I am not making the argument that Venezuela would have descended into economically destructive political conflict if it had faced a similar negative terms of trade shock in earlier years. Figure 3.4 is based on the premise that the two-player model of political competition presented in this chapter is valid, but this model assumes that both actors have the capacity to harm the economy. Yet I also argue that opposition groups had neither the international support nor the control of key institutions needed to severely affect the economy until they gained control of the legislative branch in the 2015 parliamentary elections and Donald Trump reached the White House in the 2016 US presidential election.[19]

One important characteristic of my model is that while it traces the country's descent into authoritarianism to the increases in the stakes of power built into the country's institutions through the political reforms of the turn of the century, it also explains why this descent could happen not at the time of those reforms but rather after the opposition gained control of the levers necessary to affect the economy's performance and a strong negative economic shock such as that of the mid-2010s had occurred. The model—at least evaluated at the parameters that I have used to represent Venezuela's trajectory schematically—also suggests that if the country had maintained the moderate levels of stakes of power embedded in its post-1968 institutions, Venezuelan democracy would likely have survived a negative shock of this magnitude.

The conceptual framework offered in this chapter provides an explanation for Venezuela's economic collapse that traces it to the decisions taken by political actors to adopt strategies that imposed growing economic costs on society as a by-product of their struggle for power. During the 2012 to 2016 period, an adjustment to a large negative terms of trade shock became more contractionary than it needed to have been because of the government's focus on short-term priorities. The economic contraction that resulted from this shock and the poor policy response limited the access of political actors to resources and raised their incentives to adopt scorched earth strategies in their struggle for political control of Venezuela. I now go on to develop this explanation in greater detail. I begin with the story of how Venezuela's economic policy choices during Hugo Chávez's years in power made a major economic adjustment after his death all but inevitable.

PART II

The Unraveling of Venezuela's Populist Experiment, 2012–2015

FOUR

Populism Unplugged

Unfortunately, for now, the objectives that we had set for ourselves have not been achieved.
—Hugo Chávez, 1992

BREAKING THE MIRAGE

In the same way in which almost all Americans remember where they were on 9/11, most Venezuelans remember what they were doing when they first saw Hugo Chávez on television. In the early morning of February 4, 1992, the country learned that the previous day an unsuccessful military coup attempt had taken place. The leader of the insurgency, a thirty-seven-year-old lieutenant colonel, had been allowed to speak briefly on television to ask his supporters to give up their weapons. Dressed in his army fatigues, Chávez was on the air for less than two minutes, but his words would shape the evolution of Venezuelan society for years to come. He thanked his fellow fighters for their courage, assumed responsibility for the rebellion, and let it slip into his remarks that the rebellion had been unsuccessful "for now" (*por ahora*), suggesting that it would one day achieve its objectives.

These brief words sent shock waves through the Venezuelan political system. Establishment politicians quickly condemned the uprising, assuming people would rally to the defense of one of the continent's oldest democracies. The president of Congress, David Morales Bello, from the governing Democratic Action (Acción Democrática, AD) party, launched a scathing attack on the rebels from the congressional floor, calling for "death to the coup plotters" even though the Venezuelan Constitution barred the death penalty (Morales 2017). Former president and opposition leader Rafael Caldera (1992), however, best captured the mood of the country when he called on the government to address the underlying issues, such as corruption and poverty, that created fertile terrain for the uprising. Caldera would be elected to lead the country again just one year later but proved unable to tackle these issues to the satisfaction of Venezuelans, who ultimately voted Chávez into the presidency in 1998.

Three years before Chávez made his appearance on Venezuela's political stage, the country had been racked by violent protests just as the government of Carlos Andrés Pérez, elected for a second five-year term,[1] began to implement a package of economic policy reforms and austerity measures. Although the policies varied in scope, it was the increase in gasoline prices and ensuing rise in the cost of public transportation that sparked the protests. These spread rapidly from the outskirts of the capital—whose residents were hardest hit by increased bus fares—to all the city and evolved from focused incidents into generalized looting and a complete breakdown of law and order. Official numbers said that 276 persons had died during the social explosion that came to be known as the Caracazo; later research found that the number of casualties could have been closer to one thousand (Inter-American Court of Human Rights 2002; Velasco 2015, 195).

There is a fairly small literature on the Caracazo and its causes (López-Maya 2003; Honorio 2008; Vasquez 2012; González 2014; Velasco 2015; Rivero 2016). Events involving riots and looting are very difficult to predict and even to explain after the fact (Newburn 2021). Though one can often point to deep-seated frustration and social grievances as driving factors, there are many places and times at which these do not lead to social explosions. Generally speaking, widespread looting can only happen when there is a generalized breakdown of law and order (Green 2006). A controversial reorganization of the command structure and an ongoing strike in the Caracas Metropolitan Police at the time certainly appears to have affected the organism's capacity for initial response. After looting had spread, the government decided to deploy more than nine thousand soldiers with instructions to carry out a combat plan originally designed to respond to the urban guerrilla insurgencies of the sixties. This reaction may have allowed it to contain the protests, at a large human cost (Velasco 2015, 211).

Whatever the underlying causes of the Caracazo, Venezuelans clearly had good reasons to be dissatisfied with how things were going in the country. After having risen steadily during five decades, GDP per capita collapsed during the 1980s. Measured at constant consumption prices, it fell by 24% between 1980 and 1989, the year of the Caracazo. It would fall by a further 19% between that year and when Chávez was elected in 1998, for a total decline of 39% in the 1980 to 1998 period, marking the worst performance among twenty countries in the region.[2] Poverty rates shot up, rising from 39% to 48% between 1981 and 1998.[3] Venezuelans had long gotten used to the idea that living standards would rise from one generation to another; after two decades of economic contraction, the realization began to sink in for most Venezuelans that they would almost certainly be worse off than their parents.

Chávez would ultimately come to power in 1998, when he took 56.2% of the vote in a low-turnout presidential election.[4] The country's established political parties had by then fallen into complete disarray and ended up withdrawing support for their own candidates to back a regional politician, Henrique Salas Romer, in a last-minute attempt to stop Chávez from gaining office. They also maneuvered to separate congressional from presidential elections—which had been held concurrently since 1958—in an attempt to ensure that Chávez would not have a parliamentary majority if elected (Maingón and Sontag 2000).

At the outset, Chávez's ideological leanings were unclear (Kronick, Plunkett, and Rodríguez 2023). During the campaign he courted the support of both the left and the right, going as far as visiting a former dictator Marcos Pérez Jiménez in his residence in Spain (Espinoza 1998). He refused to label himself a socialist or even a leftist, claiming instead to be inspired by the ideas of Simón Bolívar, Venezuela's nineteenth-century independence hero (Pernia 2016). Once elected, Chávez made few changes to the country's macroeconomic policy framework. He confirmed his predecessor's finance minister, Maritza Izaguirre, and slashed spending, managing to run a budget surplus during his first year in office.[5]

CHANGING THE GAME

Chávez's initial priorities seem to have been primarily political. His central campaign promise had been to "refound" the Venezuelan state by rewriting the country's Constitution. He signed a decree calling a referendum on whether to hold elections for a constitutional convention on his first day in office. He easily won the referendum, as well as the subsequent elections, with his supporters capturing 124 of the convention's 131 seats (Combellas 2003; Corrales 2018, chap. 5).

The convention, however, was not just tasked with drafting a new Constitution. It also gave itself the power to reorganize other branches of government, under the argument that voters had effectively conferred on it supraconstitutional powers. It stripped away all legislative powers and suspended sessions of the existing bicameral legislature (in which Chávez's supporters were a minority). The Supreme Court, rather than pick a fight with the Constitutional Convention and Chávez—who at the time had overwhelming popular support—decided to back the convention's interpretation and refused to strike down its decisions (Combellas 2003, 195–96).

At the end of this process, Venezuela not only had a new Constitution, but new branches of government, all of them controlled by Chávez loyalists. The 1999 Constitution created five separate branches: executive, legislative, judiciary, electoral, and accountability. Despite comfortably winning congressional elections held in August 2000 under the new Constitution, Chávez supporters fell short of the two-thirds supermajority necessary for the appointments of the heads of some of these bodies; nevertheless, they quickly moved to negotiate the needed votes with some opposition legislators, consolidating the government's control of all branches of government.

It is difficult to overstate the importance of this moment for Venezuela's political evolution. The leader of the executive branch had set in motion a process that led to the replacement of the other branches of government by his supporters, thereby effectively erasing any existing separation of powers. It's worth recalling that this was happening in a country that only seven years earlier had seen a president impeached by the nation's Supreme Court—that is, in which branches of government had in the past acted with significant levels of autonomy and independence from each other.

The idea of a constitutional convention has been used by other leftist regimes in the region, such as those of Rafael Correa in Ecuador (2007) and Evo Morales in Bolivia (2006), after winning presidential elections to consolidate power in the hands of the executive (Corrales 2018). More recently, leftist candidates such as Gustavo Petro in Colombia and Pedro Castillo in Peru proposed constitutional conventions in their bids for power. But the left does not hold a monopoly on this type of initiative: in 1992, the market-friendly government of Alberto Fujimori also called elections for a constitutional convention after dissolving the existing Congress.[6] As in Venezuela, the most important way in which these bodies reshape the existing power structure is not so much by writing a new Constitution as by appointing government loyalists to the branches of government that were meant to serve to counterbalance the power of the executive branch.

The appeal to this modality of institutional change rekindles an age-old debate in political theory going back at least to the French Enlightenment. Modern Western democratic institutions are built on the idea, articulated by Montesquieu in his 1748 *Spirit of the Laws*, that for separate branches of government to function independently, they need to have different sources of legitimization (Montesquieu 1750). A contrasting view was expressed by Jean-Jacques Rousseau, who argued that the "General Will" of the people was the primary source of political legitimacy and that the people should have the power to "appoint them [leaders] and dismiss them as it pleases" (Rousseau [1726] 2014, 434). Chávez—similar to other authoritarian leaders—was fond of Rousseau's work, often citing him in speeches and even calling himself a "Rousseauian democrat" (Wiarda 2014, 78).[7]

Not only did the 1999 Constitutional Convention allow Chavismo to take control of other branches of government at the time. It also enshrined this power in article 348 of the new Constitution, allowing the president to call elections for a constitutional convention with the authority to dissolve other branches of government at any moment.[8] This rule effectively converted Venezuela into a winner-take-all political system: if you win the presidency, you can make all other powers subordinate to you by threatening to dissolve them. Eighteen years later, Nicolás Maduro would use this same rule to deal with the governance crisis caused by massive street protests and an internal rebellion within government ranks.

Venezuela's political polarization owes a lot to the institutional design that was brought into force by the 1999 Constitution. In a winner-take-all political system, the benefits of being in power are very high—as is the cost of being out of power. Cohabitation is unlikely to work, because the winners have little to gain from sharing power with the losers. The high stakes of power encourage excessive levels of political risk taking: actors will be willing to invest large resources in strategies aimed at rapidly capturing (or keeping) control of the executive instead of consolidating their political strength over time. Political negotiations invariably revolve around zero-sum games, in which each side cares only about improving its chances of reaching power and in which bargaining is ultimately ineffective. As I argued in chapter 3, increases in the stakes of power create incentives for politicians to adopt strategies that generate severe economic externalities in society, thus sowing the seeds of a descent into economically destructive political conflict.

FROM CRISIS TO COMEBACK

Chávez would get a taste of his own medicine just a couple of years later, when a stagnant economy and a balance of payments crisis took a toll on his popular support. The economy had managed to perform decently during Chávez's first two years in office, buoyed by a recovery in oil prices from the lows hit in the aftermath of the 1997 Asian and 1998 Russian financial crises. The price of a basket of Venezuelan oil rose from a low of $8 in December 1998—the month in which Chávez won the election—to $29 in August 2000. But in the following sixteen months it would fall steadily, reaching $15 in January 2001.

Among the policies that Chávez had inherited and left largely untouched was the exchange rate regime. Venezuela's Central Bank had adopted an exchange-rate bands system in 1996 after ending the Caldera administration's experiment with exchange controls. In that system, the Central Bank intervened in the foreign exchange market only when the exchange rate moved outside of predetermined bounds. In practice, it worked as a crawling-peg system with a steady rate of depreciation.[9] Authorities, convinced that exchange rate stability was the most effective mechanism to bring down inflation, consistently lowered the Central Bank's target rate of depreciation. Domestic inflation thus outpaced depreciation, and the real exchange rate strengthened.

Such a system is ill equipped to handle negative terms of trade shocks unless authorities are willing to revise the target rate of depreciation in line with changes in fundamentals. But the Central Bank board, heavily influenced by Planning Minister Jorge Giordani—a social studies professor from the Central University of Venezuela whom Chávez had tapped to run the economy—decided to lower the target rate of depreciation even as the price of the country's largest export was falling (a policy response that, as I discuss in the following chapters, Maduro would repeat twelve years later). As a result, international reserves fell from $20 billion to $16 billion in less than three months, forcing the government to abandon the bands system and allow the currency to float in February 2002. The bolivar plummeted, losing 28% of its value in the ten days after going on the float. It would decline by an additional 42% over the following year, until the government imposed exchange controls.

In Venezuela, where the government owns the industry that generates more than nine-tenths of exports, currency depreciation is akin to a large tax increase, strengthening government revenues while lowering real incomes for most of the population. Devaluations are therefore unpopular and contractionary. Economic growth, which had reached 3.7% in 2000 and 3.4% in 2001, collapsed to -4.4% in the first quarter of 2002.[10] Inflation nearly tripled, shooting up from 12% in 2001 to 31% in 2002. Chávez's approval rating, which had been in the 60s up to the first half of 2001, fell to 34% in February 2002 (fig. 4.1).

The opposition saw an opportunity. During his three years in office, Chávez had alienated most economic and intellectual elites and had directly antagonized the leaderships of the business sector, organized labor, and the Catholic Church. By concentrating control of key institutions, he had closed the door on any power-sharing agreement with the opposition. He had created a winner-take-all political system, making it all too tempting for the opposition to take advantage of his current weakness and stage a bid to seize power. The fact that most Venezuelans

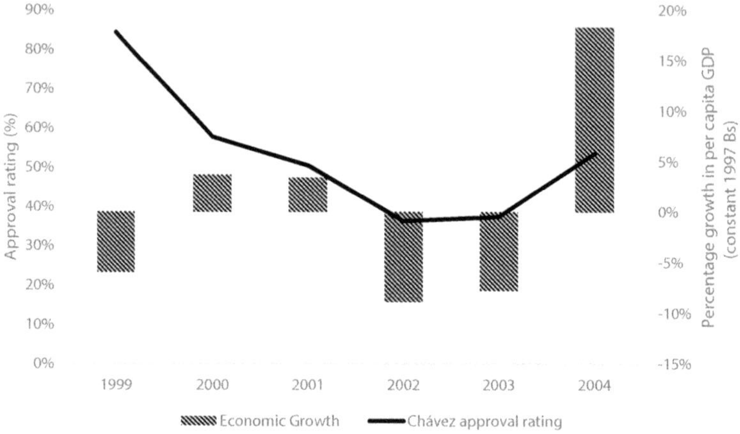

FIGURE 4.1. Chávez approval rating and per capita GDP, 1999–2004. *Source*: Author's construction using Datanálisis 2021; BCV 2023b.

now opposed him made him seem vulnerable to well-articulated political mobilization.

Shortly after taking office in 2000, the new National Assembly approved an enabling law that allowed Chávez to legislate by decree for twelve months. An enabling law is a constitutional figure through which the legislature partially transfers its power to legislate to the presidency within specific bounds that delimit the scope of the delegated authority. The figure had also existed in the 1961 Constitution and had been used by several pre-Chávez administrations.[11] Yet Chávez would use these powers aggressively, enacting forty-nine laws that radically altered existing legislation in many sectors. These included a lands law that gave the government greater authority to redistribute private agricultural lands and a public function statute that made it significantly easier for the government to fire public sector employees. Other pieces of legislation expanded the state's role in the banking, insurance, tourism, electricity, and gas sectors. A new hydrocarbons law allowed the government to sharply raise tax rates on the oil industry and extract more royalties from foreign investors. The government also moved to replace PDVSA board members with its political allies.

All these decisions created fertile ground to galvanize opposition to Chávez from many sectors affected by the reforms. Opposition groups began organizing protests and a series of one-day national strikes toward the end of 2001, culminating in a large opposition rally on April 11, 2002, that ended in violent clashes with government supporters and elements of the army. Disobeying Chávez's orders to disperse, opposition demonstrators headed to the presidential palace, and that evening several high-ranking military officers launched a successful coup. However, the ouster lasted just two days before pro-Chávez factions within the military organized a countercoup that brought him back to power on April 14.

Despite surviving the coup attempt, Chávez remained unpopular, and the opposition coalition continued its push to remove him from power. In late 2002, it began organizing a petition drive to hold early elections and launched a nationwide strike that brought the economy to a standstill for nearly two months, in December 2002 and January 2003. After the strike failed to unseat Chávez, the opposition focused its efforts on invoking one of the constitutional mechanisms available to force early elections to be held. Eventually, it overcame numerous government attempts to block these efforts, and a recall referendum was held on August 15, 2004. Surprising many observers, Chávez won with the support of 59% of voters against 41% who voted to recall him. Although the opposition claimed electoral fraud, observers from the Organization of American States (OAS) and the Carter Center vouched for the legitimacy of the vote count (OAS 2004a, 2004b; Carter Center 2005).

This was a remarkable political comeback. Chávez's popularity had been in the low 30s since 2001 but began rising steadily in the late months of 2003. By the time of the referendum, it was at 55%, and after winning the vote, it rose into the 60s. What drove this recovery? There are several competing explanations, including economic recovery, increased social spending, and changing political attitudes to the opposition. Let us consider each of them.

An extensive academic literature links economic performance, presidential approval, and incumbent electoral performance.[12] The higher economic growth is and the lower inflation is, the better incumbents and their parties perform at the polls. Chávez's approval certainly tracked economic performance very closely during this period—as well as during the rest of his administration: his approval fell into the 30s as growth collapsed in 2002 and 2003, but by the time of the referendum the economy was recovering rapidly and managed to expand by a whopping 18.3% in 2004, pushing his approval rating up to around 60% (see fig. 4.1).

Part of the rebound was automatic: the economy had contracted strongly because of the 2002–3 oil strike and recovered as the government took control of the state-owned oil company and oil output recovered to its normal levels. The expansion was also helped along by a sizable rise in oil prices, which had risen to $40 per barrel by the time of the referendum. The increase in revenues allowed the government to significantly raise spending and provided ample funding for a new set of social initiatives called the *misiones*, programs managed outside of the traditional government structure and aimed at resolving concrete problems such as illiteracy or lack of access to medical care in urban shantytowns.[13]

But there is a sense in which the contraction of 2002–3 and the 2004 recovery are atypical. Voters commonly penalize incumbents for poor economic performance when they attribute this performance to the policymaker's decisions. But when results are clearly due to causes out of the politician's control, then voters may be inclined not to punish the government at the polls. The Venezuelan case was somewhat of an anomaly: the nation's deep economic contraction was in large part the result not of anything that the government was doing but of the opposition's decision to paralyze the economy indefinitely to force Chávez from power.[14]

It is hard to overstate the deep political significance of this moment. By bringing the country's economy to a standstill, the opposition managed to convince Venezuelans of something that Chávez had not been able to on his own: its leaders didn't care much about the well-being of ordinary people. The strike lent credence to the characterization of the opposition as led by upper-class elites disconnected from the needs of ordinary Venezuelans. Those calling the strike, Chavistas charged, could afford a luxury that regular people could not: they could go several months without a paycheck. The government's 2004 referendum campaign even featured the character of a devil, representing the opposition, who tried in every way possible to make people's lives more difficult (Luiguiger 2012; Montero 2021). As we will see in the following chapters, the opposition's strategy foreshadowed its advocacy of punitive economic sanctions fifteen years later.

WINNING THE COMMODITIES LOTTERY

After recovering from the strike, the Venezuelan economy experienced strong growth, with real incomes—which had been falling for almost two decades by the time Chávez reached office—almost tripling between 1998 and 2012.[15] This was largely a result of a huge rise in oil prices: the price of a Venezuelan barrel rose from $11 to $103 during the same years. While this was generally a period of terms of trade improvement in the region, the Venezuelan positive terms of trade boom far outstripped that of any other country in the region (fig. 4.2).

This huge boom allowed Chávez to fund an economic model that no other economy in the region could have afforded. Especially after the consolidation of political power with his victory in the 2004 referendum and his 2006 reelection—which he won with a comfortable 63% of the vote—Chávez moved to increase the government's control of the economy. The government forced private oil firms that had been operating oil fields in the Orinoco Basin and that at the time produced 620 tbd—21% of the nation's production—into joint venture agreements where they would act as minority partners with the state-owned oil company PDVSA. It also took over the national telecommunications company (CANTV), the largest electricity company (Electricidad de

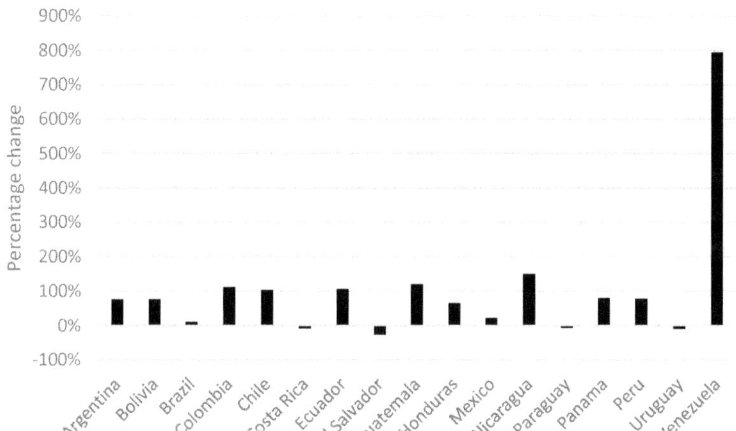

FIGURE 4.2. Change in terms of trade, 1998–2012, Latin American countries. *Source*: World Bank World Development Indicators 2021.

Caracas), and the third largest bank in the country (Banco de Venezuela) (Ruiz 2008).

In many of these cases, the government paid generous compensations to the expropriated owners. For example, it paid $1.1 billion to the Spanish bank Banco Santander for the sale of its Venezuelan subsidiary, Banco de Venezuela, as well as $0.9 billion to the American owners of Electricidad de Caracas (*El Mundo* 2007; *El Confidencial* 2009). Since the government was flush with oil revenues, money was not an issue. In the words of the then–oil czar, Rafael Ramírez, "Nationalization for us has no costs, it has an important benefit, a benefit in national sovereignty" (Hernandez 2007).

Economic controls also allowed the government to increase its political control. The government adopted exchange controls in February 2003, initially as a response to the collapse of oil revenues caused by the oil strike. Chávez had avoided exchange controls the previous year when he responded to the balance of payments crisis by floating the currency. But amid the strike, which was openly promoted by the country's main business federation, Fedecámaras, the possibility of deciding who had access to foreign exchange became an attractive political tool.

Exchange controls were thus not just a way to stop exchange rate depreciation. By deciding who would receive foreign exchange and who would not, the government would be able to punish the firms that were participating in the strike or other attempts to subvert it (Gulotty and Kronick 2021). Even after the strike, this political control proved too effective to give up. In the words of Aristóbulo Istúriz, Chávez's education minister, "Exchange controls in Venezuela are an economic, not a political measure. If we take away exchange controls, they [the opposition] will overthrow us" (Entorno58 ODH 2016).

The positive terms of trade shock not only increased government revenues from royalties and taxation of the oil industry; it also opened its access to additional sources of external finance. This often happens with resource booms: they make financial markets more willing to lend to countries benefiting from them and thus create the risk that the country will not only spend the additional resources, but end up mired in debt—a phenomenon known in economics as the "voracity effect" (Tornell and Lane 1999). Between 1998 and 2012, the public sector's external debt expanded fourfold, rising from $28 billion to $113 billion.

In some cases, the additional debt went to fund investment projects that would never be completed, such as the construction of an ambitious nationwide railway system of which only one line was ever inaugurated (*El Impulso* 2013a). In other cases, the debt would be used simply to expand consumption of imported goods. In several instances, the government and state-owned oil company issued bonds to allow Venezuelans access to foreign exchange at a cheaper rate than in the black market, thus using debt issuance as a way to maintain an overvalued currency.[16]

All in all, however, there were certain foundations of the market economy that Chávez did not interfere with excessively. One of these was the price system. Venezuela had established price controls on essential goods in the 1940s and maintained them throughout most of the postwar period. Prices had undergone a period of relative liberalization with the free-market reforms carried out in 1996. When Chávez took office in 1999, he largely left price regulation untouched. The number of goods subject to price controls was increased when Chávez imposed exchange controls in 2003—as had happened during previous episodes of exchange controls—but then remained essentially unaltered between 2004 and 2011.[17] Price adjustments were frequent and sought to maintain prices sufficiently in line with market equilibrium so as not to produce excessive levels of scarcity. The Central Bank's scarcity index, a measure of the percentage of products that are unavailable, averaged 12.8% of all products between 2003 and 2012 (Red Agroalimentaria de Venezuela 2020). The ratio between the official exchange rate and the black market exchange rate, another indicator of the extent of rationing, averaged 2.0 during the 2003 to 2012 period. Both numbers would look small relative to what would develop after 2013.

By 2012, Venezuela had an economy that had squandered a large oil boom, assumed large levels of debt, and was ill prepared to face a decline in oil prices such as what would come after 2014. But there is a sense in which the Venezuelan economy was not all that different from what had existed before Chávez came to power: it had a functioning price system, and—despite the spree of nationalizations—most economic activity remained in the hands of the private sector. Chávez's economic policies were in fact not all that different from those of many previous governments: Venezuela had imposed highly distortionary exchange controls for most of the 1980s and part of the 1990s, and the governments that ran the country during the prior oil boom of the 1970s and early 1980s had also nationalized large sectors of the economy and run up high levels of debt. Surely, the economy would have to undergo a large and painful price adjustment to accommodate a negative oil price shock—much as it did in 1983, 1989, and 1996—but there were few reasons to foresee anything that would be qualitatively different from what Venezuelans had become used to.

What had changed dramatically between 1998 and 2012 was the nature of the country's political conflict and the ability of its institutions to manage political differences. Venezuela's prior political arrangements had grown out of a 1958 pact between three of the country's largest political parties committing participants to seeking consensus policies and defending democratic stability. The 1999 Constitution and Chavismo's takeover of the leadership of all branches of government substantially raised the stakes of political conflict, leading to the systematic exclusion of the opposition from virtually all spheres of national decision making. The raising of the stakes of political conflict radically altered the incentives of the country's political actors, leading them to prioritize attempts to seize or maintain control of the all-powerful presidency and to eschew any type of cooperation. As I discuss in the following chapters, it would be this highly conflictive winner-take-all political system that would prove unable to handle the coming economic crisis.

FIVE

Enter Maduro

My opinion, firm, as full as a full moon, irrevocable, absolute, total, is that . . . you elect Nicolás Maduro as president of the Bolivarian Republic of Venezuela. I ask this of you from my heart.

—Hugo Chávez, 2012

THE ORCHESTRATED SUCCESSION

Hugo Chávez was reelected for a third six-year term in 2012, taking 55% of the vote. On the face of it, the result was not that surprising. Oil was at $103 a barrel, and the economy had grown at 5.6% that year. Incumbents rarely lose elections in Latin America: there are just five documented cases, all amid serious economic crises,[1] and this was not to be one of them. Just in case, the government wasn't about to leave it to chance and embarked on a spending spree that raised spending by 10% of GDP in the run-up to the elections.[2]

But below the facade, there were many causes for concern in government circles. To fund that spending, the government had to run a large budget deficit, which reached 12.5% of GDP in 2015. Not only had Chávez tapped international financial markets through bond issuances, but he had also engaged other lenders such as China to borrow additional resources through loans that were backed by future Venezuela oil sales. Flush with dollars, the country took imports to an all-time high, almost four times their level when Chávez reached office.[3]

By the end of 2012, the import binge had erased the country's current account surplus, and by the last quarter of the year the economy was running a sizable $2.3 billion deficit (2.4% of quarterly GDP). This was only the second time since 2001 that the economy had run a current account deficit: the previous, short-lived one had occurred during a period of abrupt decline in oil prices in 2009 after the Lehman crisis. But this time the deficit was occurring even with oil prices at their highs. Furthermore, since the private sector was accumulating financial assets abroad by around $8 billion a year, the country would have needed to run a current account surplus of at least that magnitude for the public sector to avoid depleting its assets.

At that time, the government's political leaders had an even more pressing concern in their minds: Chávez was dying. The fifty-seven-year-old president had been diagnosed with cancer during a visit to Cuba in mid-2011. Doctors had discovered a baseball-sized tumor in his pelvic area. He would undergo two surgeries and several rounds of chemotherapy and radiation therapy before claiming in mid-2012 that he was "totally free" of cancer and ready to run for reelection.

Many suspected otherwise as a leader visibly bloated by steroid treatment went on the campaign trail. Nevertheless, the ailing president once again proved a formidable campaigner. As he spoke to hundreds of thousands of supporters in his closing campaign rally under thundering rain in October 2012, it was easy to suspend disbelief and forget that the Chávez era was coming to an end. Those closest to him, however, were fully aware that they were preparing for a succession.

Running the revolution without Chávez was not going to be easy. Victory in the 2012 presidential elections was crucial, but the Venezuelan Constitution mandated that new elections must be held if the president has to leave office for whatever reason during the first four years of his term. That meant that Chávez's last reelection would have to be won resoundingly enough that the opposition would still be in sufficient disarray when a new election was called.

Then there was the issue of finding a successor. Several names came on the table, but in the end Chávez settled on his fifty-year-old foreign minister, Nicolás Maduro, a former trade union leader who had cultivated a close relationship with the Cuban regime. Chávez announced his choice to the country on December 8, 2012, less than two months after being reelected and just before traveling to Cuba for a fourth surgery, from which he would never recover. He would be brought back to Caracas, where he died on March 5. A new presidential election was scheduled for April 14.

That election would prove much closer than expected. Maduro had gone into the race with double-digit leads in the polls, benefiting from an outpouring of sympathy after Chávez's death. In the end, he would eke out victory over Capriles by a small margin of 1.5 percentage points.

SLAMMING ON THE BRAKES

One reason for Maduro's weak performance in the April 2013 election is that the economy had completely shifted gears after Chávez died. Quite simply, the government had hit the brakes on spending and import growth almost immediately after the election. This was inevitable: maintaining the rate at which spending had grown before October 2012 was not feasible. During the last three quarters of 2012, the government had burned through $16 billion in cash holdings outside of the Central Bank's international reserves. Everyone knew that the spending spree would come to an end after the elections, as in fact it did.

Imports, which had peaked at an all-time high of $5.8 billion a month in November 2012, declined strongly and by March had fallen to $3.3 billion, the lowest level in two years. Venezuela's economy grew only at an annual rate of 0.8% in the first quarter of 2013—down from 5.5% in the last quarter of 2012 and less than the country's rate of population growth.[4] By the elections, many Venezuelans were having second thoughts about whether the country was really headed in the right direction: the percentage of respondents that assessed the country's situation as positive fell from 60.8% to 50.8% between December 2012 and April 2013 (Datanálisis 2021).

On top of all this, Maduro had decided to devalue the currency just two months before the election. As I discussed in the previous chapter, devaluations are typically unpopular in Venezuela: because the government is the country's only relevant exporter, a devaluation is essentially akin to a large tax increase. If there is one unwritten rule about Venezuelan politics, it is that you shouldn't devalue before an election. Yet this was precisely what Maduro did in February 2013.

Adding insult to injury, Maduro didn't just devalue before the election. He closed one of Venezuela's two official markets for foreign exchange. Until then, Venezuelans could buy dollars legally in two markets: one in which foreign exchange was allocated for imports of goods included on a government-sanctioned list subject to strict quotas administered by the Commission for Administration of Foreign Exchange (CADIVI) and another complementary system, the System for Transactions in Foreign Currency Securities (SITME), in which individuals could access foreign exchange at a more depreciated rate for nonessential transactions with, by Venezuelan standards, virtually no red tape. The government regulated both rates and therefore rationed allocations in both subsystems. Buyers who were unable to receive allocations on these two systems could purchase foreign exchange in the black market, which, while illegal, was widely used.

The solution implemented by the government on February 8, 2013, was puzzling to many observers. It devalued the official rate by 32%, from 4.3 to 6.3 Bs/$, but completely closed SITME, which had been operating at the more depreciated 5.3 Bs/$ rate, putting nothing in its place.[5] Importers who had previously used SITME would now have to purchase dollars on the black market—which at that time was trading at 20 Bs/$, with the added complication that trading on the black market was against the law. Many firms that had been using SITME until that moment decided to simply stop importing, generating a burst of scarcity in some goods on the eve of the election.

That a devaluation was sorely needed was not in doubt. Venezuela needed to restrain import growth, which requires increasing the relative price of imports. Under exchange controls, you can do this either by devaluing the official rate or by reducing allocations of foreign exchange for imports. Relying on the latter creates a host of additional complications, such as increased goods scarcity and a larger fiscal deficit.

From a political standpoint, it is not easy to explain why the government didn't wait until after the election to announce it. One could try to explain it as reflecting the government's desire not to lose credibility with voters by carrying out a major adjustment right after the election, though this would be at odds with its later conduct. An alternative explanation is that Maduro was paying little attention to economic decisions that did not seem all that consequential, was focused on adequately handling the succession crisis, and had not yet defined internal decision-making processes for the government given Chávez's absence. It is clear that there was not much of a functioning economics cabinet in Venezuela in 2012. Jorge Giordani, who had run the Venezuelan economy almost uninterrupted since 1999, recounts that he was unable to give Chávez a document outlining economic policy recommendations that the ailing leader had requested at a late October cabinet meeting (the only one held between his reelection and death) and finally ended up handing the document to Maduro in January (Dinero 2014).

Giordani was well aware that an adjustment was needed. In his memos to Maduro, he characterized the spending increase of 2012 as a "great sacrifice" that had been necessary "for the consolidation of political power." He strongly advocated for sharp spending cuts, the same strategy that he had implemented in 2009 after the fall in oil prices that followed the Lehman crisis, together with a tightening of administrative controls in foreign exchange allocation. Maduro, who had little confidence in Giordani, followed his recommendation on the exchange controls but refused to cut spending (Dinero 2014).

Giordani also wanted to close SITME, which he saw as a hotbed for corruption, and replace it by what he believed would be a more transparent system for foreign exchange allocation using auctions. Maduro accepted this recommendation in principle. However, at the moment of the devaluation, the auctions system was not ready to be unrolled. As a result, the government closed down SITME on the same day it was devaluing the official rate without replacing it with anything else except for a somewhat opaque currency board, jointly headed by Giordani and the Central Bank president, and formally tasked with overseeing foreign exchange allocations (Imprenta Nacional 2013a). It was only on March 19, more than a month later, that the government announced that it would be launching an auction system as a complementary market for foreign exchange.

Only one auction was carried out under that system, on March 29, in which the government sold $200 million (by contrast, SITME had been selling an average of $351 million per month previous to its closing

(*El Impulso* 2013b). When results from the auction came in, authorities realized that the price that bidders were willing to offer for dollars was much higher than they had expected and decided not to publish the resulting exchange rate (Zamorano 2013). As a result, they stopped the auctions, which would not resume until July—by which time authorities had designed a system to restrict bids and effectively impede the auction from producing a market-clearing rate.

The decision to close SITME generated mayhem in the Venezuelan retail sector. Importers of nonessential goods had regularly used SITME to obtain foreign exchange; now they had to choose between going to the illegal black market or halting operations. Furthermore, the government had begun running significant arrears in CADIVI allocations, which meant that importers of essentials would often receive the dollars for their imports long after the good had been imported and sold. SITME had provided them with a licit mechanism to obtain the dollars at a reasonable cost in the meantime; now that mechanism had evaporated.

The result was increasing scarcity and inflation in both essential and nonessential goods. The Central Bank's scarcity index shot up from 14% in 2012 to 21% in 2013; inflation rose from 20% to 56% in the same period. Shortages of food and basic staples—from toilet paper to sugar—became pervasive. The shortages hit hardest in goods subject to price caps, where retailers were unable to raise prices to make markets clear at the lower supply levels.

THE MADURO ADJUSTMENT

Perhaps inadvertently, Maduro had decided to carry out a quantity adjustment rather than a price adjustment. In a standard economic adjustment (also called a price adjustment), the government would have opted for a much larger devaluation of the currency and tolerated higher transitory inflation levels as the price of imported goods adjusted to reflect the reduced availability of dollars for imports. Venezuelans would have woken up to the reality of higher prices at which many of them could not afford to buy the goods they wanted.

But in Maduro's style of adjustment, the government decided to maintain a relatively overvalued exchange rate and enforce price caps while reducing the availability of dollars for imports. While imports fell by 25% between 2012 and 2014, the increase in scarcity rates reflects that prices were not going up by as much as would have been needed for markets to clear. Instead, markets were adjusting via rationing, with demand outstripping supply at regulated prices. Instead of finding goods that they couldn't afford, Venezuelans could afford goods that they couldn't find.

Rather than recognize publicly that rationing was a mechanism to implement adjustment without forcing price increases, the government opted for blaming scarcity on hoarding and speculators. During a speech in August 2013, Maduro attributed the growth slowdown to an "economic war launched by the bourgeoisie" (Orozco 2013). According to the government's narrative, the private sector was intentionally hiding goods and raising prices to artificially create an economic crisis after the death of Chávez. It was no coincidence, government leaders claimed, that prices and the black market rate had shot up just as Chávez had taken ill after his reelection: the timing was decisive proof that the bourgeoisie had taken advantage of the leader's illness to generate economic havoc (Correo del Orinoco 2013).

The "economic war" narrative would become a mainstay of Maduro's speeches from late 2013 on. In January 2014, Maduro would tell the National Assembly that inspectors had found overpricing by more than 99% of retailers and claimed that the "sterile bourgeoisie" had "declared economic war on the whole country" and was trying to impose "neoliberalism by force" (Nodal 2014). By 2015, Maduro would be laying out a full-fledged historical narrative according to which the modality of hoarding products to create artificial scarcity crises was a replay of the strategy that right-wing groups had used against leftist leaders in the region such as Chile's Allende, Guatemala's Árbenz, the Dominican Republic's Bosch, and Brazil's Goulart (Cara de Lentes 2015).

Maduro's vision of the causes of scarcity was strongly influenced by the thinking of Alfredo Serrano Mancilla, a Spanish economist with links to his country's leftist Podemos party and head of a Quito-based think tank. Serrano, who authored a book on Chávez's economic ideas (Serrano 2014), would begin to lay out the detailed explanation for the workings of the economic war hypothesis in his writings and give a veneer of intellectual backing to Maduro's ideas. Serrano recognized structural weaknesses in Venezuela's economy but argued that actors interested in overthrowing the government exploited them to destabilize the country (Serrano 2016).

Maduro's willingness to rely on price controls to carry out the 2014 adjustment also had its genesis in the evolution of Chávez's thinking on the economy in the last years of his life. In 2011, as Chávez was getting ready for his reelection drive, he started devoting efforts to thinking about the next steps that he needed to take to transform Venezuela into a truly socialist economy. One of the ideas that caught his eye was a project to create a wide-ranging system of price controls that kept businesses from excessive profit taking.

Chávez charged Vice President Elías Jaua with drafting the legislation to do this.[6] The result was the 2011 Law of Just Costs and Prices, which significantly expanded the state's authority to impose price caps across the economy. The law created the Superintendence of Prices and Costs, granting it the authority to set prices after receiving data on each sector's cost structures; the entity could proceed to fine or close establishments if it found them in violation of the price caps. After approval of the law, which Chávez claimed would help "fight against the injustice of capitalism" and protect Venezuelans from "speculators . . . that hoard and hide and inflate prices" (MariscalVoroshilov99 2011), the government proceeded to set price caps on eighteen previously unregulated products, including soap, toothpaste, and diapers, in November 2011 (Orozco 2013).

At the time, the effects of these price caps on scarcity were limited, as the government was willing and able to maintain the flow of foreign exchange to importers to ensure adequate supply levels ahead of the election. However, when the government needed to begin cutting dollar allocations for imports at the end of 2012, the administrative structure was already in place to enforce caps. Not only was the economic war narrative a convenient one to shift the blame for scarcity onto the private sector, but it was accompanied by an emerging bureaucracy of price inspectors with the ability and opportunity to impose large costs on retailers—and the political and ideological backing to do so.

Maduro would find out how politically effective this tactic was by the end of 2013. His approval ratings had dipped throughout 2013, as increasing scarcity, inflation, and the economic slowdown started taking a toll on his popularity. The proportion of Venezuelans that approved of his job in office fell from 52% to 41% between the election in April and September 2013 (Datanálisis 2021). In the face of the close election result in April, opposition leaders started viewing Maduro as electorally vulnerable and decided to present the December 2013 municipal elections as a referendum on his government.

Maduro then made an audacious move. On Friday, November 8, he went on national television and accused the owners of Daka, one of the country's largest electronics retailers, of price gouging, claiming that they were selling products at more than 1,000% above cost. On the following morning, looting broke out at a Daka store in the city of Valencia in central Venezuela as hundreds of persons stormed the store and laid it bare (EuroNews 2013). The government proceeded to order the military occupation of three large electronics retailers, sending soldiers along with price inspectors with orders to lower prices and organize the long lines of persons who wanted to buy the electronics at reduced prices (Cawthorne 2013).

The government claimed that Daka's owners had obtained dollars at the official rate of 6.3 Bs/$ and were reselling the goods bought with these dollars at prices marked to the black market exchange rate, at the time at 104.1 Bs/$, pocketing a huge return while using subsidized state-provided dollars. How much of this was true remains uncertain. Most retailers at the time bought dollars to purchase imported goods on both the official market and the black market, so at any moment in time the goods on store shelves reflected a combination of both exchange rates. Furthermore, the government system didn't provide dollars to retailers prior to importing—it instead provided a promise to sell dollars at the official rate at some time in the future—forcing them to finance themselves on the black market anyway. Nevertheless, the last thing Daka executives could claim was that they had purchased these goods with dollars bought on the black market, as they would have been admitting that they had committed a crime.[7]

At issue were the huge arbitrage premia that were generated by the government's insistence on enforcing an overvalued official rate through exchange controls. Importers who received a dollar at the official rate and used it to import goods and resell them at black market prices could pocket an outsize return on the order of 1,600%. This also means that products sold at the official prices were seventeen times cheaper than products purchased on the black market. Firm owners who racked up prices, government officials who took bribes in exchange for foreign exchange allocations, and consumers who stood in line to purchase goods at rock-bottom prices were all trying to capture a part of the premium generated by the government selling dollars at one-seventeenth of their market price.

From the pure standpoint of electoral politics, the event that became known as the Dakazo proved to be a master stroke. For most Venezuelans, the idea that retailers should not rack up prices for goods that the government had subsidized through preferential foreign exchange access made perfect sense. Maduro's approval rating rose from 41% in September to 50% in November, a boost that helped government candidates coast to victory in the December 8 municipal elections, taking 49% of the national vote. The opposition MUD coalition took 41% of the vote and independent candidates the remaining 10%.

REWRITING THE PLAYBOOK

Doling out benefits from preferential access to foreign exchange had been part of the Venezuelan political playbook from time immemorial. But governments typically exercised some level of restraint. Throughout the Chávez administration, the ratio of the black market exchange rate to the official rate had averaged 2.1; at its highest level, it had reached 4.1. Under Maduro, it went much higher. By the end of 2013, that ratio had risen to 10.2 and would increase to a whopping average of 2,356 in 2017.

The reason previous governments had balked at letting distortions rise to the levels that Maduro was willing to toy with, despite their obvious political benefits, was that they knew that doing so would play havoc with the economy. A high black market premium means that the government is selling foreign exchange at a rate that is well below the market-clearing rate. The lower the revenue from selling foreign exchange, the larger the resulting fiscal deficit and the greater the cost for the government, which would then have to seek other forms of financing it.

By 2014, that cost was huge. In a paper published in March 2014, I estimated that the government could cut the deficit—which reached 9.0% of GDP that year—by between 7.5% and 11.7% of GDP just by unifying the exchange rate at its equilibrium level (Rodríguez 2014c). This would have required a major devaluation of the official rate of around 40%. However, given that the black market rate had already depreciated considerably, the average rate paid by consumers (including both official and black market transactions) was not all that different from the rate that the government could adopt as the unified exchange rate. Higher fiscal revenues would allow the government to curb money printing, making the inflationary effects of that policy adjustment limited.

For a moment, it looked as if that was precisely what the government was going to do. Just one day after its victory in the municipal elections, Vice President Jorge Arreaza broached the idea of adjusting heavily subsidized gasoline prices in an interview with a private television network (Correo del Caroní 2013). Two months earlier, Maduro had appointed Rafael Ramírez as economics chief. Ramírez, who had led the oil industry for nearly ten years, was an advocate of foreign exchange unification and fiscal adjustment. By March, he had launched a new complementary foreign exchange system and let the exchange rate in it rise to 50 Bs./$, nearly allowing it to fully converge with the black market rate. In mid-June, Ramírez was telling investors in London that Venezuela's multitier exchange rate system was about to come to an end (Orozco 2013).

It was not to be. Ramírez would be out by September, with the government deciding to shelve the adjustment program. Maduro would choose to keep the exchange and price controls in place rather than risk the political fallout from another major devaluation of the official rate.

Why did Maduro decide to shelve an adjustment that his policy advisers recognized as needed and whose avoidance implied a huge fiscal cost for the government? It is tempting to argue that he did so because maintaining the overvalued official rate increased the government's capacity to hand out rents to supporters in the form of access to subsidized dollars. Yet there is a problem with this line of reasoning. Giving out cheap dollars is not necessarily the most efficient way to distribute rents to cronies, because many Venezuelans over whom the government was unlikely to gain much sway would also gain access to the highly subsidized dollars.

To name just one salient example, under the country's currency controls, every Venezuelan had the right to purchase up to $3,000 a year in order to pay for expenses when traveling to another country (CADIVI

2009), an allocation that cost the government several billion dollars a year and that for the most part benefited upper- and middle-class Venezuelans who were not part of the government's political constituency.[8] As we will see in later chapters, over time the Maduro administration migrated to direct subsidy policies for which it was much easier to target and condition access on political support. The interesting question is why it chose to maintain this expensive transfer to its nonconstituents for so long, thereby also choosing to fund expenditures by printing money, a policy that would inflict severe costs on the poorest sectors of society in which government supporters were concentrated.

When the government decides to fund subsidies by printing money instead of raising taxes or cutting other expenditures, it is making a choice to appeal to alternative sources of revenues than those that it traditionally relies on. Exactly what those sources are will depend on its exchange rate policy. If the government sells enough dollars to match the increases in money supply—a monetary policy action known as sterilization—then it will deplete its wealth by either running down its assets or running up its liabilities. Once the government stops sterilizing and the money supply increases, then it will begin financing itself by taxing holders of local currency through what economists label the inflation tax. When inflation began to rise in Venezuela—from 20% in 2012 to 56% in 2013—the government was thus beginning to shift the burden of financing from future taxpayers to current holders of domestic currency. It is the choice to aggressively tap this source of taxation that needs to be explained.

Inflation taxes are temporary and highly distortionary but have a particular advantage: their benefits tend to be perceived before their costs.[9] As long as prices remain unchanged, the inflation tax is costless to contributors: real money holdings are only eroded when money printing affects prices, something that usually happens with a time lag. This makes inflation taxes particularly attractive for politicians who want to reap short-term benefits and care little about how high the associated long-term costs may be. The inflation tax is, in other words, the canonical "election tax" because politicians can spend the revenues ahead of an election, but contributors will only pay the cost in terms of increased prices after the election. Thus we expect to see governments use the inflation tax more intensively when they face competitive elections and the costs of losing those elections are high.

SURVIVAL OF THE FITTEST

There is a common thread that runs across the Dakazo, the tightening of price controls, and the decision to print money to pay for fiscally costly subsidies. All three actions had positive short-term political benefits for Maduro, and all three imposed significant long-term costs on the economy. The three actions are examples of the type of policies that we expect to see at times of intense political competition in a winner-take-all political system characterized by very high stakes of power. In this, they accord with the predictions of the single-actor model of politically induced distortions presented in chapter 3.

In this chapter, we also came across an incident that does not exactly conform to the predictions of our single-actor political economy model but that nevertheless confirms its analytical relevance. This is the February 2013 devaluation, carried out on the eve of the 2013 presidential elections, which nearly cost Chávez's successor the election for which only months before he had been considered a shoo-in. Whatever the explanation for that decision, and here I discussed some of them (desire to avoid loss of credibility by imposing a post-election adjustment, focus on political succession, undefined decision-making processes), it is clear that it imposed a significant political cost on Maduro: he came into office with a much weaker political mandate than he would have enjoyed otherwise.

It is also clear that he learned the lesson from that incident. By November 2013, Maduro was able to pull off a political master stroke by accusing one of the nation's largest retailers of price gouging and forcing it to slash prices ahead of a key election. Given the growing levels of political polarization and the high stakes of the political contest, it is not surprising that he did so. Venezuela's political game put a premium on survival and in so doing generated a bias toward short-term-oriented policies. Maduro's reticence to devalue in future years—which I discuss in greater detail in the next two chapters—was also likely strongly influenced by the understanding of the high electoral costs of devaluing the currency in election times that he gained from the February 2013 incident.

Of course, as I described in chapter 4, Chávez was also prone to populist policies. Yet given the exceptionally positive external conditions he enjoyed during his time in power, the electoral constraints were of a different nature. Chávez was fortunate to count on enough resources to keep the electorate content and ensure that voters would continue to support him at election time. It was when Maduro was forced to cut back spending that the electoral constraint became more binding. That is the moment at which we see policies turn increasingly short-term oriented.

Analysis of the Maduro administration's economic policy decisions in 2013 offers us a window into the learning process whereby politicians come to understand how to play the economy to their political advantage. At the start of the year, we find a Maduro unpreoccupied with economic policy decisions who severely miscalculated the political cost of getting the timing wrong on a policy decision that everyone around him knew was sorely needed. By the end of the year, we find him having learned to play the political game of manipulating the economy just enough to manage to stay in office.

That game was about to get much more difficult to play. Until 2013, Venezuela was a relatively buoyant oil producer capable of exporting around $90 billion a year. In the following three years, it would suffer a major external shock unlike anything that it had seen since the 1980s, its foreign currency revenue falling by more than two-thirds. I turn now to the story of that shock and its reverberations.

SIX

Living Dangerously

Venezuela is like a piece of dry leather, if I step on one side of it, it rises up on the other side.

—Antonio Guzmán Blanco, in DeLuca 2001

ADJUSTMENT IN PLAIN SIGHT

By early 2014, the Venezuelan economy had produced a significant external adjustment. Between the third quarter of 2012—just prior to Chávez's reelection—and the first quarter of 2014, the country had cut imports by more than a third.[1] Exports had suffered a small 5% decline due to some leveling of prices, but even so, the economy had been able to erase its external deficit and in fact was running a sizable $5.3 billion current account surplus (2.9% of GDP) at the start of 2014 (fig. 6.1).

A word of caution is in order with regard to interpreting these figures. In Venezuela's case, looking at the current account figures only tells us half the story about the sustainability of the country's external accounts. Venezuela's private sector has typically accumulated large stocks of foreign currency holdings abroad, so even a large current account surplus sometimes isn't enough to ensure sustainability. In fact, according to Central Bank data, Venezuela's private sector held a total of US$170 billion of currency holdings outside of the country by the end of

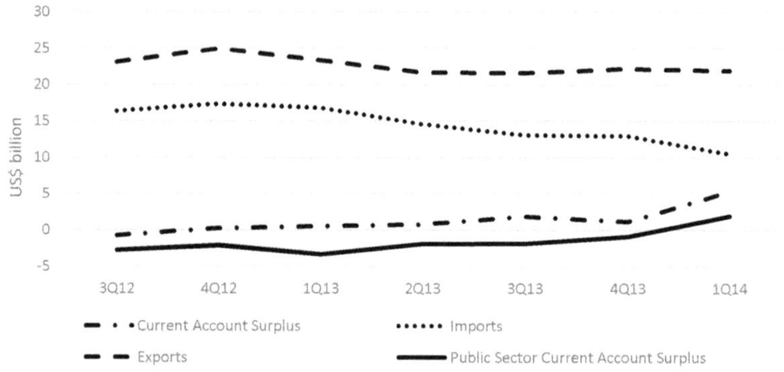

FIGURE 6.1. Current account and components, seasonally adjusted, 3Q12–1Q14. *Source*: Author's construction using BCV 2023c. *Note*: The public sector current account balance is defined as the increase in net external liabilities of the consolidated public sector.

2015—an amount larger than the country's total external debt of $151 billion. Clearly, that money was not available to policy makers.

What we really want to look at to see if a state-run economy is on an unsustainable path is the accumulation of net external liabilities by the public sector. In other words, we want to know whether the government is incurring more net external debt than it can pay for.[2] This calculation, displayed in figure 6.1, shows that between the third quarter of 2012 and the first quarter of 2014, the government had turned a $2.8 billion hard currency deficit into a $1.9 billion surplus.

In other words, by the start of 2014, Maduro's government had brought the economy down to living standards that it could afford at the oil prices and revenues of the time—in contrast to 2012, when the economy was clearly living above its means despite high oil prices. The government did not need to increase its external debt or run down its hard currency holdings further (and thus did not need to generate further cuts in imports) to sustain its finances.[3] The Venezuelan government still had a lot of economic problems, but running out of dollars wasn't one of them.

Maduro, however, had carried out this adjustment in an unconventional way. His administration had chosen to adjust quantities instead of prices. Afraid of losing the 2013 municipal elections and with the memory of the February 2013 devaluation fiasco still fresh, the government preferred to cut imports via administrative restrictions and to bring down consumption levels via rationing rather than allow imported goods to become more expensive.

Adjusting via quantities instead of prices had generated two problems that the government now had to contend with. One was a large fiscal deficit: given that the government was selling its dollars cheap, its local currency revenue was insufficient to cover its expenditures. The other problem was that the huge arbitrage rents generated by the gap between the official and black market exchange rate were completely distorting the country's economic and political incentives.

BAIT AND SWITCH

To understand how a government can be running a hard currency surplus but have a local currency deficit, it is useful to think in terms of analogies. Suppose one day you find out that your household is spending more money than it is earning. Maybe your rent has gone up, your salary or your partner's salary has declined, or you have to cover some expenses that you didn't have before. You and your partner sit down at the dinner table and decide that you are going to cut your spending. Two months later, you go through the numbers again and find that your household is now spending less than it earns. You breathe a sigh of relief: you're back on a sustainable path.

Except there's a problem. Your personal bank account continues showing lower balances month after month, so there is a sense in which *you* are running out of money. This is because a few years ago, your partner started putting a monthly amount into a savings account. So their savings are growing, but your cash holdings are declining.

This means you need to do another round of adjustment, but it's different from the previous one. In this one you aren't going to lower the level of consumption of the household as a whole. What you must convince your partner to do is stop running a surplus in their savings account at the same time that you are running a deficit in yours. Granted, that may be a difficult discussion. Maybe your partner will tell you that you should reduce your expenditures because the savings in their account are meant to pay for that Caribbean vacation you've always dreamed of. But while a cut in your consumption is one possible strategy for bringing your individual account into balance, there is no need to lower the aggregate consumption of both of you. Were you to cut your consumption, your partner would be able to increase theirs (by paying for the Caribbean vacation you would otherwise have been unable to afford) without threatening your household's sustainability because, as a household, you're already living within your means.

By the start of 2014, Venezuela had stopped importing more than it could pay for as a country. Yet the government had less revenue than necessary to fund its operations. The reason was that it was forgoing the potential revenues that it could have received from selling dollars, gasoline, and government-provided imported goods to the public at market prices by instead insisting on keeping the prices of these goods artificially low. That's why it was running a huge budget deficit despite having a current account surplus. But it wasn't paying for that deficit by running down its assets or going into debt: it was doing so by printing money, effectively levying a tax on a large part of the economy. In other words, it was imposing a huge tax on holders of local currency to transfer wealth to consumers, businesses, and importers who gained from having access to scarce yet cheap dollars, gasoline, and imported goods.

Money printing is the economic equivalent of bait and switch (marketing lingo for the practice of fooling consumers by substituting inferior goods for more expensive goods). The government lets the private sector keep a huge surplus of local currency but then erodes the value of those holdings by printing more money. In the household analogy, it is as if you went to the bank and withdrew money from your partner's account to cover your shortfall without their knowledge. You let your partner hold to the illusion that their savings are increasing. However, if your partner tries to spend that money, they will find out that there isn't as much in that account as they believed. At that time, your approval ratings will plummet.

Figure 6.2 shows the rapid rise in the rate of money creation during the end of Chávez's period in power and the Maduro government. The rate of base money growth remained stable at around 20% before 2011 and then started shooting up as the government got ready for the presidential elections. But even after the elections, when Maduro took power and began cutting imports, money printing continued to rise unabated.

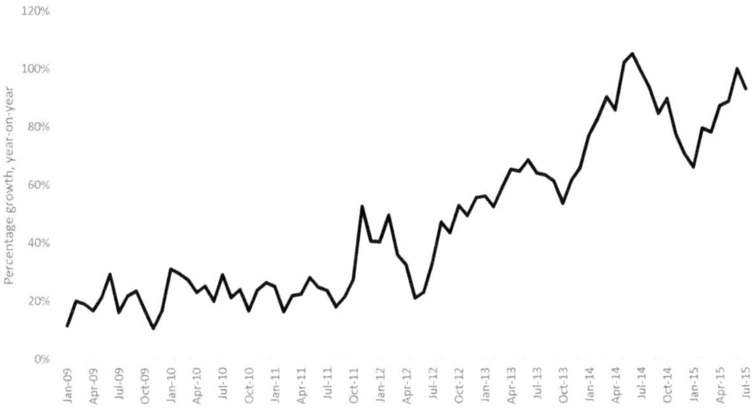

FIGURE 6.2. Base money growth, year-on-year, 2009–2015. *Source*: Author's construction using BCV 2023f.

By the end of 2013, the annual growth rate of base money had reached 66%, and by mid-2014, it would rise to 105%.

What Maduro had started to do was finance the budget deficit via money printing. Rather than tell Venezuelans that they had to pay more for their gasoline or for their imported goods, he decided to fund government spending by lowering the real value of their wages and savings through higher inflation. Seigniorage—the revenue generated for the government through money creation—which during Chávez's time in office had averaged 2.0% of GDP, rose to 8.4% of GDP by 2014 (fig. 6.3).[4]

Recall from the previous chapter that the approximate range of values by which exchange rate unification would have cut the deficit was between 8% and 12% of GDP. What figure 6.3 tells us is that Maduro had effectively decided that instead of letting Venezuelans know that they needed to pay more for imported goods, he would maintain the fiction that these goods were inexpensive and would cover the government's revenue shortfall by taxing Venezuelans' wages and savings through inflation. Note that this is very different from what was happening, say, at the end of the Chávez administration. At that time, the government was running up external debt to fund the spending boom, effectively transferring the cost of subsidies to Venezuelans in the future. By the start of 2014, the government had shifted the cost of that financing to

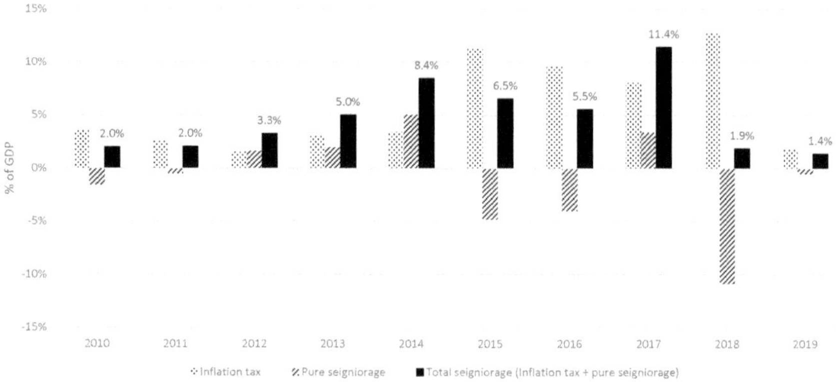

FIGURE 6.3. Seigniorage and components as % of GDP. *Source*: Author's construction based on Iyer and Rodríguez 2021.

the present, and it was making holders of money pay for the subsidies through the depletion of the real value of their cash holdings.

In short, Venezuela as a whole had brought down its consumption of imported goods to a level that was consistent with its exports, so the country was not living beyond its means. But the government didn't want to charge Venezuelans more for access to dollars and other publicly provided goods such as gasoline. So the government decided that it would tax Venezuelans in a more surreptitious way—via inflation.

Now taxing people through inflation is at least as painful as taxing them in any other way. Unanticipated inflation erodes the value of people's savings; it also makes people receive lower real wages than they planned to receive. In the end, when inflation gets out of control, people start racing to spend the money as rapidly as possible before it loses its value in a phenomenon that is traumatic for the whole economy. It is far from clear that covering a deficit through the inflation tax is in any way less painful or less popular than covering it through regular taxes.

This also means that getting out of this problem is not necessarily traumatic. To go back to the household spending metaphor, it is like coming clean to your partner and committing not to continue surreptitiously withdrawing money from your partner's account while asking your partner to give you that money to cover your shortfall. Your partner may get angry at first and perhaps won't want to do it, but the reality is that your partner won't be any worse off by giving you the money to contribute to the household expenses than if you continue to take that money out of their account without their knowledge.[5]

In other words, Venezuela had done the hard part of the adjustment, but it still needed to do something crucial to put its house in order: it needed to put the value of the exchange rate and other prices of publicly provided goods and services in line with market fundamentals. This would not necessarily have been costly politically. Surely people wouldn't like having to pay more for imported goods and gasoline, but they would no longer be having their wages and savings confiscated by the inflation tax. Furthermore, since there was no need to lower the aggregate level of consumption of the economy, the adjustment did not need to cause an economic contraction, and in fact the efficiency gains from eliminating all the price distortions in the economy could have generated a boost in growth.

That said, the economy still had two major problems. One was that what Maduro had done during his first year in office was bring its living standards to an affordable level given that oil was selling at $100 per barrel. This was indeed the price of Venezuelan oil up to late 2014. But on September of that year, prices collapsed when OPEC decided not to cut output even as the market was being inundated by growing US shale oil production. The country was completely unprepared for this collapse, which would require another major external adjustment.

The other problem was that by 2014, a set of new beneficiaries from foreign exchange and price arbitrage had emerged. One implication of carrying out a quantity adjustment via rationing is that the state ends up giving away very valuable assets to people. If the government is selling a dollar for 6 bolivars but that dollar is worth 120 bolivars in the black market, then anybody who buys it is getting a dollar at 5% of its market price. It is as if the government was selling $20 bills for a dollar. Whoever is among the lucky few selected to buy these dollars at rock-bottom prices will surely owe the government a favor and will be willing to put up a fight to defend the right to keep receiving it. As I have argued above, some of the groups benefiting from the handouts of subsidized dollars were not necessarily among the government's supporters, so it could make sense politically to take this subsidy away and instead use the funds to more directly target government constituencies (as Maduro would ultimately do). But the noise associated with a major reallocation of government benefits was something that the government was keen to avoid, particularly at moments of perceived political vulnerability.

LOOKING FOR THE EXIT

Venezuelans recognize January 23 as the birthdate of their democracy. It was on that date in 1958 that a military uprising led to the ouster of General Marcos Pérez Jimenez and his de facto government from power, leading to the emergence of what for long was one of the continent's most enduring democracies. Venezuela in fact boasted until recently the longest stream of uninterrupted competitive presidential elections in South America,[6] and it was commonly seen as the most successful example of democratization in the region. Writing in 1981, the US political scientist Peter Merkl (1981, 127) called it "a textbook case of step-by-step progress" in democratization.

January 23 was also the date chosen in 2014 by three key Venezuelan opposition leaders to launch a protest movement called La Salida (the Way Out). The three leaders were well known for their willingness to confront the government directly. María Corina Machado was a young fiery legislator who had attained notoriety when she interrupted a Chávez speech before the National Assembly to tell him that "expropriating is stealing" (Machado 2012). Leopoldo López was a charismatic Harvard-educated former mayor of Chacao, an opposition stronghold and one of the wealthiest districts in the country. Antonio Ledezma was a veteran politician from the Democratic Action (Acción Democrática, AD) party who had been able to wrest the Greater Caracas mayoralty—which includes many of the poorer districts in the nation's capital—from the government in the 2008 elections.

Ledezma, López, and Machado were well-known opposition leaders but were far from the most prominent ones. Henrique Capriles, the opposition candidate in the 2012 and 2013 elections, and his Justice First (Primero Justicia, PJ) party did not support La Salida. Nor did the leaders of AD or A New Time (Un Nuevo Tiempo, UNT)—which, together with PJ, made up the three largest opposition groups in the National Assembly at the time. López and Machado, in fact, had run in the 2012 primaries for the opposition nomination. López had withdrawn to support Capriles, while Machado had come in third with less than 4% of the vote (*El País* 2012). On the other hand, Capriles had never accepted Maduro's victory in the 2013 presidential election, requesting a full audit and manual recount (Prados 2013); while his claims did not gain much international traction at the time, they did serve as motivation for those in the opposition who believed in the legitimacy of seeking to oust Maduro from power through protests.

La Salida presented itself as a protest movement to call for a change in government. Its organizers were careful enough to clarify that "the way out" should be peaceful and constitutional, but they were vague on the specifics of how it would be achieved. Machado, for example, insisted that Maduro's resignation was a constitutional way out—undeniably true but hardly relevant (Moleiro 2015).

La Salida came on the heels of spontaneous security-related protests at two universities in western Venezuela, although the government charged that these were part of a coordinated plan to generate political instability (PSUV 2014). As student protests continued and spread to other regions, La Salida's leaders called for a massive nationwide demonstration in thirty-eight cities on February 12.

In Caracas, the February 12 demonstration headed toward the prosecutor general's office to protest the arrests of several student leaders in the demonstrations of previous days. At the close of the rally, hooded protesters began throwing rocks and setting fires at the entrance of the building. Three persons died during the clashes: a pro-government community leader and two pro-opposition demonstrators (Pardo 2014). Maduro accused the opposition of the deaths, and on the following day, a court issued an arrest warrant for López on charges of instigating violence; López turned himself in five days later. The prosecutor general initially charged López with homicide and terrorism but later lowered the charges to instigating violence (*El Mundo* 2014; *El Impulso* 2015).[7]

Protests would continue for three months across the country, leaving more than forty dead and nearly a thousand wounded, with more than three thousand arrests. Though the size of these protests would be dwarfed by the massive demonstrations that the country would see three years later, it was the first time since 2002 that the government faced large-scale prolonged demonstrations. For the purposes of my current discussion on economic policy, what is important to understand is that the onset of protests altered the government's policy decisions. A government that in mid-December was ready to discuss fiscal and exchange rate adjustments faced a country that was literally on fire only three months later.

The 2014 protests, while national in scope, were for the most part concentrated in opposition bastions, with the poorer urban Chavista strongholds relatively unaffected (Hernández 2014; Rodríguez 2018). Yet the possibility that they could extend into the poorer sectors of society was a permanent preoccupation of government leaders. We saw in chapter 4 how the Caracazo—which many Chavistas saw as the event that inspired their movement—was precipitated by protests that followed a large hike in gasoline prices. While by 2014 most government leaders understood the need to raise gasoline prices, they also thought that doing so during nationwide protests could cause these to spill over into poorer sectors and get out of control.

It was precisely at this time that some government leaders began to think that they were able to control the protests because they had not carried out a conventional orthodox adjustment. Eleazar Díaz Rangel, editor of the Caracas newspaper *Últimas Noticias* and one of the most prominent pro-government intellectuals, wrote an editorial two months into the protests in which he compared the Caracazo to La Salida and claimed that the main difference was that "back then businesses were fully stocked[,] but the poor . . . had no money to buy them. Today they can afford them, even if they have trouble finding them" (Díaz 2014).

Certainly, the government had reasons to be concerned that carrying out the adjustments in the midst of protests would play into the opposition's hands. Leopoldo López had lambasted the government in his January 23 speech for devaluing the currency on the previous day—a reference to the government's decision to raise the exchange rate paid by Venezuelan tourists abroad and airlines (Zea 2014a).[8] Several opposition leaders would go on the offensive later that year when the government hinted at the possibility of adjusting gasoline prices, saying that the government should instead stop sending subsidized oil to other countries (*Diario Qué Pasa* 2014; Prensa Gobernación de Miranda 2014; *La Voz* 2014).

That the opposition would take the government to task for doing something unpopular was to be expected; the problem was that this was happening during protests that the government felt threatened its hold on power. This made the government shift into election-year mode: it did not reject the adjustments per se but assessed their timing as inconvenient. The problem, of course, was that 2014 was the one year in which the government could expect to be unconstrained by elections, as key parliamentary elections were scheduled for 2015.

THE CASH CRUNCH

Oil prices took a nosedive in late 2014. Between June 2014 and January 2015, the price of a Venezuelan barrel of oil fell from $101 to $39; in the following twelve months, they would plunge deeper, hitting a low of $22 in mid-January 2015. The price plunge followed years of surging production of high-cost oil produced from shale rock fragments in the United States. US production rose from 5.0 to 9.5 million barrels between 2010 and 2014, due to a more than doubling of production from shale oil rigs (Doggett 2015; OPEC 2020b). Proven reserves of shale oil deposits in the United States were also reassessed dramatically, leading the market to become concerned about a potential impending oil glut. As a result, prices began dropping steadily in the third quarter of 2014: by mid-November, Venezuelan oil was selling for $71 a barrel, down from $100 just five months earlier.

On November 27, the oil ministers of OPEC, the thirteen-member cartel of oil producers that accounted at the time for more than a third of world oil production, met in Vienna to try to agree on a response. Traditionally, OPEC would have responded to a 30% decline in oil prices by cutting production to prop up prices. This was the case made by countries like Venezuela and Iran, whose inability to raise production made them strong advocates for output cuts. But they faced strong resistance from low-cost producers like Saudi Arabia, which claimed that an output cut would imply giving up market share to shale oil producers as well as non-OPEC members like Russia and Brazil (Reed 2014).

In the end, the Saudis prevailed. The decision entailed a sea change in the way in which OPEC conceptualized its relation with global oil markets. By refusing to act as a buffer to stabilize oil markets, OPEC opened the possibility that the market would start to see the much higher price volatility that typically characterizes commodity markets and that it had for decades avoided as a result of OPEC's policy of targeting price stabilization. What the Saudis had decided to do was begin a price war against US shale producers, in the hope that a prolonged period of low oil prices would drive them out of the market. For as long as this lasted, the bottom could very well fall from under oil prices, making the previously unimaginable scenario of $30 oil a real possibility.

With the benefit of hindsight, it is easy to forget how unexpected this drop was. At the end of 2013, the average forecast of Bloomberg's poll of twenty-five oil industry analysts was that a barrel of West Texas Intermediate (WTI) would be worth $97 by the end of 2014 and $96 by the end of 2015 (fig. 6.4).[9] Oil futures markets told pretty much the same story, with forward contracts pricing in $93 and $86 respectively for 2014 and 2015. Even the most pessimistic analyst in the Bloomberg survey only expected prices to drop to $83 in 2014 and $70 in 2016. By contrast, prices fell to $53 in 2014 and to $37 in 2015, before recovering to $60 by 2017 (still well below the 2013 mean Bloomberg forecast of $95 for the end of that year).

What followed was one of the largest external shocks ever suffered by Venezuela. Between June 2014 and February 2016, Venezuelan oil prices collapsed from $99 to $22 per barrel, a 76% drop. Prices eventually recovered somewhat from their early 2016 lows, yet the depth of the collapse was still huge. The average price of the country's exports measured in terms of its imports, also known as the net barter terms of trade, fell

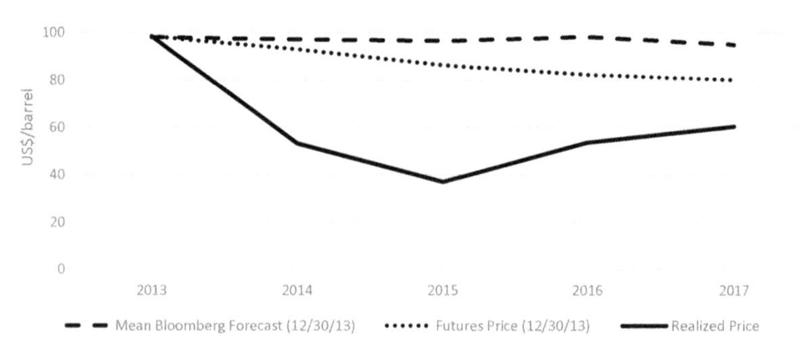

FIGURE 6.4. Oil price forecast at the end of 2013 and realized prices. *Source*: Author's construction using Bloomberg 2018a, 2018b, 2018c.

by 52% between 2012 and 2016. The only comparable episode was the 57% decline that had been observed between 1981 and 1988, the period immediately preceding the 1989 Caracazo.[10]

Measured in terms of foregone export revenue, the hit was considerably larger than that of the 1980s. While oil production had slumped at the onset of the 1980s oil shock, it had also begun recovering by the late 1980s, so that the decline in real export revenue between 1981 and 1988 was a more attenuated 53%. But in 2016, oil production began to decline as the cash crunch hit PDVSA's capacity to maintain operations (this is discussed in greater detail in chapters 2 and 9). Furthermore, near-zero gasoline prices buoyed domestic consumption and contraband trade, limiting the number of barrels that the government could export. By 2016, real export revenues were only 31% of their 2012 levels, making the decline in the purchasing power of Venezuela's exports much deeper than in the 1980s. By 2016, Maduro had to run the country with less than a third of the foreign exchange that Chávez had at his disposal.

Venezuela was particularly ill-prepared for this shock. Figure 6.5 compares the international reserves of Venezuela measured in terms of months of import coverage with those of other large oil exporters at the end of 2013. At that time, Venezuela's international reserves of $20.3 billion covered 4.3 months of imports. In contrast, Saudi Arabia's

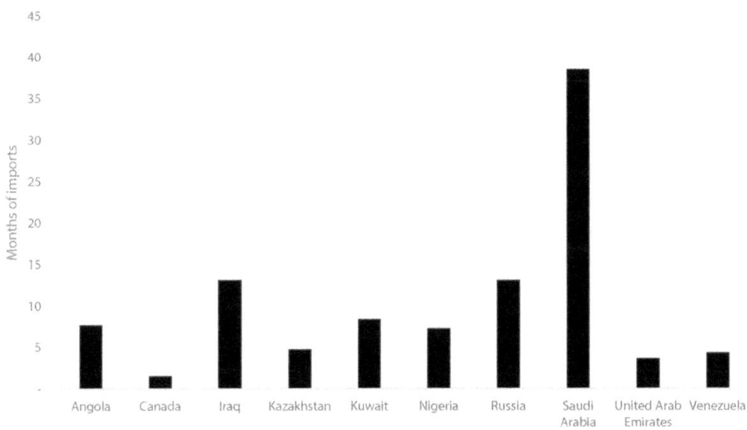

FIGURE 6.5. International reserves measured in months of imports, top 10 oil exporters, December 2013. *Source*: Author's construction using OPEC 2023; World Bank 2023b; IMF 2023a.

$738 billion reserves covered more than 3 years of imports. Oil exporting countries are used to high terms of trade volatility; therefore, most of them try to save a sizable portion of their windfalls to prepare for downturns. But in Venezuela, savings had taken a backseat to the government's spending needs and the country had emerged from the oil boom with a relatively small level of hard currency savings.[11]

CALM BEFORE THE STORM

By May 2014, La Salida had died down and the country was in relative calm. The economics chief, Rafael Ramírez, who also headed the country's oil industry, began a roadshow to present the reforms to international financial markets. On June 14, he told a group of investors in London that Venezuela's three exchange rates would "progressively converge," stating that the system of exchange controls "is no longer suitable for the economy" (*Financial Times* 2014).

On July 30, Ramírez made a formal presentation of the economic measures before the Third Congress of the governing Socialist Party, PSUV. The party congress is the close equivalent of a party convention, bringing together some eight hundred delegates, including all high-ranking government leaders as well as elected representatives from every municipality. The decision to showcase the presentation of the economic program at the congress seemed a clear signal that Maduro had given the green light and that the event would be used as an opportunity to buttress support from the party structures that would have the job of explaining the measures to their constituents.

Nevertheless, some ominous signs appeared. Maduro missed Ramírez's presentation, appearing to signal that it lacked his full endorsement. A hiatus then began during which none of the economic decisions that had been presented to investors and the PSUV congress was announced. This period of paralysis lasted a full month. On September 2, Maduro announced that he was replacing Ramírez as economics chief, moving him to the foreign ministry. In his place, Maduro appointed Rodolfo Marco Torres, a brigadier general who had previously served as national treasurer and head of a state-owned bank.

It is unclear at what time Maduro took the decision to shelve the adjustments, or what his thought process was when taking this decision. The fact that there were no signals from the new team on the direction of policy for several weeks after Ramírez's ouster suggests that the government had not made a clear decision. On September 7, the Finance Commission president, Ricardo Sanguino, said in a highly watched Sunday TV program that an increase in fuel prices and foreign exchange unification had not been discarded, showing that even high-ranking PSUV members were confused as to how to read the administration's decisions (Pitts 2014). It is even possible that Maduro decided to shift Ramírez to the foreign ministry—while ratifying him as OPEC representative—in the hope that he could help convince other OPEC members to cut output and strengthen prices, thus giving the government the breathing space that it needed to implement the policy changes.

What we do know is that the decision to delay adjustment coincided with the free fall in oil prices. The price of Venezuela's oil basket fell by $14 during the third quarter of 2014 and would then fall by $37 during the following quarter. By January 2015, Venezuelan oil was selling for under $40 per barrel. The price would fall even more during the next year (to $22 in early 2016), but even this was a huge shock by historical standards.

The shock completely changed the set of policy choices facing the government. At the start of 2014, the government had brought the economy's external accounts into balance via a quantity adjustment but had yet to carry out the price adjustment necessary to bring fiscal accounts into balance. By early 2015, it was looking at the need to carry out another huge external adjustment on top of the delayed price adjustments.

The government had depleted a great part of its political capital by then. Maduro's approval rating, which had reached 55% at the start of his term in 2013, had fallen to 23% by the end of 2014 (Datanálisis 2017). Legislative elections were scheduled for 2015, and the government began to seriously consider the risk that it could lose control of the National Assembly. The window of opportunity for carrying out the adjustments before producing a political backlash with damaging electoral consequences was closing fast.

In retrospect, one can argue that the government would have been better off carrying out the Ramírez plan and unifying the exchange rate in the second half of 2014, by which time La Salida protests had subsided. Some degree of liberalization would have increased the efficiency of resource allocation and strengthened government revenues, possibly helping it perform better than it ended up doing in the 2015 parliamentary elections (see chap. 8). Furthermore, as the government would eventually show, it could survive the loss of a parliamentary majority. A government focused on its long-term survival would have been better advised to focus on improving economic conditions before having to face other elections that implied a greater existential threat, including a post-2016 recall referendum and the 2018 presidential election, even if that meant having to live with a hostile legislature (which it would end up having to do anyway).

It is thus possible to argue that a rational-actor model of a unitary government cannot provide a satisfactory account for the 2014 decision to shelve adjustments. In two articles published in November 2014, I made the case that the delay of price and exchange rate adjustments could be understood as consequence of the government's loss of integrative capacity in the face of successive political and economic shocks (Rodríguez 2014a, 2014b). Borrowing on the behavioral economics literature that finds that individuals focused on addressing their most urgent needs lose their capacity to make and carry out long-term plans (Mullainathan and Shafir 2013), I argued that dealing with the diverse array of operational difficulties associated with handling a complex system of price and exchange controls under declining oil revenues could similarly cause a state to lose its integrative capacity to make wise long-term choices.

The focus of the Maduro government at the time on addressing the consequences of scarcity, rather than dealing with its deeper causes, was in fact striking. Virtually all major economic policy announcements made by Maduro during his first two years in office were concerned with resolving scarcity issues. The agency in charge of enforcing price controls, created in 2011, was restructured in January 2014 and had four directors between 2013 and 2014; the exchange controls agency, also reorganized in 2014, likewise had four directors in the same period. Organizations as diverse as the Central Bank, the military, and even the intelligence services were tasked with overseeing the nation's increasingly byzantine system of controls. These decisions were characteristic of a government whose reduced bandwidth drove it to focus on short-term issues and to lose the integrative capacity to consider major policy changes.

Whatever the reason for the paralysis, by the start of 2015, it had become clear that Maduro had ditched the idea of carrying out a full-fledged price adjustment. Despite the massive adverse terms of trade shock, he announced in early 2015 that he had decided to keep the preferential exchange rate of 6.3 bolivars per dollar. With inflation running in the high double digits, the official exchange rate was quickly appreciating in real terms, the exact opposite of the necessary policy response to such a shock. The government also discarded the proposal to carry out a gasoline price adjustment and decided instead to maintain the price of 9.7 Venezuelan cents for a liter of gasoline (equal to approximately 1/20th of a US cent per liter at the black market rate of the time, as opposed to an international price of around $0.60/liter at the time). Price adjustment, for now, was off the table.

CHOICE AND CONSEQUENCES

Maduro's decision to shelve proposals for price adjustments meant that the government would face the need to cut imports as a response to the terms of trade shock via tighter rationing. While this gave the government the discretion to choose among recipients of foreign exchange and essential goods, it also meant that the use of that discretion would become a salient political issue. When people can't buy dollars because they are too expensive, they may blame the government for the economic conditions that led to the depreciation of the currency but will not necessarily hold it responsible for who gets the dollars. But when it is the government instead that is deciding who will have the right to buy dollars at the official overvalued rate, the choice to favor some sectors to the detriment of others in the allocation of the rights to acquire these dollars will take center stage.

This problem was exacerbated by the government's decision to begin issuing IOUs to those whose demand for dollars it could not immediately satisfy. Rather than explicitly tighten allocation rules narrowing the conditions needed to obtain cheap dollars, the government maintained unchanged the allocation rules but began delaying the time that it would take to make those dollars available, issuing promises to provide future dollars at that exchange rate. Importers could thus rapidly obtain an "authorization to purchase foreign exchange," effectively conceived of as a green light to import the good, yet would have to wait longer and longer to receive the elusive "authorization to obtain foreign exchange."[12] By 2016, the government had run up $21.2 billion in arrears on these authorizations, almost the same as the amount of outstanding central government foreign-currency bonds at the time ($21.7 billion).[13]

From a legal standpoint, these obligations were almost completely worthless. In 1989, Venezuela's Supreme Court had ruled that the government could unilaterally revise the exchange rate at which it honored these commitments, allowing it to erase their market value at the stroke of a pen.[14] In this sense, they were very different from the foreign currency bonds issued in international financial markets and bound by New York law, where any unilateral change in the conditions of payment constitutes an event of default and confers on creditors the right to seek immediate remedies in foreign courts. Yet what is most relevant is not so much the legal strength of the obligations as the political fact that they generated a large constituency of holders who felt just as entitled to receive payments as any other of the nation's creditors.

These arrears were just one of the many internal obligations that the government racked up because of its decision not to carry out a price adjustment. Another was the massive issuance of internal debt. As we have seen, the government carried out deep imports cuts but left the official exchange rate and the price caps on many imported essentials unchanged, leaving a large fiscal gap that it could cover only by issuing internal debt bonds. In order to create demand for these bonds, the Central Bank had to print money with which they could be acquired, either by government entities or by the private sector.[15] The money printing, of course, would ensure that the real value of the newly minted internal debt would be ultimately inflated away.[16] Therefore, the government was essentially funding itself by issuing internal debt that it was sure to default on. The losers would be the Venezuelans who acquired that debt and would see the real value of their local currency savings pulverized.

As these choices became more salient, it was only a matter of time before someone would ask why the country did not also ask its foreign creditors to foot part of the bill. In a September 2014 article, two Venezuelan economists, Ricardo Hausmann and Miguel Ángel Santos, claimed that Venezuela should also consider defaulting on its external creditors, as it was patently clear that it was unable to pay all its obligations (Hausmann and Santos 2014). They pointed to growing arrears in obligations derived from the currency controls system as examples of how the country was defaulting on its other creditors while continuing to pay bondholders. They also suggested that the government's prioritization of bondholders was driven at least in part by the fact that many of these bonds were "held by well-connected Venezuelans," charging that Maduro's decision to default on millions of Venezuelans rather than on Wall Street was "a signal of its [the Maduro government's] moral bankruptcy" (Hausmann and Santos 2014).

Hausmann and Santos were not the only ones critical of the government for continuing to honor its debt payments. In 2015, the left-wing movement Marea Socialista (a group of Chavista dissidents critical of Maduro) called for a moratorium on Venezuela's debt payments (*Noticiero Digital* 2014). And of course Venezuela's left-wing parties had made calls for repealing the country's external debt in the 1980s and 1990s, with Chávez himself briefly campaigning on a moratorium promise in 1999, only to backtrack once elected president.[17] But this time, the criticism of creditors and debt markets was not coming from the left of the political spectrum but from intellectuals associated with the country's opposition.

Any government, of course, could default on its debt and free up resources to devote to addressing the needs of its people. Yet most governments try to avoid doing so unless faced by very unusual levels of stress. This is because there are good reasons to believe that defaulting on a nation's debt has adverse consequences that must be weighed against the short-term benefits derived from saving on debt service. Governments all over the world make the decision to devote toward debt service resources that could have been used to address more urgent needs; when doing so, they decide to keep their word to pay creditors to the detriment of other explicit or implicit commitments made to many of their citizens.

Financial obligations to creditors are not all that different from other commitments made by politicians, whether we choose to call them "debts" or not. Claims of one type or another on a government are created whenever a politician makes a promise; choosing which of those commitments to honor is part and parcel of a politician's job. As Niccolò Macchiavelli famously told us more than five centuries ago, a prince will never be short of good reasons to explain away a broken promise (Macchiavelli [1513] 2009, 69).

Whether Venezuela should have defaulted—or, more generally, how aggressively it should have tried to restructure its debt[18]—at the time is a complex question. Economists generally recommend that a government should try to honor its debt if its debt stock is intertemporally sustainable (i.e., paying it is feasible both today and in the future) and should attempt to restructure unsustainable debts. By these standards, there didn't seem to be a very strong argument for defaulting on Venezuela's debt at the time of Hausmann and Santos's column in mid-2014. At the end of 2013, Venezuela's total public sector external debt was $124 billion, or 55% of the country's GDP, a number that is well within the limits of traditional sustainability analyses.[19] As I argued earlier in this chapter, the public sector's external position had been brought into surplus as of the first quarter of 2014, and while an internal adjustment was needed to cut the government's local-currency deficit, the country as a whole was not using up more external resources than it was generating. Interest payments totaled $6.8 billion, which was equal to 7.6% of Venezuela's exports, a number that is also not atypical in an emerging-market context.[20] The average yield on the country's foreign currency bonds—which measures the cost of financing and thus of rolling over the debt—was 11.0%, a number that is on the high end of the emerging market spectrum, yet again not unusual for emerging market countries that continue to service their debts.[21]

These numbers would become progressively worse as oil revenues plummeted in the following years. By 2016, the same calculation yielded a debt-to-GDP ratio of 117%, with interest payments taking up 25% of exports. The reason is not that debt had gone up considerably—it had not—but that GDP measured in dollars and export revenues had fallen dramatically.[22] By 2020, after the collapse of the country's oil industry, debt accounted for 275% of GDP, and the interest that the nation would have had to pay, had it tried to remain current on its debt (without including past due interest), represented

65% of exports. As I discuss in coming chapters, while the decline in oil revenues was initially driven by falling prices, over time the dominant factor became declining oil production, which was deeply impacted by sanctions. These numbers suggest that the current unsustainability of Venezuela's debt is a consequence, rather than a driver, of the country's output collapse.

Assessing the sustainability of a country's debt and working out how it should react to large negative terms of trade shocks, some of which turn out to be temporary, isn't always easy. It is even harder when the country's terms of trade, and thereby its capacity to service external debt, are highly volatile. One reason is that it is difficult to predict how much of a given decline in export prices is permanent and to determine when it will make sense for a government to react to it as permanent. To complicate things even more, the costs of default may be considerably higher for a country in which the main debtor is a state-owned company with external assets and revenue flows, a case for which the standard sovereign immunity protections that shield restructurings of external debt from creditors' attempts to seize assets are unavailable.[23] As I discuss in chapter 10, Venezuela's default ultimately set off a scramble from creditors, some of whom successfully attached foreign facilities and subsidiaries of PDVSA, including its large US refiner, CITGO, severely hampering the prospects of regaining access to the US market in the future.[24]

As I remarked in a comment on Hausmann and Santos's article published in the *Financial Times* developing economies blog in September 2014, focusing on the country's debt service when the economy's price system was in policy-induced havoc seemed like putting the cart before the horse (Rodríguez 2014d). Dollar scarcity in Venezuela at the time was not a reflection of the country not having enough dollars but of the decision of the government to sell those dollars at an unrealistically low price. With the black market pricing dollars at ten times the official exchange rate, I argued, Venezuela's Central Bank may just as well have put a sign on its front door saying, "We sell $10 bills for $1." The fiscal payoff to adjusting the overvalued exchange rate and other out-of-sync relative prices would have dwarfed any savings from default and would also have helped stop inflation in its tracks and restart economic growth. Thinking that the country could solve its policy-induced economic problems by making external creditors foot the bill instead of addressing the economy's deep price distortions and fiscal imbalance was losing the forest for the trees.

An interesting policy discussion ensued regarding the relative costs and benefits of attempting to forcibly restructure the country's debt as opposed to other policy alternatives. Hausmann and Santos argued that debt was the problem, or at least one key problem, that impeded Venezuela's recovery. My position was that the country's dysfunctional policies were the problem and that once you cured those policies—which you needed to do anyway for the good of the country—the problem of access to international capital markets would tend to solve itself. At the very least, as I argued in a Brookings Forum held in 2016, the uncertainty regarding the market reaction to policy reforms—and the possible effect that such reforms could have on the country's financing costs—was so high that one could make a strong case to embark on policy reforms first and then decide, depending among other things on the market reaction to those reforms, whether an aggressive debt restructuring, with its associated costs, was necessary (Bahar and Strauss 2016).

Maduro did neither. He didn't try to restructure the debt, and he didn't try to fix the country's deep policy distortions. By rolling over debt at increasing financing costs and refusing to correct relative price distortions even as oil prices fell and stayed low, he made both problems worse. As oil revenues went down, the government refused to alter the official exchange rate, leading it to become even more overvalued and further distorting resource allocation. This decision impeded the economy from assigning resources to the production of alternative exportable and import-competing goods to offset its reduced capacity to purchase imported goods. Foreign exchange scarcity deepened, as did the ensuing economic contraction. Nor did Maduro revise the conditions for foreign investment in the oil sector. Instead, the growing overvaluation of the official exchange rate served as an increasing tax on oil investors at the time that the economy needed to raise incentives for them to continue investing. Investment in the oil sector slumped, and the ensuing decline in production made it more and more difficult for the country to meet its basic import needs.

Ultimately, the country was rendered incapable of servicing its debt and meeting Venezuela's basic needs, leaving it with no alternative but to default. There was nothing surprising in this outcome: to all those who were involved in the debate, it was clear that if Venezuela did not undertake the needed policy corrections in time, it would ultimately be unable to service its debt. By refusing to change the direction of the country's policies, Maduro had limited his choices to either continuing to repay the debt at the expense of lower imports or defaulting and paying the costs of losing access to financing and foreign investment.

Yet the discussion had more wide-ranging political implications than those of a purely academic debate. Opposition politicians soon latched on to the idea that they could score easy points against the government by railing against the country's creditors (Voluntad Popular 2016b). Doing so helped them appeal to the country's import-dependent private sector, which was sympathetic to the idea that cutting debt service would allow it to have greater access to dollars. And while most opposition politicians understood that the reduced access to capital markets that would follow a disorderly default could deepen the recession, they also believed that the political consequences would be borne by Maduro and not by the opposition, which was likely to do better electorally if the economy tanked.

Some of the hostility to creditors was based on misconceptions. The claim that Venezuela's bonds were mainly held by insiders, for example, was incorrect: local bond holdings in mid-2017 accounted for less than a third of all outstanding bonds, and most of them were in the hands of state-owned banks (Rodríguez 2017b). Yet such claims constituted an appealing and convenient narrative for a highly polarized environment.

As the opposition began to characterize financial markets as allies of the Maduro regime, calls for a broader repudiation of the country's debts grew, further spooking markets, restricting the country's access to finance, and forcing it to carry out deeper import cuts. The increasingly hostile language used to describe international markets would become a mainstay of opposition discourse in years to come. Hausmann, who would later go on to form part of the opposition-led interim government in 2019, would eventually coin the term "hunger bonds" to refer to the idea that repaying the nation's external debt was a driver of Venezuela's humanitarian crisis (see chap. 8). It is no coincidence that when opposition leaders first started lobbying the Trump administration for sanctions, they focused on getting the United States to restrict the government's access to debt markets. The discussions about the legitimacy of existing debt would be a harbinger of what was to come: a struggle for power in which Venezuela's links with the global economy would be at the center of the political tug-of-war.

PLAYING CHICKEN

In mid-2014, the Maduro government backtracked on a decision to unify the country's exchange rate and reduce domestic fuel subsidies. These measures would have stabilized fiscal accounts at the time and completed the adjustment initiated when the government undertook deep import cuts the previous year. They would have also left the country in much better shape to handle the major external shock that would result from the decline in oil prices that began in the second half of 2014.

The reason the government decided to shelve the adjustments and instead maintain the deeply overvalued exchange rate, funding the resulting fiscal imbalances through monetization, was not ignorance of what it needed to do. On the contrary, there was broad consensus in the administration that a policy adjustment was needed. The fact that the government began to announce these measures one day after its victory in the 2013 municipal elections suggests that it had thought through not just the design of the measures but also their political timing and that it would aim to take advantage of the two-year political window until the 2015 parliamentary elections.

That political window closed just as rapidly as it had opened. By February 2014, the country was racked by protests called by a sector of the opposition that questioned the results of Maduro's 2013 election and sought to force his ouster from power through mass demonstrations. Government leaders feared that the protests could extend to lower income areas and knew that a major devaluation and gas price hike had the potential to make them unmanageable, as had happened with the Caracazo. While they acknowledged that the adjustments were needed, they also recognized that there was an overarching priority not to do anything that could risk the government's stability.

The 2014 delay in adjustment is in broad terms consistent with the framework sketched in the single-actor model of politically induced distortions presented in chapter 3 but with a twist. What made the government hesitant to carry out the adjustments in 2014 was not the proximity of elections—there was what appeared to be a reasonable window between the 2013 municipal elections and the 2015 parliamentary elections—but rather the onset of La Salida protests. It was these demonstrations that made government leaders feel that their hold on power was under threat. The story told in this chapter fits into the framework of the single-actor model under a flexible interpretation in which governments' decisions to impose policy distortions also respond to nonelectoral threats to their hold on power.

Accepting this broader interpretation opens a host of other questions. Single-actor political economy models of electorally induced distortions were inspired by presidentialist systems like those of the United States in which the timing of elections is exogenous. Extensions that considered the case of endogenous elections typically focused on the possibility that the government could decide when to call an election, as in many European parliamentary systems (Alesina, Mirrlees, and Neumann 1989; Cargill and Hutchinson 1991; Heckelman and Berument 1998).[25] The idea that the opposition can induce an election-like moment in which the government faces a short-term incentive to shore up political support has, to the best of my knowledge, not been explored.

What we start to see in this chapter is how the opposition begins to acquire and make use of a strategy to challenge the government's hold on power by playing outside of the established rules of political competition. This in turn affected the government's incentive to adopt distortionary macroeconomic policies. While the government was trying to avoid the repeat of a Caracazo moment, the leaders promoting La Salida were preparing to take advantage of the expected unpopular adjustments to fuel the protests. The political reality that emerges during 2014 begins to acquire some of the characteristics of the two-player model of political competition introduced in chapter 3.

As I discussed in chapter 3, for economically destructive political conflict to arise, both the opposition and the government must have access to political technologies that allow them to harm the economy. Governments have access to these technologies just by virtue of being in office, but oppositions generally do not. While political movements capable of calling protests that endanger the government's stability in office can affect and manipulate the timing of political incentives, this does not mean that they have the capacity to damage the economy to the extent necessary to alter the structure of the political contest for power.

That capacity would emerge when the opposition gained control of the National Assembly at the end of 2015. As I discuss in chapter 8, its control of the legislature meant that it gained the power to hinder the government's access to external finance. The election of Donald Trump to the US presidency in late 2016 increased this power, by endowing the opposition with the support of an ally that could isolate the Venezuelan economy from global financial and goods markets.

While it would take some years for the opposition to develop this power, what we do begin to see as early as 2014 is the emergence of the ideas that will serve to underpin and justify its future drive to block the government's access to external funds. What began as an academic debate on whether Venezuela should restructure its debt rapidly spilled over into the political arena, where opposition leaders found that the questioning of the legitimacy of the country's external debt served as a rallying point to unify criticisms of the government and its allies. Once international financial markets began to be characterized as enablers of Maduro's permanence in power, the stage would be set for a strategy that called for the severing of Venezuela's financial and trade links with the world.

SEVEN

Elections, the Stakes of Power, and Economic Policies

The commonwealth is sick of their own choice.
—William Shakespeare, *Henry IV, Part 2*, 1600

WRONG DIRECTION

Maduro inherited an economy that was overextended fiscally and had saved very little of the oil boom enjoyed by Chávez. The country was thus very poorly prepared to handle a large negative terms of trade shock like the one it faced starting in late 2014. When the shock hit, Maduro ended up doing the opposite of what economic theory dictates should be the policy response. Rather than devalue the exchange rate to create incentives for import substitution and export production, he let the real exchange rate appreciate significantly while relying on state-led rationing to allocate the increasingly scarce foreign exchange. Rather than adjust the prices of goods and services provided by the public sector to the public, he monetized rising budget deficits, driving rising inflation. Rather than improve conditions for foreign partners in the oil sector to fund the investment that PDVSA no longer had the money to pay for, he maintained tight controls on the sector, forcing joint venture partners to sell their dollars into the local market at the overvalued official rate, effectively imposing a large additional tax on their operations.

In the previous chapter, I explained how the 2014 La Salida protests played a key role in incentivizing Maduro to delay the adjustment. In this chapter, I argue that the political incentives to focus on short-term benefits to shore up political support ahead of elections or during moments of political vulnerability also determined the government's decision to increase the implicit subsidy on purchases of foreign exchange in response to the collapse in oil prices.

The policy bias leading politicians to prioritize the short term and behave as if they have very high discount rates arises from incentives created by two crucial characteristics of the country's political system. First, as I have already argued, the political system embodied in the 1999 Constitution dramatically increased the stakes of power, raising both the benefits of being in power and the costs of leaving office. Second, as I explain in this chapter, it also significantly increased the frequency with which elections were held, subjecting the government to a near-permanent state of electoral exposure. The combination of high stakes of power and high electoral exposure raised the incentives for policy makers to focus on the short-term effects of policies and disregard their long-term consequences.

Deficit monetization and currency overvaluation, I argue, helped Maduro survive the near-term political contest, even if they created further problems down the road. In approximating economic policy with a short-term lens and disregarding the long-run effects of policies with an immediate political payoff, Maduro was choosing to do what it takes to prevail in the fight for power, regardless of the long-run costs to society. In this, the macroeconomic policies of the first part of the Maduro administration are the precursors of the scorched earth approach that would later be embraced by both political actors and drive Venezuela's subsequent descent into economically destructive political conflict.

ALTERNATIVE EXPLANATIONS: INCOMPETENCE, CORRUPTION, AND CONSPIRACY

The first explanation that comes to mind when trying to understand the logic behind Maduro's policy actions is that of incompetence. Perhaps the government caused a hyperinflation because it didn't know better. The government's rejection of "neoliberal" economists as well as its contempt for specialists with academic training led it to rely on policy makers with little if any formal background in economics. In contrast to the norm in other countries of the region, no economist occupied the main economics position in the cabinet; neither was the Central Bank president an economist during most of Maduro's term in office.[1] In fact, at times there was not a single economist among the seven members of the Central Bank board.

Maduro increasingly relied on a group of economic policy advisers whose ideas were on the fringe of academic thinking. Even some of the heterodox economists close to the administration, such as Rodrigo Cabezas and Jesús Faría—two academics with some policy experience—were sidelined in favor of a group led by the Spanish economist Alfredo Serrano. Serrano argued that class struggle rather than monetary policy was the main driver of inflation and that scarcity was due to intentional coordinated hoarding by business groups (Del Valle 2016).

Nevertheless, the idea that sheer ignorance drives policy failure is problematic on several dimensions. The most evident one is that a political movement that has managed to stay in power for more than two decades isn't the best candidate for a charge of being inept. Opposition negotiators involved in talks with the government, for example, regularly point to the ways in which the Maduro government has repeatedly outmaneuvered them, leading them to take decisions—such as the suspension of protests in November 2016 as a supposed goodwill gesture to initiate talks—which ended up playing in the government's favor (Romero-Castillo 2017b). And the government has not shied away from seeking top talent in other areas—such as the design of its electoral campaign strategy (EFE 2017).

Of course, there is a difference between being inept and holding on to a wrong theory. In fact, in my personal conversations with some of the Maduro government officials that defended continued deficit monetization, I found them repeatedly arguing that the data did not support the hypothesis that money creation led to inflation, a position similar to that taken by heterodox economists in the United States (e.g., Kelton 2021). (As I explained in chapter 5, this lack of correlation was due to the fact that the government was sterilizing expansions in the money supply through the depletion of international reserves.)

Rational actors have wrong beliefs all the time. They also revise these beliefs when confronted with information that disproves them. It is one thing to have believed that money creation did not cause inflation in 2013, when inflation was in the same double-digit range in which it had spent the previous three decades, and another one to deny it in 2018, when inflation had skyrocketed to six digits. The presence of nonconventional economists with fringe ideas in the teams of governments that cause hyperinflations is common, as is the fact that after hyperinflation ensues, governments almost invariably tend to replace them with more mainstream teams that proceed to implement stabilization strategies.[2]

An alternative explanation is that the policy distortions that exacerbated the country's economic crisis also served Maduro as devices to allocate rents to the military and other key power brokers without whose support he could not have stayed in power. Dorothy Kronick coined the term "arbitrage lobby" to refer to politically connected elites that made huge gains on the arbitrage from foreign currency allocations and that she argues were instrumental in blocking much-needed policy reforms (Kronick 2015; Gulotty and Kronick 2021).

While the corruption hypothesis appears intuitive, it is problematic at several levels.[3] First, while there are many corrupt governments in the world, very few of them produce the type of macroeconomic crises generated by Maduro's government. Malaysia's Prime Minister Najib Razak, to name just one example, managed to siphon $700 million to his bank accounts through a state-owned 1MDB corporation while keeping inflation at less than 4% and growth at 6% when he left office (Tan 2018; IMF 2024).

Second, there is nothing about policy distortions that makes them an efficient mechanism for distributing corruption rents. Governments typically use payments to contractors to siphon off resources to their cronies, and when—as in Venezuela—there are no effective institutions to ensure accountability and transparency in the use of public funds, this is remarkably easy to do. The amount of resources that a government can transfer to connected firms through overpriced contracts is limited only by the size of the budget. There is no need to create massive policy distortions that shrink the size of the economy and government revenues to do this.

In fact, if there is something striking about Venezuela's currency and price controls, it is the size of the rents created by the system that were going to ordinary people. Any Venezuelan that bought dollars through CADIVI at a preferential rate to travel abroad was receiving a piece of the rents created by the system, as did anyone who bought essentials at controlled prices. By 2014, Venezuela had accumulated bills of $3.8 billion with airlines arising from the sale of international tickets sold under the currency control scheme (Cardenas 2017). The beneficiaries of these tickets were not corrupt regime oligarchs; they were ordinary middle-class Venezuelans who purchased their tickets in local currency and took advantage of the opportunity to travel cheaply—a group that did not form part of the government's core political constituency.

This is not to argue that outright corruption benefiting the oligarchs was small but rather that when you redistribute oil rents through relative price distortions, the need to share them with ordinary Venezuelans impedes rent-seeking groups from capturing the totality of the rents and makes the system particularly inefficient as a way to pay for corruption. Perhaps even more important, any argument that Maduro's economic policies were designed to benefit the arbitrage lobby must explain why this lobby allowed these distortions to increase to a level where they caused a macroeconomic crisis large enough to seriously threaten its hold on power.

Another explanation for why Maduro allowed price distortions to get out of control is that doing so was part of a systematic plan to destroy the Venezuelan economy. According to this hypothesis, the rationale for the policies was political and not economic. Advocates point to the case of Cuba, where a stagnant economy has facilitated the regime maintaining itself in power for over sixty years. A weak private sector and emigration of the educated middle and upper classes may harm the economy, but they also make the country easier to control politically. Applied to Maduro's policy decisions, this argument suggests that he faced a choice in 2016: to free up the economy, which would have strengthened civil society, or to double down on controls and strengthen the state. As one defender of this thesis writes, "Yes, the catastrophe would weaken the regime; but society would weaken even faster, assuring the regime continued control"(Hausmann 2018).

To a certain extent, this hypothesis is consistent with the view presented in the previous chapters that the government was willing to impose significant policy distortions if it believed that doing so would enable it to maintain its hold on power. As the opposition strategy began to shift away from one of electoral mobilization to more intensively calling for street protests, some government leaders began to articulate the argument that the economy's crisis could have positive political effects. In a 2018 TV interview, Maduro's prisons minister, Iris Valera, expressed relief at seeing many of the activists who had participated in the previous year's protests leave the country during a massive emigration wave. "For my part, I hope they never return," said Valera (*El Nacional* 2018).

Nevertheless, the argument that the only way for Maduro to stay in power was by engineering an economic implosion and hyperinflation seems stretched. To impede the economy from entering the macroeconomic tailspin that it was in by 2016, Maduro only needed to do a few basic things: close the budget deficit by raising revenues and restraining spending and reduce excess demand of imported goods by devaluing the currency. Authoritarian governments take these measures every day; there is nothing particularly reempowering for their opponents about undergoing a devaluation or a tax hike. And while lower spending may have decreased some of the government's political clout, the collapse in real spending levels ultimately caused by hyperinflation ended up being much more harmful for the government's capacity to purchase loyalties.

What many of these hypotheses are missing is an understanding that Maduro's key policy decision between 2013 and 2016 was to pay for high levels of government spending using a particularly distortionary form of taxation, which is inflation. High spending levels certainly make the government more powerful. But there are many ways to fund a larger state. For starters, you can raise taxes and you can confiscate assets. To make its state all-powerful, Cuba installed a centrally planned economy, as did many other Communist regimes. It never ran a hyperinflation.

There is a good reason why authoritarian governments with the power to quash political dissent don't usually run hyperinflations. Hyperinflations ultimately erode the government's capacity to sustain high spending levels. They are the policy equivalent of shooting yourself in the foot. Continued deficit monetization is not a sensible choice from an intertemporal standpoint for a government that plans to stay in power for a long time. It may buy you a greater chance to stay in power today, yet at the cost of a significantly lesser chance to be in power tomorrow.

To understand the reason that a government appeals to printing money, we need to take account of the fact that one of the things that makes inflation different from other taxes is the time lag associated with its effects. There are two important time lags associated with inflationary financing. One, which I discussed in chapter 5, is the lag between the moment at which money is printed and the moment when prices go up. This gives the government the capacity to finance spending without making its cost immediately apparent to the public.

The other relevant lag is the time it takes the economy to reach rates of inflation at which the capacity of the inflation tax to fund real spending wanes. A decision to print money over and above what is necessary to keep up with rising money demand initially enables the government to increase real spending. But as this process evolves and inflation continues to increase, money demand falls so fast that real resources mobilized by the inflation tax begin to decline. Furthermore, real taxes collapse due to the lag between the moment at which they are generated and the moment at which they are collected. Once an economy is on the downward-sloping side of the inflation Laffer curve, more money printing is self-defeating as it leads to lower real levels of expenditure.[4] Ultimately, deficit monetization leaves the government less, not more, capable of financing spending than it was before it started printing money.[5]

The crux of my argument is that to understand the choice to monetize the deficit consistently over a multiyear period, we have to ask what makes the government prioritize the near term above the future so much that it systematically funds its spending through a tax that is inherently time-bound. My answer is that the combination of high stakes of power and frequent elections inclines the government toward prioritizing near-term results and that deciding to do so can severely harm the economy in the presence of large negative terms of trade shocks.

ELECTIONS, POLARIZATION, AND POLICIES

I argue that key changes in constitutional rules, particularly those that raised the frequency of elections and the stakes of power, dramatically affected the quality of economic policy making in Venezuela, raising the incentive of decision makers to defer needed economic adjustments.

These adjustments were strongly needed after the 2014 oil price shock hit, and the government's inability to enact them exacerbated the magnitude of the contraction caused by the shock.

My hypothesis thus relies on three key claims: frequent elections distort the incentives for policy making, causing policy makers to pursue more short-run-oriented policies; increased stakes of power raise the incentives for policy makers to stay in office and thus increase the likelihood that they will pursue distortionary policies ahead of an election; and the cost of pursuing short-run-oriented policies is higher the larger the macroeconomic imbalances that need to be corrected.

I have discussed the first two of these ideas at length in previous chapters. In chapter 3, I explained how both the public choice tradition and political business cycle models accounted for why governments would have a bias toward more short-term policies around the time of elections or during which they saw their hold on power otherwise threatened. I also introduced the hypothesis, central to modern theories of democratization, that high stakes of power induce political actors to undertake greater risks in their fight for power. Chapters 5 and 6 illustrated how the Maduro government began to exploit its ability to manipulate the economy by pursuing short-term objectives and delaying adjustments near elections and other perceived threats to its hold on power. I now discuss how the cost of the short-term biases induced by high stakes of power and electoral exposure are affected by the magnitude of external shocks.

The Politics of Economic Adjustment

There is a voluminous economics literature describing what countries need to do to respond to macroeconomic shocks. Economies facing a current account imbalance that cannot be financed have to engage in a combination of expenditure reduction, which lowers domestic absorption to bring it in line with disposable income, and expenditure switching, which requires moving domestic demand away from tradable goods and toward nontradable ones (Corden 1989). Expenditure reduction is often achieved by a mixture of contractionary fiscal and monetary policies, whereas expenditure switching occurs through changes in relative prices. Thus, the typical adjustment program will include fiscal expenditure cuts, tax increases, and a devaluation of the nominal exchange rate, as well as accompanying monetary policies to ensure that the nominal devaluation transfers to the real exchange rate. The magnitude of the needed price adjustments is inversely related to the economy's terms of trade, so that larger negative external shocks will require the economy to undertake larger adjustments in relative prices; when government fiscal balances depend on export revenues, so will the magnitude of expenditure adjustments.

In the absence of adjustment policies, countries will sooner or later go through a balance of payments crisis. Before that, governments attempting to maintain an overvalued exchange rate will see international reserves drop. Once reserves are low enough, it will make sense for investors to stage a speculative attack against the currency, given the knowledge that the exchange rate level is ultimately unsustainable. Once the government runs out of reserves, it has no option but to let the exchange rate drop to its equilibrium level.[6]

It is relatively straightforward to account for adjustment policies in the context of the political business cycle model discussed in chapter 2. Delaying adjustment policies is one way in which policy makers can try to fool voters into believing that they are more competent than they actually are. Voters can read the tax increases or expenditure cuts implemented in a structural adjustment program as a signal that the government is inefficient at converting taxes into public goods and thus decide to vote against the government because of these decisions.

The issue is compounded in the case in which the state is also the owner of the export sector because then the exchange rate acts as a tax. By increasing the relative price of tradables, a devaluation increases the purchasing power of the state's oil revenues and decreases the purchasing power of the private sector, which is a net importer. Therefore, both the policies that you need for expenditure reduction (tax increases and expenditure cuts) and those that you need for expenditure switching (devaluation) act as taxes on voters and can thus be read as signs of government incompetence.

There is evidence that governments try to hide the existence of serious balance of payments imbalances ahead of elections. This is not surprising, as balance of payments crises tend to be electorally costly. Broz, Duru, and Frieden (2016), for example, find that governments are much more likely to resort to capital controls and international reserve depletion ahead of elections, leaving major exchange rate adjustments and changes in trade policy until after the elections.

The above reasoning can explain why governments would resort to inflationary financing ahead of elections, allowing them to fund higher spending levels and/or lower taxes than they would otherwise. It does not explain why the government would decide to use rationing instead of price increases as an allocation mechanism. One electoral advantage of rationing is that it gives the government direct control over the identity of the recipients and thus enables the government to target these benefits to pivotal constituencies. This ability to target benefits can become much more important in times of electoral competition.

An arguably sensible assumption in modeling Venezuelan politics is that voters do not have direct information on oil price shocks or the magnitude of oil revenues. If this is the case, then policy makers will have an incentive to raise spending and lower taxes when oil prices go up prior to an election, rather than save the windfall, because this will allow voters to believe that these governments are more efficient in delivering public goods with lower taxes. But this also means that when negative terms of trade shocks occur and governments are forced to lower spending or raise taxes, voters are likely to take it as a sign that they are less competent and therefore punish them electorally.[7]

One could question the assumption that oil prices are not directly observable by voters in a country where news on oil market developments is typically in the headlines of the local press. Nevertheless, it appears reasonable to think that most voters do not have an incentive to invest in attempting to comprehend the implications of this information for the country's fiscal accounts, given the limited private returns of this understanding. Whatever the validity of the argument, it is certainly the case that approval ratings are positively related with increases in oil prices. This was not only true for the Chávez and Maduro years (fig. 7.1), but it also helps explain much of electoral performance in the pre-Chávez period. Carlos Andrés Pérez, who held office during the first oil boom, became one of the country's most popular politicians and was easily reelected to office as soon as he was legally eligible to do so; after Chávez, he remains the best-remembered president by Venezuelans today (Datanálisis 2021). In contrast, Luis Herrera Campins and

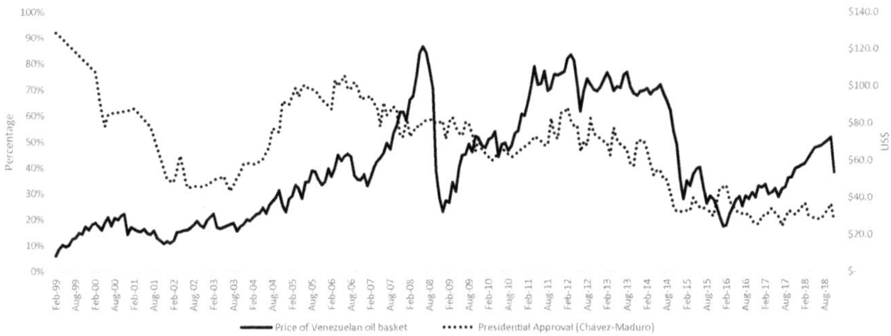

FIGURE 7.1. Presidential approval and oil prices, 1999–2018. *Source*: Author's construction using Datanálisis 2019; Bloomberg 2021b.

Jaime Lusinchi, who ruled during periods of declining oil prices, became deeply unpopular and were never considered as potential nominees by their parties when they became eligible to run again.[8]

RAISING THE STAKES

In chapter 4, I discussed how after taking office in 1999, Hugo Chávez moved to reform the country's Constitution as part of his campaign commitment to "refound" the Venezuelan state. The Constitutional Convention elected that year would not only draft a new constitutional text; it would also reorganize other branches of government, effectively ensuring Chavismo control of the whole structure of the state. In this section, I discuss in greater detail how these reforms affected the incentives of political actors.

Venezuela's political system prior to the 1999 Constitution has been labeled one of "pacted democracy" by political scholars (e.g., Karl 1987). The system emerged from a set of agreements between the nation's key political parties after the downfall of military rule in 1958 to limit interparty competition and ensure cooperation among key political players. The initial explicit documents, subscribed by the country's main political parties (with the exception of the Communists) just after the overthrow of Pérez Jimenez and before the 1958 presidential elections, provided amnesty to the military, committed all parties to support a common economic program, and guaranteed a "prolonged political truce," ensuring consultation among parties and depersonalizing political debates. Each party was guaranteed access to state jobs and contracts, a partitioning of ministries, and participation in a complex spoils system.

Some of these arrangements were later enshrined in the 1961 Constitution. The Constitution lowered the power of the executive branch by limiting presidential reelection (presidents could only aspire after ten years had elapsed since the end of their first mandate) and lowered the scope for interparty competition by apportioning seats in Congress through the principle of proportional representation with closed lists. It also limited the president's legislative prerogative: Venezuela had the lowest index of executive power in an index of legislative powers constructed by Carey and Shugart (1995).

The 1999 Constitution would change all this (Trinkunas 2002a; Combellas 2003; Corrales 2018). The presidential term was increased to six years, with one immediate reelection (in 2009, the two-term limit was eliminated). The president obtained direct control of promotions within the armed forces, scrapping the previous requirement of congressional approval for promotions for senior officer positions. The president's legislative powers were increased to include powers to activate any kind of referendum, thus effectively gaining the ability to circumvent most powers of the legislature. The share of seats allocated through majority voting rose to 60%, significantly lowering the power of political parties.

Some of these reforms rode a wave of prior public discontent with Venezuelan democracy. The 1990s had been rife with criticism of the outsized power and lack of accountability of existing political parties. The country's political system came to be derisively known as the *partidocracia* ("party-ocracy"). The shift away from proportional representation toward a mixed system began with reforms first instituted in 1989, which set the share of seats to be allocated by majority voting to 50%, with this share rising to 60% by 2000 and to 69% by 2015.[9] The climate of discontent with parties also made it easy for the 1999 reforms to abolish public financing of political parties.[10]

Increasing the powers of the presidency while lowering those of political parties significantly raised the stakes of power, making it costly not only to be part of the opposition but also to form part of dissenting factions within the government. When Chávez faced an internal rebellion from a moderate faction led by Luis Miquilena in 2001, it was easy for the government to marginalize them; when Chávez ordered the governing Fifth Republic Movement (Movimiento Quinta República, MVR) party in 2007 to dissolve itself in order to create the new PSUV, he found no opposition from party leaders.

One key change in the 1999 Constitution effectively subordinated all institutions to the presidency: the ability to call elections for a national constitutional convention with the power to restructure existing branches of government. Recall from my discussion in chapter 4 that in 1999 the Supreme Court allowed the recently elected Constitutional Convention to take over legislative powers from the existing Congress, effectively abolishing the old legislature. The new constitution would enshrine these powers, allowing a future constitutional convention to replace the heads of any existing branch of government. Furthermore, the president could not only define the timing of the elections for the constitutional convention but also propose the electoral rules, allowing him to increase the likelihood of being able to control the elected body.[11]

In a comparative study of constitutions enacted in the region between 1949 and 2009, Corrales (2018, 59) argues that Venezuela's 1999 Constitution was by far the one that expanded presidential powers the most. State funding for parties was banned, thus de facto reserving state funding for the incumbent. Military promotions went from being in hands of the eliminated Senate—which had represented the interests of states in which traditional parties were at the time strongest—to being under full control of the executive. In adopting consecutive reelection and at the same time expanding the presidential term from five to six years, Venezuela's 1999 Constitution enacted one of the broadest relaxations of presidential term limits in Latin America at the time (Corrales 2018, 125).

Even without appealing to the "nuclear option" of convening a constitutional convention, however, the new constitutional framework still allowed presidents to impose their will on other branches of government. For example, after the Supreme Court refused to try military officers for their participation in the 2002 coup attempt, Chávez supporters in Congress decided to reform the Supreme Court Law and increased the number of magistrates from twenty to thirty-two, taking advantage of the fact that the Constitution allowed them to appoint the new magistrates through a simple majority vote. This allowed them to secure a comfortable pro-Chávez majority in the court.

In other words, the new rules made it extremely easy for a popular president—and even to a certain extent, unpopular ones—to replace the heads of other branches of government, erasing one of the key restrictions necessary for effective separation of powers to prevail. They also made political parties weaker and eliminated any sharing of government positions with opposition forces. The combination of a powerful presidency, a judiciary that was subordinated to the executive, and weak political parties significantly raised the benefits of being in power as well as the costs of being out of it.

As expected, higher stakes of political competition led to deeper polarization. This was seen not only in the attempts by the government to concentrate even more power in its hands and to abuse the structure of the state to maximize its chances of winning elections, but was also reflected in the opposition's willingness to appeal to increasingly extreme means to drive the government from power. As argued by Monaldi and Penfold:

> Constitutional changes have radically increased the stakes of power and therefore have promoted a less stable democracy. . . . As a result, a significant part of the opposition has incentives to exclude itself from the regular democratic political process, and instead to invest resources in trying to overturn the regime by nondemocratic means (as observed in the April 2002 coup and the 2002–3 oil strike). This has led to a process of radical political polarization as well as a politicization of the armed forces. (2014, 307–8)

In this sense, higher political polarization and increased stakes of power became mutually reinforcing processes (Corrales and Penfold 2015, chap. 2). The higher the stakes, the more either side was willing to resort to extreme measures to preserve or attempt to gain power and the deeper the divide between Chavistas and the opposition became.

One way in which political polarization can increase the stakes of power is by raising the exit costs for the incumbent. If current government leaders feel that they face a real prospect of going to prison once they leave office, then they will try very hard to stay in it. As political polarization rose, many in the opposition began demanding not just that Chavismo leave government, but that many of its key leaders be jailed. That this was a credible threat became evident during the April 2002 coup, when Chávez as well as several of his ministers were imprisoned without charges. It also happened in other countries that had undergone similar processes of constitutional change, such as Bolivia and Ecuador, where some of Chavismo's international allies faced prosecution and prison time on leaving office. It is not surprising that after Chávez returned to power after the 2002 coup, the position of radical leaders within his administration who rejected any compromise with the opposition became stronger.

ELECTORAL COMPETITION AND THE RISE OF ELECTORAL EXPOSURE

Another of the most important institutional changes that took place in the past three decades in Venezuela was the increase in the frequency with which elections were held. This, in fact, is still a statistic often cited by government advocates: rather than a dictatorship, they claim, Venezuela has held more than two dozen elections since Chávez rose to power, in most of which voters had reaffirmed their support for the government (Wilpert 2018).

However, the start of the increase in the frequency of elections predates Chávez and has much to do with a movement to increase the accountability of Venezuela's governments by raising the number of positions filled through elections. In a hallmark 1986 report, a commission appointed by President Jaime Lusinchi (AD) tasked with studying possible reforms to Venezuela's state and political institutions recommended that state governors, who had previously been appointed by the president, should be elected directly by voters. While the proposal was rejected by the sitting government, it found strong support in public opinion, particularly among civil society organizations that were critical of the existing party system, and was ultimately embraced by the incoming president, Carlos Andrés Pérez (AD), upon taking office in 1989.

One effect of the 1989 reforms was to introduce a new set of nationwide elections that occurred at a different time from the general elections held every five years for the presidency and Congress.[12] A step in this direction had already been taken in a timid 1979 reform that had separated municipal council elections from the general elections. The 1989 reforms went much deeper, introducing the direct election of state governors as well as of mayors, a newly created figure (Lucena 2003; Penfold 2003, 197–225). Other electoral reforms allowed the election of council members through open lists, as well as the election of most state and national legislators through nominal voting (Crisp and Rey 2003).

One of the effects of these reforms was to increase the frequency with which governments had to deal with a nationwide election. Between 1958 and 1979, governments faced just one major election near the end of the presidential term. Between 1979 and 1989, governments would face an additional election near the start of their term, but in practice that new election (for municipal councils) was so close to the presidential election that governments could still expect to spend most of their terms in office without having to deal with an election.

The 1989 reforms changed this: the government would now have to contend with regional elections once every three years, in addition to the presidential and legislative election every five years. A consequence of this was that the same administration that introduced the reforms that year ended up facing elections during three of its five years in office (1989, 1992, and 1993).

The idea of having even more staggered elections gained force with Chávez's 1999 Constitution. The Constitution established periods of four years for governors and mayors as well as state legislators, five years for members of Congress, and six years for the president.[13] In practice, this meant that Chávez would not have to deal with elections during the first three years of his first presidential term under the new Constitution, but then the frequency of election years would begin to vary over time, depending on when each of the terms came to an end.

In addition, the 1999 Constitution introduced a new institution, the recall referendum, which allowed voters to recall the mandate of any elected officials through a popular vote after the first half of the official's mandate had elapsed. What this meant is that governments were exposed to a nationwide election not only whenever the terms for president, legislators, or regional governments ended but also during the last three years of the presidential term.[14] Any government could be subject to a nationwide election or recall referendum for at least half of its years in office, and a government that was unlucky enough could face elections in five of its six years in office.

I now introduce two concepts that will prove analytically useful. I define *electoral exposure* as the risk that a government will have to face a nationwide election at any time during its term in office. My measure of election exposure is the number of years of a government's term in office during which a nationwide election is held or can be called through actions initiated by the opposition (this refers to the recall referendum). I also introduce an alternative measure capturing *election insulation*, defined as the longest period that elapses in a presidential term during which no elections are held or (again in the case of the recall referendum) can be called through actions initiated by the opposition.

Both concepts capture how constrained governments are by the holding of elections during their term in office. A government that must face an election only toward the end of its term effectively enjoys low electoral exposure and high election insulation, while a government that must face elections every year will have high election exposure and low election insulation. But while the concepts are related, they are not necessarily identical. It is possible for a government to have high electoral exposure but, if all the elections are bunched up in time, also to have a relatively high period of electoral insulation. This was true for example of Chávez's second term (the first under the 1999 Constitution), which faced a sequence of consecutive election years in the second half of his term but had a four-year period at the outset of his term during which it faced no elections.[15]

The concept of electoral insulation is particularly interesting for understanding the way in which electoral institutions can affect the formation of macroeconomic policies. Electoral insulation can be understood as a measure of the length of the "window of opportunity" that a government has to implement policies and present the results of these policies to voters. A government with a five-year insulation period can reasonably implement adjustment policies that impose significant economic costs toward the start of its term and wait for these policies to deliver economic growth by the time it faces elections. A government with a one- or two-year insulation period has a much shorter time span to implement policies and deliver their results without facing a backlash at the polls.

Under the rules laid out in the 1999 Constitution, a government's election exposure would be at least 50%—that is, a government would be at risk of facing a nationwide election for at least half of its years in office—given that a recall referendum could be called during the last half of the term. But for a government that was unlucky enough, election exposure could rise to 83% or even—after electoral authorities decided to separate the election date for municipal and state elections in 2005—to 100%. Similarly, while some governments could enjoy a four-year election insulation period, others could end up having election insulation as low as one year.[16]

Figures 7.2 and 7.3 show the evolution of measures of electoral exposure and insulation throughout Venezuela's democratic history.[17] Between 1958 and 1979, governments faced one election every five years and thus had electoral exposure of 20%. When municipal elections were separated from other elections in 1979, the exposure ratio rose to 40% and increased again to 60% right after direct elections for mayors and governors began to be held. Once I include the years in which a recall referendum could be called in the measure of election exposure, I find that the two most recent presidential terms have had the largest levels of election exposure observed so far in Venezuela.

The measure of electoral insulation tells a similar story. Figure 7.3 displays the length of the maximum electoral insulation period measured in absolute number of years as well as relative to the total length of the

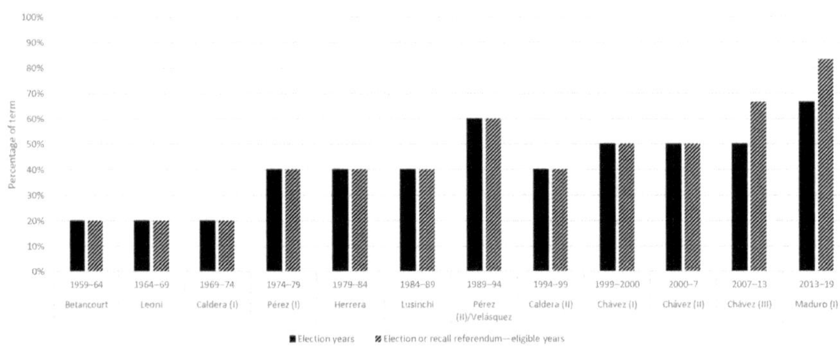

FIGURE 7.2. Electoral exposure across presidential terms, 1958–2019. *Source*: Author's construction using CNE 2023a, 2023b, 2023c; Official Gazettes.

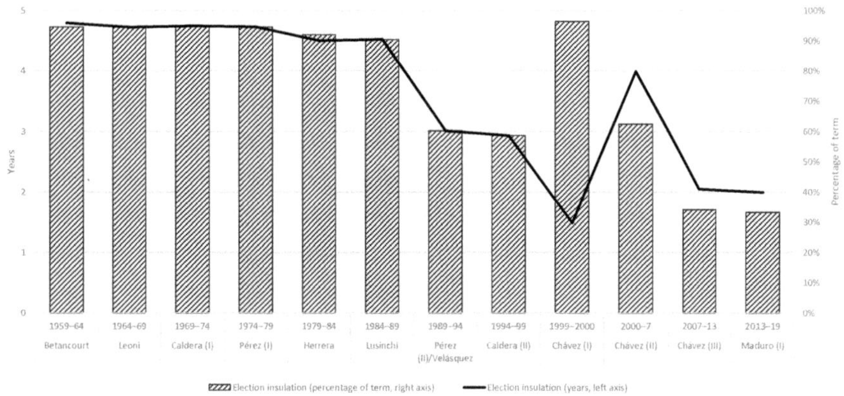

FIGURE 7.3. Electoral insulation across presidential terms, 1958–2019. *Source*: Author's construction using CNE 2023a, 2023b, 2023c; Official Gazettes.

presidential term. Up to 1989, governments had very long stretches of time without facing elections. This declined markedly after 1989 and then fell further with the 1999 Constitution. With the exception of Chávez's shortened first presidential term, which only lasted two years, the last two presidential terms have shown the lowest levels of electoral insulation in the period.

According to these measures, Nicolás Maduro's first presidential term was marked by very high levels of electoral exposure and very low electoral insulation. Because of Chávez's death, snap presidential elections were held in April 2013, during the first year of the term. But electoral authorities also ended up delaying municipal elections twice—the second time because of the scheduling of the snap presidential election—with the consequence that these were held in December 2013, one year later than originally planned.[18] The government thus faced nationwide elections during four of its six years in office (2013, 2015, 2017, and 2018) and was subject to a recall referendum drive starting in 2016. Its longest stretch of election-insulated time was thus the twenty-four-month period between the December 2013 municipal elections and the December 2015 legislative elections (see the discussion of this period in chapter 6). During his first term in office, Maduro faced the highest level of election exposure and the lowest level of relative electoral insulation seen until then by any president in Venezuela's democratic history.

TOO BIG TO DEAL WITH

The economic costs of avoiding devaluation are proportionate to the size of the gap between the economy's exchange rate and its equilibrium exchange rate. The larger this gap, the greater the drain in international reserves if the government is defending the parity and the greater the black market premium if the government is imposing exchange controls. A large black market premium will generate increased incentives for rent seeking, whereby individuals and firms devote resources to appropriating cheap foreign exchange. By forcing large swaths of the economy to function at misaligned prices, a large black market premium combined with price controls impedes resources from reallocating to the economic activities where they are most needed, thus reducing output.

A higher black market premium also entails a higher political cost of resolving the distortion by devaluing ahead of an election. Maintaining an overvalued currency is one of the mechanisms that a government has for fooling people about the economy's ability to sustain high living standards ahead of an election. Voters can interpret an overvalued exchange rate—and the associated low price of imported goods compared to local incomes—as a sign that the government is competent in generating the economic conditions that allow them to enjoy higher living standards. Conversely, a large devaluation will be interpreted by voters as a sign of the government's incompetence. The larger the devaluation, the greater the "incompetence surprise" and the greater the cost the government will pay when people go to the polls.

Nevertheless, if the government is imposing exchange controls and rationing access to goods in order to sustain the overvalued exchange rate, it will become evident to voters that the goods are not easy to find and that the government is thus not all that competent at providing cheap imported goods for everyone. Yet the government may still be able to target key constituencies through the allocation of goods, and these constituencies may come to believe that the government is capable of sustainably delivering cheap imported goods to them. Targeting specific constituencies through rationing is easier than doing so through the price system. After all, the government doesn't need to convince everybody that it is competent; it only needs to convince a majority of voters that this is the case. Being able to provide access to cheap goods to just a fraction of the population may even have the added benefit of consistency with the political message of a movement that has promised to reverse historical inequalities and empower previously disadvantaged groups.[19]

As I chronicled in chapter 6, Venezuela suffered a massive decline in oil revenues between 2014 and 2016 due first to the decline in oil prices and later to the collapse of oil production. One of the consequences of this decline was to increase the magnitude of the adjustment that the country needed to carry out to resolve the misalignment of the exchange rate and restore external sustainability.

To get a sense of the size of these effects, I estimate the level of the exchange rate that would have been needed to correct the overvaluation of the currency. My estimates are based on an econometric model in which the equilibrium real exchange rate has a long-run stable relationship with the level of per capita real oil revenues.[20] Figure 7.4 shows the results of my estimates, alongside the evolution of the country's oil export revenues.

The real exchange rate can be understood as a measure of external prices relative to domestic prices. An increase in the real exchange rate indicates that imported goods are becoming more expensive in terms of domestic goods: this is called a real depreciation.[21] The index is measured in relation to a baseline level of 100 in December 2007. At the start of

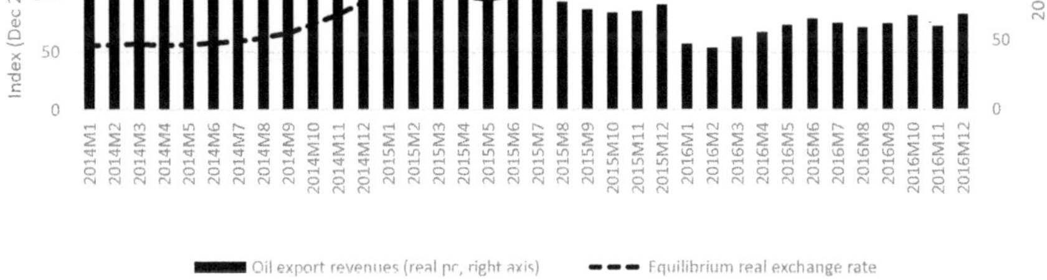

FIGURE 7.4. Oil exports and equilibrium real exchange rate, 2014–2016. *Source*: Author's construction using BCV 2023g; DolarToday 2023; US Bureau of Labor Statistics 2023.

2014, the index was at 55, or, in other words, 45% stronger than in 2007, reflecting the effects of the oil boom. By the close of the year, with the start of the decline in oil prices, it had risen to 93, and at the start of 2016, when oil prices hit their lows, it reached 243. In other words, to correct the exchange rate's misalignment, the government would have had to devalue the exchange rate to make dollars 4.4 times as expensive in terms of local goods in 2016 than in 2014.[22]

A fourfold depreciation of the real exchange implies an increase of four times in the prices of imported goods in terms of domestic goods. Since nominal wages are proportional to the prices of domestic goods, it also would imply cutting the purchasing power of wages in terms of imported goods by four-fifths.

The net effect on real wages (i.e., wages in terms of a basket of imported and domestic goods) will depend on how large the weight of imported goods is in the consumption basket of workers. A reasonable proxy for this is the share of tradable goods in the consumption basket used by the Central Bank of Venezuela to calculate the nation's Consumer Price Index (CPI), which is 48%.[23] Using this number, we can estimate the real wage that would result if the real exchange rate were allowed to reach its equilibrium, absent changes in other determinants such as productivity. The resulting series, represented in figure 7.5, shows that Venezuelans would have had to see real wages fall by 58% by the

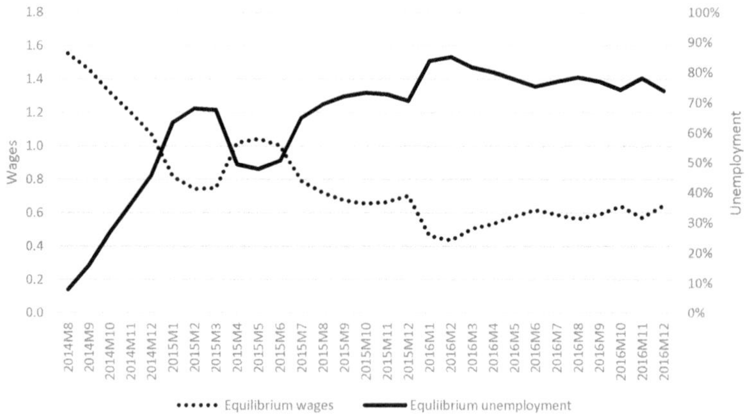

FIGURE 7.5. Wage and employment adjustments needed to restore exchange rate equilibrium. *Source*: Author's construction.

end of 2016 as a result of the depreciation of the exchange rate that would have been needed to eliminate the distortions in the exchange market. Greater details of these calculations are provided in the online appendix to this chapter.

Note that the wage represented in figure 7.5 represents the real wage under the assumption that labor markets are fully clearing and competitive. Real labor compensation fell by between 37% and 54% in this period, depending on whether we use Central Bank or National Assembly data. Measured in dollars (i.e., in tradable goods), it fell much more sharply, by 92%.[24] In other words, the government was not able to stop the slide in the exchange rate (which occurred through the parallel market) or in real wages (which occurred through inflation). What it could try to do, and in fact consistently did, was pretend to voters at election time that there was no need for this adjustment.

What would have happened if the government had neither printed money nor devalued the currency? Since equilibrium real wages would have dropped anyway as a result of the shock in external revenues, the government would have had to either cut the minimum wage or accept very high levels of unemployment. Figure 7.5 shows the unemployment rate that I estimate would have resulted had the government held the real wage constant at 2012 levels. The calculations are built on the premise that the 58% adjustment of figure 7.5 was needed to restore labor market equilibrium (as we saw above, a magnitude similar to the observed decline when we use the National Assembly CPI). The model predicts that the effort to stabilize real wages when the economy required a 58% cut in the real wage level would have required unemployment rates of more than 70% by the end of 2016.[25]

The two series represented in figure 7.5 can be seen as two extreme scenarios in terms of the policy response to a negative terms of trade shock. Either authorities let the shock transmit fully to wages and experience a massive decline in them, or they maintain the level of real wages and thus expect to see a massive rise in unemployment. Most governments (except those bound by dollarization or a currency board, which can't lower real wages through inflation) adopt a mixture of the two approaches, letting real wages drop and unemployment rise at the same time.

Venezuela opted for lower real wages. But it did so in a roundabout and distortionary way. By refusing to devalue its currency while experiencing

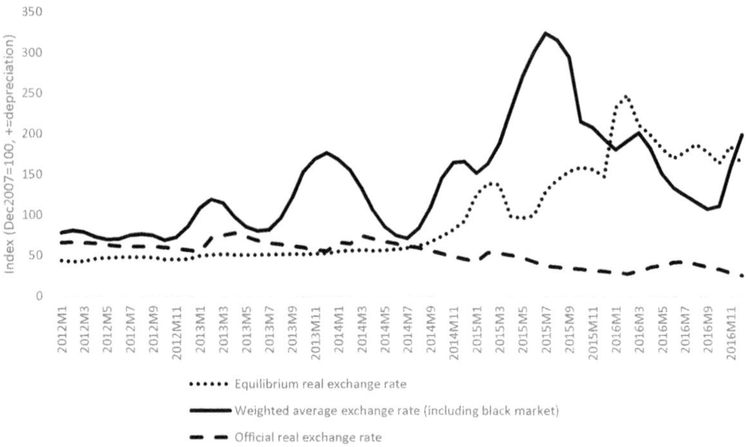

FIGURE 7.6. Equilibrium, average, and official real exchange rates, 2012–2016. *Source*: Author's construction using BCV 2023g; DolarToday 2023.

high inflation, the government let its official exchange rate appreciate at the time at which it was experiencing a negative terms of trade shock that required a real depreciation. It thus raised the gap between the official and the black market rate, with all the associated distortions. Figure 7.6 shows two measures of the exchange rate in the economy: the official exchange rate and the weighted average exchange rate over all transactions (including parallel-market transactions). Note that the government has direct control over the former but not over the latter, since the black market rate is set by market forces. In fact, the series shows that the average exchange rate inclusive of black market transactions depreciated when the decline in oil revenues led to a depreciation of the equilibrium level—implying again that on average, Venezuelans did pay more for their dollars as these became scarcer. In fact, the series suggests that the average exchange rate was undervalued through the 2012 to 2015 period, suggesting that Venezuelans were on average paying more for their dollars than they would have needed to pay had the government successfully unified at the equilibrium rate. Yet the official exchange rate was completely out of sync with this. In fact, the real official exchange rate systematically appreciates during the 2012 to 2016 period. In other words, while Venezuelans were on average paying increasingly more to buy dollars, those with access to official dollars were paying increasingly less.

Let us return to using the framework of political business cycles models to understand these decisions. Political business cycle models tell us that governments will try to delay adjustments prior to elections because voters may interpret an adjustment as a sign that the incumbent is less competent than they had previously thought. Voters suffering the wage and employment effects of the adjustment know that there is a probability that these measures are necessary because of an external shock but also attribute some probability to their reflecting the government's incapacity to deliver as many public goods as they had previously thought it capable of. The Chávez and Maduro governments had previously brushed aside criticisms of economic policies by arguing that the economy was shielded from negative shocks.[26] Adopting a major economic adjustment would have exposed these claims as deceitful.

What my estimates show is that if Maduro had undertaken the policies necessary to restore external balance and eliminate the exchange rate's overvaluation, he would have had to accept the need for real wages to drop by more than 50% or for unemployment to rise to the high double digits. The political implications of such an adjustment in the run-up to a major parliamentary election—in which the opposition could potentially obtain the power to oust Maduro from office or make the country ungovernable—would have been huge. Many voters would have concluded that the need for such an adjustment implied that Chavismo's long-standing promise to improve living standards by redistributing the country's wealth was nothing more than a blatant lie. Very few governments manage to win elections after economic adjustments, much less after an adjustment of the magnitude that faced the administration at that time. It is thus not surprising that Maduro opted for hiding the need of this adjustment from voters.

ECONOMIC DECISION MAKING WHEN THE POLITICAL CLOCK IS TICKING

In this chapter, I have argued that Venezuelan political institutions, some of which were significantly transformed in the late 1990s and early 2000s, fundamentally affected the incentives of policy makers to adopt certain economic policy decisions. By increasing the frequency of elections and raising the stakes of power, they raised the incentive for politicians to attempt to avoid electoral defeats at any cost while raising the frequency with which they had to choose between addressing economic imbalances and maintaining their hold on power. These contradictions came to a head during the Maduro administration, when an increase in electoral exposure and growing polarization coincided with a huge decline in the country's external revenues.

This analytical framework provides us with a more systematic way of reading the economic narrative of policy decisions at the start of the Maduro administration discussed in chapters 5 and 6. In each of those chapters, we saw how Maduro opted for policies with high short-term benefits when faced with elections or protests that threatened his hold on power. In this chapter, I provided an account of what made this short-term bias a pervasive characteristic of Maduro's first term in office. I argued that increasing levels of polarization and a winner-take-all political system combined with a constitutional design mandating almost-permanent nationwide elections supercharged the incentives for the government to prioritize short-term objectives over long-run goals.

This narrative of Maduro's economic policies during his first administration highlights the constraint put on his decisions by frequent elections, high polarization, and the challenge of dealing with a massive external shock. Maduro came to office with a very weak mandate, first taking over after Chávez became too ill to govern and then winning a presidential election in April 2013 by a slim margin—a victory that was never recognized by the opposition. Despite this, he undertook first steps toward adjustment by devaluing the currency two months before the election and severely curtailing imports.

His ability to go further was constrained by political realities. First, there was a very highly mobilized opposition, some of which was openly questioning the validity of the results leading to his election. Second, there was widespread skepticism about Maduro's ability to lead Chavismo to electoral success, given that his only electoral victory came riding on a widespread sympathy effect after Chávez's death in March. Third, the opposition began mobilizing around the idea of making the December 2013 municipal elections a referendum on Maduro.

The risks to the government became evident as polls showed the government lagging behind opposition candidates by large margins ahead of the 2013 municipal elections. As I discussed in chapter 5, this led the government to shelve any discussion about economic adjustments until after these elections and to decide to raise economic distortions ahead of the elections by forcing prices down during the Dakazo. The essence of the Dakazo, in fact, was convincing voters that the government was able to ensure the supply of cheap imported goods, even if the result could only be sustained for a short period ahead of the elections.

The government's proceeding to announce policy adjustments including increases in the price of gasoline on the day after the municipal elections was strong evidence that the delay of adjustments had been driven by political and electoral considerations rather than by ideology or rent seeking. The fact that the government's only serious attempt to present a coherent macroeconomic stabilization plan occurred in 2014, the only year of its term in which it did not have to face an election or possible recall referendum, is consistent with my view that elections are a deterrent to economic adjustments and that frequent elections will increase the likelihood of governments letting macroeconomic imbalances pile up.

However, it is impossible to understand the government's policy decisions in 2014 without taking account of La Salida. By calling on people to go to the streets to try to generate a change in government, the promoters of La Salida were effectively turning 2014 into something very similar to an election year. In the midst of these protests, government leaders began to see stopping the demonstrations from extending to poorer neighborhoods as their overriding strategic objective.

Protests died down in the second half of 2014, and there again we see the government seriously begin to push the Ramírez plan. They shelved the plan when oil prices went into freefall. During the last six months of 2014, the government found itself facing the need to lower real wages by more than 50% in order to adjust to the decline in the terms of trade. The shock became too large to deal with without exposing the deep economic vulnerabilities that Chavismo had tried to hide over the previous decade and a half.

By the time the government realized that oil prices were not going to recover, it was election year again.[27] And 2015 was not any election year: the National Assembly, where a supermajority of two-thirds had the constitutional power to impeach the president, was up for grabs. The opposition in fact would end up winning that two-thirds majority, leading the government to use its control of the Supreme Court to suspend the election of several legislators. In 2016, electoral authorities scuttled a drive to call a recall referendum that Maduro seemed certain to lose, leading to a significant escalation of political conflict.

I have argued that the decisions to make use of inflationary financing and let the official exchange overvalue were not irrational policy choices. They were, rather, decisions to use highly distortionary modes of taxation to convince voters that the government was better able to provide public goods than it was. Their upside is that they helped win elections; their downside is that they ultimately shrank the economy. Like their predecessor, the Dakazo, they are political strategies with potentially large political payoffs for governments and significant aggregate costs for the economy.

The story told in these chapters falls well within the framework of the single-actor model of politically induced distortions presented in the first part of chapter 3. As predicted by the model, governments increase distortions ahead of elections and have a greater incentive to adopt larger distortions the higher the stakes of power. Take a country with high levels of political polarization and winner-take-all political competition, make it face elections nearly every year, and put it against a massive external terms of trade shock, and it is not surprising to see increasingly distortionary economic policies emerge.

The dynamics sketched in this part of the book and summarized in this chapter, however, are only relevant if the incumbent government sees elections as a constraint. As we reach the end of 2016, this will begin to change. In late 2016, the government would use its control of state courts to scrap a recall referendum drive that appeared likely to lead to Maduro being voted out of office. At the same time, the government-controlled Supreme Court would begin to strip constitutional functions from the National Assembly. The opposition's decision to begin boycotting elections in 2017 also began moving the space of relevant political confrontation away from elections.

By the end of 2016, both political actors had begun to shift to a new arena of political confrontation in which their ability to appeal to the military selectorate would be much more binding than the need to prevail in elections. The opposition would also acquire the capacity to block the government's access to external funding by denying legislative approval for debt issuance and by the entry into office of a US president willing to impose economic sanctions on the Maduro government.

The structure of the political game had begun to change. The capacity to manipulate the economy for political gain was no longer solely in the hands of the government. Both the government and the opposition had begun to show increasing willingness to play outside of the established rules of political engagement. The result would be a tug-of-war between the country's political forces for control of the economy's sources of foreign exchange revenue, ultimately plunging the country into full-fledged economically destructive political conflict. I turn now to that story.

PART III

The Descent into Economically Destructive Political Conflict, 2016–2020

EIGHT

Becoming Toxic

A nation that is boycotted is a nation that is in sight of surrender. Apply this economic, peaceful, silent, deadly remedy and there will be no need for force.
—Woodrow Wilson, in Foley 1923

UNEASY BEDFELLOWS

January 15, 2016, marked the first and only time this century in which a Venezuelan president delivered a speech before an opposition-controlled legislature. During his three-hour speech—an annual message that serves as Venezuela's equivalent to the US State of the Union address—Nicolás Maduro recognized that the opposition had achieved an electoral majority ("which could be circumstantial") and acknowledged that data just released by the Central Bank pointed to a "catastrophic" economic performance, for which he blamed an "investment strike" and a "monstrous attack on the currency." He asked the opposition to help his government recover the economy while at the same time accusing the opposition of plotting to undermine it (Resumen Latinoamericano 2016).

Immediately after Maduro spoke, Henry Ramos Allup, National Assembly president and leader of the opposition Democratic Action party, took the floor to deliver a rebuttal, criticizing Maduro for keeping to an outdated economic model and demanding the government free political prisoners and allow the return of prominent exiles (Vivoplay 2016).

Although they traded barbs, both leaders listened calmly and respectfully when the other spoke and even laughed at each other's jokes. Maduro asked the Assembly to consider granting him extraordinary powers to deal with the country's economic crisis. Ramos Allup responded that the Assembly would study in detail the request with the "greatest goodwill" and promptly issue a response. Maduro was accompanied to the podium and back by a delegation of mainly opposition legislators, in keeping with the tradition of deference accorded to the head of the executive branch.

Scenes like this are common in modern democracies. One could even say that the Maduro and Ramos Allup speeches were quite civil from a comparative perspective (think of Nancy Pelosi ripping in half Donald Trump's 2020 State of the Union address or the frequent shouting matches in the British Parliament). Yet if the moment gave a glimmer of hope that Venezuela's political forces would learn to live with each other, those hopes would soon be dashed.

In the end, Venezuela's National Assembly elected in 2015 would never exert much legislative power. A first trial would come from the request for emergency powers made by Maduro. The National Assembly rejected it one week later, arguing that it would only serve to deepen the country's crisis by allowing the government to continue to pursue its misguided economic strategies.[1] Two weeks later, the Supreme Court ruled that the government could make use of those emergency powers despite the National Assembly's decision, alleging procedural errors in the Assembly's invalidation (TSJ 2016a). This would mark the start of a long string of Supreme Court decisions invalidating or rendering ineffectual nearly every decision taken by the new legislature.

The choice to go down the route of confrontation rather than seek to find mechanisms for cohabitation would have a profound effect on Venezuela's society and its economy. Over the following years, Venezuela's financial and trade links with the global economy would be progressively severed, destroying the economy's capacity to generate foreign exchange and causing a massive import and growth contraction. In this and the next two chapters, I argue that the evidence points to the politically driven process of toxification of the country's global economic relations as a key driving factor in the collapse of the country's import capacity.

THE RECOVERY THAT WASN'T

The year 2016 had every reason to be Venezuela's annus horribilis. The price of Venezuela's oil, which had stood at above $100 in June 2014, had collapsed to just $22 by the third week of 2016. Despite recovering some ground later in the year, the yearly average closed at only $36, one-third of its 2012 level. Given the strong historical correlation between export revenues and growth, it is not surprising to see that the economy contracted by 17% that year.

However, by the end of 2016, one would have had good reasons for thinking that the worst was over. Oil had recovered from its nadir, closing the year at $46, a seventeen-month high. Oil production had declined somewhat during 2016, but it would have been reasonable to expect that it would level off in a scenario of recovering oil prices. In a presentation made in November 2016 before a group of investors in New York, IPD Latin America—probably the most respected oil consultancy covering Venezuela—predicted that exports of crude petroleum and oil products, which had fallen by 12% in 2016 to 2.1 million barrels per day, would rise slightly (by 0.8%) in 2017 and then level off at similar levels for the next three years (fig. 8.1).

Financial markets certainly reflected the perception that the worst was over. Venezuela's country risk, as measured by the J. P. Morgan Emerging Markets Bond Index, had shot up from less than 1,000 basis points in mid-2016 to more than 3,600 basis points by February 2016. But in the following twelve months it declined steadily, falling to around 2,000 basis points by January 2017 (fig. 8.2). This was still a pretty high level, implying an excess cost of 20 percentage points on Venezuelan debt over and above that of US risk-free instruments. But it implied a significant decline in the probability that markets assigned to the country would default on its external debt, reflecting the effect of improving external conditions.[2]

The improvement in Venezuela's interest rate spreads with the recovery in oil prices was not surprising. Over the 2012 to 2016 period, the J. P. Morgan country risk measure showed a -0.96 correlation with

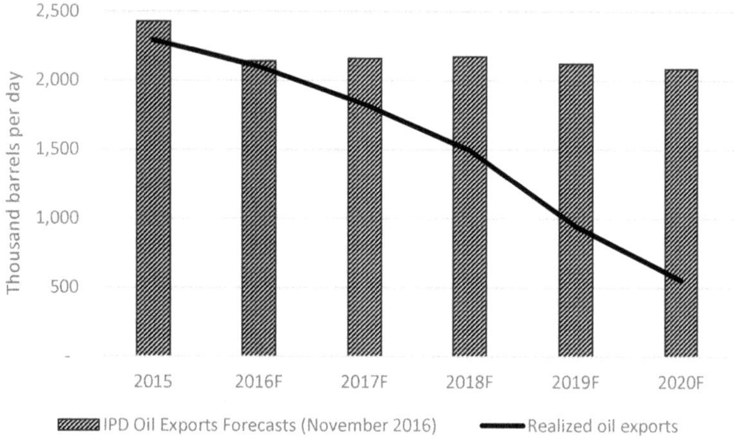

FIGURE 8.1. Oil production, forecast and realized. *Source*: Author's construction using IPD Latin America 2016; OPEC 2023. *Note*: Realized production series calculated using the annual average of the direct communication series of government-reported output published in OPEC's Monthly Oil Report, scaled to equal the IPD series in 2015.

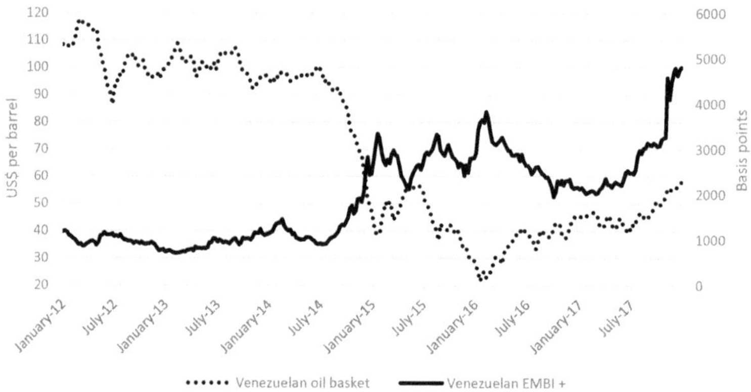

FIGURE 8.2. Oil prices and Venezuela country risk, 2012–2017. *Source*: Author's construction using Bloomberg 2021b, 2021c.

oil prices, with a one dollar increase in the price of oil leading on average to a 28.7 basis point decline in country risk. If recent history was any guide, one could well expect that if oil prices continued improving, as they in fact did in 2017 (during which they rose by $12 per barrel), the country's financing risk would continue to decline.

Of course, Venezuela's economy still had huge problems, including the pervasive exchange and price controls and huge budget deficit that I discussed in preceding chapters, and no one expected those problems to go away. But they were not too different from the problems that it had had during the preceding sixteen years and that had generated stagnant growth, high inflation, and macroeconomic volatility but nothing even remotely resembling the economic collapse that was to come.

Because of these factors, economic analysts expected the country to turn the corner sometime between 2017 and 2018. A survey of fourteen economic forecasters published by Consensus Economics in January 2017 showed average growth forecasts of -3.2% for 2017 and 0.4% for 2018—as opposed to an average growth rate of -9.2% over the preceding 2013 to 2016 period. Some analysts were even more optimistic: Ecoanalítica, one of the most prestigious local consultancies, expected the economy to post a moderate 0.3% growth in 2017 and accelerate to 2.5% in 2018 (Consensus Economics 2017).

They were all proved dead wrong. The economy shrank by 15.7% in 2017 and by 19.6% in 2018, essentially replicating for two more years the 2016 performance of -17.0%. What is even more striking is that this happened even as oil exports were recovering by even more than markets expected them to. Exports rose by 24% in 2017, from $27 billion to $34 billion. Typically, such a recovery would have led to rising imports and growth, but what we saw was the opposite: imports *fell* by 27%. The country had more money but bought much less.

How did this happen? The answer is that Venezuela's capacity to fund imports dried up. The country went from running a current account deficit of 3.9% of GDP in 2016 to a current account surplus of 8.7% of GDP in 2017.

A current account surplus means that the country is accumulating assets or reducing its liabilities, much in the same way that a person who spends less than they earn can increase their savings or pay down debt. Likewise, if a country is buying more from the rest of the world than it is selling, someone must be financing that spending, so the country must be running up its liabilities or running down its assets.

Countries, just like people, can run surpluses by choice or by circumstance. If you spend less than you earn, it may be because you have chosen to save, or it may be because no one is willing to lend you money and you are forced to pay your maturing debt. In both cases, you will see net assets increase, but they will reflect two very different situations.

For Venezuela, it clearly was an example of the latter. It was in 2017 that international credit markets closed their doors on the country. This is transparent when we look at the way in which the country's credit risk rose from less than 2,000 basis points in March to nearly 5,000 basis points by the end of the year (see fig. 8.2). Clearly, the reason that Venezuela cut imports by so much in 2017 is that no one would lend it money to continue buying goods from abroad.

What is remarkable is that this happened in the context of a strong recovery of oil prices. As figure 8.2 shows, oil prices rose continuously during 2017. But instead of oil price rises leading to falls in country risk, in 2017, both country risk and oil prices were going up at the same time. As I noted above, between 2012 and 2016, the correlation between the EMBI Venezuela Index and oil prices was -0.96. In 2017, that correlation was a *positive* 0.87. For the first time in years, oil prices were rising in tandem with the perceived risk of default.[3]

The breakdown of the negative correlation between credit spreads and oil prices suggests that there are other factors that significantly drove up Venezuela's country risk in 2017. We don't have to look very far to find them. It was in 2017 that the Supreme Court annulled the power of the National Assembly to legislate, the opposition staged massive street protests, the government convened elections for an all-powerful constitutional convention, and the United States imposed the first economic sanctions on the country. It was in 2017 that the economic crisis became political, scorched earth tactics became the norm, and Venezuela became toxic.

CAREFUL WHAT YOU WISH FOR

In December 2015, Venezuela's opposition scored a stunning political victory. For the previous fifteen years, the country's legislative power had been controlled by Chavismo, whose absolute majority in the country's unicameral legislature had effectively turned the institution into a rubber stamp. But the 2015 elections took place after two years of recession during which the economy had contracted by a cumulative 10%. Though this may seem moderate by comparison with what happened later, it was unlike anything that Venezuelans had seen in the recent past. Venezuela's economy had only suffered two previous contractions of a comparable size: in 1989, when a drastic economic adjustment led to massive street riots that left thousands dead, and in 2002–3, when a strike paralyzed the country's oil industry as well as much of the economy for months.

In the 2015 parliamentary elections, Chavismo became a victim of its own rules. Through the years, it had designed an electoral system that would amplify in seats its advantage in votes. More than two-thirds of legislators were chosen in first-past-the-post district-level elections, with the remainder chosen through a state-level proportional representation system. Since twenty of twenty-three states—as well as the Capital District—had two representatives chosen by lists, state-level proportional representation virtually ensured that each of the top two parties would get at least one legislator per state. Therefore, the balance of forces in the Assembly was essentially determined by the district-level results.

Depending on the geographic distribution of voter preferences, first-past-the-post elections can amplify the advantage of the winning party. In an extreme case in which voter preferences are equally distributed across districts, a party can win 100% of seats with only 51% of the vote. Even with a more heterogeneous distribution of preferences, it will typically be the case that the winning party will manage to pick up a much greater percentage of districts than its national vote share.

This is indeed what had typically happened. In 2010, the government party edged out the opposition coalition by less than one percentage point—48.1 to 47.2%—but managed to capture 59% of seats. In 2015, the tables turned. Popular dissatisfaction led voter support to shift to the opposition, which captured 56.2% of the vote to the government's 40.9%. This allowed the opposition to capture 112 of the Assembly's 167 seats, or exactly two-thirds of the legislature.

In Venezuela's Constitution, a two-thirds supermajority can carry out radical political changes, including the removal of Supreme Court justices, the appointment of electoral authorities, and the convening of elections for a constitutional convention (a smaller three-fifths majority is needed to fire government ministers). The result was by and large unexpected, with almost all political analysts contending that a two-thirds majority was all but impossible.[4] As a result, both the government and the opposition had put little thought into how to prepare for that scenario.

Recall from my discussion in chapter 4 that a constitutional convention has the authority to dissolve all other branches of government and replace them by temporary appointees. This power effectively turns Venezuela's political system into a winner-take-all contest (or, in terms of the models presented in chapter 3, a system where δ is close to 1), in which a popular president (as most presidents tend to be at the start of their terms) can achieve subordination of all other branches of government by convening, or even by just threatening to convene, elections for a constitutional convention. It turns out that a two-thirds majority of the National Assembly has that same authority. A legislative supermajority is thus just as powerful as the country's all-powerful president.

Taken by surprise, Chavismo did not immediately question or visibly attempt to interfere with the announcement of the electoral result. Electoral authorities announced on the following day that the opposition coalition had reached the magic number of 112 legislators, ensuring the two-thirds supermajority. Yet only ten days later, the government's campaign chief, Jorge Rodríguez, called a press conference in which he shared an audio of conversations in which a high-ranking official of the governorship of Amazonas—at the time held by the opposition—had allegedly agreed to provide funds to rig the electoral process in the state. The mechanics discussed in the call included paying persons in charge of assisting illiterate voters to ensure that their vote would be cast for the opposition candidate and bribing witnesses to allow the casting of votes representing voters who had died but were still on the voting rolls (Telesur 2015).

Shortly after Rodríguez's press conference, one of the losing Chavista candidates in that state requested that the Electoral Chamber of the Supreme Court annul the results of the Amazonas election. The chamber decided on the day immediately following the filing to approve a protective measure suspending the election of all four legislators elected in Amazonas (three of whom were from the opposition and one from the government party) pending its decision on the case. The chamber made no further advances in this case (now moot as the legislature's term has expired), leaving the state of Amazonas without parliamentary representation for all its 2016 to 2021 term (TSJ 2015).

Annulling the results of the Amazonas elections, however, was only one of the avenues through which Maduro used his institutional control to offset the opposition's power in the legislature. In December 2015, the lame-duck legislature, which was controlled by the governing Socialist Party, moved to appoint new justices to thirteen of the court's thirty-two seats, filling positions that would otherwise have been appointed by the new National Assembly (*El Nacional* 2015). Although the outgoing National Assembly had the constitutional authority to appoint justices to fill vacant Supreme Court seats, the opposition charged that the appointments had been made in violation of established procedure. For example, the terms of the outgoing magistrates were not due to expire for one more year and the legally specified time periods for consultation with civil society were not obeyed, according to the legal experts who backed the opposition's objections (Human Rights Watch 2015; Rosas 2017). At the same time, Maduro used powers to legislate by decree, which he had been granted by the outgoing Assembly, to reform sixteen laws in the last weeks of December, eliminating any powers of oversight by the National Assembly of the statutes.

Perhaps even more importantly, the Supreme Court made clear in the first months of 2016 its unwillingness to allow the National Assembly to wield any substantive power. Between January and September 2016, the Supreme Court reviewed the constitutionality of seven laws and fourteen other decisions of the National Assembly and annulled all but one of them; in the case of the only law that was not annulled (the Law of Food Bonuses and Medicines to Pensioners and Retirees), it subjected its application to budgetary approval by the executive branch (table 8.1). The grounds alleged for the annulment of these laws were varied, but the pattern was unequivocal.

These decisions effectively annulled the capacity of the National Assembly to act as a counterbalance of the executive branch. For example, Article 187 of the Constitution grants the legislature the authority to fire any cabinet member, including the vice president, with the votes of three-fifths of the legislature.[5] If used, this power would have allowed

TABLE 8.1. Supreme Court decisions dealing with acts of National Assembly, January–September 2016

Date of Supreme Court Decision	*Decision Number*	*National Assembly Decision*	*Supreme Court Chamber*	*Supreme Court Decision*
11-Jan-16	N° 1	Incorporation of Amazonas state legislators	Electoral Chamber	Orders disincorporation of Amazonas legislators
14-Jan-16	N° 3	Request for President Maduro to present Annual Report to the National Assembly	Constitutional Chamber	Annuls National Assembly's request
20-Jan-16	N° 4	Declaration of State of Exception and Economic Emergency Decree as unconstitutional	Constitutional Chamber	Rules that decree is constitutional and orders compliance
11-Feb-16	N° 7	Denial of approval of State of Exception and Economic Emergency Decree	Constitutional Chamber	Establishes that AN cannot overrule validity of decree; orders entry in effect
1-Mar-16	N° 9	Requests for high-ranking government officials to appear before the National Assembly	Constitutional Chamber	Annuls requests
17-Mar-16	N° 184	Denial of approval for renewal of State of Exception and Economic Emergency Decree	Constitutional Chamber	Extends the decree for 60 days
29-Mar-16	N° 225	Annulment of appointment of Supreme Court justices made on December 23, 2015	Constitutional Chamber	Dismisses National Assembly's annulment
31-Mar-16	N° 259	Reform of Central Bank Law	Constitutional Chamber	Annuls reform; affirms validity of previous law
11-Apr-16	N° 264	Law of Amnesty and National Reconciliation	Constitutional Chamber	Declares law unconstitutional
28-Apr-16	N° 327	Law of Food and Medicine Bonus for Pensioners and Retirees	Constitutional Chamber	Declares law constitutional but rules that fiscal viability must be coordinated with Executive

Date of Supreme Court Decision	*Decision Number*	*National Assembly Decision*	*Supreme Court Chamber*	*Supreme Court Decision*
5-May-16	N° 341	Partial Reform of Supreme Court of Justice Law	Constitutional Chamber	Declares reform unconstitutional; affirms validity of prior law
6-May-16	N° 343	Law to Grant Property Titles to Beneficiaries of the Housing Venezuela Great Mission and Other Housing Programs of the Public Sector	Constitutional Chamber	Declares law unconstitutional
19-May-16	N° 411	Rejection of State of Exception and Economic Emergency Decree	Constitutional Chamber	Declares decree valid and constitutional
9-Jun-16	N° 460	Special Law to Attend to the National Health Crisis	Constitutional Chamber	Declares law unconstitutional
14-Jun-16	N° 478	Resolution urging other national powers to abide by the constitution and democratic principles, attend to Venezuelans' needs, and allow entrance of humanitarian aid. Resolution calling on international community to defend Venezuelans using mechanisms to stop human rights violations and protect the country's democracy.	Constitutional Chamber	Finds AN is usurping presidential foreign policy functions; suspends legal effects of the resolutions
19-Jul-16	N° 614	Approval of report of commission to review Supreme Court appointments	Constitutional Chamber	Annuls the commission and the session in which the report was approved. Annuls any other possible commission aimed at annulling magistrate appointments. Annuls AN summons of Supreme Court justices and the session where it was approved.

(*continues*)

TABLE 8.1. Supreme Court decisions dealing with acts of National Assembly, January–September 2016 (*continued*)

Date of Supreme Court Decision	*Decision Number*	*National Assembly Decision*	*Supreme Court Chamber*	*Supreme Court Decision*
19-Jul-16	N° 615	Declaration that 60-day extension of State of Exception and Economic Emergency Decree is unconstitutional	Constitutional Chamber	Declares 60-day extension constitutional
2-Aug-16	N° 108	Incorporation of Amazonas state lawmakers	Electoral Chamber	Declares National Assembly in contempt of prior TSJ decisions regarding Amazonas state lawmakers. Rules the incorporation invalid, nonexistent, and legally ineffective.
11-Aug-16	N° 126	National Assembly Board of Directors requests Supreme Court set aside decision that prevented incorporation of Amazonas legislators	Electoral Chamber	Rules request is inadmissible
19-Aug-16	N° 797	National Assembly sessions from April 26 and 28 and May 3, 5, 10, 12, and 17, including among other things no-confidence vote on agriculture minister. Request for annulment from pro-government legislators.	Constitutional Chamber	Suspends the effect of contested sessions
2-Sep-16	N° 808	Partial Reform of the Organic Law That Reserves to the State the Activities of Exploration and Exploitation of Gold	Constitutional Chamber	Finds Partial Reform null and void. Finds the National Assembly is in contempt of Decision 260 (Illegality of incorporation of Amazonas state lawmakers).

Sources: Author's construction using Asamblea Nacional de Venezuela 2023b; TSJ 2023a, 2023b.

the National Assembly to bring public administration to a standstill and virtually force the government to enter into a cohabitation agreement. Nevertheless, when the Assembly tried to fire Agriculture Minister Rodolfo Marco Torres based on this provision, Maduro issued a decree "restricting and deferring" the ability of the National Assembly to approve no-confidence votes in the context of an economic emergency, while the Supreme Court invalidated the session on the argument that it had not been called according to established procedure (Imprenta Nacional 2016a; TSJ 2016a).[6]

Maduro was not the only one playing hardball. On January 5, upon being sworn in as the first speaker of the opposition-controlled Congress, the Democratic Action legislator Henry Ramos Allup promised to present "a method, a system to change the government constitutionally," within a six-month period. A two-thirds majority of the National Assembly would be able to use several constitutional avenues to do this, including calling a referendum on a constitutional reform shortening the presidential term or the convening of an all-powerful constitutional convention. Ramos Allup's statement was thus widely viewed as a commitment to use one of these means to constitutionally remove Maduro.

The new National Assembly also moved to question the appointment of Supreme Court magistrates made by the preceding legislature. A commission to review judiciary appointments was established on January 27, less than a month after the new Congress had been sworn in (Marrero 2016). On July 15, the National Assembly adopted the recommendations of the commission, invalidating the appointment of all justices made by the prior Congress during its lame-duck period (Comisión especial para el rescate de la institucionalidad del Tribunal Supremo de Justicia 2016).

Perhaps most importantly, the National Assembly refused to abide by the Supreme Court decision invalidating the Amazonas elections. On January 6, the board of the National Assembly swore in the three Amazonas legislators whose proclamation had been suspended by the Supreme Court, effectively recognizing their full rights as elected representatives. In response, the Supreme Court declared the National Assembly in contempt of court decisions, ordering the Assembly to disincorporate the legislators (TSJ 2016b). The National Assembly initially backtracked, withdrawing the recognition of the three legislators on January 13. However, after it became clear that the judiciary was unlikely to grant it any effective authority, it swore the legislators in again in July, leading the Supreme Court to reinstate the contempt order and to declare all subsequent legislative decisions invalid.[7]

In the meantime, the opposition settled on one avenue for ousting Maduro: to invoke the right of voters to request the holding of a recall referendum to determine whether an elected official can serve out the remainder of his term. As discussed in chapter 4, article 72 of the Constitution allows 20% of registered voters to request the holding of a recall referendum; if the recall option is supported by a majority of voters (and by an absolute number of voters greater than those that elected the official), then the official is removed from office. The article can only be applied after the midterm of the official's term has elapsed; this would have made possible a recall against Maduro after January 2016.

As mentioned in chapter 4, a recall referendum had been held in 2004, in which the opposition managed to collect enough signatures to invoke the provision but failed to win a majority of votes. Yet Maduro's approval rating in 2016 was lower than that of Chávez at the time of the recall, and the opposition was just coming from a major election victory. The recall route thus seemed a safe bet both from the standpoint of its chances of success and in terms of its democratic legitimacy.

As the recall attempt advanced, electoral authorities began placing roadblocks that had not been present in the prior collection drive. One of these was the requirement that to initiate the process of collecting signatures for the event, a "citizens' group" would have to register with the signatures of 1% of registered voters in each state. Following the submission of these signatures, petitioners would have to verify their signatures in public booths at which their fingerprints would be validated with a scanner that is also used during voting events. Nevertheless, the 2004 event had also been characterized by numerous impediments to signature collection, so the opposition was by and large undeterred by the roadblocks.

On August 1, electoral authorities announced that the 1% threshold had been reached in all twenty-four jurisdictions, thus complying with the initial signature collection requirement. They also claimed that some signatures had not matched the fingerprint scan and requested that an investigation be opened into those cases. Those signatures, however, were not counted toward the 1% tally. The National Electoral Council (Consejo Nacional Electoral, CNE) board published a schedule for the definitive collection of 20% of signatures, to be held at the end of October.

However, government representatives used the CNE's invalidation of signatures to allege that there had been a massive fraud in the collection process. Opposition spokespersons argued in response that the instances of alleged fraud were for the most part due to errors in data transcription (e.g., a digit altered when transcribing the manual forms into an electronic database). Nevertheless, the government pressed on with its demand. On October 20, several regional courts announced that they were invalidating the signature collection process in their states.

Even taken at face value, the case for suspending the recall was illogical. The CNE had not counted the allegedly fraudulent signatures for determining that the opposition had met the threshold. Even if some citizens had decided to forge signatures, this could not invalidate the right of those that had validly signed, which according to the CNE exceeded the required threshold. Rather than defend its decision before courts, the CNE announced the suspension of the process nationwide only hours after the court decisions came through.[8]

Opposition leaders were enraged and called for street demonstrations. These were initially well attended, with an October 26 demonstration drawing nearly half a million persons in Caracas (fig. 8.3). That same week, Maduro made a surprise visit to the Vatican, where he asked Pope Francis for his help mediating the conflict with the opposition. A Vatican spokesperson announced shortly after the meeting that negotiations would begin at the end of that week.

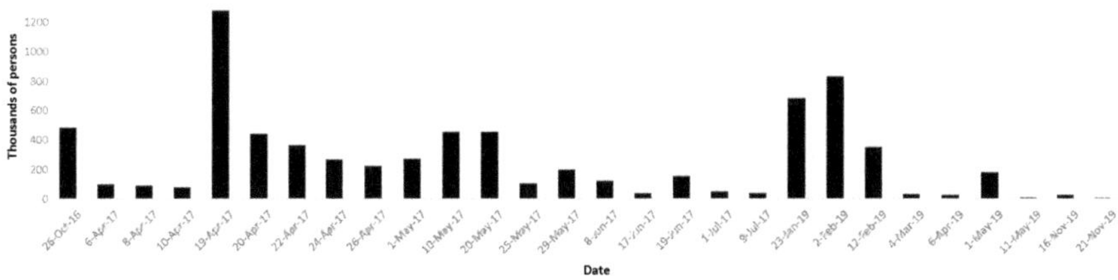

FIGURE 8.3. Attendance at opposition protests in Caracas, 2016–2019. *Source*: Author's estimate based on aerial photography collected from public sources.

Maduro had in fact been attempting to initiate dialogue with the opposition since the start of 2016 with the help of the Union of South American Countries (UNASUR), an international organism chaired by the former leftist Colombian president Ernesto Samper. The opposition had balked at participating, insisting that a precondition for talks was the activation of the recall referendum, a constitutional right that it accused the government of obstructing. The Vatican's willingness to act as mediator and the government's offer of a proposal to schedule regional and early presidential elections convinced opposition leaders that it made sense to take part in the talks.

Negotiators announced an initial agreement a few days later, on November 12, after only two rounds of talks. The agreement, which was read publicly by the Vatican's representative, spoke about resolving the National Assembly's contempt situation and holding new elections for the state of Amazonas but gave little specifics on how to achieve either objective (Pardo 2016). Both issues would have required a decision of the judiciary, which was not formally represented in the negotiations. Nevertheless, the agreement seemed to fall apart almost as soon as it was announced, with opposition negotiators reading a statement outlining a different agreement from that read by the Vatican's representative. Two hard-line opposition groups that had refused to participate in the talks issued critical statements, and even some of the opposition representatives who had participated sounded defensive once the outcome became public (Vente Venezuela 2016; Voluntad Popular 2016a).

On December 6, the opposition withdrew from the talks, charging that the government had not complied with the agreements (Voz de América 2016). By that moment, most opposition leaders felt they had been outmaneuvered into suspending street protests (Rosati and Soto 2016). They made no attempt to call new demonstrations at the time, as supporters seemed to have lost motivation and the Christmas season had begun.

It would only be a matter of time before protests got under way again. The sparks that reignited the fire were two Supreme Court decisions published in late March 2017 that further restricted the legislature's power. One decision annulled a National Assembly resolution invoking a clause from the Democratic Charter of the Organization of American States reserved for the "unconstitutional alteration of the constitutional regime that seriously impairs the democratic order in a member state" (OAS 2001). More importantly, it also stated that approval of that resolution could be considered an act of treason and that legislators who approved it could be tried. Another decision allowed the government to create and modify joint ventures in the oil sector and to reform the National Hydrocarbons Law given the National Assembly's continued contempt (TSJ 2017).

A major international reaction ensued, with the OAS secretary general and nine governments in the region issuing statements expressing concern or outright rejection of the Supreme Court decisions. Peru even went as far as to permanently withdraw its ambassador to Caracas. Yet perhaps the most surprising statement came from Prosecutor General Luisa Ortega Díaz, previously a government loyalist, who stated that the two Supreme Court decisions generated a "rupture in the constitutional order," a phrase that in Spanish is essentially a synonym for a coup d'état (Dinero 2017).

On the following day, Maduro held a hastily convened meeting of the National Defense Council, an advisory group composed of the heads of the different branches of government as well as some cabinet members. The president of the opposition-controlled National Assembly did not attend. The council issued a resolution calling on the Supreme Court to revise its decisions. On the following morning, the Supreme Court published on its Web page summaries of two new decisions revoking key elements of the prior decisions.

The strong show of international support and the willingness of National Assembly leaders to confront the government energized the opposition base. Demonstrations called in April drew an estimated 1.3 million persons to the streets of the capital, with similar numbers turning out in other cities (see fig. 8.3). Opposition protesters voiced slogans demanding elections and the resignation of the Supreme Court. Protesters clashed with security forces as they attempted to advance on central Caracas, an area where many government buildings, including the presidential palace, are located. More than one hundred persons are estimated to have died during the protests (a figure that includes government supporters and nonparticipants).[9]

Amid these tensions, Maduro stunned the nation on May 1 by announcing that he would convene elections for a national constitutional convention. In principle, a move like this would have opened the possibility for a resolution to the country's crisis, given that a constitutional convention has the authority to dissolve other branches of government (all of which were controlled by Maduro at the time). In fact, convening a constitutional convention, given its capacity to clean the slate of existing institutions, had been a preferred option of the more hard-line opposition groups before Maduro invoked it.

However, and in contrast to the case of parliamentary elections, the Constitution gives little guidance on the rules for the election of legislators to the Constitutional Convention. The government-controlled National Electoral Council proceeded to draft rules that would have allowed two-thirds of representatives to be elected by municipal-level nominal voting, with each municipality having one representative, regardless of population.[10] This decision created a significant advantage for the government given its support in sparsely populated rural districts. The other third would be elected by separate voter rolls, which divided registered voters into eight mutually exclusive sectors ranging from workers and pensioners to persons with disabilities.

The opposition decided unanimously to boycott the election; instead, it convened an alternative referendum organized by the National Assembly in which voters could choose to reject the Constitutional Convention and order the military to defend the Constitution. Organizers claimed that 7.7 million voters (39% of registered voters at the time) participated in the event, which was held in mid-July.[11] Two weeks later, the elections for the Constitutional Convention were held, with electoral authorities announcing a turnout of 8.1 million voters (42% of registered voters).

The official turnout numbers for the Constitutional Convention election seemed abnormally high. Turnout was 41.5% of voters, despite there being no candidates from nongovernment parties running. By contrast, only 32.2% of registered voters would cast votes for government candidates in the regional elections held three months later. The last time that the government had received such a high share of support among registered voters was during Chávez's 2012 reelection. The idea that more people would turn out to support the government in the highly questioned Constitutional Convention elections than had voted to elect Maduro in 2013, or than would vote for the government in any other electoral event held since, seemed a stretch.

Similar questions could be leveled at the turnout figures for the referendum convened by the National Assembly. The 6.8 million persons who turned out to vote in the territory of the country was considerably higher than the 5.0 million who would vote for MUD candidates in the gubernatorial elections held three months later.[12] However, it was lower than the 7.7 million who had supported the opposition in the 2015 parliamentary elections, so that the figure did not necessarily sound implausible at the time. The electoral process was overseen by the presidents of five universities, all of whom had maintained public positions in support of the opposition.

The apparent exaggeration in the official turnout figures, as well as a public statement by the provider of electoral technology for the CNE stating that it could not validate the result, fed into increasing suspicion that the vote count had been fabricated. According to a national survey, the approval rating for the CNE dropped from 46% in January 2016, after the announcement of the legislative election results, to 24% by October 2017 (see fig. 10.4).

Distrust and frustration with the inability to generate regime change fed into voter apathy, particularly among opposition supporters. When the government moved ahead to schedule regional elections, the opposition suffered a major defeat, winning only five of twenty-three governorships and capturing only 46% of the national vote, to the government's 54%. Opposition leaders immediately cried foul and charged the government with tampering with the results.[13]

I defer a discussion on the evidence of systematic vote tampering and other electoral irregularities in Venezuela to chapter 10. My main conclusion, explained in more detail in that chapter, is that while Venezuela's electoral playing field is clearly not level, there is little evidence, prior to 2024, of large-scale vote tampering in contested elections such as those of October 2017. Vote tampering, I argue, is plausible in an uncontested election such as the one held in 2017 for the Constitutional Convention, because the only safeguard against ballot box stuffing is the presence of opposition witnesses. In the case of the 2017 regional elections, the evidence suggests that the results were driven primarily by a decline in turnout among opposition voters (Kronick and Rodríguez 2017).

As the year came to an end, the opposition began debating what to do regarding the upcoming 2018 presidential elections. On the one hand, the opposition had been looking for an opportunity to defeat Maduro at the ballot box, and 2018 was precisely that opportunity. On the other hand, increasing distrust of electoral authorities led a large part of the leadership and the opposition base to become convinced that any election would be rigged. The results of the 2017 regional elections suggested that victory in the 2018 election was far from assured. Adding to the problems was the fact that some of the most popular opposition leaders—including Leopoldo López and Henrique Capriles—had been banned from running due to court convictions and administrative sanctions.[14] Ultimately, most of the opposition would go on to boycott the 2018 presidential elections, allowing Maduro to sail to reelection.

FIGHTING OVER PURSE STRINGS

As the country's political crisis worsened, the opposition leadership transitioned from the belief that it could defeat the government by playing within the existing institutional framework to the conviction that the rules and norms governing political confrontation were hopelessly biased in favor of the government and that to win, it would have to play outside of them. This increasingly meant opting for tactics that it would not have considered previously. Recall that in 2012 and 2013, the opposition had grudgingly come to terms with its electoral defeats in three consecutive elections.[15] Yet by the end of 2017, it was openly rejecting any process organized by electoral authorities and openly calling the elections fraudulent.

There was one dimension in which this change in tactics would have significant economic effects: the government's access to external financing. Constitutionally, a National Assembly supermajority has broad powers that allow it to block almost all the government's economic policy actions. Even a simple majority can reject approval of the government budget and debt plans, leaving the government without authorization to spend or borrow.[16] But starting in 2016, almost all those powers were rendered worthless by decisions of the judiciary. Yet there was one weapon that neither Maduro nor the Supreme Court could take away from the opposition-controlled National Assembly: its ability to affect the willingness of the rest of the world to do business with the Venezuelan government.

Blocking a government's economic decisions is a risky political move for an opposition. Maduro had charged almost from the start of his government that the economy's problems were due to the concerted actions of opposition leaders and the private sector to sabotage the economy, in what he called a process of "economic war" (see chap. 5). Certainly, there was a precedent to this strategy, and it was not good: as I discussed in chapter 4, the 2002–3 oil strike had generated a political backlash against the opposition, allowing Chávez to claim that his opponents were willing to hurt people's livelihoods to achieve their political aims.

Perhaps for this reason, the opposition began by treading carefully in this terrain. When in March 2016 the government submitted the first amendment to the budget, an authorization to transfer 21 billion Bs ($2.1 billion at the official rate at the time) to state and municipal governments, the Assembly approved it without objections (Imprenta Nacional 2016b). Even as late as September, when it discussed the decision by the state-owned oil company PDVSA to exchange $7.1 billion in maturing bonds—a decision for which the government did not consider it necessary to request the Assembly's authorization—the legislature approved a resolution that rejected the use of assets as collateral to back the bond but did not object to the legality of the issuance, abstaining from using the language customarily used in its resolutions to reject authorization requests (Asamblea Nacional de Venezuela 2016b).[17] Most importantly, no attempt was made by opposition leaders to dissuade investors from participating in the swap, which allowed the government to defer payment of $2.8 billion in maturing bonds (PDVSA 2016).

The tone would change markedly with the turn of the year. One of the reasons was legal. Government spending and debt issuance in 2016 were done under the authorization of the fiscal year budget and debt laws approved by the legislature in 2015. Yet when the time came to approve the 2017 budgets and debt laws, the Supreme Court had declared the National Assembly in contempt. Maduro therefore did not send the 2017 budget to the opposition-controlled National Assembly, instead asking the Supreme Court to fill the vacuum of power generated by the Assembly's contempt and approve the law. Thus, the opposition could make a strong legal case that debt issued from 2017 on did not comply with the Constitution.

Yet by and large the main motivation for the opposition's change of tone was political. By the end of 2016, the opposition was outraged at the government's use of the courts to cancel the recall referendum, as well as frustrated by the way in which it had apparently been outmaneuvered to suspend street protests to participate in the Vatican-mediated talks without being able to obtain any tangible concessions from the government. In fact, when the government went ahead and issued a $5 billion sovereign bond on December 29, 2016—two days before the yearly authorization issued by the previous legislature was set to expire—a prominent government legislator called the operation "totally illegal," despite there being no grounds to argue its invalidity as it was based on the 2016 budget (Armas and Vyas 2017).[18] The noise around that issuance impeded the state-owned bank that had bought the issuance from reselling it in the secondary market.

By the turn of the year, the opposition had decided to take the issue of financing head-on. When it became known that the Central Bank was involved in negotiations with Deutsche Bank to make liquid some of its gold reserves, the National Assembly president, Julio Borges, sent a letter to the bank's CEO requesting that the bank reject the deal. While the letter did put forward some legal arguments, the thrust of its case was political: entering this deal, Borges wrote, would be tantamount to acting "in favor of a government that is recognized as dictatorial by the international community." Instead, Deutsche Bank should cooperate with "the institution that today counts with the support of the Venezuelan people and that continues in the struggle to recover democratic order in our country [i.e., the National Assembly]" (Romero-Castillo 2017a).

Deutsche Bank's decision not to carry out the operation would turn out to be a wise one from a public relations standpoint. One of its competitors was far less prudent. In May 2018, Goldman Sachs's asset management arm, an independently run investment fund within the bank, decided that it wanted to raise its position in Venezuelan debt, in anticipation of a potential change of government. Instead of buying the bonds in the secondary market, where accumulating a large position could take time and push prices up, it decided to offer to buy the bonds directly from Venezuela's Central Bank at a deep discount.

The purchase, made at 31% of face value, caused an uproar. Goldman Sachs surely knew there was a risk that this would happen, as it decided to make the purchase through a little-known intermediary called Dinosaur Securities. However, it was not hard for the financial press to figure out who the ultimate buyer was, and the *Wall Street Journal* broke the story about Goldman Sachs's involvement on May 28 (Vyas and Kurmanaev 2017). Two days later, Venezuelan protesters convened at Goldman Sachs's headquarters in New York to decry the bank's helping to finance the Maduro government (Thomas 2017). Borges wrote to Goldman's CEO, Lloyd Blankfein, charging that the US bank had "decided to make a quick buck off the suffering of the Venezuelan people" and vowing that a future government would not recognize the bonds (Alvarado 2017). Interestingly, the vow to repudiate the bonds came despite there being no question as to the legality of their issuance, which had taken place in 2014.

The Goldman Sachs purchase came only days after the publication of a piece in *Project Syndicate* by the Venezuelan economist Ricardo Hausmann (2017) decrying bond investors who purchased Venezuelan debt. Venezuela's "hunger bonds" could yield high returns, Hausmann charged, only as a result of bad things happening to Venezuelan people. To service its debt, he argued, Venezuela had to cut imports, and these import cuts were behind the economy's precipitous collapse and increase in poverty. Hausmann called on Venezuela to be excluded from an influential emerging bond market index calculated by J.P. Morgan, which was used as a benchmark of returns in emerging markets by many funds and at the time included a 5% share of Venezuela bonds.

Hausmann's piece made no reference to the Goldman Sachs operation, which had not yet taken place at the time the article was published. Yet by a perhaps fortuitous coincidence, Hausmann's phrase caught on quickly and became the standard label attached to the bonds purchased by Goldman Sachs. This is somewhat of an irony, as the Goldman Sachs operation achieved the contrary of what Hausmann was criticizing Venezuela bonds for doing. Hausmann's argument was that paying the country's debt left the government without money to pay for its imports, fueling Venezuelans' hunger. But the Goldman Sachs deal did not constitute a debt payment; it was a sale of already issued debt meant to provide the government with funds to avoid even deeper import cuts. Had the government been unable to find a creditor willing to purchase these bonds, it would have been forced to carry out even deeper import cuts that year.

What is most interesting about the hunger bonds argument is that it can be leveled at any country that decides to run a primary surplus (a surplus of fiscal revenues over noninterest spending) to remain current on its debt. It will always be the case that resources paid to service debt could be put toward other, more urgent uses. In just about every contemporary society, reducing hunger among vulnerable populations is one of them. If your government runs a primary surplus, this means that it could raise its level of spending by suspending debt payments, even if this implied that it would receive no new lending. Note that standard sustainability analysis shows that countries need to run primary surpluses for their debt levels to be sustainable. By this logic, all bonds issued by countries with sustainable fiscal accounts are hunger bonds.

Despite its conceptual shortcomings, the label was politically very effective, namely, because it married the normative critique of Maduro—a government that is causing hunger—with the advocacy case for stopping the government from accessing funds. It thus provided the opposition with the conceptual and normative case to use one of its most powerful weapons against the government: its ability to hinder or block the government's access to external financing. To a certain extent, the label got right (at the emotional if not at the argumentative level) what the opposition got wrong during the 2002–3 oil strike. It allowed the opposition to put concerns for Venezuelan's hunger at the center of its discourse while at the same time actively trying to stop the Venezuelan government from having access to resources.

The groundswell of criticism against bond markets' financing of Venezuela paved the way for the consideration of economic sanctions impeding Maduro's government from access to international financing. Throughout 2017, the Trump administration had been exploring mechanisms to increase pressure on the Venezuelan government in an attempt to get Maduro to back down in its confrontation with the National Assembly. As the elections for the Constitutional Convention drew near, the White House considered the possibility of a full-fledged oil embargo, but the measure met with resistance both from policy circles and from the domestic refining business (Matthews and Córdoba 2017; Naím 2017; Penfold 2017). Sanctions on new debt, however, looked more appealing precisely because of the very strong prior advocacy effort directed against financing the regime. When the Trump administration imposed sanctions barring any new financing of the Venezuelan government or the state-owned oil company right after the elections to the Constitutional Convention, there was little criticism and even some support from groups that had previously warned against the detrimental effects of an oil embargo (Smilde and Ramsey 2017).

As the Venezuelan government became financially more toxic—in the sense of being more prone to causing regulatory and reputational harm to those who decided to do business with it—firms that had previously been willing to deal with the Maduro government decided that the benefit was no longer worth the risk. Even prior to the adoption of sanctions in August 2017, tankers carrying Venezuelan oil shipments had been stranded off US coasts, with purchasers unable to obtain letters of credit from financial institutions (Ulmer and Parraga 2017). One important casualty of financial toxification was the loss by the Venezuelan government of correspondent banking relationships enabling the execution of wire transfers and trade finance. Following the decision of large financial institutions such as Citibank to close Venezuela's correspondent bank accounts, the Maduro government started shifting its correspondent banking activity—needed to carry out wire transfers and trade-related credit operations in the United States—to small and less known financial institutions (Castro 2016). At the end of 2017, after the financial sanctions announcement, even these banks ceased providing correspondent services to the Venezuelan government, citing increased reputational risk (Pons 2017).

The August 2017 sanctions were followed by a September 2017 Financial Crimes Enforcement Network (FinCen) letter of guidance recommending that many transactions originating from Venezuela be automatically flagged as potentially criminal (FinCen 2017). The issuance of this letter implied that any entity considering deals involving financial transactions by the Venezuelan government would have to be ready to shoulder large reputational and compliance risks. Many financial institutions proceeded to close Venezuelan accounts rather than face the risk of inadvertently participating in activities that could be targeted for money laundering investigations. Venezuelan payments to creditors got stuck in the payment chain, with financial institutions refusing to process wires coming from any Venezuelan public sector institutions.

IN SEARCH OF LEVERAGE

The year 2017 was when Venezuela's political crisis became economic. That this happened was the result of the decisions by key political actors, including opposition leaders and their international allies, who concluded that economic pressure was one of the few instruments of leverage that they had on the Maduro regime. To adopt this strategy, they had to overcome concerns about the potential political backlash from voters and decide to break unwritten norms of political coexistence that preclude the use of certain instruments in the fight for power. After the government made it clear that it was not willing to play by the rules when it blocked the recall referendum and stripped the National Assembly of its powers, it was only natural that the opposition would feel justified in taking conflict to this higher level.

In 2017, Venezuela's opposition also decided to step over a red line that it had balked at crossing ever since the disastrous aftermath of the 2002–3 oil strike: to target the government's—and the nation's—access to external resources. Opposition leaders were fully aware that doing so would be unpopular, yet they chose to put aside their concerns given their expectation that this strategy would force Maduro to back down. In making this choice, they were doing something very similar to what Maduro had done in previous years when he ordered the Dakazo or flooded the economy with bolivars ahead of elections. They were adopting strategies that they saw as maximizing their chances to win the near-term contest for power, despite the effect that these strategies had on the country's long-term viability. By the end of 2017, both sides had bought into the idea of employing scorched earth strategies.

The spilling over of political conflict into the economic arena significantly harmed the economy's growth and impeded the recovery that would have naturally happened given the rebound in oil prices that began in mid-2016. Macroeconomically, 2017 is somewhat of an anomaly because it is one of the only years in recent Venezuelan history in which exports recover from a decline but the economy does not grow.[19] Yet despite higher oil revenues caused by recovering oil prices (which, that year at least, offset the effect of declining production), the economy went into another year of double-digit economic contraction. Part of the reason for this was the closure of international financing, which made the country run a current account surplus to continue servicing its debt.

Yet the magnitude of the economic contraction seen in 2017 was even higher than we would have expected given the import cuts seen that year. This suggests that the political crisis affected not just the economy's capacity to pay for imported inputs but also its ability to turn those inputs into economic output. We saw this in the growth accounting decompositions discussed in chapter 2, which start to show an increasingly severe decline in productivity from 2017 on. The coincidence of this deep contraction with the progressive withdrawal of the economy's public and private sector from access to a broad array of financial and economic transactions as a result of its toxification suggests that the quantitative estimates of the effects of financial and economic sanctions on oil production that I discuss in the next chapter may need to be seen as a lower bound for the damage done to the country's economy by the spilling over of its political conflict into the economic arena.

The escalation of Venezuela's political crisis wasn't just reflected in what Venezuela's political actors were willing to do in terms of confrontation strategies; it was also reflected in who they were willing to call and what they were willing to ask of their international allies. Starting in 2017, we will see a large part of the international community become progressively involved in Venezuela's crisis and begin to contemplate the use of new strategies that would contribute to deepening the country's economic crisis. I take up the role of these allies and the economic consequences of their involvement in the next two chapters.

NINE

Sanctioning Venezuela

I thought it was time to turn the screws and asked,
"Why don't we go for a win here?"
—John Bolton, former National Security Advisor to
President Donald Trump, 2020

UPPING THE ANTE

During the summer of 2017, a new rumor started making the rounds in Washington circles: the United States was considering imposing an oil embargo on Venezuela. On June 4, Reuters published a story stating that US authorities were contemplating slapping sectoral sanctions aimed at restricting trade between Venezuela's state-owned oil sector and the rest of the world. The proposal, the story claimed, had been "discussed at high levels of the administration as part of a wide-ranging review of U.S. options." However, US authorities were moving cautiously, as they understood that "if such an unprecedented step is taken it could deepen the country's economic and social crisis" (Gupta and Spetalnick 2017). In mid-July, President Trump threatened "strong and swift economic actions" if Maduro went ahead with the plan to convene the all-powerful National Constitutional Convention (Woody 2017).

The news found significant resistance among policy circles, many of whom foresaw the Trump administration going down the same rabbit hole as the US Cuba policy, promoting economic isolation that would only help entrench the regime. Moisés Naím, one of the foremost Venezuelan intellectuals in exile, wrote in the Spanish newspaper *El País* that prohibiting Venezuelan oil imports could "strengthen the government in Caracas, weakening the opposition and aggravating the humanitarian crisis that is devastating Venezuelans" (Naím 2017). Francisco Monaldi, a prominent Venezuelan oil industry expert, wrote that oil sanctions "would translate into an even deeper recession, a greater decline in consumption and an escalation in inflation and exchange rate depreciation" (Monaldi 2017). Others were less cautious: OAS Secretary General Luis Almagro told a US Senate hearing that "sanctions will not worsen the suffering of the Venezuelan people. . . . [W]e need more economic pressure on a government that is investing the money it earns through natural resources that belong to the people to fight and kill that very same people" (OAS 2017).

Eventually, the Trump administration shied away from imposing a full-fledged oil embargo, opting instead for more limited financial sanctions barring issuance of debt. The reasons appear to have had to do primarily with the concerns of specific US economic interests, in particular, those of refiners. The vice president of Valero Energy, the Texas-based refining behemoth, told the press that an import ban would simply rechannel Venezuelan fuel to other markets and raise domestic fuel prices in the United States (Reuters 2017b). The chief executive of the American Fuel and Petrochemical Manufacturers, a trade group, sent a letter to President Trump arguing that oil sanctions on Venezuela "would likely hurt consumers and businesses right here in the United States" (Argus Media 2017).

The US government opted instead to impose financial sanctions impeding the government and state-owned firms from accessing international credit markets. As I discussed in the previous chapter, a number of earlier controversies over financing of the Maduro regime—in particular, the Goldman Sachs scandal and the hunger bonds controversy—had given Venezuelan debt a sufficiently toxic aura so as to make it an easier target of policy. In contrast to the oil sanctions, financial sanctions that were seen as impeding the government from digging the country more deeply into debt were generally well received.

However, as I argue in this chapter, financial sanctions had a significant effect on a crucial part of Venezuela's oil industry: the joint ventures with multinationals that the government had increasingly relied on to stabilize oil production. By stopping these firms from entering into financial agreements with their foreign partners, the sanctions hit hard at what was at the time the only source of growth in Venezuelan oil output.

Over time, the Trump administration would enter a cat-and-mouse game in which it would systematically threaten the Maduro government with tighter sanctions if the regime crossed certain lines only to see those lines crossed time after time. Oil sanctions would ultimately be adopted in early 2019, followed by a ban on all transactions with the Venezuelan government later that year and sanctions on foreign firms that helped market Venezuelan oil in non-US markets in early 2020. By the end of 2020, US policy on Venezuela was totally focused on finding ways to further increase restrictions on the economic and financial transactions of the regime, premised on the assumption that greater economic pressure could ultimately cause a change in government.

MAXIMUM PRESSURE

The current Venezuela sanctions regime—with some exceptions[1]—is based on a 2015 declaration of a national emergency with respect to the situation in Venezuela issued by the Obama administration premised on the assessment that this situation constituted an "unusual and extraordinary threat" to US national security.[2] Despite being the first administration to formally impose sanctions on Venezuela, the Obama administration used the national emergency declaration somewhat selectively, sanctioning only seven individuals, six of whom were security force officers involved in human rights violations during the 2014 protests (the other was a prosecutor who had filed conspiracy charges against opposition leaders).[3] This approach would change with the Trump administration, which would use sanctions intensively as the main instrument of its Venezuela policy,

The first step taken by the Trump administration after coming into office was to increase the reach of personal sanctions by directing them at some of the highest-ranking members of the government. While Obama had designated officials linked directly to human rights violations, Trump targeted a larger number of government officials based on a broader set of considerations. These began with the designation of Vice President Tareck El Aissami in February 2017, a month after his appointment to that post, and subsequently increased to cover several cabinet members, Supreme Court justices, high-ranking PDVSA officials, as well as the president, first lady, and many of their close associates.[4] The justifications for the imposition of sanctions ranged from drug trafficking to corruption and undermining democracy.

Individual-specific sanctions are in principle not designed to affect the functioning of an economy; rather, they are supposed to be "smart sanctions" aimed at punishing wrongdoers (Cortright and Lopez 2002). In practice, their effects tend to go beyond the individuals affected, as widespread use of sanctions against actors in a jurisdiction tends to generate de-risking and overcompliance by international commercial and financial actors, often leading them to elude transactions with non-sanctioned entities in the jurisdiction (Cortright and Lopez 2002; Batmanghelidj and Moret 2022). In the case of government officials, there is an even more direct and immediate effect of the imposition of personal sanctions, which is the fact that US persons are precluded from dealing with sanctioned individuals even if they are acting only in their official capacity as government representatives (OFAC 2018). Lawyers for firms involved in dealings with Venezuela advised their clients to take care not to enter into any contracts executed by PDVSA's sanctioned CFO "as that would apparently be construed as a direct or indirect dealing with an SDN" (West P&I 2017).

Unsurprisingly, the addition to the Office of Foreign Assets Control (OFAC) list of high-ranking government officials had a chilling effect on interactions with the Venezuelan government. When the Venezuelan government invited creditors to Caracas for talks on debt renegotiations in November 2017, almost no international bondholders showed up. "For some, the meeting could land them behind bars," read a Bloomberg article published ahead of the meeting titled "The Drug Kingpin Running Venezuela's Bond Negotiations" (Laya and Rosati 2017).

The United States would take the first step in the direction of more explicit economic sanctions on August 24, 2017. On that day, President Trump issued an executive order prohibiting the purchase of new debt or equity issued by the government of Venezuela or PDVSA as well as the purchase of previously issued debt held by the government or entities under its control. It also barred dividend payments to Venezuela, impeding the government from using the profits from its offshore subsidiaries to fund its budget.

The August 2017 financial sanctions were specifically motivated by the government's decision to proceed with elections for the Constitutional Convention on July 30 of that year. Two weeks ahead of the vote, as part of a concerted effort to get Maduro to back down, Trump had promised that if the Maduro regime went ahead, the United States would respond with "strong and swift economic actions" (Reuters 2017a). The vote took place, and the Trump administration responded three weeks later with the financial sanctions.

Several weeks later, Maduro announced that he would seek to restructure Venezuela's external debt (BBC Mundo 2017). Yet sanctions not only impeded direct negotiations with sanctioned individuals—a restriction that Venezuela could in principle circumvent by appointing nonsanctioned persons to lead the restructuring negotiations. By prohibiting issuance of new debt by the government or PDVSA, the August financial sanctions also effectively prohibited any restructuring of the country's existing debt, as restructurings are implemented through the exchange of old bonds for new bonds.[5]

In November 2018, the Trump administration issued a new executive order that laid the groundwork for restricting trade, and not only financial, transactions with Venezuela. The order allowed the secretary of the treasury to determine that actors in a given sector of the economy were contributing to the national emergency generated by the Venezuelan situation. Authorities originally presented the order as aimed at restricting trade in the country's gold sector, yet the order gave the government the leeway to target any sector of the economy (*Federal Register* 2018). During the next months, the treasury secretary would determine that four broad economic sectors were contributing to the national emergency: gold (November 2018), oil (January 2019), finance (March 2019), and defense and security (May 2019) (US Department of State 2019a, 2019b, 2019c). It subsequently added several private and public sector entities belonging to these sectors to the SDN list. The designations were broad enough to essentially preclude US actors from doing business with anyone in these sectors of the Venezuelan economy.

Oil, accounting for 93% of exports and 12% of GDP at the time of the January 2019 sanctions, was by and large the most relevant sector of those targeted. The United States announced the decision to designate PDVSA as part of a major ratcheting up of pressure on the Venezuelan regime, with National Security Advisor John Bolton saying that he expected PDVSA to lose US$11 billion in export proceeds—a number equivalent to more than a third of the country's oil exports at the time—in addition to the effect of freezing $7 billion in assets (De Young, Mufson, and Faiola 2019). The decision was made public on January 28, just five days after the US had said it would recognize Juan Guaidó as the country's interim president, and its announcement included a direct exhortation to Venezuelan security forces "to accept the peaceful, democratic and constitutional transfer of power" to the new government (McClatchy 2019).

Bolton's $11 billion estimate appears to have been a simple calculation of the value of Venezuela's oil exports to the United States at the time.[6] The net effect of sanctions would of course depend on Venezuela's capacity to route that oil to other markets. For that reason, the United States immediately focused its efforts on blocking Venezuela from channeling to other destinations the oil it could not export to the United States, explicitly pressuring some of PDVSA's other clients not to increase imports from Venezuela after the US decision.[7]

As the country's political crisis dragged on without clear resolution, the United States started to mull the possibility of increasing pressure on non-US firms to cut (rather than just not increase) their purchases from Venezuela. In August 2019, it sent a strong signal that it was willing to do so by adopting a new executive order that blocked any transactions with the government of Venezuela and that also gave the executive branch the power to sanction non-US persons for having "materially assisted" the Venezuelan government or its state-owned entities.

US authorities made a point of highlighting their new powers to sanction non-US firms.[8] Speaking one day after the publication of the new order in a meeting at a summit on the Venezuelan crisis held in

Lima, Bolton said that the United States had issued this order to "deny Maduro access to the global financial system" and used the opportunity to send a stern message to third parties: "There's no need to risk your business interests in the U.S. for the purposes of profiting from a corrupt and dying government"(Kurmanaev and Jakes 2019).

Bolton, however, would leave the White House in September; he would later claim that his disagreements with Trump included the latter's indecisiveness on Venezuela.[9] Some Venezuela clients then began pushing back on US policy. In an October interview with the *Financial Times*, the finance minister of India—which, together with China, had become one of the main purchasers of Venezuelan oil after the closing off of the US market—acknowledged that the United States had tried to convince India to stop buying Venezuelan oil but said that the country also needed to maintain its own strength and strategic interests. "India is a strategic partner for the United States of America and you want a strategic partner to be strong and not weakened," the minister said he had told US representatives (Reuters 2019a).

The next turn in policy would come in February, on the heels of an international tour by Guaidó designed to showcase his global support that culminated in a visit to the White House and an appearance at Trump's annual State of the Union address. US authorities decided to ratchet up the pressure on the Maduro regime by making use of the authority to impose secondary sanctions. Administration officials said that the US government's "maximum pressure" campaign against Venezuela was only "50–60%" implemented and would continue to be ramped up as long as Maduro refused to give up power (Lawler 2020).

The key new decision was to sanction two subsidiaries of the Russian energy company Rosneft, which had been in charge of business with Venezuela (Mohsin and Millard 2020; US Department of the Treasury 2020). The United States also sanctioned two Mexican companies that had signed oil-for-food deals with Venezuela (Kassai 2020). Rosneft at the time was handling around 75% of Venezuela's oil sales as a result of other partners' caution regarding doing direct business with the country (Yagova, Aizhu, and Parraga 2019). It had also supplied almost all the gasoline imported by the country during the previous year, as Venezuela's refining infrastructure remained beset by operational problems (Argus Media 2019). Predictably, Venezuela began suffering severe gasoline shortages shortly after Rosneft halted all trade with the country and divested from its operations there in response to the sanctions.

HOW SANCTIONS AFFECTED VENEZUELA

Economic sanctions are commonly used to attempt to induce changes in the conduct of targeted nations or entities and have increasingly come to be seen as an alternative to full-fledged armed conflict (Mulder 2022). The study of sanctions forms part of a much more extensive literature on the use of economic policy as part of the foreign policy tool kit used to influence the decisions of other nations and actors, a field known as economic statecraft (Fabre 2018; Nephew 2017; Baldwin and Kapstein 2020). Although they are often imposed through multilateral bodies such as the United Nations Security Council, unilateral sanctions are also common. The use of economic sanctions has grown significantly in recent decades, with nearly a third of the world economy affected by trade sanctions imposed by the United States, Europe, or the United Nations (Rodríguez 2023).

In general, there is considerable controversy regarding the usefulness of sanctions as a policy tool. In contrast, there is much more consensus on the finding that they have adverse effects on living conditions in target countries. In Rodríguez (2023), I survey thirty-one quantitative studies of the effect of sanctions on living conditions in target countries; thirty of them find unambiguously negative effects of sanctions on indicators of living standards ranging from economic growth, health, and inequality to human and political rights. For example, Neuenkirch and Neumeier (2015) estimate that the cumulative effect of the imposition of UN sanctions on per capita income is an average decline in per capita GDP of 26%, while that of US sanctions is 13%. Gutmann, Neuenkirch, and Neumeier (2017) find that UN sanctions are associated with a decrease in life expectancy of 1.2 years for men and 1.4 years for women, while Afesorgbor and Mahadevan (2016) find that a sanctions episode increases the Gini coefficient by 1.7 points. Lucena and Apolinário (2015) estimate that the protection of rights to physical integrity (the right to life and the prohibition of torture) is 1.7 times more likely to worsen under sanctions.

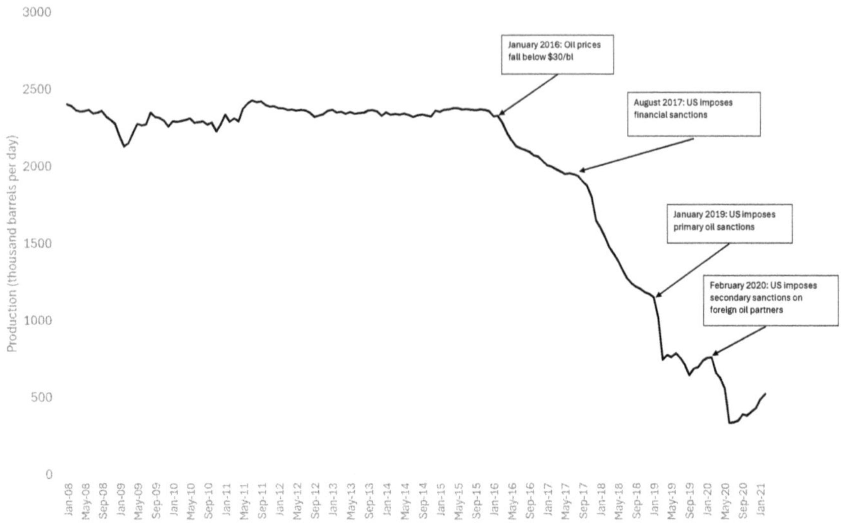

FIGURE 9.1. Venezuela's oil production, 2008–2020. *Source*: Author's construction using OPEC 2023.

As I discussed in chapter 2, the decline in Venezuela's oil revenues by 93% is the most important proximate cause of the country's growth collapse in the 2012 to 2020 period. It thus makes sense to begin my analysis of sanctions by focusing on their effect on oil revenues. Figure 9.1 plots the evolution of Venezuela's oil production between 2008 and 2020, according to data reported by secondary sources to OPEC. This series shows remarkable stability up to 2016. Production begins falling in 2016, and the rate of decline accelerates markedly after that. Venezuela's production level at the end of 2020, at around 400 tbd, was about one-sixth of its pre-2015 production and lower than the level of domestic consumption when the economy is working at full capacity.[10]

The series represented in figure 9.1 also suggests that there are three distinct periods in the evolution of Venezuela's oil production data. Production remains relatively stable at around 2.3 million barrels up to December 2015. At the start of 2016, it begins to decline and falls at a rate of 1.0% per month. Then, from September 2017 on, the rate of decline accelerates, averaging 3.1% over the following sixteen months. In the last part of the sample, it suffers two discrete jumps: a 35.2% drop

(405 tbd) between January and March 2019 and a 55.7% drop (423 tbd) between February and June 2020.

In chapter 2, I provided a discussion of the determinants of oil production growth up to 2016. To briefly recap my argument, Venezuela's oil sector significantly underperformed that of its peers in terms of production growth between 1999 and 2016, with the country's output going from accounting for 10.5% of total OPEC production in 1999 to 7.5% in 2015. I argued that Venezuela's inability to take greater advantage of its oil wealth was largely a consequence of overtaxation of the oil industry and numerous arbitrary changes over time imposed by the government on its private sector partners and providers.

Nevertheless, petrostates don't usually kill the goose that lays the golden eggs. They are, after all, interested in self-preservation. Over time, authorities came to grudgingly accept a model of oil sector management that relied significantly on joint ventures with private sector multinationals such as Chevron, Eni, and Total and state-controlled firms of allies such as China's CNP and Russia's Rosneft (Hernández and Monaldi 2016; Crooks 2017; Rosales 2018). Originally intended as vehicles to renegotiate the terms of pre-Chávez operational agreements, these joint ventures became islands of productivity in the country's oil sector. For example, between 2010 and 2015, production in fields operated solely by PDVSA fell by 28%, but production in joint ventures increased by 42% (Hernández and Monaldi 2016, table 2).

One of the mechanisms used to grant joint venture (JV) partners more control over revenues was through financing agreements whereby foreign partners would lend funds into a JV with the state-owned oil company as long as the loan could be repaid directly from the JV's production (Neuman 2014; Reuters 2015; Telesur 2016b). These mechanisms were born out of talks between PDVSA and private companies in 2013 and 2014 mediated by Venezuela's Hydrocarbons Association, a trade group representing foreign oil companies in Venezuela (Gallegos 2016). Given that Venezuelan law requires the government to be the majority shareholder in joint ventures, this design allowed foreign partners to fund most of the investment in the firms, without being formally granted a higher stake in the company. In return, partners would be paid directly from offshore accounts into which the proceeds from oil sales would flow directly before being transferred to the PDVSA-controlled entity. Between 2013 and 2016, PDVSA signed twelve special financing deals with nine private sector partners, for a total of $11.1 billion in financing (table 9.1). Partly through these arrangements, Venezuela managed to stabilize oil production at 2.4 million barrels per day.

I also discussed in chapter 2 how PDVSA cut investment in response to the 2014 oil price shock. That a decline in production ensued in 2016 is thus not surprising. But I also argued that there were no reasons to expect cuts of these magnitudes to lead to anything more than a moderate decline in production and certainly not the virtual disappearance of the country's oil industry as both financial and real indicators of investment remained within their historical range. Oil industry analysts expected oil production to stabilize or at worst decline moderately, while economic analysts were expecting the economy to turn the corner sometime between 2017 and 2018 given recovering oil prices and the expectation of recovering export revenue.

While countries like Saudi Arabia and Russia were able to ramp up production from their low-cost oil fields in 2016, high-cost and highly leveraged producers like Venezuela were particularly vulnerable to oil price declines. As a result, many of them were forced to cut back investment and suffered losses in production at the time. For example, oil output in neighboring Colombia, part of whose oil industry was also highly leveraged, saw production fall by similar levels during 2016, as did those of Argentina (which shared a similar policy framework during more than a decade) and Mexico (whose politicized national oil company is often compared to Venezuela's). Not surprisingly, this was the period of the spectacular collapse of Pacific Rubiales, a Colombian oil venture run by Venezuelan expatriates who had left their country's oil industry after Chávez's takeover (Peinado 2011; Quevedo 2016).

As figure 9.1 also shows, there was a marked acceleration in the rate of decline in oil production after August 2017. The change in trend coincides with the approval of the August 2017 executive order barring US persons from providing new financing to the Venezuelan government or PDVSA. The adoption of sanctions occurred within the broader context of financial toxification described in chapter 8, whereby it became increasingly clear that institutions that decided to enter financial

TABLE 9.1. Special financing arrangements signed by PDVSA with foreign oil partners, 2013–2018

Name	*Main Partner*	*Main Partner Nationality*	*Other Partner*	*Facility Type*	*Amount (US$ million)*	*Date*	*Maturity*	*Term*	*Rate*
Petroboscán	Chevron	United States	–	Loan	2,000	May 13	2025	12	Libor+4.5%
Petrolera Sinovensa	CNPC	China	–	Loan	4,015	Jun. 3	2023	10	Libor+5.8%
Petrozamora	Gazprom Bank	Russia	–	Loan	1,000	Dec. 13	2019	6	Libor+6.9%
Petrowarao	Perenco	UK/France	–	Loan	420	Aug. 14	2021	7	Libor+4.5%
Petrocedeño	Total	France	Statoil	Revolver	60	Oct. 14	2017	1	0.0132
Petropiar	Chevron	United States	–	Revolver	10	Jan. 15	2017	1	Libor+4.5%
Petroboscán	Chevron	United States	–	Revolver	10	Jul. 15	2017	1	Libor+4.5%
Petrodelta	HNR/CT Energía	Venezuela	–	Revolver	6	Dec. 15	2017	1	0.12
Petroquiriquire	Repsol	Spain	–	Loan	1,200	Oct. 16	2026	10	Libor+4.5%
Petrolera Indovenezolana	ONGC	India	–	Revolver	60	Nov. 16	2017	1	Libor+5.5%
Petrolera Indovenezolana	ONGC	India	–	Loan	318	Nov. 16	2019	3	Libor+5.5%
Petromonagas	Rosneft	Russia	–	Prepaid exports	1,985	Dec. 16	2021	13	Libor+5%
Petrozumano	CNPC	China	–	Loan	184	Sep. 18	N/A	N/A	N/A

Note: Table lists JVs subject to SFV arrangements, detailing financing conditions as well as main partners and their nationalities.

Source: Rodríguez 2022b.

arrangements with Venezuela would have to be willing to pay high reputational and regulatory costs.

Loss of access to credit stopped PDVSA from obtaining financial resources that could have been devoted to investment or maintenance. Of course, given the high levels of debt, it is unclear that the loss of market access should be attributed solely to sanctions. Nevertheless, countries that lose market access typically have the possibility of regaining it after entering a debt restructuring process, a door that was closed to Venezuela after the August 2017 executive order.

The January 2019 designation of PDVSA barred any US nationals from doing business with the company or any of its affiliates. Since PDVSA is the majority stakeholder in oil JVs in Venezuela's oil sector, this also effectively constituted a prohibition of purchases of Venezuelan oil, as well as of exports of oil products to Venezuela. The US decision to recognize Guaidó as the nation's legitimate interim president had the implication that bank accounts of the Venezuelan government and the Central Bank were transferred to the Guaidó administration. Guaidó appointees also were able to successfully request recognition by US courts of their appointments to the board of state-owned corporations, including PDVSA and its subsidiaries (Reuters 2019b).

As a result of the OFAC designation, Venezuela completely lost access to the US oil market and financial system. Any previous exceptions that had been carved into the financial sanctions became moot both because they were disallowed by PDVSA's SDN designation (e.g., trade credit of less than 90 days) and because the contracting entity would in any case have had to be the Guaidó administration, which lacked any real control over the oil industry. At the same time, US authorities extracted commitments from other key partners (namely, India, the most important destination for Venezuelan oil after the United States) not to increase oil purchases from Venezuela.

Oil sanctions were directly followed by a drop in oil production of a magnitude similar to that of the lost US market. Between January and March 2019, production fell by 405 tbd and stabilized at a level of around 750 tbd for the subsequent twelve months. Export data produced by Bloomberg based on loading of vessels in PDVSA docks in Venezuela and the Caribbean, as well as ship-to-ship transfers, showed total loadings dropping by 35% between January and June 2019. Exports to the United States fell to zero by February 2019, as compared to 326 tbd in the month before sanctions (and an average of 521 tbd in the twelve previous months), while exports to India and China remained stable through 2019 (Bloomberg 2021c).[11]

Likewise, the decision in 2020 to sanction Rosneft (which at the time was responsible for the marketing of approximately three-fifths of Venezuela's oil exports) and two Mexican companies involved in oil-for-food deals had a chilling effect on Venezuela's remaining foreign partners, which decided to curtail all their involvement with the country's oil sector (Parraga and Verma 2020). These actions were followed by a subsequent discrete drop in oil production, which fell by 423 tbd over the subsequent four months. In the aftermath of that decision, it became increasingly difficult for Venezuela to find any partners willing to supply it with oil products or inputs to the oil industry. Later that year, Venezuela would turn to Iran—also a target of a US "maximum pressure" sanctions campaign—for assistance fixing its refineries and importing gasoline, drawing stern warnings from the United States and the Guaidó administration (Argus Media 2020b; Reuters 2020a; Lipin 2021).

Previous Studies of the Impact of Venezuela Sanctions

Most studies of the effect of sanctions on Venezuela have focused on their impact on its oil sector.[12] Since oil accounted for 95% of Venezuelan exports prior to sanctions, it would be natural to expect any first-order effects to impact the economy through the oil sector. Previous research, discussed in greater detail in chapter 2, has documented the high level of import dependence of the Venezuelan economy, establishing a clear channel through which oil activity can impact growth: lower oil rents lead to import contraction, which drives the reduction in investment as the economy dissaves, capital flows out, and imported intermediate goods decline.

In Rodríguez (2018), I first pointed out that the adoption of financial sanctions coincided with the acceleration of the rate of decline in Venezuela's oil production, which went from 1.0% monthly in the period preceding the 2017 financial sanctions to an average of 3.1% per month in the subsequent sixteen months. I also suggested the use of neighboring Colombia, which had pre-sanctions trends in oil production similar to Venezuela, as a potential counterfactual. While Colombia saw a similar decline in output in 2016 and early 2017, possibly a common reaction to plummeting global oil prices, Colombian oil output stabilized after oil prices began recovering in 2017 while Venezuelan oil output continued declining.

Weisbrot and Sachs (2019a) used this evidence to contend that both financial and oil sanctions had led to significant declines in oil revenues and thus caused the import contraction that led to major deteriorations in socioeconomic indicators. They also argued that it is "virtually certain that the US economic sanctions made a substantial contribution" to the increase in mortality observed in 2018, associated with an additional forty thousand deaths.

In an initial reaction, Hausmann (2019) and Santos (2019) questioned the Weisbrot and Sachs analysis, alleging that the decline in Venezuela's oil output preceded the sanctions and that the Weisbrot and Sachs comparison was distorted by the use of different graphical scales for Colombia and Venezuela. In their response, Weisbrot and Sachs (2019b) argued that using Venezuela's share of OPEC production, as Hausmann did, to argue in favor of a long-run decline, implied introducing extraneous factors and that Santos's argument that oil output for two different-sized countries should be viewed in the same absolute scale made little sense if the objective was to compare growth rates.

In a more extensive response, Hausmann and Muci (2019) questioned the counterfactual assumption that oil production would not have declined in the absence of sanctions and claimed that the 2019 drops in oil output were caused by electrical blackouts. They contended that Colombia is not a good control group because the oil production series for the two countries are uncorrelated in longer-run data going back to 1999. Morales (2019) proposed the alternative hypothesis of militarization of the oil industry as an explanation for the decline in oil production. Bahar et al. (2019) argued that social indicators show strong preexisting trends before the sanctions and thus likely reflect the effect of past policies. As I already argued in chapters 2 and 8, this last argument is problematic, as recovering oil prices in the 2017 to 2019 period suggest that the Venezuelan economy should have at least stabilized in a counterfactual scenario without sanctions.

To the best of my knowledge, these authors, who wrote in early 2019, have neither revised nor restated their claims on the effect of oil sanctions after the availability of more recent data. However, given that electrical blackouts have eased from their early 2019 highs, an argument linking them with the sustained post-2019 drop in oil output would appear to be less tenable.[13] Rodríguez and Rodríguez (2019) argue that lack of diesel fuel needed to run backup thermal power plants after the United States banned diesel imports, as well as reluctance by US companies to extend credit to replace power generators after the 2017 financial sanctions, contributed to the intensity and duration of the February 2019 blackouts.

Neither is it clear that the lack of correlation between the Colombian and Venezuelan oil production series prior to 2013 is a reason that the former should not be used as a counterfactual for the latter. In the absence of an experimental setup, it is essentially impossible for the control and treatment group to be identical; what we seek is that they be sufficiently similar. A group of 35-year-old males may be an adequate control for a group of 40-year-old males, but if we stretch their pretreatment window to include their childhoods, we will find widely divergent behaviors at the start of the series due to age differences. Hausmann and Muci's (2019) suggestion of lengthening the pretreatment window to 1990 (twenty-eight years) implies a ratio of pretreatment to treatment period of 16.6, more than six times the typical ratio used in the literature (Rodríguez 2019b, 11). The danger of excessively lengthening the pretreatment period is that we may contaminate our data with variations that are irrelevant to the comparison we want to make. If we applied Hausmann and Muci's suggestion of a pretreatment to treatment window ratio of 16.6 to the landmark Abadie, Diamond, and Hainmueller (2010) study of the effects of 1980s tobacco control legislation in California, for example, we would have needed to take the sample back to 1806, more than four decades before California became a state.

Oliveros (2020) surveys the qualitative evidence of the impact of sanctions on the economy. He finds significant evidence of overcompliance and inability to use the humanitarian exceptions approved by the US government to its sanctions regime. He cites several examples of humanitarian agencies that have had payments for medical supplies blocked by financial institutions alleging sanctions-related restrictions, and he quotes business leaders claiming that the harm caused by sanctions to their productive capacity is similar to that of the 2007–8 wave of expropriations. Oliveros also presents several counterfactual exercises of what would have happened to oil production in Venezuela in the absence of sanctions based on extrapolations of prior trends. Even in the most conservative of these scenarios, he estimates that sanctions can be associated with a cumulative decline in oil production of 616 tbd. Equipo Anova (2021) uses a trend interruption analysis to estimate the break in trend in oil output at the time of sanctions and finds that it is associated with a decline of 698 tbd in oil production, or 33.1% of pre-sanctions oil output.

New Econometric Estimates

In this section, I explore the key empirical issues in identifying the effect of sanctions on the Venezuelan oil sector through three complementary approaches. First, I use a data-driven method to select an appropriate comparison group that can serve as a counterfactual for how the Venezuelan oil sector could have evolved in the absence of sanctions. Second, I use cross-national panel data to study the effect of sanctions on oil production in a panel of countries. Third, I use firm-level data from Venezuela's oil industry to assess how the impact of sanctions varied according to firms' financial exposure.[14]

Synthetic Control Estimates

The crucial identification issue for estimating the effect of sanctions on oil production refers to being able to specify an adequate counterfactual for what would have happened in the Venezuelan oil industry in the absence of sanctions. As I noted above, the original suggestion of using Colombia as a counterfactual due to its high-cost structure and similar pre-2017 performance met with criticism by those who highlighted structural dissimilarities between the oil industries of the two countries.

This type of discussion is not new to event-study analyses. Similarity is often in the eye of the beholder: no two cases are identical, and cases that may look alike to some analysts will likely look different to others.

One solution to this problem is to let the data tell you which other cases form an adequate counterfactual. This is the approach taken by Abadie and Gardeazabal (2003) and Abadie, Diamond, and Hainmueller (2010). They use a synthetic control group estimator to choose an adequate counterfactual to estimate intervention effects. This method is based on the observation that a combination of control units designed to replicate as closely as possible the evolution of the treatment group before an intervention can serve as a much better comparison for the unit exposed to the intervention than any single unit on its own. The method creates a counterfactual as a linear combination of potential control units that approximates the values of the predictors of the outcome variable of interest in the pretreatment period.

Using this method, I build a synthetic Venezuela that approximates the values of a set of control variables that serve as predictors for oil production. My set of covariates includes domestic oil consumption, refining capacity, oil reserves, political institutions, and lagged oil production 4, 8, and 12 years before treatment. I work with a 12-year window, which begins in 2005 because longer-run windows are affected by the 2002–3 oil strike, which caused a 79.8% decline in oil production within a two-month period.[15]

In applying the synthetic control method, it is particularly important to choose the donor pool from economies that are not also being treated and that share some basic similarities with the treatment group. I restrict the control group to nonsanctioned economies with an average GDP per capita of less than $40,000 in 2014 (Venezuela's was $18,000).[16] This leaves a donor pool of thirteen countries.[17]

Figure 9.2 plots the evolution of the logarithm of oil production in Venezuela and the synthetic group. The method chooses as the synthetic control group for Venezuela a combination of Mexico (55.5%), Kazakhstan (31.9%), and China (12.6%). The synthetic control reproduces the treated country very well throughout the whole pre-2017 period. Venezuela somewhat outperforms the synthetic group in 2015 and underperforms it in 2016, but in both cases the difference is within two standard deviations of the mean-squared error (MSE). These periods of under- and overperformance offset each other, so that the decline in Venezuela's oil output during the 2014 to 2016 plunge in oil prices is virtually identical to that of the control group. By August 2017, the month at the end

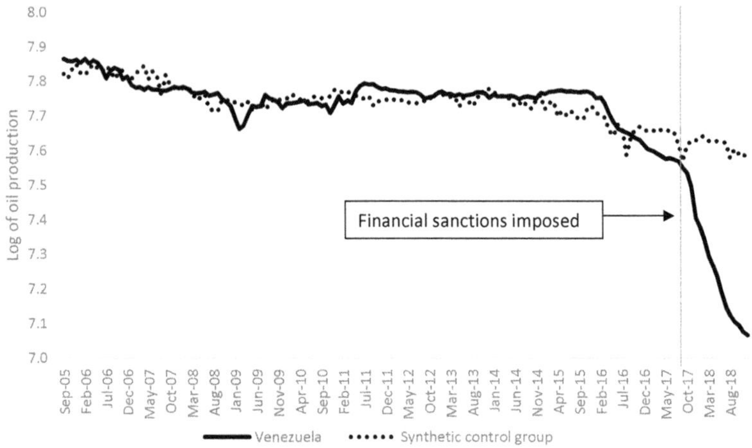

FIGURE 9.2. Venezuela and synthetic control production, 2005–2018. *Source*: Author's construction using OPEC 2023. *Note*: Chart displays the evolution of oil production in Venezuela and a synthetic control group. The synthetic control group is created by the method of Abadie, Diamond, and Hainmueller (2010). Pretreatment period begins in September 2005 and thus has a 12-year length. Controls include domestic oil consumption, per capita GDP, refining capacity, oil reserves, and the Polity Index. All variables except for the Polity Index are represented in logs. Donor pool includes all nonsanctioned countries with a per capita GDP of less than $40,000 in 2014.

of which financial sanctions were imposed, the difference between the synthetic and treatment groups was 5 log points, as opposed to an MSE of 4 log points.

This difference grows markedly after the adoption of US financial sanctions. In the month after treatment,[18] the difference between synthetic and control group production rises to 8 log points, and then in November it rises again to 13 log points, more than three standard deviations of the pre-trend difference. By the end of the sample in December 2018—just before the adoption of US oil sanctions—the difference had grown to 53 log points, or more than fourteen times the pretreatment standard deviation of the series. Taking the August 2017 level of production as the baseline, this would imply a loss of 797 tbd in production, or $17.5 billion at current oil prices.[19]

In Rodríguez (2019b), I provide a set of additional tests to assess the robustness of this result. They include placebo tests, which assess whether a similar sanctions effect could have been identified in a country chosen at random from the donor pool, as well as estimation using alternative treatment windows and donor groups. These tests confirm the conclusion of an economically and statistically significant effect of the 2017 financial sanctions, as well as the adequate power of the estimator against alternative hypotheses.

Cross-Country Panel Data

An alternative approach to using the data of oil producers to estimate the effect of sanctions is by pooling the experience of Venezuela with other producers that have been subject to sanctions. Instead of comparing a group of nonsanctioned countries with Venezuela, as I did in the previous subsection, this method considers the performance of all sanctioned oil producers relative to nonsanctioned producers and uses an estimate of that effect to calculate the incidence of sanctions on Venezuelan oil output.

Figures 9.3 and 9.4 show two examples, Iraq and Iran. In August 1990, the United Nations Security Council imposed oil sanctions on Iraq in the aftermath of its invasion of Kuwait. These sanctions were in place until the fall of Saddam Hussein in 2003 but for practical effects were considerably relaxed with the start of the UN oil-for-food program in 2006. We see a precipitous drop in output of 87% in the year of sanctions. Output remains low for several years after the war

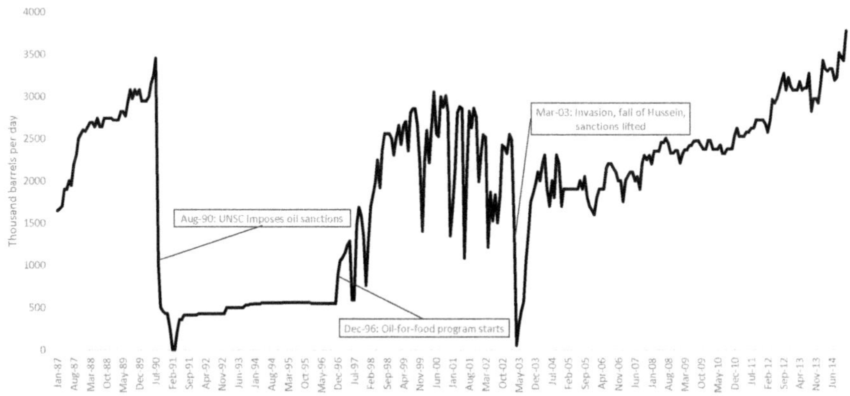

FIGURE 9.3. Iraq oil production, 1987–2014. *Source*: Author's construction using EIA 2023b.

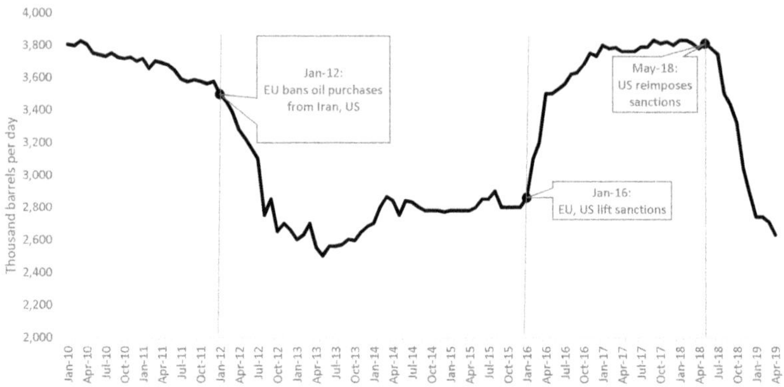

FIGURE 9.4. Iran oil production, 2010–2019. *Source*: Author's construction using Bloomberg 2022a.

and then recovers almost all the lost ground when Iraq is permitted to begin exporting oil again through the oil-for-food program. Sanctions are lifted after the US-led invasion in 2003, and production begins to recover subsequently.

In the case of Iran, multilateral sanctions were imposed in 2012 as a response to Iran's development of nuclear weapons. Output fell by approximately 20% after the European Union (EU) banned oil imports from Iran and the United States implemented secondary sanctions on countries trading with Iran. These restrictions were lifted in January 2016, and output subsequently recovered most of the lost ground. In May 2018, the United States again imposed secondary sanctions on Iranian oil sales, leading to a decline of a similar proportion.

In order to explore these results more systematically, I run a set of panel regressions on monthly data from thirty-eight oil exporting countries for the 1999 to 2020 period.[20] My base specification is

$$o_{it} = \alpha_i + \gamma_t + \pi_i t + \beta_0 X_{it} + \beta_1 S_{it} + \varepsilon_{it} \tag{9.1}$$

where o_{it} denotes oil output in country i at time t, X_{it} is a *jx1* vector of covariates, and S_{it} is an indicator variable capturing whether the country was subject to oil sanctions. α_i and γ_t respectively denote country and time-fixed effects, while t is a time trend, which is allowed to have country-specific effects.[21]

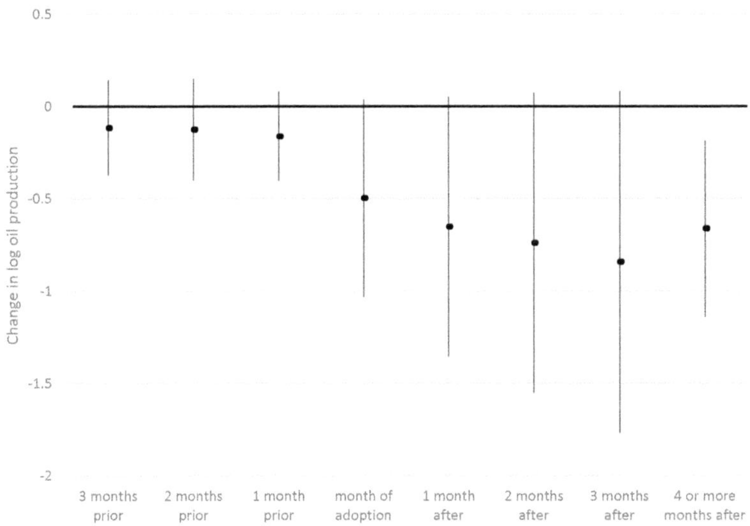

FIGURE 9.5. Estimated effects relative to timing of adoption of sanctions, panel data estimates. *Source*: Author's construction.

Figure 9.5 represents one of the specifications, in which I estimate separate coefficients for months before and after sanctions.[22] If the correlation was due to reverse causation, we would expect the data to show significant effects before the sanctions. In contrast, there are no significant effects before the sanctions, with the estimated effects becoming larger in the month of adoption and reaching their highest levels three months after adoption.[23] This is consistent with the patterns shown in figure 9.1 for Venezuela, as well as figures 9.3 and 9.4 for Iraq and Iran, in which the production effect of sanctions is quite rapid.

Numerically, the regression estimates of equation (9.1) deliver a range of -69 to -73 log points.[24] Applied to the Venezuelan economy, these effects would imply a decline of between 572 tbd and 594 tbd if we take the January 2019 production level as our starting point. Valued at current market prices, this would amount to $12.5 to $13.0 billion in foregone oil revenues. It would also represent around double the country's estimated 2020 level of imports.

Note that because financial sanctions almost always accompany oil sanctions (Venezuela being an atypical case), coefficient estimates from this model could be interpreted as proxying for the joint effect of financial and oil sanctions.[25] The results thus suggest that the financial sanctions imposed on Venezuela in 2017 had effects on the economy similar to those that could have been expected from full-fledged oil sanctions.

Firm-Level Panel Data Estimates

My third and last estimation makes use of a firm-level panel data set of monthly production levels in Venezuela's Orinoco Belt region. The Orinoco Belt is home to 262 billion barrels of oil reserves, the bulk of the country's proven reserves of 304 billion (Ministerio del Poder Popular de Petróleo 2019). It also generates around half of the country's production and more than two-thirds of its production by joint ventures. This is largely a result of the opening of Orinoco Belt to foreign investment in the late 1990s (Rodríguez 2005). During that period of low oil prices, authorities deemed the investment cost of developing these fields too high for then cash-strapped PDVSA. The contracts initially assigned in the 1990s were renegotiated by the Chávez administration in 2006. At that moment, PDVSA negotiated their conversion from operating contracts with private sector firms into joint ventures in which PDVSA held a majority stake.

Over time, the Orinoco Belt became one of the main sources of production growth in the Venezuelan oil industry. This was due in part to the greater concentration of JV arrangements with national and multinational companies in the area, which allowed foreign direct investment (FDI) inflows into an area of significant potential during a period of high oil prices. As figure 9.6 shows, Orinoco Belt production showed moderate production growth during the 2009 to 2015 period, which partially offset a trend of declining production in other areas of the country.

My estimation approach follows a difference-in-differences specification to assess the performance of firms with access to the special financing vehicle (SFV) deals shown in table 9.1 relative to those that did not have the deals before and after 2017. If the 2017 sanctions affected the oil industry by closing access to international lending, then we would expect the firms that had credit market access at the time of the sanctions to underperform those that lacked it.

My data correspond to observations of monthly production in thirty-three production blocs in the Orinoco Belt spanning the

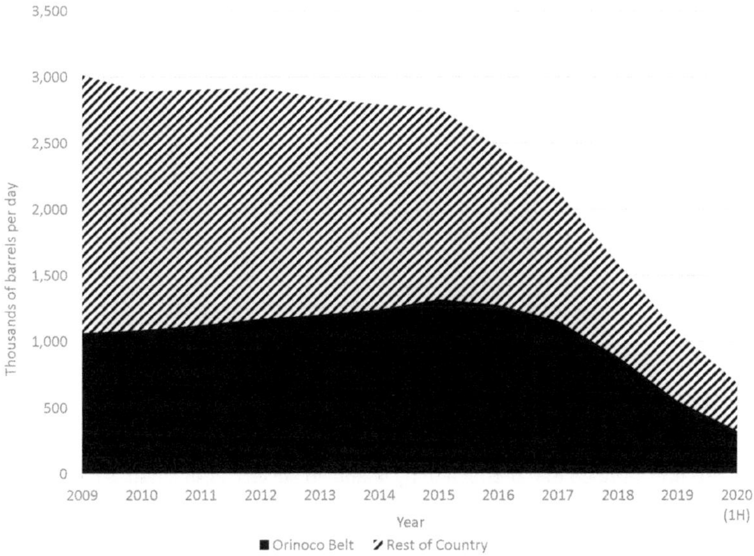

FIGURE 9.6. PDVSA production by region, 2009–2020. *Source*: Author's construction using PDVSA 2020.

twelve-and-a-half-year period from January 2008 to June 2020. The panel data regressions include time-specific treatment effects, treating the six firms with SFV agreements as of the time of the announcement of financial sanctions in August 2017 as the treatment group and the remaining twenty-six firms that did not have SFV deals at that time as the control group.[26] Therefore, the baseline specification is

$$p_{it} = \eta_i + \lambda_t + \theta(SFV_i \cdot t) + \sum_{k=T_0}^{T} \beta_k SFV_i S_k + \varepsilon_{it}, \tag{9.2}$$

where p_{it} is an indicator of production in firm i at time t, η_i denotes a firm-specific fixed effect, λ_t a month-specific fixed effect, t a time trend, S_k an indicator variable that takes the value 1 on month k and 0 on all other months, SFV_i an indicator variable that takes the value 1 for firms for which there is a special financing vehicle arrangement during my sample and 0 for those for which there is not, T_0 is the first month of sanctions (August 2017), and ε_{it} an iid error term.

Figure 9.7 shows that SFV firms were seeing positive growth prior to the sanctions, in contrast to non-SFV firms for which growth was

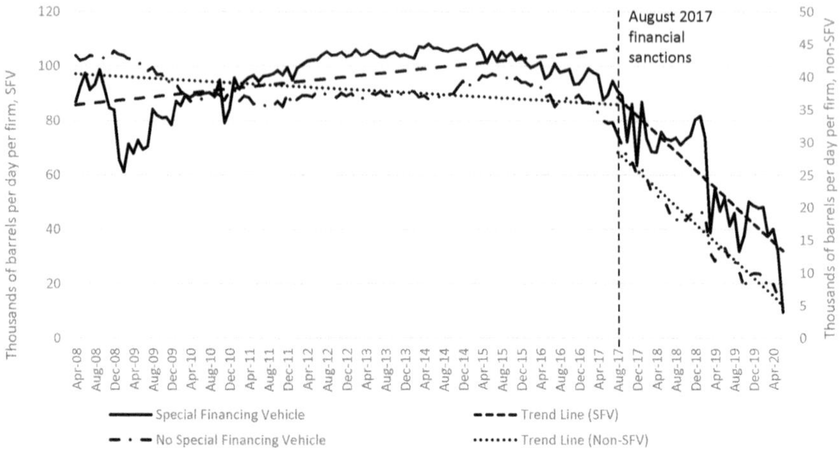

FIGURE 9.7. Orinoco Belt production by financing access, 2015–2020. *Source*: Rodríguez 2022b.

declining. After the sanctions, both groups see production decline at similar rates. At first sight, the data do not seem to have the characteristics associated with the ideal difference-in-differences specification. In the ideal framework, the control and treatment group should have similar behavior before the intervention and begin to differ after the intervention. This characteristic of the control and treatment groups is what is known as the "parallel trends" hypothesis. The difference-in-differences method can still be applied to data with no parallel pre-intervention trends, but the interpretation of the results is somewhat different: instead of testing for the effect of an intervention on the level of an outcome, we are testing for the effect on its growth rate—that is, we are attempting to capture deviations from the "parallel growth" hypothesis. Precisely for this reason, it is advisable for equation (9.2) to include a group-specific trend in this specification, whose effect is captured by the parameter θ (Bilinski and Hatfield 2018).[27]

Table 9.2 presents my estimates. I use three different measures of production because the standard measure (log of production) is biased given that a large part of the sample falls to zero production after the sanctions. When the dependent variable is the level of production (the first specification in table 9.2), I find an average treatment effect of 39.3 thousand barrels per day, which is strongly significant (p = .006). If I just calculate

TABLE 9.2. Panel regression results, firm-level data, Orinoco Belt

Average Treatment Effects	*Level of Production*	*Log of Production*	*Standardized*
SFV*Financial Sanctions	−39,314***	−0.66*	−1.736***
	−13,215	−0.329	−0.395
SFV*Financial and Oil Sanctions	−51,416***	−0.939*	−2.106***
	−16,177	−0.541	−0.453
N	4,188	4,188	4,188
Adjusted R-Squared	0.2528	0.3998	0.4801

Note: Standard errors in parentheses. Asterisks denote statistical significance: *10%, **5%, ***1%. All specifications include month-specific dummies, firm fixed effects, and post-treatment month*SFV interactions. Log of production corresponds to estimates with imputed minima to avoid the loss of zero production observations. Average Treatment Effect is the average of estimates of βk in equation (9.2).

Source: Rodríguez 2022b.

the treatment effect over the period of oil sanctions (from January 2019 until the end of the sample on June 2020), I get a somewhat stronger effect of 51.4 thousand barrels per day, or 54.2% of pre-sanctions production (p = .006). The logarithmic specification delivers a treatment effect of 66.0 log points, equivalent to a decline of 48.3% from the initial baseline, yet the statistical significance is milder (p = .053). When I use standardized levels as the dependent variable, the effect is slightly larger as a share of initial output: sanctions are associated with a 1.7 standard deviation drop in production, which evaluated at the SFV averages yields a 48.5% output drop, and statistical significance is much stronger (p = .000).[28]

In Rodríguez (2022b), I provide a battery of additional robustness tests of this specification. These include controlling for the nationality of the largest partner (which yields the interesting result that US firms were more protected from the impact of sanctions given the waivers approved by OFAC) and use of different pretreatment windows and trend specifications. All these variations produce consistent results, with several of them strengthening their statistical significance.

What do these estimates mean in terms of the economic magnitude of the effects? I estimate that sanctions can explain around 46% of the loss of production of SFV firms. SFV firms, however, accounted for only 47% of the production loss observed in the whole region, so these estimates can account directly only for around 21% of the observed loss of production in the region. Furthermore, the SFV model was much less extended in the non-Orinoco oil fields (for which the monthly data used in this estimation are not available), so this number is likely to be even smaller if applied to the country's whole oil sector. Nevertheless, it is worth highlighting that this number is far from meaningless in the current context: at current oil prices of $60 per barrel, this would represent $5.1 billion, enough money to nearly double the country's 2020 import bill of $6.5 billion.

One reason this estimate may be excessively conservative is that it assumes that the Maduro government would not have extended the SFV model more broadly in the absence of sanctions. However, given that the SFV model was yielding positive results in terms of production growth and that the Maduro government was expanding its use at the time, it seems safe to assume that in the absence of sanctions the government would have continued to make use of this type of arrangement to help offset the decline in production occurring in firms that lacked financial market access. More broadly, it is hard to imagine a scenario in which PDVSA would not have ultimately restructured its debt in the face of prohibitive financing costs for most of its production, allowing the whole firm to ultimately regain access to capital markets. A less conservative projection would be to estimate the effect of sanctions against a counterfactual in which all firms in the Orinoco Basin had obtained access to financing by adopting SFV modalities. In that case, the effect would rise to 678,000 barrels per day, or $14.8 billion at current prices.

Summary of Estimates

Table 9.3 summarizes the diverse quantitative estimates of the effects of financial and oil sanctions on Venezuela's oil production. Since many of the works cited highlight the magnitudes of losses in terms of barrels of oil production and revenue lost, it is tempting to compare these magnitudes across estimates. However, as table 9.3 shows, these methods have been applied to different samples in terms of time and sector coverage and in some cases estimate the impact of different events (e.g., financial vs. oil sanctions). Therefore, I also present a comparison across estimates in terms of the losses as a percent of pre-sanctions output and of the total observed decline in production over the sample studied.

TABLE 9.3. Summary of estimates of sanctions effects on oil production

Author	*Event*	*Estimation Technique*	*Sample*	*Period*	*Thousand Barrels per Day*	*% of Initial Output*	*% of Post-Sanctions Decline*	*% of Total Decline*
F. Rodríguez (2018)	2017 sanctions	Difference-in-differences with Colombia as a counterfactual	Whole country	August 2017 to August 2018	–468	–24.2	67.2	41.1
Rodríguez (2019b, this volume)	2017 sanctions	Difference-in-differences fixed effects regression on pairwise comparisons of Venezuela with 36 other oil-producing countries	Whole country	August 2017 to May 2019	–689	–35.6	58.7	42.6
Rodríguez (2019b, this volume)	2017 sanctions	Synthetic control	Whole country	August 2017 to December 2018	–797	–41.2	104.3	66.1
Rodríguez (2019b, this volume)	2019 sanctions	Cross-country panel data	Whole country	January 2019 to December 2020	–572	–49.7	79.5	–
Rodríguez (2019b, this volume)	2019 sanctions	Cross-country panel data	Whole country	January 2019 to December 2021	–594	–51.6	82.5	–
Oliveros (2020)	2017 sanctions	Linear extrapolation, lower bound (2% MoM decline)	Whole country	July 2017 to July 2020	–597	–30.8	37.2	29.4

(continues)

TABLE 9.3. Summary of estimates of sanctions effects on oil production (*continued*)

Author	*Event*	*Estimation Technique*	*Sample*	*Period*	*Thousand Barrels per Day*	*% of Initial Output*	*% of Post-Sanctions Decline*	*% of Total Decline*
Oliveros (2020)	2017 sanctions	Linear extrapolation, midrange (1.5% MoM decline)	Whole country	July 2017 to July 2020	−786	−40.6	49.0	38.7
Oliveros (2020)	2017 sanctions	Linear extrapolation, upper bound (1% MoM decline)	Whole country	July 2017 to July 2020	−1,012	−52.3	63.1	49.8
Equipo Anova (2021)	2017 sanctions	Trend interruption analysis	Whole country	August 2017 to December 2019	−698	−33.2	58.5	37.4
Rodríguez (2022b)	2017 sanctions	Difference-in-differences approach with firm-level data	Orinoco Basin SFVs	August 2017 to June 2020	−235	−41.4	46.1	42.0
					−276	−48.5	53.9	49.3
–	–	–	–	Median estimates	−597	−41.2	58.7	42.0

Source: Author's construction.

The range of absolute decline attributable to sanctions ranges from 235 tbd to 1,012 tbd, with an associated value of $5.1 to $22.1 billion in foregone revenues. If we use only national-level estimates, the range narrows to 468 to 1,012 tbd ($10.2–$22.1 billion). The estimated range of losses is also between 24% and 52% of pre-sanctions output. The median estimates of decline are 597 tbd ($13.1 billion) and 41% of pre-sanctions output.

What fraction of the collapse in the country's oil production can be attributed to sanctions, according to these estimates? The last two columns of table 9.3 present two estimates of this ratio. The first estimate is the fraction of the post-sanctions decline attributable to sanctions. This produces a range of 37% to 104%, with a median value of 59%.[29] However, calculating only the post-sanctions ratios disregards the decline in production that occurred prior to sanctions, which obviously cannot be attributed to sanctions. The second of these columns includes the pre-sanctions decline since 2012 in the denominator, calculating the sanctions effect as a share of the total decline observed between 2012 and the end of the sample. This provides a range of 29% to 66% for the fraction of the decline attributable to sanctions, with a median of 42%.[30] Were we reasonably certain that the effects of sanctions have been completely internalized by the end of the sample, the latter range would be the more accurate calculation. Since all these samples are truncated before the end of sanctions, the true value is likely to be somewhere in the middle of these two ranges.[31] In my calculations, I use the midpoint between these two medians, 50.3%, as an estimate of the share of oil production decline attributable to sanctions.

In sum, empirical estimates of the effect of sanctions on Venezuelan oil output produce a broad range of effects. Depending on the method used, sanctions event, sample of study, or period during which the decline is assessed, sanctions can explain between one-third and the totality of the observed decline. The central tendency of the estimates presented in table 9.3 suggests that sanctions can explain around half of the decline in oil production.

In my discussion in chapter 2, I argued that one of the main drivers of Venezuela's output decline was the reduction in the country's import capacity. This reduction was in turn caused by the decline in oil exports, as well as the loss of access to international capital markets. Oil price declines account for around two-fifths of the decline in oil revenues, with declines in production accounting for the other three-fifths. If sanctions explain around half of the decline in oil production, that means that they explain roughly one-third of the total decline in oil revenues, with nonsanctions causes explaining the other two-thirds.

I return to these numbers later. For now, it is important to bear in mind that although sanctions may explain one-third of the decline in oil revenues, it does not mean that they explain the same share of the decline in output. This is because the loss of access to international capital markets and the decline in productivity also affect output. I already presented evidence in support of the idea that sanctions were associated with the post-2016 decline in productivity in chapter 2. In the rest of this chapter, I discuss how sanctions played a key role in Venezuela's permanent loss of access to capital markets; chapter 10 develops the idea that sanctions and other politically motivated foreign policy actions led Venezuela to lose access to its offshore assets and multilateral finance. I take up the discussion of the aggregate effect of sanctions relative to that of other contributing causes in chapter 10.

Revisiting the Effect of Financial Sanctions

One popular argument among sanctions skeptics holds that the 2017 sanctions could not have affected the Venezuelan economy because the government had already lost access to international capital markets on the eve of sanctions, making an eventual default inevitable (Bahar et al. 2019; Hausmann and Muci 2019; Zambrano 2018). We can call this argument the redundancy hypothesis because it contends that financial sanctions targeted borrowing that was not accessible to the country or the oil industry at the time and were thus irrelevant.

This argument is problematic for several reasons. I have already discussed one of them: the evidence that key parts of the Venezuelan oil industry, including the joint ventures with foreign oil partners in which production was growing prior to 2017, did have access to international financing before sanctions and that prohibiting that access severely hurt them. Another reason is that even if we accept that a Venezuela default would have occurred in the absence of sanctions, sanctions precluded a restructuring of the country's debt and thus caused a much more costly permanent loss of access to capital markets. A third reason is that, given that oil prices recovered strongly in the 2017 to 2019 period, it is not difficult to map out a scenario in which the country continued to service its debt had oil revenues not been negatively affected by sanctions.

Let's return to the first of these points. While it may be true that unsecured lending to PDVSA and the Republic was not available at reasonable rates at the time sanctions were imposed, this does not mean that the country's oil industry was wholly cut off from financing access. The firm-level results on joint ventures in the Orinoco Basin discussed in the previous section demonstrate the existence of channels at the time through which an important part of the country's oil production suffered the effects of the loss of access to financing. The SFV deals described in table 9.1, some of which were concluded as late as the end of 2016, provide a clear example of financing access that was obtainable at reasonable rates and to which sanctions closed the door.

Another example regards the refinancing of commercial debt. In 2015, PDVSA began refinancing its arrears with service providers such as General Electric, Halliburton, and Schlumberger through the issuance of New York law promissory notes at 6.5% interest. By mid-2017, PDVSA had issued and remained current on at least $3.2 billion of these promissory notes. US financial sanctions had two effects on these arrangements: they stopped the company from issuing new notes, and they barred holders of these notes from trading them—unless they obtained an OFAC license to do so—thus generating large losses for the firms that had accepted to refinance PDVSA debt through these mechanisms. Blocking PDVSA's attempts to deal with provider debt was bound to influence the willingness of PDVSA's providers to continue to engage with it.

Both modalities illustrate how credit is interconnected with the production process. External finance is costly in the presence of informational asymmetries because creditors cannot easily verify whether a default occurs as a result of a project's inherent risk or the debtor's decision not to pay (Smith 1987). One way in which borrowers can resolve these informational asymmetries is by entering into joint ventures, which give external investors equity together with some level of operational control and access to information (Balakrishnan and Koza 1993). This can be done either by jointly operating production processes (as in the SFV arrangements) or by outsourcing some production processes to external suppliers (as in the suppliers paid with the New York law promissory notes). Suppliers can extend trade credit at rates that would not be agreed to by financial intermediaries because of their informational advantage and capacity to control assets that are required for production (Bernanke and Gertler 1989). An extreme way to resolve the informational asymmetry is by fully collateralizing loans, yet this is often difficult if not impossible to do for sovereign or quasi-sovereign debtors.

In other words, modern finance is commingled with a set of other activities that are essential to production. Trade credit is often a necessary by-product of relations with vendors. While the August 2017 sanctions carved out exceptions for trade credit of less than ninety days, there is substantial evidence that these exceptions were far from sufficient to protect trade-related loans. Even CITGO, the PDVSA-owned US refining arm that was immediately granted a license excepting it from sanctions, began having trouble obtaining routine trade credit after sanctions were imposed (Parraga and Ngai 2017). The short-term debt exception was also insufficient to cover part of PDVSA trade credit and completely ruled out the conversion of trade credit arrears into financial debt that was being carried out by PDVSA at the time. The exception also became moot after the January 2019 designation of PDVSA impeded any type of dealings with the firm.

However, let us for the sake of argument say that Venezuela's oil industry had no capital market access in 2017. Sanctions did not just impede the country from accessing capital markets at the time. They barred it from accessing capital markets for as long as sanctions were in place. For all relevant purposes, this meant that the Maduro government permanently lost access to capital markets, including the access necessary to restructure the country's debt to bring it in line with its capacity to pay. To argue that sanctions were redundant, one would have to argue not just that Venezuela would have eventually defaulted in the absence of sanctions. One would have to argue that it would never have restructured its debt.[32]

Such a counterfactual is particularly problematic because once governments lose access to capital markets, one of two things eventually happens: either they regain that access owing to changes in external conditions and/or policy reforms, or they enter debt restructuring negotiations that bring down their debt to levels compatible with sustainability. Scenarios in which governments spend several years shut out of capital markets are relatively rare.[33]

Thus, even if one agrees that a Venezuelan default was highly likely as of late 2017, it does not follow that the most reasonable counterfactual scenario would have included a prolonged period during which the country's oil industry would have been unable to access international financing. Sanctions ensured that absence by impeding any issuance of new debt, including the exchange of old bonds for new bonds through which debt restructurings typically occur. While the timing of sanctions is what helps us identify its effect empirically, it is the way in which they permanently sever the links between the country and international financial markets that makes them particularly damaging.

In contrast, there are clear signs that the Venezuelan government was seriously considering a debt restructuring at the time of sanctions. In September 2016, when PDVSA offered to exchange maturing unsecured debt for collateralized bonds, its president told creditors that if they did not accept the deal, the company might not be able to continue honoring its debt.[34] More explicit attempts at restructuring were put forward in subsequent years. Less than three months after the imposition of the 2017 sanctions, the Venezuelan government announced the creation of a commission to restructure Venezuela's debt. The commission produced no results, largely because US investors were legally barred from negotiating with it.[35] A September 2020 offer by the Maduro government to renegotiate existing debt bonds by waiving the statute of limitations on creditor legal actions—a move that would have been unambiguously positive for creditors—also met with a tepid response, given that from a legal standpoint any such change would have had to have been signed off on by Guaidó to be valid before US courts (Laya and Yapur 2020).

Ultimately, an even more serious problem with the redundancy hypothesis is that it is hard to explain why the United States would adopt a set of policies that had no effect on the Venezuelan government's access to resources. That is, if we believe Venezuela would have lacked access to any type of financing even in the absence of sanctions, then we must conclude that Donald Trump's August 2017 executive order, which barred transactions that would not have taken place, was essentially irrelevant. It is hard to understand why the Trump administration would have chosen to respond to Maduro's decision to conduct the 2017 elections for the Constitutional Convention with a decision that had no effect on the choice set of the Venezuelan government.

Statements by high-ranking Trump administration officials at the moment of the adoption of sanctions clearly indicate that US authorities believed that the actions significantly curtailed the Maduro regime's access to resources. At a press briefing held immediately after the publication of Executive Order 13808, National Security Advisor H. R. McMaster stated that the ban "strongly punishes the Venezuelan regime. . . . Through the President's strong action, the United States will target the means with which the Maduro dictatorship can accumulate debt to enrich its corrupt regime insiders and perpetuate its repressive behavior"(Gearan and Faiola 2017). Treasury Secretary Steven Mnuchin added that "Maduro may no longer take advantage of the American financial system to facilitate the wholesale looting of the Venezuelan economy at the expense of the Venezuelan people" (Sánchez and Goodman 2017). According to the redundancy hypothesis, these statements must reflect either ignorance or deliberate misrepresentation of the consequences of their actions by high-ranking US officials.

At least one high-ranking official of the Guaidó administration also went on record to indicate that sanctions were severely affecting the functioning of Venezuela's offshore subsidiaries. In April 2019, John Bilbao, a former PDVSA official who had been fired by Chávez in 2003, was appointed president of PDVSA-owned Monómeros, Colombia's largest producer of fertilizers, by Guaidó. On June 6, Bilbao told the *Financial Times* that his most pressing concern was getting US sanctions lifted. The company had swung from net profits of $20 million in 2016 to net losses of $23 million in 2018, after financial sanctions (and before oil sanctions) were imposed. According to Bilbao in early 2019, if sanctions were lifted, Monómeros could turn to produce a profit that same year. This, in fact, was what happened: sanctions were lifted in June, and the company posted earnings of $8 million in the second half of 2019 (Becerra 2020).

Was a Venezuela Default Inevitable? Ask Markets

Would Venezuela have defaulted anyway in the absence of sanctions? Would that default have been as traumatic as the one that took place, and what would have been its broader economic implications? Any answer to this question is fraught with speculation. Would Maduro have maintained the import cuts that had been carried out to that moment, even if he had the option of raising imports by saving on debt service? Would the government have implemented price reforms (such as those it ultimately started adopting toward the end of 2018)? Would it have engaged in a debt restructuring, and would such a restructuring have taken the country's debt to sustainable levels?

Sovereign debt analysts distinguish between a government's capacity and its willingness to service its debt. The actions taken by the Maduro government until 2017 signaled a strong willingness to pay. In fact, many of the criticisms leveled at Maduro from the opposition were due to his apparent willingness to prioritize debt payments above other obligations. Assessing capacity is a trickier question. *Ex post*, we know that the collapse in oil production would have made continuing to service the debt impossible. What we don't know is how much of that collapse would have occurred in the absence of sanctions. The estimates presented in this chapter have shown a broad range of effects, including some in which the quantity of barrels exported would not have declined significantly in the absence of sanctions.

Consider the magnitude of the recovery in oil revenues that would have been reaped if Venezuela had not seen a post-sanctions decline in oil production. Between the first half of 2017 and the second half of 2018, Venezuelan oil prices rose from $43.6 to $64.9 per barrel. Taking the August 2017 production level as a reference, this implies that Venezuela would have been able to reap $15.0 billion in additional oil revenues from increased oil prices, far more than the $9.0 billion of service on its bonds that it was scheduled to pay in 2018. Those additional oil revenues should have significantly improved the country's access to financing in 2018 in the absence of sanctions, making a default less likely, as well as improving the conditions under which the government could have refinanced or restructured its debt. Even if we assume that oil production would have declined in the absence of sanctions at 41% of its rate of eventual decline (the median estimate for the effect of sanctions in table 9.2), the government would still have reaped an increase of $8.5 billion in revenues from higher oil sales, so that it would not have had to cut imports any more in order to maintain debt service payments. If the government managed to avert default with oil prices in the $30s, one could argue, there was no reason to jump to the conclusion that a default, much less a prolonged default (i.e., one that was not followed by a successful restructuring), would have become inevitable when oil prices were in the $60s.

Another way to answer this question without relying on subjective hypothetical scenarios is by asking what probability markets would have assigned to the likelihood of default in the absence of sanctions. As I argued in chapter 8, around the time of the imposition of sanctions, the correlations between key asset prices and economic fundamentals in Venezuela broke down. While yields on Venezuelan sovereign debt typically declined with higher oil prices—reflecting the market's assessment that changes in the country's capacity to pay were a key determinant of default probabilities—this stopped being the case in 2017, as market yields rose even as oil prices recovered.

Figure 9.8 revisits this finding by looking at more precise market valuations of default probabilities through the price of five-year insurance contracts against a Venezuelan default—also called credit default swaps (CDSs). While country risk and CDS prices are obviously related, they are not identical. Bond prices can be affected by the liquidity of each instrument as well as the expected recovery values after default. For example, if the market believes that a country is under a particular type of stress that will impede it from making bond payments in the near future, yet also expects it to try to cure that default quickly, its CDS prices can shoot up much more rapidly than the return on its bonds.

CDS prices, therefore, provide us with the most precise measure of the market's expectation of a default event and can thus help us evaluate the extent to which markets saw a default as inevitable—and how this perception was influenced by oil prices. As figure 9.8 shows, investors were willing to offer insurance on Venezuelan debt for around 1,000 basis points (10% of the nominal value of the insured debt) during the period up to late 2014 when oil prices were at around $100. As oil prices fall to around $40 per barrel in early 2015, the cost of insuring against default rose sharply, spiking to more than 9,000 basis points at the

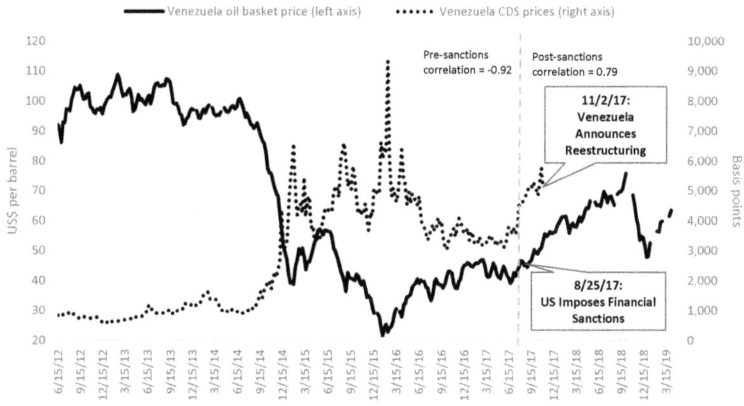

FIGURE 9.8. Venezuela oil prices and Credit Default Swap prices. *Source*: Author's construction using Bloomberg 2018d, 2021a.

moment at which oil prices reached their minimum of $22 per barrel at the start of 2016.

Yet as oil prices began to recover into the mid-$40s—and the government defeated predictions of default despite the oil price stress—CDS costs fell to around 4,000 basis points, or less than half their peaks of early 2016. This is still a high number, but $40 per barrel is also a relatively low oil price. What is interesting about the data is that prior to the adoption of US sanctions, it displays a very strong negative correlation between oil prices and perceived default probabilities, with the correlation coefficient at -.93 (similar to what we saw in chapter 8 regarding bond spreads). This correlation breaks down completely after sanctions are imposed: between August and November 2017, oil prices recover strongly, but CDS prices continue to rise, with the correlation in this period now at +.79. This suggests that the market began to see oil prices as irrelevant to the occurrence of a default after the adoption of the sanctions, as it understood that the sanctions were likely to drive the country into a default regardless of the evolution of the oil market.[36]

What the data are thus telling us is that in the absence of sanctions, one should have expected Venezuelan default probabilities and the cost of financing to the government to have declined as oil prices improved. Consider, for example, what we would have expected to happen with the CDS price if the pre-sanctions correlation of -.93 had been sustained into the post-sanctions period. By the end of 2018, as oil prices topped $70, this correlation would have predicted CDS prices to fall to around 2,500 basis points. The implicit five-year probability of default associated with a CDS price of 2,500 basis points is 36%—or an annual default probability of 8.5%.[37] While the market would have continued to be concerned about the probability of a default event, its most likely scenario would have been one in which Venezuela escaped default.

Credit market prices thus suggest that in the absence of sanctions, markets would have expected Venezuela to avoid a traumatic default once oil prices recovered. They thus are consistent with an interpretation in which the default, as well as the subsequent prolonged suspension of access to credit markets, was caused by the imposition of sanctions and the broader process of politically induced toxification of Venezuelan financial markets.

THE LIMITS TO MAXIMUM PRESSURE

A Spotty Record

Venezuela was a prominent example of what came to be known as the Trump administration's "maximum pressure" approach to sanctions. The phrase, which appears to have been originally coined to describe its initial approach to nuclear negotiations with North Korea, reflected the belief that there was a monotonic relationship between the intensity of sanctions and their effectiveness at reaching their intended ends (Pennington 2017).[38] According to this approach, sanctions policy should close off all existing loopholes and tighten restrictions, as only by making the target government pay a higher cost will it be incentivized to give up. The goal of sanctions should be to "make life as burdensome as possible for the elite" (Hausmann and Morales-Arilla 2021). The underlying premise is that sanctions create pain for the receiving regime and that increasing this pain will increase the likelihood that the target will concede.[39]

The Trump administration regularly used the phrase to refer to its approach in cases as diverse as North Korea, Iran, Syria, and Venezuela. Trump used OFAC designations much more intensively than any previous US administration, with additions to the OFAC list of SDNs growing 50% with respect to the previous four years and net designations (designations minus delistings) expanding almost tenfold (figs. 9.9, 9.10). Venezuela sanctions—which were, from a numerical and economic standpoint, negligible up to 2017—were one contributor to this increase but far from the only one.

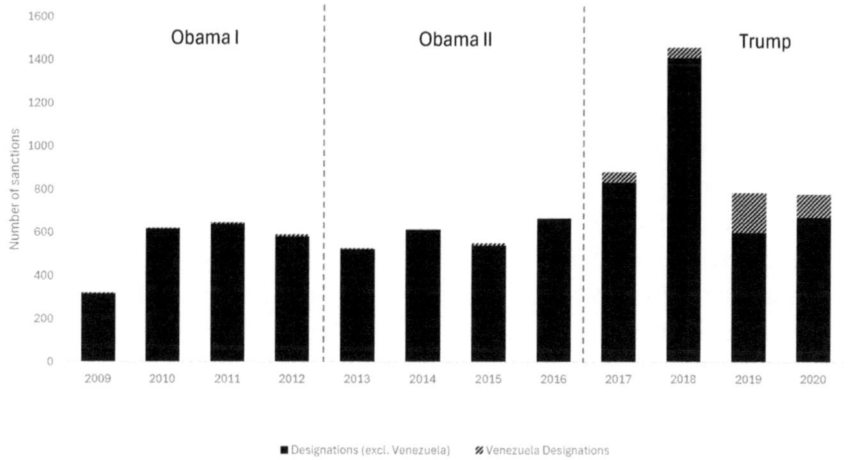

FIGURE 9.9. Global and Venezuela OFAC designations by administration, 2009–2020. *Source*: Author's construction using OFAC 2023c.

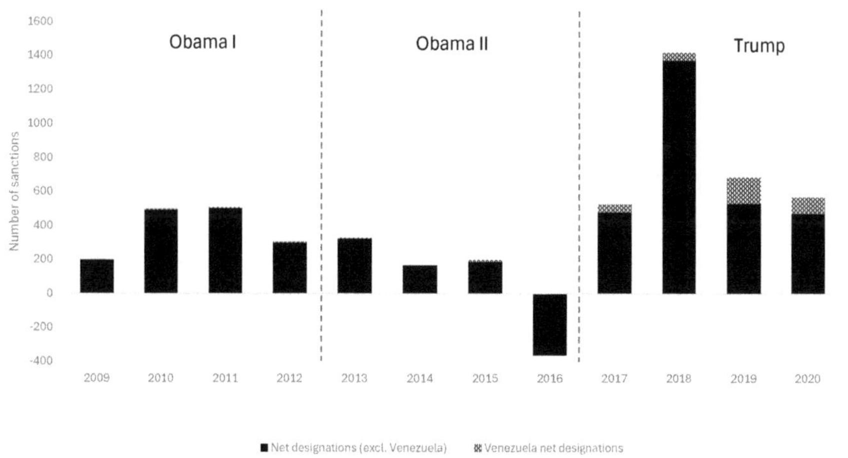

FIGURE 9.10. Global and Venezuela OFAC net designations by administration, 2009–2020. *Source*: Author's construction using OFAC 2023c.

It is by now clear that the strategy did not attain its stated objective of forcing Maduro to abandon power.[40] Of course, some hold the view that the opposition's bargaining power is higher than it would be without sanctions. Any discussion about the effectiveness of sanctions in specific cases is, in any case, a discussion about counterfactuals, and it is always possible to construct a reasonable alternative scenario in which things would be even worse if the intervention in question had not been carried out. Yet it is uncontestable that the maximum pressure approach failed to live up to the expectation that it could produce, in Senator Marco Rubio's words, "a big foreign-policy win" (quoted in Bolton 2020, 254).

The failure of the maximum pressure strategy will not come as a surprise to those familiar with the literature on the effectiveness of sanctions. By and large, cross-national studies find that while sanctions can be successful in reaching their intended ends in some instances, in most cases they fail to do so. One landmark study found that only 34% of sanctions were effective in attaining their intended policy goal (Hufbauer et al. 1990, 2007). Even this moderate indication of success has been disputed. Some scholars have argued that most of these success cases occurred amid other more relevant actions, including military interventions; once these are taken into account, the success rate declines even further.[41]

The finding of a poor success rate of sanctions is interesting, yet leaves many questions open. Ultimately a success rate is only meaningful if compared with its counterpart in a counterfactual scenario in which sanctions are not imposed. In other words, even if sanctions are successful in only one-third of cases, they may not be an unreasonable policy choice if the chances of obtaining success without sanctions is zero; alternatively, if success is obtained in a third of cases even without sanctions, then the marginal effect of sanctions could be negligible, nonexistent, or even negative. Furthermore, if the aim of sanctions is deterrence of similar actions by other actors who may be tempted to pursue them in the absence of punishment, then we may not expect to find strong results in changes in the conduct of targeted entities yet may find it in the conduct of those who were deterred by the sanctions.

Some empirical work has focused on understanding the correlates of sanctions success. It finds that sanctions are more likely to be successful when their policy goals are modest, when there are good relations between the sanctioning and the sanctioned country prior to the sanctions, when the economic cost imposed by the sanctions is large, and when the sanctioned country is more democratic (Dashti-Gibson, Davis, and Radcliff 1997; Hufbauer et al. 2007; Lektzian and Souva 2007; Kavakli, Chatagnier, and Hatipoglu 2019).

Venezuela sanctions had almost none of the characteristics of successful sanctions. Their demands were not moderate but rather maximalist. By focusing on regime change, they backed the regime into a corner, giving it little option but to do everything possible to hold on to power. The regime they were imposed on was hostile to the sanctioning country to begin with—in contrast, say, to the case of Apartheid-era South Africa, whose elite saw the United States and Europe as role models and where the imposition of anti-Apartheid sanctions forced it to rethink its view of itself. Nor was there an effective mechanism for voters to punish the sanctioned regime by voting it out of office as, say, happened with Nicaragua's Sandinistas in the 1990 election.[42]

A key conceptual problem in the maximum pressure approach regards the fact that the policy focuses on increasing the cost to the regime of the status quo but appears to disregard what happens to payoffs outside of the status quo. Making life as burdensome as possible for the members of the government elite can cause them to change their conduct only if they can remove that burden by conceding. But what if sanctions push down the payoffs of the targets both in the scenario in which they yield and in the one in which they do not? How can making Maduro's life in power more difficult convince him to step down if he is certain that he will go to jail once he gives up power? And what if sanctions, by convincing relevant stakeholders that the target has engaged in reprehensible acts, increase the likelihood that the target will be jailed *unless* he can cling to power? Perversely, sanctions may in such a scenario make the target even less likely to yield to the sanctioner's demands.[43]

A User's Guide to "Smart" Sanctions

Defenders of the maximum pressure approach may contend that it was never their intention to convince Maduro of anything. Rather, sanctions aimed at generating selective incentives for power holders to withdraw their support of the regime. This explains why personal sanctions formed such an important part of the approach and why the United States openly voiced and reiterated its willingness to lift sanctions on regime insiders who withdrew their support for Maduro.[44] Yet while it is true that targeted personal sanctions can in principle be designed to generate incentives for defection from regime loyalists, they also run the risk of having the opposite effect if they are not well calibrated.

To think through these arguments, it is useful to discuss a simple model of individual sanctions.[45] Consider an authoritarian regime in which a subgroup of the population can determine who holds power. In a democracy, this is known as the electorate, and the mechanism through which this determination occurs is that of periodic elections. In a nondemocratic state, this is what political scientists call the "selectorate" (Bueno de Mesquita et al. 2004). In order to remain in power, a leader must count on the support of a minimum winning coalition of the selectorate. Let the members of the selectorate differ in terms of their proximity to the regime. Members with greater proximity to the regime derive greater benefits from the status quo. These benefits can be economic but can also be purely political or even symbolic. What sanctions do is impose an individual-specific cost on the selectorate members who support the regime.[46]

Therefore, we can think of a sanction as a cost that is imposed on a member of the selectorate who supports the regime and that is not imposed on a member who does not support the regime. This conditionality of the reward on the member's action can happen in one of two ways. Either a selectorate member who does not support the regime avoids the sanction and its associated costs, or a member who was supporting the regime changes sides and gets the sanction lifted. From a theoretical standpoint, these choices are equivalent, as long as we can take at face value the sanctioning government's claim that sanctions are conditional on actions. In any case, the aim of sanctions is to generate a sufficiently high cost of supporting the regime to make the number of selectorate members backing the regime fall below the minimum winning coalition.

This dynamic is illustrated in figure 9.11, which represents the benefits from the status quo for selectorate members and the reward from defection implicit in the sanctions. The higher the reward, the greater the defections. Let R be the individual-specific cost of the sanction,

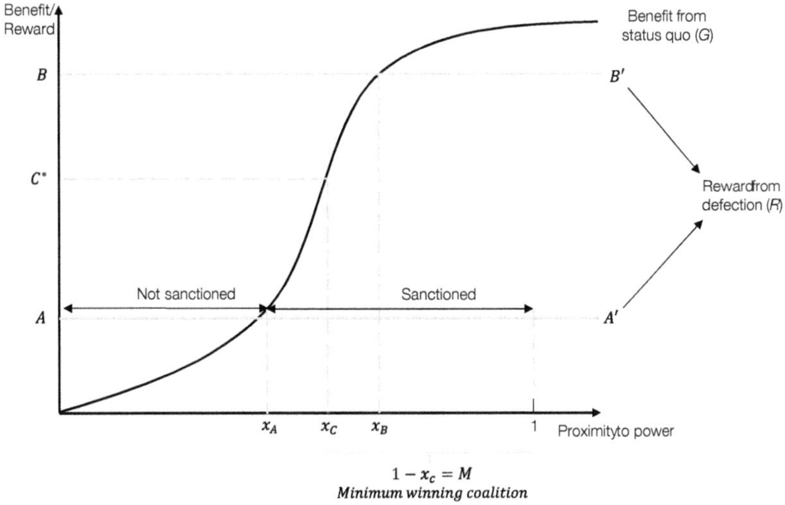

FIGURE 9.11. Effect of sanctions on members of the selectorate. *Source*: Author's construction.

and let *G* be the benefit that the individual receives from the status quo (a benefit that can only be enjoyed if they support the regime). It follows that individuals for whom $R > G$ will not support the regime and thereby avoid sanctions; individuals for whom $G > R$, in contrast, will continue supporting the regime and end up sanctioned.

I illustrate two possible sanctions levels: one (*A*) that is insufficient to force enough defections to generate regime change and another (*B*) that is large enough to provoke enough defections so as to make the regime unable to count on the support of a minimum winning coalition. *A* appears to be the equilibrium that Venezuela is stuck in: extensive use of sanctions and a regime that maintains the support of a coalition that is sufficiently large to allow it to stay in power.

Why not just raise sanctions to the level C^* or higher needed to generate a break in the minimum winning coalition and thus force the regime to abandon power? Isn't this precisely what "maximum pressure" is supposed to entail? One reason this may not be so simple is that it is costly. It requires giving a reward of *C* to X_c defectors. The total cost of this strategy, $C \cdot X_c$, may exceed the benefits that the sanctioning country would derive from regime change. Therefore, the optimal strategy for the sanctioner may be to impose sanctions at a lower level such as

A. In equilibrium, $(1 - X_A)$ members of the selectorate are sanctioned, X_A defect, and the regime manages to hold on to power as $(1 - X_A) > M$, the minimum size of the winning coalition.

To understand why this may be a valid explanation for the failure of regime change efforts, it's worth considering in more detail what the reward from defection is. As explained earlier in this chapter, the standard US sanction involves freezing of assets through inclusion in OFAC's SDN list. Avoiding these sanctions could mean maintaining access to their funds and the capacity to make transactions in the US financial system. This may be a sizable incentive for some members of the selectorate. However, government officials—or their associates—with large deposits in the US financial system are likely to have obtained these funds through corrupt practices and therefore likely to be subject to other risks independent from individual sanctions. It is thus unclear that even if they were to regain access to their funds abroad, they would be able to use them unhindered. They would likely be liable to prosecution under the Foreign Corrupt Practices Act or other laws associated with drug trafficking or money laundering. For other officials who in the absence of sanctions would not have had assets in the United States anyway (either because they are honest or because they decided to stash the money elsewhere), this reward from avoiding sanctions is negligible or irrelevant.

Of course, there may be much more than meets the eye in the rewards offered to key officials who defect. At the limit, the United States or its associates could offer them substantial economic rewards using covert funds, for example. But the challenges associated with setting up such a reward structure today are significant. For starters, public opinion is unlikely to take kindly to having monetary rewards being offered to human rights violators. The point is that raising the rewards to defectors can be not only economically but also politically costly. There is thus a limit in practice to how high R can be made.

In principle, one could also try to lower the benefits to selectorate members from the status quo. An extreme case of this is a military intervention that makes life literally impossible for regime insiders. But the costs associated with these actions—and the appetite of foreign policy makers to contemplate them—are significant. This puts us back in the territory in which the sanctioner is unwilling to pay the costs necessary to generate regime change.

In the absence of a full-scale military intervention, other tools available to reduce selectorate member benefits under the status quo are often too blunt. If the regime stays in power, a nondefecting member of the selectorate will likely enjoy significant benefits regardless of the external pressure. The government is, after all, playing essentially the same game: it is designing the benefits function to target rewards to its minimum winning coalition. Wide-ranging economic sanctions may thus limit the ability of the government to reward its coalition but at a very high cost to the population at large. Even then, it is unlikely that economic sanctions have the capacity to make a sufficiently large part of regime insiders miserable enough to lead them to prefer a situation in which they lose power.

Another reason it is difficult to raise R is because of the lack of capacity of the sanctioning country, or of the political coalition that it seeks to favor, to make credible commitments. While it may be possible to promise key regime insiders significant benefits to betray the regime, it is unclear that the sanctioner will have any incentive to live up to that promise once the regime loses power. In fact, it is probable that neither the United States nor the opposition has the capacity to stop trials against regime officials for corruption or human rights abuses from going forward in the event of a transition, even if they wanted to do so. If they had that capacity, it is not clear that they would want to use it once the regime has lost power. Rational regime insiders are likely to be able to infer this and will thus treat any promises of rewards upon defection as noncredible.

One way credible promises can be made to regime defectors is by promising them power in a transition. This, in fact, appears to have been the thinking behind US actions to support the attempted military rebellion against Maduro of April 30, 2019. Key regime insiders, including Defense Minister Vladimir Padrino and Chief Supreme Court Justice Maikel Moreno, are said to have participated (or to have claimed to be participating) in the conspiracy, which would have ensured that they could have been in a position of power after pushing Maduro out. If successful, they could have had the possibility of retaining their current roles or even having more prominent roles in the transition government. This would have given them a reasonable degree of protection against prosecution for their alleged crimes and would have offered them the prospect of key roles in a legitimate transitional government—presumably a much better agreement than their roles in the current pariah de facto government.

However, these benefits can only materialize if the conspiracy is successful. Put differently, defectors don't just have to take a personal decision to defect; they also must solve a coordination problem among themselves. This coordination problem can be very difficult to solve not just because of the inherent difficulties of these situations (e.g., incentives to free ride) but also because coordinating is potentially dangerous. Participants in a failed conspiracy can be sure that the regime will ruthlessly punish them. Potential conspirators may prefer to become regime informants than run the risk of spending the rest of their lives in the regime's torture chambers. There is very little that sanctions can do to help potential defectors solve this coordination problem.

SURGICAL STRIKE

The evidence presented in this chapter strongly supports the contention that financial and trade sanctions imposed on the Venezuelan government and state-owned entities starting from 2017 on had significant effects on the country's economic crisis. Sanctions strongly impacted the country's oil sector, hampering its capacity to fund its operations and investment and blocking access to traditional markets and inputs. The high oil dependence of the Venezuelan economy ensured that such a surgical strike against its oil sector would have catastrophic effects on the broader economy, by depriving the country of what was essentially its only source of foreign currency revenue.

That Venezuela's poor economic policies played a significant role in the country's deep recession between 2013 and 2016 is not under discussion. Because of its lack of savings and investment during the oil boom, Venezuela was particularly unprepared for a strong adverse terms of trade shock like the one it suffered in this period. It was thus inevitable that a collapse in oil prices would translate into deep import cuts and economic contraction.

The post-2017 contraction, however, is a different animal. Recovering oil prices would have typically been expected to lead to import recovery and some recovery in growth. This recovery never happened because of the ensuing collapse of oil production, which was to a significant extent driven by successive rounds of economic sanctions.

Sanctions are only one of the factors that made it increasingly costly for foreign economic actors to do business with Venezuela. Financial and commercial toxification resulted from the escalation into full-fledged economically destructive political conflict. The decision by both sides of the political spectrum to embrace scorched earth political strategies in their struggle for power would lead to the progressive severing of the country's trade and financial links to the rest of the world. Things would only get worse when global oil and financial markets weren't even able to know which government of Venezuela they were supposed to do business with. I turn now to that story.

TEN

Politicians without Borders

We can't do it alone. We face an international criminal conglomerate.
Today, we need your help.
—Juan Guaidó, Davos World Economic Forum, 2019

OF PENS AND PODIUMS

On the evening of February 6, 2018, a swarm of reporters waited expectantly in the lobby of the Dominican Republic's Ministry of Foreign Affairs for representatives of Venezuela's government and opposition. The ministry had announced hours earlier that the main conference room of its building would be the site of the signing of a political agreement that would pave the way for the opposition to participate in that year's presidential elections.

This was far from the first time that the government and the opposition had entered into formal negotiations. Some instances of past negotiations had had the support of international mediators and at times had resulted in partial agreements.[1] Yet the Dominican Republic talks were different in at least one formal aspect: they marked the first time that these talks took place outside of the country and were formally hosted by another government.

The negotiations had grown out of the attempt by UNASUR to host talks in Caracas in 2016, which I discussed in chapter 8.[2] UNASUR had enlisted the help of three respected former presidents—Spain's José Luis Rodríguez Zapatero, the Dominican Republic's Leonel Fernández, and Panama's Martín Torrijos—to lower tensions and broker an agreement. Initially, both the United States and the European Union had backed the talks (Alarcón 2016; EFE 2016).

As I discussed previously, this mediation effort had gained brief prominence when it enlisted the support of the Vatican and managed to get the sides to negotiate in November 2016, following opposition protests in response to the invalidation of the recall referendum drive. Yet those talks collapsed almost immediately amid confusions and acrimonious recriminations, with opposition leaders upset at having been outmaneuvered into suspending street demonstrations. An attempt to revive the talks was launched in September 2017, with the Dominican Republic offering to host them and four other governments in the region agreeing to act as a "group of friends" that would commit to monitoring compliance with any agreements reached (*El Comercio* 2017).

The urgency of the talks was evident given the upcoming presidential elections, constitutionally mandated to be held in 2018. In January, the government upped the ante by bringing forward the elections—which had normally been held between August and December—to no later than April 30 through a decision of the National Constitutional Convention (ANC) (BBC Mundo 2018; *El Observador* 2018; Infobae 2018). The opposition insisted that there were insufficient conditions to guarantee the transparency of the vote and demanded electoral reforms as a pre-condition for participating (América Noticias 2018).

Following weeks of negotiations, facilitators claimed that the parties had converged on an agreement. The agreement included the appointment by consensus of two new electoral council board members to the five-member board, a request to the United Nations secretary general to form an electoral observation mission, guarantees of equal access to media, technical audits using standards similar to those of the 2015 elections, and the opening of a special period for registering voters abroad. It also mentioned a tentative date of April 22 for the elections. The agreement also referred to nonelectoral issues, including the establishment of a truth commission to investigate human rights violations, joint efforts to revert unilateral economic sanctions, and a mechanism for coexistence between the National Assembly and the ANC (Ministerio del Poder Popular para la Comunicación y Información 2018; *Tal Cual* 2018a).[3]

Yet there were signs of stress in the opposition. Popular Will, the party of the former Chacao mayor Leopoldo López, who had been jailed on charges of inciting violence in the 2014 protests, had decided to sit out the talks, and some other hard-line leaders were openly critical of negotiations (EFE 2018; Florido 2018). The agreement did not comply with some opposition demands—such as lifting the bans on electoral participation by key opposition leaders including López and Capriles—which many saw as crucial. Without these figures, the opposition had not yet converged on a candidate or a mechanism to choose one. The announcement by mediators that an agreement had been reached caused some surprise and substantial anticipation.

Dominican president Danilo Medina and Spain's Zapatero arrived at the Convention Center shortly after 4:00 p.m. on February 6. They were followed a few minutes later by the Venezuelan government's delegation, led by Communications Minister Jorge Rodríguez, who confirmed to reporters that an agreement had been reached and waved a pen in the air indicating that he was ready to sign (*El Nuevo Diario* 2018). Yet as the afternoon dragged on, it was clear that something was wrong. The lead opposition negotiator, former National Assembly president Julio Borges, arrived almost two hours later and denied to reporters that an agreement had been reached. When asked about the table and pens that had been set up for the signing event, he responded, "There may be a table, there may be pens, but what's missing is the truth, which is nothing else than the rights of Venezuelans" (García 2018).

A tense calm ensued as government and opposition negotiators met behind closed doors. At around 8:00 p.m., ministry staff quietly withdrew the pens that had been placed in front of the two chairs where government and opposition representatives would have sat. At around 10:00 p.m., the foreign minister of Chile—one of the two governments selected by the opposition as its allies in the group of friends—tweeted, "Enormous pressures for the Venezuelan opposition to sign a piece of paper that does not contemplate guarantees for the presidential elections.

Pdt Maduro in campaign, opposition parties disqualified, banned candidates, etc. Would any Chilean party accept that?" (Muñoz 2018).

Just before 11:00 p.m., the head government negotiator, Jorge Rodríguez, spoke to the press showing a draft agreement, reiterating the government's claim that the document had been agreed to by both parties the previous night and accusing the opposition of backtracking due to US pressures. Rodríguez claimed that Borges had refused to sign after receiving a call from US Secretary of State Rex Tillerson, who was visiting Colombia at the time (Telesur 2018). The government delegation went on to publicly sign the draft agreement unilaterally. Around midnight, Borges spoke, saying that the opposition had never agreed to the document and warning that the opposition would not sign an agreement that sacrificed Venezuelans' constitutional rights (*Tal Cual* 2018a).

Although mediators made a last-minute attempt to revive the talks, it soon became clear that they had reached an impasse. The opposition presented a counterproposal, which more fully spelled out electoral guarantees. Its key difference with the one signed by the government was in two points: it did not mention a date for the election but deferred the setting of the schedule to after the initiation of the UN-led electoral observation mission, and it called for the immediate lifting of participation bans on López, Capriles, and their parties.[4] Two days later, Maduro formally signed the draft agreement previously subscribed to by his negotiators, while the opposition reiterated its decision to reject it, arguing that it was inconsistent with the basic conditions for free and fair elections (Europa Press 2018). Dominican president Danilo Medina said the talks had entered into an "indefinite recess" (Hernández 2017).

DITCHING ELECTORAL COMPETITION

The MUD coalition would go on to boycott the presidential vote, which took place on May 20. The decision was controversial, causing one of the MUD's main leaders, former governor Henri Falcón, to break ranks with the coalition and stage his own presidential bid with the support of some centrist parties. However, despite having the backing of a handful of prominent opposition leaders,[5] Falcón's candidacy stumbled on lack of resources and organization. Despite some favorable showings in preelection polls, Falcón's bare-bones organization was no match for Chavismo when the time came to get out the vote. Maduro was able to easily defeat Falcón, garnering 68% of the vote to Falcón's 21%, with Javier Bertucci, an evangelical pastor, taking the remaining 11% of the vote.

Maduro's large margin of victory, however, masks a significant decline in his capacity to get out votes over time (fig 10.1). In absolute terms, Maduro received 1.4 million votes less than in the 2013 presidential election—and 2.0 million fewer votes than Chávez received in his 2012 reelection. As a percentage of registered voters, the decline was even more accentuated: Maduro's 2018 vote share of 30% of registered voters was 10 percentage points lower than his 2013 performance and 13 percentage points lower than Chávez's 2012 share.[6]

These numbers pose a puzzle. The opposition would only have needed to maintain its share of registered voters at the levels it obtained in the 2012 and 2013 presidential elections to defeat Maduro in the 2018 election. If anything, there would have been plenty of reasons to expect that the opposition should have been able to get a much higher vote share than in prior elections given that the economy was by then in its fifth consecutive year of recession and second year of hyperinflation. Opinion surveys also showed that Maduro's approval rating was in the low 20s, much lower than the low 50s it had been when he won the election for his first term by a small margin in 2013 (fig. 10.2). Running against an incumbent in the midst of a major recession and runaway

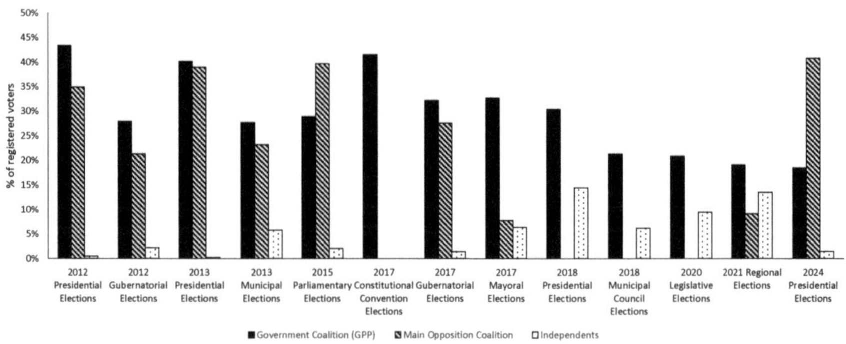

FIGURE 10.1. Coalition vote shares, percent of registered voters. *Source*: Author's construction using CNE 2023a and Comando con Venezuela 2024.

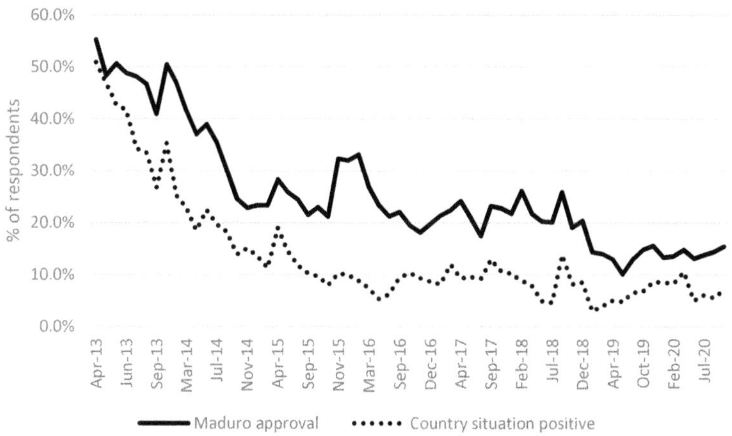

FIGURE 10.2. Presidential approval and country perception, 2013–2020. *Source*: Author's construction using Datanálisis 2021.

inflation is a typical challenger's dream. Incumbents almost invariably lose competitive elections under high inflation (table 10.1). Why, then, did the opposition decide to boycott what seemed to be its best opportunity in nearly two decades of winning the presidency from Chavismo?

In principle, electoral boycotts can make sense as part of a political strategy for various reasons (Bratton 1998; Pastor 1998; Beaulieu 2014; Buttorf and Dion 2017). One is that the threat of a boycott can force the government to grant concessions that improve the prospects for the challenger of winning the election or of gaining power after winning it. Another one is that a boycott can serve to delegitimize an electoral process and thus undermine the political sustainability of the incumbent. At the same time, the challenger must be at the very least highly uncertain about their prospects of winning an election in the absence of further concessions for a boycott to make sense. Otherwise, it would be optimal to contest the election and win it. In fact, many regime transitions occur as a result of an incumbent's attempt to tamper with the results of a vote that they have lost. The empirical evidence is at best mixed on the effectiveness of electoral boycotts, with one study arguing that their success rate is as low as 4% (Lindberg 2006; Frankel 2010; Beaulieu 2014).

Clearly the opposition's 2018 boycott aimed at delegitimization rather than extracting concessions for future electoral processes. After

TABLE 10.1. Results of elections under very high inflation since 1990

Country	*Year*	*Results*	*Election Type*
Argentina	1994	Government loses	Competitive
Bolivia	1985	Government loses	Competitive
Peru	1990	Government loses	Competitive
Brazil	1990	Government loses	Competitive
Nicaragua	1990	Government loses	Competitive
Azerbaijan	1990	Government wins	Noncompetitive
Belarus	1994	Government loses	Competitive
Ukraine	1994	Government loses	Competitive
Zimbabwe	2008	Government wins	Boycott
Yugoslavia	1992	Government wins	Boycott
Estonia	1992	Government wins	Competitive
Turkmenistan	1992	Government wins	Noncompetitive
Tajikistan	1994	Government wins	Boycott

Note: I take as the operational definition of "very high inflation" episodes in which annual inflation exceeds 1,000%.

Sources: Author's construction using Prieto 1985; Grompone 1990; Vilas 1990; US Commission on Security and Cooperation in Europe 1990; Inter-Parliamentary Union 1992; Valimised 1992; Koulinka 2014; Bojcun 1995; Muhutdinova 2007; IFFES 2008; Indeo 2016; Martín 2016.

all, the government had already shown that it was relatively unresponsive to the boycott threats carried out during the July 2017 Constitutional Convention elections and 2017 mayoral elections. And it is hard to think of what future concessions by the regime would have been necessary for it to prove optimal for the opposition to let pass the chance of defeating a highly unpopular incumbent in a presidential election.

If the aim of the decision was to delegitimize Maduro's presidency, then it probably succeeded beyond expectations. As I discuss below, at the start of 2019, the governments of fifty-seven countries decided to recognize National Assembly president Juan Guaidó instead of Maduro as Venezuela's legitimate president, a decision with few international precedents that allowed the opposition to seize control of Venezuela's offshore assets and shut the government and PDVSA off from access to the US banking system.

However, despite the international support garnered by the opposition in its attempt to question Maduro's legitimacy in government, doing so proved insufficient to dislodge him from power. In 2021, the MUD decided to lift its boycotts strategy and opted to participate in gubernatorial and mayoral elections; and in 2024 they contested, and won, a presidential vote despite facing much more adverse conditions than six year earlier—although electoral authorities would ultimately fraudulently declare Maduro to be the winner.

Surely, there were many arguments to support the contention in 2018 that Venezuela's electoral process was neither free nor fair. The pro-government majority controlling the CNE was unabashedly partisan, with the board systematically handing out decisions that were strongly biased in favor of Maduro and the PSUV. The imposition of multiple obstacles to the collection of signatures for the recall referendum drive in 2016, culminating in the invalidation of the whole petition process, as well as the announcement of likely inflated turnout numbers for the 2017 Constitutional Convention elections, were clear examples. The government had free rein to spend public resources without risking any type of sanction, even though doing so was a clear violation of electoral law. Choosing to participate in a Venezuelan election is a choice to play on an unlevel playing field.

Yet it is hard to argue that the playing field would have been any more uneven than in past elections, including some that the opposition had won. The 2018 Dominican Republic agreement that the government had been willing to sign would have allowed the opposition to gain at least one additional electoral council member and to count on the presence of international electoral observers. It also included a commitment to the same level of technical audits as the 2015 parliamentary elections, which the opposition had won by an ample margin. As I argue in the next section, Venezuela's electoral system makes it virtually impossible to tamper with the aggregate vote count without leaving a huge trail of evidence in the form of inconsistencies between tally sheets obtained by witnesses and figures published by the electoral council. Had Maduro's allies rigged the vote count, the opposition would have had massive credible evidence of vote tampering. Such an event could have served to mobilize international and domestic support, with a much stronger and legitimate claim to power than Juan Guaidó's later attempt to assume the interim presidency.[7]

To understand the opposition's choice to sit out the elections, we need to go back to October 2017. After holding the July Constitutional Convention vote—which the opposition claimed was both unconstitutional and had voting rules heavily slanted to ensure governmental control of the body—the CNE announced it would hold gubernatorial elections in October. The opposition had previously been relishing the chance to contest these elections, which the government had delayed for nearly a year.[8] Maduro's popularity had already declined precipitously, and most political analysts expected a very strong showing by the opposition.

In contrast, the electoral results were an unmitigated disaster for the opposition. Opposition candidates were able to win just five of twenty-three governorships, taking 45% of the vote against the government's 53%. Although the opposition did slightly better than in 2012, when it had taken only three governorships, it lost two important strongholds, the state of Miranda (which includes much of the Caracas metropolitan area) and the state of Lara. Most importantly, the results marked a major deterioration from its performance in the 2015 legislative election, when it had garnered 56% of the national vote.

The defeat dealt a major blow to the opposition narrative. Throughout most of 2016 and 2017, the opposition had mobilized around demands for elections to be held, on the assumption that it would be able to easily replicate or even improve on its 2015 performance. As the results from the 2017 regional elections came in, the opposition scrambled to frame an alternative interpretation in which it could claim to still represent the will of the majority, despite being unable to mobilize voters in its support.

Its decision was to claim that a major fraud had occurred. Opposition leaders charged that there were 1.6 million voters (15% of votes cast) for which the fingerprint machines had failed to provide an adequate match. It also pointed to evidence of forged tally sheets in the state of Bolívar, decisions by the electoral council to relocate voting centers in opposition strongholds, and the fact that the CNE had left on the ballot the names of some candidates who lost primaries. It further accused the government of distributing food bags near the entrance of voting centers to motivate turnout (Infobae 2017).

Some of these charges had an element of truth. The government had launched a program of subsidized food bags through the Local Committees of Supply and Production (CLAPs) and cash bonuses through its Card of the Fatherland, and there is evidence that they were distributed near approximately one-fourth of voting centers.[9] The CNE also relocated voting centers ahead of the election, although its rationale for this—that these centers had been the object of attacks during the violent protests of mid-2017 and were thus unsafe for voters and election workers—does not sound completely unreasonable. Regarding other claims, such as the number of unmatched fingerprints, the figure does not appear to have been anomalous; it appears to reflect the fact that the biometric identification database is far less than comprehensive. In the 2012 presidential elections, whose results the opposition had recognized, the percentage of votes cast without an adequate fingerprint match was slightly higher, 17% (Martínez 2017b).

Nevertheless, there is a deeper problem with the fraud story line. Both identity fraud (proxied by fingerprint match mistakes) and vote buying (through food boxes and cash bonuses) would be expected to lead to higher pro-government turnout. And while it is true that the government increased its vote share somewhat relative to previous elections, the main driver of changes in electoral performance between 2015 and 2017 was not the increase in government votes but the decline in opposition votes. If we restrict the comparison to votes in the districts that were eligible to vote in both elections, we find that the government increased its votes from 5.6 to 5.8 million (i.e., from 31.5% to 32.2% of registered voters) while the opposition votes dropped from 7.7 to 5.0 million (from 43.3% to 27.5% of registered voters).[10]

Other fraud hypotheses are numerically improbable. Voting center relocation may have been targeted at making it more difficult for opposition supporters to vote. Yet changes in turnout in the 272 relocated centers account for only 0.2 percentage points of the government's nationwide lead. Similarly, if ballot stuffing were widespread, we would expect the government to derive a large share of votes from voting centers with an anomalously high turnout. But less than five thousand votes nationwide were cast in voting machines with turnout higher than 90%. Subtract those votes from the government's total, and the overall vote share changes by four hundredths of one percentage point (Kronick and Rodríguez 2017).

In contrast, the evidence suggests that abstention grew dramatically in opposition strongholds. In the most pro-opposition precincts, abstention rose by 15 percentage points more than in the most pro-government ones (fig. 10.3). Had turnout patterns replicated those

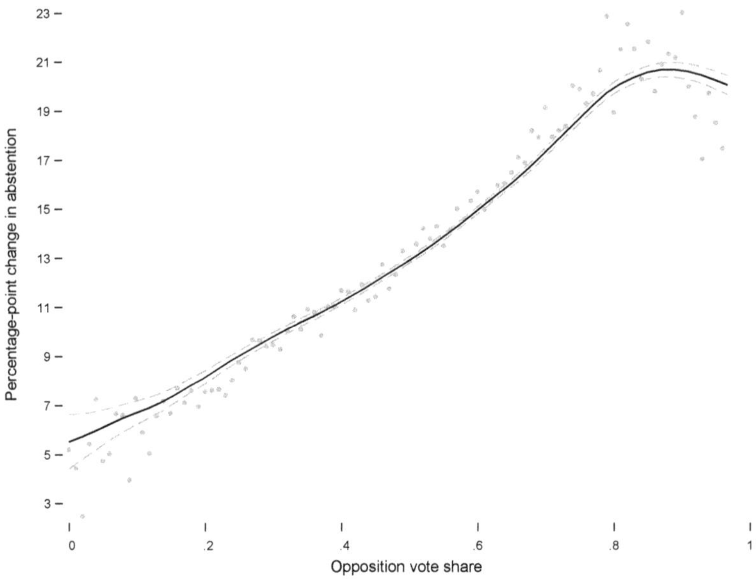

FIGURE 10.3. Abstention increase in opposition strongholds, 2017. *Source*: Kronick and Rodríguez 2017. *Note*: Each point plots the weighted mean of abstention rates across precincts in one-pp bins of 2013 opposition vote share; the line is a local linear fit to the raw precinct-level data (with 95% confidence interval).

of 2015, then the opposition would have obtained around 50% of the national vote share, a result that would have marked its best performance ever in gubernatorial elections.

Understanding the causes of the demobilization of opposition voters is a difficult and inherently speculative task. Opinion surveys show high levels of distrust in electoral institutions, which many Venezuelans see as inherently biased and pro-government. This distrust can easily explain why people may be unwilling to vote. One can also point to the deterioration in electoral transparency in the period between 2015 and 2017 as reasons for declining confidence in electoral authorities. Certainly, the decision to cancel the recall referendum process in October 2016 and the announcement of a highly questioned turnout figure of 8.1 million voters in the July 2017 Constitutional Convention elections should have served to undermine the credibility of the CNE.

On the other hand, there is no evidence that Venezuelans' views of their electoral authorities changed much with these two events. The

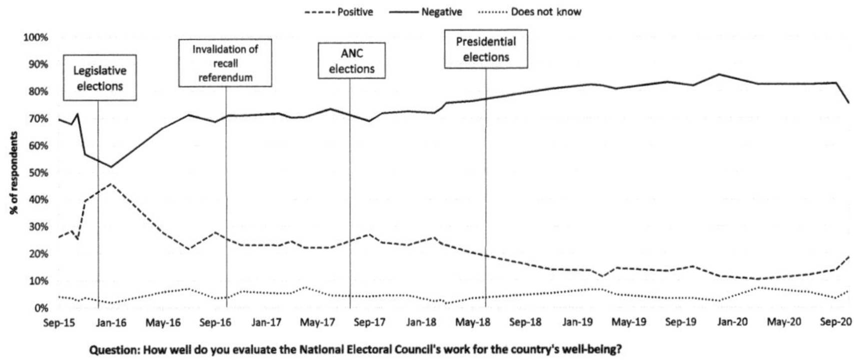

FIGURE 10.4. Views on National Electoral Council, 2015–2018. *Source*: Author's construction using Datanálisis 2017, 2018, 2021.

share of Venezuelans who assessed the CNE's work as positive at the time of the election (24%) was not very different from its levels in mid-2016 prior to the invalidation of the recall referendum request. Nor were they all that different from their levels in mid-2015, although trust in the electoral board does seem to have increased just before the 2015 elections, perhaps due to efforts by the opposition to build confidence in the effectiveness of voting as part of their campaign for the legislative elections (fig. 10.4).

There are other, more complex explanations for increasing voter apathy, some of which don't fall that clearly into the opposition story line. For one, the opposition seems likely to have lost a significant number of voters to emigration: approximately three million persons are estimated to have left the country between 2015 and 2017, of which around two million are likely to have been of voting age.[11] Only a small share of emigrants register to vote abroad and in any case are not eligible to vote in regional elections.[12] The scant existing evidence shows that the diaspora is very strongly pro-opposition, so it is probable that opposition voters were overrepresented in this exodus (University of North Florida 2020).

Alternatively, it is possible that voters who had bought into the opposition promise of rapid change in 2015 may have felt unmotivated by the opposition's inability to fulfill its promises. A prominent opposition TV spot ahead of the 2015 elections claimed that lining up to vote in the 2015 elections would be "la última cola" (the last queue), in a reference to the prevalent lines that Venezuelans put up with in the midst of generalized scarcity of basic goods at regulated prices (Venezuela Quiere Cambio 2015). As voters found their expectations of rapid change unfulfilled, they may have felt increasingly alienated from the political process.

Understanding which of these reasons is behind opposition demobilization is a complex task and one that may well prove intractable. At the very least, it requires a deep study of public attitudes, which is beyond the scope of this work. Yet the indeterminacy in itself is useful in helping understand the emergence of different competing narratives about Venezuelan institutions. If the key driver of voter apathy is distrust of electoral authorities, this points to the existence of an important democratic gap that should be addressed through greater transparency; if, on the other hand, the problem lies in voters' increasing distrust and skepticism of politicians in general, then the failure is not so much one of democracy as it is one of opposition leadership to present an attractive project of political change.

Yet the electoral results made one thing clear for the opposition: victory in the 2018 presidential elections was far from assured. If they were to defeat Maduro, they would at the very least have to convince voters to turn out in their favor again. Perhaps this would be possible if they achieved major changes in the electoral system, such as the appointment of a highly credible and impartial CNE board. But if opposition supporters were so distrustful of electoral authorities that they decided to stay home in the 2017 regional elections despite their leaders' call to vote, there was no guarantee that they would behave any differently in 2018.

RIGGED ELECTIONS?

In 2020, US secretary of state Mike Pompeo referred to Venezuela's legislative elections as "a political farce intended to look like legislative elections" (Reuters 2018). Two years earlier, he had written on Twitter that "sham elections change nothing," in reference to the country's presidential elections (Pompeo 2018). A *Washington Post* editorial published days after the 2020 elections called them "an unmitigated farce" and said they were "blatantly rigged" (*Washington Post* 2020). After the 2021 regional elections, in which opposition forces won 3 of 22 governorships and 125 of 325 mayoralties, the State Department issued a statement claiming,

"The Maduro regime deprived Venezuelans yet again of their right to participate in a free and fair electoral process. . . . [T]he regime grossly skewed the process to determine the result of this election long before any ballots had been cast" (US Department of State 2021).

Given these statements, one may be forgiven for thinking that Venezuela's election results prior to 2024 were cooked up in an office in the presidential palace. Reality is much more complex. Prior to 2024, there had not been a convincing accusation of alteration of the vote count in a contested Venezuelan national election, and some of the claims of fraud that had been made have been strongly questioned on methodological grounds. Partisan electoral authorities have certainly skewed the rules in favor of the government and made it more difficult for the opposition to compete. Yet partisan decisions by politicized electoral authorities are far from new in Venezuelan or Latin American politics.

Venezuela is one of only four countries that use automated voting machines for virtually all their electorate (Ropek 2020). Venezuela's voting machines produce a verifiable paper trail, allowing voters to ascertain that the vote processed by the machine is the same one they cast. In contrast, as of 2020, eight US states still used paperless voting machines offering no such possibility of verification. In Venezuela, a random audit of more than 50% of voting booths is made in the presence of witnesses from each side to verify that the vote totals reported by the electronic system are in line with the paper votes (Torre 2023).[13]

These characteristics of the country's automated voting system make undetected tampering of the aggregate vote tally virtually impossible in a contested election.[14] Any attempt to modify the aggregate tally will generate inconsistencies with the records of individual voting centers, which representatives of all sides have immediate access to. As long as the CNE publishes results disaggregated by voting booth, it is straightforward to demonstrate any alteration of vote totals by national authorities. Audits carried out in the context of the European Union's Electoral Observation Mission to the 2021 regional elections concluded that "the automated voting system offered enough guarantees of integrity and secrecy of the vote and were one of the most important measures of transparency of these elections" (EU 2021).

Note that I have not claimed that tampering with the vote totals in Venezuelan elections is impossible or that it has not happened. In fact,

I will argue below that that is precisely what took place in 2024. And there are at least two cases prior to that in which there appeared to be evidence that some tampering occurred. These are the 2017 Constitutional Convention elections and the 2017 elections for the governorship of Bolívar.[15] In the former, the national turnout numbers indicating that 42% of the electorate had voted appear implausible, as I discussed in chapter 8. And in the latter, the opposition candidate, Andrés Velásquez, published tally sheets that were inconsistent with the voting aggregates published by the electoral council (Moreno 2017). The votes allegedly altered would have been enough to give Velásquez the victory in that election, which he lost by 1,471 votes (0.26% of the total vote).

What I have claimed instead is that aggregate vote tampering is detectable and can be documented and proven in contested elections, as occurred in 2024. To detect fraud in Venezuela's electoral system, you need witnesses who can participate in the audits of the paper trails and collect copies of the tally sheets in each electoral center to prove that they differ from those published by the CNE in its aggregate vote tallies. When there are no opposition witnesses—say, because the opposition decides to boycott the election—there is nothing impeding electoral authorities from altering the vote totals.

The Bolívar case serves as an example of how attempts by electoral authorities to alter results are detectable as long as elections are contested. It is only because the Velásquez campaign had witnesses in the voting centers where he alleged tampering that he was able to present tally sheets at odds with the results reported by national authorities. It is also important to note that the contested tally sheets in Bolívar came from thirteen voting booths in which electoral machines did not transmit their results electronically to the CNE's central processing system due to connectivity failures (Martínez 2017). In those cases, tally sheets were taken to the regional electoral council, where they were put into the system manually. Velásquez claimed that the results that the regional electoral authorities put into the system were different from those of the tally sheets in his possession.[16] To the best of my knowledge, prior to 2024 there had been no claims of inconsistencies between results published by the CNE and tally sheets in cases in which machines have transmitted their results electronically to the CNE's central processing system.[17]

Accurate tallying of votes is only one aspect of what makes an election free and fair. Interfering with the way in which voters cast their votes is another. This can be done by interfering with the exercise by voters of their right to vote or by allowing votes to be cast by those who do not legally have that right. Vote buying, or the offering of selective incentives conditioned on the act of voting, is an example of the former. Vote buying is not uncommon in Latin America and has been documented in numerous elections across the region.[18] Recall that the Maduro government accused the opposition of vote buying in the 2015 elections for Amazonas legislators.

Whether large-scale identity fraud occurs in Venezuela is less clear.[19] One marker of identity fraud is found in statistically anomalous turnout patterns. If the government has total control over some voting booths and can turn a blind eye to identity fraud, then we would expect a large share of voting booths to show very high turnout rates—as the government allows its supporters to vote in place of absent voters. In that case, we would expect to see clusters of voting booths concentrated at very high turnout rates. Yet the percentage of voting booths with more than 90% turnout—1.7% in the 2015 parliamentary elections and less than 0.1% on the 2018 presidential elections—is neither unusually high nor large enough to alter the results of most elections. By comparison, the share of voting booths with more than 90% turnout in Argentina's 2019 general election—an election with turnout similar to Venezuela's 2018 election—was a much higher 7.0%.[20] Similarly to Argentina's, the Venezuelan vote turnout histograms show no evidence of bimodality or the clustering near some threshold that would be indicative of decentralized attempts at large-scale stuffing (figs. 10.5, 10.6).[21]

Perhaps due to the lack of evidence of aggregate vote tampering, criticisms of Venezuela's elections prior to 2024 have centered on irregularities in the voting process that restrict the scope of political competition. Among the most often-cited electoral irregularities are the disqualification of opposition candidates and the banning of opposition parties (OAS 2018; US Department of State 2021; Polga-Hecimovich 2022; Corrales 2023).

Let us consider these objections in the context of the 2018 presidential elections. Venezuelan law grants the Comptroller General the ability to bar candidates from running for elected office for up to fifteen

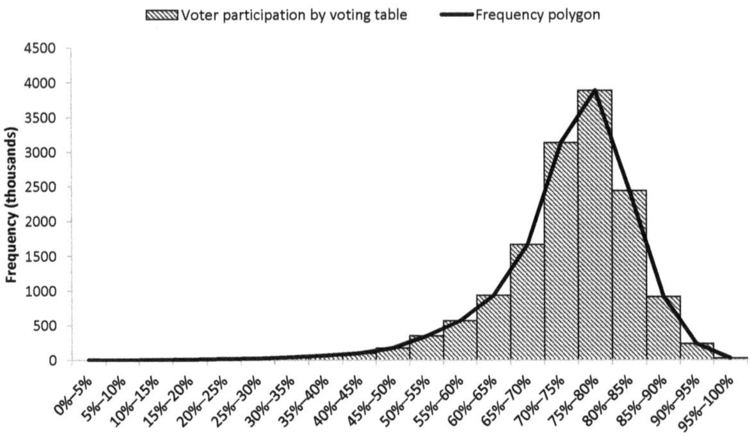

FIGURE 10.5. Distribution of voter participation per voting booths, Venezuela's 2015 legislative elections. *Source*: Author's construction using CNE 2015. *Note*: Histogram represents distribution of voting booths by turnout rate with bin size equal to 5%. The line represents frequency polygon.

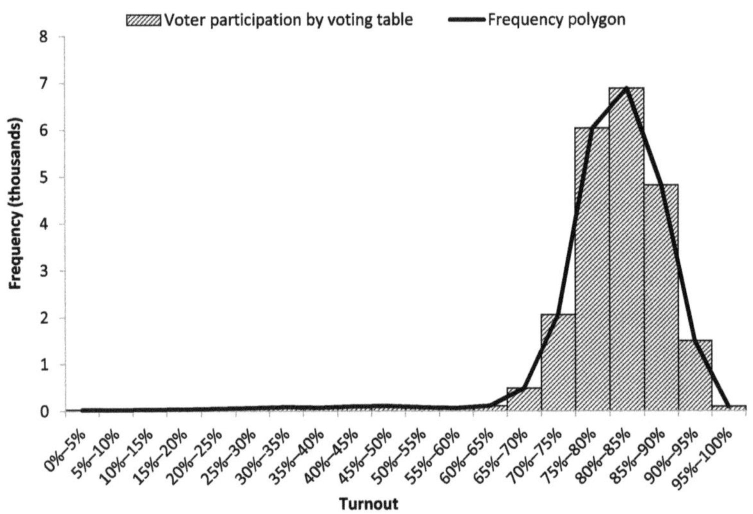

FIGURE 10.6. Distribution of voter participation per voting booths, Argentina's 2019 presidential elections. *Source*: Author's construction using Dirección Nacional Electoral Argentina 2019. *Note*: Histogram represents distribution of voting booths by turnout rate with bin size equal to 5%. The line represents frequency polygon.

years if they are determined to have incurred administrative irregularities when they held office in the past (Asamblea Nacional de Venezuela 2023b).[22] Although nominally part of an independent branch of government, the Comptroller General's Office has almost invariably been held by government loyalists appointed by the pro-government majority in the National Assembly. In 2017, the Comptroller General disqualified a former presidential candidate, Henrique Capriles, from running for office for the maximum of fifteen years due to administrative irregularities that it found Capriles incurred during his tenure as governor of the state of Miranda. Venezuela's Constitution also bars anyone serving a prison term after having been convicted of a crime from running for office. Leopoldo López, one of the leaders of La Salida (see chap. 6), had been sentenced to a thirteen-year term for his role in the protests that had ended in the burning of the Prosecutor General's Office building in 2014. The inability of Capriles and López, among the most popular opposition leaders at the time, to run for the presidency certainly curtailed the space of political competition ahead of the 2018 elections.

Regarding the claim that opposition parties were barred from participating in the election, things were a bit murkier. Venezuelan law states that parties that have received less than 1% of the vote in national elections need to renew their registration by collecting signatures of at least 0.5% of the electoral registry in twelve states (*Gaceta Oficial* 2007b). After the 2017 municipal elections, which were boycotted by several opposition parties, the Constitutional Convention decreed that parties that did not participate in that election would also have to renew their registration. One of the main opposition parties, Popular Will (Voluntad Popular, VP), refused to participate in the process, claiming that it was unconstitutional, while another one, PJ, failed to collect enough signatures (Martínez 2018b). Other opposition parties that formed part of the MUD, including UNT and Progressive Advance (Avanzada Progresista, AP), had participated in the 2017 municipal elections and thus could keep their registration active.

Therefore, as of January 2018, two key parties in the MUD coalition, VP and PJ, had lost their registration and would thus not appear on the ballot. A parallel Supreme Court decision had also decided that the MUD could not be registered as a political party independently from its constituent member parties, as doing so would violate a prohibition on double party membership. Therefore, an opposition presidential candidate in 2018 would not have been able to appear on the ballots on the VP, PJ, or MUD tickets.

However, as of 2018, three opposition parties that were members of the MUD—AP, UNT, and AD—maintained valid registration. The first two of these had not boycotted the 2017 municipal elections, while the third had been able to collect enough signatures to validate the party's registration. Therefore, any candidate chosen by the MUD would have been able to register for the elections with the support of any or all these three parties. It would not have been the first time that the symbols of opposition parties did not appear on the ballot. In 2015, the opposition had decided to omit all party symbols except for that of the MUD coalition from the ballot and had nevertheless won a resounding victory.

Both the disqualification of key opposition leaders from the election and the suspension of the registration of two opposition parties are examples of how the Maduro government used its control over institutions to generate obstacles to opposition participation and tilt the electoral playing field in its favor. However, neither of them appears to be systematically different from politically biased decisions by the judiciary or electoral authorities that are frequently taken in other countries in the region and that are often evident expressions of the political bias of institutions whose function is to impartially regulate or oversee elections.

Consider, for example, the August 2018 decision by a Brazilian electoral court to ban former president Luiz Inácio Lula da Silva from running in the country's presidential election held later that year. Like Leopoldo López, Lula had been convicted in a case that many observers saw as problematic and deeply politicized. The UN Human Rights Committee found that Lula's investigation and prosecution violated his right to be tried by an impartial tribunal, as well as his right to privacy and his political rights (OHCHR 2022). In 2021, Brazil's Supreme Court would find that Sergio Moro, the judge who had investigated and tried the case, lacked jurisdiction and was not impartial. Moro would later serve as justice minister in the administration of President Jair Bolsonaro, Lula's political rival.

Consider, alternatively, the 2020 decision by an Ecuadorean court to condemn former president Rafael Correa to eight years in prison, barring him from a spot on the presidential ticket for that year's election

(España 2020). Supporters of the former president allege that the court sped up its consideration of charges to make sure that the verdict would be in place in time to stop Correa from registering for that year's elections (Pérez 2020). In 2018, an electoral court had handed to President Lenin Moreno, who had broken with Correa after being elected with his support, control over Alianza País, the party founded by Correa. Electoral authorities would later bar the registration of another pro-Correa party, Fuerza Compromiso Social (*El Comercio* 2020). All these decisions were taken after Moreno had obtained through a referendum the power to appoint the members of the Council of Citizen Participation and Social Control, an institution with the power to appoint and fire electoral authorities and prosecutors (CPCCS 2023).

In sum, Venezuelan elections clearly occur in a context in which the control by the government party over key institutions serves to slant the playing field in its favor. Yet there is also strong evidence that the country's electronic voting system guarantees that any large-scale manipulation of the vote totals will be easy to detect in any contested election in which the opposition is able to field witnesses in a sufficiently large share of voting centers, as occurred in 2024. And while electoral authorities and the judiciary have certainly taken decisions that have restricted the ability of certain candidates to register, manipulated the dates of elections, and suspended the registration of certain political parties, none of these restrictions impeded the opposition coalition from running candidates in the 2018 or 2020 elections. Nor does the politicization of key judicial and electoral decisions seem systematically different from what occurs in some elections across the region.

The purpose of the foregoing is not to argue that Venezuelan elections (or Brazilian or Ecuadorean elections) held prior to 2024 conformed to a given standard of fairness or transparency. My aim in this work is not to make a normative assessment of the country's institutions but rather to understand the decisions of its key political actors and assess how they contributed to the country's economic collapse. What I view as important and relevant about this discussion is that it helps us characterize the choice faced by opposition actors in the run-up to the 2018 presidential election.

At the start of 2018, Venezuela's opposition faced a choice between boycotting or participating in the upcoming presidential election.

Maduro's unpopularity and the country's deep economic crisis meant that it had a good chance of winning the election. And while it was certainly possible that Maduro would decide to tamper with the result rather than accept defeat, Venezuela's electoral system pretty much guaranteed that were this to happen, the opposition would have copies of the tally sheets that evidenced its victory. Even if one took as given that Maduro would not leave power willingly, it is hard to imagine a better way of delegitimizing him than by showing the world the smoking gun evidence that he had stolen an election.

Nevertheless, that decision carried some risks. The most obvious one was that the opposition could lose the election. The results of the 2017 gubernatorial races had demonstrated that victory was far from assured. By accusing the government of rigging those elections, the opposition had again begun to box itself into a familiar corner, where a narrative of fraud discouraged opposition supporters from turning out to vote. If neither López nor Capriles could run, the opposition nomination appeared to be between AD's Henry Ramos Allup and AP's Henri Falcón. But opinion polls suggested that Ramos Allup was a weak candidate who could lose against Maduro, and many opposition supporters distrusted Falcón because of his Chavista past.

Furthermore, even if the opposition were to win the election and assume the presidency, it was far from clear that everything would be smooth sailing after that. While it had a solid majority in the National Assembly, it would have had to coexist with a hostile Supreme Court and prosecutor general—not to mention the all-powerful Constitutional Convention, most state governorships, and other key institutions, including the military leadership that would remain under the control of Chavismo. It would not be unreasonable to imagine a scenario in which Chavismo used the control of those institutions to ensure that the country remained ungovernable and to position itself to reclaim power in a future election.

Its other alternative was to sit out the election and attempt to use the boycott to delegitimize Maduro's reelection. Ideally, the prospect of facing an election alone would force Maduro to back down and grant the opposition more concessions. But if that did not happen, the opposition knew that it could rely on a strong ally in the White House who was willing to pursue a policy of increasing pressure on the Maduro regime. Ultimately, the prospect of economic isolation could generate a break in the governing coalition, leading the military to abandon Maduro rather than become international pariahs. Were Maduro to be ousted in a military coup, it would prove much easier to ensure the exit of some of his loyalists from other state institutions.[23] Were this strategy to prove successful, the upside would be much higher than that of simply winning a presidential election.

We will likely never know whether the Dominican Republic talks broke down, as Maduro's representatives claim, after the opposition negotiator Julio Borges received a call from Secretary of State Rex Tillerson, who was then visiting Colombia, telling him not to sign the agreement (Aporrea 2018). But it is hard to imagine that the opposition did not at the very least consult with the US government, which by then had become one of its strongest allies, on its decision about what to do regarding the talks. And given what we know about later US decisions, it seems probable that Trump administration officials conveyed to the opposition the view that they had no need to take what they felt was a bad and risky deal with Maduro. After all, it wouldn't be long before top US officials would publicly transmit very high levels of confidence in the ability of their maximum pressure strategy to drive Maduro from power.

By deciding to boycott the 2018 election, the opposition was also deciding to raise the stakes of the political game. Rather than play for a chance at sharing power with Chavista-controlled institutions in case of winning an uncertain presidential race, they opted for a winner-take-all strategy with the support of a very powerful international ally. Opting for a nonelectoral strategy promised a very high return, if successful. If it failed, however, it ran the risk of leading the country into economic isolation and severely deepening its recession.

The results and aftermath of the 2024 presidential election are consistent with our story. Prior to the election, the Maduro government tried many of the tactics that it had used in the past to suppress opposition participation. These included banning prominent opposition politicians, fostering opposition divisions, and restricting voter registration. Despite all of this, the opposition decided to contest the election, and massively won the vote.

The government-controlled electoral council, however, proceeded to announce that Maduro had won by a margin of 52.0% to 43.2% over MUD challenger Edmundo González (Efecto Cocuyo 2024). The opposition was able to produce overwhelming evidence that the official result did not reflect the actual vote. It collected and published electronic tally sheets corresponding to 83.5% of voting booths, which showed González ahead of Maduro 67.1% to 30.5% (Comando con Venezuela 2024). The tally sheets were consistent with abundant anecdotal evidence, including numerous videos of the vote count in specific voting centers, that showed González easily defeating Maduro even in localities that had traditionally supported the government. Independent analyses found the opposition data to be internally consistent and not showing any indication of tampering (Kronick 2024; Mebane 2024). The electoral council, in turn, did not publish disaggregated results as required by law, and even its aggregate numbers appeared to show statistical evidence of manipulation (Gelman 2024).

The 2024 results confirm that the Venezuelan electoral system made it possible for the opposition to clearly show that the government had tampered with the vote count to steal an election. It also demonstrated that the opposition could overcome the numerous obstacles that the government put in its way with the intent of suppressing the opposition vote. And while none of this stopped the government from ultimately stealing the election, its decision to do so severely tarnished any claim by Nicolás Maduro to democratic legitimacy.

With the benefit of hindsight, the opposition's decision to sit out the election six years earlier looks like a grave miscalculation. Yet it also underscores the extent to which the opposition in 2018 was willing to take very high risks to opt for a strategy of full-fledged regime change—instead of the negotiated transition that could have resulted from an electoral victory. Venezuela's 2018 opposition was confident that Maduro would be unable to survive the effects of an electoral boycott. To understand why it believed this, we have to bring into the picture what the opposition's international allies were willing to do to help its cause.

THINKING LOCALLY, ACTING GLOBALLY

As Venezuela's crisis deepened, it also began garnering growing international attention. Partly this was expectable: the country was undergoing a spectacular output collapse, millions of Venezuelans were arriving in other countries, and a stable democracy was spiraling into political chaos. Yet partly this also responded to the growing effort by the opposition to seek the aid of its international allies in opposing the Maduro regime.

The opposition found a ready ear in the Trump administration. Trump had made clear to his foreign policy team that he favored a tougher stance on Venezuela, broaching the idea of invading Venezuela as early as mid-2017.[24] He was also more willing to pursue key foreign policy issues unilaterally, without feeling the need to coordinate with Europe's more guarded approach.[25] Perhaps most importantly, Trump kept a keen eye on the politics of Florida, which had been crucial to his 2016 victory. That meant courting the support of Florida's Hispanic voters and key leaders such as Republican senator Marco Rubio, who strongly favored a hard-line stance on Cuba and Venezuela.

The regional context was also strongly supportive of Venezuela's opposition. Partly this reflects the ebbing of the "pink tide" resurgence of leftist movements that had dominated Latin American politics during the previous two decades. In key countries, leftist movements lost power through elections (Argentina in 2017 and Chile in 2018), impeachment (Brazil in 2016), or defections (Ecuador in 2017). In others, conservative movements were already in power (Mexico, Paraguay), and in some, there was a clear turn to the right as centrist leaders were succeeded by more conservative ones (Colombia in 2018). The result was a regional politics dominated by center-right leaders.

In mid-2017, twelve of these governments led an effort to create a regional group that would take a stronger stance toward the Maduro regime.[26] The Lima Declaration, approved on August 8—a week after the Constitutional Convention elections—condemned the rupture of the democratic order in Venezuela, ratified its solidarity with the National Assembly, and announced the decision not to recognize the Constitutional Convention (Grupo de Lima 2017). At the same time, some of these governments moved to disband UNASUR, whose decision mechanism would have required coordination with leftist governments such as Bolivia. OAS Secretary General Luis Almagro also became a staunch critic of the Maduro government, pushing for an investigation of human rights abuses committed by Venezuelan authorities and advocating for tighter sanctions on the country (Deutsche Welle 2017; Faus 2018).

What emerged was a regional policy approach focused on using external pressure to try to change the conduct of the Maduro regime. This strongly contrasted with the Zapatero-UNASUR search for a negotiated solution between the government and the opposition. Almagro and other Lima Group leaders explicitly condemned the November 2017 resumption of talks, warning the opposition that it would be a mistake to enter into an agreement on electoral conditions with the government (Lugo 2017). The new OAS–Lima Group position was clearly aligned with the Trump administration's approach, marking a rare instance of regional multilateralism.

Much like the opposition, Maduro went in search of international support. In September he would embark on an international trip that would take him to Algeria, Belarus, Turkey, and Russia, culminating in a face-to-face meeting with President Vladimir Putin where the latter praised Maduro for managing to "establish some kind of contact with the political forces that are opposing you" (Kremlin 2017). Maduro would also visit China in September 2018 (Pons and Shepherd 2018). China and Russia both agreed to refinance Venezuelan debts and signed new oil deals. The battle lines were clearly drawn for the legitimacy crisis of 2019.

RECOGNITION AND ITS DISCONTENTS

Nicolás Maduro was sworn in by the Supreme Court for a second six-year term on January 10, 2019. His government went to significant lengths to ensure the attendance of representatives from as large a number of countries as possible, including the heads of state of six countries; representatives from China, Russia, Turkey, Mexico, Uruguay, Belarus, Iran, and Palestine, the African Union, and the League of Arab States; and OPEC's secretary general (Blanchard and Ulmer 2018; Ministerio del Poder Popular para la Comunicación y Información 2019). Nevertheless, the event was overshadowed by the condemnation of the United States, the Lima Group, and the European Union, which stated that they did not consider that his election had been free or fair and refused to send their diplomatic envoys to the ceremony (Bolton 2019; Consejo Europeo 2019; Ministerio de Relaciones Exteriores, Comercio Internacional y Culto Argentina 2019).

Five days before, the National Assembly had elected thirty-five-year-old legislator Juan Guaidó to its presidency. Guaidó's election was the by-product of an agreement to rotate the legislature's presidency among the largest parties; for 2019, the position fell on Leopoldo López's VP party, of which Guaidó was a junior member. By that time, most of VP's leaders were in exile, so the position went to one of their least-known members.

What the next step should be for the opposition at the time was a controversial topic. Despite sanctions and international condemnation, Maduro had forged ahead undeterred. The high levels of mobilization reached during the 2017 protests had ebbed, and it was unclear that there was much that could be done to pressure the government further. After the board of the National Assembly issued a statement saying that there was no legitimate president in Venezuela (Asamblea Nacional de Venezuela 2019b), many opposition leaders were skeptical of taking the conflict any further. A previous 2017 attempt by the National Assembly to declare that Maduro had abandoned his position as president had no tangible consequences and was largely perceived as a strategic blunder.

On January 23, Guaidó would surprise much of the country's political establishment by announcing before a crowd of supporters that he would assume the powers of the presidency by invoking an article of the Constitution that regulates how to fill permanent absences of the executive branch. Although there was some speculation that legislators had not been informed of the decision and had not planned to support it,[27] it would shortly become clear that the move had substantial support from key international allies. Less than half an hour after Guaidó's announcement, the White House's official Twitter account announced that President Trump was recognizing Guaidó;[28] this was quickly followed by recognition statements of thirteen countries (eleven of them from the Lima Group) on the same day. Over the next few weeks, the countries formally recognizing Guaidó reached fifty-seven, a number that included most of Europe and Latin America (fig. 10.7).

Although the convergence around Guaidó's recognition among most Western democracies seemed to be a rare instance of multilateralism, some key differences in policies between the United States and other nations emerged. Most European nations would eventually refuse to accept the

FIGURE 10.7. Countries by formal announcement of recognition decision at the end of 2020. *Source*: Author's construction based on WOLA 2020; Oil for Venezuela 2021.

credentials of Guaidó's ambassadors, treating them as personal envoys while continuing to interact formally with the Maduro regime (fig 10.8). They would also refuse to go along with Washington's policy of economic sanctions, imposing only personal sanctions limiting financial transactions and physical movement in their territories of Maduro regime leaders.

Deciding to recognize a government without some degree of de facto control over its territory was a substantial and unusual break with diplomatic traditions. The far-removed precedents were the US recognition of the Kuomintang government of China until 1979 and the recognition of the governments-in-exile of most Nazi-occupied countries during World War II (Meyer and Lourie 1943; Bell and Dennen 1944; Brown 1979). Most Western governments had evolved toward the tradition of recognizing "states, not governments," allowing them to maintain diplomatic relations with governments without necessarily recognizing their legitimacy of origin (Talmon 1998).

FIGURE 10.8. Countries by status of diplomatic relations at the end of 2020. *Source*: Author's construction based on WOLA 2020; Oil for Venezuela 2021.

One of the most important legal implications of a recognition decision is that it allows the recognized government to represent the legal interests of the state, including the management of its assets in the host country. Shortly after the announcement of Guaidó's recognition, the US secretary of state determined that Guaidó had authority over the bank accounts of the country's government and Central Bank (Wong 2019). Guaidó quickly moved to appoint a new board of the state-owned oil company PDVSA, ensuring control over the accounts of the company, including its US refining arm, CITGO Petroleum (Asamblea Nacional de Venezuela 2019c, Runrun.es 2019).

The transfer of the control of assets to Guaidó came almost simultaneously with the designation of PDVSA under the sanctions regime—a decision that is typically referred to as the imposition of oil sanctions as it barred US oil trade with Venezuela (see chap. 9). Yet in and of itself, Guaidó recognition would have been enough to lock Venezuela out of the US oil market. While Maduro retained control over the country's territory and therefore over its capacity to produce oil, Guaidó had gained control over the capacity to invoice that oil. Maduro could sell the oil, but only Guaidó could get paid for it.

In fact, the implications were much broader. A simple ban on oil would have precluded Maduro from selling to the US market, but the State Department's determination barred Maduro from using the US financial system to sell to any buyer, even outside of the United States. It also blocked Maduro from accessing the Venezuelan government's financial assets in the United States, which US authorities estimated at $7 billion at the time.[29]

The resulting de facto ban on financial transactions was particularly pernicious given the relevance of the US financial system for global trade. A Colombian company exporting to Venezuela, say, is more likely to request payments to a US bank account than to a local financial institution. Even a bank transfer between non-US banks often moves through US intermediary or correspondent banks (McDowell 2019). After January 2019, no US institution was authorized to process such a transaction involving the Maduro regime.

Access to the European financial system was also complicated by the political crisis. Although no European Union member made a determination analogous to the State Department's, the legal uncertainty caused by the unusual recognition decision was enough to compel most banks to similarly restrict transactions involving the Maduro regime. Financial institutions have a broad level of discretion regarding what transactions to process; in practice, it made little sense to them to process a transaction that could create significant legal and regulatory risks and liabilities.

In May 2019, Deutsche Bank asked a London court to initiate an arbitration process to determine how it should handle $120 million in proceeds from a gold swap transaction with the Central Bank of Venezuela concluded in 2017. Deutsche Bank had received conflicting instructions from the Maduro- and Guaidó-appointed Central Bank boards regarding the funds. Since the contract was governed by English law and provided for arbitration disputes to be resolved in London, it was up to the court to resolve the dispute. The court ordered the funds to be transferred to a receiver and initiated a legal process to determine who had control over them. The case was later heard together with a larger, $2 billion dispute over gold holdings at the Bank of England. As of this writing, the process is ongoing, and the funds are still in receivership (Royal Courts of Justice 2020a, 2020b).

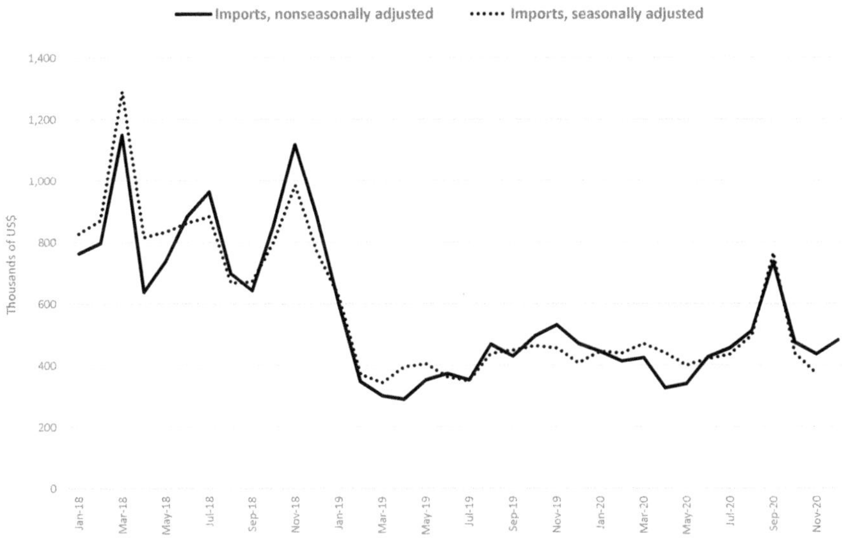

FIGURE 10.9. Monthly imports reported by trading partners, seasonally adjusted and nonseasonally adjusted, 2018–2020. *Sources*: Trading partners' institutes of statistics; author's calculations.

Not surprisingly, imports plummeted immediately after the announcement of the sanctions and recognition decision, falling 43% in February with respect to January (57% when compared to February of the previous year; see fig. 10.9). Note that while exports fell dramatically in the same month due to the effect of the sanctions, one would not expect to have seen an immediate effect of lower export revenue on the capacity to pay for imports, as the standard Venezuelan oil contract is paid with a ninety-day lag, so that the revenue effects of the sanctions should not have been felt until May. Nevertheless, the effects of the broader set of restrictions on the country's capacity to trade was felt immediately, explaining the quick decline in imports.

The recognition decision also made most exceptions to the sanctions regime, including the much-touted humanitarian exceptions, essentially irrelevant. While OFAC formally codified the authorization for the Venezuelan government to import agricultural goods, medicines, and medical supplies (US Department of the Treasury 2019), these authorizations applied to the Guaidó and not the Maduro government. Maduro was nothing more than a former Venezuelan president—who also happened to be on OFAC's SDN list—with no more authority than any other individual to conduct (or appoint persons to conduct) transactions on behalf of the Venezuelan state.

The problem extended not just to the use of the financial system but also to the signing of any relevant contracts with the Venezuelan state—such as, for example, contracts for provision of COVID vaccines. Such contracts are commonly governed by foreign law, ensuring that multinationals can use the US or European courts or arbitration mechanisms to resolve legal disputes. Yet the only ones entitled to sign a contract on behalf of Venezuela in these jurisdictions were the representatives of the recognized government, which was that of Guaidó.[30] While companies could choose to write the contracts to be governed by Venezuelan law, that would essentially have entailed giving up any right of enforcement to Maduro-controlled courts. Even so, any transaction emanating from such deals would be legally and reputationally problematic, given that Maduro was transacting with what were technically, at least from the standpoint of US law, stolen funds. In practice, no major multinational chose to continue transacting with the Maduro regime.[31]

The decisions thus caused a peculiar conundrum: even if all economic sanctions were lifted, Venezuela would still not be able to sell oil, purchase inputs, or issue debt in the United States, at least in the absence of an agreement between the Guaidó and Maduro administrations. Any transaction would have to be subscribed to by the Guaidó government; otherwise, the Guaidó government would have the legal right to seize any payments related to those transactions. Guaidó had not gained control of the country, but he had gained the ability to impede Maduro from controlling an important part of the country's economy.[32]

DOUBLING DOWN

In a surprisingly frank comment made shortly after announcing that he was stepping down, Guaidó's first PDVSA president said that the interim government's strategy to protect Venezuelan assets abroad had been decided on "in a context where it was believed that political change would arrive soon" (Hernández 2020). Such thinking was prevalent in policy circles throughout most of 2019 and likely accounts for the willingness of many countries to forgo diplomatic tradition and recognize Guaidó.

A major push ensued in early 2019 to create the type of public opinion pressure that it was believed could cause Maduro's military support to crumble. Two weeks after his swearing-in, Guaidó issued an order requesting that the military open the border to the entry of humanitarian aid, setting a deadline of February 23.[33] On that day, activists massed at the border demanding that the military admit the convoys. The military was unmoved, and the crowds were dispersed with tear gas. The military leadership would remain loyal to Maduro through this and other confrontations, including an open call to military insurrection that coincided with the defection from the Maduro government of the head of intelligence services (Faiola 2019).

Perhaps the best quantitative indication of the attention being captured by Venezuela among US authorities was in how often they used the Twitter social media platform to refer to that country. Figure 10.10 shows the evolution of tweets on Venezuela by four top US government leaders (Senator Marco Rubio, National Security Advisor John Bolton, Secretary of State Mike Pompeo, and Vice President Mike Pence). The

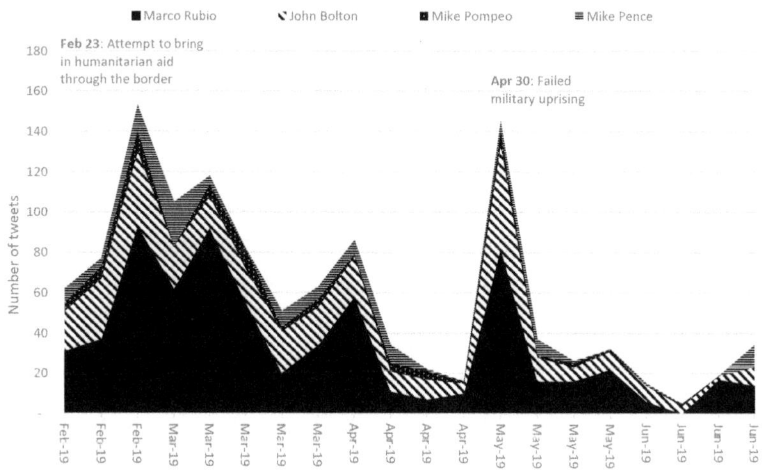

FIGURE 10.10. Tweets on Venezuela by top US officials. *Source*: Author's construction using Twitter.

peak of the series was achieved in the week of February 23, when the officials issued 153 Venezuela-related tweets, accounting for 77.3% of all their tweets. Another peak occurred around the time of the failed military insurrection on April 30, when they accounted for 62% of all tweets.

By the end of 2019, it was clear to many observers that the attempt at overthrowing Maduro was not succeeding. The government had begun to find ways to market its oil with the help of the Russian oil company Rosneft. Oil production began to inch up, rising by 18% between August and February. Imports had also begun recovering and by February were 19% higher than they had been in the same month of the previous year, just after sanctions had been imposed. Remittances from the country's large exodus had begun flowing in, causing a mini-consumption boom in some areas of the country (Amaya 2019). A relieved Maduro would refer to the emerging process of spontaneous dollarization as "an escape valve" that had served to fuel economic recovery, adding, "Thank God dollarization exists" (Infobae 2019).

Yet there would be at least one last push: after Guaidó organized an international tour that culminated in a meeting with President Trump and an invitation to the State of the Union address, the United States announced that it would implement secondary sanctions on non-US firms assisting PDVSA in selling its oil, including Rosneft, which at the time handled around 75% of Venezuela's oil sales and all of its gasoline imports.

The pandemic then hit. COVID-19 had two effects on the Venezuelan economy. On the one hand, as in the rest of the world, lockdowns and social distancing led to significant declines in economic activity. On the other hand, it caused a collapse in oil prices, with the basket of Venezuelan oil falling from \$58 in 2019 to \$32 in 2020. Yet even that decline likely understates the drop in oil sales, as it captures the official reference price and not the actual sales contract price. Because of the fear of secondary sanctions, PDVSA was forced to sell barrels at a deep discount, reducing the price of Venezuelan oil by as much as an additional \$23 per barrel (Parraga and Cohen 2020).

Somewhat unexpectedly, Venezuela does not appear to have been among the countries most hit by the pandemic. As of June 2023, Venezuela had documented 552,695 cases of and 5,856 deaths due to COVID-19. This makes it the country with the third lowest infection rate of thirty-three countries in Latin America and the Caribbean in per capita terms. The extent to which low COVID incidence and mortality reflects underreporting and lack of testing or whether it is genuine and due to aggressive lockdowns, climate, or lack of incidence of comorbidities is not altogether clear. What is true is that Venezuela had less and later access to vaccines than comparable countries, in part due to funding and banking overcompliance with sanctions.[34] According to data from the World Health Organization, as of February 2023, Venezuela had a vaccination rate of 133.1 vaccines per 100 people, making it the country with the fifth lowest vaccination rate in the region.

Venezuela was unique in the world in not having access to any type of financing sources to fund the response to the pandemic. In a context of increasing worldwide deficits, Venezuela's deficit is estimated to have fallen during 2020 as a result of lack of internal and external financing, as well as the erosion of real seigniorage caused by continued hyperinflation (Yapur 2020). As a result of its governance crisis, Venezuela also lacked access to emergency financing from multilateral organisms.

The IMF, for example, more than doubled assistance to member states during the pandemic, increased limits for access to its condition-free Rapid Financing Instrument (RFI) and Rapid Credit Facility (RCF), and issued $650 billion in Special Drawing Rights primarily intended to provide developing countries with enough liquidity to deal with the crisis. These mechanisms would have given Venezuela access to $12.8 billion, or more than a fifth of its 2020 GDP, in emergency financing not subject to program conditionality. Yet the IMF refused to consider Venezuela's requests for these funds (Devex 2021). According to a spokesperson who explained the decision, "IMF engagement with member countries is predicated on official government recognition by the international community. . . . There is no clarity on recognition at this time" (Goodman 2020). Other multilaterals have taken similar positions (Oil for Venezuela 2021).

The pandemic generated the only existing instance of cooperation between the Guaidó and Maduro governments, which in June 2020 created a joint committee of the 2015 National Assembly and Maduro's Ministry of Health to coordinate efforts to attend to the pandemic. This committee produced an agreement to buy 340,000 antigen tests and a deal to use offshore funds controlled by the Guaidó administration to fund the payment for vaccines through the World Bank's COVAX system (Vasquez 2021). Both efforts broke down ultimately, with the opposition accusing the government of not administering the antigen tests effectively and the government insisting on making the COVAX payments on its own and refusing authorization for the Astra-Zeneca vaccine (Yapur 2021).

Constraints on access to the international payments system also severely restricted the country from carrying out a conventional macroeconomic stabilization program to exit hyperinflation. Such programs typically rely on having a monetary authority that can intervene in foreign exchange markets to stabilize the currency and break inflationary expectations. Yet it is virtually impossible for Venezuela's Central Bank to carry out large-scale intervention in the foreign exchange market because foreign banks are not willing to process payments originating in a Central Bank transaction. Thus, even if the Central Bank can find the dollars to sell to the Venezuelan public, whoever tries to use those dollars runs the risk of having their bank account frozen. For this reason, the Central Bank shifted to carrying out intervention in the foreign exchange market through cash transactions (Pons and Armas 2019).

By the end of 2020, Venezuela was mired in an intractable political and economic crisis. Not only had the country's links to the global economy been severed; its authorities had been left without the tools to rebuild them. Venezuela was precluded from using its external assets, seeking private sector or multilateral financing, restructuring its obligations, selling oil to much of the world, and using a large part of the international financial system to make payments. The country was trapped in a tragic stalemate, in which both sides of the political divide had accumulated enough strength to block each other's actions but not enough to decisively prevail in the fight for control of the country's economy.

QUANTIFYING DESTRUCTIVE CONFLICT

In these pages, I have argued that Venezuela's economic collapse can be explained as a consequence of the adoption by political actors of strategies in their fight for power that generated severe negative economic externalities. In chapters 5 through 7, I showed how Maduro began to increasingly appeal to economic policy decisions with strong distortionary effects on the economy as a response to political incentives. I argued that the holding of very frequent nationwide elections in a context of very high stakes of power and declining external revenues made it increasingly difficult for Maduro to satisfy the electorate in the same way in which Chávez had done during the oil price boom. In chapters 8 through 10, I argued that after the opposition gained control of the National Assembly and the support of the hawkish Trump administration, it began to seek ways to impede the government's access to international financial and trade markets. It is this adoption by both sides of scorched earth strategies capable of inflicting severe damage on the economy that is behind Venezuela undergoing the largest output collapse ever documented outside of wartime.

In this section, I try to provide a quantitative approximation of the effect of the adoption of some of these scorched earth strategies on the country's economy. Such an exercise, I feel compelled to warn at the outset, is indicative and suggestive at best. There are many channels through which political strategies can affect the economy, and attempting to identify and quantify all of them can rapidly turn intractable. How can we estimate, for example, the effect of the 2013 Dakazo (Maduro's accusation of price gouging by retailers that led to the looting and military takeover of electronics stores, discussed in chap. 5) on private sector investment decisions? And how can we construct a reasonable counterfactual to indicate what price control policies would have been at the time in the absence of the political incentives generated by high stakes of power and the proximity of the 2013 municipal elections? While there may be imaginative research designs that will allow us to answer these questions, it is inevitable that many of them will remain open at this stage of research.

I therefore focus on three sources of what I argue are some of the most important politically driven causes of output decline. The first one is the decline in oil production caused by economic sanctions. The second one is the decline in access to external sources of funding caused by the withdrawal of recognition of the Maduro government. The third one is the decline in productivity that can be associated with the intensification of political conflict after 2016. It is important to note that these three impacts are far from a complete and exhaustive list of the economic distortions generated by the adoption of scorched earth strategies by political actors. My estimates should thus be read as a conservative lower bound for the effect of politically induced distortions on the country's economic growth. Table 10.2 summarizes my estimates of these effects.

Consider first the effect of economic sanctions on oil output. In chapter 9, I surveyed a set of alternative estimates of the contribution of sanctions to the reduction in oil output. I showed that the median estimate of the decline in output was equal to 42.0% of the post-2012 decline in production and 58.7% of the post-sanctions decline in production; given the truncation of sanctions effects at the end of the sample covered in these studies, the midpoint between these two estimates offers a reasonable approximation of the effect of sanctions on oil production. I thus attribute 50.3% of the decline in oil output to sanctions.

The sanctions-induced decline in oil output affects GDP through two channels. First, since oil accounted for 11% of GDP prior to the collapse, there is a direct contribution of the sanctions to the GDP decline through reduced oil output. This represents a loss of 4.2 percentage points of initial (2012) GDP. Second, there is an indirect effect through the losses in non-oil GDP caused by reduced import capacity. In chapter 2, I estimated that reduced import capacity can explain 59.8% of the decline in GDP (see table 2.3). Applying this ratio to non-oil GDP, I conclude that 37.7 percentage points of the GDP decline is due to loss in import capacity.[35] Of this, around three-fifths is due to lower production, with the other two-fifths due to price declines, implying that an additional 10.2 percentage points of the loss of GDP can be attributed to reduced import capacity caused by sanctions.[36]

I propose to quantify the politically induced loss of access to credit by considering three sources of funding that the country would have surely made use of had it been able to. These are the Special Drawing Rights issued by the IMF in its 2021 general allocation, which were valued at $5.0 billion; the IMF's non-program Rapid Financing Instrument facility, which would have given the country access to 150% of its IMF quota, or $7.8 billion; and its Central Bank gold and other reserve assets blocked at the Bank of England, valued at $2.1 billion. I assume that in 2020 the country would have spent one-third of these assets in higher imports. Using again the estimated contribution of reduced import capacity to GDP from table 2.3, this means that the politically

TABLE 10.2. Decomposition of 2012–2020 economic growth in politically induced and other drivers

Concept	*Cumulative percent decline, 2012–2020*	*Percentage contribution*
Change in per capita GDP	−71.5	100.0
Oil GDP	−8.4	11.7
Sanctions effect	−4.2	5.9
Other causes	−4.2	5.9
Non-oil GDP	−63.1	88.3
Import capacity	−37.7	52.8
Oil exports	−34.5	48.3
Oil price	−14.3	20.1
Oil production	−20.2	28.2
Sanctions effect	−10.2	14.2
Other causes	−10.0	14.0
Permanent loss of access to credit	−3.2	4.5
TFP	−19.2	26.7
Sanctions and toxification effects	−14.8	20.7
Other causes	−4.3	6.0
Factor Accumulation	−6.3	8.8
Sanctions and toxification effects	−4.9	6.9
Other causes	−1.4	2.0

Aggregates Effects	*Cumulative percent decline, 2012–2020*	*Percentage contribution*
Change in per capita GDP	−71.5	100.0
Sanctions and toxification effects	−37.5	52.2
Other causes	−34.2	47.8

Source: Author's construction.

induced loss of access to external funding sources accounts for a loss of 3.2 percentage points of GDP.

Last, I address the effects of sanctions on total factor productivity. Productivity affects GDP both directly and indirectly by inducing changes in factor accumulation. I use the difference between the post-2016 decline in productivity (15.4% annual) and the 1999 to 2016 decline in productivity (1.7%) to estimate the share of productivity in the 2017 to 2020 period that is attributable to sanctions and other politically induced toxification effects. In contrast, I assume that all of the decline in productivity in 2012–16 is due to causes other than sanctions and toxification. This delivers an estimate of 14.8 percentage points of

2012 GDP attributable to the direct effect of sanctions and toxification on productivity, with another 4.9% attributable to the indirect effects through factor accumulation.

The sum of all these effects is 37.2% of 2012 GDP, or 52.2% of the decline in output observed in the 2012 to 2020 period. Of this loss, 53% is attributable to direct and indirect productivity effects, 39% to sanctions effects on oil production, and 9% to loss of access to external funding sources. It is worth emphasizing that this is most likely a lower bound approximation. For example, it is almost certain that if the country had not lost access to international capital markets, it would have been able to fund higher imports through borrowing by much more than one-third of its access to IMF funds and reserve assets blocked in the United Kingdom. The inherent uncertainty about the possible access to funding sources other than those leads me to adopt a conservative estimate of this effect.

The numerical approximation offered in this section thus suggests that approximately half of the decline in GDP observed in Venezuela between 2012 and 2020 can be attributed to politically induced causes, including economic sanctions, the loss of access to external funding sources, and the politically induced toxification of relations with the Venezuelan economy. One way to think about this number is by noting that it implies that in the absence of these economic effects of political conflict, Venezuela's economy would have contracted by 34.2% in the 2012 to 2020 period. Such a contraction would have been more in line with the magnitude of other large contractions in developing countries, as well as in past Venezuelan history, induced by a combination of external shocks with prior unsustainable macroeconomic policies, as discussed in chapter 2.

In other words, if we ask how much of Venezuela's economic contraction between 2012 and 2020 can be attributed to the country's economically destructive political conflict, the results in this section suggest that the answer is around half. But if we ask why Venezuela suffered such an unusually large collapse, a good case can be made that the cause is the country's descent into economically destructive political conflict. Without the adoption of scorched earth tactics that led to the severing of the country's trade and financial links with the global economy, Venezuela would still have undergone a major economic crisis after the collapse in oil prices. But not only would that crisis have been much smaller than what we observed; it would also not have been atypical given the magnitude of the terms of trade decline and the country's exposure to external shocks. Had Venezuela's income declined by around a third after seeing a fall of more than two-thirds in oil prices, not many observes would have considered the result unusual and this book would probably not have been written. The fact that Venezuela suffered an economic collapse of a much greater order of magnitude than that is what makes the country's experience atypical. The country's excess contraction over and above what would have usually been the response to a large negative terms of trade shock cannot be explained without bringing in the phenomenon of economically destructive political conflict.

PART IV

Extending the Framework

ELEVEN

Scorched Earth Politics beyond Venezuela

What is lacking now is goods on the shelves. That's all.
—Robert Mugabe, in Holland 2008

In the preceding pages, I argued that Venezuela's economic collapse is a consequence of the nation's descent into a particularly destructive form of political conflict. While politically induced distortions are common to many political settings, governments generally stop far short of severely undermining the productive basis of their economies. Yet under conditions of very high stakes and effective contestation of power, such as those present in Venezuela in the 2010s, political actors may find it optimal to adopt strategies that impose severe negative externalities on the rest of society. It is this adoption of scorched earth strategies that causes the descent into the type of political conflict capable of destroying an economy.

At the center of my argument is the idea that the structure of political competition is a crucial determinant of political and economic outcomes. Winner-take-all political systems raise the incentives for political actors to play outside of established rules of competition and increase the likelihood that they opt for the pursuit of strategies that severely harm society. Despite their destructiveness, these strategies make political sense from the standpoint of participants in the high-stakes contest for political power.

This chapter argues that the scorched earth framework can help us understand the role that political conflict plays in determining economic outcomes in other settings. I claim that the capacity to manage and restrain political conflict to impede it from spilling over into the economy is a central characteristic of most functioning political systems. This means that when the arrangements governing political conflict break down, we can expect to see nations pay significant economic costs. Likewise, if we consider cases in which political actors had the capacity to harm the economy but decided not to do so, we may understand the nature of the rules and agreements that serve to restrain destructive conflict.

I explore these hypotheses with four examples. I begin with two cases of peacetime economic collapses: Zimbabwe at the turn of the twentieth century and Weimar Germany in the interwar years. I show that in both cases we see shifts in political strategies toward those that generate more severe negative economic externalities. I also argue that in both cases, the decision to adopt scorched earth strategies was a response to increases in the stakes of power or in the effective contestability of that power. I then turn to two examples of countries that did not—or have not—suffered economic collapses, despite their political actors having access to scorched earth technologies. These are Poland at the end of communism and the United States today. I explore the reasons that politicians decided not to make use of their ability to harm the economy and show that the existence or prospects of reaching cohabitation agreements allowing contending sides to share in the benefits from power played a key role in restraining political actors from turning their economies into political battlefields.

ZIMBABWE'S DESTRUCTIVE LANDGRAB

In February 2000, Robert Mugabe suffered a stunning political defeat. His government had put before voters a proposal for a new Constitution to replace the 1979 Lancaster House Agreements that had brought an end to the civil war between Black insurgents and a white-rule government. The proposal, which would have significantly strengthened presidential powers, was rejected by 55% of voters. Four months later, the opposition Movement for Democratic Change (MDC) captured 57 of

120 seats in a very close parliamentary election in which it garnered 47% of the popular vote to 49% for Mugabe's Zimbabwe African National Union (ZANU-PF). These results pointed to a remarkable change from the situation in the prior (1995) elections, in which ZANU-PF had been unchallenged and captured 118 of the 120 seats in Parliament.

Right after the referendum defeat, the government decided to focus its parliamentary campaign on a promise of increased land redistribution, exemplified by the slogan, "Land Is the Economy; the Economy Is Land" (Human Rights Watch 2002). One month after the parliamentary elections, it announced a "fast track" resettlement program. Over the next seven months, it would mark 2,706 farms covering more than six million hectares for compulsory redistribution (Ministry of Lands, Agriculture, and Rural Resettlement Zimbabwe 2002). The state began sponsoring land invasions on a large scale, with a mix of government forces and vigilante groups forcibly taking over white-owned land. Land occupations were often carried out by armed gangs and in several instances led to the killing of white owners. After the Supreme Court ruled the invasions illegal in December 2000, Mugabe expanded the court in July 2001, appointing three new judges to ensure a loyal majority that would reverse the decision (New Humanitarian 2001; Zimbabwe Human Rights NGO Forum 2010).

The drop in agricultural production was staggering. Maize farming, which yielded more than 1.5 million tons annually before 2000, dropped to 500,000 tons by 2003. Wheat production fell from 309,000 tons in 2000 to 27,000 tons in 2003, and tobacco production fell from 265,000 tons in 2000 to 66,000 tons in 2003. These three crops accounted for 70% of the country's agricultural production before 2000 (Power 2003). Agricultural production growth was negative throughout these eight years, and virtually every crop was affected (World Bank 2019).

Driven by falling agricultural production, the economy shrank for nine consecutive years, living standards collapsed, and the country entered hyperinflation. The currency lost all its value, virtually disappearing from use. More than five million people were thrust into poverty, more than two million emigrated, and over half a million lost formal sector jobs. By 2010, Zimbabwe had the lowest Human Development Index (HDI) of 169 countries ranked by the United Nations Development Programme and was one of only three countries in the world to see

TABLE 11.1A. Sources of growth decomposition, Zimbabwe, 1982–1996 (pre-collapse)

Sources	*GDP*	*Capital*	*Human Capital*	*TFP*
Growth (%)	3.2	0.9	1.6	–
Contribution (%)	3.2	0.3	1.0	1.9
Percentage contribution	100.0	10.4	31.3	58.3

TABLE 11.1B. Sources of growth decomposition, Zimbabwe, 1996–2008 (collapse)

Sources	*GDP*	*Capital*	*Human Capital*	*TFP*
Growth (%)	–3.6	–1.3	1.2	–
Contribution (%)	–3.6	–0.5	0.8	–3.9
Percentage contribution	100.0	13.6	–20.8	107.2

Source: Rodríguez and Imam 2022.

a decline in its HDI since 1970 (UNDP 2010, 3, and Statistical Annex table 1). The portion of the population living below US$1 a day stood at more than 80% in 2006, up from 36% in 1990. Life expectancy collapsed from 59 years in 1990 to 37 years in 2005 and was among the lowest in the world (World Bank 2007; Besada and Moyo 2008).

Table 11.1 presents the results of a growth accounting exercise for Zimbabwe from 1982 to 2008. As I did for Venezuela, I distinguish between the pre-collapse period (1982–96) and the collapse period (1996–2008). As occurred in Venezuela, the period of collapse witnessed a slump in TFP. The rate of drop in TFP (-3.9% annual) exceeds the drop in GDP (-3.6). A similar pattern is present if we adjust for import externalities.

As in the case of Venezuela, Zimbabwe's economic contraction intensified precisely after the government suffered an electoral setback that put in danger its hold on power. Venezuela in 2015 and Zimbabwe in 2000 were not fully fledged authoritarian states. Rather, they were states in which the political system was sufficiently competitive to make power effectively contested. An initial adverse shock (2012–16 in Venezuela, 1997–2000 in Zimbabwe) led to a deterioration in the government's electoral competitiveness. Electoral victories or near-victories by the opposition ensued in both cases, putting the government's hold on power at risk.

Faced with the risk of losing power in a winner-take-all political system, the Mugabe government decided to play a scorched earth strategy. This implied an about-face in its land reform strategy. For the previous two decades, Mugabe had been pursuing land reform policies under a model in which land transfers were being done through voluntary sales. The system had worked fairly well, redistributing four million hectares to around seventy thousand families (Human Rights Watch 2002). Under the voluntary land reform system, Zimbabwe saw positive economic growth of nearly 1% per year during a period in which sub-Saharan Africa as a whole was contracting. It is not that Mugabe did not know how to do a land reform that was compatible with economic efficiency. It is that the pre-2000 strategy did not serve his political aims as well as the post-2000 model did.

In contrast to Venezuela, Zimbabwe never faced a trade embargo from its main trading partners. Yet sanctions did block Zimbabwe's access to international financial institutions, which could have played a role in helping Zimbabwe weather its economic crisis. In December 2001, the US Congress prohibited its representatives at international financial institutions from voting in favor of extending loans or grants to Zimbabwe, de facto blocking the debt restructuring of Zimbabwe's arrears (Matyszak 2019). The EU followed suit in 2002, strengthening the pariah status of Zimbabwe. Development program assistance was reduced, ending budgetary support, and visa bans and asset freezes were adopted. The growing isolation was compounded by suspension from the Commonwealth in the same year.

In contrast to Venezuela's opposition, Zimbabwe's MDC was much more guarded in its support for sanctions, drawing a line between personal sanctions, which it fully supported, and economic sanctions, which it publicly claimed to oppose—although this didn't stop the government from accusing the MDC of secretly lobbying for them. Zimbabwe's political history may have had an impact, as the War of Independence was still raw in the minds of the population, and outside interference would always be attacked by ZANU-PF as neocolonialism. Yet even if MDC formally opposed economic sanctions, it did little to nothing to try to get them reversed.

In practice, selective sanctions did have a chilling, even if perhaps unintended, consequence. Not only did they create a pariah status and de facto block international reengagement, but they complicated international banking, creating sometimes unsurmountable obstacles for the business environment (Matyszak 2019). Most international operators—for fear of inadvertently violating sanctions—treat Zimbabwe with extreme caution, minimizing any risks of falling foul of penalties.

Zimbabwe's economic collapse thus fits well into the framework of economically destructive political conflict. A government that sees its hold on power threatened makes use of increasingly distortionary policies to avoid losing office, while the opposition and its international allies react by imposing additional restrictions on the economy's functioning that interfere with its international insertion. Economic contraction is driven by productivity losses in the sector that is at the center of the political tug-of-war. As the political threat recedes, the government adopts policy reforms, including a macroeconomic stabilization program, and embraces dollarization.

WEIMAR GERMANY'S SLIDE INTO HYPERINFLATION

Between 1913 and 1923, Germany's per capita GDP fell by 25%. During this same period, the per capita incomes of its neighbors France and Belgium grew respectively by 8% and 7%.[1] This occurred even though the physical devastation from World War II appears to have been much greater in France and Belgium—which suffered from German occupation through most of the war. In contrast to its neighbors, Germany did not experience a postwar recovery but saw instead a continued income decline, macroeconomic instability, and ultimately hyperinflation in the postwar years.

Germany's currency collapsed in the aftermath of the war, falling from a value of 7.4 German marks to the US dollar at the signing of the Armistice in 1918 to 4.2 trillion marks per US dollar at the end of the hyperinflation in December 2023 (Taylor 2013, 403–12). Traditional analyses of the German hyperinflation, many of them inspired by Keynes's ([1919] 2012) initial reaction to the 1919 Versailles Treaty, emphasize the unviability of the reparations payments demanded by the Allies, which required Germany to pay 132 billion gold marks, or more than three times its net national product, in compensation for war damages and debts incurred by the Entente countries.[2] However, while Germany's Reichsbank did at times print marks to purchase hard currency to make reparations payments, the weight of any actual payments made by Germany ended up being much smaller than originally foreseen, and it is unclear that they were large enough to explain the country's contraction in and of themselves (Marks 1978, 2013; Kolb 2004).

In contrast, a more pressing problem for the Weimar government was how to deal with the 154 billion marks ($21 billion, or four times net national product) in war debt that it owed, a large share of which was in the form of war bonds held by German citizens. Hyperinflation was the main mechanism through which the Weimar Republic defaulted on that debt, whose value was inflated away to 15.4 pfennigs of a new mark, or 3.7 cents of a US dollar (Taylor 2013, 382). As in the case of Venezuela, hyperinflation served for the government to default on some obligations that it lacked the legal power to renege on, including wage demands.

Following the abdication of Kaiser Wilhelm II in November 1918, leaders from the Social Democratic Party of Germany (MPSD) proclaimed a Republic. Although they initially backed the new government, more radical leftist groups soon split off and tried to install a Communist government during the short-lived Spartacist uprising of January 1919. The uprising was put down with the aid of right-wing Freikorps militias, consolidating the alliance of the MPSD and conservative elements of demobilized armed forces that would later be subsumed into Nazism.

Because of its origins in and support from the organized labor movement, MPSD leaders felt bound to honor their commitments to building a welfare state that the insolvent postwar German state could ill afford. This included promises of increased wages, unemployment insurance, an eight-hour workday, and rights to unionize (Potthoff and Miller 1987; Treue 1954, 97–102). Honoring these commitments while dealing with the country's outstanding debt obligations would require serious fiscal reforms. Finance Minister Matthias Erzberger succeeded in pushing some of these through the National Assembly in 1919, including the centralization of taxes in the federal government, the introduction of income and inheritance taxes, and the imposition of an emergency one-off war wealth levy. Erzberger became the focus of the animosity of Germany's growingly radicalized right, which blamed him for imposing tax reforms to pay reparations to the Allies (Eichengreen 1992; Patton 1996; Hefeker 2001). As a result, he was forced to resign from the ministry and give up his seat in the National Assembly. There would be two assassination attempts on Erzberger; the second, which took place in August 1921, would be successful (Fergusson 2010, chap. 4).

Erzberger's reforms contributed to stopping the slide in the currency, which managed to remain stable against the dollar between the approval of the federal income tax and Erzberger's assassination in August 1921. Later that year, Germany would lose control of the key industrial area of Upper Silesia to Poland, and one year later France and Belgium would invade and occupy the Ruhr region to enforce reparations. In response, Weimar authorities instituted the policy of "passive resistance" in which Germans refused to cooperate with the production, loading, or transport of coal by France (Global Nonviolent Action Database 1923; Fischer 2003a, 2003b). In practice, this meant that the German government continued to pay the salaries of virtually all the industrial population of the region. Near the peak of the hyperinflation in August 1923, 59% of government expenditures corresponded to payments for the Parliament-mandated Ruhr struggle (Feldman 1997, 711). The government finally put an end to the passive resistance policy at the end of September and was able to successfully stabilize prices by introducing a new currency backed by land mortgages, the rentenmark, in October. A decree published that month authorized the government to dismiss 25% of civil servants, marking the government's virtual abandonment of its commitment to protect workers' rights.

While monetary and fiscal reforms were successful in stabilizing prices, the Nationalist right seized on the abandonment of passive resistance to accuse the Social Democrats of treason, reinforcing the "stab in the back" narrative that claimed that Germany could have won World War I if leftist politicians hadn't forced it to sign the Armistice. Bavaria essentially seceded from the Republic when it unilaterally transferred national executive powers to its local government (Landauer 1944). The government handed over control of the Rentenbank—the bank that issued the new rentenmark—to industrialists and bankers and forcibly removed the Communist-Socialist government of Saxony, further consolidating its turn to the right (Feldman 1997, chap. 15). Contractionary adjustment led to persistently high unemployment, sowing the seeds for the future growth of radical nationalist movements.

Germany's interwar crisis fits well into the framework of economically destructive political conflict. As Social Democrats, Communists, and Nationalists clashed for power, they increasingly appealed to political positions that generated severe costs for the German economy. Initially unable to block tax reforms in Parliament, Nationalists opted for terrorizing, and often killing, key government figures. Both the left and the right boxed the centrist government into paying for passive resistance in the Ruhr, a policy that would lead to the final demise of the currency. The Social Democrats, in turn, felt they could not stabilize public finances without reneging on promises to their labor constituents. When they finally did so and pacted with industrial and agricultural interests, they saw their electoral support wane, paving the way for the rise of right-wing nationalism.

—I now turn to discussing cases in which the descent into destructive conflict, while conceivable and perhaps even seemingly predictable, did not occur. I focus on two cases of societies marked by high levels of polarization and in which both the government and the opposition had scorched earth strategies at their disposal. This focus allows us to envision counterfactual scenarios in which political actors could have wreaked havoc on the economy, and it allows us to explore the motivations that drove them not to do so.

HOW POLAND AVOIDED DESTRUCTIVE CONFLICT

I begin with Poland's transition from a centrally planned Communist one-party state to a multiparty democratic market economy. The 1980s saw two groups with seemingly irreconcilable differences face off against each other for control of the country. Despite the potentially high stakes of political conflict, these groups proved able to effectively lead a coalition government that engineered a successful economic stabilization and transition to democracy.

Controlling Poland, a country with a fierce nationalist tradition, was never easy for the Soviet Union. Poland's four and a half decades of Communist rule were racked by persistent protests and often-brutal repression, denying political stability to many of the Soviet-backed governments. As early as 1970, unrest following the repression of protests against the raising of prices of basic foodstuffs led to the ouster of Władysław Gomułka, first secretary of the Soviet-supported Polish United Workers' Party (Polska Zjednoczona Partia Robotnicza, PZPR) (Fajfer 1993; Kramer 1995).

Some incipient forms of social organization nevertheless took hold. In August 1980, the termination of a shipyard operator less than two months before her retirement as punishment for her activism in support of trade unions ignited a strike movement in support of workers' rights (Staniszkis 1981; Majchrzak 2017). The popularity of the strike movement, which called for the acceptance of free trade unions independent of the Communist Party, respect for the right to strike, and compliance with the constitutional guarantee of freedom of speech, led to the creation of Solidarity, the first independent labor union in a Soviet bloc country (Mason 1989; Kubow 2013). The government grudgingly yielded and allowed its legalization in September 1980. Under the leadership of a shipyard electrician, Lech Wałęsa, the union's official membership skyrocketed, increasing to almost ten million people by 1981—41% of Poland's adult population at the time—turning it into a formidable political movement (Berend 1996, 258).

Threatened by Solidarity's increasing influence, the Polish army seized power in 1981, with the defense minister, Wojciech Jaruzelski, heading the new government. Jaruzelski moved to declare martial law, claiming that doing so was necessary to avoid a Soviet invasion. The new government prohibited trade unions and detained hundreds of Solidarity leaders, including Wałęsa, but failed to dissolve the movement. Other activists soon filled leadership positions and managed to reorganize underground (Bartkowski 2009). Martial law remained in place for almost two years. By 1984, the government had released all political prisoners and lifted martial law, yet its international legitimacy was severely tarnished.

A political stalemate ensued. Western governments refused to resume normal economic relations, calling on the government to negotiate with Solidarity. In 1985, Mikhail Gorbachev assumed power in the USSR and took a stance against his country's military intervention in other European Communist countries, rejecting what had become known as the Brezhnev doctrine (Skórzyński 2010; Phlipot 2010).

The economy deteriorated strongly. Poland had accumulated a large amount of debt, turning it into one of the only Soviet bloc countries to suffer from the debt crisis triggered by the increase in US interest rates in the early 1980s. The economy shrank by 14% and inflation soared from 8% to 104% between 1978 and 1982.[3] Growth then stagnated as the government struggled to make debt service payments and resorted to money printing, causing inflation to rise to 245% in 1989. As the USSR crumbled and demand for Polish exports fell, strikes multiplied, leading the weakened government to reengage with Solidarity.

One remarkable difference between Solidarity and the Venezuelan opposition was the stance taken by Solidarity against economic sanctions. During his Nobel Peace Prize acceptance speech, Wałęsa called on the United States to lift sanctions, arguing that "Poland ought to be helped and deserves help" (Saikowski 1983). The appeal, which was seconded by the Polish-born pope John Paul II, led President Ronald Reagan to lift various sanctions in 1984 and to ultimately lift all sanctions in 1987, stating that it was never his intention to hurt the Polish people (Kamm 1982; Goshko 1984; Reagan 1987). The lifting of all sanctions preceded by two years the Roundtable Agreement of 1989 that led to that year's elections and formation of a unity government, suggesting that the sanctions may not have been necessary and could even have been an obstacle to reaching a negotiated agreement. Under Wałęsa's leadership, Solidarity took an explicit decision not to employ a scorched earth strategy, a decision that may explain its sustained electoral strength during and after the transition.

Wałęsa was also open to a cohabitation agreement, and by 1989, the government and Solidarity reached what became known as the Roundtable Agreement, in which the Communists allowed the legalization of trade unions and the creation of the President's Office, and the opposition agreed to participate in semi-open elections to the Sejm, the unicameral parliament. These elections, however, were designed so as not to risk the Communists losing power. The government reserved 300 seats for the ruling party and allies, allowing the opposition to compete for the remaining 260 seats, with the parliament in turn electing the president. It also included an additional offer to persuade Solidarity to agree: the return to a bicameral system, with totally free elections for the new Senate seats.

The results made evident the unpopularity of the military government and the huge support for Solidarity. The opposition won all contested Sejm seats and 99 of 100 seats in the Senate (Biskupski, Pula, and Wróbel 2010, 273). Despite this crushing defeat, parliament moved to appoint Jaruzelski as president in a vote in which the opposition abstained. Initially, Wałęsa rejected any participation in a Communist-led government. He then made a risky gambit, offering a coalition to two parties hitherto allied with the Communists that their leaders accepted. This forced the government to accept a transition in which it kept the Defense and Internal Affairs Ministries (Krok-Paszkowska 2001).

In September 1989, the new parliament approved the provisional government cabinet with Wałęsa's adviser, Tadeusz Mazowiecki, as prime minister. Mazowiecki took advantage of Solidarity's popularity and credibility to present radical economic reforms aimed at starting the transition from central planning to a free-market economy (Krok-Paszkowska 2001). The plan got rid of price controls and subsidies, privatized state-owned businesses, created a stable convertible currency, and restrained wage increases to reduce inflation (Blanchard 1994; Sachs 1994; Balcerowicz 1996). The PZPR ultimately dissolved itself, with some of its leaders forming a social democratic party that would also perform poorly. In December 1990, Wałęsa won a runoff presidential election with 74% of the votes, effectively completing the transition.

The transition government's economic policies successfully stabilized Poland's consumer goods market, increased exports, and restored the government's finances (Buzek 2009). Since 1989, Polish GDP per capita has more than tripled, posting the strongest economic performance of any country in the European Union. Poland was the only economy in Europe to avoid a recession during the global financial crisis (Piatkowski 2013) and saw one of the lowest economic contractions in the OECD during the COVID-19 pandemic (Bukowski and Paczós 2021).

Why did Solidarity and the Communists not descend into economically destructive political conflict? Why didn't the Communists try to block or torpedo economic reforms? Why did Solidarity not push for harsher economic sanctions but instead advocate for their lifting? Why did Communist Poland—in contrast to Venezuela, Zimbabwe, and Weimar Germany—never enter full-fledged hyperinflation? Why were the sides to Poland's political conflict able to enter into, and make work, a cohabitation agreement?

One important characteristic of Solidarity is that it had its origins as a trade union movement. While it ultimately morphed into a broad social movement and political party, its organizational power came from the mobilization of factory workers. In contrast to the Venezuelan and Zimbabwean oppositions, Solidarity's initial demands were primarily related to workers' rights instead of political reforms. For example, in the twenty-one demands published by the Interfactory Strike Committee in August 1980 that eventually led to the Gdansk agreement, there was no mention of political freedoms other than the right to strike and the constitutional guarantee of free speech. Therefore, a great part of the negotiations between it and the Jaruzelski government during the 1980s focused on improvements in wages and working conditions rather than on political reforms.

Solidarity's trade union base meant that the movement was highly sensitive to changes in current economic conditions. This was particularly true of anything that affected the external demand for Polish goods or the country's import capacity. Poland's shipyard industry, the birthplace of the Solidarity movement, was particularly hit by declining demand for its products from Soviet bloc countries in the 1980s. Attempts to access Western markets were hampered by sanctions, and the sector saw the number of new ships per year decline by 8.3% between 1975 and 1980 and 2.7% between 1981 and 1985 (Majchrzak 2017; Maritime Institute n.d.). Polish exports fell by 19% between 1980 and 1985, while the suspension of credit forced the country to cut its current account deficit, leading to an even larger 30% decline in imports.[4]

Not unlike other sanctions-affected governments, the Jaruzelski government made use of these results to carry out a public relations campaign blaming sanctions for the country's economic conditions (Daodi and Dajani 1985). Interestingly, Solidarity leaders recognized in private as early as 1983 that these claims had gained traction in public opinion, leading to a decision by the movement's leadership that "for the good of the trade union, it would be better to appeal for the withdrawal of the economic sanctions before the beginning of the next year [1984]" (Domber 2014, 121).

Another important difference between Poland and some of the other cases that I have discussed is the fact that the leadership of Solidarity remained firmly in the hands of more moderate sectors that favored negotiated coexistence with the Communist leadership. Of course, there were other sectors in the Polish opposition that favored a more hard-line stance—indeed, some of these sectors were harshly critical of Wałęsa, whom they accused of collaborationism (Ost 1990, 134). But Wałęsa's international prestige, possibly in itself a consequence of how the movement became known around the world through the Gdansk shipyard protests, as well as the movement's control of the not inconsiderable amount of international funding that came with it, all but ensured that the moderates would remain at its helm (Domber 2014, 283–88).

Moderates also played an important role in the Communist government, which only imposed martial law in 1981, after strong Soviet pressure, and maintained permanent back-channel communication with the US government. By the second half of the 1980s, the Jaruzelski government had already initiated market reforms, similar to those being implemented under Perestroika in the Soviet Union. There were thus many fewer policy differences, and a greater possibility for policy convergence, between the Communists and Solidarity at the time (Mason 1988, 437–39). US authorities saw sanctions as an inducement that they could use to move the Jaruzelski government to reforms rather than to try to topple it. The Reagan administration, which was in general wary of the overuse of sanctions and had tried to impede or reduce their use in other contexts,[5] was concerned that an economic collapse of Poland would force Soviet intervention and end up consolidating Poland as a Soviet satellite (Domber 2007, 40).

US corporate interests may also have played a role in making the Reagan administration more prone to supporting a negotiated solution that could lead to a rapid lifting of sanctions. In a move that was strongly criticized by the Democrats, the Reagan administration committed to lend $613 million to Poland so that it wouldn't default on its debt—part of which was owed to private US banks (*New York Times* 1982). While the AFL-CIO strongly opposed lifting sanctions, other lobby groups with corporate membership or support, such as the Polish American Congress, supported it (Erdmans 1995; Goddeeris 2007).

The sway of moderates willing to accept cohabitation in both the government and opposition camps made the stakes of power in Poland much lower than in other cases studied in this book. In fact, the eventual transition saw many of the outgoing Communists reintegrate into the country's social and political life with little risk of prosecution.[6] The decline of the Soviet Union and the start of Perestroika—with the implication that the Polish government could not expect to continue receiving large subsidies from the bankrupt Soviet economy—also meant that the Jaruzelski government did not have the necessary support to withstand an all-out confrontation. The unwillingness of the Reagan administration to maintain harsh sanctions over time, as well as the cost that these sanctions were having on Solidarity's base of support among trade unions, meant that the opposition also lacked access to a scorched earth strategy that it could adopt without severely damaging itself.

AMERICA'S BUDGET CRISIS THAT WASN'T

In the spring of 2023, the administration of President Joe Biden faced off against legislators from the opposition Republican Party over the refusal of the latter to unconditionally raise the country's debt ceiling. The standoff sent short-term yields on Treasury bonds rising to their highest level in more than twenty years (Mosolva, Kerr, and Lockett 2023). Failure to reach a deal likely would have led to an unprecedented default on the country's financial debt, producing a recession comparable to that caused by the 2008 financial crisis (White House 2023a; Zandi, Karmins, and Yaros 2023).

The US Constitution grants Congress the sole power to borrow money on behalf of the United States. In use of this authority, Congress directly authorized all debt issuance until 1917; in that year, the Second Liberty Loan Act established a $15 billion aggregate limit on the amount of government bonds issued to finance the war effort. Since 1960, Congress has acted seventy-nine separate times to permanently raise, temporarily extend, or revise the definition of the debt limit. These approvals tended to be granted almost automatically until the 2010s. In 2011, a standoff between the Republican-controlled Congress and the administration of Barack Obama was resolved only days before the projected default date (also known as the X date), leading S&P to downgrade the US credit rating from AAA to AA+ for the first time in history (Brandimarte and Bases 2011).

In 2023, the Speaker of the Republican-controlled House, Kevin McCarthy, demanded that the government conduct major spending cuts to bring the growth in the nation's debt under control. Republicans pointed to the large increase in the federal debt, which stood at 95% of GDP, more than double the ratio fifteen years before.[7] The United States ran a budget deficit of 5.4% of GDP in 2023 and has not seen a primary surplus since 2001. There is a broad consensus that US fiscal policy is unsustainable: according to the US of the Treasury Department (2022), were fiscal policy to continue on its path, the share of debt held by the public would grow to 228% of GDP by 2050 and 566% of GDP by 2097.

President Biden characterized the Republican position as "reckless" and claimed that it was Congress's responsibility to unconditionally extend the debt limit. According to the administration, since all spending carried out by the federal government had already been approved by past congressional appropriation decisions, Congress had an obligation to allow the government to incur the debt needed to pay for its past decisions (Biden 2023). Biden had also submitted a budget proposal contemplating cuts of $300 billion a year, or 1.1% of current GDP, over the course of the next decade. Republicans countered with a plan of $450 billion a year in cuts, or 1.8% of GDP, over the same period. Both plans would have been insufficient to stabilize the US debt, for which cuts of at least $840 billion a year (3.3% of GDP) would be needed (CFRB 2023).

Biden and McCarthy announced that they had reached a deal on May 28, and a bipartisan bill was passed in Congress on June 1, four days before the Treasury Department's estimated X date. The compromise bill suspended the debt limit for eighteen months, capped discretionary spending for the following two years, ended a moratorium on student debts, and introduced work requirements for some welfare recipients. The bill is estimated to reduce the deficit by $152 billion a year over the 2024 to 2033 period (0.6% of GDP).

Hard-liners on both the Republican and Democrat sides criticized the bill. The House Freedom Caucus, a group of ultraconservative Republican legislators, tried to block the vote and vowed to seek to replace McCarthy as Speaker. Progressive Caucus Whip Greg Casar referred to the bill as "a ransom deal" (Karni 2023; Trudo 2023). Senator Bernie Sanders, who lost the race for the Democratic nomination against

Biden in 2020, opposed the bill, urging Biden to invoke an interpretation of the Fourteenth Amendment to the Constitution—which specifies that the validity of the public debt should not be questioned—as granting the government the authority to issue debt in excess of the debt ceiling (Gans 2023).

Why did the sides reach a compromise? And how were they able to generate enough support among legislators to pass it? Twenty-eight percent of legislators in the House and 36% in the Senate—including 63% of Senate Republicans—either voted against the bill or abstained. Influential voices on both sides favored continued confrontation. Former president Donald Trump—at the time the frontrunner in the race for the Republican nomination—said to Republican legislators that "if they don't give you massive cuts, you're going to have to do a default" (Calia 2023). Nobel laureate Paul Krugman spelled out proposals to deal with what he termed the Republicans' "extortion" in a *New York Times* article published only three days before a deal was reached: invoking the Fourteenth Amendment, issuing perpetual bonds, or printing a commemorative $1 trillion coin. Biden himself said the lawyers he had consulted claimed that invoking the Fourteenth Amendment would be "legitimate" (White House 2023b).

Just after the 2011 deal that averted a similar budget crisis and that also ended in symbolic concessions to Republicans, then Senate minority leader Mitch McConnell said that the deal was made possible due to the support of moderate Republicans who did not want to see themselves blamed for causing a default on the national debt. "I think some of our members may have thought the default issue was a hostage you might take a chance at shooting," McConnell told the *Washington Post*. "Most of us didn't think that" (Fahrenthold, Montgomery, and Kane 2011).

In 2023, as in 2011, it was the Republican leadership that appears to have backed down. While they received some symbolic concessions, the cuts were only one-third of those that they had demanded initially, and the rate of desertion among Republican legislators who refused to back the deal was much greater than on the Democrats' side. One important factor may have been the uncertainty about the public reaction to a default. Though recessions tend to favor challengers in elections, 39% of respondents to a poll taken at the time of negotiations said that they would blame Republicans for a default—slightly higher than the 36% that said they would blame Biden. Most importantly, 58% agreed with Biden that debt payment and the federal spending cuts should be handled separately. In contrast, only 26% said they agreed with the view that Congress should let government pay its debts only if the administration agrees to spending cuts (Langer 2023).

Despite having access to scorched earth strategies, the Republican leadership was aware that pursuing them would have a high electoral cost. Not ready to ditch electoral competition, they decided to avoid the potential blowback from throwing the government into default. And while the United States has become increasingly polarized politically in recent times, its political system continues to be characterized by moderate stakes of power, including the potential for a parliamentary minority to block legislation using filibuster tactics. It doesn't appear coincidental that the faction of the party that has disavowed election results and whose leader was facing the possibility of a criminal conviction was the one that was most in favor of a scorched earth approach.

TWELVE

Venezuela beyond Scorched Earth Politics

We accept that our country is being consumed by conflict, and that a scorched earth is not in anyone's interest.
—Willie Esterhuyse, South African academic and negotiator, 2012

This concluding chapter returns to Venezuela to ask how the framework offered in this book can inform attempts to find ways out of the country's crisis. I argue that most existing attempts at resolving Venezuela's economic, humanitarian, and political crisis have paid scant attention to the structure of political incentives behind it. By focusing on increasing the cost to the government of the status quo or facilitating political negotiations over zero-sum outcomes, conventional strategies have missed the forest for the trees. I argue that attempts to resolve Venezuela's crisis should instead focus on changing the structure of political incentives to reduce the stakes of power and lower the incentives for political actors to continue adopting strategies that damage the economy in their fight for power.

The preceding chapters laid out an analytical narrative of Venezuela's economic collapse that traces it to the incremental adoption by the country's political actors of scorched earth strategies. This process began during the 2013 to 2016 period when the Maduro administration adopted increasingly distortionary economic policies in response to political incentives. With its weak initial mandate, and facing a particularly intense calendar of elections and a large adverse external shock, the government decided to prioritize short-run objectives instead of long-term growth to shore up popular support when faced with upcoming elections or other threats to its stability in power. Tight enforcement of price controls, massive monetization of budget deficits, and the maintenance of exchange rate overvaluation followed the electoral cycle, with distortions increasing markedly when the government faced tangible threats to its hold on power.

The increasing appeal to policy distortions by a government that was seeing its electoral competitiveness eroded can be explained in the context of single-actor models of politically induced distortions first introduced into neoclassical economics by the Virginia public choice school of economics. As Venezuela entered the second part of the 2010s, however, the structure of political competition began to change. When the opposition gained control of the National Assembly and a team of foreign policy hawks came into office with Donald Trump in the United States, the opposition gained the ability to do what is typically only an option open to governments: manipulate economic conditions in its favor by impairing the country's access to international trade and financial markets.

This change in the political technologies that the opposition had access to necessitates a conceptual framework that goes beyond the one-actor model of politically induced distortions that is standard in the traditional political economy literature. In chapter 3, I introduced a two-actor model in which both the government and the opposition could adopt strategies that generated negative economic externalities on society in their fight for power. This framework helped characterize the conditions under which political actors adopt scorched earth tactics. When the stakes of power are very high and the value of the economy's endowments decline, a descent into full-fledged economically destructive political conflict with both actors adopting strategies that damage the economy becomes more likely.

The acceleration of Venezuela's economic implosion despite recovering oil prices in the post-2016 period fits well into the framework of the two-player model of economically destructive political conflict. I documented how the conflict over the purse strings affected the government and oil industry's access to international financing, ultimately leading to the imposition of financial and trade sanctions that barred the government from restructuring its debt, accessing oil markets in Europe and the United States, and using its offshore assets to offset the decline in export revenues. A numerical approximation provided in chapter 10 suggests that approximately half of the country's economic contraction since 2012 is attributable to oil sanctions, the loss of access to external funds, and the productivity effects of politically induced toxification. In the absence of its political crisis, I argue, Venezuela would have seen a decline of around one-third percent in its GDP, similar to its response to large negative terms of trade shocks in the past. Because of the descent into economically destructive political conflict, that crisis grew in magnitude to one that saw the country lose nearly three-quarters of its income and suffer the largest decline in per capita incomes ever documented outside of wartime.

In sum, Venezuela's economic and political crises are deeply interconnected. The country suffers an economic and humanitarian catastrophe because its political elites are locked in an all-out struggle for political power. The country is likely to remain mired in crisis unless the structure of political incentives changes to reduce the stakes of the political contest and lower the benefits from pursuing scorched earth strategies.

This vision contrasts with much conventional thinking about Venezuela, according to which changes in government and economic policies are necessary and sufficient conditions for the country's economic recovery (e.g., Obuchi, Lira, and Raguá 2016; Halff et al. 2017; Bahar, Piccone, and Trinkunas 2018; Asamblea Nacional de Venezuela 2019a; Abuelafia and Saboín 2020). My argument goes beyond the oft-repeated truism that policies are endogenous to the political process. I contend that growth-inducing policies are not a political equilibrium for Venezuela given the high stakes embodied in the country's structure of political competition. Put politicians who espouse reasonable policy ideals into this competition, I argue, and they will do their best to block their implementation when they are out of office and ditch them once they reach office. Poor policies are less a reflection of the convictions of those in power and more a reflection of what they feel compelled to do to survive politically.

The collapse of Venezuela is thus not so much the consequence of the failure of an economic model—though the model that its governments tried to impose during the past two decades was certainly not a good one—as it is the result of a failure of its political system to manage the conflicts inherent to a polarized society. At a fundamental level, Venezuela is trapped in a catastrophic stalemate between forces that are not powerful enough to prevail over each other but are powerful enough to impede the other one from governing effectively.

This chapter discusses the implications of this vision for thinking about how to chart a way out of Venezuela's crisis. I begin by reviewing the history of initiatives aimed at resolving Venezuela's political stalemate through facilitated negotiations or external pressure. I show that many of these initiatives have systematically ignored or underestimated the role of the structure of political incentives and that their failure to generate change can be traced to their inability to alter the zero-sum nature of political competition. I then go on to discuss a range of possible reforms that would alter the structure of political payoffs. These include proposals for constitutional changes, power-sharing agreements, and multiparty negotiations, as well as changes in sanctions policy and opposition coordination.

THE ROAD TO NOWHERE

Table 12.1 presents a summary of negotiation initiatives involving government and opposition representatives in Venezuela since 1999. I identify ten major negotiation initiatives since 2002. Five of these broke down or were suspended without the signing of an agreement; the remaining five led to the signing of partial agreements. In three of these cases, the agreements broke down on implementation, with one of the sides accusing the other of having violated the terms. In only one case—also the only one not to involve the mainstream opposition coalition[1]—was a partial agreement implemented. The remaining case is that of negotiations that were being conducted at the time of writing.

The first two negotiation initiatives occurred in the context of the 2002–3 oil strike discussed in chapter 4. That event was a clear precursor of the use of scorched earth tactics, as it involved the opposition leadership calling for the paralysis of oil production in an attempt to force the government from power. Given the strong support for the opposition

TABLE 12.1. History of negotiations between government and opposition since 1999

Start of Talks	*End of Talks*	*Description*	*Parties*	*Facilitators/ Mediators*	*Outcome*	*Comments*
Nov 2002	Late 2005	Boston Group (I)	Government and opposition lawmakers from the National Assembly	Delegation of US Congressmen	Parties suspended the talks without signing an agreement.	After two meetings, the Boston Group lost traction after the opposition boycotted the 2005 parliamentary elections. Group sought to discuss improvements in democratic conditions and poverty levels.
May 2003	Aug 2004	Negotiation and Agreement Roundtable	Government of Venezuela, Democratic Coordinator	United Nations Development Programme (UNDP), OAS Secretary-General César Gaviria, and Carter Center	Parties signed an agreement.	Negotiations led to the 2004 Presidential Recall Referendum. Opposition denounced irregularities and alleged fraud in the vote count.
Feb 2014	Apr 2014	National Peace Conference	Government of Venezuela, Democratic Unity Roundtable	Union of South American Nations (UNASUR)	Parties signed a partial agreement.	Initial agreement included creation of a Truth Commission to investigate violence related to protests, as well as the designation of new members of the CNE and TSJ. Opposition abandoned talks alleging continuation of government repression of protests and persecution of opposition leaders.
Oct 2016	Dec 2016	National Dialogue for Peace	Government of Venezuela, Democratic Unity Roundtable	Union of South American Nations (UNASUR) and the Vatican	Parties signed initial declaration, failed to reach agreement.	Opposition and government presented different texts of the agreement that they claimed both sides had subscribed to. Opposition abandoned talks alleging that the government did not comply with the agreement.

(*continues*)

TABLE 12.1. History of negotiations between government and opposition since 1999 (*continued*)

Start of Talks	*End of Talks*	*Description*	*Parties*	*Facilitators/ Mediators*	*Outcome*	*Comments*
Dec 2017	Feb 2018	Dominican Republic talks	Government of Venezuela, Democratic Unity Roundtable	Dominican President Danilo Medina and Spanish Prime Minister José Luís Rodríguez Zapatero	Parties suspended the negotiations without signing an agreement.	Government accepted and signed proposal of one of the facilitators focused on conditions for the 2018 elections (Zapatero). Government claims opposition agreed to sign, then backtracked. Opposition claimed electoral guarantees were insufficient. Facilitators then said that negotiations had gone into "prolonged recess."
May 2019	Aug 2019	Oslo/Barbados talks	Government of Venezuela (Maduro), Interim Government of Venezuela (Guaidó)	Norwegian government	Parties suspended the talks without signing an agreement.	Opposition proposed national unity government with both Maduro and Guaidó stepping down. Government suspended participation after US issued executive order banning transactions with the government of Venezuela in August 2019.
Sept 2019	Dec 2020	National Dialogue Roundtable	Government of Venezuela (Maduro), centrist opposition parties	None	Parties signed an agreement.	Agreements included freeing of political prisoners, government legislators rejoining the National Assembly, and establishment of oil-for-food program. The latter was never implemented in practice as it would have required agreement of international actors.

Start of Talks	*End of Talks*	*Description*	*Parties*	*Facilitators/ Mediators*	*Outcome*	*Comments*
Nov 2019	–	Boston Group (II)	Opposition, government, civil society	Former Venezuelan legislators	No official agreement has been signed.	Two proposals emerged from the group: an agreement through which regional multilateral bank CAF would lend funds for the recovery of Venezuela's electrical grid (2019) and an oil-for-food program with the participation of the United Nations (2021). The opposition-controlled National Assembly created a commission to study the former, but the commission never produced a report.
Jun 2020	Jun 2021	Health care agreements due to COVID-19 pandemic	Health care advisers of the Maduro and Guaidó governments	Pan American Health Organization	Two agreements were signed.	The June 2020 agreement focused on coordinating purchase and distribution of health care–related goods as part of the COVID-19 response. In January 2021, the opposition claimed that the government was violating the agreement by distributing tests in violation of agreed guidelines. A February 2021 agreement created a roundtable for the procurement of vaccines. Roundtable has not met since June 4.
Sep 2021	–	Negotiation and Dialogue Process, Mexico/ Barbados	Government of Venezuela (Maduro), Unitary Platform	Norway, Russia, Netherlands	Parties signed partial agreements.	Process ongoing at time of writing. September 2021 agreements focused on backing territorial claims on Guyana and creating commissions to study social assistance initiatives. October 2023 agreements included electoral conditions and defense of external assets.

Sources: Author's construction; Smilde and Ramsey 2020.

among oil industry managers at the time, the strike was successful in bringing oil production to a standstill for several months. The first initiative, the Boston Group, was an informal Track II diplomacy initiative that aimed to bring together some legislators and civil society representatives to find common ground amid the crisis.[2] The group lost relevance after the opposition boycotted the 2005 parliamentary election.

The talks facilitated by OAS, UNDP, and the Carter Center, formally known as the Negotiation and Agreements Roundtable (Mesa de Negociación y Acuerdos), were initiated a month before the start of the oil strike. After the government recovered control of the oil industry and oil production began to rise again, the opposition accepted an agreement that foresaw a resolution to the country's crisis through the holding of a recall referendum, with the eventual possible participation of the three facilitators as observers (OAS 2003; Martínez Meucci 2010). The agreement broke down on implementation after the opposition charged the 2004 referendum results were fraudulent, despite the fact that the OAS (2004b) and the Carter Center (2005) issued statements validating the official results.

The failure of the 2002 to 2004 OAS–UNDP–Carter Center effort is consistent with my view that there are structural incentives for the losers of Venezuelan elections not to recognize the results. The 2004 referendum initiated an almost endless cycle of nonrecognition of results by the losers in nationwide elections. The opposition boycotted elections in 2005, 2017, 2018, and 2020, alleging that they were neither free nor fair. When it participated in elections, it claimed that final results did not reflect the actual vote in 2006, 2013, and 2017. On the government's side, the refusal to abide by the results of elections has also been prominent, even if did not take the form of overt disavowal of official returns. In 2004 and 2016, the government party alleged that CNE-supervised signature collection events to invoke recall referendums had been marred by fraud. It appealed to courts to annul the results of the 2015 parliamentary elections in Amazonas, the 2016 recall referendum drive, and the 2021 gubernatorial elections in Barinas. And in the only two elections that it lost prior to 2024, it used all means at its disposal to make the results irrelevant—by calling a new referendum in 2009 and by rendering powerless the opposition-controlled National Assembly elected in 2015. When it lost the presidency by a landslide in 2024, as discussed in chapter 10, it used its control of electoral authorities to alter the election result and declare Maduro the winner.

This pattern suggests that agreements that focus on the holding of elections under international monitoring are insufficient to achieve an enforceable negotiated solution to Venezuela's crisis. It is consistent with the view that I have laid out in this volume in which political actors have structural incentives not to accept playing even by rules that they have previously agreed on. The framework developed in this volume suggests that this conduct is a consequence of the high-stakes nature of the country's political conflict, which all but ensures that political actors will prefer to try their luck at nonelectoral modes of confrontation rather than accept the implications of having been on the losing side of an election.

The winner-take-all framework can also help us explain the failure of the 2016 UNASUR- and Vatican-facilitated talks and the 2017–18 Dominican Republic negotiations. Both sets of talks were focused on establishing conditions for elections that could potentially have led to either a change in government or the validation of the legitimacy of the incumbent government. While other nonelectoral demands were also discussed, the holding of elections took center stage in both cases. Yet both the government and the opposition torpedoed any agreement that they saw as leading to an election that they could lose. Similarly, the 2019 Oslo-Barbados talks reached a standstill when the opposition focused its demands on the holding of new elections.

None of these outcomes is surprising. Negotiations over electoral conditions focus on defining the specifics of a mechanism to decide who will occupy Venezuela's all-powerful presidency. Changes in electoral conditions will imply changes in the probability of each side prevailing in this contest. Any agreement that leads to improvements in the likelihood of one side prevailing will obviously lead to its rejection by the other side.[3] In 2016, the government saw a high probability that it would lose the recall referendum and decided to block it. In 2018, the opposition saw a high risk that it could lose that year's presidential election, thought that internationally delegitimizing Maduro offered a better chance to generate a change in regime, and thus decided to boycott the elections instead of signing the agreement proposed in the Dominican Republic talks.

Foreign governments have not just acted as facilitators of electoral agreements. As discussed extensively in preceding chapters, they have also actively tried to alter the bargaining power of both sides. The United States and other allies of the mainstream opposition have used economic and personal sanctions, government recognition decisions, and direct control of funding sources with the objective of weakening the Maduro government and strengthening the hand of some sectors in the opposition. Maduro allies such as China, Russia, and Iran have increased purchases of Venezuelan oil, rescheduled debts, and provided economic and operational assistance.

As I discussed in detail in chapter 9, it is unclear that sanctions have significantly changed Venezuela's political situation, and they may have inadvertently strengthened the government's bargaining power and helped solidify its resolve. The framework offered in this volume provides an explanation for this outcome. Altering the relative payoffs to the sides in conflict will do little to improve the chances for a negotiated solution if the contest for power continues to revolve around a zero-sum structure of outcomes. Increasing the cost of the status quo for the government will only lead to a higher probability of a negotiated solution if the costs of accepting a negotiated solution do not also increase in tandem. Yet the evidence suggests that a sanctions-focused approach has significantly increased exit costs to Chavismo. Sanctions may thus have made Chavismo less willing to accept a negotiated solution that significantly risks its prospects of remaining in power.

Interestingly, some of the talks that have produced more progress have had less ambitious goals. For example, in June 2020, the 2015 National Assembly and Maduro's Ministry of Health created a joint commission to coordinate efforts to attend to the COVID-19 pandemic. The commission produced an agreement to buy 340,000 antigen tests, as well as a deal to use offshore accounts controlled by the Guaidó administration to fund paying for vaccines through the World Bank's COVAX system for vaccine acquisition for low-income countries (Vasquez 2021). Both efforts broke down ultimately, with the opposition accusing the government of not administering the antigen tests effectively and the government insisting on making the COVAX payments on its own and refusing authorization for the Astra-Zeneca vaccine, alleging concerns about its side effects (Yapur 2021). Yet the commission was created and operated at the time at which the Barbados talks had been suspended and neither side was expressing interest in their resumption. Despite the absence of high-level talks, both sides agreed to let their representatives elaborate and even begin to implement an agreement focused on solving an urgent yet specific problem not directly related to the competition for control of government.

Similarly, in November 2022, the Unitary Platform (PU) and the Maduro government subscribed to a partial agreement to direct \$3.2 billion in funds in blocked offshore accounts to use in social expenditures overseen by the United Nations (ReliefWeb 2022).[4] At the time of this writing, the agreement has not yet been implemented, though there appear to be advances in resolving some of the main impediments.[5] This agreement builds on a principle included in the initial 2021 Memorandum of Understanding, which specified that partial agreements could be reached on urgent issues even in the absence of an overall deal (Regjeringen 2021).

An altogether different experience was the National Dialogue Roundtable (Mesa de Diálogo Nacional, MDN) created in September 2019 by the Maduro government and centrist opposition parties outside of the mainstream opposition coalition. Its launch came shortly after the suspension of the Barbados talks between Maduro and Guaidó representatives and at a moment in which the Guaidó government's official position was that negotiations had been "exhausted" (BBC Mundo 2019). The MDN, whose candidates had jointly garnered 31% of the national vote in the 2018 election boycotted by the MUD, was decried by mainstream opposition representatives as forming part of a Maduro plan to create a "fabricated opposition" (Borges 2019). Nevertheless, the talks generated several agreements, which included the freeing of jailed opposition leaders, the reincorporation of PSUV legislators in the 2015 National Assembly, and the appointment of a new electoral council.

Two of these agreements were immediately implemented: PSUV legislators rejoined the National Assembly, and the prosecutor general announced the release of twenty-four political detainees (Europa Press 2019b; *Tal Cual* 2019). Among those released was the vice president of the National Assembly, a key member of the Guaidó coalition who had been arrested for his participation in a failed military uprising in April of that year (Sánchez 2019). A new CNE was appointed in June 2020, with two of five board members representing opposition MDN parties (between 2006 and 2020, the opposition had had one member). The last of these agreements appears to have survived to this day: CNE boards appointed in 2021 and 2023 also included two opposition members (one from the MUD and one from the MDN parties), instead of the one opposition representative they had had since 2005.

Clearly, the actors involved were facing different incentives in these last three negotiations. In the COVID and Social Roundtable Assistance Agreements, the fact that the government's hold on power was not directly under discussion appears to have made it easier for both it and the opposition to acquiesce to a deal. In the case of the MDN talks, there was clearly an interest by the government in strengthening the nonmainstream opposition. The outcome of these cases suggests that incorporating new actors and separating the humanitarian dimension from political negotiations may play an important role in reaching viable and enforceable agreements that can, under some conditions, lead to concrete improvements in institutions and living conditions.

At the time of writing, the round of negotiations initiated in 2021 in Mexico, which were later moved to Barbados, is ongoing. In October 2023, the Maduro government and the PU signed an agreement establishing plans for a competitive presidential election in mid-2024 (Government of Norway 2024). Both the government and the opposition have accused each other of not complying with the agreement, although the MUD ultimately decided to participate in the elections. The agreement was also accompanied by an easing of sanctions agreed to in separate bilateral US-Venezuela talks hosted by Qatar; the easing was partially reversed in April 2024 after US authorities claimed that the Maduro government was not complying with its commitments, including the holding of transparent elections (Ministry of Foreign Affairs of Qatar 2023; US Department of State 2024).

RETHINKING CHANGE

If sanctions and negotiations have both failed to produce a way out of Venezuela's conflict, then what—if anything—could work? The framework developed in this book suggests an alternative way of thinking about Venezuelan political transformation that emphasizes the need to alter the structure of political competition. I have argued that the decision by political actors to disregard democratic rules and adopt scorched earth strategies can be traced back to the winner-take-all political game embedded in the country's formal and informal institutions for political competition. If this is the case, then attempts at overcoming the country's political and economic crisis should center on reforms that aim to tackle this structure of incentives.

Deriving policy implications from political economy analyses is always a thorny issue. In contrast to traditional normative economics, political economy approaches assume that policy-maker actions are endogenous. Taking a stance on what politicians should do can lead to interesting debates on moral philosophy. Yet if our theories are right, these discussions will be ineffective in altering the conduct of political actors. Nevertheless, normative policy analysis is ubiquitous in part because decision makers want to know how to make choices that help them successfully pursue their objectives. For the same reason, it should be possible to think about actions that can help reshape the structure of Venezuelan incentives and reduce the likelihood that the country continues to be mired in destructive conflict.

Broadly speaking, we can think of three different types of initiatives aimed at reducing the stakes of power in Venezuela. One set of initiatives would aim at changing the agenda of negotiations so that it can focus partially or totally on different issues from the winner-take-all contest for power. For example, the government and the opposition could decide to conduct negotiations on constitutional reforms, a power-sharing agreement, or sectoral humanitarian initiatives. Another set of initiatives would aim to change the set of actors involved in the discussion, either by including more actors through multistakeholder talks or by reframing intracoalition competition. Last, there are recommendations aimed at international actors such as the United States and Europe, which could revise their strategy of sanctions and economic statecraft or their involvement in domestic politics. Table 12.2 presents a schematic description of these alternatives.

TABLE 12.2. Varieties of initiatives to reduce stakes of power

Reforms	*Key Actors Involved*	*Examples*	*Benefits*	*Risks*
Constitutional reforms	Maduro government, mainstream opposition	Eliminate authority of Constitutional Convention to dissolve branches of government. Firmly establish supermajority requirements for key appointments and organic laws. Guarantee post-2024 recognition of heads of judiciary and accountability branches.	Constitutional reforms are difficult to revert. Approval referendum could imply strong mandate.	Referendum defeat could deepen instability. Constitutional Court could distort interpretation of new norms.
Power-sharing agreements	Maduro government, mainstream opposition	Opposition and experts to manage PDVSA, central bank, and finance ministry. Chavismo maintains control of national security, interior, and foreign affairs ministry.	Facilitates international economic support for economic stabilization and reforms. Lowers risk of post-transition judicial persecution and lawfare.	Political instability and policy paralysis.
Multistakeholder negotiations	Maduro government, mainstream opposition, other opposition groups, civil society actors	Expansion of talks to include nonainstream opposition, labor unions, business associations, and church.	Increases legitimacy of talks. Benefits from credibility of nonpolitical actors.	Increased chance of negotiations gridlock.

Reforms	*Key Actors Involved*	*Examples*	*Benefits*	*Risks*
Sectoral agreements	Maduro government, mainstream opposition, international organizations	Oil-for-essentials program. UN-administered social fund using blocked assets.	Generates concrete improvements in living standards of most vulnerable groups. Greater willingness of political actors to cooperate given separation of sectoral and political negotiations.	Political actors could block implementation if they perceive that their opponents capture the bulk of the political benefits.
Reforming sanctions and economic statecraft	United States, Europe, United Nations	Unilateral lifting of US economic sanctions. Reforms to reduce overcompliance and increase effectiveness of targeted sanctions.	Spurs economic growth. Economic recovery could strengthen civil society groups vis-à-vis government. Facilitates multilateral coordination.	Likely to be strongly opposed by opposition hard-line groups and their international allies.
Reframing intra-opposition competition	Mainstream opposition, other opposition groups	Hold direct elections for party leaderships. Choose presidential nominee in two-round or second-degree elections.	Broadens opposition coalitions and lowers risks of defection. Moves opposition platform to center, making it more attractive to nonaligned voters.	Likely to be resisted by current party leaders and hard-line sectors.

Source: Author's construction.

Legal and Constitutional Reforms

In previous chapters, I argued that Venezuela's 1999 Constitution is a key determinant of the high-stakes structure of political competition. It gives the executive branch the power to subordinate the complete structure of the state to it through the convening of a constitutional convention with the authority to dissolve other branches of government. The constitutional framework also puts inordinate amounts of power in parliamentary supermajorities, which can be as powerful as the very strong presidency. Its provisions for staggered elections together with the recall referendums generate a setting of electoral hypercompetitiveness in which governments have little opportunity to implement policy reforms that can produce results of value for the electorate before their mandate can be taken away in an election.

A first set of constitutional reforms could aim at reducing the power of both the government and parliamentary supermajorities to interfere with the functioning of the judiciary and accountability branch. The power of the constitutional convention to dissolve existing branches of government should be eliminated. At the same time, a constitutional reform could introduce explicit rules requiring supermajorities for major legal reforms, thus allowing sufficiently large political minorities to block legislative changes that fundamentally affect the structure of payoffs. A reformed constitutional text could also explicitly delineate the decision-making process to be followed when required supermajorities are not achieved.

Many of these reforms would be aimed at reversing interpretations of the constitutional text made by the Constitutional Court over the past decades that have reduced supermajority requirements. For example, in 2004, the Constitutional Court ruled that a supermajority was not required for reforming so-called organic (i.e., constitutional framework) laws.[6] This allowed the National Assembly to approve a Supreme Court law enabling the appointment of new justices through a simple majority (Human Rights Watch 2004).

Other reforms could tackle the redesign of the electoral system to ensure a greater representation of political minorities and create a high bar for any political group to obtain a powerful supermajority (Abdul et al. 2020). Venezuela's system for apportioning legislative seats is extremely problematic, as it allows the winning party to easily capture an oversized share of seats with only a slim plurality of popular support. Reintroducing a bicameral legislature with a Senate in which all states have equal representation could also reduce the stakes of power by protecting political movements that perform better electorally in more rural areas. The Senate could also be assigned specific prerogatives such as appointing the prosecutor general and initiating impeachment procedures (Aveledo 2019).

The power of Venezuela's executive branch, of course, is not just political. As Venezuela is a petrostate, the government handles enormous resources that allow it, under normal conditions, to become the predominant actor in the nation's economy—a reality that has political consequences. By creating massive off-budget funds such as the National Development Fund and the Chinese Fund, the Chávez administration ensured that the government would be able to spend these resources with next to no institutional oversight. Reforms could limit the ability of the government to route spending through these off-budget funds and restrain its capacity to generate additional funds through predatory extraction of natural resources (Rosales 2019; Ebus 2022). The legislative branch should be granted the authority to confirm appointees to the Central Bank and the PDVSA board and should maintain oversight over any discretionary mechanisms for the allocation of foreign exchange.

Negotiations focused on such an institutional redesign would of course not occur in a political vacuum. The outcome of such negotiations would have to be acceptable to the current government, which by virtue of holding power today also has the most to lose from abandoning the status quo. The simplest way to lower the stakes of power from upcoming presidential and/or parliamentary elections is to ensure that there is no doubt as to the permanence in office of the current heads of the other branches of government—which, in Venezuela, include not just the judiciary but also the electoral authority and accountability branches. Explicit transitory constitutional provisions could ensure that the current heads of these branches remain in office for the duration of their terms and suspend the authority of the National Assembly to initiate procedures to remove the heads of these branches of government.

Some of these reforms could, in principle, be implemented through legal instead of constitutional reforms. Given the ample power of simple majorities to reform existing laws in the judiciary's current interpretation of the 1999 Constitution, however, any legal reforms implemented now could easily be reversed in the future; therefore, a constitutional reform would likely be required to unequivocally affirm supermajority requirements. However, an additional benefit of a constitutional reform process is that it requires approval by popular vote in a referendum.[7] The holding of a referendum on a constitutional reform born out of the negotiation process could go a long way toward forging a national consensus and endowing the new institutions with significant national and international legitimacy.

Power-Sharing Agreements

Power-sharing agreements are a common proposal in post-conflict settings, particularly in cases in which there is no clear winner at the moment of a peace deal. These agreements can take the form of apportioning or rotation between parties of political offices such as cabinet positions in the executive branch and reservation of seats in the legislative branch (Hartzell and Hoddie 2007; Sisk 2013; McCulloch and McGarry 2017).

Rodríguez and Sachs (2019a, 2019b) proposed a power-sharing deal for Venezuela roughly modeled on the Polish transition discussed earlier in this chapter. An interim government of experts would have a limited mandate for economic stabilization and recovery, while Chavismo would retain control over the military and security forces. While it initially had demanded that Maduro unconditionally hand over power to Guaidó, the Trump administration proposed in March 2020 a "Democratic Transition Framework," which contemplated the creation of a Council of State composed of two representatives each of the PSUV and MUD, with a fifth member selected by the other four and serving as interim president until a new presidential election were held (US Department of State 2020). This framework appears to have informed the design of negotiations with representatives of the judiciary and military prior to the failed April 2019 coup attempt. I have proposed (Rodríguez 2024a) going back to the Democratic Transition Framework to design an agreement that could help solve the impasse over the result of the 2024 presidential election.

Power-sharing agreements are sometimes unstable and can lead to policy paralysis (Mandler 2000; Vaishnav and Smogard 2014). It may be very difficult to get candidates to agree to such a deal before a presidential election in a high-stakes setting. However, in the aftermath of an election, a commitment by the winner to form a national unity government with representatives of all sides could be a viable mechanism for providing guarantees to the losers. During the campaign for the 2024 presidential election, a centrist candidate made a commitment to retain Chavismo's defense minister if elected (*El Nacional* 2023a). Power-sharing should also be on the table to avoid another legitimacy crisis in case the results of the elections are disputed.

There is a sense in which Venezuela's current constitutional arrangements could force the sides to the country's conflict to enter into cohabitation agreements if an opposition leader is able to assume the presidency in 2025. In that case, the new president would be forced to cohabitate with the PSUV-controlled National Assembly until early 2026. The new president would also have to coexist with the PSUV-appointed Supreme Court and members of the accountability branch, including the powerful prosecutor general, for all of the presidential term.[8] A key question would be how to avoid that coexistence turning into a repeat of the constitutional legitimacy crisis caused by the conflict of powers between the National Assembly and the Supreme Court that began in 2017. As discussed above, constitutional reforms would likely be needed to stop the new president from convening a new constitutional convention to dissolve the PSUV-appointed branches of government.

Sectoral Agreements

By "sectoral agreements," I refer to those that result from negotiations aimed at cooperatively solving specific problems of society and are not conditioned on an overarching political agreement. Sectoral negotiations have direct value to Venezuelans over and above the instrumental use for solving other problems. Sectoral agreements should be distinguished from partial agreements, which are those in which the sphere of negotiation only has instrumental value in addressing a more complex problem.[9]

The fact that sectoral agreements have value for people in and of themselves implies that there are potential gains from the parties to the country's conflict cooperating through them. Political leaders from both factions that participate in agreements to improve public health services, for example, could strengthen their aspirations to occupy important elected roles in the future under diverse political scenarios. It is easier to find immediate gains from cooperation in sectoral agreements than in partial or global political agreements because sectoral agreements require actors to run much lesser risks and allow them to build up credibility over time in the context of repeated interactions.

An oil-for-essentials agreement could allow the Venezuelan oil industry to regain access to US and global oil markets currently restricted by primary and secondary oil sanctions. Even a conservative assessment of the potential for recovery in Venezuelan oil production through the lifting of oil sanctions suggests that the country could increase sales by around 400 tbd—the size of the US market for Venezuelan oil that was closed off in January 2019 (see chap. 9). At current oil prices of $60 per barrel, these sales would represent approximately $8.8 billion in additional export revenue (14% of GDP and 108% of exports in 2020). Cooperative agreements could allow the country to tap the use of funds currently blocked in the international financial system to tackle the country's humanitarian crisis (see the discussion in chap. 10).

In separate work, I have proposed concrete institutional arrangements that would allow the country to tap these resources as part of a political agreement. One initial step toward the use of these resources would be the appointment of a consensus Central Bank board (Oil for Venezuela 2021). Since the Central Bank is the owner of several of the funds under legal dispute, this would allow the country to access these resources. The Central Bank is also the designated fiscal agent of Venezuela before the IMF, empowering it to initiate requests for financing and use of Special Drawing Rights.

A similar arrangement could be set up to administer the proceeds from an oil-for-essentials program (Oil for Venezuela 2019; Banca y Negocios 2021; Martínez 2021; Atlantic Council 2022; Rodríguez 2022a). An administrative board jointly appointed by the opposition and government could oversee procurement and distribution of essential imports, as well as subscribe oil sales contracts under the supervision of an international organism. An international oversight board could monitor compliance with the agreement and be empowered to suspend it in case any of the parts violate it. Distribution could be carried out primarily by the private sector, with the program's revenues used to fund a voucher system for Venezuelans to purchase the essentials. The program should be designed in a way to avoid the problems of the Iraq oil-for-food scheme, for example, by ensuring that oil sales contracts are subject to review by the supervisory body.

One reason that humanitarian sectoral agreements may be feasible is that they may be able to count on the support of key international actors. It is unlikely that the opposition, which depends for its bargaining power on international recognition and sanctions, would refuse to go along with an initiative strongly supported by the United States and Europe. For roughly the same reasons, it is also unlikely that Maduro would refuse to go along with an initiative that China and Russia strongly support. And while it may not be feasible to reach an agreement between the United States, the EU, China, and Russia on the design of a grand political transition of power in Venezuela, it may be much more feasible for such an agreement to emerge around an initiative to address the country's economic and humanitarian crisis. A UN Security Council unanimous resolution in support of a cooperative humanitarian agreement in Venezuela would be very hard for either Maduro or the opposition to reject.

As noted earlier in this chapter, the Mexico talks have at the time of writing produced a tentative sectoral agreement to fund expenditures agreed on in the Social Assistance Roundtable. While funds have yet to be disbursed, some of the main impediments to implementation appear to have been resolved, and it appears that as of the time of writing, the Biden administration is cautiously supporting implementation of the agreement. This is not the case with oil-for-essentials programs, which received support from neither the Biden nor the Trump administration.

In fact, the easing of oil restrictions begun toward the end of 2022 explicitly avoided an oil-for-essentials design. This easing began with the granting of a license to Chevron in November 2022 to sell Venezuelan oil in the United States and continued with the issuance in October 2023 of a six-month license authorizing PDVSA to sell oil in the United States. Both licenses were issued in support of agreements signed in the Mexico-Barbados framework between the government and Unitary Platform. While the United States partly reversed the October 2023 easing in April 2024, it has left the door open to replacing it with tailored one-off authorizations with similar economic and market implications. The reluctance to formally accept oil-for-essentials initiatives may reflect concerns with the stigma associated with the corruption scandals of the Iraq oil-for-food program in the 1990s.[10]

Multistakeholder Negotiations

With the exception of the 2019 MDN dialogues, all other formal negotiations carried out in Venezuela have confronted representatives of the Chávez/Maduro governments and the mainstream opposition coalition at the time. While the Maduro government has recently advocated for the incorporation of other groups and claimed that bilateral talks with the Unitary Platform are only one of its multiple attempts to engage with diverse opposition sectors, the mainstream opposition has remained staunchly opposed to the inclusion of other opposition groups in the talks (Europa Press 2019a; Voz de América 2019). This reflects a concern that the presence of other groups would dilute the mainstream coalition's bargaining power and the belief that nonmainstream groups have been co-opted by the government.

Nevertheless, over time the claim to representativeness of the mainstream opposition coalition began to be questioned. In the 2021 regional elections for governors and mayors, the MUD only garnered 42% of votes not cast for the government, with the remaining 58% going to non-MUD candidates, most of them from centrist parties opposed to sanctions (table 12.3). The second largest opposition coalition, the Democratic Alliance (Adem), obtained 38% of the opposition vote.[11] In October 2023, María Corina Machado, whose Come Venezuela (Vente Venezuela, VV) party had remained outside of the MUD coalition, allowing her to present herself as a political outsider, swept the opposition primaries for the presidential nomination with 93% of the vote.

The opposition was able to unify around the candidacy of former ambassador Edmundo González, who was supported by Machado, in the 2024 presidential election. González obtained two-thirds of the

TABLE 12.3A. Distribution of votes by coalition in 2017, 2020, and 2021 elections

Coalition	*2017 Votes*	*2017 Percent Valid Votes*	*2020 Votes*	*2020 Percent Valid Votes*	*2021 Votes*	*2021 Percent Valid Votes*	*2024 Votes*	*2024 Percent Valid Votes*
Great Patriotic Pole (GPP)	6,321,610	53.7	4,321,975	69.1	4,040,054	45.8	3,959,345	30.5
Democratic Unity Roundtable (MUD)	5,111,524	43.4	–	–	1,917,748	21.7	8,731,653	67.2
Democratic Alliance (Adem)	–	–	1,667,959	26.7	1,746,855	19.8	–	–
Democratic Alliance (Unitary candidates)	–	–	1,387,696	22.2	1,458,953	16.5	–	–
Other	345,360	2.9	261,146	4.2	1,117,702	12.7	311,262	2.4

TABLE 12.3B. Turnout and abstentions in 2017, 2020. and 2021 elections

Voter Decision	*2017 Votes*	*2017 Percent Valid Votes*	*2020 Votes*	*2020 Percent Valid Votes*	*2021 Votes*	*2021 Percent Valid Votes*	*2024 Votes*	*2024 Percent Valid Votes*
Turnout	11,778,494	59.7	6,251,080	30.2	8,822,359	41.7	13,002,260	60.8
Abstention	7,943,573	40.3	14,459,341	69.8	12,337,487	58.3	8,390,204	39.2
Total	19,722,067	100.0	20,710,421	100.0	21,159,846	100.0	21,392,464	100.0

Sources: Author's construction using CNE 2017, 2020, 2021 and Comando con Venezuela 2024.

national vote while the vote share of non-MUD opposition parties collapsed to the low single digits.[12] This followed an implosion of the Adem coalition that saw some of its former prominent leaders throw their support toward González, marking the return to a broad-based coalition under the MUD. Yet both the process to choose González as nominee and the aftermath of the election highlighted key fissures in the MUD coalition, suggesting that a split in the coalition could well resurface, particularly if it proves unsuccessful in driving Maduro from power.

Perhaps even more importantly, opinion studies regularly highlight low approval ratings for the majority of politicians over most of this period, regardless of what sector of the government or opposition they belong to—with Machado in 2024 being an important exception.[13] In contrast, the data show high approval ratings for broad nonpolitical sectors such as business and the Catholic Church (table 12.4). This suggests that a negotiation process could gain significantly from broadening representation to include civil society organizations.

Multistakeholder negotiations have proven successful in tackling complex conflicts such as those of South Africa and Northern Ireland (Berman and Abdollahian 1999; Mnookin 2003; Hancock 2008). Through a broadening of participation and inclusion, multistakeholder approaches can also help the negotiations process gain greater legitimacy in society. By including groups that are not directly competing for political power but have a direct stake in the improvement of economic and social conditions, the negotiations are more likely to be able to converge to agreements that are positive-sum for many participants.

One common concern is that the multiplicity of stakeholders may produce gridlock. This need not be the case, if decision rules are designed to ensure that participants do not have veto power (Austen-Smith et al. 2019). In practice, some groups will inevitably opt out of the negotiation at one stage of the process, but the remaining group of participants may be ample enough to allow the process to be perceived as legitimate by most of society. Ideally, the agreements reached in any negotiations process would be put before voters in a referendum. The participation of organizations with broad legitimacy among voters in the negotiations and in the presentation of the agreement before voters should increase the likelihood of its subsequent approval.

TABLE 12.4A. Public opinion on leadership, 2022

Candidate/Institution	*Approval Ratio in 2022 (%)*	*Approval Ratio in 2024 (%)*
Nicolás Maduro	22.0	25.4
Manuel Rosales	28.6	23.1
María Corina Machado	21.7	57.1
Benjamín Rausseo	31.1	26.4
Henrique Capriles	17.5	11.1
Edmundo González	–	34.1
Hugo Chávez	60.8	–
Leopoldo López	16.1	–
Juan Guaidó	16.1	–
Henri Falcon	18.3	–
Diosdado Cabello	13.9	–
Entrepreneurs	58.9	61.6
Catholic Church	55.9	61.2

Note: The original question was, "How do you evaluate the work of [candidate/institution] for the well-being of the country?"

TABLE 12.4B. Public opinion on sanctions and negotiations, 2022

Question	*Yes (%)*	*No (%)*	*Don't Know/ Didn't Answer (%)*
Do you agree with the oil sanctions imposed by the United States on Venezuela?	15.4	74.5	8.8
Do you agree with easing the economic sanctions on Venezuela?	75.1	15.8	9.1
Do you agree with resuming negotiations between the government and the opposition?	64.8	25.1	10.1

TABLE 12.4C. Public opinion on sanctions and negotiations, 2022 (interviewees' political self-definition)

Question	*Ruling Party Supporter (%)*	*Unaligned (%)*	*Opposition Supporter (%)*	*Don't Know/ Didn't Answer (%)*
Within Venezuelan politics, do you consider yourself . . . ?	17.8	54.8	25.3	2.1

Note: Observation refers to average value of four recent surveys at the time of writing, which range from February 2022 to November 2022.

Sources: Author's construction using Datanálisis 2022a, 2022b, 2022c, 2022d, 2024.

Reframing Intracoalition Competition

There is somewhat of a paradox in Venezuelan politics. Public opinion studies systematically tend to find that most Venezuelans are in favor of negotiations between the government and the opposition and would like to see economic sanctions lifted, even among self-identified opposition supporters (see table 12.4). These studies also suggest that there is broad support for sectoral agreements aimed at channeling external resources to address the humanitarian crisis. However, those who have led the mainstream opposition in recent years have maintained much more hard-line positions on these issues. Mainstream opposition leaders have strongly advocated for more severe economic sanctions, conditioned any sanctions relief on political concessions, and opposed or blocked some sectoral humanitarian agreements.[14]

The framework developed in this book suggests that the reason the parties do not converge to the type of negotiated solutions that most Venezuelans want is that, prior to 2024, political actors had not been primarily engaged in electoral politics. Catering to the desire of the electorate, I have argued, has taken a backseat to pleasing important selectorates, including the military and foreign governments. However, my framework is premised on the idea that there are two competing political sectors that are engaged in a struggle over the spoils of power. While extending the framework to a multiplayer setting is beyond the scope of this book, the question of why other actors with different policy preferences have not emerged remains highly relevant for making sense of the country's political dynamics.

Absent the force of electoral competition, both sides may also have an interest in maintaining high barriers to entry into political competition. There is certainly no shortage of efforts on the sides of both Maduro and the mainstream opposition to stamp down internal dissent, including through judicial persecution on the government side and through the imposition of personal sanctions on opposition dissidents by the United States and Europe.[15] While Maduro's control of regulatory agencies allows him to have broad control of the local media, the greater financing capacity of organized diaspora groups may give hard-liners an edge in the control of social media influence.[16] Despite this barrier, parties unaffiliated with either the MUD or PSUV obtained 32.5% of the votes in the 2021 regional elections—although they were unable to maintain that support into the 2024 presidential elections (see table 12.3).

Internal coalition dynamics may also privilege control by more hard-line groups. The creation of the interim government reproduced the winner-take-all dynamics inside the opposition, as the movement's capacity to fund itself depended in large part on control of government funds managed by Guaidó appointees.[17] Since control of resources depended on renewal of OFAC licenses, opposition politicians acquired an incentive to prioritize lobbying Washington for its continued support rather than focus on mobilizing resources and support within the country. The high number of defections suffered by the Guaidó coalition in 2019 and 2020 suggests strong levels of disaffection within many groups, particularly those that did not belong to the traditional Caracas elites.[18]

In October 2023, the mainstream opposition carried out a first-past-the-post direct primary vote to elect its presidential candidate. According to the organizers, 2.4 million Venezuelans voted in the primary, representing 12% of the current electorate. The primary resulted in the election of Machado, one of the most hard-line figures in the opposition, as presidential candidate. Despite winning the primaries, Machado was not allowed to run in the elections on a prior decision of the comptroller general (Contraloría General de la República 2023). Opinion surveys show that the majority of Venezuelans do not align with Machado's views on key issues such as negotiations and sanctions (see table 12.4). Electing a candidate without renewing party leaderships could have exacerbated the winner-take-all problem by endowing the candidate with high levels of legitimacy vis-à-vis political parties. Choosing the nominee through second-degree elections or a two-round system, in contrast, could have served to facilitate the internal negotiations among parties needed for effective coalition building. Edmundo González, in contrast, was appointed as MUD nominee initially as a stand-in candidate, and was only reaffirmed as nominee after the government blocked other potential replacements for Machado. His moderate candidacy nevertheless appears closer to what one would expect to have emerged from an internal negotiation instead of an open primary.

That presidential primaries lead to the selection of more hard-line leaders should not surprise us. Only 25% of Venezuelans self-identify as pro-opposition or anti-Chavista, as opposed to 18% who identify as pro-government or Chavista and 55% who do not identify with either side. Opposition sympathizers are also more likely to back sanctions and oppose negotiations than are neutral or pro-government voters.[19] Interestingly, some leaders of the MUD coalition who are now vocal opponents of sanctions chose to either not participate in or withdraw from the primaries (Reyes 2022; *El Nacional* 2023b). This appears to signal that presidential primaries were more effective in mobilizing hard-line voters with extreme positions on some of these issues.

The 2023 primaries organized by the opposition had only 4,688 voting booths, much fewer than the 33,783 booths deployed in the last presidential elections, raising concerns about the representativeness of the electorate that chose the opposition nominee. One way to address the potential nonrepresentativeness of primaries is by having them organized by the national electoral authority with the same infrastructure used in national elections. Turnout can also be incentivized by having all party primaries held on the same day. Compulsory voting on national primary day (as is the case in Argentina) or holding primaries concurrently with another national election (as is the case in Colombia) can increase voter turnout and representativeness of primary elections. Reintroducing compulsory voting in national elections—which was eliminated in the 1999 Constitution—could also help ensure that the composition of the electorate better reflects the views of the population instead of privileging groups with superior mobilization capacity (Birch 2009; Chapman 2019; Singh 2019).

After electoral authorities refused to let Machado register as a candidate and reportedly blocked other potential nominees, the MUD nominated González as her replacement.[20] Interestingly, González's campaign made a distinct emphasis on coexistence and refused to endorse sanctions, lending support to my point that electoral competition leads candidates to adopt more centrist platforms (Núñez and Kolster 2024; Paredes 2024; VPITV 2024).[21] Nevertheless, while this convergence to the center is present at times of electoral campaigns, my view is that it is likely to be replaced by the adoption of more extreme postures once electoral competition recedes. Given my contention that presidential elections are unlikely in and of themselves to yield a stable solution to the country's governance crisis, I expect nonelectoral competition and the accompanying polarization to continue to be the dominant trend in Venezuelan politics absent reforms to meaningfully lower the stakes of political competition.

Foreign governments and political actors should restrain their inclination to become involved in internal opposition politics, including disputes between the mainstream opposition and centrist political parties. Picking political winners is always tricky, and throwing one's support behind specific opposition factions runs the risk of having the bet go wrong and in the process antagonize important political forces. Perhaps even more importantly, doing so introduces perverse incentives for the opposition leadership to attempt to mimic the preferences of foreign and diaspora constituencies that may be very different from those of voters in Venezuela.

Reforming Sanctions and Economic Statecraft

As I documented in previous chapters, a variety of measures of economic statecraft imposed primarily by the United States, including financial and oil sanctions and the recognition of an opposition-led government, have contributed to considerably worsening Venezuela's economic crisis. My framework suggests two reasons, over and above their direct economic effects, that these measures have contributed to the exacerbation of Venezuela's political conflict. By endowing the opposition with a powerful scorched earth technology, the US willingness to impose sanctions helped precipitate the descent into economically destructive political conflict. And by making the economy considerably poorer, they may have also contributed to making democratic institutions less sustainable.

This reasoning suggests that the unilateral lifting of US economic sanctions may produce the opposite effects of their imposition and thus contribute to a democratic transition. By spurring domestic growth, the lifting of sanctions could allow the strengthening of loci of economic and political power distinct from those under direct control of the government, reinforcing civil society and opposition movements. Since economic sanctions are highly unpopular among Venezuelans (see table 12.4), lifting them would take away a powerful political argument from Maduro, who regularly uses them to rally popular support and to lambast the opposition for willfully harming Venezuelans. A lifting of economic sanctions could also help efforts to coordinate with Europe and other allies that have refused to impose economic sanctions in designing a truly multilateral strategy centered on the strategic use of targeted personal sanctions (see chap. 9). Similar arguments apply to the use of recognition decisions to block the government's access to funds. The October 2023 decision to ease oil sanctions, which was accompanied by the first explicit recognitions by US officials that the prior sanctions strategy had not worked and needed to be revised, could reflect a movement in this direction (*Americas Quarterly* 2023).

Of course, there are normative reasons that in and of themselves would support the unilateral lifting of economic sanctions. Sanctions with broad-ranging effects on economic conditions are arguably akin to the targeting of civilians during armed conflict. As argued by the political philosopher Cecile Fabre, while there are strong human rights arguments that favor the use of targeted sanctions subject to the principles of proportionality, necessity, and effectiveness, "[we] should be correspondingly very reluctant to resort to more comprehensive sanctions that are likely to inflict considerable harm on individuals who, we also have strong evidence to believe, do not contribute to those wrongdoings" (Fabre 2018, 75). Whether sanctions approved outside of the United Nations Security Council are valid under international law is a controversial issue (Shagabutdinova and Berejikian 2007; United Nations 2019; Schmidt 2022).

Targeted sanctions could also be better calibrated to minimize collateral effects on nontargeted entities and increase effectiveness. Reforms that reduce overcompliance and de-risking include the publication of enhanced compliance guidelines for private and nonprofit sectors, simplified licensing processes and broader standing exemptions, and the creation of protected banking processes, alternative remittance channels, and stand-alone humanitarian banks (Moret 2021). The effectiveness of sanctions is often blunted by the confusion between sanctions that are used strategically (i.e., to generate an incentive for a change in conduct of the target) and nonstrategically (as a substitute for inexistent or coopted judiciaries in target jurisdictions). Clearer signaling to distinguish strategic from nonstrategic sanctions could serve to improve the incentive structure generated by the former.

PARTING SHOTS

While electoral authorities declared Nicolás Maduro the winner of the 2024 elections, the opposition and a significant part of the international community are demanding that González be allowed to take office. For all I know, by the time you reach this page, the country will have a new president and begun a complex political transition. Alternatively, by that time Maduro could have begun his third term in office. Perhaps it is wisest to stop speculating. History teaches us that spelling out future scenarios in detail simply makes us look foolish when they do not materialize.

Nevertheless, the story that I have told in these pages suggests that regardless of who occupies Venezuela's presidency in January 2025, the country is unlikely to become a stable and prosperous democracy. Unless, that is, it embarks on a process of deep institutional reforms that lower the stakes of political conflict and set the grounds for coexistence of its dueling political forces. Venezuela's current institutional structure, I have argued, is preprogrammed to generate destructive conflict and convergence toward authoritarianism. Throw even the most decent and measured politicians into the boxing ring of Venezuelan politics, and they will find a way not only to destroy each other but also to bring down the country's economy with them.

I also have no idea how the politics of the United States will have evolved by the time these pages are published. Yet the story that I have told here reaffirms my fear that the country where I now live and teach may not be that far from becoming another casualty to destructive conflict. As I watched the debt ceiling cliffhanger play out in 2023 with my University of Denver students, my mind kept conjuring up images from Philip Roth's dystopic 2005 masterpiece, *The Plot Against America*. It takes the genius of Roth to demonstrate, more convincingly than any mathematical theorem or econometric estimate ever could, that human and social tragedies are often just a roll of the historical dice away.

My fears and apprehensions, of course, may simply be reflections of my own lived experience. Having been born into the most prosperous and democratic nation in Latin America and having seen it descend into an economic and political version of Dante's *Inferno*, I could be forgiven for seeing a fire in every spark. Perhaps that is the reason Simón

Bolívar, Venezuela's founding hero, cautioned us that revolutions should be observed up close but judged from afar.[22] Writing from a city that, despite being three thousand miles from my birthplace, sees more than a hundred Venezuelan migrants arrive each day,[23] it is hard to shake the feeling that I may still be too close. And too far.

NOTES

PREFACE

1. Calculations based on the variable XRCOMP (Competitiveness of Executive Recruitment) in the Polity5 data set (Integrated Network for Social Conflict Research 2020). Only Brazil, Costa Rica, and Uruguay had competitive elections as of 1957. Venezuela, Argentina, and Chile held competitive presidential elections in 1958. All those countries except Costa Rica and Venezuela would fall to military dictatorships in the 1960s or 1970s.

CHAPTER ONE

1. As discussed in chapter 2, the resource curse literature of course presents explanations for why resource-abundant economies may experience slower growth and remain poorer than those without natural resources, but this is different from accounting for why some countries experience absolute declines in living standards.

2. Although Venezuela did suffer a major terms of trade shock in the 2014 to 2016 period, most of that shock had been reverted by 2018, and Venezuela had withstood similar shocks in the past without suffering a growth collapse of comparable magnitude. In chapters 6 and 7 I argue that while this initial shock was an important trigger, it was its interaction with key features of the political system that led to the change in political strategies that drove the collapse.

3. Note that, as I show in chapter 2, the decline in import capacity induced by declining oil revenues does not explain the totality of the collapse in per capita incomes. Declining productivity, both in the pre- and post-sanctions period, also plays an important role.

4. In general, death sentences in the United States can only be imposed by juries and not by judges (577 U.S. 2016). Nevertheless, some states continue

to permit judges to impose death sentences under certain conditions, such as when there are deadlocked juries (Death Penalty Information Center 2023). I refer to judges making the sentencing decision in this example for expositional simplicity.

5. The judge's decision is one cause but not necessarily the only cause of the death sentence. There are several other factors that may play a role in determining the criminal's death. Some of them may affect the likelihood of death directly (e.g., a decision by the governor to pardon the convict, death by other causes) while others may affect it indirectly through their effect on the judge's sentence (e.g., whether the criminal committed the crime, whether evidence of the crime was found by police and deemed admissible by the court, whether the jury felt that such evidence established culpability beyond a reasonable doubt). The fact that both the judge's sentencing and the crime can be characterized as endogenous variables does not disprove their causal role; it does imply that it is possible to restate the causal effects in terms of the determinants of the endogenous variable, some of which may also be adequately described as endogenous. This type of complex links is common in causal identification problems associated with controversial moral choices.

6. See Bates et al. 2000 for the concept of analytical narratives and Rodrik 2004 for an application of the concept to studies of economic growth.

CHAPTER TWO

1. The most recent official national accounts data published by the Central Bank of Venezuela (BCV) is for the first quarter of 2019. For later time periods, I use the average estimates across analysts surveyed in FocusEconomics (2023). The World Bank has not published PPP-adjusted data for Venezuela since 2011, the last year for which it is possible to calculate survey-based relative prices based on the organization's International Comparisons Program (ICP) surveys. The Penn World Table (PWT) publishes an estimate that puts the 2012–20 PPP-adjusted contraction at 99.0%, by far the largest in the data set. Given that all GDP component and relative price data for the last years of this series are extrapolated, the figure should be taken with a grain of salt.

2. Measured as constant-price GDP. The number is slightly higher (74.4%) if we measure the collapse from its 2013 level of GDP, given that the economy grew moderately in that year. However, since 2013 growth was slightly below that year's population growth, per capita incomes peaked in 2012. As my focus is on living standards, I consider the period between 2012 and 2020 for the baseline quantification of the magnitude of the collapse.

3. See Rodríguez and Imam 2022 for a formal definition. Calculations use PWT 10.0 (University of Groningen 2021) national accounts constant price GDP data, as recommended by Feenstra, Inklaar, and Timmer (2015), when the purpose is to compare growth performance across economies. PWT data are used for all countries, except Cuba, for which I use the World Bank series, and Venezuela for 2019 and 2020, for which I use the FocusEconomics forecasts (PWT uses IMF for 2019 and has no data for 2020). Data are not uniformly available from 1950 for all countries, as some series start at later years.

4. Hausmann and Rodríguez (2014) provide an overview and discussion of the explanations for the collapse in output between 1977 and 1998.

5. According to the conventional Cagan (1956) definition, an economy enters hyperinflation when its monthly inflation rate surpasses 50% and exits it when the monthly rate falls below the threshold and spends the subsequent 12 months below it. Venezuela spent 37 months in hyperinflation by that standard according to data published by BCV and 40 months according to a competing index published by the opposition-controlled National Assembly elected in 2015. In both cases it is the third longest documented hyperinflation, after Nicaragua (70 months) and Greece (68 months) and above that of Azerbaijan (36 months).

6. The Central Bank published a press release in 2022 with GDP growth estimates for the first three quarters of 2022 (BCV 2022), and some high-ranking Venezuelan officials have referred to growth numbers in speeches (EFE 2022; D. Rodríguez 2023), but the last official data series published on the Central Bank website is for 1Q19.

7. As noted previously, the one existing data series adjusted for PPP, the PWT's expenditure-side real GDP at chained PPP, displays a staggering contraction of 99.0% between 2012 and 2020. Despite a slight conceptual preference for this series, which I use for an earlier time period in chapter 4, I am hesitant to use an estimate that is ridden with evident estimation problems for more recent years. The problem comes from the fact that Venezuela's most recent price data in the International Comparisons Program used to construct these series dates from 2011; estimates after that date are based on extrapolations that are very likely inaccurate given the deep structural changes experienced by the economy.

8. See R4V 2021. Many sources used in these estimates, with the important exception of Colombia, omit estimates of irregular migration.

9. I.e., $(1-.261)^4-1 = -.702$.

10. See Rodríguez 2006 for a discussion of Adriani's proposals, which were only adopted in very watered-down versions.

11. Calculations based on Bolt and van Zaden 2020.

12. By 2018, this ratio had fallen to 91%, largely as a result of the collapse of oil production and an increase in gold exports.

13. The average share of oil to total GDP in national accounts data from 1Q97 to 1Q19 is 14.3%. That share had declined through the 2000s, so that in the last four quarters of available data (2Q18–1Q19) it averages 12.1%.

14. As a result of the massive migration exodus discussed above, the country has begun to receive significant remittance inflows. Nevertheless, these numbers were still minor relative to oil revenues for most of the period covered by my discussion. According to official statistics, net current transfers were $2.0 billion in 2018 (up from $0.2 billion in 2016), as opposed to $29.8 billion in oil exports. However, given the collapse in oil revenues and continued emigration, it is probable that remittances became as large if not larger than net oil exports by 2020.

15. Barro and Sala-i-Martin (2004, chap. 12) find a positive effect of terms of trade shock on growth in a baseline panel regression but show that this coefficient is not stable across time periods or robust to changes in specification.

16. These numbers rise to 0.84 and 0.25, respectively, if I use year-on-year log changes in the nonseasonally adjusted data and maintain their strength if I use export levels or export prices as instrumental variables. My argument does not rely on a claim of causality between imports and growth, both of which are in principle endogenous—although, as I argue below, a good case can be made that for Venezuela over most of this period, this correlation likely does reflect a causal link. Nevertheless, my point is that models that appropriately describe oil-exporting economies should predict a high correlation between imports and growth.

17. All dollar ($) amounts in the text refer to US dollars.

18. In contrast to many other potentially spurious correlations in economics time series, reverse causation isn't a great concern in this case: the bulk of variations in import capacity is caused by changes in global oil market conditions that are exogenous to the domestic economy. Reverse causation could arguably begin to play a role in the post-2016 period, where it could be argued that the decline in per capita incomes led to an exodus of specialized workers that negatively affected the productivity of the oil industry. In chapter 9, I address reverse causation hypotheses of the oil collapse and apply a variety of quasi-experimental methods to show that economic sanctions were a key driving factor in the decline in oil production after 2016. Nevertheless, my story does embody one channel of reverse causation, as I argue that the

negative terms of trade shock of 2014–16 could have caused the change in political strategies that led political actors to target the oil sector in their struggle for power.

19. Formally, if $y = \alpha + \beta xz$, with y representing the dependent variable, x and z both independent variables, and α and β both parameters, then the effects of x and z are said to be nonseparable. Since $\frac{dy}{dz} = \beta x$ and $\frac{dy}{dx} = \beta z$, the partial effects of both x and y depend on the level of the other variable and cannot be meaningfully distinguished. That said, it is common in retrospective analysis to decompose variations in y into the variations of the explanatory variables. For example, if z is a measure of institutions and x a measure of oil revenues, and only the latter changes between $t = 0$ and $t = 1$, we could write $y_1 - y_0 = \beta z_0 (x_0 - x_1)$ and attribute the totality of changes in y to changes in x because no changes in z were observed. While such decompositions are common, they don't necessarily have a causal interpretation, since the initial level of $z = z_0$ also helps determine changes in the level of income. For example, if $z_0 = 0$, then changes in oil revenues would have no effect on incomes because institutions have managed to insulate the economy from the effects of oil revenues.

20. The idea that nonseparabilities are inherent to the growth process is explicit in theories of the takeoff into sustained growth harking back to Rostow (1960). For modern evidence on nonlinearities in growth empirics, see Rodríguez and Shelton 2013.

21. Even this is almost surely a gross overestimate of the change in the economy's net asset position, given that many government holdings were essentially in assets that could only be recovered at a deep markdown. For example, in 2015, the government sold back to the Dominican Republic and Jamaica debt issued under the Petrocaribe cooperation agreement, obtaining respectively 52 and 46 cents on the dollar. See Fieser 2015a, 2015b.

22. For the role of intermediate inputs in growth accounting, see Hulten 1978, 2009; Syrquin 1987. The canonical model of growth as increasing varieties of intermediate inputs is due to Romer (1987, 1990). For a review of these models and their implication for growth accounting, see Barro and Sala-i-Martin 2004, chaps. 6, 10. The idea that oil served as a source of modernization for the country, deeply seated in Venezuelan contemporary thinking (Uslar Pietri 1947; Coronil 1997; Baptista and Mommer 1999; Tinker Salas, Joseph, and Rosenberg 2009), suggests that technological externalities of imports had a tangible influence in the economy.

23. This is the implication of the Matsuyama (1992) model discussed earlier in this chapter and highlights the inherent tension between Dutch disease

models and models that seek to explain the contribution of oil revenues to growth through an import externalities channel.

24. Between 1954 and 1977, Venezuela's per capita GDP grew at a yearly rate of 2.3%, while the capital stock grew at 2.9%; between 1977 and 1998, the growth rates fell to -1.0% and 0.1%, respectively.

25. The classic reference is Friedman 1953. Much of modern growth theory assumes a closed capital account; models with an open capital account tend to generate immediate convergence to the steady state and thus are not useful as descriptions of the development process. See Barro and Sala-i-Martin 2004, sec. 3.3, for a discussion.

26. The choice to invest oil export revenues domestically rather than save them externally was a conscious decision by policy makers during the first oil boom of the 1970s and was premised on the view, inspired by "Big Push" development model, that massive domestic investment was needed to allow the economy to embark on the road to development. See Rodríguez 1986 for a discussion.

27. Rodríguez and Sachs (1999) also provide a multisector model that shows that the overshooting effect is preserved. They calibrate that model to the Venezuelan economy and find that it explains adequately the decline in growth during the 1980s and 1990s.

28. Allowing consumers to own part of the capital stock makes no difference to the model's results, aside from slightly complicating the algebra.

29. By equation (2.12), imports are equal to g, which is an exogenous variable. Ceteris paribus, import expansions lead to increases in the capital stock and output via the production function in the Rodríguez-Sachs model. In contrast, in Hausmann and Rigobón (2003) import expansions have no effect in the economy's production but are solely a consequence of the economy's greater wealth.

30. There are, of course, other factors aside from oil revenues that may impact the savings rate. The purpose of figure 2.4 is not to claim that the model explains all the variations in the savings rate but rather to make the more limited claim that movements over time in the savings rate are consistent with the predictions of the model. One driving factor in the decline in the savings rate in addition to oil revenues may be falling productivity, which I discuss in the next subsection.

31. See Barro and Sala-i-Martin 2004, chap. 10, for an explanation of these methods. I use data from Penn World Table 10.0 (University of Groningen 2021). There is a slight difference between the aggregate growth numbers and those presented earlier in this section because the PWT uses the

IMF forecast for 2019 (-35.0%), while I used the FocusEconomics estimate (-31.2%).

32. This number is different from that presented at the beginning of this section because it goes only up to 2019 and uses Penn World Table GDP estimates (which rely on IMF projections).

33. Venezuela's productivity decline shown in table 2.4 (14.2% a year, 63.0% cumulative) is slightly different from that shown in table 2.3 (14.1% a year, 62.7% cumulative) because the approximation used to construct the PWT capital stock numbers uses yearly data, whereas I use data for the time periods indicated in the table. Since the discrete-time approximation used in constructing the figures relies on beginning- and end-period factor shares, estimation over different time periods implies weighting by slightly different factor shares. This reflects the fact that the discrete-time formula is only an approximation to the continuous-time growth dynamics that I am trying to estimate (Thörnqvist 1936).

34. Hulten (1978) shows that TFP at the aggregate level consists of the residual of aggregate production growth on the share-weighted growth of primary (and not intermediate) inputs. Recall that payments to intermediate inputs (as opposed to payments to capital and labor) are not part of value-added. Therefore, their inclusion in the aggregate production function is premised on the idea that there is some externality based on their use, such as learning from the superior foreign technology embodied in the inputs, quality-ladder effects from higher-quality imports, or variety effects from an enlarged set of available inputs.

35. This is the average estimate found across four studies in the literature (Amiti and Konings 2007; Kasahara and Rodrigue 2008; Halpern, Koren, and Szeidl 2015; Ahn and Choi 2020).

36. The phrase was coined by Abramovitz (1956).

37. Note that the period labeled "2016–19" in table 2.3 takes as a starting point 2016 levels of GDP and factor inputs and thus can capture the effects of changes in growth determinants that occur on or after 2017.

38. Bull and Rosales (2020) also argue that increasing informalization and criminalization of the economy are a by-product of sanctions and economic isolation. Corrales (2020) suggests that these attitudes are all part of a larger trend of adjustments to secure regime survival. For a contrasting view on the role of crime and corruption in the governance model, see López-Maya 2018.

39. See chapter 9 for a discussion of trends among different data sources of Venezuelan oil production.

40. See Bahar et al. 2019; Hausmann and Muci 2019. The former, for example, document trends in socioeconomic indicators since before the sanctions and find significant worsening in these trends before sanctions were imposed in August 2017. This leads the authors to claim that "in the presence of these strong pre-trends, it is impossible to attribute the current performance of these socio-economic indicators to the sanctions" (1). The temporal precedence argument also gained wide appeal in public debate. For example, in response to the visit by UN Special Rapporteur Alena Douhan to document the impact of unilateral coercive measures on human rights, a group of nongovernmental organizations launched a campaign to position the hashtag #LaCrisisFuePrimero (The Crisis Came First) to counter government claims about the negative impact of sanctions.

41. Venezuela currently holds 304 billion barrels of proven crude oil reserves (OPEC 2020a). Some industry experts claim that this is an overestimate given technical, economic, political, and institutional difficulties associated with actually extracting and selling the oil (J. Rodríguez 2020). Nevertheless, my argument is precisely that the low ratio of production to proven reserves is indicative of the absence of the policies and institutional reforms that would be needed to exploit that productive capacity.

CHAPTER THREE

1. Other attempts to provide a conceptual framework for the analysis of Venezuela's political conflict include Dunning 2008; Smilde 2014; Corrales and Penfold 2015; López-Maya 2016; Gamboa Gutiérrez 2016; and Jiménez 2021.

2. These results do not necessarily mean that elections are bad for the overall quality of policy. This is because there are two separate effects of elections on economic performance: on the one hand, they allow voters to pick more competent politicians; on the other, they introduce incentives for governments to carry out more distortionary policies at election time.

3. See Barro 1996; Tavares and Wacziarg 2001; Knutsen 2012.

4. For example, the Democracy-Dictatorship database of Cheibub, Gandhi, and Raymond (2010) requires that an alternation in power under electoral rules identical to the ones that brought the incumbent into office must have taken place to label a country a democracy.

5. There is an extensive literature on the effects of campaign spending on election outcomes. See Austen-Smith 1987; Baron 1994; Levitt 1994. For the use of contest success functions to model the effect of spending on election outcomes, see Klumpp, Mialon, and Williams 2015; Avis et al. 2017.

6. The literature on democratic backsliding discussed in the previous section focuses on this type of decision by incumbents to use the powers of the office achieved through an election to weaken democratic checks and balances and increase the returns from being in office.

7. There are two destructiveness assumptions: global destructiveness, which ensures that any conflict at positive levels of P results in some destruction of the pie, and local destructiveness, which ensures that when both forces increase their levels of P in a conflict equilibrium, the size of the pie declines. For more details, see Rodríguez and Imam 2022.

8. Proofs of all propositions and corollaries can be found in the online appendix (https://franciscorodriguez.net/wp-content/uploads/2024/10/online-appendix.pdf) as well as in Rodríguez and Imam 2022.

9. If we restrict to functions in which $\partial C(P_i,P_j)/\partial P_i > 0$, then the condition for a contested SSPNE is reduced to $P^{**} = \overline{L}$.

10. See, e.g., the discussion in Rasmusen 2006, chap. 3.

11. For similar interpretations in other contexts, see Maskin and Tirole 1988; Norman 2009; Wang 2009.

12. See Hale 2005 for an application of this idea of political regime cycles to the post-Soviet transition process.

13. The example is more than hypothetical. In 2021, mercenaries assassinated Haitian president, Jovenel Moïse (Turkewitz and Kurmanaev 2021). One year earlier, the Venezuelan government foiled a plot by mercenaries who claimed to have been hired by the Guaidó administration to kidnap Maduro (Neuman 2022, 273–78).

14. For the purposes of this discussion, I focus on parameter ranges consistent with pure-strategy SSPNEs and do not consider the area of very low stakes of power $\delta < \tilde{\delta}$. While quantification of δ is obviously an empirical issue, my working assumption is that $\delta < \tilde{\delta}$ corresponds to very low stakes of power usually seen in power-sharing agreements.

15. My argument in no way relies on the assumption that Venezuelan elections are free or fair. Unfair elections are one of the ways in which the stakes of power are raised in my model. But even in unfair contests, there is a reward to the loser from participating in that contest (e.g., control of some local governments and seats in the legislature). My point, developed in greater detail in chapter 10, is that the opposition decided not to participate in those contests and to eschew accepting that reward because it saw a trade-off between doing so and pursuing an all-out battle for absolute power.

16. I present data on Venezuelans' attitude toward sanctions, showing that nearly three-quarters of the population are opposed to oil sanctions, in chapter 12, table 12.4b.

17. Jiménez (2021) suggests that the lack of opposition unity is a response to greater state repression. My model is consistent with that hypothesis—repression is, after all, a reflection of the government's decision to play outside of the democratic arena—but views it as embedded in a broader explanation of the change of strategies by both actors.

18. I take as the starting point 1968, the last year of the Broad Base coalition governments under the 1958 Punto Fijo accords. See Magallanes 1997; Quintero 1997.

19. However, the model of economically destructive political conflict could be applied to understanding the 2002–3 oil strike. At that time, pro-opposition forces controlled significant parts of the oil industry's leadership, giving it the capacity to bring oil production to a standstill. The government of George W. Bush was also strongly supportive of the opposition, as shown by its decision to almost immediately recognize the de facto government of Pedro Carmona installed during the short-lived 2002 coup attempt.

CHAPTER FOUR

1. Under the 1961 Constitution, Venezuelan presidents could not seek immediate reelection but had to wait for ten years after the end of their term in office to seek the presidency again. Pérez, who had ruled the country during the first oil boom in 1974–79, ran for a second term in 1988 and had been sworn in less than a month before the protests.

2. For this comparison, I use expenditure-side real GDP adjusted for PPP from the June 2021 update of the Penn World Table 10.0 (Feenstra, Inklaar, and Timmer 2015; University of Groningen 2021). This series adjusts for internationally comparable consumption prices and thus allows comparisons of living standards across countries and over time. The series is distinct from the national accounts-based constant-price GDP data that I use in chapter 2, which is more appropriate for comparing the growth performance of economies over time. See Feenstra, Inklaar, and Timmer 2015 for a discussion of the appropriate uses of each series. The national accounts series (shown in chap. 2, fig. 2.1) peaks earlier and also sees a large decline between that peak in 1977 and 1998 of 18.4%, the third worst performance of twenty economies in the region during that period.

3. Data refer to share of the population living on less than \$6.85 at 2017 prices from World Bank (2022). Other poverty line thresholds show increases of similar or larger proportions for the same time period. Poverty head count ratios actually declined in the 1981–89 period and then rose markedly in the

1989–98 period, likely reflecting the effect of unsustainable fiscal and exchange rate policies during the 1980s.

4. Turnout was 63.4%, much lower than the average 87% turnout of the previous presidential elections held since the start of Venezuela's democracy in 1958. Of those who turned out to vote, 6.5% cast null votes, so that Chávez was effectively elected with the support of only 33.4% of the electorate. See Kronick, Plunkett, and Rodríguez 2023 for more details on Chávez's electoral support.

5. The consolidated public sector moved from a deficit of 4.5% of GDP in 1998 to a surplus of 0.7% of GDP in 1999; for the central government, the deficit went from 4.0% to 1.7%. Primary spending fell from 18.9% of GDP to 17.0% in the central government and from 25.7% to 22.8% of GDP in the consolidated public sector. See MPPEF 2018.

6. Social Democrat Hipólito Mejía also pushed successfully for a constitutional reform to void term limits in 2002, yet lost his reelection bid two years later after a major banking crisis. See Ortiz 2016.

7. Chapter 13 of Wiarda 2014 contains an in-depth discussion of the links between Chávez's thinking and Rousseau's political doctrine.

8. Article 347 of the Constitution states that the people of Venezuela, as "depository of the original constituent power," have the authority to convene the convention, while article 348 grants the president—as well as two-thirds supermajorities of the National Assembly or municipal councils, or a petition signed by 15% of registered voters—the "initiative to convene" the convention. Some legal scholars interpret this language as requiring the proposal for a constitutional convention to be subject to referendum before elections for delegates to the convention can be held (Acceso a la Justicia 2017; Mónaco 2017; Transparencia Electoral 2017), although the Supreme Court took a different view in 2017 (TSJ 2017). Regardless of whether a prior referendum is required, in principle only a sufficiently popular president whose supporters can be sure of winning the election for delegates to the convention can use this clause to subordinate other branches of power to their authority. In chapter 8, I discuss how Maduro was able to use this rule to consolidate power in 2017 despite his unpopularity at the time.

9. A crawling peg is an exchange rate system in which the exchange rate is fixed yet depreciates at a steady, predetermined rate. An exchange-rate bands system is one in which the exchange rate is allowed to float until it hits predetermined upper or lower bounds, at which time the Central Bank intervenes to maintain it within those bounds. See IMF 2003.

10. Unless otherwise noted, all growth data refer to national accounts constant-price GDP as published by the Central Bank of Venezuela (BCV).

11. These include Rómulo Betancourt in 1959, Carlos Andrés Pérez in 1974, Jaime Lusinchi in 1984, Ramón Velásquez in 1993, and Rafael Caldera in 1994.

12. For literature reviews, see Lewis-Beck and Stegmaier 2013; Stegmaier, Lewis-Beck, and Park 2017. Dassonneville and Lewis-Beck (2014) estimate that a 1 percentage increase in growth leads to a 0.7 percentage point increase in incumbent support. For evidence more specific to Latin America, see Remmer 2003; Lora and Olivera 2005; Singer and Ramalho 2012.

13. Corrales and Penfold (2015) emphasize the spending channel and argue that popularity over this period is strongly correlated with growth in public spending. It is hard, however, to distinguish using time-series data between the effect on popularity of spending and that of economic growth more generally, given their high correlation.

14. Estimates produced by the Economic and Financial Advisory Office to the National Assembly, which I headed at the time, attributed 9.0 percentage points of the GDP decline to the combined effects of the national strikes carried out by the opposition in 2002 and 2003. See Rodríguez 2003.

15. Data again from Penn World Table. Expenditure-chained GDP per capita rose by 174%, from $7,015 to $19,196.52, between 1998 and 2012.

16. Between 1999 and 2012, the government would issue a total of $43 billion in foreign currency bonds. Of these, twenty issuances for $34 billion would be offered directly in the local currency market, where locals could acquire them using local currency at an implicit rate that would generally be higher than the official exchange rate yet lower than the black market rate.

17. The list of regulated categories of products would rise from 87 in 2003 to 98 in 2008 and would be subsequently cut to 91 by 2011. See BCV 2012, 76.

CHAPTER FIVE

1. Those were Daniel Ortega in 1990 in the midst of the Nicaraguan hyperinflation, Hipólito Mejía in 2004 after the Dominican Republic's banking crisis, Mauricio Macri in Argentina in 2019 after a deep recession, Jair Bolsonaro in 2022 in Brazil after the COVID-19 pandemic, and Nicolás Maduro in Venezuela in 2024. Evo Morales in Bolivia resigned in 2019 before the runoff could be held; discussions on fraud allegations refer to whether he won the presidency outright in the first round, as official results claimed, or whether a second round needed to be held. See Idrobo, Kronick, and Rodríguez 2020 for a discussion.

2. See F. Rodríguez 2019a, 5. Expanded public sector spending—the broadest available category of government for Venezuela—rose from 40.5% of GDP in 2010 to 51.6% in 2012.

3. Real per capita imports (deflated by the US Producer Price Index) rose by 281% in that period.

4. Unless otherwise noted, all references to annualized quarterly economic growth figures are in year-on-year terms, i.e., in relation to the same quarter of the previous year.

5. I use "Bs" to refer to the Venezuelan currency in use at the time. Technically, Venezuela has had four currencies during the past two decades: the Venezuelan bolivar (Bs), used between 1879 and 2007; the strong bolivar (*bolívar fuerte*, Bs.F), in use between January 1, 2008, and August 19, 2018; the sovereign bolivar (*bolívar soberano*, Bs.S), in use between August 20, 2018, and September 30, 2021; and the digital bolivar (*bolívar digital*, Bs.D), in use since October 1, 2021. For simplicity, I will refer simply to bolivars (Bs) unless otherwise noted.

6. Venezuela's vice president is appointed and removed by the president. Jaua served as vice president between January 2010 and October 2012, when he was replaced by Maduro.

7. Persons who transacted more than $20,000 a year in the black market could be imprisoned for two to six years and fined an amount equal to twice the exchanged dollars. See Imprenta Nacional 2010.

8. The precise number is hard to pin down but is definitely on the order of magnitude of billions of dollars. Venezuela had a deficit of $17.0 billion in its services balance in 2013, of which travel accounted for $2.3 billion according to BCV balance of payments statistics. Given the 90% subsidy to travel in the official exchange rate, this implies that the opportunity cost of subsidizing international airline travel in that year was at least $2.1 billion, or 0.9% of GDP. This is just the cost of subsidizing international airline tickets and excludes the cost of subsidizing travelers' expenses while abroad, which is subsumed in other services. In a January 2014 press conference, economics chief Rafael Ramírez claimed that the "other concepts" category of foreign exchange allocations, which included travel, outgoing remittances, students abroad, airlines, pensions, and private external debt, had added up to $8.9 billion in 2013 (3.9% of GDP) and that the government would strive to lower it to $5.2 billion in 2014 (Zea 2014a).

9. Milton Friedman (1972) is credited with having first observed that monetary policy takes much longer to affect prices than output, estimating that the peak effect of expansions in the quantity of money on inflation took around two years to materialize. His hypothesis has been confirmed in more recent works in both developed and developing countries (see Friedman 1972; Carlson 1980; Bernanke, Gertler, and Gilchrist, 1999; Gerlach and Svensson 2001; Batini and Nelson 2003; Havranek and Rusnak 2013; Havranek, Horvath, and Zeynalov 2016).

CHAPTER SIX

1. Unless otherwise noted, all quarterly external accounts data cited in this chapter are seasonally adjusted.

2. Standard sustainability analysis centers on the government (or public sector) fiscal accounts for assessing the sustainability of the public sector and on the nation's external accounts for the economy as a whole for analysis of an economy's external sustainability. See Milesi-Ferretti and Razin 1996; Milesi-Ferretti and Lane 2005; IMF 2006. Both analyses can be made in Venezuela, and their results are unsurprising, as well as of limited relevance for the period in question. In 2013, external sustainability analyses found a strongly sustainable economy given the current account surplus and unsustainable public finances given the double-digit budget deficit. The former is of limited relevance for the reasons explained in the text, while the latter tells us little about the government's capacity to service foreign obligations given that it can inflate domestic liabilities at will. The intermediate concept of public sector external accounts, defined as the accumulation of net external liabilities by the public sector, seems more appropriate to study an economy with these characteristics. See Rodríguez 2013 for a more in-depth discussion of the concept of public sector external accounts and its relationship to conventional analyses.

3. If we take exports and the private sector current account balance (the net accumulation of external assets by the private sector) as given, then there will be a one-to-one relation between imports and the public sector current account. However, the private sector current account is ultimately determined by the investment decisions of individuals, which may depend on the actions of the government. Increases in the government's surplus may lead private actors to demand less external assets as they perceive less need to hedge against a future devaluation.

4. Economists distinguish between seigniorage and the inflation tax. Seigniorage is the total revenue that the government obtains through money creation; the inflation tax is the loss in the value of people's real money holdings as a result of inflation. The difference between them is the increase in real money holdings that people are willing to have, also known as pure seigniorage. For example, in an economy with zero inflation and positive real growth, demand for money will increase over time as a result of people's need to carry out more economic transactions, so that real money holdings will increase and seigniorage will be positive even though there is no inflation.

5. Stopping high inflation may be difficult for reasons different from those for changing the distribution of taxes between inflation tax and other

taxes, which is what the household example is meant to highlight. If inflationary expectations are embedded in current contracts, then ending high inflation will require producing a recession to reduce nominal wages to a level consistent with lower than expected prices and labor market equilibrium. Whether this would have been an issue for Venezuela at the time is an open question. Since around 40% of the Venezuelan labor force was in the informal sector at the time, a large part of labor markets was highly flexible and thus not subject to the wage stickiness that is determinant of the real effects of monetary policy.

6. See note 1 of preface.

7. Investigations by independent media and the Prosecutor General's Office later found that security forces had been responsible for the three deaths, including that of the pro-government leader (Boon 2015; *El Impulso* 2015).

8. Economics chief Rafael Ramírez had announced on the previous day that travelers abroad and airlines would pay the more depreciated 11.3 Bs/$ auctions rate instead of the official 6.3 Bs/$ rate (BBC Mundo 2014).

9. The price of West Texas Intermediate oil, light sweet oil traded among Texas and Oklahoma refineries, is a commonly used reference price for describing oil market conditions.

10. Calculations based on data from UNCTAD (2021).

11. Venezuela also had another $21.3 billion in foreign currency holdings outside of the Central Bank, according to its International Investment Position statistics at the end of 2013. This was for the most part composed of deposits in PDVSA, the National Development Fund FONDEN, and accounts used for the disbursement of Chinese loans. Especially once one includes these funds in the picture, Venezuela's level of reserves was not atypical for a developing country, but it was low in comparison to other countries that had benefited from the oil boom, putting the country in a difficult position to face the large terms of trade shock that took place in 2014.

12. In Spanish, Autorización de Adquisición de Divisas (AAD) and Autorización de Liquidación de Divisas (ALD).

13. See Rodríguez 2019a. Another $24.3 billion in bonds had been issued by state-owned corporations, including PDVSA.

14. Venezuelan legal precedent from before the Chávez era had upheld the prerogative of the government to modify the exchange rate applying to foreign exchange arrears of the exchange controls agency, effectively allowing it to devalue them away. In 1989, the incoming Carlos Andrés Pérez administration lifted exchange controls and refused to recognize letters of credit issued during the previous administration at the prior exchange rate. It imposed a sliding

scale whereby letters of credit issued after a certain date would be recognized only at the postdevaluation rate. Venezuelan courts upheld the government's decision against a lawsuit by the private sector association CONINDUSTRIA (see Naím 1993, 92 n. 34; Garnica de López 1991). More recently, foreign exchange agreements Nos. 25 and 27 devalued old foreign exchange authorizations to the SICAD I and II rates (Imprenta Nacional 2013b, 2014). However, there is one case of a firm that was able to enforce these awards in international courts. In 2017, Air Canada filed an arbitration claim before the International Centre for Settlement of Investment Disputes (ICSID) alleging that Venezuela had breached its duties under the Canada-Venezuela bilateral investment treaty by devaluing the rate at which it would honor its AADs. The tribunal ruled in favor of Air Canada, granting it an award of $21 million, well below Air Canada's request of $213 million. To date, this is the only partially successful attempt, and it appears unlikely to be replicated given that it requires the existence of a bilateral investment treaty with an ICSID arbitration clause in which the statute of limitations has not expired. See *Air Canada v. Bolivarian Republic of Venezuela*, No. ARB(AF)/17/1 (January 13, 2017).

15. Money printing is the mechanism that the government uses to ensure that there will be demand for the new internal bonds. Venezuela's Central Bank cannot directly purchase bonds issued by the central government but can lend bolivars to private banks or to state-owned enterprises to acquire them.

16. Venezuela's Central Bank maintained regulatory interest rate caps during this period, ensuring that creditors would not be able to internalize the expectation of depreciation through higher nominal interest rates. Banks, on the other hand, had no problem acquiring the government-issued local currency bonds despite their negative real interest rates because interest rate caps ensured that they could pay depositors even lower nominal rates and thus continue to turn a profit.

17. Chávez would later explain that the risks of having the country shut off from international capital markets would in his view have outweighed the benefits of savings on debt service. See Harnecker 2002, 134–40.

18. Almost invariably and unless precluded by legal impediments, debt defaults tend to be followed by negotiations with creditors to restructure the outstanding debt. Technically, a default in the sense of a suspension of payments need not take place for renegotiations, although many analysts treat the two as synonymous as any renegotiation leading to net present value creditor losses has to be backed by at least an implicit threat of nonpayment. Therefore, there is a broad range of choices typically available to debtors, ranging from the offer of voluntary debt exchanges such as the one carried out by PDVSA

in September 2016 to the more aggressive suspension of payments followed by a take-it-or-leave-it offer to creditors, such as was done by Argentina in 2001.

19. My estimates are based on data from BCV (2021) plus an adjustment for liabilities caused by expropriation subject to international arbitration. The number is higher than the one shown in figure 2.9 ($112 billion) because of the estimated arbitration claims.

20. Data from BCV (2023d).

21. The figure corresponds to the unweighted average over all sovereign bonds for 2013. In August 2014, just before the publication of Hausmann and Santos's (2014) work, that number had risen only moderately to 11.9%.

22. Between 2013 and 2016, external debt inclusive of ICSID obligations rose by 8.3% while GDP measured in US dollars fell by 49%. The decline in GDP thus accounts for 92% of the increase in the debt-to-GDP ratio in that period.

23. The principle of sovereign immunity as codified in the United States Foreign Sovereign Immunities Act of 1976 protects assets of foreign governments from being seized by creditors. However, there is an exception for the case of assets that are used in commercial activities. Therefore, a government that sells oil or any other goods abroad is not immune from a lawsuit in foreign courts that attempts to seize the proceeds from its commercial oil sales. Furthermore, state-owned companies are legal entities distinct from the state and can therefore be sued in foreign courts without having recourse to the claim of sovereign immunity. For most state-owned entities, this is not a binding constraint because they do not do business internationally. However, state-owned commodity exporters are particularly vulnerable. For example, in 2005, an English High Court judge allowed two creditors of Congo to seize oil shipments and freeze funds in the French bank BNP Paribas to collect on debt issued by the Congolese government in the 1980s (Goldhaber 2008).

24. The sale is currently halted because US sanctions impede asset transfers—including attachments—yet a Delaware court has ordered that the mechanics of the sale be defined so as to proceed with the sale pending issuance of a license by the Department of the Treasury (Reuters 2021).

25. See also Alesina, Cohen, and Roubini 1993; Heckelman and Berument 1998.

CHAPTER SEVEN

1. During Maduro's first term in office (2013–19), the Central Bank of Venezuela had six presidents. Of these, one was a mathematician (Nelson

Merentes) and two were industrial engineers (Edmeé Betancourt and Calixto Ortega, though the latter had a master's degree in economic policy). Of the three economists, two were professional politicians (Ricardo Sanguino and Ramón Lobo), while only one (Eudomar Tovar) was a Central Bank staff member.

2. See, e.g., Carbonetto et al. 1987.

3. See Corrales and Penfold 2015; Kronick 2015; and López-Maya 2018 for alternative views of the role of corruption during the Chávez and Maduro eras.

4. The Laffer curve is a hump-shaped relationship between tax revenue and tax rates (Fullerton 2008). Given the assumptions that tax revenue must be zero when the tax rate is zero as well as when the tax rate is prohibitively high and that tax collection is positive for some intermediate levels of the tax rate, then there must be a revenue-maximizing level of the tax rate. The same logic applies to inflation taxes, implying that there is a downward-sloping segment over which inflation tax revenue declines in the level of inflation (Bali and Thurston 2000).

5. For a more detailed discussion of Venezuela's slide into hyperinflation, see Iyer and Rodríguez 2021.

6. See Krugman 1979 for the classic presentation of this mechanism.

7. There is an underlying assumption in my argument that governments are credit constrained, so the positive shock allows them to raise spending and negative shocks force them to bring down spending. In practice, positive shocks also tend to improve access to capital markets, allowing the government to raise spending by more than the magnitude of the shock, while negative shocks tend to be associated with the closing-off of market access and thus deeper spending contractions.

8. The 1961 Constitution had a two-term ban on immediate reelection, making Pérez eligible for reelection in 1988 (which he won); Herrera Campins, in 1993; and Jaime Lusinchi, in 1998.

9. This share is set by law, so it has varied over time independently of constitutional changes. See Molina 2009.

10. For a description of the constitutional reforms of 1999 in contrast to the institutions of pacted democracy, see Monaldi and Penfold 2012.

11. In 1999, the president proposed a set of electoral rules together with the proposal for holding a constitutional convention to voters, who approved both in an initial referendum. In a controversial interpretation used by Maduro to elect the 2017 Constitutional Convention, the National Electoral Council set the electoral rules based on a proposal submitted by the president. See chapter 8 for a more detailed discussion.

12. Throughout this chapter, I refer to any election in which all or a large majority of the country's voters are eligible to participate as a "nationwide election," including local and regional elections held across the country as well as presidential recalls, and reserve the term "general election" for those in which the president and national legislature are elected concurrently.

13. The Constitution did not specify the length of the period for municipal council members, but the Law of the Municipal Public Power set it at four years.

14. I do not count in this assessment the years in which officials other than the president could be subject to recall. In practice, these recalls were hard to invoke and infrequently carried out. My focus is on nationwide elections that have the potential for significantly changing the national political balance and threatening the government's hold on power.

15. From August 19, 2000, when Chávez was elected, to August 15, 2004, when the recall referendum was held. I take the length of this period as the relevant one to calculate electoral insulation in subsequent presidential terms, on the assumption that if the opposition had successfully called a referendum during these terms, it would have faced delays similar to those seen in 2004 between the beginning of the midterm, when the president effectively becomes eligible to face the referendum, and the date at which such a referendum would have been held.

16. From 1958 to 1973, all five nationwide elections (for the president as well as national-, state-, and municipal-level legislative bodies) were held on the same date. Starting in 1979, elections for municipal councils were held roughly six months after the presidential election, lowering the electoral insulation period from 5 to 4.5 years.

17. For purposes of my measure, I take into account only elections that are scheduled by constitutional rules. I do not count referendums or elections for constitutional conventions, such as those held in 1999 and 2017, as these are initiated by the government and can thus be understood as an "electoral option" that the government can decide to invoke. The fact that the government can decide whether to call these contests implies that it can choose not to do so if they are an obstacle to the implementation of its policy agenda. However, once the Constitution was passed in 1999, new elections were scheduled to "relegitimize" all branches of government in 2000. I count the 2000 elections in my measure as these are set in observance of constitutional rules.

18. The possibility of manipulating the timing of elections implies that it is not necessarily exogenous. Authorities can in principle use this power to lengthen the windows of opportunity to enact unpopular policies. This does

not appear to have been a major factor in the delay of the 2013 municipal elections. That said, the political costs associated with manipulating the timing of elections are far from trivial, and there are instances in which the politically optimal move may be to move elections forward (as in May 2018), thus reducing electoral insulation.

19. Of course, foreign exchange controls can do just the opposite, by allowing politically connected groups to build large fortunes on the basis of arbitrage. But this is much less visible and thus harder for voters to take into account at election time.

20. I build an estimate of the equilibrium real exchange rate using cointegration techniques following Baffes, Elbadawi, and O'Connell (1999). See Rodríguez 2014c for alternative estimation methods. I model the logarithm of the real exchange rate as a function of log real per capita oil exports. Dickey-Fuller tests do not reject the unit root hypothesis for either variable for the 1957–2016 period. Johansen tests reject the hypothesis of no cointegrating vectors but cannot reject the hypothesis of at most one cointegrating vector between both variables, with the optimal lags selected by minimization of the Hannan-Quinn and Schwarz Bayesian information criterion. I use the Johansen estimate of that cointegrating vector as the estimate of the equilibrium real exchange rate.

21. I follow a convention widely used among Latin American economists—but not in other regions—of representing the real exchange rate as the relative price of imported to domestic goods. Therefore, a higher value of the exchange rate corresponds to a weaker or more depreciated exchange rate.

22. In retrospect, this may have been an overadjustment since the equilibrium real exchange rate strengthened as oil prices recovered from their lows. Because per capita oil exports follow a unit root, their current level is the best predictor of future levels and their subsequent recovery could not have been foreseen when they hit their early 2016 lows.

23. Although I have distinguished between imported and domestic goods in the text for the purposes of exposition, analytically the correct distinction is between tradable and nontradable goods, as the prices of tradable goods, regardless of whether or not they are produced domestically, are determined internationally.

24. Calculations use labor compensation from national accounts data, defined as remuneration of employees plus a share of mixed income equal to the share of labor in nonmixed income. This is divided by occupied workers according to National Institute of Statistics employment data and deflated by the respective price measures. A good case can be made that the dollar wage is a better indicator than the CPI-deflated real wage given the prevalence of

regulated goods in both the Central Bank and the National Assembly CPI baskets. Put differently, a real wage deflated by prices of goods that are hard to find does not take into account the opportunity cost of the time invested in finding the goods or the welfare losses from substituting other goods for them. Applied to the statutory minimum wage, the calculations yield 2012–16 changes of -12.7% at the BCV's price index, -30.0% at the National Assembly's price index, and -87.4% in dollars.

25. These calculations assume that all employment in the economy is subject to the minimum wage. Since around 40% of the labor force is employed in the informal sector, which does not observe minimum wage legislation, the government would have been unable to avoid a decline in real wages regardless of what level of the minimum wage it targeted. The calculations in this stylized model are meant to serve as indicators of the choices that the government faced at the time by comparing two extreme scenarios of complete and zero wage flexibility.

26. For example, shortly after the 2012 elections, Planning and Finance Minister Jorge Giordani told reporters that setting the price of oil in the 2013 budget at $55, around half its market price at the time, "is the best way we have found to shield our economy" (Ministerio del Poder Popular para la Comunicación y Información 2012). The truth is that underestimating oil prices in the budget did not lead to lower spending, as the government also underestimated spending and many government offices depended on additional spending allocations approved during the budget year based on the higher-than-budgeted oil prices. If the higher oil prices did not materialize, the government was forced to come up with other revenue sources (e.g., from devaluation) to fulfill spending commitments, a large part of which were nondiscretionary.

27. Recall from chapter 6 the discussion of OPEC's decision not to curtail output on November 27, 2014. In the run-up to that decision, Venezuela lobbied strongly for an output cut. Therefore, it only became clear that oil prices were going into freefall after the supporters of maintaining production levels carried the day in the November 2014 OPEC meeting.

CHAPTER EIGHT

1. The decree gave the president the power to redirect budgetary resources, reform tax administration, and suspend administrative procedures without prior National Assembly authorization. It also granted the government the power to direct the use of privately owned food transport or storage units in order to ensure adequate food supply. See Maduro 2016.

2. In chapter 9 I discuss in greater detail the relationship between default probabilities and the closest asset-price proxy for default risk, which is the price of credit-default swaps. In January 2017, Venezuela five-year credit default swap (CDS) spreads were pricing in a 49.1% probability of a default occurring over the next five years, equivalent to a 12.6% annual probability of default over the five-year period. While markets were obviously concerned about the risk of a Venezuelan default, they were not yet treating it as a foregone conclusion.

3. This had only happened in two of the preceding thirteen years. One was in 2007, when a spate of nationalizations carried out by Chávez in the aftermath of the 2006 reelection led to increasing perceptions of country risk despite rising oil prices. The other was in 2011, when the downgrade of the United States by Standard and Poor's (S&P) had an amplified effect on developing country risk unrelated to commodity prices. In other words, while it was not impossible for certain events to break the negative Venezuela oil price–country risk correlation, it was unusual.

4. A summary of preelection seat forecasts can be found in Wikipedia (2021). Only three of twenty-two firms publishing forecasts had the opposition winning a two-thirds majority in its forecast range.

5. Venezuela's vice president is appointed by the president and coordinates the cabinet, serving a role that is similar to that of a prime minister in parliamentary systems. The president can dissolve a National Assembly that has approved three no-confidence votes against the vice president and call for new legislative elections, but there is no limit on the number of ministers that can be fired through this procedure.

6. Article 338 of the Constitution allows the government to issue an economic emergency decree for sixty days, renewable for the same period of time, but requires the National Assembly to approve it within eight days. The Supreme Court has allowed the government to extend the decree twenty-eight times, for a total duration of 4 years and 8 months as of this writing. Regarding National Assembly authorization, the Supreme Court's Constitutional Chamber ruled in a February 2016 decision that the legislative branch of power only has "political" control over emergency decrees and has no capacity to render them null. Note that the Constitution does not grant any authority to the executive to suspend no-confidence votes under an economic emergency and explicitly states that an economic emergency decree "cannot interrupt the functioning of the organs of public power" (Brewer-Carías 2016, 233).

7. The National Assembly again moved to disincorporate the legislators in January 2017. The Supreme Court ruled that this decision was not valid given that it was taken by a board that was elected while in contempt (TSJ 2017).

8. Eubank and Kronick (2021) use cell phone data on the location of petition signatories to estimate the effect of social sanctioning on the likelihood of signing the petition. They found that those whose behavior was more easily observed by peers were much more likely to protest and much more likely to sign a political petition than otherwise similar people in less visible social network positions.

9. Foro Penal (2018), a local NGO, reported at least 102 direct killings during protests, at least 73% of which occurred during the intervention of security forces or pro-government paramilitary groups. The government routinely accused the opposition protests of violence. In a highly publicized case, a man was burned alive during an opposition protest; he would later die as a result of the burns. The government said that he was burned after being accused of being a government spy, while some demonstrators claimed that he was a pickpocket. No apology was ever issued by opposition leaders for this incident (*Guardian* 2017).

10. The exceptions were state capitals, which received two legislators, and the national capital, which received seven legislators (Rodríguez 2017b).

11. No final tally appears to have been publicly announced by the electoral commission appointed by the National Assembly to oversee the process. In its last public statement, the commission announced a turnout of 7.5 million votes with 99% of votes tallied (Mesa de la Unidad Democrática 2017). On July 18, Baruta mayor Gerardo Blyde announced via his Instagram account that the final figure amounted to 7,676,894 votes with 100% of votes tallied, a figure that was reported by several media sources (e.g., El Cooperante 2017).

12. Turnout numbers from Mesa de la Unidad Democrática 2017.

13. The National Assembly president, Julio Borges, denounced a major fraud, assuring that multiple voting affected the results in at least ten states and that 1.6 million people had trouble identifying their fingerprints: "The group of people who have possibly been able to vote more than once is several times the difference by which those elections were supposedly lost. . . . We are not talking about a number that does not alter the final result; on the contrary, the problem of fingerprints that do not coincide with effective voters may have altered the result" (VPITV 2017).

14. López and Capriles had been banned from running for office as a result of decisions by the Comptroller General's Office, which had found evidence of administrative irregularities in their role as elected officials. In December 2009, the Inter-American Court found that the restriction on López violated the American Convention on Human Rights given that it was not made by a competent court, as required by the convention (Pulido 2021). López was later sentenced for the crime of instigating violence in the February

2014 protests at the building of the Prosecutor General's Office (see chap. 6), a decision that was affirmed in 2017 by the Supreme Court. According to article 227 of the Constitution, persons against whom a firm judgment has been handed down are disqualified from holding the office of the presidency. See chapter 10 for a discussion of the bans on participation of parties in the 2018 elections.

15. To be precise, Capriles never recognized the defeat in the 2013 presidential election against Maduro, in which he requested a full and comprehensive vote audit. Yet even in that case, the MUD never withheld formal recognition of Maduro as president and continued to advocate for contesting elections.

16. Article 313 of the Constitution specifies that if the National Assembly does not approve a budget law for a given fiscal year, then the government will continue to use the previous year's budget. Doing so freezes spending in nominal levels and thus forces a significant real spending contraction in the context of moderate or high inflation.

17. In 2019, the Guaidó administration decided to default on this bond and sought a New York court to overturn the granting of the collateral on the argument that the bond had not been duly authorized. Its argument was based on the claim that the National Assembly's 2016 resolution's language rejecting the use of PDVSA's offshore assets as collateral should be construed as a denial of authorization even though such a denial was not formally issued. Defendants—the collateral agent and trustee for the bonds—claimed that even if the National Assembly resolution was interpreted in this way, PDVSA is legally exempted from the requirement of National Assembly authorization for bond issuances and asset pledges. This is probably why no political leaders issued statements at the time of the swap in 2016 warning investors not to participate in the exchange, and the language of the resolution differs significantly from that of other resolutions in which it did intend to block authorization, as was the case with mining concessions (Asamblea Nacional de Venezuela 2016a). In October 2020, the US District Court for the Southern District of New York denied the Guaidó request, concluding that "the Republic's submission does not provide significant support for the proposition that the September 2016 Resolution either characterized the Exchange Offer as a contract of national public interest or declared the Exchange Offer as null and void" (*Petróleos de Venezuela S.A.* v. *MUFG Union Bank* [2020], 40). However, the court affirmed the validity of the issuance based on New York law considerations, and in February 2024 the New York Court of Appeals ruled that the district court should have directly considered the validity of the issuance under Venezuelan law.

18. Although the National Assembly in principle has the authority to approve all debt issuances, there is an exception for the case of PDVSA and the Central Bank, among other state entities, codified in the Organic Law of Financial Administration of the Public Sector. In the case of debt issued directly by the sovereign, the National Assembly's right to authorize is exercised through the setting of a debt ceiling in the Annual Indebtedness Law, approved concurrently with the Budget Law. The Guaidó administration's contestation of the legality of the PDVSA 2020 bond was based on the argument that while a PDVSA bond issuance did not require National Assembly authorization, a pledge of a national asset like CITGO did. The sovereign Venezuela 2036 bond issued on December 29, in contrast, was neither secured by an asset pledge nor issued without authorization, as it was covered by the 2016 Indebtedness Law. There was thus no legal argument against its validity, and no attempt has been made to legally contest it.

19. In the previous thirty years, this had only occurred three times: (i) 1999, Chávez's first year in office, when investor concerns with the new administration combined with Chávez's decision to carry out a fiscal adjustment caused a recession despite recovering oil revenues (see chap. 4); (ii) 2003, during which oil revenues rose moderately on rising prices, yet the decline in oil and non-oil output directly caused by the oil strike caused a plunge in GDP; and (iii) 2010, in the immediate aftermath of the Lehman crisis, when the economy spent a second year in recession even though oil revenues recovered relative to 2009.

CHAPTER NINE

1. Venezuelans associated with the regime have been added to the list of sanctioned individuals, also known as Specially Designated Nationals (SDN), as far back as 2008 for providing assistance to terrorist organizations like Hezbollah or for drug-related offenses.

2. As is the case with most US sanctions regimes, Venezuela sanctions are based on the US government's capacity to restrict interactions with certain actors that are seen as posing a threat to US national security. This authority stems from legislation first adopted during World War I aimed at granting the president the power to restrict trade and financial interactions with the country's enemies during wartime. In its most recent iteration, which dates from 1977, the International Emergency Economic Powers Act allows the president to declare the existence of a national emergency when an "unusual and extraordinary threat" to national security originates outside of the United States (Office of the Law Revision Counsel 1977).

3. It is not unusual for some experts to date the start of Venezuelan sanctions as far back as 2005, the year that the Bush administration declared Venezuela a major drug transit country (e.g., United Nations Human Rights Council 2021, 3). This seems hard to justify, as the designation had little practical effect and included twelve other Latin American nations, some of which, such as Colombia, Peru, and Mexico, were strong US allies at the time. A stronger case could be made for dating the start of sanctions as of the determination that the country was not fully cooperating with antiterrorism efforts in 2006, which led to the imposition of an arms embargo. Venezuelans associated with the Chávez government were first added to the SDN list in 2008 for providing assistance to terrorist organizations like Hezbollah or for drug-related offenses. See Executive Order 13382, OFAC 2005; MacAskill 2006. However, it was not until 2015 that a specific Venezuela sanctions regime was created through the issuance of the Obama administration's executive order declaring a national emergency with respect to the situation in Venezuela (White House 2015). In total, the Obama administration issued twenty designations of Venezuelan individuals or entities. However, only seven were issued within the framework of the 2015 national emergency declaration. The remaining designations were issued within the framework of antiterrorism or antidrug regulations (Barlett and Ophel 2021).

4. While El Aissami's 2017 designation was done in the context of the Kingpin Act related to drug-trafficking activities, most other designations were done within the framework of Obama's national emergency declaration.

5. Some have argued that a default would have occurred in the absence of sanctions, yet it is clear that the announcement of the intent to restructure the debt was not due to the government's having run out of money, for the simple reason that the government made a large payment of $1.1 billion in maturing bonds at the time that it announced the restructuring on November 2 (BBC Mundo 2017). The payment appears to have been intended as an olive branch to creditors to convince them to lobby the US government to withdraw sanctions. Venezuela would only go into default in the sense of not making scheduled payments on November 13 for its PDVSA bonds and November 14 for its sovereign bonds.

6. According to US Energy Information Administration (EIA) data, Venezuela exported on average 514,000 barrels per day of crude oil to the United States, which valued at the price of the Venezuelan oil basket on the week prior to the announcement (US$56) gives $10.5 billion.

7. Reliance Industries, Venezuela's largest customer in India, announced in March 2019 that its US subsidiary had stopped all business with Venezuela (as required by sanctions) and that its global parent "has not increased crude purchases." This happened after consultations with US authorities and a direct

warning from the Indian government (Chakraborty and Kassai 2019; Gordon, Gupte, and Bambino 2019).

8. Most entities of the Venezuelan public sector, including all its oil industries, had already been blocked at the time as a result of past actions or decisions. Most importantly, the assets of the Central Bank and the government had been transferred to the Guaidó administration in January 2019 and courts had subsequently confirmed the power of Guaidó appointees over US-based subsidiaries. The power of the United States to sanction third parties had also already been established for PDVSA—if not for the government as a whole—by the firm's January SDN designation. Nevertheless, the US government publicized the order highly so that it would serve as a signal of its willingness to punish third parties that did business with the Venezuelan government.

9. Bolton claimed that efforts to topple the Maduro regime were partly derailed by Trump's wavering, including his desire to meet with Maduro and his request that the Guaidó administration guarantee preferential access to US oil companies (Bolton 2020).

10. There are several data series for oil production in Venezuela. All of them show a break in trend in the second half of 2017, as well as in the initial months of 2019 and 2020. Data produced by secondary agencies tend to show stability in the 2008–15 period, while data produced by the Venezuelan government tends to show a pre-2016 decline. Most oil industry experts are distrustful of the official data, which becomes highly volatile in the post-sanctions period. It is possible that the pre-2016 decline in the official series is an artifact of changes in the magnitude by which the government decided to exaggerate output.

11. Data from the US EIA (2024) tell a similar story, with imports averaging 514 tbd during 2018 and falling to zero by June 2019.

12. An exception is Bull and Rosales (2020), who focus on the incentives for informalization and criminalization of the Venezuelan economy created by sanctions.

13. Throughout 2019, Venezuela suffered a series of nationwide blackouts, with two major outages: the first lasting 105 hours and beginning in March 7 and the second lasting 95 hours and beginning in March 25. Two more major blackouts occurred in April and July, for a total of 235 hours of blackout, or 9.8 days. Since then, despite the poor electric coverage and rolling blackouts in some regions, particularly rural regions, no major nationwide blackouts have occurred. See Rodríguez 2019c.

14. The synthetic control and panel data estimates are updated results of research originally published in Rodríguez 2019b. The firm-level analysis summarizes results published in Rodríguez 2022b.

15. Although production never returned to its pre-strike levels, the data suggest that most of the effect of the strike was gone by 2005. Because of how atypical (and idiosyncratic) the oil strike plunge and subsequent recovery are, no other country will replicate the Venezuelan data over this period. While using a longer window does not qualitatively change my results, it does diminish the capacity of the synthetic control group to replicate the pretreatment data.

16. The last year of Venezuelan GDP data in the World Bank's World Development Indicators Database is 2014.

17. Algeria, Argentina, Azerbaijan, Brazil, China, Colombia, Egypt, India, Indonesia, Kazakhstan, Malaysia, Mexico, and Vietnam. Eleven countries are excluded from the donor group by the income criterion (Australia, Canada, Denmark, Kuwait, Norway, Oman, Qatar, Saudi Arabia, UAE, the United Kingdom, and the United States), three by the sanctions criterion (Iran, Iraq, and Russia), and eight because of insufficient data in either the dependent variable or the covariates (Angola, Ecuador, Equatorial Guinea, Gabon, Libya, Nigeria, Sudan, and Syria).

18. October 2017.

19. I use a current oil price of $60 for Venezuelan oil exports.

20. My oil production variable is taken from several sources: OPEC's "Monthly Oil Market Report" (OPEC 2023), the US EIA's International Energy Statistics (EIA 2023a), Bloomberg's crude oil production data (Bloomberg 2023), and Colombia's National Hydrocarbons Agency's data set (ANH 2023). I choose the series with the highest coverage for each country. See Rodríguez 2019b for more details.

21. Venezuela's case is atypical in the presence of financial sanctions without oil sanctions. Typically, both financial and oil sanctions are imposed and removed simultaneously, impeding us from empirically estimating the effects separate from each other. Therefore, the coefficient estimates in this section could be interpreted as the joint effect of oil and financial sanctions.

22. This follows Autor's (2003) idea to use Granger causality tests to study whether sanctions effects precede or are preceded by changes in oil production.

23. When estimated separately, the coefficients on individual months are significant at $p < .1$ but not at $p < .05$ for the first three months after adoption and become significant at $p < .05$ for four or more months. When estimated jointly, the post-sanctions coefficient is significant at $p < .05$ for all specifications.

24. That is, the imposition of sanctions would lead to a decline of between 48% and 52% in output. See Rodríguez 2019b for a discussion and a full set of regression tables. The coefficient drops in a specification with controls for

a number of industry covariates to -20 log points, yet remains strongly statistically significant. Nevertheless, as I discuss there, the reduction in coefficient magnitude is due to the loss of observations, which include some cases of sanctioned economies.

25. Attempts to separately estimate a financial sanctions effect in these regressions yielded unstable coefficient estimates, which makes sense given the high level of collinearity with the oil sanctions variable. However, the coefficient on oil sanctions remained robust to the inclusion of a control for financial sanctions.

26. Time-specific treatment effects are necessary so that the treatment group trend does not pick up variation over time in the treatment effect (Wolfers 2006). I refer indistinctly to firms and blocs in my discussion for ease of exposition. While each firm operated by a JV is operated by a distinct firm (even if the foreign partner is the same), the ten blocs wholly operated by PDVSA are operated by a single firm, a PDVSA subsidiary known as the Corporación Venezolana de Petróleo (CVP).

27. There is another way to look at the data that also yields an appealing interpretation. This is to think of the sanctions as the end of the treatment rather than their beginning. This squares well with the idea that our treatment group was different from our control group before the sanctions but not after them. The reason is that by closing off access of all public sector firms to international financing, the sanctions made SFV firms, which previously had access, similar to non-SFV firms, which previously lacked them. In this interpretation, we would expect trend growth rates to be parallel after the sanctions and not before them. This is indeed the pattern displayed in the data.

28. Alternative specifications of the scaled variable, such as those using production as a percentage of average pre-sanctions or of August 2017 production, deliver similarly strong results.

29. Estimates above 100% indicate a counterfactual in which oil production would have recovered in the absence of sanctions, possibly as a result of higher oil prices.

30. I exclude the cross-country panel data estimates, which are the only estimates that focus solely on the 2019 oil sanctions, from this last calculation. To the extent that the aim of this exercise is to understand the relative weight of sanctions to nonsanctions influences on the production decline, only estimates of the effect of all sanctions, which begin in 2017, can be used to establish that weight.

31. To illustrate, suppose that production falls from 100 to 90 before the onset of sanctions and then falls from 90 to 60 after sanctions are imposed.

Assume that the pre-sanctions decline lasts one year and that our data on the sanctions episode last two years. Were we to estimate that 100% of the post-sanctions decline is attributable to sanctions, then we would also conclude that 75% of the total decline is attributable to sanctions. But if sanctions were to continue for another two years after the end of our sample and continued to cause the same proportionate decline over time, then production would fall by another third, to 40, and the weight of sanctions in the total decline would be 83% instead of 75%. This point is particularly important because some of the estimates in table 9.3 were truncated well before production bottomed out, suggesting that they only partially captured the impact of sanctions.

32. My use of the words *never* and *permanently* in referring to loss of capital markets access in this section should be read as referring to the time span during which sanctions are being kept in place, which runs up at least to the time of writing. That is, to argue that sanctions were completely redundant between their imposition and today, one would have to argue that in their absence the country would not have restructured its debt as of the time at which the statement is made.

33. Sturzenegger and Zettelmeyer (2006) present case studies of eight restructuring events. In four of them, no payments were missed prior to the time of the restructuring. In the remaining four, the time periods between the initial default and the eventual restructuring range from a few days (Ukraine) to three years (Argentina).

34. This type of statement is not unusual in distressed debt exchanges and essentially reflects the fact that conceptually "voluntary" debt swaps are not necessarily all that different from explicitly negotiated debt restructurings. For these reasons, S&P classified the debt offer as a "distressed debt exchange" after concluding that if the exchange were not to be carried out, the firm would be unlikely to meet its obligations (Chinea and Ellsworth 2016).

35. Although there is no legal impediment for institutions in other countries to participate in such a restructuring, non-US creditor groups have shied away from any action that would impose restrictions on their capacity to do business in the United States and that would leave them with bonds that would not be tradable in US markets. Furthermore, after January 2019, any changes to existing bonds would have had to be approved by the Guaidó administration, recognized by the US government at the time as the legitimate representation of the Venezuelan state, to be valid under US laws.

36. Bahar et al. (2019) argue that the lack of increase in the sovereign spread after sanctions suggests that the market did not perceive the default as relevant. However, they fail to consider that the relevant counterfactual in the

absence of sanctions would be that spreads would have fallen, given the strong recovery experienced by oil prices in the second half of 2017.

37. This calculation assumes a recovery value of 30%. This is a very conservative estimate of recovery values for Venezuela given what we know about the experience *ex post*. Given that current bond prices have turned out to hover in the single digits, one could argue that recovery value of the bonds in net present value as of 2017 should have been much lower. This only strengthens our argument: for a given CDS spread, lower recovery rates imply that one is insuring against a costlier event and that the perceived probability of default is thus lower. At a recovery rate of 10%, for example, a 2,500 basis point CDS price would imply a 28% five-year probability of default and an annual probability of 6.3%.

38. See Davari 2020 for a discussion of the strategy in the Iran context.

39. Recently, Nephew (2017) has popularized the characterization of the use of sanctions as the exertion of pain (see his discussion, pp. 9–10), although his conclusions are nuanced with respect to the required intensity of sanctions to reach specific objectives.

40. Although initial demands from the Trump administration focused on reverting or impeding decisions by Maduro that were seen as undermining democracy, by 2019 it became clear that the United States would not consider as acceptable any solution in which Maduro did not abandon power. On February 25, Vice President Mike Pence told a Lima Group meeting that "what brings us together today is the recognition, by all the nations gathered here, that Nicolas Maduro is a usurper with no legitimate claim to power, and Nicolas Maduro must go" (US Mission OAS 2019). Even in the "Framework for a Peaceful Democratic Transition in Venezuela," published by the United States on March 2020, when it was clear that the strategy had been unable to wrest power from the Maduro regime, the United States proposed the creation of a Council of State (to replace the interim government) of which neither Maduro nor Guaidó would form part, and whose secretary general would serve as interim president until new elections were held. See Office of the Spokesperson 2020.

41. Pape (1997) argues that once one controls for these other factors, the success ratio falls to as low as 5%. Other scholars are less pessimistic but still derive success ratios well under 50%. See Bapat and Morgan 2009; Bapat et al. 2013; Morgan, Bapat, and Kobayashi 2014; Biersteker and Hudáková 2015; Biersteker and Van Bergeijk 2015; Weber and Schneider 2019; Felbermayr et al. 2020.

42. Months before the publication of this book, the mainstream Venezuelan opposition coalition participated in a presidential election, reversing the

strategy of boycotts that characterized its strategy during my period of study. This occurred concurrently with a change in sanctions policy that saw a significant easing of oil sanctions. I discuss these recent developments in chapter 12.

43. In fact, the use of sanctions to cope with highly salient issues such as regime change might not only fail but also become counterproductive by further deteriorating political freedoms in the target. See Wood 2008; Peksen 2009; Peksen and Drury 2010; Adam and Tsarsitalidou 2019.

44. The only important case in which sanctions have been lifted from a former regime collaborator is that of Christopher Figuera, former director general of the Bolivarian Intelligence Service (SEBIN). Figuera assisted Guaidó during an April 2019 attempted coup against the Maduro government and was forced to leave the country after the affair turned sour. Following his escape, sanctions were removed on May 7, 2019 (US Department of the Treasury 2019).

45. For a more detailed elaboration of similar ideas, see Lektzian and Souva 2007. Kaempfer and Lowenberg (2007) provide a game-theoretic model where both the target group and its domestic opposition are utility-maximizing agents with utility functions characterized by diminishing returns. Both perceive the sanctions as costs; thus sanctions are only effective when the opposition's willingness to pay is higher than the target group's. But there are many perverse equilibria in which sanctions end up hurting the opposition much more than the targeted government.

46. Personal sanctions are typically specified as punishments conditional on an individual's actions to support the regime. In fact, the United States usually goes out of its way to signal that sanctions are dependent on conduct and can be lifted. Note, for example, this statement on the Treasury Department's sanctions page on filing petitions for removal from OFAC lists: "The power and integrity of the Office of Foreign Assets Control (OFAC) sanctions derive not only from its ability to designate and add persons to the Specially Designated Nationals and Blocked Persons List (SDN List) but also from its willingness to remove persons from the SDN List consistent with the law. *The ultimate goal of sanctions is not to punish but to bring about a positive change in behavior*. Each year, OFAC removes hundreds of individuals and entities from the SDN List" (OFAC 2024; emphasis added).

CHAPTER TEN

1. The most important predecessor were the 2002–3 talks between the government and the opposition mediated by OAS secretary general César

Gaviria, which had concluded in a formal agreement that paved the way for the 2004 recall referendum (Rodriguez Olivari 2014). Maduro had also called for talks in April 2014, after La Salida protests, with the cooperation of UNASUR (BBC Mundo 2014).

2. UNASUR is a regional organization created in 2008 formed by the governments of the twelve independent nations of South America. The creation of the body was strongly promoted by Chávez, who saw it as a counterweight to the influence of Washington in the Organization of American States.

3. The new CNE appointments would have replaced temporary appointees named by the Supreme Court in December 2016. Constitutionally, electoral board members are supposed to be politically unaligned; in practice, they invariably side with one of the parties. Of the remaining board members, two were perceived as pro-government and one as pro-opposition. Assuming the consensus choice of the new members would have delivered one representative for each side, the agreement would have resulted in a 3–2 pro-government majority, as opposed to the prior 4–1 pro-government majority.

4. See chap. 8, note 14.

5. These included COPEI's 1988 presidential candidate, Eduardo Fernández; AD's 1993 presidential candidate, Claudio Fermin; and the AN's 2016 First Vice President Enrique Márquez. Other leaders, such as former MUD secretary general Jesús Torrealba (2014–17), did not openly campaign for Falcón but did explicitly support voting in the election.

6. As a share of voters actually residing in the country, Maduro's vote share is somewhat more stable, given the significant population exodus that took place over this period. Maduro's votes amounted to 32% of the voting-age population residing in Venezuela in 2018, as opposed to 39% in 2013 (and 42% for Chávez on 2012). Venezuelans abroad can vote in presidential elections, although not in regional or legislative elections; however, the share of voters registered to vote abroad is small (0.5% of the electoral registry in 2018).

7. One can make the argument that the CNE's conduct had become more partisan in 2016–17 than in previous years, particularly in the 2005–12 period. This argument relies on the observation that the CNE had never previously outright canceled a recall referendum petition, as it did in 2016, nor did it appear to have inflated turnout numbers, as in the 2017 Constitutional Convention election. Of course, it is hard to compare the conduct of the pro-government majority in the CNE during a period in which the government was electorally strong and heavy-handed tactics were not needed (2005–12) with one in which the government was much weaker electorally

(2016–17). The CNE's actions in the latter period appear comparable with those of 2001–4, when electoral authorities imposed several roadblocks to the collection of signatures for the recall referendum, serving to delay the event until the economy had recovered enough for the government to appear likely to win (Hsieh et al. 2011). Furthermore, the Dominican Republic draft agreements offered the possibility of bringing the CNE closer to balance, as two pro-government members in the five-member board would be replaced by two new members chosen by consensus, while the pro-opposition member would remain on it. This would have given the opposition effective veto power over the appointment of the CNE majority, making the resulting board the most balanced one since at least 2003.

8. Governors and mayors serve four-year terms and the last election had been held in December 2012, so these elections should have been held in December 2016. The CNE explained its decision to delay regional elections on the improbable excuse that it was busy with the recall referendum process.

9. Note that this estimate derives from a study of the 2017 mayoral elections, which occurred three months later. It is reasonable to expect that the incidence in the October elections must not have been very different from that of the December contest. If anything, since the programs were both relatively new, the practice may have been even less widespread in October than in December (Rodríguez and Navarro 2018).

10. Libertador district, home to the country's capital, does not have a governor (much like the District of Columbia) and thus did not vote in the 2017 gubernatorial elections.

11. We have no comprehensive data on the age structure of emigration. According to the National Institute of Statistics, 66.2% of Venezuelans in 2020 were nineteen or older.

12. Of the 4 million Venezuelans living abroad, only 107,000 are registered to vote abroad (Bello 2018).

13. Hausmann and Rigobón (2004) claim that the selection of the 1% of audited tally sheets for the 2004 recall referendum was neither random nor representative. Weisbrot, Rosnick, and Tucker (2004) claim that the results of Hausmann and Rigobón most likely stem from model misspecification. After the 2004 referendum, electoral authorities changed the size and modality of the audit, to ensure that it would cover more than 50% of voting booths and would be randomly selected at the voting center, thus putting to rest concerns about nonrandomness of the audit sample in contested elections in which opposition witnesses can ensure that regulations mandating a random choice of voting machines for the audit are complied with.

14. For more details on the verification mechanisms used to identify possible inconsistencies in the different phases of the election, which include voting receipts with watermarks, security ink, unique non-sequential identifier, fixed and removable memory of the voting machines, minutes, and votes sent to the totalization center and tally and totalization minutes, see González, del Nogal, and Müller 2012. According to the Electoral Observation Mission of the EU, Venezuela's audit of paper receipts has characteristics that meet the most advanced international electronic voting standards (Misión de Observación Electoral Unión Europea 2006, 32).

15. The December 3, 2023, Essequibo referendum would appear to be another case. Similarly to the 2017 Constitutional Convention elections, no disaggregate results by voting booth have been published for the event, which was intended to lend support to the Venezuelan state's territorial claim over the Essequibo region currently under control of Guyana. The turnout numbers, at 51% of registered voters, appeared implausible given that large sectors of the opposition opposed the vote. As in the 2017 vote, the fact that no opposition forces fielded witnesses made infeasible the verification of results that occurs in contested elections.

16. The Bolívar case opens up another set of concerns, which is about how we can know that a candidate's claim of alteration of tally sheets is truthful. The answer is that we cannot, because it is not difficult to create a document that looks like an authentic tally sheet. An impartial forensic investigation may be able to ascertain whether the document in question is false. In the case of Bolívar, this investigation appears not to have been conducted. The lack of institutions capable of carrying out such investigations and credible enough for the public to believe in their findings is doubtless one of Venezuela's most important institutional deficiencies, and one that makes it very difficult to restore full credibility to the electoral system in the eyes of a large number of voters.

17. Although there is no published data on the frequency of these failures, my conversations with electoral experts suggest that it is very small. One expert claimed that in the 2021 elections there had been transmission failures in 165 voting booths, or 0.6% of the 30,106 voting booths used in the election. The delay in the announcement of results in the 2021 disputed election for governor of Barinas, which the Supreme Court ultimately ordered a repeat of, was also due to three tally sheets that were tallied manually.

18. Stokes (2005) finds empirical evidence that Argentinian parties can selectively condition access to benefits on individuals' actual voting behavior. Serra (2016) shows evidence that all major parties attempted to condition access to government social programs in Mexico on voter support.

19. As Toro (2012, 2015) argues, lack of opposition witnesses is also a necessary condition for identity fraud to take place in a voting center.

20. Turnout in 2015 was 74% in Venezuela, while in 2019 it was 80% in Argentina.

21. Bimodality would be a consequence of the fact that large-scale ballot box stuffing is only feasible in those voting centers in which the opposition cannot field witnesses. Therefore, we would expect the distribution of votes in centers vulnerable to fraud to be different from that in those that are not vulnerable. Other work on election forensics applied to Venezuela include Levin et al. (2009), who find no evidence that the government manipulated vote figures to win the 2009 recall referendum, and Jiménez and Hidalgo (2014), who argue that voting tallies show increasing anomalies after 2004. However, the statistical patterns identified by Jiménez and Hidalgo frequently arise in fair elections and are not in and of themselves sufficient evidence of fraud (Reuters 2020b; Groharing and McCune 2022).

22. The constitutionality of this provision has been challenged, as the Constitution states that political rights may only be restricted as a result of a definitive conviction; the Supreme Court has upheld the law on the argument that limiting the ability to hold elected office is not a violation of political rights.

23. There was certainly no shortage of conspiracies at the time and even an apparent assassination attempt in a drone attack on August 2018, though the level of international involvement prior to 2019 is unclear (Daniels and Zúñiga 2017).

24. Former FBI director Andrew McCabe claimed that Trump said during a July 2017 briefing that Venezuela was "the country we should be going to war with," since "they have all that oil and they're right on our back door" (McCabe 2019, 136). This comment would have been made roughly one month before Trump first mentioned publicly the possibility of a "military option" for Venezuela on August 12 (*New York Times* 2017). The emphasis on the relevance of oil wealth as a determinant of US military intervention would be consistent with Trump's stated policy positions on past Middle East conflicts, where he criticized previous administrations for not asserting US claims on oil deposits in Iraq and Libya (*Wall Street Journal* 2011).

25. On Trump's unilateralist foreign policy stances, see Pascal 2019. On the rift with Europe on key policy issues, see Bilal and Imran 2019.

26. This is not to say that all governments in the Lima Group were center-right. Chile's Socialist government and Colombia's centrist government (which had recently signed a peace agreement with its leftist guerrilla

movement) were also part of the group. Yet there were notable absences among left-of-center governments such as those of Ecuador and Uruguay.

27. This speculation has been fed by the observation that non-VP legislators at the event, including the AN's first and second vice presidents, did not raise their hands when Guaidó called on supporters to do so, nor did they applaud; others left the stage. To the best of my knowledge, however, no legislator has confirmed this dissent in on-the-record comments. See video of event at VPITV (2018).

28. Guaidó's announcement and the White House's tweet were respectively at 12:43 p.m. and 1:08 p.m. Washington time (White House 45 Archived 2019).

29. The figure comes from a statement by National Security Advisor John Bolton on January 2 (ILKHA 2019). Rodríguez (2019a) estimates that between CITGO Holding cash and accounts of PDVSA-controlled joint venture companies there were $8.4 billion in liquid financial assets. On top of this, the Guaidó administration later identified and transferred or used an additional $414 million, bringing the total figure to $8.8 billion (PDVSA 2019; Asamblea de Venezuela Nacional 2020).

30. In the case of the United States and the United Kingdom, there is established jurisprudence according to which courts defer to the executive branch in the matter of recognition of governments (Houghton 1929). In the United Kingdom, the matter is made more complex because of the decision of the British government to interact with the Maduro regime, which led the High Court to raise the issue of whether there is implicit de facto recognition of Maduro (Royal Courts of Justice 2020a, 2020b).

31. A workaround was designed for the oil sector, where transactions could be carried out with PDVSA-controlled JV firms because Guaidó decided not to appoint their boards of directors. As long as the old directors remained in place, they continued to be the legal representatives of these entities for the purposes of US and European law. Guaidó initially moved to make the appointments, with the National Assembly approving the designation of an ad hoc board of directors for the PDVSA subsidiary overseeing joint ventures (Corporación Venezolana de Petróleo, CVP) in October 2019. However, that board never took action with respect to the individual company boards and in fact did not even present an annual report before the legislature, as other Guaidó-appointed ad hoc boards did. It appears probable that the failure to follow through on company appointments was due to lobbying by oil multinationals that would have been seriously impacted by such appointments. See *Diario Las Américas* 2019 for the initial CVP appointment. To the best of my knowledge, this workaround has not been implemented in any other relevant area of state activities.

32. The United States began to ease sanctions in November 2022, when it issued a license allowing Chevron to sell Venezuelan oil in the United States (OFAC 2022). It issued a similar authorization for all oil companies in October 2023 (OFAC 2023a). Because the United States continues to recognize the opposition-controlled National Assembly elected in 2015 as the legitimate representative of the Venezuelan state, oil companies wishing to make use of these authorizations have to purchase the oil from Venezuela (or obtain it in exchange for debt repayment or services provision) and resell it directly in the United States (OFAC 2023b).

33. During the 2016 talks, Venezuela's opposition had proposed including the issue of humanitarian aid in the agenda of negotiations. The Maduro government's initial reaction was to deny that Venezuela was suffering through a humanitarian crisis and to assert that the government was capable of handling the situation on its own. In an open letter to the American people, Maduro wrote, "Due to our immense oil and mineral resources, and other great wealths, they have promoted an international coalition headed by the imperialist government of the United States to commit the severe insanity of militarily attacking Venezuela under the false excuse of a non-existent humanitarian crisis" (Maduro 2019).

34. For example, in June 2021, the Swiss bank UBS notified Venezuela that it had blocked and placed under investigation four transfers made by the country to access the COVID-19 Vaccines Global Access (COVAX) system for the distribution of vaccines to developing countries. The payments would later be processed by the bank. Nevertheless, Venezuela had to carry out a set of complex financial interactions to make these transfers in Swiss francs due to its lack of access to the US dollar or Euro accounts used by COVAX. See Arreaza 2021; Rodríguez 2022c.

35. As we have only capital stock—and therefore productivity—estimates for the whole economy, I assume that this ratio applies equally to oil and non-oil GDP. This assumption appears reasonable as the decline in per capita oil production (71.2%) is very similar to the decline in per capita total GDP (71.5%) in this period.

36. I use the average price and imports of 2019–21 for these calculations.

CHAPTER ELEVEN

1. Calculations based on Groningen Growth and Development Centre 2022.

2. Germany's 1919 NNP estimated by combining the estimates of Burhop and Wolff (2005) and Bolt and van Zanden (2020).

3. GDP data from University of Groningen 2021; inflation from World Bank 2022.

4. Calculations based on IMF 2023a.

5. Reagan campaigned on a promise to ease grain sanctions on the Soviet Union imposed by the Carter administration that he argued were hurting American farmers (Garthoff 1994, 45–46; Batmanghelidj and Rodríguez 2022). Milton Friedman, who served as Reagan's economic adviser, was strongly critical of sanctions (Friedman 1980). Reagan also vetoed sanctions against South Africa, a veto that was ultimately overridden (Hoffman 1986).

6. Eventually, some of the guarantees given to the outgoing regime were lifted, allowing for the prosecution of regime figures more than twenty years after the transition. See Kulish 2012; Wilczek 2020.

7. Data correspond to 2022. See FRED St. Louis 2023. Total outstanding public debt is higher, at 121%, given the large holdings of government debt by the Social Security Administration and other government agencies.

CHAPTER TWELVE

1. Throughout this chapter, I use the term "mainstream opposition coalition" to identify the largest opposition coalition as measured by share of votes obtained by the coalition or its member parties in the most recent prior non-boycotted election. This includes the Democratic Coordinator between 2002 and 2004, the Mesa de Unidad Democrática from 2008 to 2018, the Frente Amplio Venezuela Libre in 2018, the parties backing the interim government of Juan Guaidó from 2019 to 2020, and the Unitary Platform/Democratic Unity Roundtable from 2021 on.

2. In contrast to official, or Track I, diplomacy, which involves formal negotiations involving official state and non-state actors, Track II diplomacy involves unofficial, informal interaction between members of adversary groups or nations that aims to develop approaches that might help resolve their conflict. See Ziegler 1984; Diamond and McDonald 1996.

3. In the language of game theory, all Nash equilibria in two-player zero-sum games are equivalent in having the same payoffs for both players. See Burger 1963, 47–48.

4. The PU is an opposition alliance created in 2021 to replace the MUD at a time when the latter was barred from participating in elections and has served as the formal vehicle for participation in the Mexico/Barbados process.

5. In January 2023, Maduro accused the US government of blocking the disbursement of funds to comply with the agreement (Crónica Uno 2023). In

May 2023, Reuters reported that the US government had assured the United Nations that it would shield the fund from creditors (Spetalnick, Sequera, and Armas 2023).

6. Organic laws are those that develop fundamental political or human rights or the organization of branches of government. Many constitutions require supermajorities to modify organic laws, which are common in legal systems derived from the French and Spanish constitutional traditions (Szentgáli-Tóth 2020). In 2004, Venezuela's Supreme Court ruled that the supermajority requirement for organic laws in article 203 of the Constitution only applies to the granting of organic status to laws not explicitly considered as such in the Constitution (TSJ 2003).

7. See articles 341 and 344 of the 1999 Constitution.

8. According to their current terms of appointment, the majority of now-serving Supreme Court justices would remain in office until at least 2034. The current prosecutor general's constitutional term expires in August 2024; were a new one appointed, that person would serve in office until 2031 (*Gaceta Oficial* 2017; Ministerio del Poder Popular para la Comunicación y Información 2017).

9. The appointment of electoral authorities would be an example of a partial agreement, as it has no meaningful direct value to members of society except for its contribution to a process that does have value (the capacity to exercise the political freedom to elect government officials). An agreement to increase spending in health and food assistance, in contrast, is a sectoral agreement in that it solves a specific problem and has value for Venezuelans even if other issues are not addressed.

10. On the problems of the Iraq program, see Volcker, Goldstone, and Pieth 2005; Duelfer 2004.

11. Of the votes obtained by non-MUD parties in 2021, 34.8% went to candidates of parties in which the Supreme Court had previously ruled in favor of centrists opposed to the hard-line positions of the MUD leaders in disputes over control of the party. This raises the possibility that some voters may have been "fooled" into voting for these parties believing that they represented the more hard-line views of the MUD. It is hard to test this hypothesis without direct evidence on voter beliefs. However, the results were consistent with pre-election surveys indicating that a high share of the vote was expected to go to non-MUD opposition parties. For example, in a survey carried out by Datanálisis one month ahead of the election (Datanálisis 2021), 25.4% of voters indicated that they would support candidates who were either independent or from the Democratic Alliance, as opposed to 21.0% who claimed that they would support candidates from the MUD coalition.

12. These estimates use the partial vote tallies published by Comando con Venezuela (2024), which, as I explained in chapter 10, I consider to be a credible reflection of actual votes cast.

13. Machado's approval numbers rose significantly in 2024, making her distinctly more popular than any other politician in the country. Machado was barred from running for elected office after a controversial decision by the Comptroller General's Office in July 2023 (TSJ 2023c). González also reached relatively high approval numbers ahead of the election. A similar phenomenon occurred with National Assembly president Juan Guaidó after the opposition claimed that he was the legitimate interim president in early 2019.

14. For example, Guaidó reacted to the announcement of the imposition of sanctions on Rosneft in February 2020 by stating that "this news is a victory!" (Guaidó 2020a). VP legislator Manuela Bolivar dismissed oil-for-food proposals in July 2019, claiming that "this scheme does not guarantee that people receive food because you have a structure of incentives to steal" (Cohen 2019). In December 2019, the opposition-controlled National Assembly decided to reject an initiative of the United Nations and CAF, a regional multilateral bank, to repair the country's electricity infrastructure (Sequera and Ellsworth 2020).

15. The EU and the United States have imposed personal sanctions on key dissidents from the opposition that did not back Guaidó's bid to be reelected president of the National Assembly in 2020, as well as on those who contested the mainstream opposition's control of political parties in Venezuelan courts (OFAC 2023c). The EU also sanctioned the two centrist opposition representatives to the CNE in 2021 (European Union Council 2021).

16. See Esberg and Siegel 2023 for evidence that Venezuelan exile groups maintain more hard-line positions. Kustra (2022) argues that diasporas' electoral importance in swing states is an important driver of US sanctions policy.

17. On the use of interim government funds to subsidize activists of the MUD political parties, see Morales 2021.

18. For example, of the eighteen opposition legislators who backed dissident Luis Parra in his bid to become National Assembly president in 2020, none was from the capital region. In stark contrast, both Guaidó and his two highest-ranking parliamentary appointees at the time (Foreign Minister Julio Borges and UN Representative Miguel Pizarro) were legislators from Greater Caracas districts. The most prominent leaders of three of the four largest parties in Guaidó's coalition—Henry Ramos Allup of AD, Henrique Capriles of PJ, and Leopoldo López of VP—had also held elected positions in Greater Caracas (Ramos as Capital District legislator, Capriles and López as mayors

of Caracas municipalities). The fourth leader, Manuel Rosales, was a former mayor of Maracaibo, the country's second largest city. See F. Rodríguez 2020.

19. Twenty-eight percent of opposition supporters are in favor of oil sanctions, as opposed to 13% neutral and 3% pro-government respondents. Thirty percent of opposition supporters are against resuming negotiations, as opposed to 25% neutral and 19% pro-government voters (Datanálisis 2023a, 2023b, 2023c).

20. The MUD has claimed that the CNE did not allow it to register the candidacy of Corina Yoris, a philosophy professor whom Machado initially anointed as her replacement candidate (*Tal Cual* 2024; Unidad Venezuela 2024). These allegations, which I view as credible, have been denied by the CNE and government officials (CNE 2024; Martínez 2024).

21. This is also consistent with the predictions of the classic Downs (1957) model of electoral competition. In Rodríguez (2024b), I found evidence that the government used food program benefits to target centrist voters ahead of a key regional repeat election in 2022.

22. Simón Bolívar's letter to Pedro Gual, dated February 10, 1815. Published in O'Leary 1888, 35.

23. See Riccardi 2023 for data on Venezuelan arrivals in Denver.

REFERENCES

Abadie, Alberto, Alexis Diamond, and Jens Hainmueller. 2010. "Synthetic Control Methods for Comparative Case Studies: Estimating the Effect of California's Tobacco Control Program." *Journal of the American Statistical Association* 105(490): 493–505.

Abadie, Alberto, and Javier Gardeazabal. 2003. "The Economic Costs of Conflict: A Case Study of the Basque Country." *American Economic Review* 93(1): 113–32.

Abdul, Roberto, Egleé González, Luis Lander, Eugenio Martínez, and Benigno Alarcón. 2020. "Misión de Estudio IDEA-UCAB sobre las condiciones del proceso electoral parlamentario 2020 en Venezuela." Centro de Estudios Políticos y de Gobierno–UCAB, Caracas. https://politikaucab.files.wordpress.com/2020/11/informe-idea-version-final-11102020-5-2.pdf?&utm_source=newsletter&utm_medium=email&utm_campaign=lea_el_ultimo_informe_sobre_condiciones_electorales_de_la_mision_de_estudio_idea_ucab&utm_term=2021-08-26.

Abramovitz, Moses. 1956. "Resource and Output Trends in the United States since 1870." *American Economic Review* 46: 5–23. https://www.nber.org/system/files/chapters/c5650/c5650.pdf.

Abuelafia, Enmanuel, and José Saboín. 2020. "A Look to the Future of Venezuela." IBD Discussion Paper, No. IBDDP-798. http://dx.doi.org/10.18235/0002621.

Acceso a la Justicia. 2017. "Sin pueblo no hay Constituyente." https://accesoalajusticia.org/el-fraude-de-la-constituyente/.

Acemoglu, Daron. 2021. "US Institutions after Trump." https://www.project-syndicate.org/commentary/repairing-us-institutions-after-trump-by-daron-acemoglu-2021-01.

Acemoglu, Daron, Simon Johnson, and James Robinson. 2001. "The Colonial Origins of Comparative Development: An Empirical Investigation." *American Economic Review* 91(5): 1369–1401.

Acemoglu, Daron, Suresh Naidu, Pascual Restrepo, and James Robinson. 2019. "Democracy Does Cause Growth." *Journal of Political Economy* 127(1): 47–100.

Acemoglu, Daron, and James Robinson. 2005. *Economic Origins of Dictatorship and Democracy*. Cambridge: Cambridge University Press.

———. 2012. *Why Nations Fail: The Origins of Power, Prosperity and Poverty*. New York: Currency.

———. 2019. *The Narrow Corridor: States, Societies, and the Fate of Liberty*. London: Penguin.

Adam, Antonis, and Sofia Tsarsitalidou. 2019. "Do Sanctions Lead to a Decline in Civil Liberties?" *Public Choice* 180(34): 191–215.

Adriani, Alberto. 1946. *Labor venezolanista: Venezuela, la crisis y los cambios*. Caracas: Tipografía Garrido.

Afesorgbor, Sylvanus, and Renuka Mahadevan. 2016. "The Impact of Economic Sanctions on Income Inequality of Target States." *World Development* 83(C): 1–11.

Agence France-Presse (AFP). 2019. "Tribunal Constitucional de Bolivia avala a Jeanine Áñez como presidenta interina." *El Universo*, November 12. https://www.eluniverso.com/noticias/2019/11/12/nota/7601600/tribunal-constitucional-bolivia-avala-jeanine-anez-como-presidenta/.

Agencia Nacional de Hidrocarburos (ANH). 2023. "Datos y estadísticas." https://www.anh.gov.co/es/operaciones-y-regal%C3%ADas/datos-y-estadisticas/.

———. 2021. "Secretaría general de OEA advierte sobre 'abuso de mecanismos judiciales' en Bolivia." Gestión. https://gestion.pe/mundo/internacional/secretaria-general-de-oea-advierte-sobre-abuso-de-mecanismos-judiciales-en-bolivia-noticia/.

Ahn, Daniel, and Rodney Ludema. 2020. "The Sword and the Shield: The Economics of Targeted Sanctions." *European Economic Review* 130: 103587.

Ahn, Jaebin, and Moon Choi. 2020. "From Firm-Level Imports to Aggregate Productivity: Evidence from Korean Manufacturing Firms Data." *Japan and the World Economy* 56. https://doi.org/10.1016/j.japwor.2020.101038.

Alarcón, Ignacio. 2016. "El consejo apoya el papel de mediación de Zapatero en Venezuela." http://www.aquieuropa.com/noticia/61427-el-consejo-apoya-el-papel-de-mediacion-de-zapatero-en-venezuela.

Alesina, Alberto, and Allan Drazen. 1991. "Why Are Stabilizations Delayed?" *American Economic Review* 81(5): 1170–88.

Alesina, Alberto, Gerald D. Cohen, and Nouriel Roubini. 1993. "Electoral Business Cycle in Industrial Democracies." *European Journal of Political Economy* 9(1): 1–23.

Alesina, Alberto, and Guido Tabellini. 1990. "A Positive Theory of Fiscal Deficits and Government Debt." *Review of Economic Studies* 57(3): 403–14.

Alesina, Alberto, James Mirrlees, and Manfred J. M. Neumann. 1989. "Politics and Business Cycles in Industrial Democracies." *Economic Policy* 4(8): 55–98.

Al Jazeera. 2008a. "African Body Scorns Mugabe Win." https://www.aljazeera.covenezue2008/6/30/african-body-scorns-mugabe-win.

———. 2008b. "Mugabe Avoids Criticism at AU talks." https://www.aljazeera.cvenezus/2008/7/1/mugabe-avoids-criticism-at-au-talks.

Alvarado, Angel (@AngelAlvaradoR). 2017. "Carta de @JulioBorges presidente de la @AsambleaVE a CEO de @GoldmanSachs por compra de bonos #PDVSA22, apoyando la DICTADURA y la REPRESIÓN." Twitter, May 29, 11:02 a.m. https://twitter.com/AngelAlvaradoR/status/869207429128605699.

Álvarez, Jorge A., Marco Arena, Alain Brousseau, Hamid Faruqee, Emilio William Fernández Corrugedo, Jaime Guajardo, Gerardo Peraza, and Juan Yepez. 2022. "Regional Spillovers from the Venezuelan Crisis: Migration Flows and Their Impact on Latin America and the Caribbean." International Monetary Fund. Working Paper DP/2022/019.

Amanat, Abbas. 2017. *Iran: A Modern History*. New Haven, CT: Yale University Press.

Amaya, Victor. 2019. "Flexibilidad en controles generó una 'burbuja' pero la economía sigue mal." https://talcualdigital.com/flexibilidad-en-controles-genero-una-burbuja-pero-la-economia-sigue-mal/?web=1&wdLOR=c8278F297-E9B8-4F92-A892-0A38CD5DFBF3.

América Noticias. 2018. "Oposición venezolana regresa al diálogo con el gobierno." https://www.americateve.com/mundo/oposicion-venezolana-regresa-al-dialogo-el-gobierno-n979525.

Americas Quarterly. 2023. "The White House's Juan Gonzalez on the Venezuela-U.S. Deal." AQ Podcast, October 30. 30:18. https://www.americasquarterly.org/article/aq-podcast-the-white-houses-juan-gonzalez-on-the-venezuela-u-s-deal/.

Amiti, Mary, and Jozef Konings. 2007. "Trade Liberalization, Intermediate Inputs, and Productivity: Evidence from Indonesia." *American Economic Review* 975: 1611–38. https://doi.org/10.1257/aer.97.5.1611.

Aporrea. 2018. "JV Hoy 2 110218 entrevista Jorge Rodríguez." YouTube video, 26:19. February 19. https://youtube/CfJ6ha9HLhc?si=czLLf-xefnGzdv6E.

Arauz, Andrés, Mark Weisbrot, Andrew Bunker, and Jake Johnston. 2019. "Bolivia's Economic Transformation: Macroeconomic Policies, Institutional

Changes, and Results." Center for Economic and Policy Research. https://cepr.net/images475enezues/reports/bolivia-macro-2019-10.pdf.

Arcelus, Francisco, and Allan H. Meltzer. 1975. "The Effect of Aggregate Economic Variables on Congressional Elections." *American Political Science Review* 69(4): 1232–39.

Argus Media. 2017. "Refiners Ask US Not to Block Venezuelan Crude." https://www.argusmedia.com/ru/news/1493622-refiners-ask-us-not-to-block-venezuelan-crude?amp=1.

———. 2019. "Scant Imports Leave Venezuela Bereft of Motor Fuel." https://www.argusmedia.com/en/news/2033597-scant-imports-leave-venezuela-bereft-of-motor-fuel?backToResults=true%3Futm_source%3Dtwitter&utm_medium=social&utm_content=news-free&utm_term=pro&utm_campaign=free-content.

———. 2020a. "US Turns Screws on Venezuela as Florida Beckons." October 29. https://www.argusmedia.com/en/news/2155041-us-turns-screws-on-venezuela-as-florida-beckons.

———. 2020b. "Venezuela Gets Iranian Help to Fix Its Refineries." https://www.argusmedia.com/en/news/2100198-venezuela-gets-iranian-help-to-fix-its-refineries.

Armas, Mayela, and Anatoly Kurmanaev. 2016. "Venezuela's Nicolás Maduro Looks to a Marxist Spaniard for an Economic Miracle." https://www.wsj.com/articles/venezuelas-nicolas-maduro-looks-to-a-marxist-spaniard-for-an-economic-miracle-1470678805.

Armas, Mayela, and Corina Pons. 2019. "Banco Central venezolano obliga a bancos a vender millones de euros en efectivo." https://www.reuvenezuela article/venezuela-divisas-idLTAKCN1S91EE.

Armas, Mayela, and Kejal Vyas. 2017. "Venezuela Sells $5 Billion in New Bonds." https://www.venezuelarticles/venezuela-sells-5-billion-in-new-bonds-1483403525.

Arreaza, Jorge (@jaarreaza). 2021. "Como lo acaba de denunciar la Vicepresidenta @delcyrodriguezv, #Venezuela ha pagado LA TOTALIDAD de sus compromisos con el mecanismo #COVAX para adquirir las vacunas. Sin embargo, el Banco ha 'bloqueado' arbitrariamente los últimos pagos y están bajo 'investigación.' ¡Un crimen!" Twitter, June 10. https://twitter.com/jaarreaza/status/1403036779238862853?s=20.

Asamblea Nacional de Venezuela. 2016a. "Acuerdo sobre el decreto de creación de la zona de desarrollo estratégico nacional Arco Minero del Orinoco." https://www.asambleanacionalvenezuela.org/actos/detalle/acuerdo-sobre-el-decreto-de-creacionde-la-zona-de-desarrollo-estrategiconacionalarco-minero-del-orinoco-178.

———. 2016b. "Acuerdo sobre la situación financiera actual de Petróleos de Venezuela S.A." https://www.asambleanacionalvenezuela.org/actos/detalle/acuerdo-sobre-la-situacion-financiera-actual-de-petroleos-de-venezuela-sa-234.

———. 2019a. "Plan País el día después." https://angelalvaradorangel.com/wp-content/uploads/ACUERDOS-PLAN-PAI%CC%81S-EL-DI%CC%81A-DESPUE%CC%81S-DIC2019.pdf.

——— (@AsambleaVE). 2019b. "Pronunciamiento de la junta directiva de la #AsambleaVe al país y toda la Comunidad Internacional." Twitter, January 10, 2:49 p.m. https://twitter.com/AsambleaVE/status/1083435678715785216.

——— . 2019c. "Asamblea Nacional nombra junta directiva de Citgo." https://www.asambleanacionalvenezuela.org/noticias/asamblea-nacional-nombra-junta-directiva-de-citgo

——— (@AsambleaVE). 2020. "#ResumenAN | Condenamos las sistemáticas violaciones de DDHH por parte del régimen usurpador contra la disidencia política, la prensa y la sociedad en el marco de la pandemia del COVID-19." Twitter, April 15, 4:01 p.m. https://twitter.com/AsambleaVE/status/1250514482952011778.

———. 2023a. "Gaceta Legislativa." https://www.asambleanacionalvenezuela.org/gacetas.

———. 2023b. "Ley Orgánica de la Contraloría General de la República y del Sistema Nacional de Control Fiscal." https://www.oas.org/juridico/spanish/mesicic2_ven_anexo_34_sp.pdf.

Atlantic Council. 2021. "New Atlantic Council Poll: Insights on Venezuelan and Cuban American Sentiments regarding US Policy toward Venezuela." Adrienne Arsht Latin America Center. March 4. https://www.atlanticcouncil.org/in-depth-research-reports/report/insights-on-venezuelan-and-cuban-american-sentiments-regarding-us-policy-toward-venezuela/.

———. 2022. "Exploring Humanitarian Frameworks for Venezuela." https://www.atlanticcouncil.org/wp-content/uploads/2022/03/Exploring_humanitarian_frameworks_for_Venezuela.pdf.

Austen-Smith, David. 1987. "Interest Groups, Campaign Contributions, and Probabilistic Voting." *Public Choice* 54(2): 123–39.

Austen-Smith, David, Wioletta Dziuda, Bård Harstad, and Antoine Loeper. 2019. "Gridlock and Inefficient Policy Instruments." *Theoretical Economics* 14: 1483–1534.

Autor, David. 2003. "Outsourcing at Will: The Contribution of Unjust Dismissal Doctrine to the Growth of Employment Outsourcing." *Journal of Labor Economics* 21(1): 1–42.

Auty, Richard. 1990. *Resource-Based Industrialization: Sowing the Oil in Eight Developing Countries*. Oxford: Oxford University Press.

———. 2001. *Resource Abundance and Economic Development*. WIDER Studies in Development Economics. Oxford: Oxford University Press.

Aveledo, Ramón Guillermo. 2019. *El Senado experiencia comparada y utilidad para la democracia en Venezuela*. Caracas: Universidad Católica Andrés Bello.

Avis, Eric, Claudio Ferraz, Frederico Finan, and Carlos Varjão. 2017. "Money and Politics: The Effects of Campaign Spending Limits on Political Competition and Incumbency Advantage." *American Economic Journal: Applied Economics* 14(4): 167–99.

Ayres, Ian, and Steven Levitt. 1998. "Measuring Positive Externalities from Unobservable Victim Precaution: An Empirical Analysis of Lojack." *Quarterly Journal of Economics* 113(1): 43–77.

Azariadis, Costas, and John Stachurski. 2004. "A Forward Projection of the Cross-Country Income Distribution." KIER Working Papers No. 570. https://www.academia.edu/63487868/A_forward_projection_of_the_cross_country_income_distribution?uc-sb-sw=59938293.

Baffes, John, Ibrahim Elbadawi, and Stephen O'Connell. 1999. "Single-Equation Estimation of the Equilibrium Real Exchange Rate." In *Exchange Rate Misalignment: Concept and Measurement for Developing Countries*, ed. L. E. Hinkle and P. J. Montiel, 405–64. Oxford: Oxford University Press.

Bahar, Dany, Sebastian Bustos, José Morales-Arilla, and Miguel Santos. 2019. "Impact of the 2017 Sanctions on Venezuela: Revisiting the Evidence." https://www.brookings.edu/research/revisiting-the-evidence-impact-of-the-2017-sanctions-on-venezuela/.

Bahar, Dany, Ted Piccone, and Harold Trinkunas. 2018. "Venezuela: A Path out of Misery." https://www.brookings.edu/wp-content/uploads/2018/10/FP_20181023_venezuela.pdf.

Bahar, Dany, and Sebastian Strauss. 2016. "The Future of Venezuela: Are Reforms Enough to Guarantee Solvency?" https://www.brookings.edu/blog/up-front/2016/11/02/the-future-of-venezuela-are-reforms-enough-to-guarantee-solvency/.

Baker Hughes. 2023. "International Rig Count: International Rig Counts for April 2023." https://rigcount.bakerhughes.com/intl-rig-count/.

Balakrishnan, Srinivasan, and Mitchell Koza. 1993. "Information Asymmetry, Adverse Election and Joint Ventures." *Journal of Economic Behavior and Organization* 20(1): 99–117.

Balcerowicz, Leszek. 1996. *Socialism, Capitalism, Transformation*. Oxford: Oxford University Press.

Baldwin, David, and Ethan Kapstein. 2020. *Economic Statecraft*. New ed. Princeton, NJ: Princeton University Press.

Bali, Turan G., and Thom Thurston. 2000. "Empirical Estimates of Inflation Tax Laffer Surfaces: A 30-Country Study." *Journal of Development Economics* 63(2): 529–46. doi:10.1016/S0304-3878(00)00106-1.

Banca y Negocios. 2021. "Grupo de Boston propone destinar US$50 millones mensuales de exportaciones petroleras para fines humanitarios." https://www.bancaynegocios.com/grupo-de-boston-propone-destinar-us50-millones-mensuales-de-exportaciones-petroleras-para-fines-humanitarios/.

Banco Central de Venezuela (BCV). 2012. *Informe Económico*. http://www.bcv.org.ve/publicaciones/informe-economico-2012.

———. 2022. "El PIB de la economía venezolana creció 17,73% en el período enero–septiembre 2022." https://bcv.org.ve/notas-de-prensa/el-pib-de-la-economia-venezolana-crecio-1773-en-el-periodo-enero-septiembre-de-2022.

———. 2023a. "Balanza de Pagos." https://bcv.org.ve/estadisticas/balanza-de-pagos.

———. 2023b. "Base Monetaria Anual." https://bcv.org.ve/estadisticas/base-monetaria.

———. 2023c. "Cuentas consolidadas de la nación: Ahorro neto." https://bcv.org.ve/estadisticas/cuentas-consolidadas-de-la-nacion.

———. 2023d. "Deuda externa, servicio causado por sectores público y privado e instrumentos–Serie 1997–2018. Banco Central de Venezuela." https://bcv.org.ve/estadisticas/deuda-externa.

———. 2023e. "Posición de inversión internacional: Activos y pasivos." https://bcv.org.ve/estadisticas/posicion-de-inversion-internacional.

———. 2023f. "Producto interno bruto y sus componentes: Precios corrientes y constantes." https://bcv.org.ve/estadisticas/producto-interno-bruto.

———. 2023g. "Tipo de Cambio de Referencia." https://www.bcv.org.ve/estadisticas/otras-monedas.

Bapat, Navin, Tobias Heinrich, Yoshiharu Kobayashi, and Clifton Morgan. 2013. "Determinants of Sanctions Effectiveness: Sensitivity Analysis Using New Data." *International Interactions* 39(1): 79–98.

Bapat, Navin, and Clifton Morgan. 2009. "Multilateral versus Unilateral Sanctions Reconsidered: A Test Using New Data." *International Studies Quarterly* 53(4): 1075–94.

Baptista, Asdrúbal. 2011. *Bases cuantitativas de la economía venezolana, 1830–2008*. Caracas: Fundación Artesano Group.

Baptista, Asdrúbal, and Bernard Mommer. 1999. *El petróleo en el pensamiento económico venezolano*. 2nd ed. Caracas: Ediciones IESA.

Barlett, Jason, and Megan Ophel. 2021. "Sanctions by the Numbers: Spotlight on Venezuela." https://www.cnas.org/publications/reports/sanctions-by-the-numbers-3.

Baron, David. 1994. "Electoral Competition with Informed and Uninformed Voters." *American Political Science Review* 88(1): 33–47.

Barro, Robert. 1996. "Democracy and Growth." *Journal of Economic Growth* 1(1): 1–27.

Barro, Robert, and Xavier Sala-i-Martin. 2004. *Economic Growth*. Cambridge, MA: MIT Press.

Bartkowski, Maciej. 2009. "Poland's Solidarity Movement 1980–1989." https://www.nonviolent-conflict.org/wp-content/uploads/2016/04/Poland%E2%80%99s-Solidarity-Movement-1980-1989.pdf.

Bates, Robert, Avner Greif, Margarte Levi, Jean-Laurtent Rosenthal, and Barry Weingast. 2000. "The Analytical Narrative Project." *American Political Science Review* 94(3): 696–702.

Batini, Nicoletta, and Edward Nelson. 2003. "The Lag from Monetary Policy Actions to Inflation: Friedman Revisited." *International Finance* 4(3): 381–400.

Batmanghelidj, Esfandyar, and Erica Moret. 2022. "The Hidden Toll of Sanctions: Why Washington Must Reckon with the Devastating Inflation Its Policies Cause." https://www.foreignaffairs.com/articles/world/2022-01-17/hidden-toll-sanctions.

Batmandhelidj, Esfandyar, and Francisco Rodríguez. 2020. "Sanctions Are Driving Iran and Venezuela into Each Other's Arms." https://foreignpolicy.com/2020/09/17/iran-teaching-venezuela-maduro-how-to-withstand-us-sanctions/.

———. 2022. "The Danger of Sanctions." https://www.noemamag.com/the-danger-of-sanctions/.

BBC Mundo. 2014. "Venezuela introduce nuevo control de cambio que devalúa parcialmente el bolívar." https://www.bbc.com/mundo/ultimas_noticias/2014/01/140122_ultnot_venezuela_modifican_sistema_cambio_l.

———. 2016a. "El Tribunal Supremo de Venezuela declara válido y vigente el decreto de emergencia económica." https://www.bbc.com/mundo/noticias/2016/02/160211_venezuela_decreto_emergencia_economica_dp_bd.

———. 2016b. "Venezuela: El CNE paraliza el referendo revocatorio a Nicolás Maduro." https://www.bbc.com/mundo/noticias-america-latina-37723172.

———. 2017. "Nicolás Maduro 'decreta' la reestructuración de la deuda externa de Venezuela aunque ordena pagar los US$1.121 millones en bonos de

PDVSA que se vencen esta semana." https://www.bbc.com/mundo/noticias-america-latina-41853548.

———. 2018. "La Asamblea Constituyente de Venezuela aprueba celebrar elecciones presidenciales antes de mayo y Maduro formaliza su candidatura." https://www.bbc.com/mundo/noticias-america-latina-42796683.

———. 2019. "Crisis en Venezuela: Juan Guaidó anuncia el fin del diálogo en Barbabos, auspiciado por Noruega, debido a la prolongada ausencia del gobierno de Maduro." https://www.bbc.com/mundo/noticias-america-latina-49711112.

BBC News. 2008. "Opposition Reunites in Zimbabwe." http://news.bbc.co.uk/2/hi/africa/7371823.stm.

———. 2020. "'Bay of Piglets': A 'Bizarre' Plot to Capture a President." https://www.bbc.com/news/stories-53557235.

Beaulieu, Emily. 2014. *Electoral Protest and Democracy in the Developing World.* Cambridge: Cambridge University Press.

Becerra, Laura. 2020. "Monómeros se recuperó en 2019 con $7.844 millones en ganancias en segundo semestre." https://www.larepublica.co/empresas/monomeros-se-recupero-en-2019-con-7844-millones-en-ganancias-en-segundo-semestre-2993750#:~:text=Mon%C3%B3meros%20se%20recuper%C3%B3%20en%202019%20con%20%247.844%20millones%20en%20ganancias%20en%20segundo%20semestre,-viernes%2C%2017%20de.

Becker, Gary. 1976. *The Economic Approach to Human Behavior.* Chicago: University of Chicago Press.

Becker, Torbjorn, and Paolo Mauro. 2006. "Output Drops and the Shocks That Matter." IMF Working Paper WP/06/172. https://www.imf.org/external/pubs/ft/wp/2006/wp06172.pdf

Bell, Daniel, and Leon Dennen. 1944. "The System of Governments in Exile." *Annals of the American Academy of Political and Social Science* 232: 134–47.

Bello, Camille. 2018. "¿Por qué solo cerca del 3% de los millones de venezolanos en el extranjero va a votar?" https://es.euronews.com/2018/05/17/-por-que-solo-cerca-del-3-de-los-millones-de-venezolanos-en-el-extranjero-va-a-votar-.

Berman, Dianne, and Mark Andrew Abdollahian. 1999. "Negotiating the Peaceful Expansion of the South African Electorate." *Journal of Conflict Resolution* 43(2): 229–44.

Bernanke, Ben, and Mark Gertler. 1989. "Agency Costs, Net Worth, and Business Fluctuations." *American Economic Review* 79(1): 14–31.

Bernanke, Ben, Mark Gertler, and Simon Gilchrist. 1999. "The Financial Accelerator in a Quantitative Business Cycle Framework." In *Handbook of Macroeconomics*, ed. J. B. Taylor and Michael Woodford, 1341–93. Amsterdam: North Holland

Bernanke, Ben S., Thomas Laubach, Frederic S. Mishkin, and Adam S. Posen. 2001. *Inflation Targeting: Lessons from the International Experience*. Princeton, NJ: Princeton University Press.

Berend, Ivan. 1996. *Central and Eastern Europe, 1944–1993*. Cambridge: Cambridge University Press.

Besada, Hany, and Nicky Moyo. 2008. "Zimbabwe in Crisis: Mugabe's Policies and Failures." Centre for International Governance Innovation. Working Paper No. 38.

Biden, Joe (@POTUS). 2023. "We've come a long way in two years. And now, the biggest threat to our recovery is House Republicans' reckless talk on default. We should be building on our progress–not going backward by defaulting on our debt." Twitter, March 13, 11:30 p.m. https://twitter.com/POTUS/status/1635483388261060609?s=20.

Biersteker, Thomas, and Zuzana Hudáková. 2015. "On Sanctions and Peace Negotiations: Possibilities for Complementarity." Oslo Forum Papers, No. 004.

Biersteker, Thomas, and Peter Van Bergeijk. 2015. "How and When Do Sanctions Work? The Evidence. On Target? EU Sanctions as Security Policy Tools." *ISSReport*, no. 25: 17–28.

Biglaiser, Glen, and David Lektzian. 2020. "The Effects of Economic Sanctions on Targeted Countries' Stock Markets." *International Interactions* 46(3): 1–25.

Bilal, Asma Sana, and Nabiya Imran. 2019. "Emerging Contours of the Transatlantic Relationship under the Trump Administration." *Policy Perspectives* 16(1): 3–21.

Bilinski, Alyssa, and Laura A. Hatfield. 2018. "Nothing to See Here? Non-Inferiority Approaches to Parallel Trends Model Assumptions." ArXiv: Methodology, Semantic Scholar.

Birch, Sarah. 2009. *Full Participation: A Comparative Study of Compulsory Voting*. Manchester: Manchester University Press.

Biskupski, M. B. B., James S. Pula, and Piotr J. Wróbel. 2010. *The Origins of Modern Polish Democracy*. Athens: Ohio University Press.

Blanchard, Ben, and Alexandra Ulmer. 2018. "Venezuela Hands China More Oil Presence, but No Mention of New Funds." https://www.reuters.com/article/usvenezuelanezuela/venezuela-hands-china-more-oil-presence-but-no-mention-of-new-funds-idUSKCN1LU1EV.

Blanchard, Olivier Jean. 1994. "Transition in Poland." *Economic Journal* 104(426): 1169–77.

Bloom, David, David Canning, and Jaypee Sevilla. 2003. "Geography and Poverty Traps." *Journal of Economic Growth* 8: 355–78.

Bloomberg. 2018a. "Crude Oil, WTI. Bloomberg Composite Forecast." Bloomberg Terminal.

———. 2018b. "Crude Oil, WTI. Futures." Bloomberg Terminal.

———. 2018c. "Crude Oil, WTI." Bloomberg Terminal.

———. 2018d. "5-year CDS prices, Venezuela." Bloomberg Terminal.

———. 2021a. "Bloomberg Venezuela's Oil Basket." Bloomberg Terminal.

———. 2021b. "Bloomberg Venezuela's EMBI." Bloomberg Terminal.

———. 2021c. "CUVEEXUS Index—Venezuelan Exports by Destination." Bloomberg Terminal.

———. 2022a. "Bloomberg OPEC Crude Oil Production Output Data–Iran." Bloomberg Terminal.

———. 2022b. "Bloomberg OPEC Crude Oil Production Output Data–Venezuela." Bloomberg Terminal.

———. 2023. "Bloomberg Crude Oil Production Output Data." Bloomberg Terminal.

Boix, Carles. 2003. *Democracy and Redistribution*. Cambridge: Cambridge University Press.

Bojcun, Marko. 1995. "The Ukrainian Parliamentary Elections in March-April 1994." *Europe-Asia Studies* 47(2): 229–49. http://www.jstor.org/stable/152609.

Boldrin, Michelle. 1990. "Dynamic Externalities, Multiple Equilibria and Growth." Discussion Paper No. 918. https://www.kellogg.northwestern.edu/research/math/papers/918.pdf.

Bolivia Information Forum. 2008. "Behind the News from Bolivia." http://www.boliviainfoforum.org.uk/documents/535424538_BIF%20Bulletin%20Special%20edition%20May%202008.pdf.

Bolt, Jutta, and Jan Luiten van Zanden. 2020. "Maddison Style Estimates of the Evolution of the World Economy. A New 2020 Update." Maddison Project Working Paper, WP-15. https://www.rug.nl/ggdc/historicaldevelopment/maddison/publications/wp15.pdf.

Bolton, John (@AmbJohnBolton). 2019. "The people of Venezuela have courageously spoken out against the corruption of the regime, the shortage of food and medicine, and absence of the rule of law." Twitter, January 23, 2:35 p.m. https://x.com/AmbJohnBolton/status/1088143207773409281?s=20.

———. 2020. *The Room Where It Happened*. New York: Simon & Schuster.

Boon, Liseth. 2015. "La investigación que desarmó la historia oficial sobre el 12F." https://runrun.es/investigacion/186376/la-investigacion-que-desarmo-la-historia-oficial-sobre-el-12f/.

Borges, Julio (@JulioBorges). 2019. "La Unión Soviética y Cuba también fabricaron su oposición a la medida y esta complicidad siempre terminó en un gran fracaso. Quienes se prestan para esta maniobra no representan al pueblo venezolano, nuestra agenda sigue firme: la salida de la dictadura." Twitter, September 16. https://twitter.com/JulioBorges/status/1173654681970757633?s=20.

Brandimarte, Walter, and Daniel Bases. 2011. "United States Loses Prized AAA Credit Rating from S&P." https://www.reuters.com/article/us-usa-debt-downgrade/united-states-loses-prized-aaa-credit-rating-from-sp-idUSTRE7746VF20110806.

Bratton, Michael. 1998. "Second Elections in Africa." *Journal of Democracy* 9(3): 51-66.

Braumann, Benedikt. 2000. "Real Effects of High Inflation." IMF Working Paper No. 00/85.

Breen, Emmanuel. 2021. "Corporations and US Economic Sanctions: The Dangers of Overcompliance." In *Research Handbook on Unilateral and Extraterritorial Sanctions*, ed. Charlotte Beaucillon, 255–64. Northampton, MA: Edward Elgar.

Brender, Adi, and Allan Drazen. 2005. "Political Budget Cycles in New versus Established Democracies." *Journal of Monetary Economics* 52(7): 1271–95.

Brewer-Carías, Allan. 2016. *Dictadura judicial y perversión del estado de derecho*. 2nd ed. Colección de Estudios Políticos, no. 13. Caracas: Editorial Jurídica Venezolana International.

Brown, Harold. 1979. "Memorandum from Secretary of Defense Brown to the President's Assistant for National Security Affairs (Brzezinski)." https://history.state.gov/historicaldocuments/frus1977-80v13/d179.

Broz, Lawrence, Maya Duru, and Jeffry Frieden. 2016. "Policy Responses to Balance-of-Payments Crises: The Role of Elections." *Open Economies Review* 27(2): 204–27.

Buchanan, James. 1968. "What Kind of Redistribution Do We Want?" *Economica*, n.s., 35(138): 185–90.

Buchanan, James, and Gordon Tullock. 1962. *The Calculus of Consent: Logical Foundations of Constitutional Demcoracy*. Indianapolis: Liberty Fund.

Bukowski, Paweł, and Wojtek Paczós. 2021. "Why Is Poland's Economy Emerging So Strongly from the Pandemic? A Comparison with the UK." https://blogs.lse.ac.uk/europpblog/2021/05/19/why-is-polands-economy-emerging-so-strongly-from-the-pandemic-a-comparison-with-the-uk/.

Bull, Benedicte, and Antulio Rosales. 2020. "Into the Shadows: Sanctions, Rentierism, and Economic Informalization in Venezuela." *European Review of Latin American and Caribbean Studies* 109: 107–33.

Bueno de Mesquita, Bruce, Alastair Smith, Randolph M. Siverson, and James D. Morrow. 2004. *The Logic of Political Survival.* Cambridge, MA: MIT Press.

Burger, Ewald. 1963. *Introduction to the Theory of Games*. Englewood Cliffs, NJ: Prentice-Hall.

Burhop, Carsten, and Guntram B. Wolff. 2005. "A Compromise Estimate of German Net National Product, 1851–1913, and Its Implications for Growth and Business Cycles." *Journal of Economic History* 65(3): 613–57.

Buttorff, Gail, and Douglas Dion. 2017. "Participation and Boycott in Authoritarian Elections." *Journal of Theoretical Politics* 29(1): 97–123.

Buzek, Jerzy. 2009. "The Transformation of Poland since 1989." *European View* 2009(8): 187–90.

CADIVI. 2009. "Providencia mediante la cual se establecen los requisitos, controles y trámites para la solicitud de autorización de adquisición de divisas destinadas al pago de consumos en el extranjero." https://www.venelogia.com/uploads/PDF/cadivi-providencia-99.pdf.

Cagan, Phillip. 1956. "The Monetary Dynamics of Hyperinflation." In *Studies in the Quantity Theory of Money*, edited by Milton Friedman. Chicago: University of Chicago Press, 25–117.

Caldera, Rafael. 1992. "Discurso Rafael Caldera–Golpe 4 febrero 1992." https://www.retoricas.com/2010/05/discurso-rafael-caldera-golpe-4-febrero.html.

Calia, Mike. 2023. "Trump Urges GOP to Let Catastrophic Debt Default Happen If Dems Don't Accept Cuts." https://www.cnbc.com/2023/05/11/trump-endorses-debt-ceiling-default.html.

Calvert, Randall. 1985. "Robustness of the Multidimensional Voting Model: Candidate Motivations, Uncertainty, and Convergence." *American Journal of Political Science* 29(1): 69–95.

Cara de Lentes. 2015. "Mensaje completo de Nicolás Maduro a la Asamblea Nacional, 21 de enero 2015." YouTube video, 2:16. https://www.youtube.com/watch?v=QOmuAnQtKp0.

Carbonetto, Daniel, M. Ines Cabellos, Oscar Dancourt, Cesar Ferrari, Daniel Martinez, Jaime Mezzera, Gustavo Saberben, Javier Tantalean, and Pierre Vigier. 1987. *El Perú heterodoxo: Un modelo económico*. Centro de Economía Aplicada. Lima: Ediciones El Virrey.

Cardenas, Estefani. 2017. "Crisis de aerolíneas: Venezuela se distancia cada vez más del mercado aéreo internacional." http://globovision.com/article/los-motivos-de-las-aerolineas-que-han-abandonado-venezuela.

Carey, John, and Matthew Shugart. 1995. "Incentives to Cultivate a Personal Vote: A Rank Ordering of Electoral Formulas." *Electoral Studies* 14(4): 417–39.

Cargill, Thomas F., and Michael M. Hutchinson. 1991. "Political Business Cycles with Endogenous Election Timing: Evidence from Japan." *Review of Economics and Statistics* 73(4): 733–39.

Carlson, Keith. 1980. "The Lag from Money to Prices." *Federal Reserve Bank of St. Louis* 62(October): 3–10.

Carrión, Julio. 2015. "Democracy and Populism in the Andes: A Problematic Coexistence." In *Latin American Democracy: Emerging Reality or Endangered Species?*, 2nd ed., ed. R. L. Millett, J. S. Holmes, and O. J. Pérez, 166–97. London: Routledge.

Carter Center. 2004. "Report on an Analysis of the Representativeness of the Second Audit Sample, and the Correlation between Petition Signers and the Yes Vote in the Aug. 15, 2004 Presidential Recall Referendum in Venezuela." https://www.cartercenter.org/news/documents/doc1690.html.

———. 2005. "Observing the Venezuela Presidential Recall Referendum—Comprehensive Report." https://www.cartercenter.org/documents/2020.pdf.

Cass, David. 1966. "Optimum Growth in an Aggregative Model of Capital Accumulation: A Turnpike Theorem." *Econometrica* 34(4): 833–50.

Castro, Maoilis. 2016. "Citibank cerrará las cuentas del Banco Central de Venezuela." https://elpais.com/internacional/2016/07/12/actualidad/1468311643_987605.html.

Cawthorne, Andrew. 2013. "Venezuela Arrests Looters, Store Bosses in 'Economic War.'" https://www.reuters.com/article/us-venezuelaeconomy/venezuela-arrests-looters-store-bosses-in-economic-war-idUSBRE9A90G520131111.

Centellas, Miguel. 2008. "From 'Parliamentarized' to 'Pure' Presidentialism: Bolivia after October 2003." *Latin Americanist* 52(3): 5–30.

Centro de Comunicación Nacional (@Presidencia_VE). 2019. "Propuesta que el Presidente legítimo, @jguaido, presentó en el mecanismo de Oslo y que el régimen bloque." Twitter, September 19, 3:07 p.m. https://twitter.com/Presidencia_VE/status/1173674861773938689.

———. 2021. "Embajador de EEUU, James Story, respaldó Acuerdo de Salvación Nacional presentado por Guaidó." https://presidenciave.com

/internacional/embajador-de-eeuu-james-story-respaldo-acuerdo-de-salvacion-nacional-presentado-por-guaido/.

Cerra, Valerie, and Sweta Saxena. 2008. "Growth Dynamics: The Myth of Economic Recovery." *American Economic Review* 98(1): 439–57.

Chakraborty, Debjit, and Lucia Kassai. 2019. "India's Reliance Caps Venezuelan Oil Buying on U.S. Pressure." https://www.bloomberg.com/news/articles/2019-03-13/india-s-reliance-caps-venezuelan-oil-buying-on-u-s-pressure.

Chakravarty, Sudip. 1992. "Review: Democracy and the Market: Political and Economic Reforms in Eastern Europe and Latin America." *Bulletin of Latin American Research* 11(2): 231–33.

Chan, Stephen, and Julia Gallagher. 2017. *Why Mugabe Won: The 2013 Elections in Zimbabwe and Their Aftermath*. Cambridge: Cambridge University Press.

Chapel, Bill, and Jaclyn Diaz. 2021. "Myanmar Coup: With Aung San Suu Kyi Detained, Military Takes over Government." https://www.npr.org/2021venezue962758188/myanmar-coup-military-detains-aung-san-suu-kyi-plans-new-election-in-2022.

Chapman, Emilee Booth. 2019. "The Distinctive Value of Elections and the Case for Compulsory Voting." *American Journal of Political Science* 63: 101–12. https://doi.org/10.1111/ajps.12393.

Chauvet, Lisa, and Paul Collier. 2009. "Elections and Economic Policy in Developing Countries." *Economic Policy* 24(59): 509–50.

Chávez, Hugo. [1992] 2015. "4 de febrero de 1992: "Por ahora los objetivos no fueron logrados." BancoAgrícolaVE. YouTube video, 0:05, February 2, 2015. https://www.youtube.com/watch?v=_QqaR1ZjldE.

———. 2012. "Chávez pide a Venezuela respaldar al Vicepresidente Nicolás Maduro en caso de su ausencia." NTN24. YouTube video, 1:14, December 9. https://www.youtube.com/watch?v=9XZnWJCvvbM.

Cheatham, Amelia, Diana Roy, and Rocio Cara. 2021. "Venezuela: The Rise and Fall of a Petrostate." https://www.cfr.venezuelarounder/venezuela-crisis.

Cheibub, José, Jennifer Gandhi, and James Raymond. 2010. "Democracy and Dictatorship Revisited." *Public Choice* 143: 67–101.

Chinea, Eyanir, and Brian Ellsworth. 2016. "S&P Says PDVSA Bond Swap Offer 'Tantamount to Default.'" Reuters. https://www.reuters.com/article/us-venezuela-pdvsa-debt/sp-says-pdvsa-bond-swap-offer-tantamount-to-default-idUSKCN11Q05F.

Clausewitz, Carl von. [1832] 1997. *On War*. Trans. J. J. Graham. Wordsworth Classics of World Literature. Ware, UK: Wordsworth Editions.

CNN. 2013. "Maduro y Capriles echan un pulso en las elecciones municipales en Venezuela." https://cnnespanol.cnn.com/2013/12/05/maduro-y-capriles-echan-un-pulso-en-las-elecciones-municipales-en-venezuela/.

———. 2016. "Proceso del revocatorio, suspendido tras anulación de firmas de primera fase." https://cnnespanol.cnn.com/2016/10/20/anulan-firmas-de-la-primera-fase-del-revocatorio-en-varios-estados-de-venezuela/.

———. 2020. "Evo Morales, imputado por terrorismo: Fiscalía de Bolivia pide su detención preventiva." https://www.youtube.com/watch?v=xterLwQL4To.

Coate, Stephen, and Stephen Morris. 1995. "On the Form of Transfers to Special Interests." *Journal of Political Economy* 103(6): 1210–35.

———. 1996. "Policy Conditionality." PIER Working Paper No. 97-013. https://dx.doi.org/10.2139/ssrn.305155.

Cohen, David, and Zoe Weinberg. 2019. "Sanctions Can't Spark Regime Change." https://www.foreignaffairs.com/articles/united-states/2019-04-29/sanctions-cant-spark-regime-change.

Grimsley, Mark, and Clifford J. Rogers. 2008. *Civilians in the Path of War*. Lincoln: University of Nebraska Press.

Cohen, Luc. 2019. "Opositor presenta propuesta de plan 'petróleo por alimentos' al estilo Irak para Venezuela." https://www.reuters.com/article/venezuela-politica-petroleo-idLTAKCN1UK36W.

Collier, Paul. 2000. "Economic Causes of Civil Conflict and Their Implications for Policy." World Bank. https://people.umass.edu/educ870/PostConflict/resources/CausesofConflict-CollierWB.pdf.

Collister, Keith. 2015. "Was the PetroCaribe Buyback a Good Deal for Jamaica?" https://www.jamaicaobserver.com/business/Was-the-PetroCaribe-buyback-a-good-deal-for-Jamaica-_19221616.

Comando con Venezuela. 2024. "Resultados CON VZLA." August 5. https://resultadosconvzla.com/.

Combellas, Ricardo. 2003. "El proceso constituyente y la Constitución de 1999." *Politeia* 30: 183–208.

El Comercio. 2017. "Venezuela: Gobierno y oposición crean grupo de países amigos para el diálogo." https://elcomercio.pe/mundo/latinoamerica/venezuela-gobierno-oposicion-crean-grupo-paises-amigos-dialogo-noticia-457990-noticia/?ref=ecr.

———. 2020. "CNE suspende a movimiento político del correísmo y a tres organizaciones." https://www.elcomercio.com/actualidad/cne-suspension-fuerza-compromiso-correismo.html.

Comisión especial para el rescate de la institucionalidad del Tribunal Supremo de Justicia. 2016. "Informe Final: Asamblea Nacional de Venezuela."

https://supremainjusticia.org/wp-content/uploads/2016/07/INFORME-FINAL-COMISION-ESPECIAL-PARA-EL-RESCATE-DEL-TSJ.pdf.

Committee for a Responsible Federal Budget (CFRB). 2023. "Meeting Fiscal Goals under CBO's May 2023 Baseline." https://www.crfb.org/blogs/meeting-fiscal-goals-under-cbos-may-2023-baseline.

El Confidencial. 2009. "Filial del Grupo Santander en Venezuela pasó a manos del Gobierno de Chávez." https://www.elconfidencial.com/mercados/2009-07-04/filial-del-grupo-santander-en-venezuela-paso-a-manos-del-gobierno-de-chavez_1039396/.

Congressional Research Service. 2009. "Zimbabwe: The Power Sharing Agreement and Implications for U.S. Policy." https://www.files.ethz.ch/isn/110028/Zimbabwe.pdf.

———. 2018. "Shutdown of the Federal Government: Causes, Processes, and Effects." RL34680. https://sgp.fas.org/crs/misc/RL34680.pdf.

———. 2021. "Past Government Shutdowns: Key Resources." R41759. https://crsreports.congress.gov/product/pdf/R/R41759.

Consejo de Participación Ciudadana y Control Social (CPCCS). 2023. "Lineamientos generales para la planificación estrategica del CPCCS." http://www.oas.org/juridico/PDFs/mesicic4_ecu_lin.pdf.

Consejo Europeo. 2019. "Declaración de la Alta Representante, en nombre de la UE, sobre el nuevo mandato del presidente Maduro." https://www.consilium.europa.eu/es/press/press-releases/2019/01/10/declaration-by-the-high-representative-on-behalf-of-the-eu-on-the-new-mandate-of-president-maduro/.

Consejo Nacional Electoral (CNE). 2013a. "Elecciones presidenciales 2013." http://www.cne.gob.ve/resultado_presidencial_2013/r/1/reg_010000.html.

———. 2013b. "Manual de funcionamiento de la Mesa Electoral." http://www.cne.gob.ve/web/normativa_electoral/elecciones/2013/municipales/documentos/Manual_Miembro_Mesa.pdf.

———. 2015. "Elecciones Asamblea Nacional 2015." http://www.cne.gob.ve/resultado_asamblea2015/r/0/reg_000000.html?.

———. 2016. "Poder Electoral acata medidas cautelares ordenadas por tribunales de la República." http://www.cne.gov.ve/web/sala_prensa/noticia_detallada.php?id=3483.

———. 2017. "Elecciones regionales y municipales 2017." http://www.cne.gob.ve/resultados_regionales2017/.

———. 2018. "Elecciones presidenciales 2018." http://www.cne.gob.ve/ResultadosElecciones2018/.

———. 2020. "Elecciones Asamblea Nacional 2020." https://www2.cne.gob.ve/an2020.

———. 2021. "Elecciones regionales y municipales 2021." https://www2.cne.gob.ve/rm221.

———. 2023a. "Elecciones 1989–2000." Accessed December 8, 2023. http://www.cne.gob.ve/web/documentos/estadisticas/e009.pdf.

———. 2023b. "Elecciones presidenciales. Cuadro comparativo (1958–2000)." Accessed December 8, 2023. http://www.cne.gob.ve/web/documentos/estadisticas/e006.pdf.

———. 2023c. "Estadísticas—Resultados electorales." Accessed December 8, 2023. https://www.cne.gob.ve/web/estadisticas/index_resultados_elecciones.php.

——— (@CNEesvenezuela). 2024. "COMUNICADO OFICIAL en rechazo, de manera categórica, los insolentes y falsos cuestionamientos, del Departamento de Estado de los EEUU sobre el CNE, con el objeto de desprestigiar una de las instituciones más sólidas de la robusta democracia venezolana." Twitter 2:04 pm, March 28. https://twitter.com/cneesvzla/status/1773410742860956042.

Consensus Economics. 2017. "Latin American Consensus Forecast: Latin America." January

Contra Punto. 2019. "Guaidó informó lo que contenía el acuerdo que quedó sin firmar en la mesa de Barbados." https://contrapunto.com/nacional/guaido-hablara-este-lunes-16-sep-sobre-el-contenido-del-acuerdo-que-quedo-sin-firmar-en-barbados/.

Contraloría General de la República. 2023. "Oficio N°: DGPE-23-08-00-008." https://drive.google.com/file/d/1LIqg-E04rRHPLMCIDGjkbMTfOFq11OSI/view?pli=1.

El Cooperante. 2017. "¡Revocado Maduro! 7.676.894 venezolanos participaron en la consulta contra la ANC." https://elcooperante.com/revocado-maduro-7-676-894-venezolanos-participaron-en-la-consulta-contra-la-anc/.

Corden, Warner. 1984. "Booming Sector and Dutch Disease Economics: Survey and Consolidation." *Oxford Economic Papers* 36(3): 359–80.

———. 1989. "Macroeconomic Adjustment in Developing Countries." *World Bank Research Observer* 4(1): 51–64.

Corden, Warner Max, and J. Peter Neary. 1982. "Booming Sector and De-Industrialisation in a Small Open Economy." *Economic Journal* 92(368): 825–48.

Coronil, Fernando. 1997. *The Magical State: Nature, Money, and Modernity in Venezuela*. Chicago: University of Chicago Press.

Corrales, Javier. 2005. "In Search of a Theory of Polarization: Lessons from Venezuela 1999–2005." *European Review of Latin American and Caribbean Studies* 79: 105–18.

———. 2018. *Fixing Democracy: Why Constitutional Change Often Fails to Enhance Democracy*. Oxford: Oxford University Press.

———. 2020. "Authoritarian Survival: Why Maduro Hasn't Fallen." *Journal of Democracy* 31(3): 39–53.

———. 2023. *Autocracy Rising: How Venezuela Transitioned to Authoritarianism*. Washington, DC: Brookings Institution Press.

Corrales, Javier, and Michael Penfold. 2015. *Dragon in the Tropics: Hugo Chávez and the Political Economy of Revolution in Venezuela*. Washington, DC: Brookings Institution Press.

Correo del Caroní. 2013. "Gobierno estudia en serio aumentar precio de la gasolina." https://issuu.com/correodelcaroni/docs/13-12-2013.

Correo del Orinoco. 2013. "Presidenta del BCV Edmée Betancourt: Guerra de la derecha afectó el crecimiento económico de Venezuela." http://www.correodelorinoco.gob.ve/guerra-derecha-afecto-crecimiento-economico-venezuela/.

Cortez, Josafat. 2014. "El tribunal constitucional plurinacional de Bolivia: Cómo se distribuye el poder institucional." *Boletín Mexicano de Derecho Comparado* 47(139): 297–96.

Cortright, David, and George A. Lopez. 2002. *Smart Sanctions: Targeting Economic Statecraft*. Lanham, MD: Rowman & Littlefield..

Council of the European Union. 2021a. "Council Conclusions on Venezuela (25 January 2021)." senezu-en21.pdf (europa.eu).

———. 2021b. "Council Decision (CFSP) 2021/276. 2021." https://eur-lex.europa.eu/legal-content/EN/TXT/PDF/?uri=CELEX:32021D0276&rid=4.

Crisp, Brian, and Juan C. Rey. 2003. "The Sources of Electoral Reform in Venezuela." In *Mixed-Member Electoral Systems: The Best of Both Worlds?*, ed. Matthew Soberg Shugart and Martin P. Wattenberg, 173–93. Comparative Politics. Oxford: Oxford University Press.

Crónica Uno. 2023. "Maduro aseguró que EE. UU. no ha dado los pasos para liberar fondos de acuerdo social." https://cronica.uno/maduro-aseguro-que-ee-uu-no-ha-dado-los-pasos-para-liberar-fondos-de-acuerdo-social/.

Crooks, Ed. 2017. "Foreign Oil Companies Feel the Strain." https://www.ft.com/content/3264b33e-d680-11e7-a303-9060cb1e5f44.

Daniels, Joe, and Mariana Zúñiga. 2017. "Venezuela's Nicolás Maduro Survives Apparent Assassination Attempt." https://www.theguardian.com/world/18/aug/04/nicolas-maduros-speech-cut-short-while-soldiers-scatter.

Daodi, M. S., and M. S. Dajani. 1985. "Poland: The Politactics of Sanctions." *Polish Review* 30(2): 149–66.

Dashti-Gibson, Jaleh, Patricia Davis, and Benjamin Radcliff. 1997. "On the Determinants of the Success of Economic Sanctions: An Empirical Analysis." *American Journal of Political Science* 41(2): 608–18. https://doi.org/10.2307/2111779.

Dassonneville, Ruth, and Michael Lewis-Beck. 2014. "Macroeconomics, Economic Crisis and Electoral Outcomes: A National European Pool." *Acta Politica* 49: 372–94. https://doi.org/10.1057/ap.2014.12.

Datanálisis. 2017. Encuesta Nacional Ómnibus.

———. 2018. Encuesta Nacional Ómnibus.

———. 2019. Encuesta Nacional Ómnibus. October.

———. 2021. Encuesta Nacional Ómnibus. October.

———. 2022a. Encuesta Nacional Ómnibus. February.

———. 2022b. Encuesta Nacional Ómnibus. August.

———. 2022c. Encuesta Nacional Ómnibus. September.

———. 2022d. Encuesta Nacional Ómnibus. November.

———. 2024. Evaluación de Aprobación (Popularidad). July.

Davari, Arash. 2020. "US-Iran Relations under Maximum Pressure: A Narrow Path to Negotiations," Middle East Brief, Crown Center for Middle East Studies. https://www.brandeis.edu/crown/publications/middle-east-briefs/pdfs/101-200/meb137.pdf.

De Alba, Mariano. 2019. "¿Qué son las sanciones secundarias?" https://prodavinci.com/que-son-las-sanciones-secundarias/.

Death Penalty Information Center. 2023. "When Jurors Do Not Agree, Should a Death Sentence Be Imposed?" https://deathpenaltyinfo.org/news/when-jurors-do-not-agree-should-a-death-sentence-be-imposed.

DeLong, Bradford. 2022. *Slouching towards Utopia: An Economic History of the Twentieth Century*. New York: Basic Books.

Del Valle, Sofia. 2016. "Alfredo Serrano: El cerebro de la economía venezolana." http://www.dinero.com.ve/din/actualidad/alfredo-serrano-el-cerebro-de-la-econom-venezolana.

De Young, Karen, Steven Mufson, and Anthony Faiola. 2019. "Trump Administration Announces Sanctions Targeting Venezuela's Oil Industry." *Washington Post*, January 28. https://www.washingtonpost.com/national/health-science/trump-administration-announces-sanctions-targeting-venezuelas-oil-industry/2019/01/28/4f4470c2-233a-11e9-90cd-dedb0c92dc17_story.html.

Deutsche Welle. 2017. "Almagro pide sanciones más duras contra Venezuela." https://www.dw.com/es/almagro-pide-sanciones-m%C3%A1s-duras-contra-venezuela/a-40681249.

———. 2018. "Oposición niega haber alcanzado acuerdo con el Gobierno." https://www.dw.com/es/oposici%C3%B3n-venezolana-niega-haber-alcanzado-acuerdo-con-el-gobierno/a-42474965.

Devex. 2021. "IMF Board Backs $650B Allocation of Special Drawing Rights." https://www.devex.com/news/imf-board-backs-650b-allocation-of-special-drawing-rights-100342.

Diamond, Louise, and John McDonald. 1996. *Multi-Track Diplomacy: A Systems Approach to Peace*. 3rd ed. Kumarian Press Books for a World That Works. West Hartford, CT: Kumarian Press.

Diario Las Américas. 2019. "Asamblea Nacional autoriza a Guaidó para designar junta ad-hoc de filial de PDVSA." https://www.diariolasamericas.com/asamblea-nacional-autoriza-guaido-designar-junta-ad-hoc-filial-pdvsa-n4186242.

Diario Qué Pasa. 2014. "Matta y Ledezma rechazan aumento de la gasolina." https://www.quepasa.com.ve/politica/matta-y-ledezma-rechazan-aumento-de-la-gasolina/.

Díaz, Eleazar. 2014. "Los barrios no bajan." https://questiondigital.com/los-barrios-no-bajan/.

Di John, Jonathan. 2009. *From Windfall to Curse? Oil and Industrialization in Venezuela, 1920 to the Present*. University Park: Pennsylvania State University Press.

Di John, Jonathan, and James Putzel. 2009. "Political Settlements." https://core.ac.uk/download/pdf/103642.pdf.

Dinero. 2014. "Carta de Giordani a Nicolás Maduro tras su salida del gabinete." http://www.dinero.com.ve/din/destacados/carta-de-giordani-nicol-s-maduro-tras-su-salida-del-gabinete#:~:text=%20Carta%2ªde%20Giordani%20a%20Nicol%C3%A1s%20Maduro%20tras,p%C3%BAblico%20que%20en%20lo%20productivo%20dominara...%20More%20.

———. 2017. "Fiscal Luisa Ortega Díaz advierte ruptura del orden constitucional." http://www.dinero.com.ve/din/actualidad/fiscal-luisa-ortega-d-az-advierte-ruptura-del-orden-constitucional.

Dirección Nacional Electoral Argentina. 2019. "Elecciones 2019." https://www.argentina.gob.ar/dine/resultados-electorales/elecciones-2019.

Di Stasio, Alessandro. 2016. "¿Qué ha sucedido en Venezuela desde la suspensión del revocatorio?" https://efectococuyo.com/politica/que-ha-sucedido-en-venezuela-desde-la-suspension-del-revocatorio/.

Dixit, Avinash, and Victor Norman. 1980. *Theory of International Trade: A Dual, General Equilibrium Approach*. Cambridge Economic Handbooks. Cambridge: Cambridge University Press.

Doggett, Tom. 2015. "U.S. Oil Production Growth in 2014 Was Largest in More Than 100 Years." https://www.eia.gov/todayinenergy/detail.php?id=20572.

DolarToday. 2023. "Tasa de cambio bolívar/dólar." https://web.archive.org/web/20230701110023/https://dolartoday.com/.

Domber, Gregory F. 2007. "Supporting the Revolution: America, Democracy, and the End of the Cold War in Poland, 1981–1989." ACES–EU Center of Excellence, Research Grants and Working Paper Series No. 8. http://aei.pitt.edu/id/eprint/59042.

———. 2014. *Empowering Revolution: America, Poland, and the End of the Cold War*. Chapel Hill: University of North Carolina Press.

Dornbusch, Rudiger, and Sebastián Edwards. 1992. *Macroeconomía del populismo en la América Latina*. Mexico City: Fondo de Cultura Económica.

Downs, Anthony. 1957. *An Economic Theory of Democracy*. New York: Harper and Row, 1957.

Drazen, Allan. 2000. *Political Economy in Macroeconomics*. Princeton, NJ: Princeton University Press.

Duelfer, Charles. 2004. *Comprehensive Report of the Special Advisor to the DCI [Director of Central Intelligence] on Iraq's WMD [Weapons of Mass Destruction]*. 3 vols. Washington, DC: Central Intelligence Agency.

Dunning, John, and Sarianna Lundan. 2008. "Institutions and the OLI Paradigm of the Multinational Enterprise." *Asia Pacific Journal of Management* 25: 573–93.

Dunning, Thad. 2008. *Crude Democracy: Natural Resource Wealth and Political Regimes*. Cambridge: Cambridge University Press.

Durlauf, Steven. 1993. "Nonergodic Economic Growth." *Review of Economic Studies* 60(2): 349–66.

Easterly, William. 2006. "Social Cohesion, Institutions, and Growth." Center for Global Development. Working Paper No. 94.

Ebus, Bram. 2022. "Exploiting Venezuela's Uncertain Future: Resource Conflicts and the Environment." Wilson Center Latin American Program.

Economist. 1977. "The Dutch Disease." https://www.uio.no/studier/emner/sv/oekonomi/ECON4925/h08/undervisningsmateriale/DutchDisease.pdf.

EFE. 2016. "Kerry telefonea a Zapatero para apoyar su mediación al diálogo en Venezuela." https://www.lavanguardia.com/politica/20160527/402093626971/kerry-telefonea-a-zapatero-para-apoyar-su-mediacion-al-dialogo-en-venezuela.html.

———. 2017. "Esposa de Joao Santana dice Maduro le pagó 11 millones de dólares sin declarar." Primer Momento. http://primermomento.com/?p=290055.

———. 2018. "Ledezma y Machado tildan de locura y burla diálogo en República Dominicana." *El Nacional*, January 14. https://www.elnacional.com/noticias/politica/ledezma-machado-tildan-locura-burla-dialogo-republica-dominicana_218722/.

———. 2021. "Evo Morales recuerda a Hugo Chávez 'como uno de los más grandes patriotas.'" https://www.swissinfo.ch/spa/venezuela-ch%C3%A1vez_evo-morales-recuerda-a-hugo-ch%C3%A1vez-como-uno-de-los--m%C3%A1s-grandes-patriotas-/46424290.

———. 2022. "Maduro asegura que Venezuela finaliza el año 2022 con avances indiscutibles." Swissinfo. https://www.swissinfo.ch/spa/venezuela-econom%C3%ADa_maduro-asegura-que-venezuela-finaliza-el-a%C3%B1o-2022-con--avances-indiscutibles-/48144292.

Efecto Cocuyo. 2024. "CNE ratifica proclamación de Nicolás Maduro en segundo boletín." August 2, 2024. https://efectococuyo.com/politica/cne-ratifica-victoria-de-nicolas-maduro-en-segundo-boletin/.

Eichengreen, Barry. 1992. *Golden Fetters: The Gold Standard and the Great Depression, 1919–1939*. Oxford: Oxford University Press.

Elster, Jon. 1985. *Making Sense of Marx*. Cambridge: Cambridge University Press.

ENCOVI. 2020. *Encuesta Nacional de Condiciones de Vida*. Caracas: Universidad Católica Andres Bello.

———. 2022. *Encuesta Nacional de Condiciones de Vida*. Caracas: Universidad Católica Andres Bello.

Engels, Friedrich, and Karl Marx. [1848] 2015. *Manifesto of the Communist Party*. Little Black Classics. London: Penguin.

Entorno58 ODH. 2016. "Aristóbulo Istúriz reitera: Si quitamos el control de cambio nos tumban." YouTube video. 0:35. October 11. https://www.youtube.com/watch?v=xtKpSeuP9OY.

Equipo Anova. 2021. "Impacto de las sanciones financieras internacionales contra Venezuela: Nueva evidencia." https://thinkanova.org/wp-content/uploads/2021/02/Anova-Policy-Brief-Sanciones.pdf.

Ercolani, Antonella. 1994. "Las relaciones entre los Estados Unidos y Francia en 1940: La misión secreta de Rebe de Chambrun." *Revista de Estudios Políticos*, n.s., no. 85 (July). http://www.cepc.gob.es/publicaciones/revistas/revistaselectronicas?IDR=3&IDN=242&IDA=16883.

Erdmans, Mary. 1995. "Conflict and Cooperation: Pomost and the Polish American Congress." *Polish American Studies* 52(1): 51–69.

Eriksen, Mette. 2004. "Venezuela: Recall Referendum." Norwegian Centre for Human Rights. Report 13. https://www.jus.uio.no/smr/english/about/programmes/nordem/publications/2004/13.pdf.

Erikson, Robert S. 1990. "Economic Conditions and the Congressional Vote: A Review of the Macrolevel Evidence." *American Journal of Political Science* 34(2): 373–99.

Esberg, Jane, and Alexandra Siegel. 2023. "How Exile Shapes Online Opposition: Evidence from Venezuela." *American Political Science Review* 117(4): 1361–78.

España, Sara. 2020. "La Corte de Ecuador inhabilita a Rafael Correa como candidato a vicepresidente." https://elpais.com/internacional/2020-09-07/la-corte-de-ecuador-inhabilita-a-rafael-correa-como-candidato-a-vicepresidente.html.

Espinoza, Javier. 1998. "Chávez propone el regreso a Venezuela de Pérez Jiménez." https://www.elmundo.es/elmundo/1998/diciembre/08/internacional/chavez.html.

Esterhuyse, Willie. 2012. *Endgame: Secret Talks and the End of Apartheid.* Cape Town: Tafelberg.

Eubank, Nicholas, and Dorothy Kronick. 2021. "Friends Don't Let Friends Free Ride." *Quarterly Journal of Political Science* 16: 533–57.

EuroNews. 2013. "Watch: Looting in Venezuela after Government Launches Attack on 'Bourgeois Parasites.'" https://www.euronews.com/2013/11/12/watch-looting-in-venezuela-after-government-launches-attack-on-bourgeois-paras.

———. 2019. "Maduro: No existe crisis humanitaria en Venezuela." https://es.euronews.com/2019/02/08/maduro-no-existe-crisis-humanitaria-en-venezuela.

Europa Press. 2018. "Maduro firma el acuerdo de paz y reitera su disposición a continuar con el diálogo en República Dominicana." https://www.europapress.es/internacional/noticia-maduro-firma-acuerdo-paz-reitera-disposicion-continuar-dialogo-republica-dominicana-20180208052601.html.

———. 2019a. "Destacados opositores rechazan la 'parodia' de acuerdo entre el Gobierno y partidos minoritarios en Venezuela." https://www.europapress.es/internacional/noticia-destacados-opositores-rechazan-parodia-acuerdo-dialogo-gobierno-partidos-minoritarios-20190916222816.html.

———. 2019b. "Maduro confirma que los diputados del PSUV se reincorporarán este martes a la Asamblea Nacional." https://www.europapress.es/internacional/noticia-cargo-oficialista-asegura-diputados-psuv-reincorporaran-martes-asamblea-nacional-20190924000058.html.

European External Action Service (EEAS) Press Team. 2020. "Venezuela: International Contact Group Statement on the Venezuelan National Assembly Elections Held on 6 December 2020." https://eeas.europa.eu/headquarters/headquarters-homepage_en/90136/Venezuela%20:%20International%20Contact%20Group%20statement%20on%20the%20Venezuelan%20National%20Assembly%20elections%20held%20on%206%20December%202020.

———. 2021. "Venezuela: Declaración del Grupo Internacional de Contacto." https://eeas.europa.eu/headquarters/headquarters-homepage_es/101711/Venezuela:%20Declaraci%C3%B3n%20del%20Grupo%20Internacional%20de%20Contacto%20*.

European Union (EU). 2021. "Misión de Observación Electoral Venezuela 2021 Informe final. EU." https://www.eeas.europa.eu/sites/default/files/eu_eom_ven_2021_fr_es.pdf.

European Union Council. 2021. "Council Decision (CFSP) 2021/276. 2021." https://eur-lex.europa.eu/legal-content/EN/TXT/PDF/?uri=CELEX:32021D0276&rid=4.

Fabre, Cécile. 2018. *Economic Statecraft.* Cambridge, MA: Harvard University Press.

Fahrenthold, David, Lori Montgomery and Paul Kane. 2011. "In Debt Deal, the Triumph of the Old Washington." https://www.washingtonpost.com/politics/in-debt-deal-the-triumph-of-the-old-washington/2011/08/02/gIQARSFfqI_story.html.

Faiola, Anthony. 2019. "El exjefe de inteligencia de Maduro llega a EE.UU. con acusaciones en contra del gobierno venezolano." https://www.washingtonpost.com/world/the_americas/el-exjefe-de-inteligencia-de-maduro-llega-a-eeuu-con-acusaciones-en-contra-del-gobierno-venezolano/2019/06/24/497f40ca-96d2-11e9-9a16-dc551ea5a43b_story.html.

Fajfer, Luba. 1993. "The Polish Military and the Crisis of 1970." *Communist and Post-Communist Studies* 26(2): 205–25.

Falcón, Henri (@HenriFalconLara). 2018. "EN DIRECTO en #Periscope: Presentación del programa de gobierno para la gran transformación hacia la Venezuela del . . . " Twitter, April 23, 12:20 p.m. https://twitter.com/HenriFalconLara/status/988452504152178689?ref_src=twsrc%5Etfw%7Ctwcamp%5Etweetembed%7Ctwterm%5E988452504152178689%7Ctwgr%5E7a501fb517a36012edf8bbdac1eefdc4c42e7d09%7Ctwcon%5Es1_&ref_url=https%3A%2F%2Fwww.telesurtv.net%2Fnews%2Fcandidato-opositor-henri-falcon-propuestas-gobierno-20180423-0030.html.

Farnsworth, Eric. 2018. "Venezuela's Humanitarian Crisis." https://www.univision.com/univision-news/opinion/venezuelas-humanitarian-crisis?hootPostID=51cd45090666682b9e0940d9813a9b11.

Faus, Joan. 2018. "La OEA pide a la Corte Penal Internacional investigar delitos de lesa humanidad en Venezuela." https://elpais.com/internacional/2018/05/30/america/1527699615_569077.html.

Fearon, James. 1995. "Rationalist Explanation for War." *International Organization* 49(3): 379–414.

———. 2011. "Self-Enforcing Democracy." *Quarterly Journal of Economics* 126(4): 1661–1708.

Federal Register. 2018. "Executive Order 13850 Blocking Property of Additional Persons Contributing to the Situation in Venezuela." *Federal Register* 83: 213. https://www.govinfo.gov/content/pkg/FR-2018-11-02/pdf/2018-24254.pdf.

———. 2019. "Declaring a National Emergency Concerning the Southern Border of the United States." https://www.federalregister.gov/documents/2019/02/20/2019-03011/declaring-a-national-emergency-concerning-the-southern-border-of-the-united-states.

Feenstra, Robert C. 2015. *Advanced International Trade: Theory and Evidence*. 2nd ed. Princeton, NJ: Princeton University Press.

Feenstra, Robert, Robert Inklaar, and Marcel Timmer. 2015. "The Next Generation of the Penn World Table." *American Economic Review* 105(10): 3150–82. www.ggdc.net/pwt.

Felbermayr, Gabriel, Aleksandra Kirilakha, Constantinos Syropoulos, Erdal Yalcen, and Yoto Yotov. 2020. "The Global Sanctions Data Base." https://voxeu.org/article/global-sanctions-data-base#:~:text=To%20facilitate%20progress%2C%20we%20developed%20a%20novel%20data,change%20their%20behaviour%20or%20to%20constrain%20their%20actions.

Feldman, Gerald. 1997. *The Great Disorder: Politics, Economics, and Society in the German Inflation, 1914–1924*. Oxford: Oxford University Press.

Fergusson, Adam. 2010. *When Money Dies: The Nightmare of Deficit Spending, Devaluation, and Hyperinflation in Weimar Germany*. New York: Public Affairs.

Fernandez, Raquel, and Dani Rodrik. 1991. "Resistance to Reform: Status Quo Bias in the Presence of Individual-Specific Uncertainty." *American Economic Review* 81(5): 1146–55.

Fieser, Ezra. 2015a. "Jamaica Seeks Agreement to Pay off Venezuelan Oil Debt." https://www.bloomberg.com/news/articles/2015-03-11/jamaica-seeks-deal-to-pay-off-venezuelan-oil-debt-minister-says.

———. 2015b. "Venezuela Gets $1.9 Billion as Dominican Republic Pays Debt." https://www.bloomberg.com/news/articles/2015-01-30/dominican-republic-taps-1-9-billion-to-pay-venezuelan-oil-debt.

Financial Crimes Enforcement Network (FinCen). 2017a. Advisory. "FIN-2017-A006." https://www.fincen.gov/sites/default/files/advisory/2017-09-20/FinCEN%20Advisory%20FIN-2017-A006-508%20Compliant.pdf#:~:text=FIN-2017-A006September%2020%2C%202017%20Advisory%20on%20Widespread%20Public%20Corruption,financial%20system.%20This%20Advisory%20should%20be%20shared%20with%3A.

———. 2017b. "Reports from Financial Institutions Are Critical to Stopping, Deterring, and Preventing the Proceeds Tied to Suspected Venezuelan Public Corruption from Moving through the U.S. Financial System." FinCen FIN-2017-A006. https://www.fincen.gov/resources/advisories/fincen-advisory-fin-2017-a006.

———. 2019. "FIN-2019-A002." https://www.fincen.gov/sites/default/files/advisory/2019-05-03/Venezuela%20Advisory%20FINAL%20508.pdf#:~:text=FIN-2019-A002May%203%2C%202019%20Updated%20Advisory%20on%20Widespread%20Public,perpetuating%20the%20humanitarian%20crisis%20of%20the%20Venezuelan%20people.

Financial Times. 2014. "Venezuela Signals Relaxation of Foreign Exchange Regime." https://www.ft.com/content/463b6740-f4a2-11e3-a143-00144feabdc0.

Fischer, Conan. 2003a. "The End of Passive Resistance." In *The Ruhr Crisis 1923–1924*, 182–219. Oxford: Oxford University Press.

———. 2003b. *The Ruhr Crisis 1923–1924*. Oxford: Oxford University Press.

Fitch Ratings. 2023. "Fitch Downgrades the United States' Long-Term Ratings to 'AA+' from 'AAA'; Outlook Stable." https://www.fitchratings.com/research/sovereigns/fitch-downgrades-united-states-long-term-ratings-to-aa-from-aaa-outlook-stable-01-08-2023.

Florido, Luis (@LuisFlorido). 2018. "#ANUNCIO @VoluntadPopular tante incumplimientos del régimen de Maduro y convocatoria a elecciones anticipadas por la fraudulenta ANC, NO PARTICIPAREMOS en reunión del 29 en RD. Ratificamos nuestro compromiso unitario de todos los q se oponen a la dictadura del hambre y la corrupción." Twitter, January 27. https://twitter.com/LuisFlorido/status/957331328873136128?s=20.

FocusEconomics. 2023. "LatinFocus Consensus Forecast: Latin America." July.

Foley, Hamilton. 1923. *Woodrow Wilson's Case for the League of Nations*. Princeton, NJ: Princeton University Press.

Forero, Juan, and Kejal Vyas. 2019. "Venezuela's Opposition Came Close to Ousting the President—but the Plan Fell Apart." https://www.wsj.com/articles/how-plan-to-oust-venezuelan-leader-fell-apart-11556926683.

Foro Penal. 2018. "Reporte sobre la represión en Venezuela en 2017." https://foropenal.com/reporte-la-represion-venezuela-2017/.

Frankel, Matthew. 2010. "Threaten but Participate: Why Election Boycotts Are a Bad Idea." https://www.brookings.edu/research/threaten-but-participate-why-election-boycotts-are-a-bad-idea/.

FRED St. Louis. 2023. "Federal Debt Held by the Public as Percent of Gross Domestic Product." https://fred.stlouisfed.org/series/FYGFGDQ188S#0.

Freitez, Anitza. 2018. *Espejo de la crisis humanitaria venezolana.* Caracas: Universidad Católica Andres Bello.

Friedman, Milton. 1953. "The Methodology of Positive Economics." In *Essays in Positive Economics*, 3–43. Chicago: University of Chicago Press.

———. 1972. "Have Monetary Policies Failed?" *American Economic Review* 62: 11–18.

———. 1980. "Economic Sanctions." https://miltonfriedman.hoover.org/internal/media/dispatcher/214231/full.

Fullerton, Don. 2008. "Laffer Curve." In *The New Palgrave Dictionary of Economics*, 1-4. London: Palgrave Macmillan. https://doi.org/10.1057/978-1-349-95121-5_2088-1.

Gaceta Oficial. 2007a. "Gaceta Oficial No. 38.785 de la República Bolivariana de Venezuela."

———. 2007b. "Gaceta Oficial No. 27.725. 1965. Ley de Partidos Políticos, Reuniones Públicas y Manifestaciones." https://pdba.georgetown.edu/Parties/Venezuela/Leyes/LeyPartidos.pdf.

———. 2009. "Gaceta Oficial No. 39.173. Ley de Partidos Políticos, Reuniones Públicas y Manifestaciones." http://historico.tsj.gob.ve/gaceta/mayo/070509/070509-39173-1.html

———. 2017. "Gaceta Oficial No. 6.322 de la República Bolivariana de Venezuela." https://pandectasdigital.blogspot.com/2017/08/gaceta-oficial-de-la-republica_59.html.

Gallegos, Raúl. 2016. *Crude Nation: How Oil Riches Ruined Venezuela.* Lincoln, NE: Potomac Books.

Galor, Oded. 2022. *The Journey of Humanity: The Origins of Wealth and Inequality.* New York: Random House International.

Gamboa, Suzanne, and Carmen Sesin. 2020. "Trump's Gains among Latino Voters Shouldn't Come as a Surprise. Here's Why." NBC News. https://www.nbcnews.com/news/latino/trump-s-gains-among-latino-voters-shouldn-t-come-surprise-n1246463.

Gamboa Gutiérrez, Laura. 2016. "Opposition at the Margins: The Erosion of Democracy in Latin America." PhD dissertation, University of Notre Dame.

Gans, Jared. 2023. "Sanders to Vote against Debt Bill, Says Biden Should Invoke 14th Amendment." *The Hill*. https://thehill.com/homenews/senate/4028921-sanders-to-vote-against-debt-bill-says-biden-should-invoke-14th-amendment/.

Garay, Cristian, and Juan E. Mendoza. 2014. "El choque de dos imaginarios geopolíticos en Bolivia: La 'Guerra del Gas.'" *Si Somos Americanos, Revista de Estudios Transfronterizos* 25(1): 115–39.

García, Madelein (@madeleintlSUR). 2018. "Acá lo que dijo Julio Borges a su llevada a la sede de cancillería 'no hay acuerdo.'" Tweet. 6:54 p.m. February 6. https://twitter.com/madeleintlSUR/status/961010303004749824.

Garfinkel, Michelle, and Stergios Skaperdas. 2007. "Economics of Conflict: An Overview." *Handbook of Defense Economics* 2: 649–709.

Garnica de López, Elizabeth. 1991. "La economía venezolana, algunos aspectos del programa de ajuste." *Economía* 16(6): 7–49.

Garthoff, Raymond. 1994. *The Great Transition: American-Soviet Relations and the End of the Cold War*. Washington, DC: Brookings Institution Press.

GASTAT. 2023. "Shares in Gross Domestic Product (GDP)." https://database.stats.gov.sa/home/indicator/436.

Gearan, Anne, Josh Dawsey, John Hudson, and Seung Min Kim. 2019. "A Frustrated Trump Questions His Administration's Venezuela Strategy." https://www.washingtonpost.com/politics/a-frustrated-trump-questions-his-administrations-venezuela-strategy/2019/05/08/ad51561a-71a7-11e9-9f06-5fc2ee80027a_story.html.

Gearan, Anne, and Anthony Faiola. 2017. "Trump Tightens Venezuela's Access to U.S. Financial System." https://www.washingtonpost.com/world/national-security/trump-administration-moves-to-restrict-venezuelan-access-to-us-financial-system/2017/08/25/18b22a5e-89ad-11e7-a50f-e0d4e6ec070a_story.html.

Geddes, Barbara. 1999. "What Do We Know about Democratization after Twenty Years?" *Annual Review of Political Science* 2: 115–44.

Gelb, Alan. 1988. *Oil Windfalls: Blessing or Curse*. Oxford: Oxford University Press.

Gelman, Andrew. 2024. "Decisions of Parties to Run Moderate or Extreme Candidates." September 11. https://statmodeling.stat.columbia.edu/.

Gerlach, Stefan, and Lars E. O. Svensson. 2003. "Money and Inflation in the Euro Area: A Case for Monetary Indicators?" *Journal of Monetary Economics* 50(8): 1619–72.

Gerring, John, Phillip Bond, William T. Brandt, and Carola Moreno. 2005. *Democracy and Economic Growth: A Historical Perspective*. Cambridge: Cambridge University Press.

Gil Fortoul, José. [1907] 1954. *Historia constitucional de Venezuela*. Caracas: Ministerio de Educación.

Global Nonviolent Action Database. 1923. "Germans Defend Ruhr Valley from French and Belgian Invasion (Ruhrkampf)." https://nvdatabase.swarthmore.edu/content/germans-defend-ruhr-valley-french-and-belgian-invasion-ruhrkampf-1923.

Goddeeris, Idesbald. 2007. "Western Trade Unions and Solidarność: A Comparison from a Polish Perspective." *Polish Review* 52(3): 305–29.

Goldhaber, Michael D. 2008. "Vulture Culture—Kensington International Litigated around the World to Collect on Bad Debt from the Congo Republic." *The American Lawyer*. September 1.

Gollin, Douglas. 2002. "Getting Income Shares Right." *Journal of Political Economy* 110(2): 458–74.

Gonda, Violet. 2013. "Constitutional Court Upholds Mugabe's July 31st Poll Date." http://www.cfuzim.com/2013/07/05/constitutional-court-upholds-mugabe-s-july-31st-poll-date/.

González, José, José del Nogal, and Roger Müller. 2012. "Venezuela: El voto electrónico. Auditorías y legitimidad del sistema automatizado de votación." *Espacio Abierto* 21(2): 305–21.

González, Juan. 1978. "Estados Unidos reconoce a China y rompe con Taiwan, en un cambio histórico de su política internacional." https://elpais.com/diario/1978/12/17/internacional/282697206_850215.html.

González, Luis. 2014. "27 de febrero de 1989: 25 años de un ciclo de conmoción social." *Reflexión Política* 16(32): 36–49.

González Deluca, María Elena. 2001. *Negocios y política en tiempos de Guzmán Blanco*. Caracas: Universidad Central de Venezuela.

Goodman, Joshua. 2020. "IMF Rejects Maduro's Bid for Emergency Loan to Fight Virus." https://apnews.com/article/420afb1fa856dedcc4cb3eddcd8ac0a2.

Gordji, Madjid, Gholamreza Askari, and Hamed Abdi. 2018. "Why Is a Boycott of the Elections a Bad Idea?" https://www.researchgate.net/publication/327099075_Why_Is_a_Boycott_of_the_Elections_a_Bad_Idea.

Gordon, Joy. 2011. "Smart Sanctions Revisited." *Ethics and International Affairs* 25(3): 315–35.

Gordon, Meghan, Eklavya Gupte, and James Bambino. 2019. "Dueling US Oil Sanctions Give India Unexpected Leverage." http://www.spglobal

.com/platts/en/market-insights/latest-news/oil/031419-analysis-dueling-us-oil-sanctions-give-india-unexpected-leverage.

Goshko, John. 1984. "Reagan Eases Polish Sanctions after Appeal from Walesa." https://www.washingtonpost.com/archive/politics/1984/01/20/reagan-eases-polish-sanctions-after-appeal-from-walesa/c72ff3f7-d0ea-4a80-85b2-9acc863ebac0/.

Government of Norway. 2024. "The Venezuelan Negotiation Process." https://www.regjeringen.no/en/topics/foreign-affairs/peace-and-reconciliation-efforts/norways_engagement/venezuela_negotiations/id2674295/

Graham, David. 2021. "This Is a Coup: A Mob Has Stormed the U.S. Capitol, Using Violence to Stop the Lawful Certification of the Electoral College Vote." https://www.theatlantic.com/ideas/archive/2021/01/attempted-coup/617570/.

Green, Adam. 2012. "Morgan Tsvangirai, Prime Minister of Zimbabwe." This Is Africa Online. https://web.archive.org/web/20130623055049/http:/www.thisisafricaonline.com/Policy/Morgan-Tsvangirai-Prime-Minister-of-Zimbabwe.

Green, Stuart. 2006. "Looting, Law, and Lawlessness." *Tulane Law Review* 81. Hurricane Katrina Symposium Issue.

Grimsley, Mark, and Clifford J. Rogers. 2008. *Civilians in the Path of War*. Lincoln: University of Nebraska Press.

Groharing, Brooks, and David McCune. 2022. "Benford's Law and County-Level Votes in US Presidential Elections." *CHANCE* 35(2): 4–10.

Grompone, Romeo. 1990. "Perú: La vertiginosa irrupción de Fujimori. Buscando las razones de un sorprendente resultado electoral." *Revista Mexicana de Sociología* 52(4): 177–203.

Groningen Growth and Development Centre. 2022. "Maddison Project Database 2020." University of Groningen. https://www.rug.nl/ggdc/historicaldevelopment/maddison/releases/maddison-project-database-2020.

Grossman, Herschel, and Minseong Kim. 1995. "Swords or Plowshares? A Theory of the Security of Claims to Property." *Journal of Political Economy* 10(36): 1275–88.

Grupo de Lima. 2017. "Declaración de Lima." Cancillería de la República de Colombia. https://www.cancilleria.gov.co/newsroom/news/declaracion-lima-8-agosto-2017.

Guaidó, Juan (@jguaido). 2020a. "Ha sido sancionada la petrolera rusa Rosneft Trading S.A. por ser cómplice de la dictadura. ¡Esta noticia es una victoria! Quien apoye al dictador, sea quien sea, venga de donde venga, deberá asumir las consecuencias. Serán bienvenidos quienes colaboren con la democracia." Twitter, February 18. https://twitter.com/jguaido/status/1229800340993794048?s=20.

———. 2020b. "Juan Guaidó PRESIDENTE DE VENEZUELA en el Foro Económico Mundial Davos 2020 / DISCURSO COMPLETO." YouTube, 1:17, January 23. La Nación Costa Rica. https://www.youtube.com/watch?v=oxh9WtM76Cg.

———. 2021. "Nuestro objetivo es salir de la tragedia y recuperar la democracia. En eso debemos mantener el foco. Nuestro adversario hoy es la brutal dictadura que enfrentamos. Este es mi mensaje al país." Twitter, May 11, 12:59 p.m. https://twitter.com/jguaido/status/1392162453195218947?s=20.

Guardian. 2017. "Venezuela: Man Set on Fire during Anti-Government Protests." May 21. https://www.theguardian.com/world/2017/may/22/venezuela-man-set-on-fire-during-anti-government-protests.

Guerra, José. 2021. *Venezuela: Anatomía de una catástrofe—Las políticas económicas de los gobiernos de Venezuela 1920–2020*. Caracas: Dahbar.

Gulotty, Robert, and Dorothy Kronick. 2021. *The Arbitrage Lobby: Theory and Evidence on the Political Economy of Dual Exchange Rates*. Cambridge: Cambridge University Press.

Gupta, Girish, and Matt Spetalnick. 2017. "U.S. Considers Possible Sanctions against Venezuela Oil Sector." https://www.reuters.com/article/us-usa-venezuela-pdvsa-exclusive/exclusive-u-s-considers-possible-sanctions-against-venezuela-oil-sector-officials-idUSKBN18V08P.

Gutmann, Jerg, Matthias Neuenkirch, and Florian Neumeier. 2017. "Sanctioned to Death? The Impact of Economic Sanctions on Life Expectancy and Its Gender Gap." ILE Working Paper Series 11. University of Hamburg, Institute of Law and Economics. https://www.econstor.eu/bitstream/10419/172437/1/ile-wp-2017-11.pdf.

Haggard, Stephan, and Robert Kaufman. 2021. *Backsliding: Democratic Regress in the Contemporary World*. Cambridge Elements in Political Economy. Cambridge: Cambridge University Press.

Hale, Henry. 2005. "Regime Cycles: Democracy, Autocracy, and Revolution in Post-Soviet Eurasia." *World Politics* 58(1): 133–65.

Halff, Antoine, Francisco Monaldi, Luisa Palacios, and Miguel Ángel Santos. 2017. "Apocalypse Now: Venezuela, Oil and Reconstruction." Center on Global Energy Policy, Columbia University.

Halpern, László, Miklós Koren, and Adam Szeidl. 2015. "Imported Inputs and Productivity." *American Economic Review* 105(12): 3660–3703.

Hancock, Landon. 2008. "The Northern Irish Peace Process: From Top to Bottom." *International Studies Review* 10(2): 203–38.

Harnecker, Marta. 2002. *Sin tierra: Construyendo movimiento social*. Madrid: Siglo XXI.

Harris, Sydney. 1986. *Clearing the Ground*. Boston: Houghton Mifflin Harcourt.

Hartzell, Caroline, and Matthew Hoddie. 2007. *Crafting Peace: Power-Sharing Institutions and the Negotiated Settlement of Civil Wars*. University Park: Pennsylvania State University Press.

Harvard Kennedy School. 2020. "Understanding the Venezuelan Crisis with Ricardo Hausmann." https://www.hks.harvard.edu/wiener-conference-calls/ricardo-hausmann.

Hausmann, Ricardo. 2017. "The Hunger Bonds." https://www.project-syndicate.org/commentary/maduro-venezuela-hunger-bonds-by-ricardo-hausmann-2017-05.

———. 2018. "The Venality of Evil." https://www.project-syndicate.org/commentary/venezuela-collapse-a-deliberate-choice-by-ricardo-hausmann-2018-07?barrier=accesspaylog.

——— (@ricardo_hausman). 2019. "Why did Venezuela oil production decline? Sachs and Warner believe that it was caused by the sanctions imposed on Venezuela in August 2017. The graph below shows the share of Venezuela in OPEC. Hint: Chavez came in 1999, dismissed 20,000 workers in 2003 & expropriated oil firms." Twitter, April 27, 8:36 a.m. https://twitter.com/ricardo_hausman/status/1122117200251367431.

Hausmann, Ricardo, and José Morales-Arilla. 2021. "What Should Biden Do about Venezuela?" https://www.project-syndicate.org/commentary/biden-strategy-on-venezuela-by-ricardo-hausmann-and-jose-morales-arilla-2021-03.

Hausmann, Ricardo, and Frank Muci. 2019. "Don't Blame Washington for Venezuela's Oil Woes: A Rebuttal." https://www.americasquarterly.org/article/dont-blame-washington-for-venezuelas-oil-woes-a-rebuttal/.

Hausmann, Ricardo, and Roberto Rigobón. 2003. "An Alternative Interpretation of the 'Resource Curse': Theory and Political Implications." In *Fiscal Policy Formulation and Implementation in Oil-Producing Countries*, ed. Jeffrey M. Davis, Rolando Ossowski, and Annalisa Fedelino, 13–44. Washington, DC: International Monetary Fund.

———. 2004. "En busca del cisne negro: Análisis de la evidencia estadística sobre fraude electoral en Venezuela." https://sumate.org/Elecciones/2004Revocatorio/20040903_analisis_evidencia_estadistica_fraude_electoral_venezuela_haussman_rigobon.pdf.

———. 2011. "In Search of the Black Swan: Analysis of the Statistical Evidence of Electoral Fraud in Venezuela." *Statistical Science* 26(4): 543–63.

Hausmann, Ricardo, and Francisco Rodríguez. 2014. *Venezuela before Chávez: Anatomy of an Economic Collapse*. University Park: Pennsylvania State University Press.

Hausmann, Ricardo, Francisco Rodríguez, and Rodrigo Wagner. 2006. "Growth Collapses." Center for International Development at Harvard University. CID Working Paper 136. https://wcfia.harvard.edu/files/wcfia/files/hausmann_growth.pdf.

Hausmann, Ricardo, and Miguel Santos. 2014. "Should Venezuela Default?" https://www.project-syndicate.org/commentary/ricardo-hausmann-and-miguel-angel-santos-pillory-the-maduro-government-for-defaulting-on-30-million-citizens--but-not-on-wall-street.

Havranek, Tomas, Roman Horvath, and Ayaz Zeynalov. 2016. "Natural Resources and Economic Growth: A Meta-Analysis." *World Development* 88(C): 134–51.

Havranek, Tomas, and Marek Rusnak. 2013. "Transmission Lags of Monetary Policy: A Meta-Analysis." *International Journal of Central Banking* 9(4): 39–75. https://www.ijcb.org/journal/ijcb13q4a2.pdf.

Heckelman, Joe C., and Hakan Berument. 1998. "Political Business Cycles and Endogenous Elections." *Southern Economic Journal* 64(4): 987–1000.

Hefeker, Carsten. 2001. "The Agony of Central Power: Fiscal Federalism in the German Reich." *European Review of Economic History* 5(1): 119–42.

Helliwell, John F. 1994. "Empirical Linkages between Democracy and Economic Growth." *British Journal of Political Science* 24(2): 225–48.

Hernández, Alejandro. 2020. "Si no hubiésemos demandado los bonistas habrían hecho una fiesta y tomado Citgo." https://lagranaldea.com/2020/11/16/si-no-hubiesemos-demandado-los-bonistas-habrian-hecho-una-fiesta-y-tomado-citgo/.

Hernandez, Clodovaldo. 2007. "Chávez se libra de las grandes empresas estadounidenses." https://elpais.com/diario/2007/07/01/economia/1183240802_850215.html.

Hernández, Igor, and Francisco Monaldi. 2016. "Weathering Collapse: An Assessment of the Financial and Operational Situation of the Venezuelan Oil Industry." CID Working Paper 327. https://www.hks.harvard.edu/centers/cid/publications/faculty-working-papers/venezuelan-oil-industry.

Hernández, Osmary. 2017. "Diálogo entre oposición y Gobierno de Venezuela queda en receso indefinido." https://cnnespanol.cnn.com/video/danilo-medina-dialogo-venezuela-republica-dominicana-indefinido-osmary/.

Hernández, Vladimir. 2014. "Venezuela: Cómo se ven las protestas en los bastiones chavistas." https://www.bbc.com/mundo/noticias/2014/02/140221_venezuela_crisis_bastiones_chavismo_az.

Hill, Fiona. 2021. "Yes, It Was a Coup Attempt. Here's Why." *Politico*. https://www.politico.com/news/magazine/2021/01/11/capitol-riot-self-coup-trump-fiona-hill-457549.

Hinich, Melvin, and Michael Munger. 1997. *Analytical Politics*. Cambridge: Cambridge University Press.

Hirshleifer, Jack. 1989. "Conflict and Rent-Seeking Success Functions: Ratio vs. Difference Models of Relative Success." *Public Choice* 63(2): 101–12.

Hobbes, Thomas. [1651] 2017. *Leviathan: Or the Matter, Forme and Power of a Commonwealth, Ecclesiastical and Civil*. Repr. Penguin Classics. London: Penguin Books.

Hoffman, David. 1986. "Reagan Vetoes Sanctions against South Africa." https://www.washingtonpost.com/archive/politics/1986/09/27/reagan-vetoes-sanctions-against-south-africa/af009ab1-2ed2-4e72-ab46-52fc2ec2d7e6/.

Holland, Heidi. 2008. *Dinner with Mugabe: The Untold Story of a Freedom Fighter Who Became a Tyrant*. New York: Penguin Books.

Honorio Martínez, José. 2008. "Causas e interpretaciones del Caracazo." *Historia Actual Online* 16: 85–92.

Houghton, N. D. 1929. "The Position of Unrecognized Governments before the Courts of Foreign States." *Indiana Law Journal* 4(8): 519–32.

Hsieh, Chang, Edward Miguel, Daniel Ortega, and Francisco Rodríguez. 2011. "The Price of Political Opposition: Evidence from Venezuela's Maisanta." *American Economic Journal: Applied Economics* 3(2): 196–214.

Hufbauer, Gary, Jeffrey Schott, Kimberly Elliott, and Barbara Oegg. 1990. *Economic Sanctions Reconsidered*. 2nd ed. Washington, DC: Peterson Institute for International Economics.

———. 2007. *Sanctions Reconsidered*. 3rd ed. Washington, DC: Peterson Institute for International Economics.

Hulten, Charles. 1978. "Growth Accounting with Intermediate Input." *Review of Economic Studies* 45(3): 511–18.

———. 2009. "Growth Accounting." NBER Working Paper No. W15341. https://www.nber.org/papers/w15341.

Human Rights Watch. 2002. "Zimbabwe: Fast Track Land Reform in Zimbabwe." HRW Africa Division, vol. 14, no. 1 (A). https://www.hrw.org/reports/2002/zimbabwe/ZimLand0302.pdf.

———. 2004. "Manipulando el estado de derecho: Independencia del poder judicial amenazada en Venezuela." https://www.hrw.org/es

/report/2004/06/16/manipulando-el-estado-de-derecho/independencia-del-poder-judicial-amenazada-en.
———. 2008. "Bullets for Each of You: State-Sponsored Violence since Zimbabwe's 29 March Elections." https://www.hrw.org/.
———. 2009. "False Dawn—the Zimbabwe Power-Sharing Government's Failure to Deliver Human Rights Improvements." https://www.hrw.org/report/2009/08/31/false-dawn/zimbabwe-power-sharing-governments-failure-deliver-human-rights.
———. 2015. "Venezuela: Curb Plan to Pack Supreme Court." https://www.hrw.org/news/2015/12/10/venezuela-curb-plan-pack-supreme-court.
Humphreys, Macartan, Jeffrey Sachs, and Joseph E. Stiglitz. 2007. *Escaping the Resource Curse*. Initiative for Policy Dialogue at Columbia: Challenges in Development and Globalization. New York: Columbia University Press.
Idrobo, Nicolas, Dorothy Kronick, and Francisco Rodríguez. 2020. "Do Shifts in Late-Counted Votes Signal Fraud? Evidence from Bolivia." University of Munich, MPRA Paper 105118. https://ssrn.com/abstract=3621475 or http://dx.doi.org/10.2139/ssrn.3621475.
ILKHA. 2019. "US Freezes Venezuela's $7 Billion Assets." https://ilkha.com/english/world/us-freezes-venezuelas-7-billion-assets-4883.
Imperiale, Johnpatrick. 2020. "Sanctions by the Numbers, U.S. Sanctions Designations and Delistings, 2009–2019." https://www.cnas.org/publications/reports/sanctions-by-the-numbers.
Imprenta Nacional. 2010. "Gaceta Oficial Extraordinaria N° 5.975." http://www.tsj.gob.ve/gaceta-oficial#.
———. 2013a. Decreto N° 9.381. Gaceta Oficial No. 40108. http://spgoin.imprentanacional.gob.ve/cgi-win/be_alex.cgi?Documento=T028700027761/0&Nombrebd=spgoin&CodAsocDoc=1709&t04=1&t05=png&SFmt=&TipoDoc=GCTOF&Sesion=427204265.
———. 2013b. Convenio Cambiario N° 22, Gaceta Oficial No. 40199. https://pandectasdigital.blogspot.com/2017/04/convenio-cambiario-n-22.html.
———. 2014. Convenio Cambiario N° 25, Gaceta Oficial No. 6122. http://spgoin.imprentanacional.gob.ve/cgi-win/be_alex.cgi?Documento=T028700013804/0&Nombrebd=spgoin&CodAsocDoc=798&t04=1-1&t05=png&Sesion=1302840233.
———. 2016a. Gaceta Oficial Extraordinaria 6225. https://mega.nz/file/vZ1GSbZR#ZEhmfOHdZUwtBu37u2DyHO35Ls0oZqBi8GrtV0BqLmk.
———. 2016b. Gaceta Oficial 40870 del 16 de marzo de 2016. https://mega.nz/file/yB920Trb#LoeTJKNWM_vZIA4Sq9fR-M9M94BL_-qVhmdal_viAHc.

El Impulso. 2013a. "Denuncian paralización de las obras del ferrocarril." August 21. https://www.elimpulso.com/2013/08/21/denuncian-paralizacion-de-las-obras-del-ferrocarril/.

———. 2013b. "Empresarios siguen esperando alternativa para obtener divisas." March 13. https://www.elimpulso.com/2013/03/13/empresarios-siguen-esperando-alternativa-para-obtener-divisas/.

———. 2015. "Balance de la Fiscalía sobre hechos de violencia entre febrero y junio 2014." https://www.elimpulso.com/2015/02/10/balance-de-la-fiscalia-sobre-hechos-de-violencia-entre-febrero-y-junio-2014/.

Indeo, Fabio. 2016. "Independent Turkmenistan in the Reshaped Geopolitical Scenario: Foreign Policy, Energy Strategy and Security Issues." *Il Politico* 81, no. 3 (243): 165–94. http://www.jstor.org/stable/45426844.

Infobae. 2017. "Oposición venezolana denunció que hay 1.600.000 votos en los que las huellas digitales no coinciden con las personas que sufragaron." https://www.infobae.com/america/venezuela/2017/10/23/oposicion-venezolana-denuncio-que-hay-1-600-000-votos-en-los-que-las-huellas-digitales-no-coinciden-con-las-personas-que-sufragaron/.

———. 2018. "La Constituyente de Maduro convocó a elecciones presidenciales antes del 30 de abril." https://www.infobae.com/america/venezuela/2018/01/23/la-constituyente-de-maduro-convoco-a-elecciones-presidenciales-antes-del-30-de-abril/.

———. 2019. "Nicolás Maduro: Gracias a Dios existe la dolarización." https://www.infobae.com/america/venezuela/2019/11/17/nicolas-maduro-gracias-a-dios-existe-la-dolarizacion/.

Integrated Network for Social Conflict Research. 2020. "Data Page." https://www.systemicpeace.org/inscrdata.html.

Inter-American Court of Human Rights. 2002. "El Caracazo Case, Judgment of November 11, 1999." University of Minnesota Human Rights Library. http://hrlibrary.umn.edu/iachr/C/58-ing.html.

International Foundation for Electoral Systems (IFFES). 2008. "Election for Zimbabwean Presidency." https://www.electionguide.org/elections/id/2076/.

International Monetary Fund (IMF). 2003. "Classification of Exchange Rate Arrangements and Monetary Policy Frameworks." https://www.imf.org/external/np/mfd/er/2003/eng/1203.htm.

———. 2006. "Methodology for CGER Exchange Rate Assessments." November 8. https://www.imf.org/external/np/pp/eng/2006/110806.pdf.

———. 2014. "Islamic Republic of Iran 2014 Article IV Consultation–Staff Report; Press Release; and Statement by the Executive Director for the

Islamic Republic of Iran." IMF Country Report No. 14/93. https://www.imf.org/external/pubs/ft/scr/2014/cr1493.pdf.

———. 2017. "Debt Sustainability Analysis." https://www.imf.org/external/pubs/ft/dsa/.

———. 2018. "Challenges to Steady Growth: World Economic Outlook." https://www.imf.org/-/media/Files/Publications/WEO/2018/October/English/mainreport/Text.ashx.

———. 2022. "IMF-WHO COVID-19 Vaccine Tracker." https://www.imf.org/en/Topics/imf-and-covid19/IMF-WHO-COVID-19-Vaccine-Tracker.

———. 2023a. "IMF Data: Balance of Payments and International Investment Position (BOP/IIP)." https://data.imf.org/?sk=7a51304b-6426-40c0-83dd-ca473ca1fd52.

———. 2023b. "World Economic Outlook Databases." https://www.imf.org/en/Publications/SPROLLs/world-economic-outlook-databases#sort=%40imfdate%20descending.

———. 2024. "World Economic Outlook database: April 2024." https://www.imf.org/en/Publications/WEO/weo-database/2024/April/weo-report?c=548,&s=NGDP_RPCH,PCPI,PCPIPCH,&sy=2014&ey=2029&ssm=0&scsm=1&scc=0&ssd=1&ssc=0&sic=0&sort=country&ds=.&br=1.

International Criminal Court (ICC). 2021. "ICC Prosecutor, Mr Karim A.A. Khan QC, Opens an Investigation into the Situation in Venezuela and Concludes Memorandum of Understanding with the Government." https://www.icc-cpi.int/news/icc-prosecutor-mr-karim-aa-khan-qc-opens-investigation-situation-venezuela-and-concludes.

Inter-Parliamentary Union. 1992. "Yugoslavia Parliamentary Chamber: Vece Gradjana. Elections held in 1992." http://archive.ipu.org/parline-e/reports/arc/2355_92.htm.

IPD Latin America. 2016. "Venezuela's O&G Industry: 2017 and Beyond." Presentation.

Iyer, Lakshmi, and Francisco Rodríguez. 2021. "Hyperinflation in Venezuela." University of Notre Dame. https://keough.nd.edu/publications/hyperinflation-in-venezuela/.

Jafari, Peyman. 2013. "Reasons to Revolt: Iranian Oil Workers in the 1970s." *International Labor and Working-Class History* 84, Special Issue 1.

Jarstad, Anna, and Desirée Nilsson. 2018. "Making and Keeping Promises: Regime Type and Power-Sharing Pacts in Peace Agreements." *Peace Change* 43(2): 178–204.

Jiménez, Maryhen. 2021. "Contesting Autocracy: Repression and Opposition Coordination in Venezuela." *Political Studies* 71(1): 47–68.

Jiménez, Raúl, and Manuel Hidalgo. 2014. "Forensic Analysis of Venezuelan Elections during the Chávez Presidency." *PLoS One* 9(6): e100884. doi:10.1371/journal.pone.0100884.

Johnston, Jake, and David Rosnick. 2020. "Observing the Observers: The OAS in the 2019 Bolivian Elections." Center for Economic and Policy Research. https://cepr.net/report/observing-the-observers-the-oas-in-the-2019-bolivian-elections/.

Jones, Lee. 2015. "South Africa: Sanctioning Apartheid." In *Societies under Siege: Exploring How International Economic Sanctions (Do Not) Work*, 52–90. Oxford: Oxford University Press.

Kaempfer, William, and Anton Lowenberg. 2007. "The Political Economy of Economic Sanctions." *Handbook of Defense Economics* 2: 868–905.

Kamm, Henry. 1982. "Pope Appears Set against Sanctions." *New York Times*, February 20. https://www.nytimes.com/1982/02/20/world/pope-appears-set-against-sanctions.html.

Kang, Songman. 2014. "Inequality and Crime Revisited: Effects of Local Inequality and Economic Segregation on Crime." *Journal of Population Economics* 29: 593–626.

Karl, Terry Lynn. 1987. "Petroleum and Political Pacts: The Transition to Democracy in Venezuela." *Latin American Research Review* 22(1): 63–94.

———. 1997. *The Paradox of Plenty: Oil Booms and Petro-States*. Studies in International Political Economy. Berkeley: University of California Press.

Karni, Annie. 2023. "House Is Paralyzed as Far-Right Rebels Continue Mutiny against McCarthy." *New York Times*, June 7. https://www.nytimes.com/2023/06/07/us/politics/mccarthy-house-republicans-mutiny.html.

Kasahara, Hiroyuki, and Joel Rodrigue. 2008. "Does the Use of Imported Intermediates Increase Productivity? Plant-Level Evidence." *Journal of Development Economics* 87(1): 106–18.

Kasparov, Garry. 2020. "Russian Democracy Is a Farce. Putin Wants the Same Fate for America." https://edition.cnn.com/2020/07/05/opinions/russian-democracy-is-a-farce-kasparov/index.html.

Kassai, Lucia. 2020. "U.S. Slaps Sanctions on Mexican Companies Helping Venezuelan Oil." https://www.bloomberg.com/news/articles/2020-06-18/u-s-slaps-sanctions-on-mexican-companies-helping-venezuelan-oil.

Kavakli, Kerim, John Chatagnier, and Emre Hatipoglu. 2019. "The Power to Hurt and the Effectiveness of International Sanctions." *Journal of Politics* 82(3): 1–17. https://www.researchgate.net/publication/337433176_The_Power_to_Hurt_and_the_Effectiveness_of_International_Sanctions.

Kelton, Stephanie. 2021. *The Deficit Myth.* New York: Public Affairs.

Key, Ramón. 2010. "La política petrolera, su interacción con la política económica y la incidencia del sector petrolero en la actividad económica interna en Venezuela." *Nueva Economía* 32: 153–94.

Keynes, John. M. [1919] 2012. *The Economic Consequences of the Peace.* Repr. Scotts Valley, CA: CreateSpace Independent Publishing Platform.

Kindleberger, Charles. 1991. "The Economic Crisis of 1619 to 1623." *Journal of Economic History* 51(1): 149–75.

Klumpp, Tilman, Hugo Mialon, and Michael A. Williams. 2015. "Leveling the Playing Field? The Role of Public Campaign Funding in Elections." *American Law and Economics Review* 17(2): 361–408.

Knutsen, Carl. 2012. "Democracy and Economic Growth: A Survey of Arguments and Results." *International Area Studies Review* 15(4): 393–415.

Kolb, Eberhard. 2004. *The Weimar Republic.* Trans. P. S. Falla and R. J. Park. London: Routledge.

Koneska, Cvete. 2014. *After Ethnic Conflict: Policy-Making in Post-Conflict Bosnia and Herzegovina and Macedonia.* Farnham: Ashgate.

Koopmans, Tjalling. 1965. "On the concept of optimal economic growth." In *Econometric Approach to Development Planning* 4: 225–87. Amsterdam: North-Holland.

Koulinka, Natalia. 2014. "Belarus and Its Flight from Democracy: Political Discourse and the People's Choice at the 1994 Presidential Elections." *Plural* 2: 33–53. https://ibn.idsi.md/sites/default/files/imag_file/33_53_Belarus%20and%20its%20Flight%20from%20Democracy_Political%20Discourse%20and%20the%20People%E2%80%99s%20Choice%20at%20the%201994%20Presidential%20Elections.pdf.

Koyama, Mark, and Jared Rubin. 2022. *How the World Became Rich: The Historical Origins of Economic Growth.* Cambridge: Polity.

Kraay, Aart, and Claudio Raddatz. 2005. "Poverty Traps, Aid, and Growth." World Bank Policy Research Working Paper 3631. https://papers.ssrn.com/sol3/papers.cfm?abstract_id=756944.

Kramer, Gerald H. 1971. "Short-Term Fluctuations in U.S. Voting Behavior, 1896–1964." *American Political Science Review* 65(1): 131–43.

Kramer, Mark. 1995. "Polish Workers and the Post-Communist Transition, 1989–93." *Europe-Asia Studies* 47(4): 669–712.

Kreike, Emmanuel. 2021. *Scorched Earth: Environmental Warfare as a Crime against Humanity and Nature.* Princeton, NJ: Princeton University Press.

Kremlin. 2017. "Russian-Venezuelan Talks." http://en.kremlin.ru/events/president/news/55769.

Krok-Paszkowska, Ania. 2001. "'Divided Government in Poland.'" In *Divided Government in Comparative Perspective*, ed. Robert Elgie, 127–45. Comparative Politics. New York: Oxford University Press.

Kronick, Dorothy. 2015. "Why Would a President Wreck the Economy before an Election?" *Washington Post*, December 4. https://www.washingtonpost.com/news/monkey-cage/wp/2015/12/04/why-would-a-president-wreck-the-economy-before-an-election/.

———. 2019. "A Backup Plan Is Needed to Prevent Venezuelan Famine." *New York Times*, February 28. https://www.nytimes.com/2019/02/28/opinion/venezuela-maduro-famine.html.

———. 2024. "On the Validity of Vote Counts Published by the Venezuelan Opposition." August 22. https://dorothykronick.com/28J.pdf.

Kronick, Dorothy, Barry Plunkett, and Pedro Rodríguez. 2023. "Backsliding by Surprise: The Rise of Chavismo." *Political Science Research and Methods* 11(4): 838–54.

Kronick, Dorothy, and Francisco Rodríguez. 2017. "15O: Fraud or Fatigue?" *Venezuelan Politics and Human Rights*. https://www.venezuelablog.org/15o-fraud-fatigue/.

———. 2023. "The Rise and Fall of the Venezuelan Economy." In *Roots of Underdevelopment: A New Economic (and Political) History of Latin America and the Caribbean*, ed. Felipe Valencia, 317–46. London: Palgrave Macmillan.

Krueger, Anne. 1974. "The Political Economy of the Rent-Seeking Society." *American Economic Review* 64(3): 291–303.

Krugman, Paul. 1979. "A Model of Balance-of-Payments Crises." *Journal of Money, Credit and Banking* 11(3): 311–25.

Kubow, Magdalena. 2013. "The Solidarity Movement in Poland: Its History and Meaning in Collective Memory." *Polish Review* 58(2): 3–14.

Kulish, Nicholas. 2012. "Poland Leads Wave of Communist-Era Reckoning." *New York Times*, February 21. https://www.nytimes.com/2012/02/21/world/europe/poland-leads-wave-of-communist-era-reckoning-in-europe.html.

Kurmanaev, Anatoly. 2019. "Venezuela's Collapse Is the Worst Outside of War in Decades, Economists Say." *New York Times*, May 17. https://www.nytimes.com/2019/05/17/world/americas/venezuela-economy.html.

Kurmanaev, Anatoly, and Lara Jakes. 2019. "With Tougher U.S. Sanctions on Venezuela, Bolton Says 'Now Is the Time for Action.'" *New York Times*, August 6. https://www.nytimes.com/2019/08/06/world/americas/venezuela-sanctions-bolton-maduro.

Kustra, Tyler. 2022. "Sanctioning the Homeland: Diasporas' Influence on American Economic Sanctions Policy." *Journal of Conflict Resolution* 66(3): 443–72.

Landauer, Carl. 1944. "The Bavarian Problem in the Weimar Republic: Part II." *Journal of Modern History* 16(3): 205–23.

Langer, Gary. 2023. "Blame Breaks Evenly If Government Defaults on Debt, Despite Preference for Biden's Position: POLL." https://abcnews.go.com/Politics/blame-breaks-evenly-government-defaults-debt-despite-preference/story?id=99085759.

Law 360. 2020. "PDVSA S.A., PDVSA Petróleo S.A., PDV Holding, INC, MUFG Union Bank, N.A, Americas LLC Case 1:19-cv-10023-KPF." https://www.law360.com/cases/5db8af143f4a3c044bb0461f.

Lawler, Dave. 2020. "U.S. Targets Russian Oil Giant in Escalating Campaign vs. Venezuela." https://www.axios.com/us-sanctions-rosneft-russia-venezuela-oil-exports-abe6f4ce-eebc-485d-86af-904921ed5306.html.

Laya, Patricia, and Andrew Rosati. 2017. "The Drug Kingpin Running Venezuela's Bond Negotiations." https://www.bloomberg.com/news/articles/2017-11-06/drug-kingpin-leading-venezuelan-bond-talks-has-a-violent-streak.

Laya, Patricia, and Nicolle Yapur. 2020. "Venezuela Reaches Out to Bondholders after Months of Silence." https://www.bloomberg.com/news/articles/2020-09-15/venezuela-reaches-out-to-bondholders-after-months-of-silence.

Lederman, Daniel, and William Maloney. 2008. "Does What You Export Matter?" World Bank. https://www.imf.org/external/np/seminars/eng/2013/spr/pdf/malo2.pdf.

Leebaw, Bronwyn. 2014. "Scorched Earth: Environmental War Crimes and International Justice." *Perspectives on Politics* 12(4): 770–88.

Lektzian, David, and Mark Souva. 2007. "An Institutional Theory of Sanctions Onset and Success." *Journal of Conflict Resolution* 51(6): 848–71.

Levitsky, Steven, and Daniel Ziblatt. 2018. *How Democracies Die*. New York: Crown Publishing Group.

Levin, Inés, Peter Ordeshook, R. Michael Alvarez, and Gabe Cohn. 2009. "Detecting Voter Fraud in an Electronic Voting Context: An Analysis of the Unlimited Reelection Vote in Venezuela." MIT Voting Technology Project. Working Paper 83.

Levitt, Steven D. 1994. "Using Repeat Challengers to Estimate the Effect of Campaign Spending on Election Outcomes in the U.S. House." *Journal of Political Economy* 1024: 777–98.

Lewis-Beck, Michael S., and Mary Stegmaier. 2013. "The VP-Function Revisited: A Survey of the Literature on Vote and Popularity Functions after Over 40 Years." *Public Choice* 157(3): 367–85.

Lindberg, Staffan. 2006. "Why Do Opposition Parties Boycott Elections?" *Journal of Contemporary African Studies* 24(1): 123–38.

Lipin, Michael. 2021. "US 'Monitoring' as Iran Sends Fuel Tankers to Venezuela in Defiance of Sanctions." https://www.voanews.com/a/usa_us-monitoring-iran-sends-fuel-tankers-venezuela-defiance-sanctions/6204325.html.

Lizzeri, Alessandro, and Nicola Persico. 2004. "Why Did the Elites Extend the Suffrage? Democracy and the Scope of Government, with an Application to Britain's 'Age of Reform.'" *Quarterly Journal of Economics* 119(2): 707–65.

López-Maya, Margarita. 2003. "The Venezuelan Caracazo of 1989: Popular Protest and Institutional Weakness." *Journal of Latin American Studies* 35(1): 117–37.

———. 2016. "La crisis del chavismo en la Venezuela actual." *Estudios Latinoamericanos* 38: 159–85.

———. 2018. "Populism, 21st-Century Socialism and Corruption in Venezuela." *Thesis Eleven* 149(1): 67–83.

Lora, Eduardo, and Mauricio Olivera. 2005. "The Electoral Consequences of the Washington Consensus." *Economía* 5(1): 1–61.

Lucas, Robert. 1988. "On the Mechanics of Economic Development." *Journal of Monetary Economics* 22(1): 3–42.

Lucena, Cristiane, and Laerte Apolinário. 2015. "Targeted versus Conventional Economic Sanctions: What Is at Stake for Human Rights?" *International Interactions* 42(4): 565–89. doi:10.1080/03050629.2015.1036989.

Lucena, Tibisay. 2003. "Las reformas en el sistema electoral venezolano y sus consecuencias políticas: 1988–1998." *Revista de Comunicação, Cultura e Política* 36: 245–65.

Lugo, Luis. 2017. "Almagro critica a la oposición venezolana por dialogar con Maduro." https://apnews.com/article/c7f8c518b6434c6fac55736a56b93847.

Luiguiger. 2012. "Comercial del Diablo en el Referendum Revocatorio 2004 Venezuela." YouTube video, 1:00. https://www.youtube.com/watch?v=i-yo-1TZDZM.

MacAskill, Ewen. 2006. "Bush Bans Arms Sales to Chávez." https://www.theguardian.com/world/2006/may/16/usa.venezuela.

Macchiavelli, Niccolò. [1513] 2009. *The Prince*. Ed. Tim Parks. Repr. Penguin Classics. London: Penguin.

Machado, María C. 2012. "María Corina Machado a Chávez: Expropiar es 'robar.'" Talentovenezuelaful, January 14. YouTube video, 2:57. https://www.youtube.com/watch?v=1kfs3T3mBJY.

Maduro, Nicolas. 2016. "Decreto N° 2.184. Gaceta Oficial de La República Bolivariana de Venezuela." https://elucabista.com/wp-content/uploads/2016/02/decreto-de-emergencia-econmica.pdf.

——— (@NicolasMaduro). 2019. "Comparto la "Carta Abierta al Pueblo de los EE.UU.," que está siendo firmada por el pueblo libre de Venezuela y elm undo. Vamos a entregarla en la Casa Blanca para exigir el respeto a nuestro derecho irrenunciable a la Paz." Twitter. February 7, 9:23 p.m. https://twitter.com/NicolasMaduro/status/1093681593875660801?s=20.

Magallanes, Manuel. 1997. "Leoni, Raúl, gobierno de." In *Diccionario de historia de Venezuela*, 2nd ed., 2:931–32. Caracas: Fundación Polar.

Magee, Stephen, William Brock, and Leslie Young. 1989. *Black Hole Tariffs and Endogenous Policy Theory*. Cambridge: Cambridge University Press.

Maingón, Thaís, and Heinz Sontag. 2000. "Los resultados de las elecciones de 1998 en Venezuela: ¿hacia un cambio politico?" *Revista de Ciencias Sociales* 6(1): 35–63.

Majchrzak, Sarah Graber. 2017. "The Gdańsk Shipyard: Production Regime and Workers' Conflicts in the 1970s and 1980s in the People's Republic of Poland." In *Shipbuilding and Ship Repair Workers around the World: Case Studies 1950–2010*, ed. Raquel Varela, Hugh Murphy, and Marcel Linden, 65–96. Amsterdam: Amsterdam University Press.

Manby, Brownen. 1992. "South Africa: The Impact of Sanctions." *Journal of International Affairs* 46(1): 193–217.

Mandler, Michael. 2000. "Interpersonal Comparisons of Utility and the Policy Paralysis Problem." *Social Choice and Welfare* 17(1): 95–115.

MariscalVoroshilov99. 2011. "Chávez aprobó Ley Habilitante de Costos y Precios Justos." YouTube video, 0:06. July 15, 2011. https://www.youtube.com/watch?v=HBFXhC8aduU.

Maritime Institute. n.d. "Maritime Economy—Statistic Review." Maritime Institute, Gdańsk.

Marks, Sally. 1978. "The Myths of Reparations." *Central European History* 11(3): 231–55.

———. 2013. "Mistakes and Myths: The Allies, Germany, and the Versailles Treaty, 1918–1921." *Journal of Modern History* 85(3): 632–59.

Marrero, Roberto (@Robertomarrero). 2016. "Este será el Orden del Día para mañana martes 26 de enero a las 2:00pm." Twitter, January 25, 12:21 p.m. https://twitter.com/robertomarrero/status/691664756411895808.

Martín, Eduardo. 2016. "Voto económico y comportamiento electoral en Argentina y Brasil (1985–2013)." *ACADEMO Revista de Investigación en Ciencias Sociales y Humanidades* 3(1): 1–27.

Martínez, Deisy. 2024. "Diosdado Cabello asegura que la oposición miente al decir que no pudo inscribir candidato." https://efectococuyo.com/politica/cabello-oposicion-plataforma-unitaria-candidato-cne/.

Martínez, Eugenio. 2017a. "Sobre los dos casos de fraude electoral denunciados ante el CNE; por Eugenio Martínez." https://historico.prodavinci.com/blogs/sobre-los-dos-casos-de-fraude-electoral-denunciados-ante-el-cne-por-eugenio-martinez/.

——— (@puzkas). 2017b."Se debe recordar que en presidencial de 2012 el 17% de electores (2.6 millones) votaron sin que de reconocieran sus huellas." Twitter, October 23, 12:25 p.m. https://twitter.com/puzkas/status/922499339943112705?s=20.

———. 2018a. "¿Qué propuestas discutieron el gobierno y la oposición en República Dominicana?" https://prodavinci.com/que-propuestas-discutieron-el-gobierno-y-la-oposicion-en-republica-dominicana/.

———. 2018b. "Sobre la ilegalización de partidos en Venezuela." https://prodavinci.com/sobre-la-ilegalizacion-de-partidos-en-venezuela/.

Martínez, Ibsen. 2021. "Venezuela: ¿petróleo por alimentos?" https://www.nytimes.com/es/2021/01/19/espanol/opinion/biden-venezuela-petroleo.html.

Martínez Meucci, Miguel Ángel. 2010. "La Mesa de Negociación y Acuerdos (2002–2003) y el proceso de facilitación de la OEA y el Centro Carte." *Politeia* 33(44): 47–88.

Masaka, Dennis. 2010. *Zimbabwe's Government of National Unity (GNU): A Panacea to an Economy in a State of Crisis?* London: Lambert Academic Publishing.

Maskin, Eric, and Jean Tirole. 1988. "A Theory of Dynamic Oligopoly, II: Price Competition, Kinked Demand Curves, and Edgeworth Cycles." *Econometrica* 56(3): 571–99.

Mason, David S. 1988. "Glasnost, Perestroika and Eastern Europe." *International Affairs* 64(3): 431–48.

———. 1989. "Solidarity as a New Social Movement." *Political Science Quarterly* 104(1): 41–58.

Matsuyama, Kiminori. 1992. "Agricultural Productivity, Comparative Advantage, and Economic Growth." *Journal of Economic Theory* 58(2): 317–34.

Matthews, Christopher, and José Córdoba. 2017. "U.S. Weighs Sanctions against Venezuela's Oil Industry." https://www.wsj.com/articles/u-s-weighs-sanctions-against-venezuelas-oil-industry-1501441035.

Matyszak, Derek. 2010. "Everything You Ever Wanted to Know (and Then Some) about Zimbabwe's Indigenisation and Economic Empowerment Legislation but (Quite Rightly) Were Too Afraid to Ask." Research and Advocacy Unit.

———. 2019. "Sanctions: The EU, US and Post-Mugabe Zimbabwe." http://www.veritaszim.net/node/3800.

Mayorga, Fernando. 2008. "El gobierno de Evo Morales: Cambio político y transición en Bolivia." In *Tendencias políticas actuales en los países andinos*, 21–39. Kyoto: Kyoto University.

McCabe, Andrew. 2019. *The Threat.* New York: St. Martin's Press.

McClatchy. 2019. "Bolton Announces U.S. Sanctions on Venezuela's State-Owned Oil Company." https://www.mcclatchydc.com/news/nation-world/world/latin-america/article225199605.html.

McCulloch, Allison, and John McGarry. 2017. *Power-Sharing: Empirical and Normative Challenges.* Routledge Studies on Challenges, Crises and Dissent in World Politics. New York: Routledge.

McDowell, Daniel. 2019. "How 'Sanctions Overreach' Could Undermine the U.S. Dollar's Dominance." https://www.worldpoliticsreview.com/articles/28418/ofac-sanctions-and-the-new-dollar-diplomacy.

McKeever, Amy, and David Beard. 2021. "The U.S. Capitol's Turbulent History of Bombings, Assassination Attempts, and Violence." https://www.nationalgeographic.com/history/article/united-states-capitol-building-turbulent-history-bombings-assassination-attempts-violence.

Mebane, Walter. 2024. "eforensics Analysis of the Venezuela 2024 Presidential Election." August 5. https://websites.umich.edu/~wmebane/Venezuela2024.pdf.

Mendoza, Mónica. 2017. "Guillermo Lasso insiste en un fraude y habla de 'gobierno ilegítimo.'" https://www.elcomercio.com/actualidad/guillermo lasso-fraude-resultados-electorales-oea.html.

Mendoza, Potellá, Carlos. 2017. *Nacionalismo petrolero venezolano en cuarto décadas*. Caracas: Banco Central de Venezuela.

Meneses, Juan, and Jose Saboin. 2021. "Growth Recoveries from Collapses." IADB Discussion Paper No. IDB-DP-880. https://observatoriodefinanzas.com/wp-content/uploads/Growth-Recoveries-from-Collapses.pdf.

Mercado, Edward. 2006. "Hugo Chavez 4 de Febrero 1992." YouTube video, 1:10, March 24. https://www.bing.com/videos/search?q=hugo+chavez+4f+1992&&view=detail&mid=000278CE272BBC2A11B2000278CE272BBC2A11B2&&FORM=VDRVSR.

Merkl, Peter H. 1981. Review of *Democratic Development, Breakdowns, and Fascism*, by A. James Gregor, Anthony James Joes, Charles Tilly, Gino Germani,

Juan J. Linz, Alfred Stepan, Raymond Grew, Reinhard Bendix, and S. N. Eisenstadt. *World Politics* 34 (1): 114–35. https://doi.org/10.2307/2010153.

Mesa de la Unidad Democrática. 2017. "En la consulta popular de este domingo participaron 7.535.259 venezolanos." https://web.archive.org/web/20170718053405/http:/www.unidadvenezuela.org/2017/07/la-consulta-popular-este-domingo-participaron-7-535-259-venezolanos/.

Meyer, Max, and Samuel Lourie. 1943. "Governments-in-Exile and the Effect in Their Expropiatory Decrees." *University of Chicago Law Review* 11(1): 26–48.

Milesi-Ferretti, Gian M., and Philip Lane. 2005. "A Global Perspective on External Positions." IMF Working Paper 05/161. https://www.nber.org/system/files/chapters/c0122/c0122.pdf.

Milesi-Ferretti, Gian M., and Assaf Razin. 1996. *Current Account Sustainability: Selected East Asian and Latin American Experiences.* NBER Working Paper 5791. https://www.nber.org/papers/w5791.

Ministerio de Relaciones Exteriores, Comercio Internacional y Culto de Argentina. 2019. "Reconocimiento del Presidente Encargado Juan Guaidó." https://www.cancilleria.gob.ar/es/actualidad/noticias/reconocimiento-del-presidente-encargado-juan-guaido.

Ministerio de Relaciones Exteriores del Peru. 2021. "Declaración del Grupo de Lima." https://www.gob.pe/institucion/rree/noticias/323547-declaracion-del-grupo-de-lima.

Ministerio del Poder Popular de Economía, Comercio y Finanzas (MPPEF). 2018. "Gobierno Central Presupuestario serie 1998–2009."

Ministerio del Poder Popular de Petróleo. 2019. "Ascienden reservas probadas de petróleo y gas de Venezuela." http://www.minpet.gob.ve/index.php/es-es/27-noticias-slider/912-ascienden-reservas-probadas-de-petroleo-y-gas-de-venezuela.

Ministerio del Poder Popular para la Comunicación y Información. 2012. "Giordani: La economía venezolana tiene potencial para crecer 10%." http://www.minci.gob.ve/giordani-la-economia-venezolana-tiene-potencial-para-crecer-10/.

———. 2017. "ANC juramenta a Tarek William Saab como nuevo Fiscal General de la República." http://www.minci.gob.ve/anc-juramenta-a-tarek-william-saab-como-nuevo-fiscal-general-de-la-republica/.

———. 2018. "Gobierno y oposición: Acuerdo de Convivencia Democrática por Venezuela (+PDF)." http://www.minci.gob.ve/gobierno-y-oposicion-acuerdo-de-convivencia-democratica-por-venezuela-pdf/.

———. 2019. "Presidentes y delegaciones del mundo llegan a Venezuela a la toma de posesión del Presidente Maduro." http://www.minci.gob.ve

/presidentes-y-delegaciones-del-mundo-llegan-a-venezuela-a-la-toma-de-posesion-del-presidente-maduro/.

Ministry of Foreign Affairs of Qatar. 2023. "Qatar Announces Successful Mediation between US and Bolivarian Republic of Venezuela on Prisoner Swap Deal." https://mofa.gov.qa/en/qatar/latest-articles/latest-news/details/1445/06/08/qatar-announces-successful-mediation-between-us-and-bolivarian-republic-of-venezuela-on-prisoner-swap-deal.

Ministry of Lands, Agriculture, and Rural Resettlement Zimbabwe. 2002. Land Reform and Resettlement Programme: Revised Phase II.

Misión de Observación Electoral Unión Europea. 2006. "Informe Final Elecciones Parlamentarias Venezuela 2005." https://aceproject.org/ero-en/regions/americas/VE/venezuela-ue-moe-final-parlamentarias-2005/view.

Mittal, Sonia, and Barry Weingast. 2013. "Self-Enforcing Constitutions: With an Application to Democratic Stability in America's First Century." *Journal of Law, Economics and Organization* 29(2): 278–302.

Mnookin, Robert. 2003. "Strategic Barriers to Dispute Resolution: A Comparison of Bilateral and Multilateral Negotiations." *Journal of Institutional and Theoretical Economics (JITE) / Zeitschrift für die gesamte Staatswissenschaft* 159(1): 199–220.

Modeni, Sibanda. 2014. "SADC Mediation in Zimbabwe's Global Political Agreement GPA: A Reflection on Opportunities and Complexities." *Africa's Public Service Delivery and Performance Review* 2(2): 21–51.

Mohsin, Saleha, and Peter Millard. 2020. "U.S. Sanctions Second Rosneft Subsidiary for Backing Maduro." https://www.bloomberg.com/news/articles/2020-03-12/u-s-sanctions-rosneft-subsidiary-for-backing-venezuela-s-maduro.

Moleiro, Alonso. 2015. "Nicolás Maduro debe renunciar a la Presidencia: Una entrevista a María Corina Machado por Alonso Moleiro." https://historico.prodavinci.com/2015/03/17/actualidad/nicolas-maduro-debe-renunciar-a-la-presidencia-una-entrevista-a-maria-corina-machado-por-alonso-moleiro/.

Molina, José. 2009. "La reforma informal del sistema electoral venezolano: De la representación proporcional al sistema mayoritario sin alterar una coma." In *Reforma del sistema electoral chileno*, ed. Arturo Fontaine, Cristián Larroulet, Jorge Navarrete, and Ignacio Walker, 139–64. Santiago: PNUD, CEP, Libertad y Desarrollo, Proyectamérica y Cieplan.

Mónaco, Miguel. 2017. "¿Por qué el presidente de la república no puede válidamente convocar a una constituyente?" https://elucabista.com/2017/05/02/presidente-la-republica-no-puede-validamente-convocar-una-constituyente/.

Monaldi, Francisco. 2017. "¿Llegó el lobo? Las sanciones petroleras y sus posibles consecuencias; por Francisco Monaldi." https://historico.prodavinci.com/blogs/llego-el-lobo-las-sanciones-petroleras-a-venezuela-y-sus-posibles-consecuencias-por-francisco-monaldi/.

Monaldi, Francisco, Igor Hernández, and José La Rosa. 2021. "The Collapse of the Venezuelan Oil Industry: The Role of Above-Ground Risks Limiting Foreign Investment." *Resources Policy* 72(C): 1–11.

Monaldi, Francisco, and Michael Penfold. 2014. "Institutional Collapse: The Rise and Breakdown of Democratic Governance in Venezuela." In *Venezuela before Chávez: Anatomy of an Economic Collapse*, ed. Francisco Rodríguez and Ricardo Hausmann, 285–320. University Park: Pennsylvania State University Press. https://doi.org/10.1515/9780271064628-012.

Montero, Daniel. 2021. "Comercial NO al Referendum Revocatorio contra Hugo Chávez en Venezuela 2004." YouTube video, 0:37, April 2. https://www.youtube.com/watch?v=-791uESUxO0.

Montesquieu, Charles. 1750. *The Spirit of Laws.* In *Complete Works*, vol. 1. London: T. Evans. First published in French as *De l'esprit des loix*, 1748.

Morales, David. 2017. "¡Mueran los golpistas! Discursos, ensayos y entrevistas del doctor David Morales Bello." https://davidmoralesbelloblog.files.wordpress.com/2017/10/mueran_los_golpistas.pdf.

Morales, Evo. 2006. "Adhesión de Bolivia al Alba." https://portalalba.org/documentos-alba/adhesion-de-bolivia-al-alba/.

Morales, Jose. 2019. "Sanciones: ¿causa o consecuencia de la crisis?" https://prodavinci.com/sanciones-causa-o-consecuencia-de-la-crisis/.

Morales, Maru. 2021. "Gobierno encargado depositó bono a 16.290 activistas de oposición en 2020 para defensa de la democracia." https://cronica.uno/gobierno-encargado-deposito-bono-a-16-290-activistas-de-oposicion-en-2020-para-defensa-de-la-democracia/.

Moreno, Vanessa. 2017. "Andrés Velásquez publica actas para demostrar que ganó gobernación de Bolívar." https://efectococuyo.com/politica/andres-velasquez-publica-actas-para-demostrar-que-gano-gobernacion-de-bolivar/.

Moret, Erica. 2021. "International Sanctions: Improving Implementation through Better Interface Management." Working Paper 01. https://www.swp-berlin.org/publications/products/arbeitspapiere/WP_International_Sanctions.pdf.

Morgan, Clifton, Navin Bapat, and Yoshiharu Kobayashi. 2014. "Threat and Imposition of Economic Sanctions 1945–2005: Updating the TIES dataset." *Conflict Management and Peace Science* 31: 5.

Mosolva, Daria, Jaren Kerr, and Hudson Lockett. 2023. "US Debt Ceiling Fears Knock Stock and Bond Markets." https://www.ft.com/content/89a3069d-f9ab-4c50-9be1-9494ffac668e.

Muhutdinova, Raissa. 2007. "Tajikistan." https://www.refworld.org/pdfid/4756ad5cd.pdf.

Mulder, Nicholas. 2022. *The Economic Weapon: The Rise of Sanctions as a Tool of Modern War*. New Haven, CT: Yale University Press.

Mullainathan, Sendhil, and Eldar Shafir. 2013. *Scarcity: Why Having Too Little Means So Much*. New York: Macmillan.

El Mundo. 2007. "El gobierno venezolano anuncia la adquicisión y nacionalización de la Electricidad de Caracas." https://www.elmundo.es/elmundo/2007/02/09/internacional/1170979956.html.

———. 2014. "Retiran los cargos de terrorismo y homicidio a Leopoldo López." https://www.elmundo.es/internacional/2014/02/20/53062e43e2704ed0468b457a.html.

Muñoz, Heraldo (@HeraldoMunoz). 2018. "En contacto permanente con Rep Dominicana. Enormes presiones para q Oposición venezolana firme papel que no contempla garantías elecciones presidenciales. Pdte Maduro en campaña, partidos opositores no validados, candidatos inhabilitados, etc. Algún partido chileno aceptaría eso?" Twitter, February 6, 10:56 p.m. https://twitter.com/HeraldoMunoz/status/961071019204202498.

Murphy, Kevin, Andrei Shleifer, and Robert Vishny. 1989. "Industrialization and the Big Push." *Journal of Political Economy* 97(5): 1003–26.

Murphy, Neil. 2020. "A 'very Fowle Warre': Scorched Earth, Violence, and Thomas Howard's French and Scottish Campaigns of 1522–1523." *War in History* 28(4): 715–35.

El Nacional. 2006. "Proclamado Hugo Chávez con 7.167.657 votos." https://web.archive.org/web/20061205233453/http:/www.el-nacional.com/Articulos/DetalleArticulo.asp?idSeccion=64&id=93586.

———. 2015. "En gaceta nuevos magistrados del TSJ." https://www.elnacional.com/venezuela/politica/gaceta-nuevos-magistrados-del-tsj_35603/.

———. 2018. "Iris Varela: Que no regresen nunca los venezolanos que se han ido del país." http://www.el-nacional.com/noticias/politica/iris-varela-que-regresen-nunca-los-venezolanos-que-han-ido-del-pais_223364.

———. 2023a. "Antonio Ecarri mantendría a Vladimir Padrino López como ministro de Defensa si gana las elecciones presidenciales." https://www.elnacional.com/venezuela/antonio-ecarri-mantendria-a-vladimir-padrino-lopez-como-ministro-de-defensa-si-gana-las-elecciones-presidenciales/.

———. 2023b. "Manuel Rosales pidió que eliminen sanciones para reactivar el sector industrial." https://www.elnacional.com/venezuela/manuel-rosales-pidio-que-eliminen-sanciones-para-reactivar-el-sector-industrial/.

Naím, Moisés. 1993. *Paper Tigers and Minotaurs: The Politics of Venezuela's Economic Reforms*. Washington, DC: Carnegie Endowment for International Peace.

———. 2017. "Así podría salvar Trump a Maduro." https://elpais.com/elpais/2017/07/22/opinion/1500736448_801513.html.

Naím, Moisés, and Francisco Toro. 2018. "Venezuela's Suicide: Lessons from a Failed State." https://www.foreignaffairs.com/south-america/venezuelas-suicide.

National Democratic Institute (NDI). 2023. "E-Voting Audits in Venezuela." https://www.ndi.org/e-voting-guide/examples/e-voting-audits-venezuela.

Neary, Peter, and Sweder van Wijnbergen. 1985. "Natural Resources and the Macroeconomy: A Theoretical Framework." UCD Centre for Economic Research Working Paper Series, 36. https://cepr.org/publications/books-and-reports/natural-resources-and-macroeconomy.

Nephew, Richard. 2017. *The Art of Sanctions*. New York: Columbia University Press.

Neuenkirch, Matthias, and Florian Neumeier. 2015. "The Impact of UN and US Economic Sanctions on GDP Growth." *European Journal of Political Economy* 40(A): 110–25.

Neuman, William. 2014. "Venezuela, in a Quiet Shift, Gives Foreign Partners More Control in Oil Ventures." https://www.nytimes.com/2014/10/10/world/venezuela-in-a-quiet-shift-gives-foreign-partners-more-control-in-oil-ventures.html.

———. 2022. *Things Are Never So Bad That They Can't Get Worse: Inside the Collapse of Venezuela*. New York: St. Martin's Press.

Newburn, Tim. 2021. "The Causes and Consequences of Urban Riot and Unrest." *Annual Review of Criminology* 4: 53–73.

New Humanitarian. 2001. "Mugabe Appoints Three New Judges." https://www.thenewhumanitarian.org/report/24020/zimbabwe-mugabe-appoints-three-new-judges.

New York Times. 1982. "U.S. to Pay Part of Polish Debt." https://timesmachine.nytimes.com/timesmachine/1982/02/01/162170.html?pageNumber=1.

———. 2017. "Trump Alarms Venezuela with Talk of a 'Military Option.'" https://www.nytimes.com/2017/08/12/world/americas/trump-venezuela-military.html.

Niskanen, William. 1971. *Bureaucracy and Representative Government*. New York: Routledge.

Nodal. 2014. "Maduro anunció nuevas medidas económicas: 30% será el margen de ganancia para cualquier actividad." https://www.nodal.am/2014/01/maduro-anuncio-nuevas-medidas-economicas-30-sera-el-margen-de-ganancia-para-cualquier-actividad/.

Nordhaus, William. 1975. "The Political Business Cycle." *Review of Economic Studies* 42(2): 169–90.

Norman, Thomas. 2009. "Cycles versus Equilibrium in Evolutionary Games." *Theory and Decision* 69: 167–82.

North, Douglas C., William Summerhill, and Barry R. Weingast. 1999. *Order, Disorder and Economic Change: Latin America vs. North America*. New Haven, CT: Yale University Press.

Noticiero Digital. 2015. "Marea Socialista: Venezuela debe declarar una mora en el pago de la deuda externa." https://web.archive.org/web/20210310185009/http://htr.noticierodigital.com/2015/02/marea-socialista-venezuela-debe-dejar-de-pagar-la-deuda-externa-de-manera-planificada/.

Notimerica. 2016. "Maduro declara 'en sesión permanente' al Consejo de Defensa de Venezuela." https://www.notimerica.com/politica/noticia-venezuela-maduro-declara-sesion-permanente-consejo-defensa-venezuela-20161026192756.html.

Nuclear Threat Initiative (NTI). 2020. "Global Health Security Index." https://www.ghsindex.org/.

El Nuevo Diario. 2018. "Gobierno venezolano dice que alcanzó acuerdo con oposición y que hoy se firma." https://www.elnuevodiario.com.ni/internacionales/455068-gobierno-venezolano-dice-que-alcanzo-acuerdo-oposi/.

Núñez, Adriana, and Kolster, Nicole. 2024. "'El chavismo tendrá en nuestro gobierno una puerta para participación,' candidato presidencial de Venezuela." Voice of America, May 22. https://www.vozdeamerica.com/a/chavismo-tendra-en-nuestro-gobierno-puerta-para-participacion-edmundo-gonzalez-candidato-presidencial-venezuela-/7622068.html.

Nuzzi, Laura, and Michael Dodson. 1999. "Political Bargaining and Democratic Transitions: A Comparison of Nicaragua and El Salvador." *Journal of Latin American Studies* 31(1): 99–127.

El Observador. 2018. "Asamblea Constituyente adelantó elecciones en Venezuela para antes del 30 de abril." https://www.elobservador.com.uy/nota/asamblea-constituyente-adelanto-elecciones-en-venezuela-para-antes-del-30-de-abril-201812315120

Obuchi, Richard, Bárbara Lira, and Daniel Raguá. 2016. "Microeconomic Binding Constraints on Private Investment and Growth in Venezuela." Center for International Development, Harvard University.

O'Donnell, Guillermo, and Phillipe Schmitter. 1986. *Transitions from Authoritarian Rule: Tentative Conclusions about Uncertain Democracies*. Baltimore: Johns Hopkins University Press.

Oeschlin, Manuel. 2014. "Targeting Autocrats: Economic Sanctions and Regime Change." *European Journal of Political Economy* 36: 24–40.

Office of Foreign Assets Control (OFAC). 2005. "Executive Order 13382." https://ofac.treasury.gov/media/8581/download?inline.

———. 2013. "Zimbabwe Sanctions Program." https://home.treasury.gov/system/files/126/zimb.pdf.

———. 2018. "505. If an official of the Government of Venezuela is designated as a Specially Designated National (SDN), does that mean that the Government of Venezuela is blocked? What are the prohibitions on U.S. persons dealing with a designated government official?" https://ofac.treasury.gov/faqs/505.

———. 2022. "General License No. 41." https://ofac.treasury.gov/media/929531/download?inline.

———. 2023a. "General License No. 44." https://ofac.treasury.gov/media/932231/download?inline.

———. 2023b. "General License No. 42." https://ofac.treasury.gov/media/931696/download?inline.

———. 2023c. "Recent Actions." https://ofac.treasury.gov/recent-actions.

———. 2024. "Filing a Petition for Removal from an OFAC List." https://ofac.treasury.gov/specially-designated-nationals-list-sdn-list/filing-a-petition-for-removal-from-an-ofac-list.

Office of the High Commissioner for Human Rights (OHCHR). 2019. "Preliminary Observations of the United Nations Special Rapporteur on the Right to Food, Ms. Hilal Elver, on Her Official Visit to Zimbabwe from 18–28 November 2019." https://www.ohchr.org/EN/NewsEvents/Pages/DisplayNews.aspx?NewsID=25348&LangID=E.

———. 2022. "Brazil: Criminal Proceedings against Former President Lula da Silva Violated Due Process Guarantees, UN Human Rights Committee Finds." April 28. https://www.ohchr.org/en/press-releases/2022/04/brazil-criminal-proceedings-against-former-president-lula-da-silva-violated.

Office of the Law Revision Counsel. 1977. "International Emergency Economic Powers Act (IEEPA)." Public Law 95–223, 50 U.S.C. §§ 1701–1706. U.S.C 50, Chapter 35. Office of the Law Revision Counsel. https://uscode.house.gov/view.xhtml?hl=false&edition=prelim&path=%2Fprelim%40title50%2Fchapter35&req=granuleid%3AUSC-prelim-title50-section1651&num=0&saved=L3ByZWxpbUB0aXRsZTUwL2NoYXB0ZXIzNQ%3D%3D%7CZ3JhbnVsZWlkOlVTQy1wcmVsa

W0tdGl0bGU1MC1jaGFwdGVyMzU%3D%7C%7C%7C0%7Cfalse%7Cprelim.

Office of the Spokesperson. 2020. "Democratic Transition Framework for Venezuela." https://2017-2021.state.gov/democratic-transition-framework-for-venezuela/index.html.

Oil for Venezuela. 2019. "A Humanitarian Oil Agreement for Venezuela: An Emergency Program to Protect Venezuelans from the Collateral Impact of the Country's Political Conflict." https://en.oilforvenezuela.org/wp-content/uploads/2022/02/Humanitarian-Oil-Agreement-PDF.pdf.

———. 2021. "Tackling Venezuela's Humanitarian Crisis." https://en.oilforvenezuela.org/wp-content/uploads/2021/04/OIL-FOR-VENEZUELA-2021-1.pdf.

O'Leary, Daniel Florencio. 1888. *Memorias del General O'Leary*. Caracas: Imprenta y Litografía del Gobierno Nacional.

Oliveros, Luis. 2020. "The Impact of Financial and Oil Sanctions on the Venezuelan Economy." October. WOLA. https://www.wola.org/wp-content/uploads/2020/10/Oliveros-report-summary-ENG.pdf.

Olson, Mancur. 1965. *The Logic of Collective Action: Public Goods and the Theory of Groups*. Cambridge, MA: Harvard University Press.

OPEC. 2020a. "Annual Statistical Bulletin." Organization of the Petroleum Exporting Countries.

———. 2020b. "Annual Statistical Bulletin, Section 3—Oil Data: Upstream, Table 3.5: World Crude Oil Production by Country." https://asb.opec.org/data/ASB_Data.php.

———. 2023. "Monthly Oil Market Report." https://www.opec.org/opec_web/en/publications/338.htm.

Organization of American States (OAS). 2001. Inter-American Democratic Charter. https://oas.org/charter/docs/resolution1_en_p4.htm#:~:text=In%20the%20event%20of%20an,situation%20and%20to%20take%20such.

———. 2003. "Acuerdo entre la representación del gobierno de la República Bolivariana de Venezuela y los factores políticos y sociales que lo apoyan y la coordinadora democrática y las organizaciones políticas y de la sociedad civil que la conforman." http://www.oas.org/OASpage/eng/Venezuela/Acuerdo052303.htm.

———. 2004a. "Auditoría de resultados del procesos de Referéndum Revocatorio Presidencial Venezuela." http://www.oas.org/documents/Venezuela/Referendo-OEA-CCarter.pdf.

———. 2004b. "Declaración de la Mision de Observación Electoral de la OEA sobre el referendo presidencial en Venezuela." https://www.oas.org/es/centro_noticias/comunicado_prensa.asp?sCodigo=C-003/04.

———. 2004c. "Jefe de la Misión de Observación Electoral de la OEA en Venezuela presenta informe sobre resultados del referendo." https://www.oas.org/es/centro_noticias/comunicado_prensa.asp?sCodigo=C-133/04.

———. 2017. "Statement of OAS Secretary General Luis Almagro to U.S. Senate Hearing on Venezuela." https://www.oas.org/en/media_center/press_release.asp?sCodigo=S-020/17.

———. 2018. "IACHR Warns about Lack of Adequate Conditions to Hold Free and Fair Elections in Venezuela." https://www.oas.org/en/iachr/media_center/PReleases/2018/112.asp.

———. 2019. "Electoral Integrity Analysis General Elections in the Plurinational State of Bolivia." http://www.oas.org/fpdb/press/Audit-Report-EN-vFINAL.pdf.

Orozco, José. 2013. "Venezuela Economy's 2Q Results to Show Growth, Tovar Says." Bloomberg Terminal.

Ortega, Daniel, and Francisco Rodríguez. 2008. "Freed from Illiteracy? A Closer Look at Venezuela's Robinson Literacy Campaign." *Economic Development and Cultural Change* 57(1): 1–30.

Ortiz, Roberto. 2016. "Hipólito Mejía Domínguez." https://www.cidob.org/biografias_lideres_politicos/america_central_y_caribe/republica_dominicana/hipolito_mejia_dominguez.

Ost, David. 1990. *Solidarity and the Politics of Anti-Politics: Opposition and Reform in Poland since 1968*. Labor and Social Change. Philadelphia: Temple University Press.

El País. 1990. "Vargas Llosa: 'México es la dictadura perfecta.'" https://elpais.com/diario/1990/09/01/cultura/652140001_850215.html.

———. 2009. "Chávez nacionaliza todos los negocios ligados al petróleo." https://elpais.com/internacional/2009/05/09/actualidad/1241820002_850215.html.

———. 2011. "El nuevo presidente anuncia elecciones legislativas en un año." https://elpais.com/internacional/2002/04/12/actualidad/1018562402_850215.html.

———. 2012. "Henrique Capriles gana las primarias de la oposición venezolana." https://elpais.com/internacional/2012/02/13/actualidad/1329101950_177206.html.

Pape, Robert. 1997. "Why Economic Sanctions Do Not Work." *International Security* 22(2): 90–136.

Pardo, Daniel. 2014. "Venezuela: Dentro de las protestas del #12F en Caracas." https://www.bbc.com/mundo/noticias/2014/02/140213_venezuela_caracas_violencia_protesta_12f_dp.

———. 2016. "Venezuela: En qué consiste el acuerdo anunciado en el diálogo entre gobierno y oposición (y por qué causó polémica)." https://www.bbc.com/mundo/noticias-america-latina-37965250.

Paredes, Norberto. 2024. "'Confiamos en que la magnitud de nuestra victoria será tan importante que abrirá incluso negociaciones con el gobierno': Edmundo González, candidato de la oposición en Venezuela." BBC Mundo, June 13.

Parra, Gastón. 1998. *De la nacionalización a la apertura petrolera: Derrumbe de una esperanza*. Zulia: Editorial de la Universidad del Zulia.

Parraga, Marianna, and Luc Cohen. 2020. "Venezuela ofrece grandes descuentos en medio del colapso de precios del petróleo: Operadores." https://www.reuters.com/article/venezuela-petroleo-descuentos-idLTAKBN20X36O?edition-redirect=in.

Parraga, Marianna, and Catherine Ngai. 2017. "Venezuela State Oil Firm's Credit Woes Spread to U.S. Unit CITGO." https://www.reuters.com/article/us-oil-citgo-pete-credit-exclusive/exclusive-venezuela-state-oil-firms-credit-woes-spread-to-u-s-unit-citgo-idUSKCN1BP2P2.

Parraga, Marianna, and Nidhi Verma. 2020. "PDVSA's Customers Schedule Last Oil Cargoes amid U.S.-Imposed Wind-Down." https://www.reuters.com/article/venezuela-oil-sanctions/exclusive-pdvsas-customers-schedule-last-oil-cargoes-amid-u-s-imposed-wind-down-sources-idUSKCN26E2YO.

Pascal, Alex. 2019. "Against Washington's 'Great Power' Obsession." https://www.theatlantic.com/politics/archive/2019/09/multilateralism-nearly-dead-s-terrible-news/598615/.

Pastor, Robert A. 1998. "Mediating Elections." *Journal of Democracy* 9(1): 154–63.

La Patilla. 2013. "Empresarios aún esperan sistema para obtener divisas tras eliminación del Sitme." https://www.lapatilla.com/2013/03/13/empresarios-aun-esperan-sistema-para-obtener-divisas-tras-eliminacion-del-sitme/.

Patton, Craig D. 1996. "Economics, Politics and Labor Protest in the German Inflation: The Tax Strikes of 1920 in the Chemical Industry." *Central European History* 29(1): 61–91.

PDVSA. 2016. "PDVSA anuncia el vencimiento y los resultados finales de sus ofertas de Canje de Bonos Senior de 5,250 con vencimiento en el 2017 y los Bonos Senior de 8,50% con vencimiento en el 2017 por Nuevos Bonos Senior Garantizados de 8,50% con vencimiento en el 2020." http://www.pdvsa.com/templates/pdvsa/img/bonos/bonopdvsa2017/Anuncio%20de%20resultados%20(PDF).PDF.

———. 2019. "The Ad Hoc Administrative Board of Petróleos de Venezuela, S.A. Announces Payment of the PDVSA 2020 Coupon." http://pdvsa-adhoc.com/notice3/.

———. 2020. "Histórico de producción 2008–2020."

Peinado, Fernando. 2011. "La diáspora venezolana que enriqueció a Colombia." https://www.bbc.com/mundo/noticias/2011/06/110607_colombia_venezuela_petroleo_fp.

Peksen, Dursun. 2009. "Better or Worse? The Effect of Economic Sanctions on Human Rights." *Journal of Peace Research* 46(1): 59–77.

Peksen, Dursun, and Cooper Drury. 2010. "Coercive or Corrosive: The Negative Impact of Economic Sanctions on Democracy." *International Interactions* 36(3): 240–64.

Peltzman, Sam. 1988. "How Efficient Is the Voting Market?" *Journal of Law and Economics* 33(1): 27–63.

Penfold, Michael. 2003. "Institutional Electoral Incentives and Decentralization Outcomes: State Reform in Venezuela." In *Federalism and Democracy in Latin America*, ed. Edward Gibson, 197–226. Baltimore: Johns Hopkins University Press.

———. 2017. "Could Economic Sanctions against Venezuela Backfire?" https://www.wilsoncenter.org/article/could-economic-sanctions-against-venezuela-backfire.

———. 2018. "Food, Technology, and Authoritarianism in Venezuela's Elections." https://www.wilsoncenter.org/sites/default/files/media/documents/misc/penfold_venezuela_elections_final.pdf.

Pennington, Matthew. 2017. "Trump Strategy on NKorea: 'Maximum Pressure and Engagement.'" https://apnews.com/article/china-ap-top-news-north-korea-asia-pacific-pyongyang-86626d21ea2b45c79457a873a747c452?utm_campaign=socialflow&utm_source=twitter&utm_medium=ap_politics.

Pennycook, Andres. 2013. "Movilizando identidades nacionales: De la Guerra del Gas a La Haya." *Acta Bioethica* 19(1): 71–86.

Pérez, Cecilia. 2020. "La inhabilitación de la candidatura de Rafael Correa generó reacciones de rechazo en la región." https://ladiaria.com.uy/politica/articulo/2020/9/la-inhabilitacion-de-la-candidatura-de-rafael-correa-genero-reacciones-de-rechazo-en-la-region/.

Pernia, Noé. 2016. "Chávez en 1998: Mi gobierno no será ni de izquierda ni de derecha." YouTube video, 9:13, February 4. https://www.youtube.com/watch?v=4jU9PrEWXSI.

Persson, Torsten, and Guido Tabellini. 2002. *Political Economics: Explaining Economic Policy*. Cambridge, MA: MIT Press.

Phlipot, Constance. 2010. "The Polish Case Comments from a Diplomatic Perspective." https://community-democracies.org/app/uploads/2016/09/The_Polish_Case_PDF.pdf.

Piatkowski, Marcin. 2013. "Poland's New Golden Age Shifting from Europe's Periphery to Its Center." World Bank. Policy Research Working Paper 6639.

Pindula. 2018. "Global Political Agreement." https://www.pindula.co.zw/Global_Political_Agreement.

Pitts, Pietro. 2014. "Venezuela Not Discarding Ramirez-Proposed Measures: Sanguino." Bloomberg Terminal.

Polga-Hecimovich, John. 2022. "Coaliciones reformistas y tipo de régimen: Una teoría del cambio electoral aplicada al Ecuador." *Revista Ecuatoriana de Ciencia Política* 1(1): 81–100.

Politicsweb. 2008. "Text of Zimbabwe Memorandum of Understanding." https://www.politicsweb.co.za/news-and-analysis/text-of-zimbabwe-memorandum-of-understanding.

Pons, Corina. 2017. "Exclusive: Small Puerto Rican Bank Halts Venezuela Correspondent Services: Source." https://www.reuters.com/article/us-venezuela-debt-bank-exclusive-idUSKBN1DM2QV.

Pons, Corina, and Christian Shepherd. 2018. "Venezuela's Maduro Travels to China in Search of Fresh Funds." https://www.reuters.com/article/us-venezuela-china-idUSKCN1LS2UL.

Pons, Corina, and Mayela Armas. 2019. "Banco Central Venezolano obliga a bancos a vender millones de euros en efectivo." *Reuters*, April 29. https://www.reuters.com/article/business/banco-central-venezolano-obliga-a-bancos-a-vender-millones-de-euros-en-efectivo-idUSKCN1S91ED.

Potthoff, Heinrich, and Susanne Miller. 1987. *The Social Democratic Party of Germany 1848–2005*. Bonn: Verlag J. H. W. Dietz Nachf.

Power, Samantha. 2003. "How To Kill a Country." https://www.theatlantic.com/magazine/archive/2003/12/how-to-kill-a-country/302845/.

Prados, Luis. 2013. "Maduro se atribuye la victoria y Capriles no reconoce los resultados." https://elpais.com/internacional/2013/04/14/actualidad/1365972053_885888.html.

Prensa Gobernación de Miranda. 2014. "Capriles: Si no hay problemas de divisas ¿Por qué aumentar la gasolina?" http://www.primerojusticia.org.ve/cms/index.php?view=item&cid=158:en-la-prensa&id=16419:capriles-si-no-hay-problemas-de-divisas-por-que-aumentar-la-gasolina&pop=1&tmpl=component&print=1&option=com_flexicontent&Itemid=500.

Presidential Commission on the Supreme Court of the United States. 2021. "Draft Final Report." https://www.whitehouse.gov/wp-content/uploads/2021/12/SCOTUS-Report-Final.pdf.

Prieto, Martín. 1985. "El general golpista Bánzer gana las elecciones a la presidencia de Bolivia." https://elpais.com/diario/1985/07/16/internacional/490312808_850215.html.

Przeworski, Adam. 1991. *Democracy and the Market: Political and Economic Reforms in Eastern Europe and Latin America*. Cambridge: Cambridge University Press.

———. 2008. "Democracy as an Equilibrium." *Public Choice* 1233(4): 253–73.

Przeworski, Adam, Michael Alvarez, Jose A. Cheibub, and Fernando Limongi. 1996. "What Makes Democracy Endure?" *Journal of Democracy* 7(1): 39–55.

PSUV. 2014. "Héctor Rodríguez condena plan fascista de sectores de oposición por ir contra la paz." http://www.psuv.org.ve/temas/noticias/hector-rodriguez-condena-plan-fascista-sectores-oposicion-por-ir-contra-paz/.

Pulido, Bernardo. 2021. "When Someone Decides before the Voter: Inadmissible Restrictions to the Right to Stand for Election." University of Notre Dame Law School.

Quah, Danny. 1996. "Empirics for Economic Growth and Convergence." *European Economic Review* 40(6): 1353–75.

Quevedo, Norbey. 2016. "La agonía de Pacific." https://www.elespectador.com/investigacion/la-agonia-de-pacific-article-612413/.

Quintero, Inés. 1997. "Amplia Base, Gobierno de." In *Diccionario de historia de Venezuela*, 2nd ed., vol. 2. Caracas: Fundación Polar.

Ramsey, F. P. 1928. "A Mathematical Theory of Saving." *Economic Journal* 38(152): 543–59.

Rasmusen, Eric. 2006. *Games and Information: An Introduction to Game Theory*. 4th ed. Hoboken, NJ: Wiley-Blackwell. 20.

Ratcliffe, Susan. 2011. *Oxford Treasury of Sayings and Quotations*. New York: Oxford University Press.

Reagan, Ronald. 1987. "Thursday, February 19, 1987." https://www.reaganfoundation.org/ronald-reagan/white-house-diaries/diary-entry-02191987/.

Red Agroalimentaria de Venezuela. 2020. "Resumen evolución la limitación del acceso a los alimentos por escasez. Red Agroalimentaria de Venezuela." http://redagroalimentaria.website/Dispon%20Demas/Res%20Acceso%20Escasez.pdf.

Reddy, Sanjay, and Camelia Minoiu. 2009. "Development Aid and Economic Growth: A Positive Long-Run Relation." IMF Working Paper. WP/09/118.

Reed, Stanley. 2014. "OPEC Holds Production Unchanged; Prices Fall." https://www.nytimes.com/2014/11/28/business/international/opec-leaves-oil-production-quotas-unchanged-and-prices-fall-further.html.

Regjeringen. 2021. "Memorando de Entendimiento." https://www.regjeringen.no/contentassets/d62443bc624041238af2902d356f949c/memorando-de-entendimiento.pdf.

ReliefWeb. 2022. "Segundo Acuerdo Parcial para la Protección Social del Pueblo Venezolano." https://reliefweb.int/attachments/62c7fbae-2c12-4bcb-a0c8-eac0479669ae/221126-26-november-agreements-merged.pdf.

Remmer, Karen L. 2003. "Elections and Economics in Contemporary Latin America." In *Post-Stabilization Politics in Latin America*, ed. Carol Wise and Riordan Roett, 31–55. Washington DC: Brookings Institution Press.

Resumen Latinoamericano. 2016. "El presidente Nicolas Maduro emitió su mensaje anual desde la Asamblea Nacional." https://www.resumenlatinoamericano.org/2016/01/15/32446/.

Reuters. 2015. "Venezuela, Russia's Rosneft Agree on $14 Billion Oil, Gas Investment." https://www.reuters.com/article/us-venezuela-russia/venezuela-russias-rosneft-agree-on-14-billion-oil-gas-investment-idUSKBN0OC2YF20150528.

———. 2017a. "Trump Threatens Sanctions If Venezuela Creates Constituent Assembly." https://www.reuters.com/article/us-venezuela-politics-usa-idUSKBN1A22EJ.

———. 2017b. "Valero Says Import Ban Would Send Venezuelan Crude to Other Markets." https://www.reuters.com/article/us-refineries-operations-valero-venezuel/valero-says-import-ban-would-send-venezuelan-crude-to-other-markets-idUSKBN1AC2E7.

———. 2018. "U.S.'s Pompeo Says Venezuelan Elections Were 'Political Farce.'" https://www.reuters.com/article/venezuela-election-usa/u-s-s-pompeo-says-venezuelan-elections-were-political-farce-idUSKBN28H212.

———. 2019a. "India Cannot Sacrifice Economic Strength to Comply with U.S. Sanctions: Finance Minister." https://www.reuters.com/article/us-india-economy/india-cannot-sacrifice-economic-strength-to-comply-with-u-s-sanctions-finance-minister-idUSKBN1WU31J.

———. 2019b. "U.S. Court Grants Stay in PDVSA Debt Cases Due to Venezuela 'Political Situation.'" https://www.reuters.com/article/us-venezuela-politics-debt-idUSKCN1SC29T.

———. 2020a. "Venezuela's Guaido Says Iran Fuel Shipment Ought to Alarm Latin America." https://www.reuters.com/article/venezuela-gasoline-iran-guaido/venezuelas-guaido-says-iran-fuel-shipment-ought-to-alarm-latin-america-idUSL1N2D2157.

———. 2020b. "Fact Check: Deviation from Benford's Law Does Not Prove Election Fraud." https://www.reuters.com/article/idUSKBN27Q3A9/.

———. 2021. "U.S. Judge Authorizes Sale of Citgo Parent Shares Despite Treasury Ban." https://www.reuters.com/business/energy/us-judge-authorizes-sale-citgo-parent-shares-despite-treasury-ban-2021-01-15/.

Reyes, Luz. 2015. "Así fue la 'noche más linda' de la oposición venezolana, en 17 año." https://efectococuyo.com/politica/asi-fue-la-noche-mas-linda-de-la-oposicion-venezolana-en-17-anos/.

———. 2016. "Fiscal Ortega Díaz reporta 97 detenciones con motivo de #LatomadeVenezuela." https://efectococuyo.com/la-humanidad/fiscal-ortega-diaz-reporta-97-detenciones-con-motivo-de-latomadevenezuela/.

Reyes, Reymar. 2022. "Capriles asegura que las sanciones fracasaron y se debe cambiar la estrategia." https://efectococuyo.com/politica/capriles-asegura-que-las-sanciones-fracasaron-y-se-debe-cambiar-la-estrategia/.

R4V. 2021. "Refugiados y migrantes venezolanos en la región." https://www.r4v.info/sites/default/files/2021-06/R4V_Stock_Jun21_Esp.pdf.

Riccardi, Nicholas. 2023. "Border Pressures Migrate North as Venezuelans Head to Denver." https://www.kunc.org/news/2023-01-10/border-pressures-migrate-north-as-venezuelans-head-to-denver.

Rivas, Federico. 2020. "Evo Morales responde a su inhabilitación electoral en Bolivia: 'No está garantizada una elección transparente.'" https://elpais.com/internacional/2020/02/21/america/1582310544_799603.html.

Rivero, Mirta. 2016. *La rebelión de los Náufragos*. Caracas: Editorial Alfa.

Rodríguez, Delcy (@delcyrodriguezv). 2023. "Entre los importantes logros de un 2022 de resistencia y grandes avances, Venezuela cerró con un crecimiento económico de alrededor del 15% del #PIB, el mayor de América Latina, impulsándose además la diversificación de la economía nacional." Twitter, January 14, 5:55 p.m. https://twitter.com/delcyrodriguezv/status/1614380737700012033?lang=es.

Rodríguez, Francisco. 2003. "Las consecuencias económicas de la revolución bolivariana." *Nueva Economía*, año XII, 19: 85–142.

———. 2006. "Caudillos, políticos y banqueros un ensayo sobre el surgimiento e incidencia de las instituciones económicas venezolanas." In *Crecimiento económico en Venezuela: bajo el signo del petróleo*, ed. Jose Gregorio Pineda and Francisco Sáez, 91–126. Caracas: Banco Central de Venezuela.

———. 2008. "An Empty Revolution: The Unfulfilled Promises of Hugo Chávez." *Foreign Affairs* 87(2): 49–58.

———. 2013. "Red Matter." Report. Bank of America Merrill Lynch.

———. 2014a. "Bandwidth and Bondholders." Report. Bank of America Merrill Lynch.

———. 2014b. "Low-Bandwidth Government." Report. Bank of America Merrill Lynch.

———. 2014c. "Venezuela Red's Adjustment." Report. Bank of America Merrill Lynch.

———. 2014d. "Why Venezuela Should Not Default." https://www.ft.com/content/6e350887-8b55-3150-9eb2-b17ae10fa6b0.

———. 2017a. "Venezuela This Week: Bond Wars." Report. Torino Capital.

———. 2017b. "Venezuela This Week: Where Are the Bonds." Report. Torino Capital.

———. 2018. "Crude Realities: Understanding Venezuela's Economic Collapse." https://www.venezuelablog.org/crude-realities-understanding-venezuelas-economic-collapse/.

———. 2019a. "Red Book: 1H2019." Report. Torino Economics.

———. 2019b. "Sanctions and the Venezuelan Economy: What the Data Say." LatAm Economics Viewpoint, Torino Economics. https://torinocap.com/wp-content/uploads/2019/06/Sanctions-and-Vzlan-Economy-June-2019.pdf.

———. 2019c. "Venezuela in the Dark." LatAm This Week, Torino Economics.

———. 2020. "What Is the True Balance of Forces in Venezuela's National Assembly?" https://franciscorodriguez.net/2020/01/11/what-is-the-true-balance-of-forces-in-venezuelas-national-assembly/.

———. 2021. "Toxic Conflict: Understanding Venezuela's Economic Collapse." Kellogg Institute for International Studies. https://kellogg.nd.edu/sites/default/files/working_papers/Rodriguez%20WP%20446%20FINAL3_0.pdf.

———. 2022a. "Es hora de aliviar las sanciones: Cuidado cómo lo haces." https://franciscorodriguez.net/2022/03/12/es-hora-de-aliviar-las-sanciones-cuidado-como-lo-haces/.

———. 2022b. "Sanctions and Oil Production: Evidence from Venezuela's Orinoco Basin." *Latin American Economic Review* 31: 6.

———. 2022c. "Sanctions, Economic Statecraft, and Venezuela's Crisis." Fourth Freedom Forum, Sanctions and Security Research Project. https://sanctionsandsecurity.org/publications/sanctions-economic-statecraft-and-venezuelas-crisis/.

———. 2022d. "Who Benefits from OFAC's Chevron License?" November 29. https://franciscorodriguez.net/2022/11/29/who-benefits-from-ofacs-chevron-license123/.

———. 2023. "The Human Consequences of Economic Sanctions." *Journal of Economic Studies* 51(4): 942–63.

———. 2024a. "A Deal That Could Save Venezuela." *New York Times*, August 7. https://www.nytimes.com/2024/08/07/opinion/venezuela-deal-political-crisis.html.

———. 2024b. "How Clientelism Works: Evidence from the Barinas Special Election." *World Development* 184 (2024): 106734.

Rodríguez, Francisco, and Adam Gomolin. 2009. "Anarchy, State, and Dystopia: Venezuelan Economic Institutions before the Advent of Oil." *Bulletin of Latin American Research* 28(1): 102–21.

Rodríguez, Francisco, and Guillermo Guerrero. 2020. "Toward Sustainable Human Development in Venezuela: Diagnosis, Challenges and Economic Strategy." *Revista Tempo do Mundo*, 23.

Rodríguez, Francisco, and Patrick Imam. 2022. "Political Growth Collapses." https://ssrn.com/abstract=4153885.

Rodríguez, Francisco, and Pilar Navarro. 2018. "¿Cómo moviliza votos el chavismo?" https://prodavinci.com/como-moviliza-votos-el-chavismo/.

Rodríguez, Francisco, and Jorge Rodríguez. 2019. "Venezuela's Powerless Revolution." https://www.nytimes.com/2019/03/26/opinion/venezuela-maduro-blackout.html.

Rodríguez, Francisco, and Jeffrey Sachs. 1999. "Why Do Resource-Abundant Economies Grow More Slowly?" *Journal of Economic Growth* 4(3): 277–303.

———. 2019a. "How to Avoid War in Venezuela." https://www.project-syndicate.org/commentary/plan-to-avoid-war-in-venezuela-by-jeffrey-d-sachs-and-francisco-rodriguez-2-2019-02.

———. 2019b. "An Urgent Call for Compromise in Venezuela." https://www.nytimes.com/2019/02/02/opinion/venezuela-juan-guaido-maduro.html.

Rodríguez, Francisco, and Cameron Shelton. 2013. "Cleaning up the Kitchen Sink: Specification Tests and Average Derivative Estimators for Growth Econometrics." *Journal of Macroeconomics* 38(B): 260–73.

Rodríguez, Gumersindo. 1986. *¿Era posible la Gran Venezuela?* Caracas: Editorial Ateneo de Caracas.

Rodríguez, Javier. 2020. "Venezuela: De los recursos a las reservas, de las reservas a la producción." http://www.debatesiesa.com/venezuela-de-los-recursos-a-las-reservas-de-las-reservas-a-la-produccion/.

Rodríguez, Jesus. 2005. "La apertura petrolera en Venezuela (1992–1999)." Thesis, Universidad de Los Andes, Mérida, Venezuela.

Rodríguez, Ronny. 2018. "Ortega Díaz: 'Me presionó Diosdado Cabello' para encarcelar a Leopoldo López." https://efectococuyo.com/politica/ortega-diaz-me-presiono-diosdado-cabello-para-encarcelar-a-leopoldo-lopez/.

Rodriguez Olivari, Denisse. 2014. "The Role of the Organization of American States in Promoting Democracy." https://www.idea.int/sites/default/files/publications/the-role-of-the-organization-of-american-states-in-promoting-democracy.pdf.

Rodríguez, Valmore. 1940. "Construyamos un país." Diario Panorama.

Rodrik, Dani. 1999. "Democracies Pay Higher Wages." *Quarterly Journal of Economics* 114(3): 707–38.

———. 2004. "Growth Strategies." John F. Kennedy School of Government. https://drodrik.scholar.harvard.edu/files/dani-rodrik/files/growth-strategies.pdf?m=1435073927/.

Roemer, John. 2006. *Political Competition: Theory and Applications*. Cambridge, MA: Harvard University Press.

Rogoff, Kenneth, and Anne Siebert. 1988. "Elections and Macroeconomic Policy Cycles." *Review of Economic Studies* 55(1): 1–16.

Romer, Paul. 1986. "The Economic Implications of Learning by Doing!" *Review of Economic Studies* 29(3): 155–73.

———. 1990. "Endogenous Technological Change." *Journal of Political Economy* 98.5: S71–102. http://www.jstor.org/stable/2937632.

Romero-Castillo, Evan. 2017a. "Deutsche Bank pone en riesgo su reputación." https://www.dw.com/es/deutsche-bank-pone-en-riesgo-su-reputaci%C3%B3n/a-38541387.

———. 2017b. "Venezuela y el concilio truncado de 2016." https://www.dw.com/es/venezuela-y-el-concilio-truncado-de-2016/a-40688746.

Ropek, Lucas. 2020. "Despite Risks, Some States Still Use Paperless Voting Machines." https://www.govtech.com/elections/despite-risks-some-states-still-use-paperless-voting-machines.html.

Ros, Jamie. 2000. *Development Theory and the Economics of Growth*. Ann Arbor: University of Michigan Press.

Rosales, Antulio. 2018. "Pursuing Foreign Investment for Nationalist Goals: Venezuela's Hybrid Resource Nationalism." *Business and Politics* 20(3): 438–64.

———. 2019. "Radical Rentierism: Gold Mining, Cryptocurrency and Commodity Collateralization in Venezuela." *Review of International Political Economy* 26(6): 1311–32.

Rosas, Pedro. 2017. "How Venezuela's Supreme Court Triggered One of the Biggest Political Crises in the Country's History." https://www.vox.com/world/2017/5/1/15408828/venezuela-protests-maduro-parliament-supreme-court-crisis.

Rosati, Andrew, and Noris Soto. 2016. "Venezuela Opposition Cancels Protest, Delays Political Trial." https://www.bloomberg.com/news/articles/2016-11-01/venezuela-opposition-calls-off-protest-delays-political-trial.

Rostow, Walt. 1959. "The Stages of Economic Growth." *Economic History Review*, n.s., 12(1): 1–16.

———. 1960. *The Stages of Economic Growth: A Non-Communist Manifesto*. Eastford, CT: Martino Fine Books.

Rousseau, Jean-Jacques. [1762] 2014. *The Social Contract*. Repr. n.p.: CreateSpace Independent Publishing Platform.

Royal Courts of Justice. 2020a. "Approved Judgement, in the High Court of Justice Queen's Bench Division Commercial Court, Cases Number CL-2019-000303, CL-2020-000304." https://www.italaw.com/sites/default/files/case-documents/italaw170681.pdf.

———. 2020b. "Approved Judgement, Court of Appeal (Civil Division). Cases Number A4/2020/1200 and A4/2020/1201." https://www.judiciary.uk/judgments/deutsche-bank-ag-london-branch-ors-v-central-bank-of-venezuela/.

Ruiz, Alejandro. 2008. "Chávez y la nacionalización del Banco de Venezuela." https://www.aporrea.org/actualidad/a61403.html.

Runrun.es. 2012. "Bocaranda lo cuenta todo: 'Hay un juego macabro de decir que Chávez gana.'" http://www.notiactual.com/bocaranda-lo-cuenta-todohay-un-juego-macabro-de-decir-que-chavez-gana/.

———. 2019. "Asamblea Nacional nombra junta directiva de Citgo." https://runrun.es/noticias/373983/asamblea-nacional-nombra-junta-directiva-de-citgo/.

Sachs, Jeffrey. 1994. *Poland's Jump to the Market Economy: Lionel Robbins Lectures*. Cambridge, MA: MIT Press.

———. 1999. "Resource Endowments and the Real Exchange Rate: A Comparison of Latin America and East Asia." In *Changes in Exchange Rates in Rapidly Development Countries: Theory, Practice, and Policy Issues*, ed. Ito Takatoshi and Anne Krueger, 133–54. Chicago: University of Chicago Press.

———. 2005. *The End of Poverty: Economic Possibilities for Our Time*. New York: Penguin Press.

———. 2020. *The Ages of Globalization: Geography, Technology, and Institutions*. New York: Columbia University Press.

Sachs, Jeffrey, and Andrew Warner. 1995. "Natural Resource Abundance and Economic Growth." NBER Working Paper W5398. https://www.nber.org/papers/w5398.

Sachs, Jeffrey, John W. McArthur, Guido Schmidt-Traub, Margaret Kruk, Chandrika Bahadur, Michael Faye, and Gordon McCord. 2004. "Ending Africa's Poverty Trap." *Brookings Papers on Eonomic Activity* 1: 117–24.

Saikowski, Charlotte. 1983. "US Reviews Sanctions on Poland after Lech Walesa's Call for Aid." https://www.csmonitor.com/1983/1214/121442.html.

Sala-i-Martin, Xavier, Gernot Doppelhofer, and Ronald Miller. 2004. "Determinants of Long-Term Growth: A Bayesian Averaging of Classical Estimates (BACE) Approach." *American Economic Review* 92(4): 813–35.

Sala-i-Martin, Xavier, and Arvind Subramanian. 2003. "Addressing the Natural Resource Curse: An Illustration from Nigeria." NBER Working Paper 9804. https://www.imf.org/external/pubs/ft/wp/2003/wp03139.pdf.

Sánchez, Fabiola. 2019. "Detienen al vicepresidente de Asamblea Nacional venezolana." https://apnews.com/article/0d2a77c2337040b680ff427a87c59d8a.

Sánchez, Fabiola, and Joshua Goodman. 2017. "Venezuela's Maduro Vows to Punish Opponents for US Sanctions." https://apnews.com/article/27a9d02c27aa46028e310c4f97e31a9e.

Santos, Miguel (@miguelsantos12). 2019. "The 'systematic evidence' presented by Weisbrot and Sachs includes a chart 'showing' pre-sanctions Venezuela and Colombia's 'parallel trajectories' in oil output. Except that they altered the scale, to make them look similar. Here is the same info, on the same scale." Twitter, April 26, 6:51 p.m. https://twitter.com/miguelsantos12/status/1121909801750020096.

Sarkees, Meredith Reid, and Frank Wayman. 2010. *Resort to War: 1816–2007*. Washington DC: CQ Press.

Schmidt, Julia. 2022. "The Legality of Unilateral Extra-Territorial Sanctions under International Law." *Conflict & Security Law* 27(1): 53–81.

Schumpeter, Joseph. 1909. "On the Concept of Social Value." *Quarterly Journal of Economics* 23(2): 213–32.

Secretary Pompeo (@SecPompeo). 2018. "Watching #Venezuela today. Sham elections change nothing. We need Venezuelan people running this country . . . a nation with so much to offer the world. We call on the government to free #JoshHolt." Twitter, May 20, 1:31 p.m. https://twitter.com/SecPompeo/status/998254964408545283?ref_src=twsrc%5Etfw%7Ctwcamp%5Etweetembed%7Ctwterm%5E998254964408545283%7Ctwgr%5E0606282f97a01a295d6fc74686524540c353ea90%7Ctwcon%5Es1_&ref_url=https%3A%2F%2Fwww.cbsnews.com%2Fnews%2Fvenezuela-elections-nicolas-maduro-dismissed-by-us-donald-trump-admin-as-sham%2F.

Sequera, Vivian, and Brian Ellsworth. 2020. "Líder opositor Guaidó busca que Europa frene tráfico de 'oro de sangre' venezolano." https://www.reuters.com/article/venezuela-politica-guaido-idLTAKBN1Z82HT.

Serra, Gilles. 2016. "Comprar, coaccionar y desinformar al votante: Problemas duraderos de la democracia mexicana." *Política y Gobierno* XXIII(2): 409–35.

Serrano, Alfredo. 2014. *Pensamiento económico de Hugo Chávez*. Quito: Editorial IAEN.

———. 2016. "Venezuela frente a la emergencia económica." https://www.celag.org/venezuela-frente-a-la-emergencia-economica-por-alfredo-serrano-mancilla/.

Shabani, Rachel. 2020. "Venezuela: Socialism, Hyperinflation, and Economic Collapse." https://www.aier.org/research/venezuela-socialism-hyperinflation-and-economic-collapse/amp/?gclid=CjwKCAiA3KefBhByEiwAi2LDHLktr67mCERb_T7n_Wlci8ix8ZM1XG4uJOQFLJ2bNgFxIOUZ33vbKhoCun0QAvD_BwE.

Shagabutdinova, Ella, and Jeffrey Berejikian. 2007. "Deploying Sanctions While Protecting Human Rights: Are Humanitarian 'Smart' Sanctions Effective?" *Journal of Human Right* 6(1): 59–74.

Shakespeare, William. [1600] 2009. *Henry IV, Part 2*. Ed. Barbara Mowat and Paul Werstine. Oxford: Oxford University Press.

Shi, Min, and Jakob Svensson. 2006. "Political Budget Cycles: Do They Differ across Countries and Why?" *Journal of Public Economics* 90(8–9): 1367–89.

Shugart, Mathew, and John Carey. 1995. *Presidents and Assemblies: Constitutional Design and Electoral Dynamics*. Cambridge: Cambridge University Press.

Simpson, Mark, and Tony Hawkins. 2018. *The Primacy of Regime Survival*. London: Palgrave Macmillan.

Singer, Matthew, and Gabriela Ramalho. 2012. "Voter Behavior in Latin America." *Oxford Research Encyclopedia*. Oxford: Oxford University Press.

Singh, Shane P. 2019. "Compulsory Voting and Parties' Vote-Seeking Strategies." *American Journal of Political Science* 63: 37–52.

Sisk, Timothy D. 2013. "Power-Sharing in Civil War: Puzzles of Peacemaking and Peacebuilding." *Civil Wars* 15(1): 7–20.

Skórzyński, Jan. 2010. "From Solidarity to Freedom: Democratic Systemic Transformation in Poland." Permanent Secretariat of the Community of Democracies. http://www.community-democracies.org/app/uploads/2016/09/The_Polish_Case_PDF.pdf.

Smilde, David. 2014. "From Partial to Full Conflict Theory: A Neo-Weberian Perspective on Post-Neoliberal Venezuela." https://amc.sas.upenn.edu/sites/default/files/Smilde%20-%20From%20Partial%20to%20Full%20Conflict%20Theory.pdf.

Smilde, David, and Geoff Ramsey. 2017. "Reactions to New US Economic Sanctions on Venezuela." https://www.venezuelablog.org/reactions-new-us-economic-sanctions-venezuela/.

———. 2020. "International Peacemaking in Venezuela's Intractable Conflict." *European Review of Latin American and Caribbean Studies* 10(9): 157–79.

Smith, Adam. [1776] 1982. *An Inquiry into the Nature and Causes of the Wealth of Nations*. Repr. Indianapolis: Liberty Fund.

Smith, Benjamin, and David Waldner. 2021. *Rethinking the Resource Curse*. Elements in the Politics of Development. Cambridge: Cambridge University Press.

Smith, Janeth. 1987. "Trade Credit and Informational Assymetry." *Journal of Finance* 42(4): 863–72.

Solow, Robert. 1956: "A Contribution to the Theory of Economic Growth." *Quarterly Journal of Economics* 70(1): 65–94.

Sosa Abascal, Arturo. 1995. *Rómulo Betancourt y el Partido del Pueblo*. Caracas: Editorial Fundación Rómulo Betancourt.

Spetalnick, Matt, Vivian Sequera, and Mayela Armas. 2023. "US Tells UN It Will Shield Venezuela Humanitarian Fund from Creditors." https://www.reuters.com/world/americas/us-tells-un-it-will-shield-venezuela-humanitarian-fund-creditors-sources-2023-05-18/.

Splinter, Melody, and Jeroen Klomp. 2021. "Do Sanctions Cause Economic Growth?" *NL ARMS: Netherlands Annual Review of Military Studies*, 115–32.

Staniszkis, Jadwiga. 1981. "The Evolution of Forms of Working-Class Protest in Poland: Sociological Reflections on the Gdansk-Szczecin Case, August 1980." *Soviet Studies* 33(2): 204–31.

Stegmaier, Mary, Michael S. Lewis-Beck, and Beomseob Park. 2017. "The VP-Function: A Review." In *The SAGE Handbook of Electoral Behaviour*, 584–605. London: SAGE Publications.

Stigler, George. 1971. "The Theory of Economic Regulation." *Bell Journal of Economics and Management Science* 2(1): 3–21.

Stokes, Susan. 2005. "Perverse Accountability: A Formal Model of Machine Politics with Evidence from Argentina." *American Political Science Review* 99(3): 315–25.

Sturzenneger, Federico, and Jeromin Zettelmeyer. 2006. *Debt Defaults and Lessons from a Decade of Crises*. Cambridge, MA: MIT Press.

Svolik, Milan. 2019. "Democracy as an Equilibrium: Rational Choice and Formal Political Theory in Democratization Research." *Democratization* 26(1): 40–60.

Swann, T. W. 1956. "Economic Growth and Capital Accumulation." *Economic Record* 32(2): 334–61.

Syrquin, Moshe. 1987. "Growth Accounting with Intermediate Inputs and the Transmission of Technical Change." *Journal of Development Economics* 26(1): 17–23.

Szentgáli-Tóth, Boldizsar. 2020. "Organic Laws and the Principle of Democracy in France and Spain." *Pro Futuro* 9(4): 61–76.

Tal Cual. 2018a. "Este es el acuerdo que la oposición se negó a firmar en República Dominicana." https://talcualdigital.com/este-es-el-acuerdo-que-el-gobierno-queria-que-firmara-la-oposicion/.

———. 2018b. "Primero Justicia no logra validarse y llama a hacerlo en proceso de reparos." https://talcualdigital.com/primero-justicia-no-logra-validarse-y-llama-a-hacerlo-en-proceso-de-reparos/.

———. 2019. "Gobierno de Maduro excarceló a varios presos políticos este #17Oct." https://talcualdigital.com/ministerio-publico-anuncia-liberacion-de-24-presos-politicos/.

———. 2024. "Machado y Plataforma Unitaria: Persiste bloqueo para postulación de candidata Yoris." https://talcualdigital.com/machado-y-plataforma-unitaria-persiste-bloqueo-para-postulacion-de-candidata-yoris/.

Talmon, Stefan. 1998. *Recognition of Governments in International Law: With Particular Reference to Governments in Exile.* Oxford: Clarendon Press.

Tan, Andrea. 2018. "Goldman Lunch at Taste Paradise Sets Table for 1MDB Money Probe." *Bloomberg*, June 27. https://www.bloomberg.com/news/articles/2018-06-27/goldman-lunch-at-taste-paradise-sets-table-for-1mdb-money-probe.

Tatum, Jeffrey. 1999. *The Patrician Tribune: Publius Clodius Pulcher.* Chapel Hill: University of North Carolina Press.

Tavares, José, and Romain Wacziarg. 2001. "How Democracy Affects Growth." *European Economic Review* 45(8): 1341–78.

Taylor, Fred. 2013. *The Downfall of Money: Germany's Hyperinflation and the Destruction of the Middle Class.* London: Bloomsbury.

Telesur. 2015. "PSUV pide investigar compra de votos de la oposición." https://www.telesurtv.net/news/Gobierno-venezolano-revela-delitos-electorales-de-la-oposicion-20151216-0035.html.

———. 2016a. "El presidente Nicolás Maduro recurrió a la Constitución de Venezuela y convocó a los poderes públicos de ese país a una reunión el próximo miércoles." https://www.telesurtv.net/news/Consejo-de-Seguridad-de-Venezuela-evaluara-intento-de-golpe-20161025-0046.html.

———. 2016b. "Venezuela e India firman acuerdos en materia de hidrocarburos." https://www.telesurtv.net/news/Venezuela-e-India-firman-acuerdos-en-materia-de-hidrocarburos-20161104-0026.html.

———. 2018. "Declaraciones de Jorge Rodríguez, 6 febrero 2018: Borges no firmó tras llamada de Rex Tillerson, Luigino Bracci Roa–Situación en

Venezuela." Youtube video, 14:08. February 7. https://www.youtube.com/watch?v=vcpkBvQDczU.

Thomas, Landon, Jr. 2017. "Goldman Buys $2.8 Billion Worth of Venezuelan Bonds, and an Uproar Begins." https://www.nytimes.com/2017/05/30/business/dealbook/goldman-buys-2-8-billion-worth-of-venezuelan-bonds-and-an-uproar-begins.html.

Thörnqvist, Leo. 1936. "The Bank of Finland's Consumption Price Index." *Bank of Finland Monthly Bulletin* 10: 1–8.

Tinker Salas, Miguel, Gilbert M. Joseph, and Emily S. Rosenberg. 2009. *The Enduring Legacy: Oil, Culture, and Society in Venezuela*. Durham, NC: Duke University Press.

Todo Chávez en la Web. 1999. "Toma de posesión del Comandante Presidente Hugo Rafael Chávez Frías." http://todochavez.gob.ve/todochavez/3013-toma-de-posesion-del-comandante-presidente-hugo-rafael-chavez-frias.

Tollison, Robert. 1988. "Public Choice and Legislation." *Virginia Law Review* 74(2): 339–71.

Tornell, Aaron, and Philip Lane. 1999. "The Voracity Effect." *American Economic Review* 89(1): 22–46.

Toro, Francisco. 2012. "About Fraud." https://www.caracaschronicles.com/2012/08/13/about-fraud/.

———. 2015. "Hate CNE? Love a Witness." https://www.caracaschronicles.com/2015/05/12/hate-cne-then-love-a-witness/.

———. 2016. "Chávez, Maduro and the Ascendancy of the Arbitrageur Kleptolobby." https://www.caracaschronicles.com/2016/02/11/maduro-and-the-triumph-of-the-arbitrage-lobby/.

———. 2017. "The Great Currency Swindle." *World Today*, October–November, 30–31.

Torre, Mario. 2014. "Bolivia: Nuevo sistema electoral presidencial y coordinación política de los partidos." *Perfiles Latinoamericanos* 4(3): 77–102.

———. 2023. "¿Cómo dejar de temer en el sistema de voto automatizado y utilizarlo para el beneficio de la alternativa democrática?" https://puzkas.com/dejar-temor-sistema-voto-automatizado-alternativa-democratica/.

Transparencia Electoral. 2017. "'Consideraciones sobre una Constituyente' por Vicente Díaz." https://transparenciaelectoral.org/consideraciones-sobre-una-constituyente-por-vicente-diaz/.

Treue, Wolfgang. 1954. *Deutsche Parteiprogramme 1861–1954*. Gottingen: Musterschmidt.

Tribunal Supremo de Justicia (TSJ). 2003. Sala Constitucional V.s. Exp. Nº. 03-2109.

———. 2015. "Sentencia N° 260, Exp N° 2015-000146, Sala Electoral." http://historico.tsj.gob.ve/decisiones/selec/diciembre/184227-260-301215-2015-2015-000146.html.

———. 2016a. "Declarada la nulidad de los actos de la Asamblea Nacional por desacato a fallo del máximo juzgado." http://www.tsj.gob.ve/-/declarada-la-nulidad-de-los-actos-de-la-asamblea-nacional-por-desacato-a-fallo-del-maximo-juzgado.

———. 2016b. "Sentencia N° 1 Exp. N° AA70-X-X2016-000001, Sala Electoral." http://historico.tsj.gob.ve/decisiones/selec/enero/184253-1-11116-2016-X-2016-000001.html.

———. 2017. "Sentencia N° 1 378, Exp. N° 2017-0519." http://historico.tsj.gob.ve/decisiones/scon/junio/199712-441-7617-2017-17-0519.html.

———. 2023a. "Decisiones de la Sala Electoral." http://www.tsj.gob.ve/decisiones#3.

———. 2023b. "Decisiones de la Sala Constitucional." http://www.tsj.gob.ve/decisiones#1.

———. 2023c. "Sentencia N° 1 244, Exp 23-0722." https://accesoalajusticia.org/la-sc-rechazo-revision-constitucional-solicitada-contra-la-inhabilitacion-politica-de-maria-corina-machado/.

Trinkunas, Harold. 2002a. "The Crisis in Venezuelan Civil-Military Relations: From Punto Fijo to the Fifth Republic." *Latin American Research Review* 37(1): 41–76.

———. 2002b. "The Re-emergence of the Venezuelan Armed Forces as a Political Actor." *Journal of Iberian and Latin American Studies* 8(2): 165–72.

Trouillot, Michel-Rolph. 2015. *Silencing the Past: Power and the Production of History*. Boston: Beacon Press.

Trudo, Hanna. 2023. "Progressives Vent Frustration as Debt Limit Bill Nears Final Vote." https://thehill.com/homenews/house/4028920-progressives-vent-frustration-as-debt-limit-bill-nears-final-vote/.

Tsebelis, George. 2002. *Veto Players: How Political Institutions Work*. Princeton, NJ: Princeton University Press.

Tullock, Gordon. 1980. "Efficient Rent Seeking." In *Toward a Theory of the Rent-Seeking Society*, ed. J. M. Buchanan, R. D. Tollison, and G. Tullock. College Station: Texas A&M University Press.

———. 1983. *Economics of Income Redistribution*. Kluwer-Nijhoff Studies in Human Issues. Leiden: Kluwer-Nijhoff.

Turkewitz, Julie, and Anatoly Kurmanaev. 2021. "Behind the Haiti Assassination, Colombia's Growing Mercenary Industry." https://www.nytimes.com/2021/08/07/world/americas/haiti-assassination-colombia-mercenaries.html.

Ulmer, Alexandra, and Marianna Parraga. 2017. "U.S. Sanctions on Venezuela Oil Company CFO Tangle Financial Deals: Sources." https://www.reuters.com/article/venezuela-oil-sanctions-idINL2N1LA19T.

Unidad Venezuela (@UnidadVenezuela). 2024. "DENUNCIA Ya han transcurrido más de 54h desde el inicio del lapso de postulación sin que se nos permita el acceso al sistema para poder postular a la Dra. Corina Yoris. @yorisvillasana. Lo repetimos una vez más: nada ni nadie nos sacará de la ruta electoral para lograr con la fuerza del voto de la mayoria el cambio para nuestra Venezuela." Twitter, March 23, 12:23 p.m. https://twitter.com/unidadvenezuela/status/1771573414987211047.

United Nations. 2019. "Negative Impact of Unilateral Coercive Measures on the Enjoyment of Human Rights." General Assembly, Human Rights Council, Forty-Second sess. https://www.ohchr.org/en/documents/thematic-reports/ahrc4246-negative-impact-unilateral-coercive-measures-enjoyment-human.

United Nations Development Programme (UNDP). 2010. "Human Development Report 2010." https://hdr.undp.org/content/human-development-report-2010.

United Nations Human Rights Council. 2021. "Visit to the Bolivarian Republic of Venezuela, Report of the Special Rapporteur on the Negative Impact of Unilateral Coercive Measures on the Enjoyment of Human Rights, Alena Douhan." United Nations Human Rights Council Forty-Eighth Session of the General Assembly, A/HRC/48/59/Add.2. https://documents-dds-ny.un.org/doc/UNDOC/GEN/G21/269/56/PDF/G2126956.pdf?OpenElement.

United Nations Inter-Agency Group for Child Mortality Estimation (UN IGME). 2021. "Child Mortality Estimation." https://childmortality.org/.

United Nations Trade and Development (UNCTAD). 2021. "Data Center–Merchandise: Trade Value, Volume, Unit Value, Terms of Trade Indices and Purchasing Power Index of Exports, Annual." https://unctadstat.unctad.org/wds/TableViewer/tableView.aspx?ReportId=184185.

University of Groningen. 2021. "Penn World Table Version 10.0." Groningen Growth and Development Centre. https://www.rug.nl/ggdc/productivity/pwt/?lang=en.

University of North Florida. 2020. "Venezuela 2020 Survey." https://www.unf.edu/uploadedFiles/aa/coas/porl/2020VenezuelaReport.pdf.

US Bureau of Labor Statistics. 2023. "Data: Consumer Price Index (Monthly)—Venezuela, RB." January 1957–May 2023. https://www.bls.gov/cpi/home.htm.

US Commission on Security and Cooperation in Europe. 1990. "Report on the Supreme Soviet Election in Azerbaijan." https://www.csce.gov/sites/helsinkicommission.house.gov/files/Report%20on%20the%20Supreme%20Soviet%20Elections%20in%20Azerbaijan.pdf.

US Department of State. 2019a. "Sanctions against PDVSA and Venezuela Oil Sector." https://2017-2021.state.gov/sanctions-against-pdvsa-and-venezuela-oil-sector/index.html.

———. 2019b. "The United States Sanctions Venezuela's Defense and Security Sector." https://2017-2021.state.gov/the-united-states-sanctions-venezuelas-defense-and-security-sector/index.html.

———. 2019c. "The United States Sanctions Venezuela's State-Affiliated Bank." https://2017-2021.state.gov/the-united-states-sanctions-venezuelas-state-affiliated-bank/index.html.

———. 2020. "Democratic Transition Framework for Venezuela." https://2017-2021.state.gov/democratic-transition-framework-for-venezuela/index.html.

———. 2021. "Venezuela's Flawed November 21 Elections." https://www.state.gov/venezuelas-flawed-november-21-elections/.

———. 2024. "Venezuela Sanctions Relief: Expiration of General License 44." https://www.state.gov/venezuela-sanctions-relief-expiration-of-general-license-44/.

US Department of the Treasury. 2014. "Entities Owned by Blocked Persons (50% Rule)." https://home.treasury.gov/policy-issues/financial-sanctions/faqs/400.

———. 2017. "Treasury Sanctions Eight Members of Venezuela's Supreme Court of Justice." https://www.treasury.gov/press-center/press-releases/Pages/sm0090.aspx.

———. 2019. "Treasury Removes Sanctions Imposed on Former High-Ranking Venezuelan Intelligence Official after Public Break with Maduro and Dismissal." https://home.treasury.gov/news/press-releases/sm684.

———. 2020. "Treasury Targets Russian Oil Brokerage Firm for Supporting Illegitimate Maduro Regime." https://home.treasury.gov/news/press-releases/sm909.

———. 2022. "Executive Summary to the Fiscal Year 2022. Financial Report of U.S. Government." https://www.fiscal.treasury.gov/reports-statements/financial-report/unsustainable-fiscal-path.html.

———. 2023. "Venezuela-Related Sanctions." https://home.treasury.gov/policy-issues/financial-sanctions/sanctions-programs-and-country-information/venezuela-related-sanctions.

US Energy Information Administration (EIA). 2021. "Weekly Preliminary Crude Imports by Top 10 Countries of Origin (Ranking Based on 2019 Petroleum Supply Monthly Data)." https://www.eia.gov/dnav/pet/pet_move_wimpc_s1_w.htm.

———. 2023a. "Annual Petroleum and Other Liquids Production." https://www.eia.gov/international/data/world/petroleum-and-other-liquids/annual-petroleum-and-other-liquids-production.

———. 2023b. "Crude Oil Including Lease Condensate Production Iraq Monthly." https://www.eia.gov/opendata/qb.php?sdid=INTL.57-1-IRQ-TBPD.M.

———. 2023c. "International Energy Statistics." https://www.eia.gov/international/data/world.

———. 2024. "Open Data." https://www.eia.gov/opendata/.

US Mission OAS. 2019. "Remarks by Vice President Pence to the Lima Group, US Mission to the Organization of American States." https://usoas.usmission.gov/remarks-by-vice-president-pence-to-the-lima-group-bogota-colombia/.

Uslar Pietri, Arturo. 1947. *De una a otra Venezuela*. Caracas: Ediciones Mesa Redonda.

Vaishnav, Milan, and Danielle Smogard. 2014. "A Devil Called Policy Paralysis." https://carnegieendowment.org/2014/05/17/devil-called-policy-paralysis-pub-55624.

Valimised. 1992. "Election of the President of the Republic in 1992." https://www.valimised.ee/en/archive/president-republic-estonia-elections/election-president-republic-1992.

La Vanguardia. 2006. "El candidato de la oposición Manuel Rosales reconoce su derrota." https://www.lavanguardia.com/internacional/20061204/51295025744/el-candidato-de-la-oposicion-manuel-rosales-reconoce-su-derrota.html.

Van Wijnbergen, Sweder. 1984. "The 'Dutch Disease': A Disease After All?" *Economic Journal* 94(373): 41–55.

Vasquez, Alex. 2021. "A Rare Maduro-Guaidó Deal Could Unlock Vaccines for Venezuela." https://www.bloomberg.com/news/articles/2021-03-19/a-rare-maduro-guaido-deal-could-unlock-vaccines-for-venezuela.

Vasquez, Paula. 2012. "El Caracazo 1989 y la tragedia 1999 economía moral e instrumentalización política del saqueo en Venezuela." *Cuadernos Unimetanos* 30: 5–15.

Velasco, Alejandro. 2015. *Barrio Rising: Urban Popular Politics and the Making of Modern Venezuela*. Berkeley: University of California Press.

Venezuela Quiere Cambio. 2015. *La última cola.* YouTube video, 1:05, November 20. https://www.youtube.com/watch?v=TXeMn2sBqis.

Vente Venezuela. 2016. "Estos no son momentos para ceder, ¡son momentos para avanzar!" https://www.ventevenezuela.org/2016/11/01/vente-venezuela-estos-no-momentos-ceder-momentos-avanzar/.

Vilas, Carlos M. 1990. "Especulaciones sobre una sorpresa: Las elecciones en Nicaragua." *Desarrollo Económico* 30(118): 255–76. https://doi.org/10.2307/3466870.

Vile, John. 2002. *Presidential Winners and Losers: Words of Victory and Concession.* Washington, DC: CQ Press.

Villarreal, Karina. 2022. "Encuesta Frequency58 | Esto opinan los venezolanos sobre las sanciones y la negociación." https://www.elnacional.com/venezuela/encuesta-frequency58-esto-opinan-los-venezolanos-sobre-sanciones-y-la-negociacion/.

Vivoplay. 2016. "Video completo del discurso de Henry Ramos Allup y las caras que no pudiste ver, solo por VIVOplay." YouTube video, 35:06, January 16. https://www.youtube.com/watch?v=bPh7urGq9tw.

Voice of America (VOA). 2009. "African Union Calls for National Unity Government in Zimbabwe." https://www.voanews.com/archive/african-union-calls-national-unity-government-zimbabwe.

Volcker, Paul. A., Richard J. Goldstone, and Mark Pieth. 2005. "Manipulation of the Oil-for-Food Programme by the Iraqi Regime." Independent Inquiry Committee into the United Nations Oil-for-Food Programme. https://www.files.ethz.ch/isn/13894/ManipulationReport.pdf.

Vollaard, Ben, and Jan C. van Ours. 2011. "Does Regulation of Built-in Security Reduce Crime? Evidence from a Natural Experiment." *Economic Journal* 12(1): 485–504.

Vollan, Kare. 2008. "Zimbabwe: The Elections on 29 March and the Later Runoff Event and By-Elections on 27 June 2008. NORDEM Report." https://www.jus.uio.no/smr/english/about/programmes/nordem/publications/2008/0808.pdf.

Voluntad Popular. 2016a. "¿Dónde quedó el derecho a elegir de los venezolanos que originó el diálogo? ¡Debemos retomar la calle!" https://voluntadpopular.com/voluntad-popular-donde-quedo-el-derecho-a-elegir-de-los-venezolanos-que-origino-el-dialogo-debemos-retomar-la-presion-popular-de-calle-para-rescatarlo/.

———. 2016b. "Freddy Guevara: Nosotros no seremos corresponsables del desfalco a la nación." https://voluntadpopular.com/freddy-guevara-nosotros-no-seremos-corresponsables-del-desfalco-a-la-nacion/.

Von Soest, Christian, and Michael Wahman. 2014. "Are Democratic Sanctions Really Counterproductive?" *Democratization* 22(6): 957–80.

La Voz. 2014. "Borges se pregunta ¿Qué harán con el dinero de la gasolina?" August 5. https://diariolavoz.net/2014/08/05/borges-se-pregunta-que-haran-con-el-dinero-de-la-gasolina/.

Voz de América. 2016. "Oposición venezolana se retira del diálogo con el gobierno." https://www.vozdeamerica.com/a/venezuela-dialogo-retiro-varticano-nunciatura-reunion/3625213.html.

———. 2019. "Guaidó critica acuerdo de diálogo de parte de la oposición con Maduro." https://www.vozdeamerica.com/a/juan-guaido-critica-acuerdo-dialogo-parte-oposicion-con-nicolas-maduro/5086656.html.

VPITV. 2017. "Julio Borges denuncia incidencias que contribuyeron al fraude electoral." YouTube video, 9:00, October 23. https://www.youtube.com/watch?app=desktop&v=OOyeoVIGx_o&embeds_referring_euri=http%3A%2F%2Fwww.cubademocraciayvida.org%2F&feature=emb_imp_woyt.

———. 2018. "Así se juramentó Juan Guaidó como Presidente Interino de Venezuela." YouTube video, 1:30, January 23. https://www.youtube.com/watch?v=SOHvqV_DpoQ.

———. 2024. "Edmundo González Urrutia conversa con el periodista Isnardo Bravo en ¿Qué Propone?" YouTube video, 25:31, April 25. https://www.youtube.com/watch?v=RaN6Cr3nyDo&t=1526s.

Vyas, Kejal, and Pedro Kurmanaev. 2017. "Goldman Sachs Bought Venezuela's State Oil Company's Bonds Last Week." https://www.wsj.com/articles/goldman-sachs-bought-venezuelan-oil-co-bonds-last-week-1496020176.

Wall Street Journal. 2011. "Trump: We Should Take Libya's Oil." Video. 4:05. April 19. https://www.wsj.com/video/trump-we-should-take-libya-oil/7E12BC15-38AE-465F-949A-CDB65ED6DC75.html.

Wang, Zhongmin. 2009. "Mixed Strategy in Oligopoly Pricing: Evidence from Gasoline Price Cycles Before and Under a Timing Regulation." *Journal of Political Economy* 117(6): 987–1030.

Wantchekon, Leonard. 2002. "Why do Resource Dependent Countries Have Authoritarian Governments?" *Journal of African Finance and Economic Development* 2: 57–77.

Washington Office on Latin America (WOLA). 2020. "Interactive Map: Degrees of Diplomatic Recognition of Guaidó and Maduro." https://www.venezuelablog.org/interactive-map-degrees-of-diplomatic-recognition-of-guaido-and-maduro/.

Washington Post. 2020. "Opinion: Venezuela's Blatantly Rigged Election Poses a Test for Biden." https://www.washingtonpost.com/opinions/global-opinions/venezuelas-blatantly-rigged-election-poses-a-test-for-biden/2020/12/07/a00f6644-38b2-11eb-bc68-96af0daae728_story.html.

Watts, Edward. 2018. *Mortal Republic*. New York: Basic Books.

Weber, Patrick, and Gerald Schneider. 2019. "Post–Cold War Sanctioning by the EU, the UN, and the US: Introducing the EUSANCT Dataset." *Conflict Management and Peace Science* 39(1): 1–18.

Weingast, Barry R. 1997. "Political Foundations of Democracy and the Rule of Law." *American Political Science Review* 91(2): 245–63.

Weisbrot, Mark, David Rosnick, and Todd Tucker. 2004. "Black Swans, Conspiracy Theories, and the Quixotic Search for Fraud: A Look at Hausmann and Rigobon's Analysis of Venezuela's Referendum Vote." Center for Economic and Policy Research. CEPR Briefing Paper. https://cepr.net/report/black-swans-conspiracy-theories-and-the-quixotic-search-for-fraud/.

Weisbrot, Mark, and Jeffrey Sachs. 2019a. "Economic Sanctions as Collective Punishment: The Case of Venezuela." Center for Economic and Policy Research. https://cepr.net/images/stories/reports/venezuela-sanctions-2019-04.pdf.

———. 2019b. "Economists Use 'Fuzzy Graphs' to Challenge Data on the Human Cost of Trump Sanctions on Venezuela." Center for Economic and Policy Research. https://cepr.shorthandstories.com/venezuela-sanctions-response/index.html.

West P&I. 2017. "Venezuela—US Sanctions." https://www.westpandi.com/publications/news/venezuela-us-sanctions/.

White House. 2015. "FACT SHEET: Venezuela Executive Order." https://obamawhitehouse.archives.gov/the-press-office/2015/03/09/fact-sheet-venezuela-executive-order.

———. 2023a. "The Potential Economic Impacts of Various Debt Ceiling Scenarios." https://www.whitehouse.gov/cea/written-materials/2023/05/03/debt-ceiling-scenarios/#_ftn1.

———. 2023b. "Remarks by President Biden on Meeting with Congressional Leaders." https://www.whitehouse.gov/briefing-room/speeches-remarks/2023/05/09/remarks-by-president-biden-on-debt-ceiling-negotiations/.

White House 45 Archived (@WhiteHouse45). 2019. "President @realDonald Trump has officially recognized the President of the Venezuelan National Assembly, Juan Guaido, as the Interim President of Venezuela." Twitter, January 23, 2:08 p.m. https://twitter.com/WhiteHouse45/status/1088136422320689152.

Wiarda, Howard. 2014. *Dispatches from the Frontlines: Studies in Foreign Policy, Comparative Politics, and International Affairs*. Lanham, MD: University Press of America.

Wikipedia. 2021. "Anexo: Encuestas de las elecciones parlamentarias de Venezuela de 2015." https://es.wikipedia.org/wiki/Anexo:Encuestas_de_las_elecciones_parlamentarias_de_Venezuela_de_2015.

Wilczek, Maria. 2020. "Poland Removes Statute of Limitations on Communist Crimes." https://notesfrompoland.com/2020/07/20/poland-lifts-statute-of-limitations-on-communist-crimes/.

Williams, Jack, and John Curiel. 2020. "Analysis of the 2019 Bolivia Election." https://cepr.net/report/analysis-of-the-2019-bolivia-election/.

Wilpert, Greg. 2018. "Venezuela's Highly Unusual Presidential Election." https://newint.org/features/web-exclusive/2018/05/15/venezuela-presidential-election.

Wittman, Donald. 1973. "Parties as Utility Maximizers." *American Political Science Review* 67(2): 490–98.

Wolfers, Justin. 2006. "Did Unilateral Divorce Laws Raise Divorce Rates? A Reconciliation and New Results." *American Economic Review* 96(5): 1802–20.

Wong, Edward. 2019. "Venezuelan Opposition Leader Guaidó Controls U.S. Bank Accounts, State Dept. Says." https://www.nytimes.com/2019/01/29/us/politics/venezuela-bank-accounts-guaido-pompeo.html.

Wood, Reed. 2008. "A Hand upon the Throat of the Nation: Economic Sanctions and State Repression, 1976–2001." *International Studies Quarterly* 52(3): 489–513.

Woody, Christopher. 2017. "'All Options Are on the Table' for Trump to Go after Venezuela, but the Side Effects Could Be Severe." https://www.businessinsider.com/humanitarian-economic-political-effect-of-us-sanction-on-venezuela-oil-2017-7.

World Bank. 2007. *The Little Data Book on Africa*. Washington, DC: World Bank.

———. 2019. "Zimbabwe: Public Expenditure Review with a Focus on Agriculture." Washington, DC.

———. 2022. "World Development Indicators." https://databank.worldbank.org/reports.aspx?source=world-development-indicators.

———. 2023a. "GDP (current US$)." https://data.worldbank.org/indicator/NY.GDP.MKTP.CD.

———. 2023b. "Imports of Goods and Services (Current US$)." https://data.worldbank.org/indicator/NE.IMP.GNFS.CD.

World Health Organization (WHO). 2020. "COVID-19 Virtual Press Conference." https://www.who.int/publications/m/item/covid-19-virtual-press-conference-transcript-14-december-2020.

Worsnip, Patrick. 2008. "Russia and China Veto U.N. Zimbabwe Sanctions." https://www.reuters.com/article/us-zimbabwe-crisis-un-idUSN0917887320080712.

Wright, Gavin, and Jesse Czelusta. 2004. "The Myth of the Resource Curse." *Challenge* 47(2): 6–38.

Wróberl, Krzysztof, and Jan Frankowski. 2016. "Fall and Rise of Polish Shipbuilding Industry." *TransNav: International Journal on Marine Navigation and Safety of Sea Transportation* 10(1): 151–56.

Yagova, Olga, Chen Aizhu, and Marianna Parraga. 2019. "Rosneft Becomes Top Venezuelan Oil Trader, Helping Offset U.S. Pressure." https://www.reuters.com/article/us-russia-venezuela-oil-idUSKCN1VC1PF.

Yapur, Nicole. 2020. "Venezuela Is Almost Alone in Slashing Its Deficit amid Covid-19." https://www.bloomberg.com/news/articles/2020-09-22/venezuela-is-almost-alone-in-slashing-its-deficit-amid-covid-19.

———. 2021. "Venezuela's Access to Vaccines Imperiled by Seized Virus Tests." https://www.bloomberg.com/news/articles/2021-01-21/venezuela-s-access-to-vaccines-imperiled-by-seized-virus-tests.

Zambrano, Omar (@Econ_Vzla). 2018. "El problema es que Venezuela a finales de AGO 2017 ya había perdido todo acceso a mercados financieros internacionales, antes del inicio de las sanciones. La razón es sencilla y es omitida deliberadamente en el análisis de @frrodriguezc: Venezuela estaba al borde del default." Twitter, September 21, 6:24 p.m. https://twitter.com/Econ_Vzla/status/1043264679945138178.

Zamorano, Abraham. 2013. "Merentes, el arquitecto del tipo de cambio más complejo del mundo." https://www.bbc.com/mundo/noticias/2013/07/130715_venezuela_economia_sicad_control_cambios_merentes_az.

Zandi, Mark, Adam Kamins, and Bernard Yaros. 2023. "Debt Limit Scenario Update." https://www.moodysanalytics.com/-/media/article/2023/debt-limit-scenario-update.pdf.

Zea, Sendai. 2014a. "Estos fueron los anuncios del Vicepresidente para el Área Económica, Rafael Ramírez." https://runrun.es/la-economia/economia/100258/estos-fueron-los-anuncios-del-vicepresidente-para-el-area-economica-rafael-ramirez/.

———. 2014b. "López y Machado llaman a la calle para debatir #LaSalida de Maduro." https://runrun.es/nacional/venezuela-2/100458/lopez-y-machado-llaman-la-calle-para-debatir-lasalida-de-maduro/.

Ziegler, David W. 1984. *War, Peace, and International Politics*. 3rd ed. Boston: Little, Brown.

Zimbabwe Human Rights NGO Forum. 2010. "Land Reform and Property Rights in Zimbabwe." https://reliefweb.int/sites/reliefweb.int/files/resources/F83EDE2320A923844925779F001CDC97-Full_Report.pdf.

INDEX

FRANCISCO RODRÍGUEZ is the Rice Family Professor of the Practice of International and Public Affairs at the University of Denver's Josef Korbel School of International Studies.

www.ingramcontent.com/pod-product-compliance
Ingram Content Group UK Ltd.
Pitfield, Milton Keynes, MK11 3LW, UK
UKHW020222290926
15470UKWH00001B/338

9 780268 209018